Prix
Ars Electronica
2024

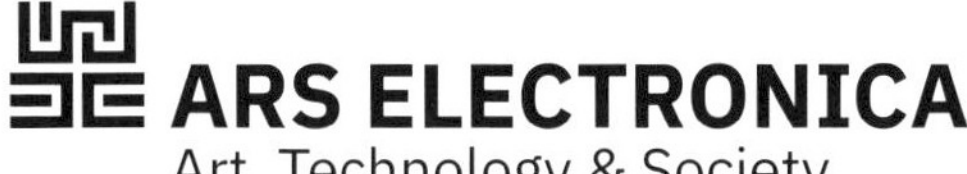

HATJE
CANTZ

Gerfried Stocker · Markus Jandl

Prix
Ars Electronica
2024

Prix Ars Electronica 2024
New Animation Art
Interactive Art+
AI in Art Award
u19–create your world

Ars Electronica Award for Digital Humanity

European Union Prize for Citizen Science
The Grand Prize for Citizen Science of the European Union recognizes outstanding achievements in the advancement of knowledge through the empowerment of civil society and citizens in the development of the future

S+T+ARTS Prize'24
Grand Prize of the European Commission honoring Innovation in Technology, Industry, and Society stimulated by the Arts

S+T+ARTS Prize Africa
Grand Prize of the European Union promoting a S+T+ARTS approach to digital innovation in Africa

Contents

Contents

Contents

Contents

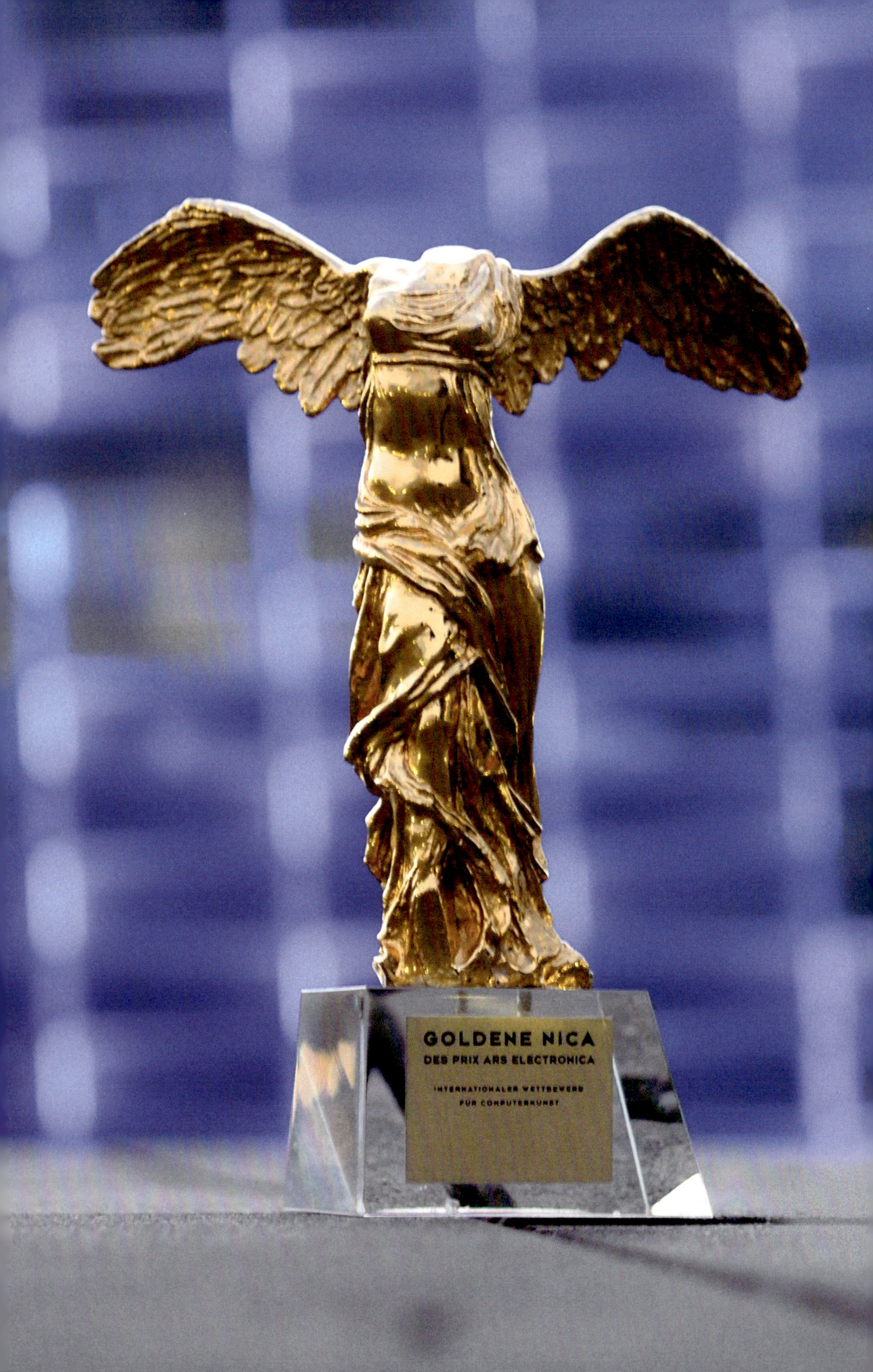

GOLDENE NICA
DES PRIX ARS ELECTRONICA
INTERNATIONALER WETTBEWERB
FÜR COMPUTERKUNST

Prix Ars Electronica 2024

Gerfried Stocker, Markus Jandl

In the second year after Chat-GPT rocked the world, in the second year after Russia invaded Ukraine, in the midst of maximum escalation of the central Middle East conflict, and 45 years after the first global climate summit took place in 1979, no prophetic talent is needed to find out which topics artists around the world are currently most concerned about. The trends that clearly manifested themselves this year have already been announced in recent years, as they have always been in the 37-year career of the Prix Ars Electronica, which was founded in 1987: democracy, free and fair forms of society, opposition to totalitarian currents, reflection on a newly gained global perspective, coming to terms with mistakes and damage from the past and, of course, dealing with the questions that the massive emergence of machine learning and so-called AI has for society and in particular for the role and self-image of art and artists raises.

Although the topics themselves are not new, the large number of projects and the range of engagement with these topics is a significant novelty. The enthusiasm for and interest in the new technical developments was quickly joined by skepticism as to what effect the one-sided balance of power would have in the development and definition of AI systems and their applications, as well as skepticism about what's actually behind the hyped-up promises.

What is most noticeable this year is the demand for participation and co-creation: in the formulation of standards and rules for AI, in the further development of AI models in order to prevent them from degenerating into mainstream monocultures which do not reflect the true diversity of our world and of course also in the monetary value creation, which in this case is based not only on technical, scientific achievements, but especially on the intellectual, cultural achievements of many generations of authors, artists, and scientists.

A claim that is not only raised, but also introduced, in new cooperation models, in the development and communication of speculative scenarios and in prototypical implementations. This is also reflected in the high number of artistic projects in which work is not done with the AI systems of the big tech giants, but rather with set-ups adapted to the respective artistic intentions based on open source. This shows once again that the prevailing idea in the current numerous discussions about art and AI is that for AI art you just have to "press the button" and the "work" will automatically appear on the computer screens and/or loudspeakers is due to the general superficiality of these debates, but certainly does not represent the prevailing artistic practice.

The Prix Ars Electronica has been reacting to these developments for many years, trying in particular to trace and take into account the differentiated debate and the advanced use of AI in artistic work. This started with the transformation of the Prix category "Hybrid Art" into a category for "Artificial Intelligence and Life Art" in 2019. A hybrid combination that focuses not so much on technological categorization but on phenomenological and epistemological intentions. A perspective typical of artistic work, in which the work on the genetic, biological foundations of life and the attempt to digitally recreate the foundations of thinking, of the mind, are suddenly very similar, in the wishes and expectations, but also in the dangers and fears associated with it. A separate category for AI art was discussed and rejected again and again, as it quickly became clear that this new tool is found equally across the entire cross-section of artistic genres and, at least so far, no new category or genre of digital arts has emerged, a distinction between digital Art with or without AI would not do justice to the prevailing artistic practice.

It cannot be denied that a fork in the road is emerging at which much will change for artistic work due to the fundamentally different way of generating content, changes in production conditions and the economic framework. In particular, with all due caution, the astonishing universal achievement of generative AI systems of being able to transform free language directly into texts, images, videos, music, code, no longer through a codified, programmed specification, but through a new type of statistical associative ability.

Where this fork in the road will lead is still unclear in many ways. Therefore, this year (in the tradition of the Prix Ars Electronica) a "side step" with a special Golden Nica and two Awards of Distinction for "AI in ART", not for the technical development, but for the exceptional achievements of the artists and to pay tribute to the important role of active participation, involvement, and intervention through art.

What particularly distinguishes the Prix Ars Electronica in its current form is not just the unique legacy of the previous prize winners. As an international platform, the Prix impressively illustrates the enormous importance and range of the different forms of development in the liaison between art and science, creativity and technology.

The basis for this is an extraordinary partner network with the S+T+ARTS Prize, which has been expanded this year in an extremely exciting way with the S+T+ARTS Prize Africa, the highly endowed prize for Citizen Science from the European Commission and the Digital Humanity Award, which the Austrian Ministry (BMEIA) gives for projects that are dedicated to perhaps the most important task in the current digital world, namely putting people at the center, exploring how we can develop and use technology to support people and not just see them as passive users and consumers.

In 2024 the Interactive Art + category received the largest number of submissions (1,428), followed by New Animation Art with 1,160 submissions. The u19–create your world category for Young Creatives (under age fourteen) and Young Professionals (age fourteen to nineteen), open for entries from all over Austria, recorded a total of 362 entries. The AI in ART award-winning projects have been selected from among all the submissions from the Prix Ars Electronica, the S+T+ARTS Prize, and the European Union Prize for Citizen Science.

In addition to the four Golden Nicas of Prix Ars Electronica 2024, the Ars Electronica Award for Digital Humanity, initiated by the Austrian Federal Ministry for European and International Affairs, was awarded for the fourth time as part of Prix Ars Electronica. This award is endowed with €10.000 prize money. The State of the ART(ist) Prize, also initiated by the Austrian Federal Ministry for European and International Affairs, provides additional prize money totaling €12,000.

In 2024, for the ninth time, the Prix Ars Electronica includes the S+T+ARTS Prize, which Ars Electronica awards on behalf of the European Commission. S+T+ARTS Prize '24 is part of the joint S+T+ARTS Ec(h)o project by: Ars Electronica, French Tech Grand Provence, INOVA+, Media Solutions Center Baden-Württemberg, Salzburg Festival, Sónar, T6

Ecosystems, Kustodie–TUD Dresden, University of Technology, and High-Performance Computing Center Stuttgart. This prize, endowed with a total of €40,000, recognizes innovative projects at the nexus of Science, Technology, and Arts (S+T+ARTS) and is awarded by the European Commission as part of the Horizon Europe funding program for research and innovation.

For the first time this year, Ars Electronica, in collaboration with its partners INOVA+, GLUON, and PiNA, successfully launched the inaugural S+T+ARTS Prize Africa as part of the European Union's STARTS4AFRICA project. The partnership with Africa is a key priority for Europe. As its closest neighbor, Africa shares not only a (grim) historical connection with European countries but also common values and interests. By targeting artists, creative professionals, and organizations from Africa, the STARTS Prize Africa aims to expand everyone's horizons and highlight novel ideas with significant potential to drive positive change and tackle shared challenges. This African edition of the renowned S+T+ARTS Prize awards continental best-practice examples in the field of creative practices at the intersection of science, technology, and arts and is endowed with a total prize money of €30,000.

Along with the European Union Prize for Citizen Science, an additional €100,000 in prize money is awarded this year.

This means that a total of €228,600 in prize money was awarded to artists in this year's Prix Ars Electronica.

The Prix Ars Electronica, organized by Ars Electronica Linz GmbH & Co KG, is being staged for the 38th time in 2024. This has been made possible by the City of Linz, which has funded Ars Electronica since 1979 and the Prix Ars Electronica since 1987. Special Thanks for additional support go to the Austrian Federal Ministry for European and International Affairs, the Austrian Federal Ministry of Education, Science and Research, OeAD, and to ORF OOE for the collaboration.

Gerfried Stocker (AT) is a media artist and an engineer for communication technology and has been artistic director and co-CEO of Ars Electronica since 1995. In 1995/96 he developed the groundbreaking exhibition strategies of the Ars Electronica Center with a small team of artists and technicians and was responsible for the setup and establishment of Ars Electronica's own R & D facility, the Ars Electronica Futurelab. He has overseen the development of the program for international Ars Electronica exhibitions since 2004, the planning and the revamping of the contents for the Ars Electronica Center, which was enlarged in 2009, since 2005; the expansion of the Ars Electronica Festival since 2015; and the extensive overhaul of Ars Electronica Center's contents and interior design in 2019. Stocker is a consultant for numerous companies and institutions in the field of creativity and innovation management and is active as a guest lecturer at international conferences and universities. In 2019 he was awarded an honorary doctorate from Aalto University, Finland.
Markus Jandl (AT) has been Chief Financial Officer (CFO) since September 2020 and, together with Gerfried Stocker as co-CEO, manages the business of Ars Electronica Linz GmbH & Co KG and Ars Electronica International GmbH. He has held various positions at Ars Electronica over many years, most recently as Head of Corporate Finance and authorized signatory for both Ars Electronica companies. Born in Linz, he studied Economics at Johannes Kepler University Linz and spent nine months at Ivey Business School in London/Ontario, Canada. Jandl specialized in corporate accounting during his studies and wrote his diploma thesis in this field.

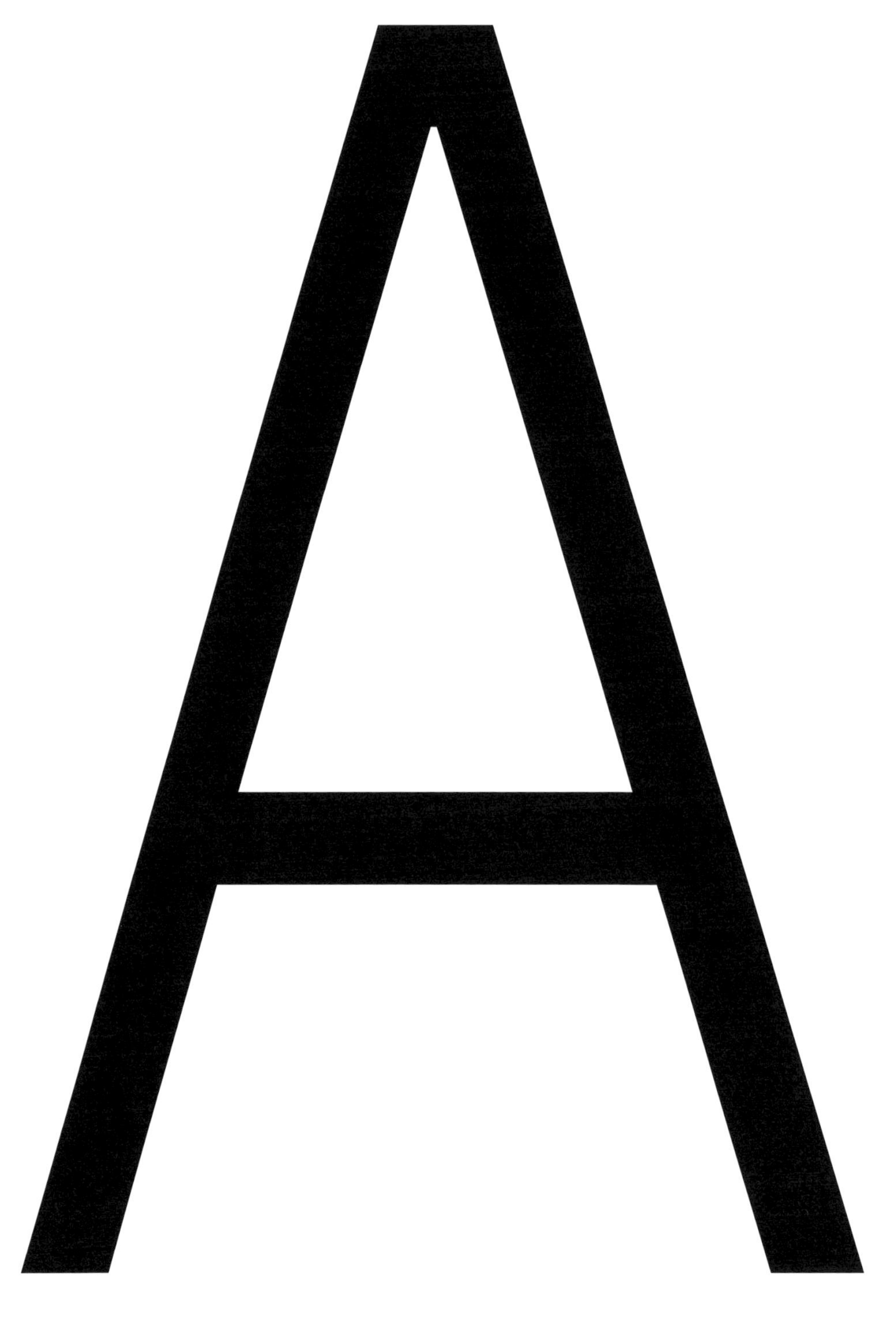

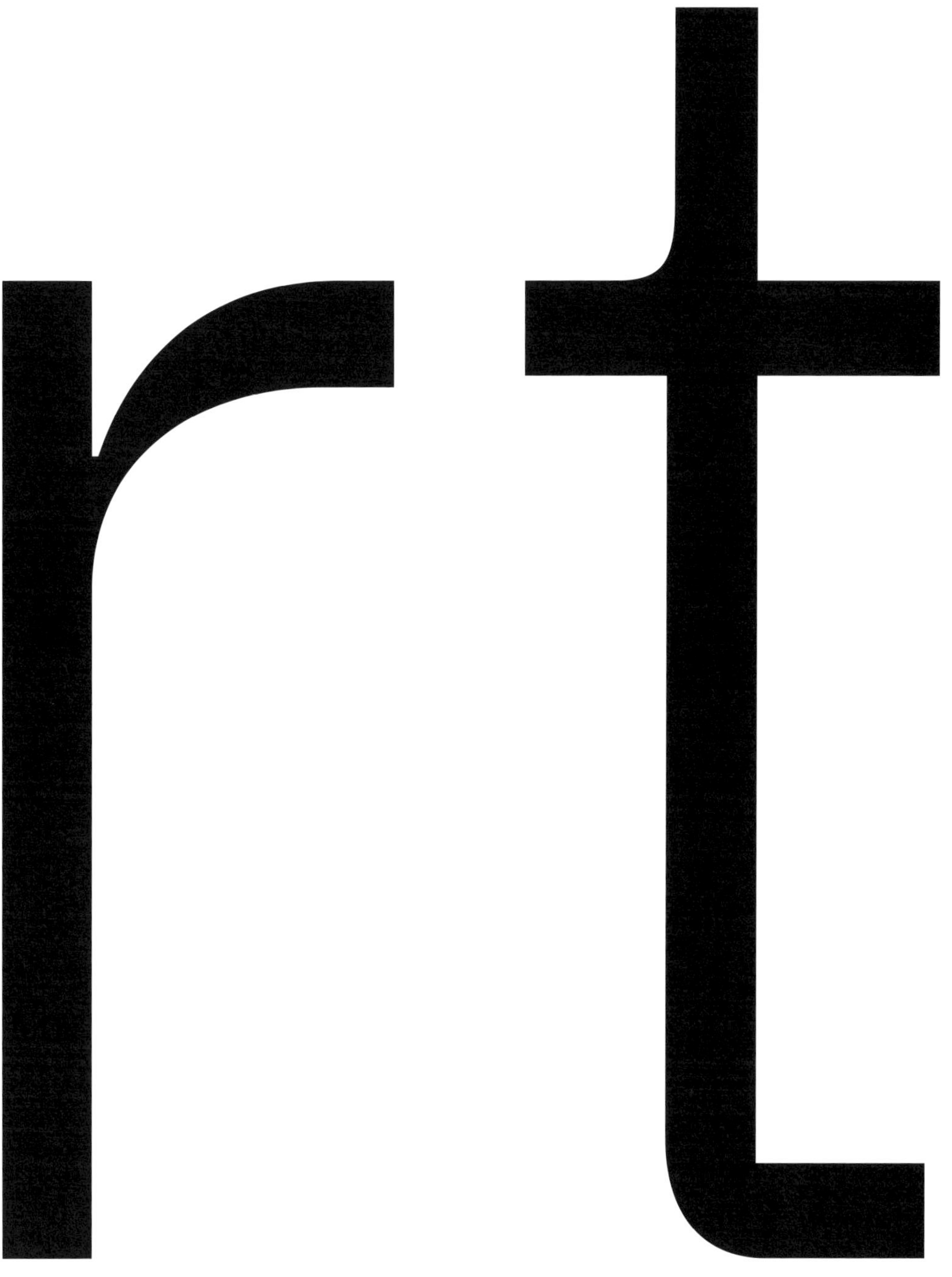

New Animation Art

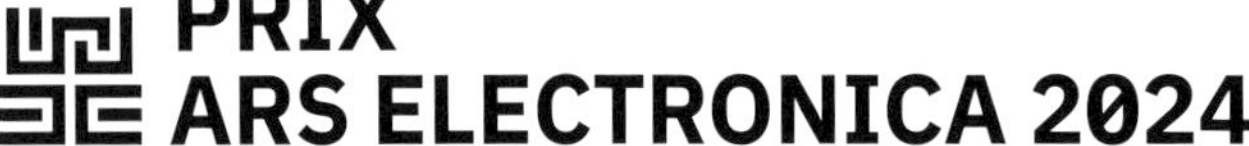

Critical Imaginaries for Animate Futures

Kalina Borkiewicz, Fanni Fazakas, Ari Melenciano,
Georgy Molodtsov, Chris Salter

The etymology of the word animation derives from the late 16th century Latin *animatio*—"the action of imparting life to". Indeed, this concept of imparting life to images through new technological tools and thinking provides the basis for the winning selections in New Animation Art for the 2024 Prix Ars Electronica. Given the explosion of new forms of animation and the sheer number of entries (some 893), the jury faced a formidable task. Submitted projects ran the gamut from static and moving images using generative AI, to short films produced with game engines such as Unity 3D or Unreal, scientific data visualizations, performance projects employing motion capture, and VR/AR works. At the same time, the jury detected a range of emerging critical socio-political themes: climate transformation, dataveillance, decolonization, gender discrimination, and political oppression, as well as playful commentaries on the nature of the moving image itself. Such works all operate in an age not only of technical reproduction but also of technical simulation, which is successfully erasing the boundary between reality and its digital double.

In grappling with these heterogeneous submissions, the jury's deliberations oscillated between one of the oldest debates in aesthetics: that of form vs. content/expression. For example, in the context of numerous "generative AI" works, the jury was struck by the unresolved tension between creators using emerging applications like Stable Diffusion, Midjourney, DALL-E, Runway, or ChatGPT as tools (akin to the early use of commercial software such as Photoshop) versus those using such models to produce critical commentary on the socio-technical nature of these systems themselves. This tension led to intense discussion about the role of AI in enabling new forms of animation, particularly when *motion*—a key characteristic—is generated by the technical specificity of a mathematical model like a neural network. The jury grappled with whether works produced with/by AI tools relied primarily on the unedited output of these tools versus creators who attempted to integrate these outputs into larger ideas that were not purely reliant on AI capabilities.

A similar debate arose around the increasing use of game engines to produce new kinds of CGI-based short films. Such tools allow for an unprecedented level of visual production that just a few years ago was only available to the likes of animators working at ILM or Disney. Yet the jury was interested in how creators could go beyond existing forms in order to transcend traditional Hollywood-driven storytelling. The jury was focused on how well creatives were able to use these technologies to tell captivating stories and how successful they were in utilizing the most appropriate technology to tell the story effectively. At the same time, many works submitted under the "hybrid form" label brought up long standing debates in media studies and art history such as the mediating power of technical images, whether scientific visualization should be "true to nature" or artistically autonomous in regards to its original data sets as well as the role of human authorship in what Joanna Zylinska terms "non-human photography"—images that are increasingly produced by algorithmically driven processes outside of human comprehension.

Given the social, technical, and ethical complexity of understanding how similar sets of tools could yield vastly different genres and forms of artistic expression, the jury developed a set of criteria to allow comparison between the different submitted works. Chief among these criteria involved balancing technical innovation with artistic impact together with the possibility of works transcending our particular technological moment—just as pioneering animators like Mary Ellen Bute or John Whitney had done with the tools of their time. Another key criterion was explicitly demonstrated novelty arising through the merging or mixing of different genres and forms. Extra credit was given to projects that explicitly used new technological possibilities to create compelling socio-political commentary while points were deducted for works that ignored the ethical concerns around the technologies being deployed. This was particularly relevant in the context of some generative AI submissions that used datasets containing the images of other creators without acknowledging the larger legal and ethical issues involved. Finally, in narrowing its selection down to the top 15 works, the jury unanimously agreed that the winning projects had to reflect diverse viewpoints in all manner of the word, from thematic and medium to cultural, racial, gender, and geographic contexts, including age

(emerging, mid and senior career), and whether the project was developed by a single creator or produced with a large team. Overall, the Golden Nica, Awards of Distinction and Honorary Mentions met many (if not all) of these criteria. The three winners (*Smoke and Mirrors, I'm Feeling Lucky,* and *Stained*) also demonstrate ways of using new technologies to make acute observations on the core wicked problems of our time: climate emergency, data capture in surveillance capitalism, and new visions of culture, nature, and space. These works thus prove that new animation as a creative form is not only a product of the technical times in which they are produced but also serve as critical imaginaries for futures that have not yet come to pass.

Golden Nica

Smoke and Mirrors
Beatie Wolfe

Smoke and Mirrors is a scientific visualization that confronts us with the ever-increasing tension between scientific facts about global warming and ideological positions denying such science. An emissions clock at the top of the screen rapidly counts the amount of methane in parts per billion as the 3D globe image starts to emit a pinkish smoke: a data visualization of methane density since 1970. As the Earth slowly turns and fills up with smoke, a series of still-to-this-day shocking headlines unfurls across the screen: "Oil pumps Life," "Unsettled Science," and "Doomsday is Cancelled." These headlines demonstrate six decades of climate denialism and misinformation in the public sphere from Big Oil corporations. *Smoke and Mirrors* is inspired by the path-breaking work of Harvard historians of science Naomi Oreskes and Geoffrey Supran, who have extensively examined how fossil fuel companies have long strategized to shift responsibility for global warming away from the fossil fuel industry and onto consumers while also depicting climate change as a "risk," rather than a reality. *Smoke and Mirrors* impressed the jury not only through its stark message but also in its reimagining of scientific data visualization. Visualization pioneer Edward Tufte popularized the notion that data should speak for itself, minimizing the influence of the designer. *Smoke and Mirrors* takes a deliberate departure from this traditional approach. Instead of letting the data stand alone, it boldly incorporates historical headlines that are in direct opposition of scientific facts, inviting the viewer to question prevailing narratives about environmental responsibility and accountability. This deliberate strategy compels the audience to confront the misalignment between scientific data and advertisement-driven public perception, emphasizing the magnitude of the climate crisis in a thought-provoking manner. Rather than being just a pure data visualization, this piece is a data "visceralization", intentionally evoking feelings of discomfort and awe. In *Data Feminism*, Catherine D'Ignazio and Lauren Klein highlight the importance of acknowledging subjectivity and emotion in data work, arguing that data practices should engage with complexity and challenge existing power structures. In this vein, *Smoke and Mirrors* exemplifies how data can be wielded not just to inform but to disrupt narratives, urging viewers to reconsider their perspectives on urgent societal issues.

Awards of Distinction

I'm Feeling Lucky
Timothy Thomasson
In *I'm Feeling Lucky* by Canadian artist Timothy Thomasson, a historically and geographically ambiguous 3D virtual landscape is generated in real-time with game engine technology and populated with figures from Google Street View. Processed by a deep neural network, thousands of anonymous figures taken from all over the world are randomly selected to inhabit the landscape. The work is based on 19th century panoramas: all-encompassing circular paintings that featured spectacular natural landscapes or battle scenes that completely surrounded the viewer. The panoramas' immersive scale aimed to condition and mediate perception, thus linking the spectacle and scale of the time with the contemporary scales of imaging and data collection undertaken by Google. Images in the work are continually produced in run time as a virtual camera rotates around the space endlessly and at times almost imperceptibly, thus creating a disjunction between the stillness of landscape painting and the expectation of high frame rate digital images. The jury was impressed with how *I'm Feeling Luck* subtly links histories of geography and historical media technology with current issues around mass data collection.

Stained
Jeremy Kamal
Stained is a CGI short film created by American trained landscape architect, Jeremy Kamal. The film is one of a series of 3D animations depicting a future where America's landscapes are transformed by Black culture. The film follows a sensitive tea master named Demetrius, a member of the Crimson Needles gang that uses colored flora to mark territory. Haunted by the voice of his elder, O.G. Bump, Demetrius relives the memory of being reprimanded for his fascination with a blue plant; forbidden by the red gang to which he belongs. Based in a world where symbiotic relationships with technology allow Black Americans to transform "natural" and synthetic environments, the film is a small glimpse into the intimate life of one of its many inhabitants. *Stained* imagines an alternative ecology that foregrounds under-explored narratives. It re-frames gang culture as a landscape phenomenon and recasts those affiliated as environmental caretakers and tea makers. Beyond its unique and captivating story, Kamal beautifully renders and acoustically designs a world experienced concisely yet incredibly viscerally.

Honorary Mentions

ATUA
FAFSWAG
ATUA is an XR (extended reality) installation created by FAFSWAG, a queer Indigenous art collective based in New Zealand. The main goal of this project is to revive stories of indigenous cultures by bringing AR (augmented reality) sculptures to life. These sculptures are designed based on the pan-Pacific deities of the Moana and can only be accessed through a digital portal. One notable deity, Tekore, is reimagined in human form, a

departure from its conventional representation as space itself. This unconventional choice not only challenges cultural norms but also highlights the limitations of available digital assets, as the character's body mesh was custom-created due to the absence of non-binary representation. Through this, *ATUA* offers commentary on the binary nature of technology in art, advocating for greater inclusivity and representation.

Chuly? Chuly / Чули? Чули
Letta Shtohyrn

This work is an artistic exploration between gaming and live performance that brings us to new frontiers of visual art. Centering the story around the body swap of the two faceless characters, the work gives both participants and outside viewers a change of perspective, raising critical questions around issues of embodiment and agency. The hybridization between game engine aesthetics and mechanics, live performance with motion capture and the exchanging of roles of performers on stage suggests new possibilities for live performance incorporating the techniques of virtual production.

DUCK
Rachel Maclean

DUCK is a daring deepfake short film, set in the instantly recognizable world of a famous British Spy Thriller. Like many of Maclean's films, *DUCK* explores the fragility and malleability of identity, the slipperiness of reality, and the ramifications of gender-based power dynamics. Society is entering an increasingly more powerful inflection point through the role and impact of more AI. Through this, *DUCK* satirically reflects on such a moment with a time-bending cultural resonance, reminding us that the issues we fear are also issues we have dealt with in other forms.

EMPEROR
Ilan J. Cohen, Marion Burger

EMPEROR is a personal experience that leverages the imperfections of VR technology to emphasize the struggles of the main protagonist of the story. Using analog, pencil-style technique in the 3D space, the work creates a unique combination of the well-optimized experience which perfectly fits the narrative. This approach brilliantly guides us through the narrative, enabling us to feel the story rather than merely being told about the family's struggles. The artistic style of the work, where objects suddenly appear or images jump from one scene to another seamlessly, aligns with the theme of fading memories, directing our focus towards the most poignant aspects of this journey.

F*ckai? (Famous)
Jordan Clarke

This ironic animation project uses a simple base idea of creating the most generic story by ChatGPT itself, but quickly turns into a magnificent journey of the struggling artist. Playing around meme culture and the most predictable evolution of the character together with clever comments on the appropriation of art historical images, Clarke shows his own excellence in animation and filmmaking.

I stitch my skin to the ground
Naomi Usami

Usami's work transcends traditional game design by using interactivity to spotlight the serious problem of sexual harassment in Japan's public spaces and its effect on the survivors. It uniquely portrays survivors' disconnection from their bodies, rendering visceral imagery of characters leaving their own skin. By defying conventional gameplay norms, users symbolically rebuild their avatars, evoking 'reparative play'—a psychoanalytic concept of empowerment amid trauma. The experience prompts users to confront uncomfortable truths and fosters collective understanding, healing, and renewal through its blend of unconventional gameplay and narrative.

ITERATIVE BODY SYNTHESIS
Michael Wallinger

ITERATIVE BODY SYNTHESIS is a technical project, a social experiment, and a work of art in itself. It explores the human form and what it means for a body to not only be beautiful, but even to be acceptable in our modern digital world, filled with photoshopped images of picture-perfect bodies. The project offers a critical commentary on the invisibility of certain body types in digital spaces, perpetuated by invisible black box algorithmic decisions that shape our media realities and, in turn, our perceptions of ourselves and those around us.

New Animation Art
Jury Statement

Mid Tide #3
Ryu Furusawa

Mid Tide #3 is a captivating installation that reimagines the concept of spacetime through an innovative visual lens, offering a meditative and visually striking exploration of temporal dimensions. This work challenges traditional linear narratives by presenting multiple cross-sections of time, continuously evolving and looping in a mesmerizing three-dimensional space. It is aesthetically beautiful and conceptually thought-provoking, encouraging viewers to consider how we navigate and understand the fabric of time. *Mid Tide #3* stands as a testament to the power of art to reshape our understanding of fundamental concepts.

No Se Van Los Que Se Aman
Matar a un Panda

This live performance project by the Chilean artist collective Matar a un Panda (Carla Redlich and Jean Didier) examines issues of individual and collective memory. It explores the experience of more than 1,200 detainees who passed through the Chacabuco concentration camp (a former mining town) in the Northern Chilean desert between 1973 and 1975 in the first years of the military dictatorship. Combining live movement, recorded bodies that are projection mapped onto architectural structures in the actual town with narrative testimonies of survivors, *No Se Van Los Que Se Aman* successfully employs minimal means to reflect on the brutality of political oppression in Pinochet-era Chile and its continued resonances within the next generation.

Random Acts of Flyness—Season 2, Episode 4—Fourth Dimension: Spacetime/bodyspirit
Kordae Henry

Fourth Dimension: Spacetime/bodyspirit is the fourth episode in the second season of the groundbreaking and unparalleled *Random Acts of Flyness* TV series. Created by renowned writer, director, and producer Terence Nance, we witness a poignant exploration into the beauty and complexities of contemporary American life. Leveraging advanced visual storytelling techniques, VFX-artist Kordae Henry (aka Tafa) creates captivating and surreal computer animations that reflect the narratives exploring space, time, and ancestral remedies. Within this animated segment, characters traverse life stages as water, vines, and the sea, connecting us through layers of dimensions.

Thank you for your souvenir, UK!
Los

The film explores the experience of a Chinese international student who spends a year in the UK and sheds light on the challenges of identity, belonging, and cultural displacement. The artist behind this personal film raises a crucial question of whether international students are being exploited as resources or are genuinely benefiting from the system. Although the film focuses on a specific narrative, it delves into broader themes of immigration and outsiderhood. By showcasing the struggle of identical closed-eyed ragdolls pushed through the system, the film urges viewers to examine the complexities of the system and its implications. The film's raw and honest portrayal will resonate with anyone who has ever felt like an outsider.

Unknown Label
Nicolas Gourault

Unknown Label captivated the jury with its innovative approach to documentary storytelling, seamlessly integrating animation as the core narrative medium and redefining the documentary film format. The animation is more than mere illustration, it is integrated as the very essence of its narrative; the documentary could not exist without it, and it is an exemplar for the New Animation Art category of Prix Ars Electronica. The film opens with a simple, single-color animation illustrating the process of segmentation, introducing viewers to the unseen individuals who label training data for AI vision systems. As the story delves deeper into the complexity of their work, social dynamics, and the discrimination faced by these workers, the animated visuals evolve in complexity as well. The narrative crescendos with a city-scale 3D data visualization, revealing the staggering amount of invisible human labor that goes into training our AI systems. The documentary navigates complex themes with clarity and empathy, elevating the discourse on AI ethics and globalization.

Smoke and Mirrors

Beatie Wolfe

Smoke and Mirrors uses art to communicate six decades of climate data, specifically rising methane levels, set alongside the verbatim advertising slogans deployed by the Big Oil industry to "Deny, Doubt and Delay" the climate data and awareness through the decades, e.g.

1970   "Out to clean the air" by Amoco/Standard Oil at 1351.7 ppb CH4

1984   "Lies they tell our children" by Mobil at 1644.9 ppb CH4

1991   "Doomsday is cancelled" by Informed Citizens for the Environment at 1724.8 ppb CH4

1993   "Apocalypse no" by Mobil at 1736.5 ppb CH4

2000   "Unsettled Science" by ExxonMobil at 1773.2 ppb CH4

2004   "Your Carbon Footprint" by BP at 1777.1 ppb CH4

2017   "Oil Pumps Life" by American Petroleum Institute at 1849.6 ppb CH4

2023   "Net-Zero" by Shell at 1911.8 ppb CH4

This evocative visualization, based on NASA's Blue Marble image and produced in collaboration with Parliament, is set to *Oh My Heart,* which was released as the world's first bioplastic record by Beatie Wolfe, Michael Stipe, and Brian Eno's Earth-Percent. *Smoke and Mirrors* follows Wolfe's multi-award winning CO_2 visualization, *From Green to Red,* which was unveiled at the Nobel Prize Summit and was the largest art piece at COP26. *Smoke and Mirrors* was influenced by the work of Geoffrey Supran and Naomi Oreskes and sources data from NOAA and the European Environment Agency.

Artist's Statement

I had the idea for *Smoke and Mirrors* a few years ago, after my CO_2 project *From Green to Red* came out, and I saw how effectively it helped people to see climate data differently and to absorb it via the power of art. Realizing that a crucial piece of the climate puzzle (how we got to this critical point) has been the fossil fuel industry's response to the emerging environmental awareness of the 1970s and that methane emissions (30 times more potent than carbon for trapping heat) are increasingly linked with that industry, I wanted to illuminate this key parallel timeline.

While *From Green to Red* visualized 800,000 years of rising CO_2 levels, *Smoke and Mirrors* focuses on fifty years of methane data set alongside the Big Oil advertising campaigns that were running during this critical period in human history. *Smoke and Mirrors* is about visualizing not just the methane data (smoke) in a way people can really absorb but also the disinformation campaign

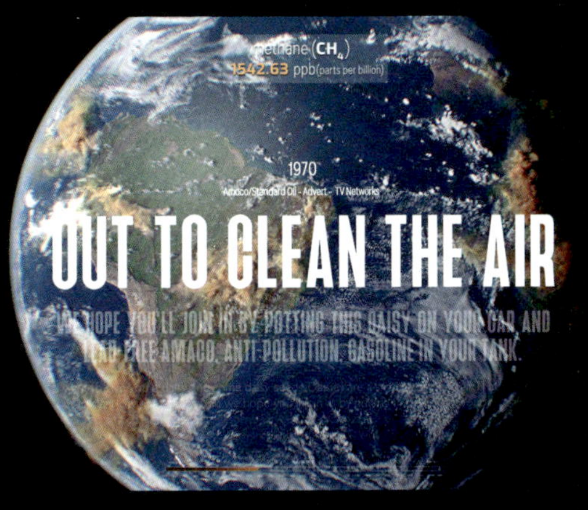

methane (CH₄)
1542.63 ppb (parts per billion)
1970
Amoco/Standard Oil - Advert - TV Networks
OUT TO CLEAN THE AIR

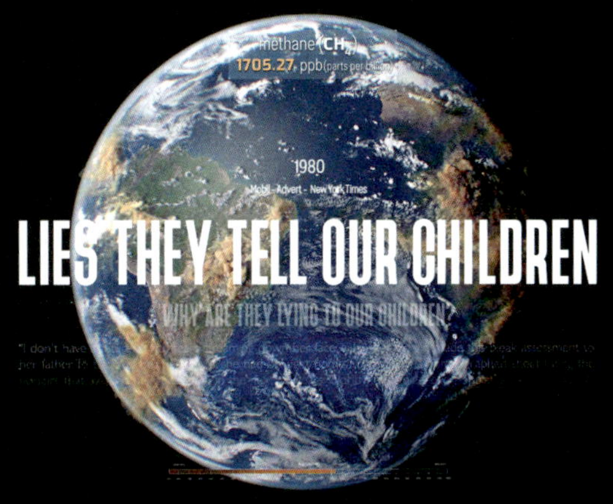

methane (CH₄)
1705.27 ppb (parts per billion)
1980
Mobil - Advert - New York Times
LIES THEY TELL OUR CHILDREN

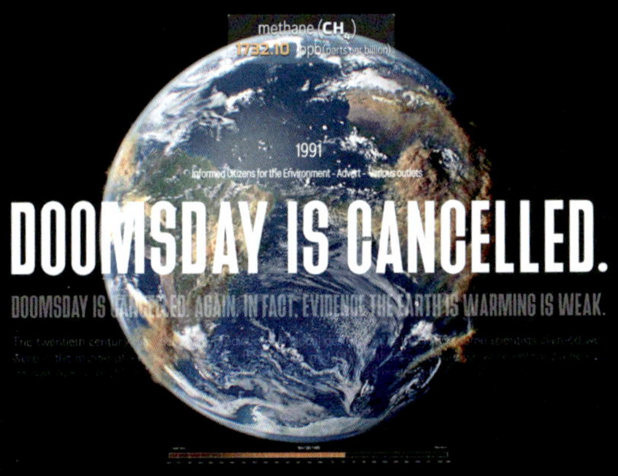

methane (CH₄)
1732.10 ppb (parts per billion)
1991
Informed Citizens for the Environment - Advert - Various outlets
DOOMSDAY IS CANCELLED.
DOOMSDAY IS CANCELLED. AGAIN. IN FACT, EVIDENCE THE EARTH IS WARMING IS WEAK.

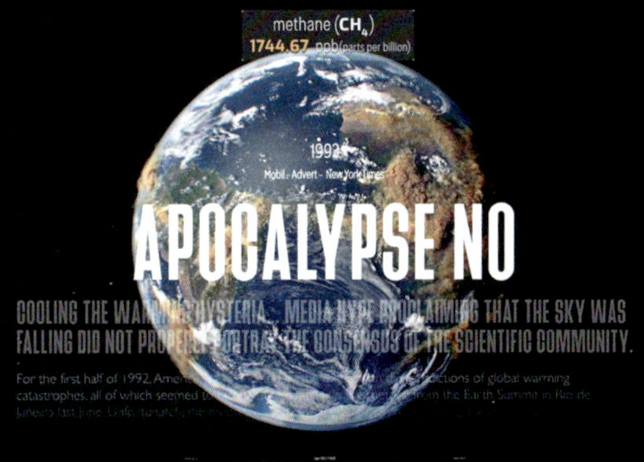

methane (CH₄)
1744.67 ppb (parts per billion)
1992
Mobil - Advert - New York Times
APOCALYPSE NO
COOLING THE WARMING HYSTERIA... MEDIA HYPE PROCLAIMING THAT THE SKY WAS FALLING DID NOT PROPERLY PORTRAY THE CONSENSUS OF THE SCIENTIFIC COMMUNITY.

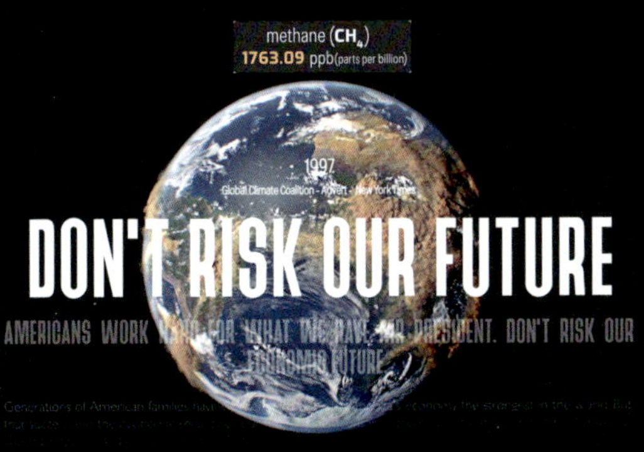

methane (CH₄)
1763.09 ppb (parts per billion)
1997
Global Climate Coalition - Advert - New York Times
DON'T RISK OUR FUTURE
AMERICANS WORK HARD FOR WHAT THEY HAVE, MR. PRESIDENT. DON'T RISK OUR ECONOMIC FUTURE.

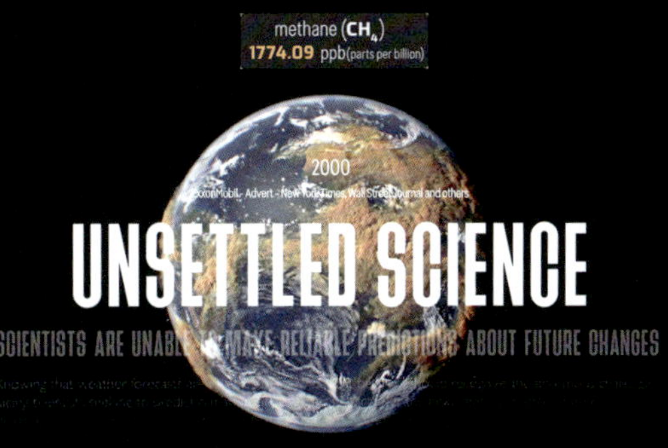

methane (CH₄)
1774.09 ppb (parts per billion)
2000
Exxon/Mobil - Advert - New York Times, Wall Street Journal and others
UNSETTLED SCIENCE
SCIENTISTS ARE UNABLE TO MAKE RELIABLE PREDICTIONS ABOUT FUTURE CHANGES

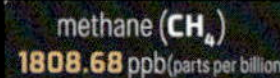

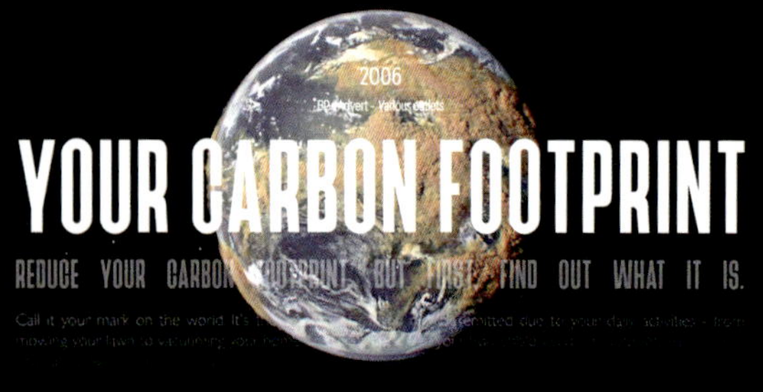

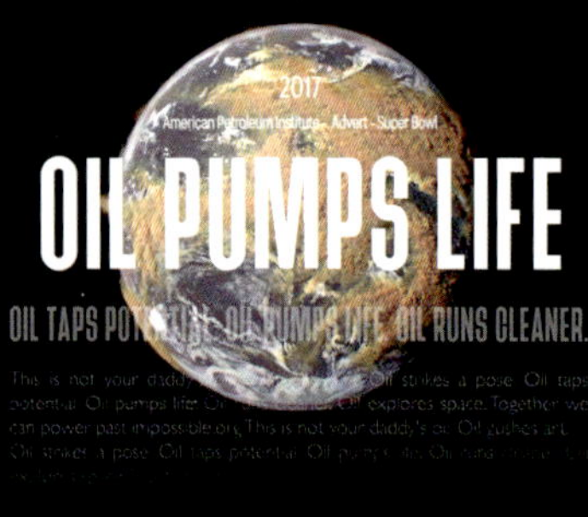

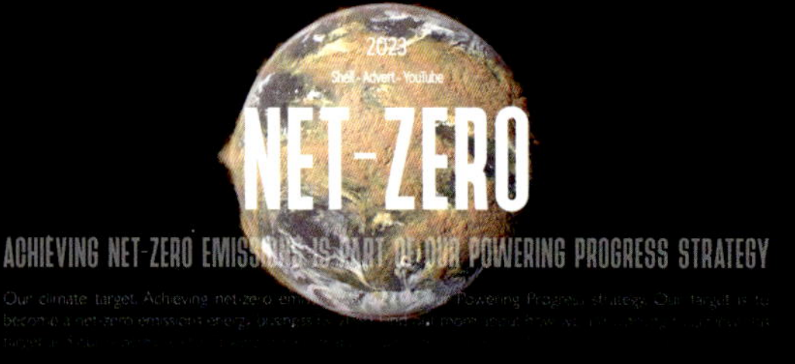

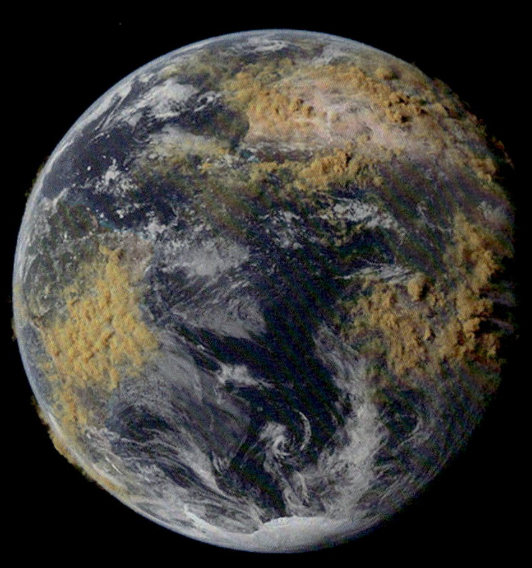

Advert - British Petroleum
- Various publications, 2006

YOUR CARBON FOOTPRINT

REDUCE YOUR CARBON FOOTPRINT. BUT FIRST, FIND OUT WHAT IT IS.

Call it your mark on the world. It's the amount of carbon dioxide emitted due to your daily activities - from mowing your lawn to vacuuming your home. Find out the size of your household's carbon footprint, learn how you can reduce it, and see how we're reducing ours at bp.com/carbonfootprint. It's a start. beyond petroleum. Amount of carbon dioxide emit (mirrors) that has caused the data to be denied, doubted, and delayed through the decades. *Smoke and Mirrors* begins in 1970, which was also the year we had our first 'Earth Day,' so I chose to base the visualization on the iconic and deeply embedded NASA Blue Marble photograph (taken in 1972) that allowed us to see our planet for the first time. This was a key point in our timeline for both emerging environmental awareness and the backlash against it.

Like *From Green to Red,* which was set to the song I wrote as a teenager after seeing *An Inconvenient Truth,* this visualization is set to a similarly inter-linked track, *Oh My Heart,* which was released as the world's first bioplastic record with the music in both cases helping to activate and humanize the data.

There was extensive research involved with building out this project, which stands apart from the video and is viewable on the website, including: compiling the ice core and atmospheric methane data along with the Big Oil advertising campaigns from 1970 until present day. It was then about choosing which campaigns to highlight to help illustrate the full spectrum of "Deny, Doubt and Delay" in just 4m30s.

Using Houdini's dynamic simulation and high-end rendering capabilities, *Smoke and Mirrors* employs detailed fluid and particle effects to map the methane data and its atmospheric flow to illustrate the emission's slow but inexorable spread across the decades. This project was rendered in a region using 100% renewable energy, one of the only data centers in the world that does this.

https://u.aec.at/943302DB

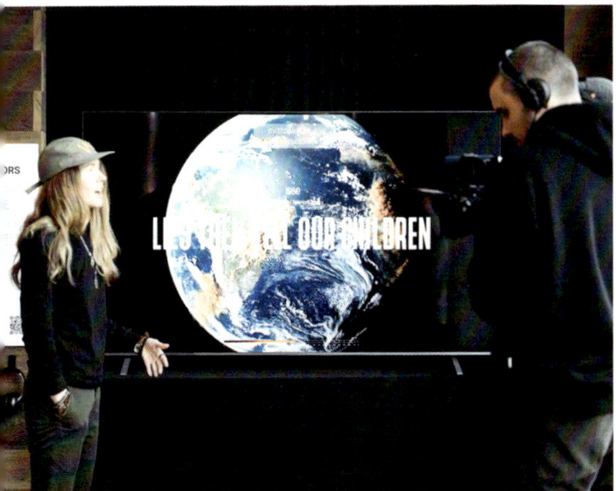

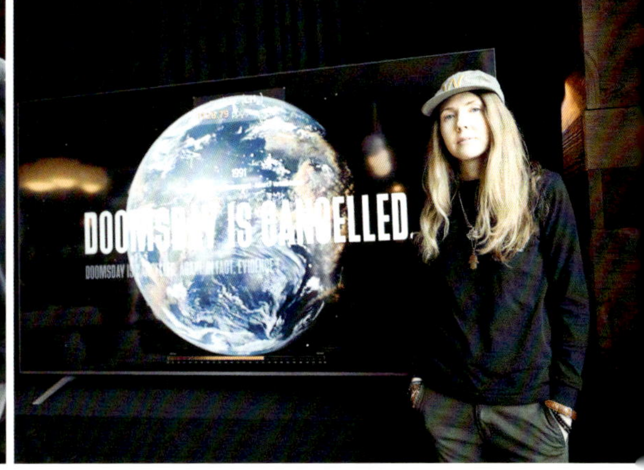

Beatie Wolfe (GB), "musical weirdo and visionary" *(VICE* magazine) has beamed her music into space, been appointed a UN role model for innovation, and held a solo exhibition of her 'world first' designs at the V&A Museum. Named by *WIRED* as one of "22 people changing the world," Wolfe is at the forefront of pioneering new formats that bridge the physical and digital. Wolfe's latest innovations include a visualization of 800,000 years of CO_2 data, which premiered at the Nobel Prize Summit, and a Brain Installation which was exhibited at the London Design Biennale in Somerset House. Other recent projects include the world's first bioplastic record with Michael Stipe and new work with Brian Eno. Wolfe is also the co-founder of a groundbreaking research project looking at the power of music for dementia.

I'm Feeling Lucky

Timothy Thomasson

I'm Feeling Lucky is a real-time computer-generated animation that questions relationships to image, geography, virtual space, historical media technology, and mass data collection systems. The work features a 3D virtual landscape that is both historically and geographically ambiguous, generated in real-time using game engine technology. This virtual landscape is then populated with thousands of figures sourced from the vast pool of 360-degree image data collected by Google Street View. These figures are processed through a deep neural network, so they become three-dimensional models in the virtual space, each frozen in their captured pose. The work interrogates mass image collection systems, as many of these individuals may not have been aware that their photo was taken by Google, let alone anticipate being placed in this new, strange setting. Many thousands of figures sourced from all over the world are randomly selected to inhabit the endless landscape together.

The work takes into consideration the panorama paintings of the 19th century as objects of historical, cultural, and perceptual significance, and situates them within contemporary media contexts. Panoramas are rotunda structures in which large 360 degree paintings depict sublime natural landscapes, battle scenes, religious events, or large cityscapes, characterized by their lack of framed boundaries and the inability to be viewed in their entirety with a single gaze. These panorama structures are theorized as part of the lineage of immersive media technologies and can be analyzed as proto-cinematic/virtual reality forms.

With *I'm Feeling Lucky,* the virtual environment is generated and populated procedurally, so the panoramic image becomes infinite as the virtual camera slowly pans across the landscape endlessly, portraying the stillness of painting at odds with the expectation of fast, high-speed movement and technical progression of digital imagery.

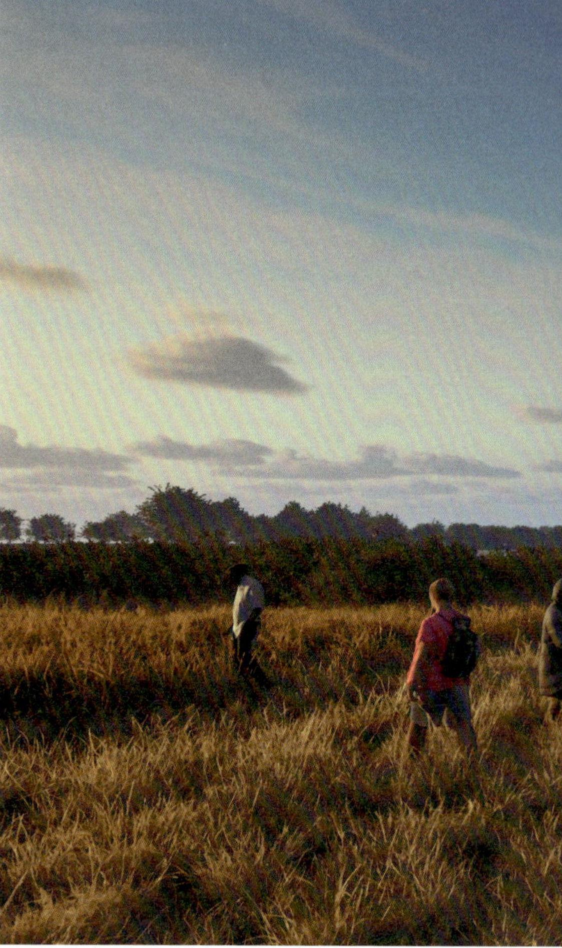

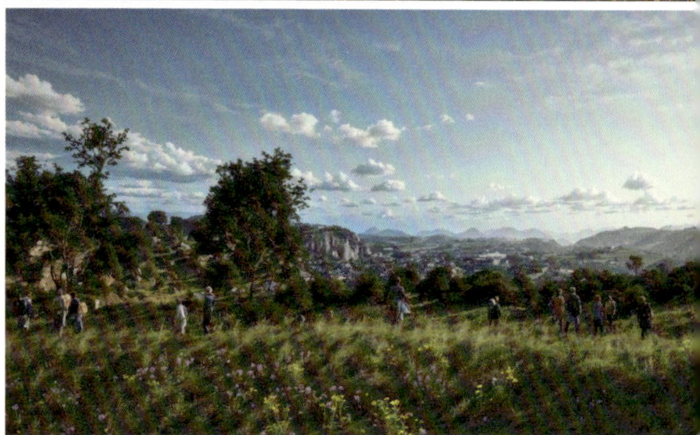

Sound design & composition: Tatum Wilson
With support from: Canada Council for the Arts,
Société des arts technologiques (SAT) Residency
Program, Canadian Cultural Center Paris

https://u.aec.at/D029590C

**New Animation Art
Award of Distinction**

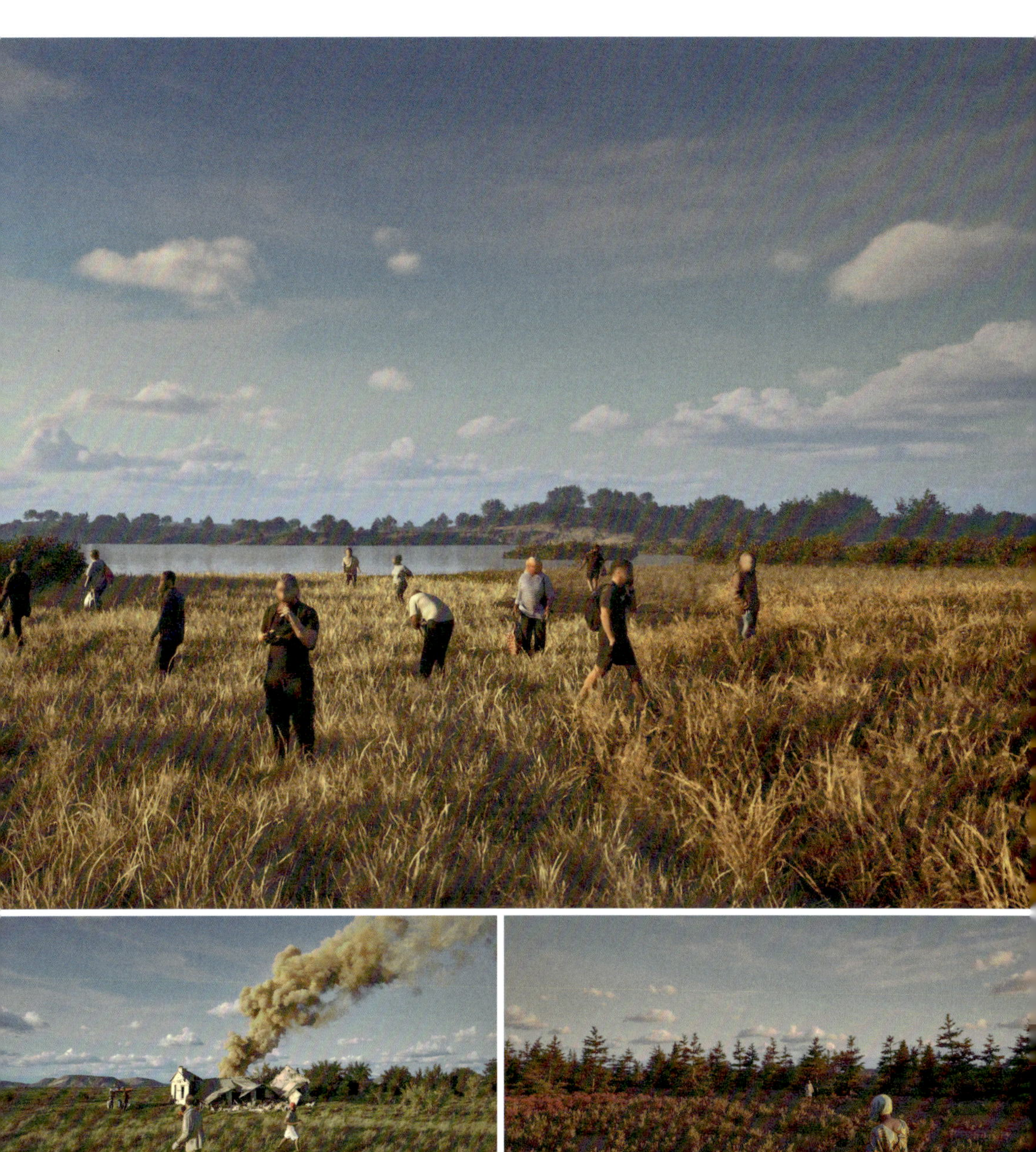

Timothy Thomasson (CA) is a Montreal-based artist. His work questions the ways in which moving images are produced and consumed in historical and contemporary contexts, looking particularly at the effects of computer-generated images and emerging technologies on society, culture, aesthetics, and perception. His work has been exhibited at numerous galleries and media festivals internationally.

Stained

Jeremy Kamal

"Blood in the soil, blood in the leaves. Blood in the pollen, blood in the seeds. May the red wash all and leave no blue. We stay true to the crimson hue."

Bump (The Crimson Oath)

Stained, a CGI short film is one of a series of 3D animations depicting a future where America's landscapes are transformed by Black culture. The film follows a sensitive tea master named Demetrius, a member of the Crimson Needles gang that uses colored flora to mark territory. Haunted by the voice of his elder, O.G. Bump, Demetrius relives the memory of being reprimanded for his fascination with a blue plant; forbidden by the red gang to which he belongs. Based in a world where symbiotic relationships with technology allow Black Americans to transform "natural" and synthetic environments, the film is a small glimpse into the intimate life of one of its many inhabitants. *Stained* imagines an alternative ecology that foregrounds underexplored narratives. It re-frames gang culture as a landscape phenomenon and recasts those affiliated as environmental caretakers and tea makers.

The film takes place in the narrative world of Mojo, a fictional future I created as a way of bridging the disparities between the contemporary Black experience and landscape discourse. It is a response to my experience in landscape architecture where we were taught to see, study, and interpret landscapes from a limited point of view. It embraces the friction and harmony that emerges when green agendas (climate activism, environmentalism, ecological study) and contemporary Black experience collide. In their collision, I mine for new rituals, mythologies, and landscapes that challenge our conventional understanding of "nature" and space.

Created by Jeremy Kamal
Music: Nathan Buttel & Jeremy Kamal
AI creative direction: Case Miller
Additional AI work: Jonathan Penvose

https://u.aec.at/1720F126

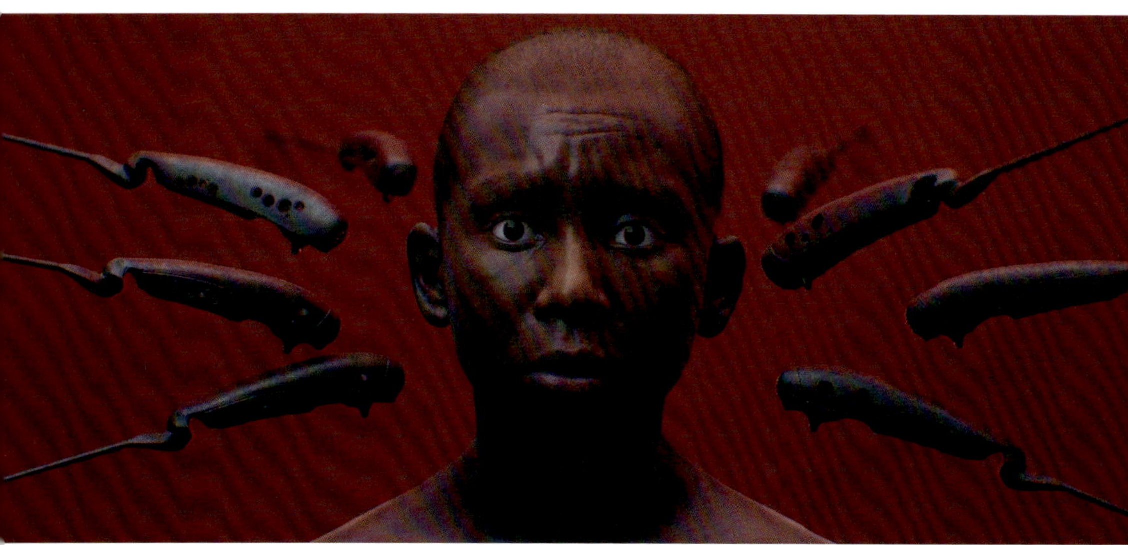

**New Animation Art
Award of Distinction**

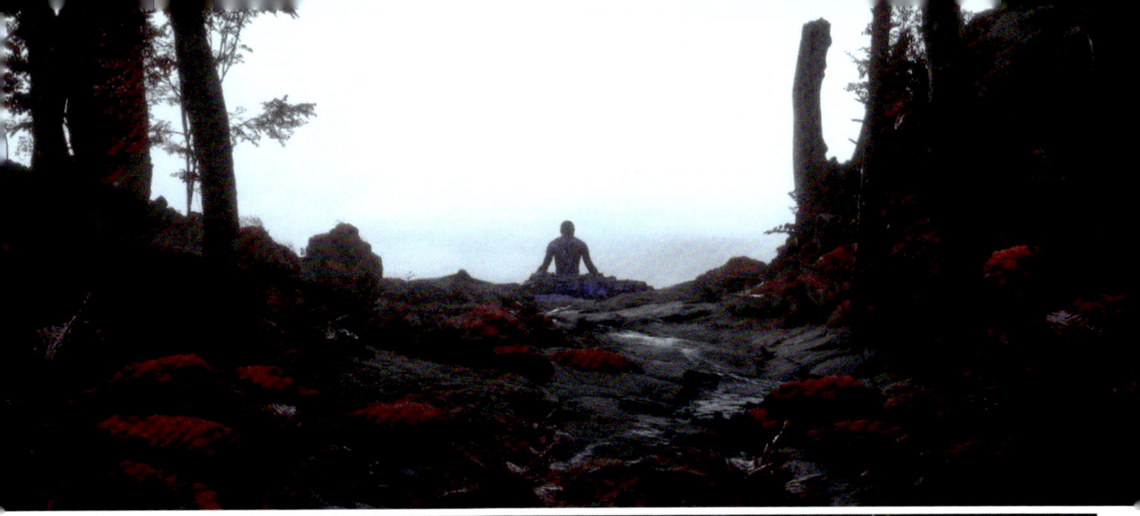

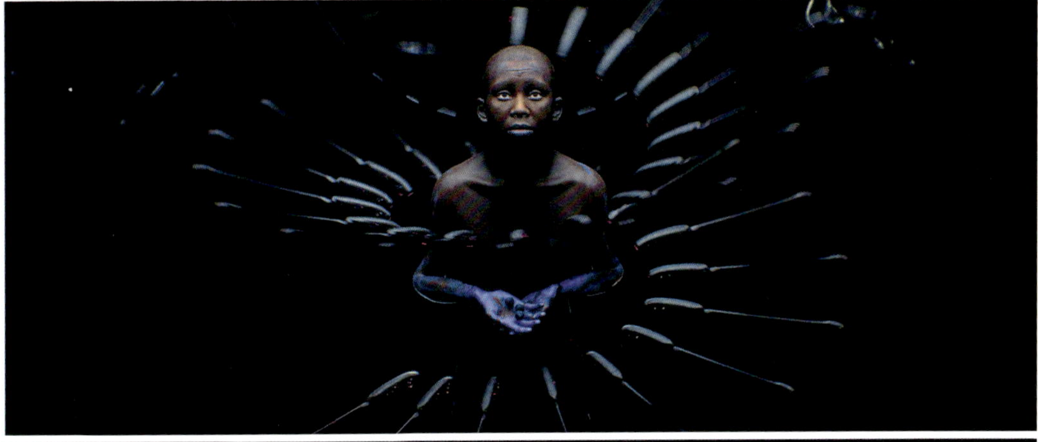

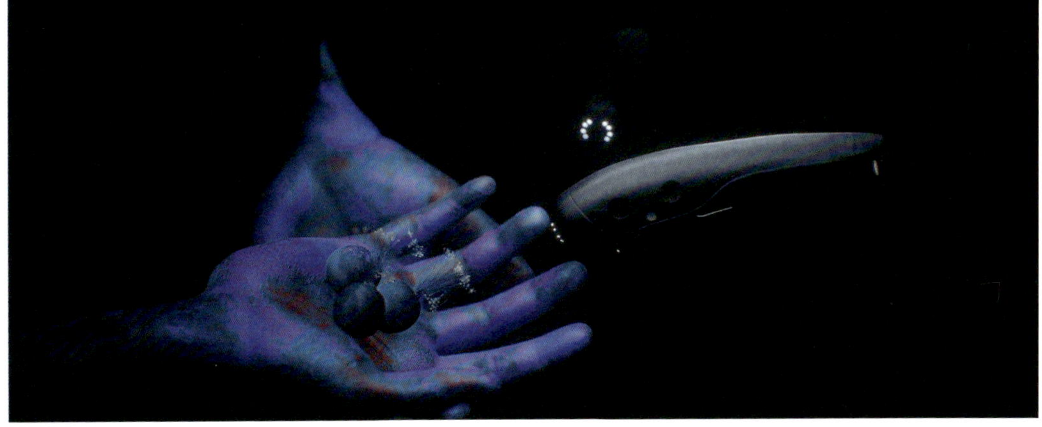

Jeremy Kamal (US) is a filmmaker and game developer creating speculative landscape mythologies through animation, sound, and video games. His geomyths explore the rituals, technologies, and ecologies that emerge when overlooked cultural values shape landscapes. Combining the design rigor of landscape architecture with the accessibility of pop culture, his 3D environments host speculative narratives that introduce landscape discourse to a broader audience. He is an Onassis ONX fellow and design faculty at the Southern California Institute of Architecture. As a freelance 3D generalist, he has collaborated on projects for Marine Serre, The North Face, Gucci, Trippie Redd, Yo Gotti, and Lil Miquela.

ATUA
FAFSWAG

ATUA reimagines the realm of Pacific gods in this new sculptural AR experience, claiming space for gender diverse identities impacted by colonial first contact and creating an intimate portal for users to see themselves reflected as vital to their pan Pacific cultural heritage and an intrinsic part of the cosmos. Become immersed in an expansive tale of time and space, in this intimate user experience that reframes Pacific cosmology through a Queer Indigenous lens.

Enabled through IOS devices, the *ATUA* experience begins with Te Kore—the Void, a space of abundance and limitless potential. Activated through the power of Augmented Reality, you can witness Te Kore being manifested into a physical form as a cosmic being, forged from ancestral memory and adorned in cultural navigation.

The digital sculpture is composed of a physical or digital pou (landmark), from which an Augmented Reality deity leaps when viewed through handheld devices. Designed to be used in a museum-based setting, we needed to be able to orient the Augmented Reality system without being 'set up' each time. We implemented a hybrid approach of image and world-based tracking so that each viewer perceives the right orientation of the experience, regardless of which angle the pou is being viewed from.

Cultural Context

"Atua" is a term that derives from the pan-Pacific pantheon and shared elemental, spiritual, cultural, and ethereal gods that make up and occupy the cosmos and Pulotu—the underworld. These forces, and sometimes beings, are considered our ancient gods. In some cultures, colonial contact played a significant role in erasing some of these cultural knowledge systems, and they were often mythologized throughout the course of human history and dismissed as pagan belief systems. However, in recent years the practice of decolonization has inspired Indigenous folk to reclaim these systems and their old gods.

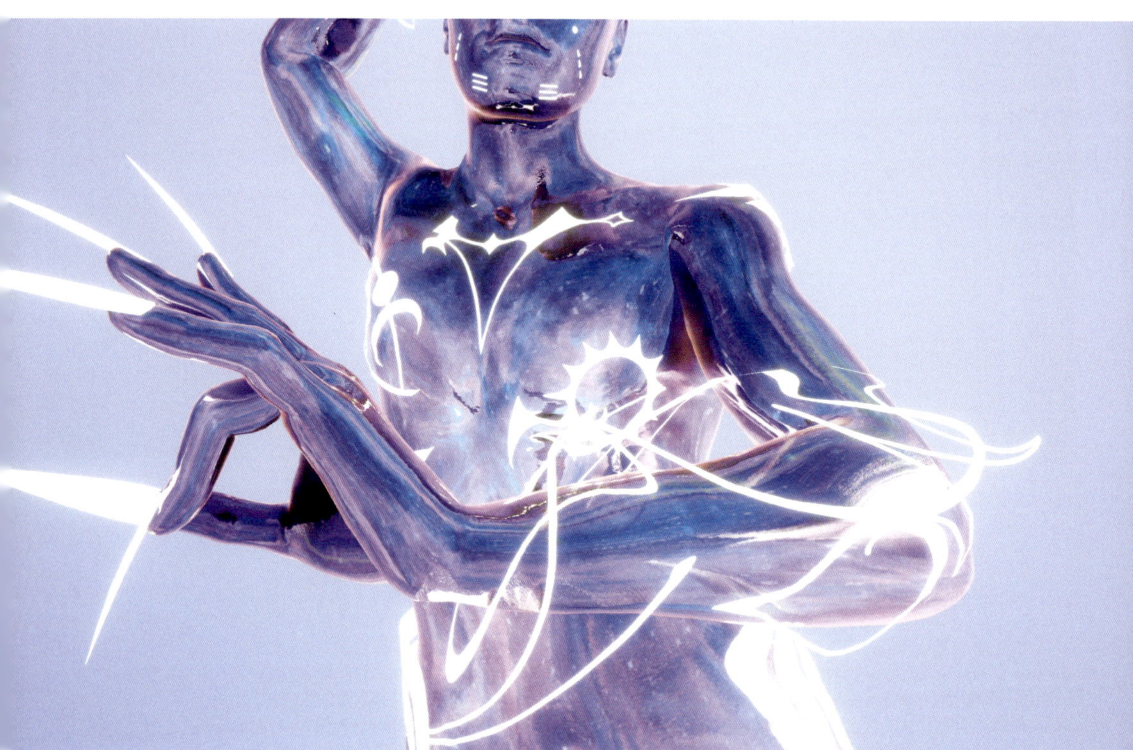

**New Animation Art
Honorary Mention**

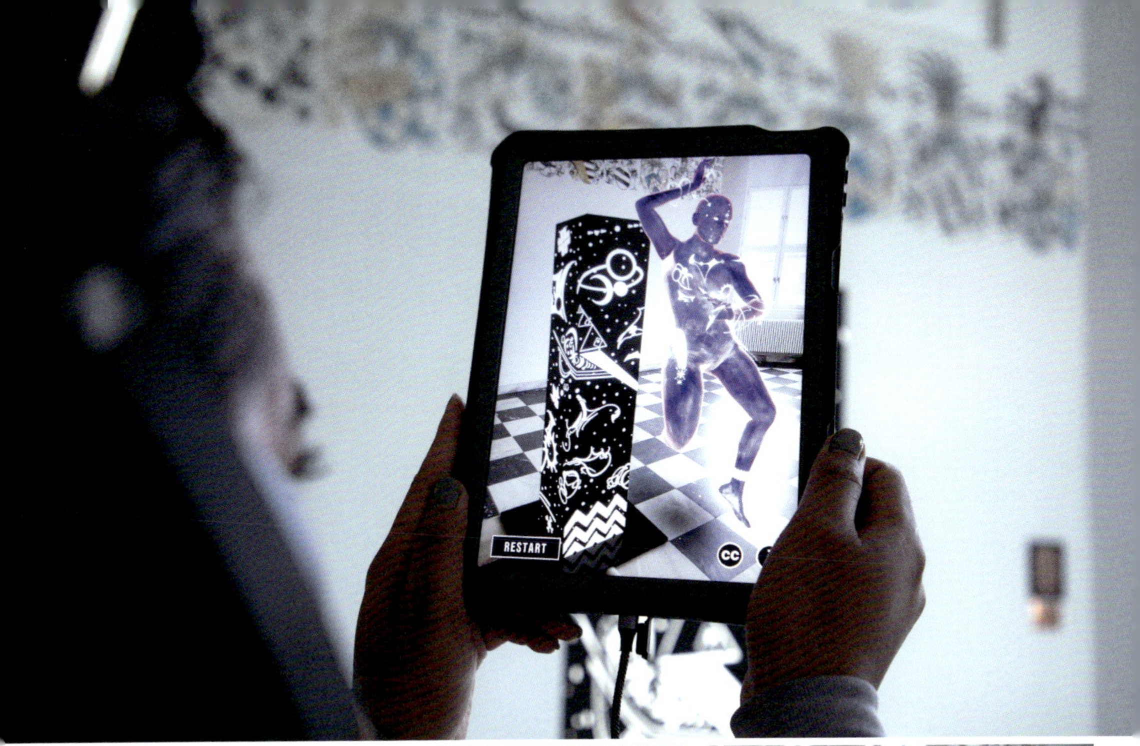

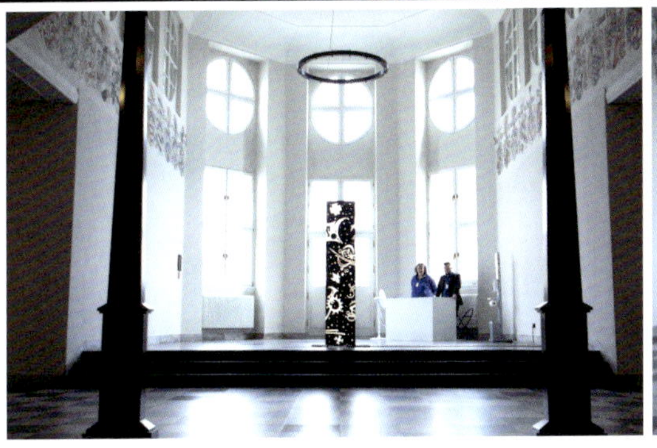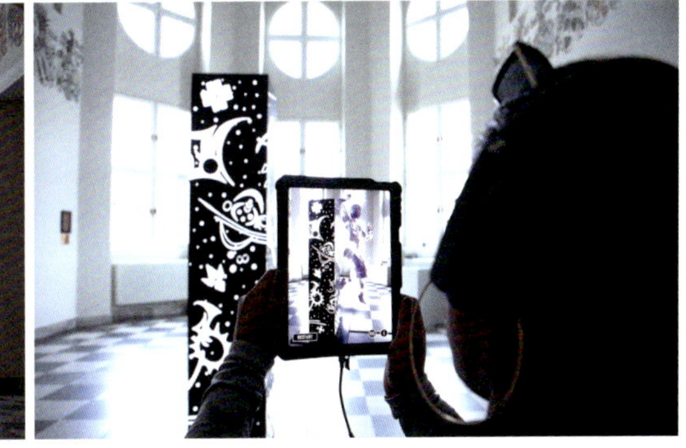

Lead artists: Tanu Gago, Māhia Jermaine Dean
Key collaborators: Kat Lintott, Carthew Neal,
Nacoya Anderson
Voice artist: Nathaniel Lees
Creative collective: FAFSWAG
Skin markings designers: Tanu Gago, Māhia Jermaine
Dean, Pati Solomona Tyrell, Jaimie Waititi
Production company: Piki Films
Interactive development: Wrestler
Interactive producer: Ben Dunn
Interactive artists: Jeff Jones, Tim Crossley,
Stan Brown, Imery Watson, Chris Ward, Eugene Park
Pou creator: Kereama Taepa

This work was created by artists Tanu Gago of
FAFSWAG Arts Collective with support from Piki films,
Wrestler studio, and the New Zealand Film Commission.
It premiered in 2022 at the Sundance International Film
Festival. Developed in association with the New Zealand
Film Commission's Interactive Development Fund.

https://u.aec.at/4C61969F

FAFSWAG (NZ) (Tanu Gago) is an interdisciplinary artist, queer activist, filmmaker, and Member of the New Zealand Order of Merit for services to Pacific arts and the LGBTQIA+ community. Gago was a Samoan immigrant who was raised in South Auckland and is co-founder of the Queer Indigenous Arts Collective FAFSWAG, working at the intersections of film, Queer activism, moving image, animation and AR interactivity. Gago has exhibited globally and won awards—2020 Arts Foundation Laureate and CNZ Pacific Arts Contemporary Artist recipient, and the 2022 McCahon House artist in residence. In 2022, along with FAFSWAG, Gago presented Alteration, a mixed media exhibition in Kassel, Germany as part of Documenta 15, and will feature new works at MIF 2025.

Chuly? Chuly /
Чули? Чули

Letta Shtohryn

The project *Чули? Чули* (Chuly? Chuly), translating from Ukrainian as "Have you heard? We've heard/ Have you felt it? We've felt it", merges performative video gameplay with choreography to delve into manipulative narratives and the embodiment of online personas. It engages with narratives shaped by human-led troll farms and AI, anchored in a speculative story from a woman who once saw giants. Her narrative, twisted by ChatGPT to reflect online misinformation tactics, indirectly guides the player through the environment, yet never reveals the discussed cave and giants. This work looks at today's giants—enormous, planetary, interconnected, and mostly invisible entities; AGIs, pandemics, secret weapons, and disinformation itself; some engineered and run by humans, others self-materializing, shapeshifting.

By setting expectations for perfection with AAA-game-like realistic worlds, the project intentionally subverts these expectations by working with the limitations of inertial motion capture suits. The susceptibility of these suits to electromagnetic interference becomes a core part of the choreography. The dancer's movements, distorted by the suit's gradual calibration loss, create choreography that embraces digital imperfection, disentangling the digital persona from its body, and exploring errors as part of liveness.

Eventually, the dancer and player exchange the motion capture suit band for a game controller, inverting their roles. Now the player becomes a calibrated Non-Player Character, even though the rest of the MoCap body is left behind, while the dancer takes control of the world camera. This purposeful acceptance of technological imperfections blurs the distinctions between player, performer, and NPC, crafting a complex narrative that encourages reflection on the intricacies of XR entanglement, roles, identity, and the portrayal of the digital self online.

Concept, CGI, environment, avatars, animation, motion capture, environment sound: Letta Shtohryn
Player, performer, dramaturg: Julie-Michele Morin
Choreography, dance: Junjian Wang
Voice narration: Emma Beard
Text/voice processing: ChatGPT, 11Labs
Sound: Lena Horse, Junjian Wang, Letta Shtohryn
3D models of life forms, rocks and meteorites: Natural History Museum Vienna
Conceptualization, prototype at IT:U x Ars Electronica FOUNDING LAB
Dramaturgy, choreography at Realities in Transition residency at iMaL Brussels

https://u.aec.at/85CBB537

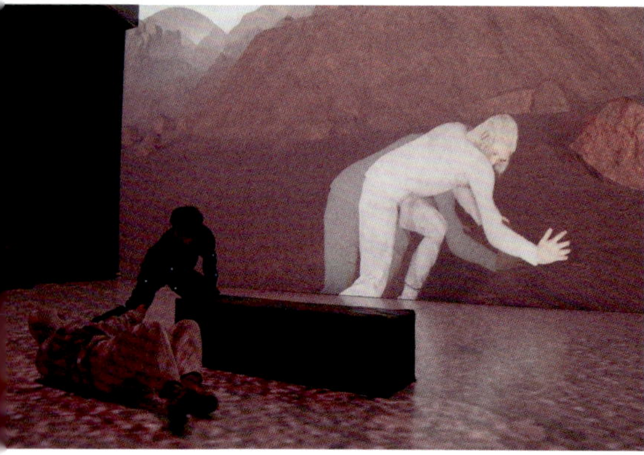

NINC Media

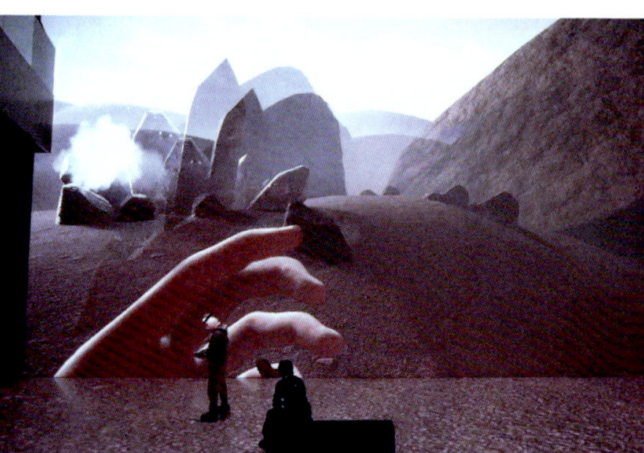

New Animation Art
Honorary Mention

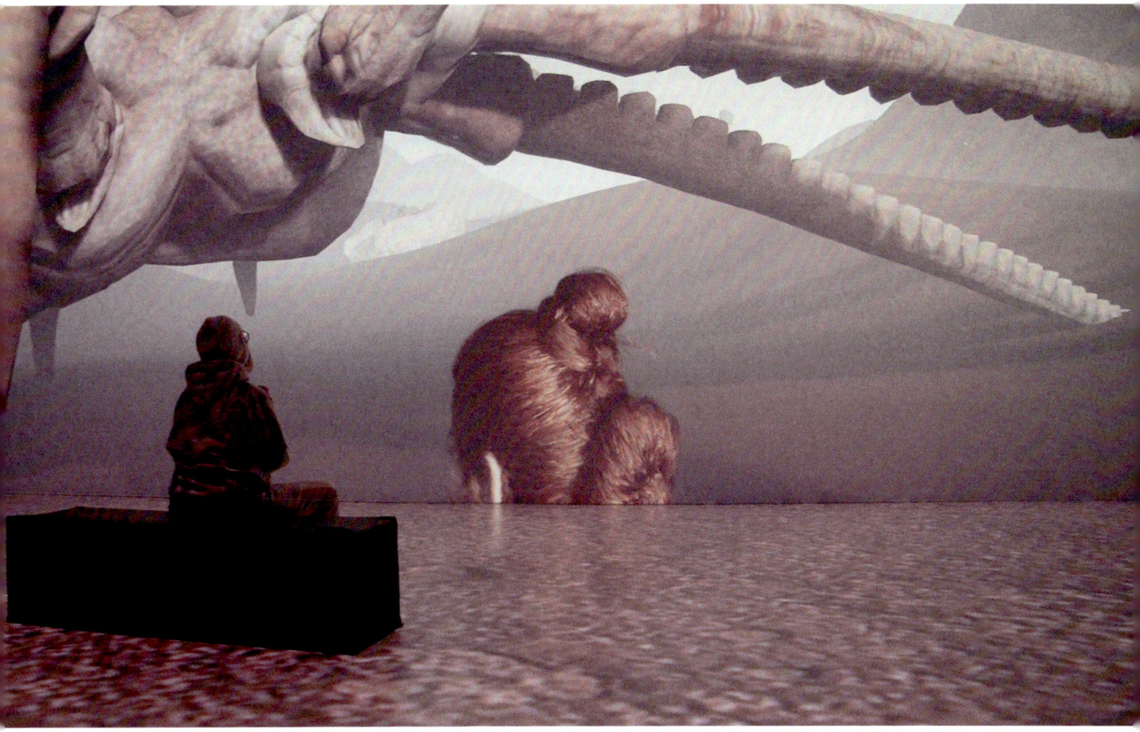

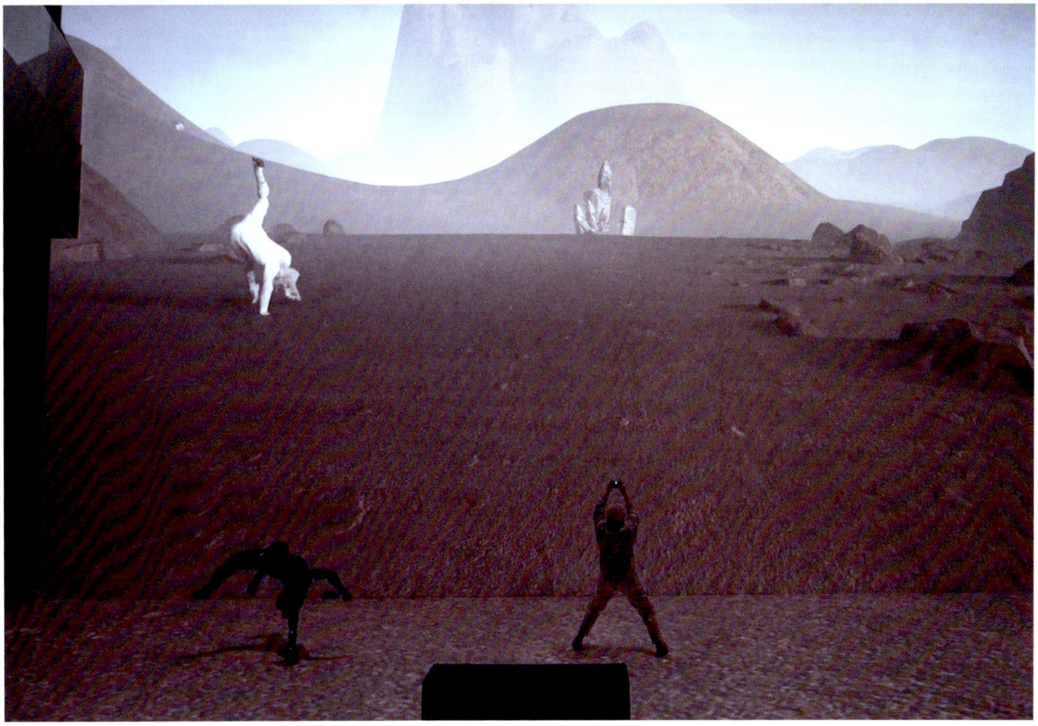

Letta Shtohryn (UA/EU) works with XR, CGI, MoCap, machinima, and video games. Her academic background is in philosophy and media art. Through a post-humanist perspective, she explores notions of embodiment with avatars, aliens, monsters, and ghosts. Since her MoCap Streamer residency at Goldsmiths, University of London in 2022, Letta has been working with Motion Capture systems. Her works have been showcased at Ars Electronica Festival (AT), Goldsmiths University of London (UK), Centre Pompidou (FR), Milan Machinima Festival (IT), Frieze Art Fair (NYC), among others.

DUCK
Rachel Maclean

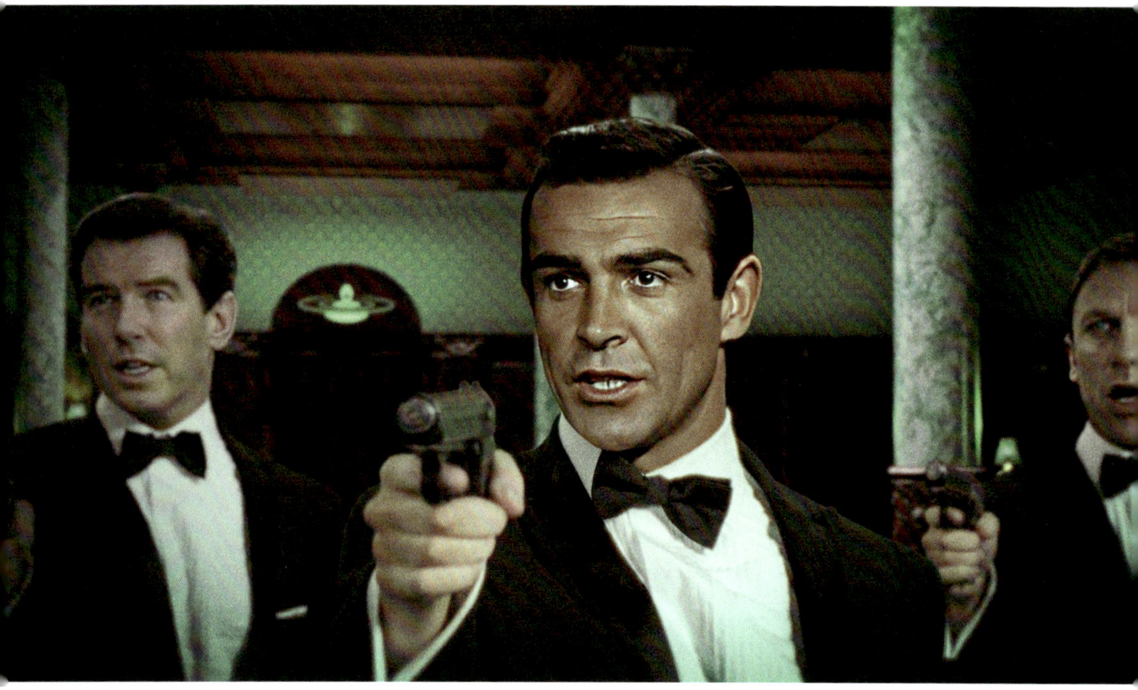

DUCK is a daring deepfake short set in the instantly recognizable world of a British Spy Thriller. The film's main protagonist—a deepfake Sean Connery—plays out the role he knows all too well: collecting clues, wrongfooting assailants, and eliminating the femme fatale—only to find that all is not what it seems. A conspiracy is at play, and as the behaviors of those around him become increasingly paradoxical, his grip on reality loosens.

Marilyn Monroe is the glamorous siren and a thorn in Connery's side. Unlike him, Monroe understands the power that comes with being just an image—an appropriation of femininity and sexuality largely defined by men—and uses her endlessly mutable image for her own manipulative gain.

Like many of Maclean's films, *DUCK* explores the fragility and malleability of identity, the slipperiness of reality, and the ramifications of gender-based power dynamics. Deepfake, a technology considered to be inherently duplicitous, is the perfect mechanism by which to pose questions not just about AI, but about how veracity is perceived in images and film more generally.

Maclean's *DUCK* is a multifaceted, self-aware film that aims to satirize some of the more histrionic narratives pushed by the media regarding deepfakes and their contribution to the 'decline of truth'.

DUCK was directed and written by Rachel Maclean and jointly produced by Forest of Black and Too Happy Studios. The film was shot entirely on green screen and funded by Newcastle University through a NUAcT Research Scholarship with additional support from Edinburgh University's Creative Informatics Department.

Director: Rachel Maclean
Writer: Rachel Maclean
Cast: Rachel Maclean
Producer: Beth Allan from Forest of Black
Producer: Ciara Dunne from Too Happy Studios
Director of photography: Jamie Quantrill
Editor: Ciaran Lyons
Composer: Julian Corrie
Sound designer: William Aikman

https://u.aec.at/E329A710

**New Animation Art
Honorary Mention**

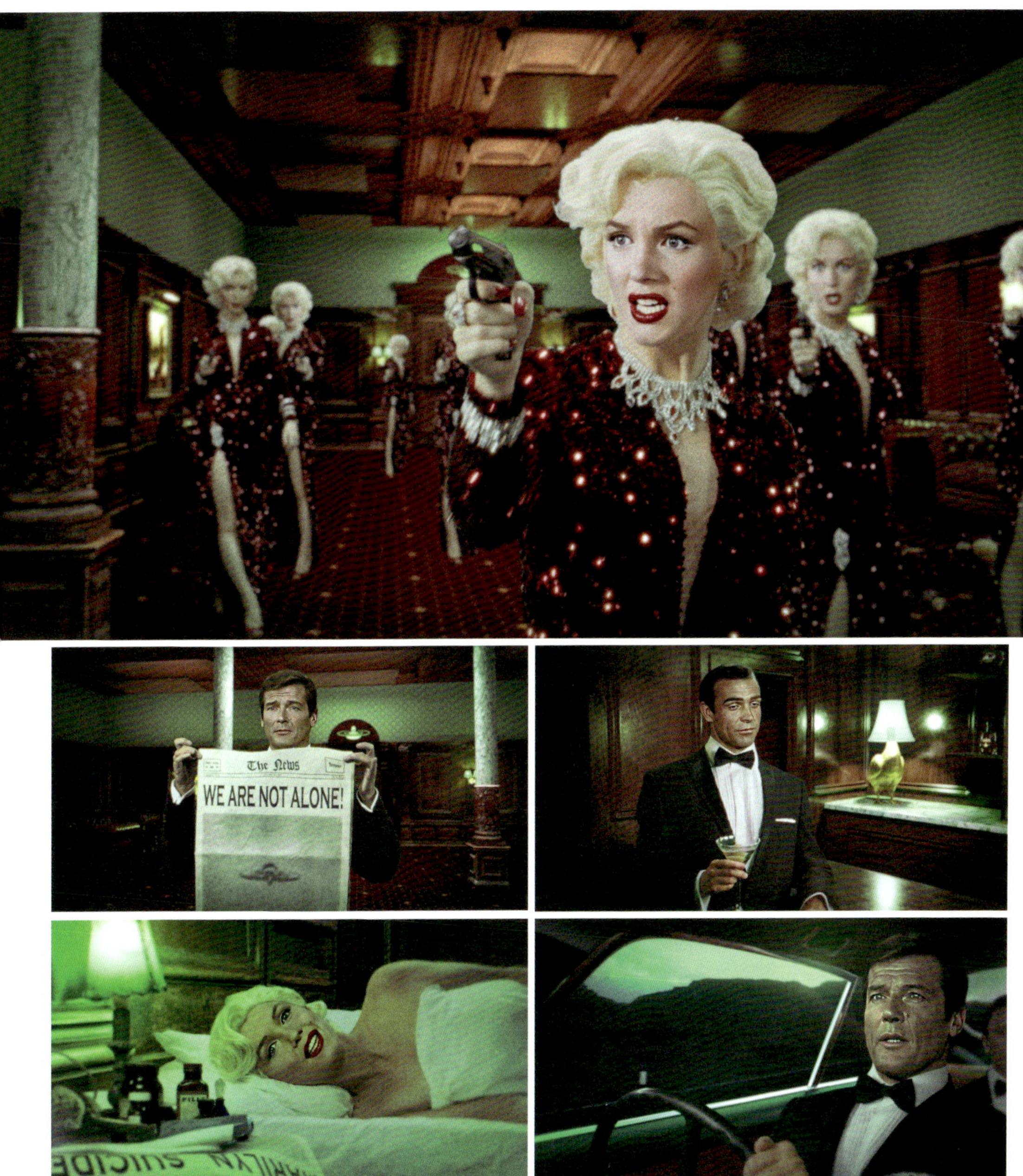

Rachel Maclean (GB) is an established artist and filmmaker whose films have shown widely in galleries, museums, film festivals, and on television. She has screened work at numerous festivals in the UK and internationally such as IFFR, Fantasia and BFI London Film Festival. In 2017 she represented Scotland at Venice Biennale with her film *Spite Your Face*. Her work *A Whole New World* (2014) won the prestigious Margaret Tate Award in 2013. She has twice been shortlisted for the Jarman Award, and achieved widespread critical praise for *Feed Me* at the British Art Show in 2016.

EMPEROR
Marion Burger, Ilan J. Cohen

EMPEROR is an interactive and narrative experience in virtual reality, which invites the user to travel inside the brain of a father who is suffering from aphasia. It is the story of a man who's lost his ability to speak, and of the daughter trying to communicate with him. It is the story of a woman, who wasn't given the chance to know the man behind her father, now obscured by this illness. As she tries to piece together what remains of his language, she discovers that his relationship to words is connected to his memories. The memories of an entire lifetime... Step by step, clue after clue, we will dive alongside her into the inner world of this man, in an attempt to decipher the story he can no longer tell us.

In a monochrome aesthetic, close to traditional animation, this personal story is told as a journey with surreal overtones, offering to explore aphasia as a distant country. *EMPEROR* is a poetic experience of the loss of one's faculties, of the passing of time, and of the bonds which, through it all, remain.

Directors' Statement

EMPEROR is based on a true story—the story of Marion's father, who has been suffering from aphasia for the past fifteen years. He confuses words, and stumbles over each syllable. He understands everything, but can no longer make himself understood.

More than the medical aspect of his condition, she was interested in the poetry of some of the absurd situations which she had sometimes encountered. One day she found herself comparing aphasia to a distant country. She could see him lost in this faraway land, trying to find his bearings, attempting to be understood. This idea helped her imagine his distress, and a bridge to try to reach him. But in order to grasp what he was trying to say, she'd have to delve into the man he had once been.

EMPEROR is at once a deeply personal story, and a universal reminder of the frail threads which keep us tethered to one another.

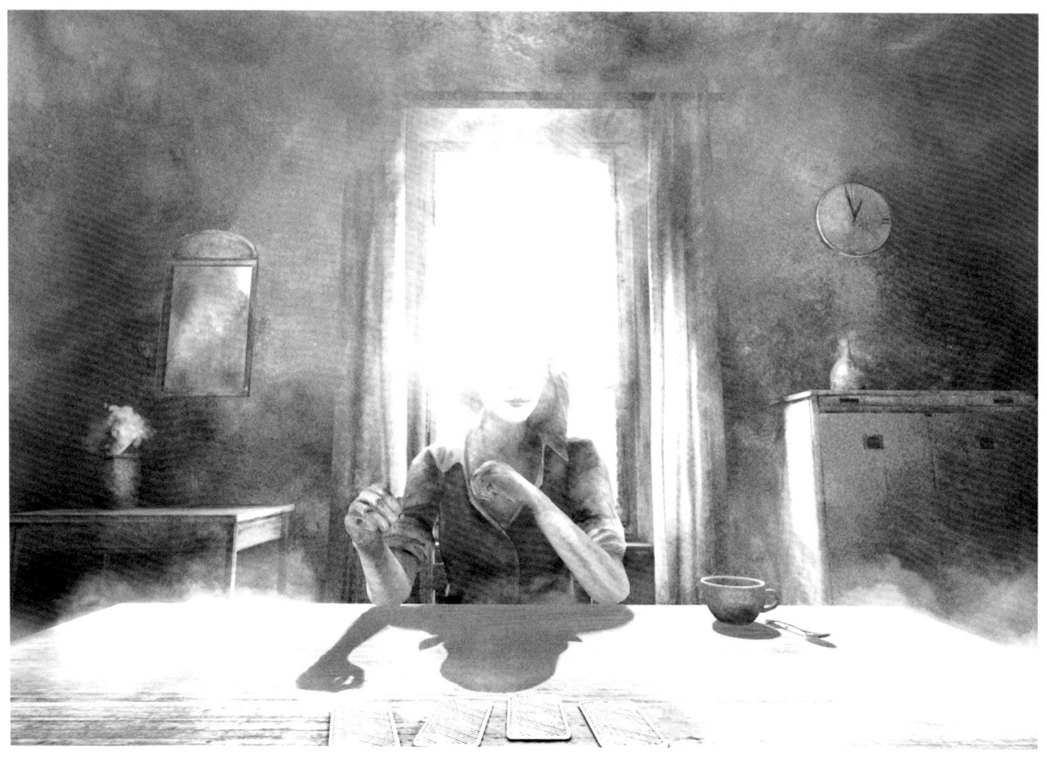

**New Animation Art
Honorary Mention**

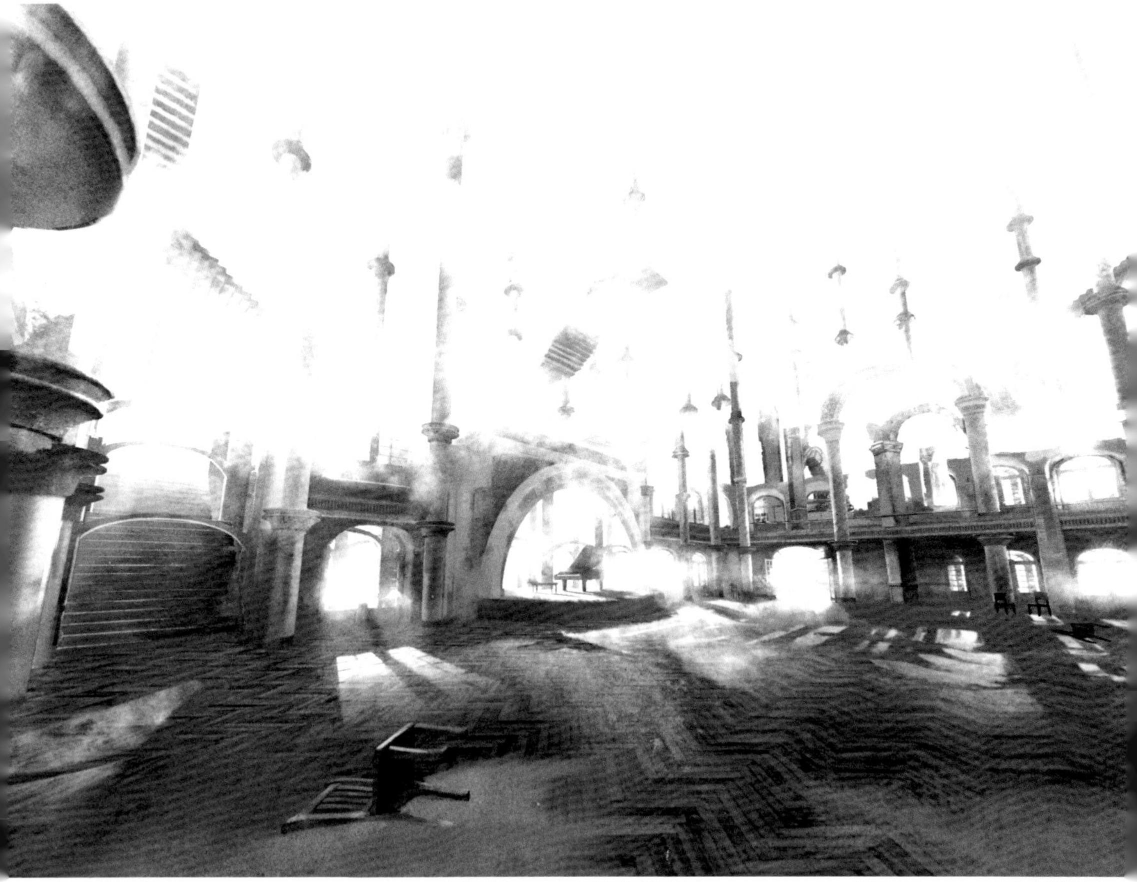

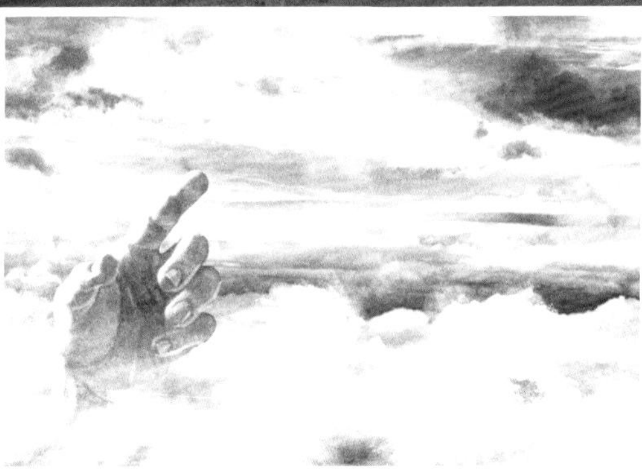

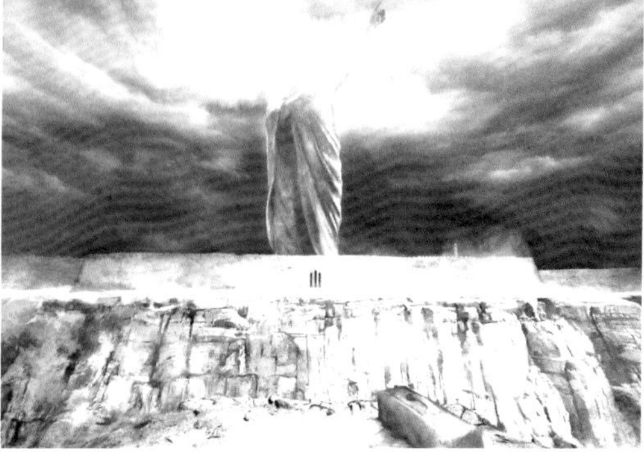

Direction: Marion Burger, Ilan J. Cohen
Production: Oriane Hurard (Atlas V),
Katharina Weser (Reynard Films),
Jeanne Marchalot (France Télévisions)

https://u.aec.at/945F5175

Marion Burger (FR) (*1987) is a production designer, who has worked on several feature films including *Divines* by Houda Benyamina (Caméra d'or 2016), *Gagarine* by Jérémy Trouilh and Fanny Liatard (Cannes 2020), and *Mother and Son* by Léonor Serraille (Cannes 2022), for which she was awarded the Young Film Technician Prize. Based on her personal story, *EMPEROR* marks her directorial debut. **Ilan J. Cohen** (FR) (*1984) has been working as a first assistant director since 2008 (including Noaz Deshe's *White Shadow*, Lodge Kerrigan's *Rebecca H.*, and Bertrand Bonello's *Sarah Winchester*) while pursuing his own screenwriting and directing music videos (Rone, Gaspar Claus).

F*ckai? (Famous)

Jordan Clarke

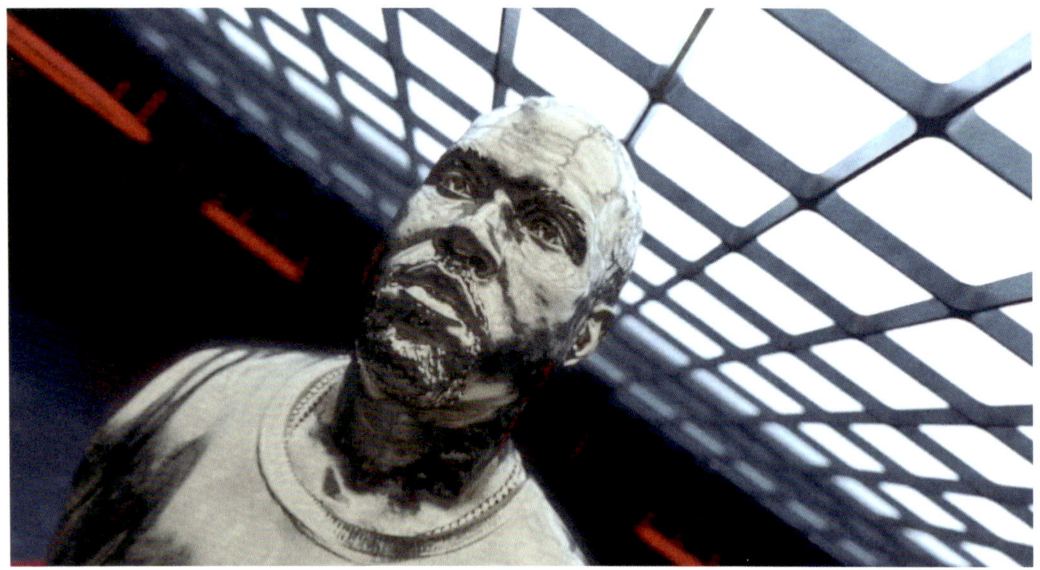

Interview first published: https://www.stashmedia.tv/jordan-clarke-meets-an-ai-who-wants-to-be-famous/

Jordan Clarke:

This is a story about an A.I. that wanted to be famous, also written and performed by an A.I. (paraphrased and edited by a human) and visualized by a human (me), flipping the norm of what we see in the AI-driven art world today.

I knew from the start that I wanted complete control over absolutely everything, which meant doing everything myself from the writing/prompting to all the animation and compositing, as well as the sound and editing.

I feel like, until recently, this unilateral control would not have been possible. However, the tools (both AI and traditional) are getting to the point where a single person is now able to achieve what only a team and render farm could have just a few years ago.

On top of this, my budget was minimal and my timeframe was somewhat limited as my subject matter was very current and I wanted to get this project made and out within a couple of months so that it was still a part of the *zeitgeist.*

A lot of people in the creative field are worried about the effect that AI will have, but I feel it will allow more individuals to create exactly what is in their head without a budget or the need to hire a team. I think it's very exciting.

From a technical perspective, the resources and tutorials online allowed me to achieve exactly what I wanted for each shot and corresponding script. If you type 'how to make a person crumble into particles' into YouTube, you will find a Houdini tutorial for it. This is why I suggest learning at least a bit of Houdini, as it can literally make almost anything you envision possible.

Another technique that I found super useful was editing in DaVinci Resolve before even starting the project. I take my story and type it out in text blocks as shots in Resolve. I then start editing the written work to the music.

From there I start blocking out shots in Cinema 4D with basic mocap and replacing the written words in Resolve. I'm basically editing the video throughout the entire animation and design process.

I think being the editor and the writer, as well as an animator and 3D artist, is a huge advantage as it allows me to take advantage of little gems and new techniques I find while working in Cinema 4D along the way and incorporate them into the story. This would not be possible in the same way if I was working with a team.

A lot of people in the creative field are worried about the effect that AI will have, but I feel it will allow more individuals to create exactly what is in their head without a budget or the need to hire a team. I think it's very exciting.

Written, directed, animated: by Jordan Clarke
NFT bro: Adam Kirschner
Music: Des Hume
Special thanks: Amie Bennett

https://u.aec.at/794D8445

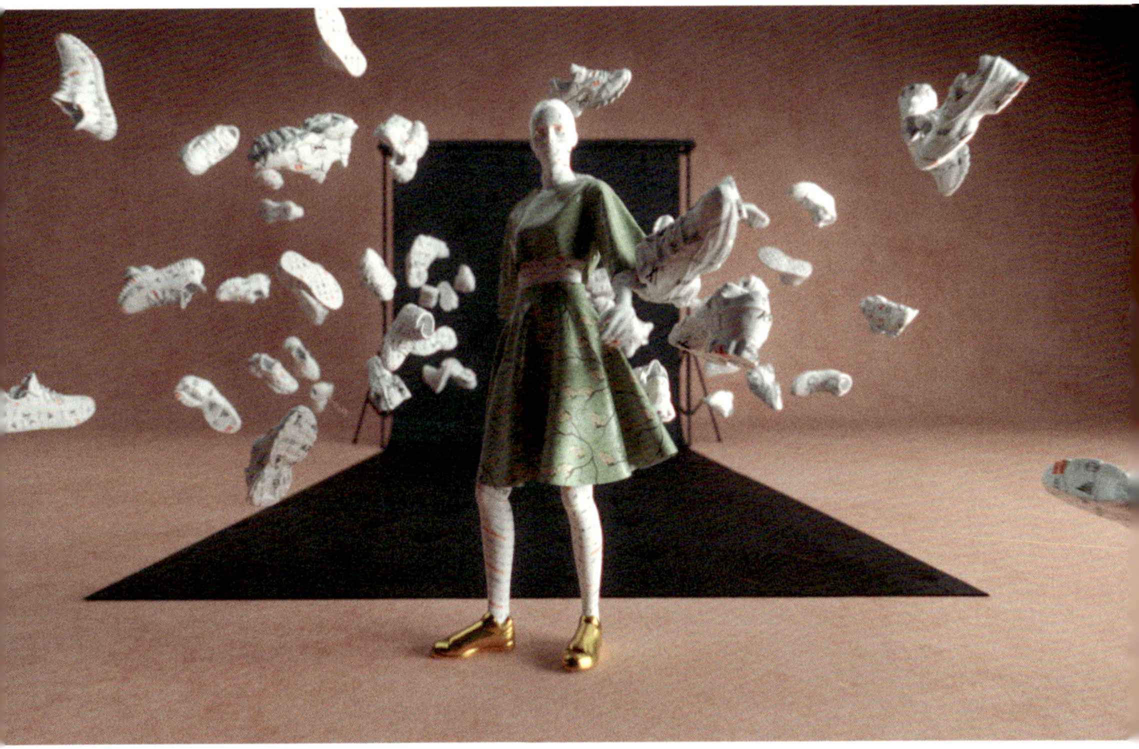

Jordan Clarke (CA) Jordan's work is constantly evolving, as he employs cutting-edge tools and techniques to create visuals that are entirely new. His background in VFX enables him to contribute a comprehensive understanding of the entire production process. Whether shooting on 35mm film or utilizing the latest AI, motion capture, or 3D animation tools, Jordan has the skills to maximize creative potential while saving time and resources. His 3D art feels organic, surreal, and tangible.

I stitch my skin to the ground

Nao Usami

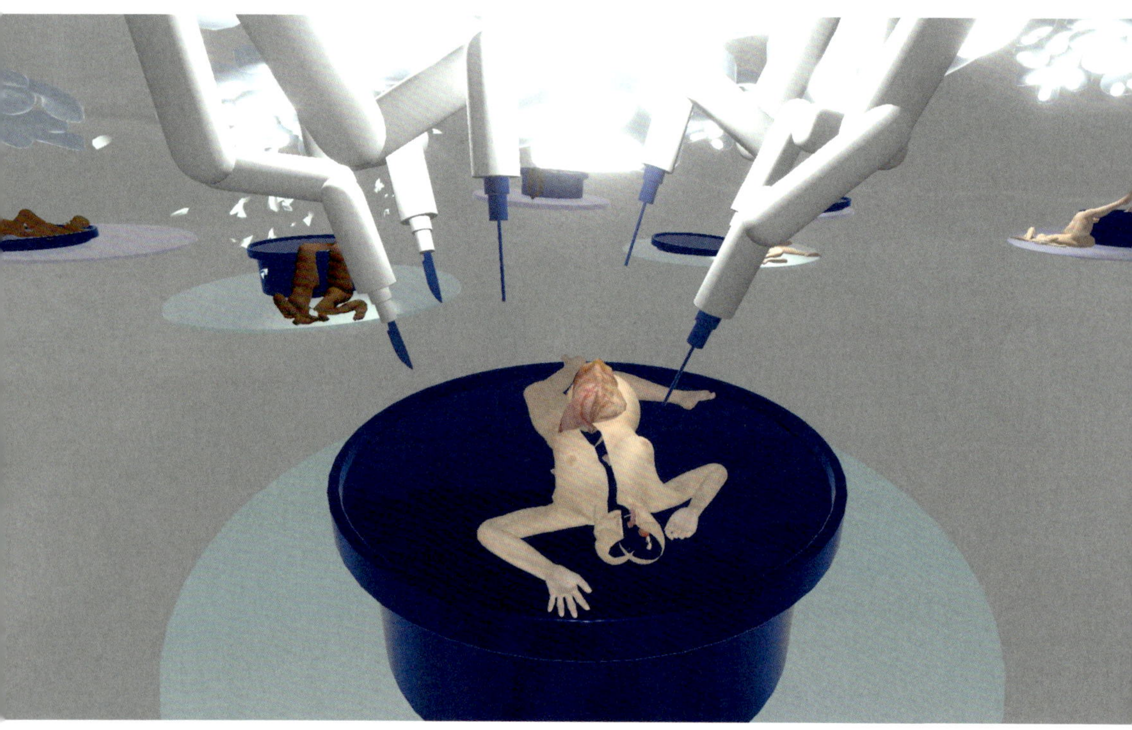

This project is composed of two video games *Replay over and over* (2023) and *Ambiguous Lucy* (2021). The story is based on accounts of people who have experienced sexual violence in the past that turned their bodies into "objects". They embark on journeys to look for new bodies.

Replay over and over (2023) has an important interaction. If the main character is harmed, the operation is disabled, and the character becomes unable to move. The discordance between the player's intention (the operation of the controller) and the character's behavior turns into a realistic experience of sexual abuse. This physical reaction is called "tonic immobility". Just like a victim of sexual abuse, the player is forced into the unreasonable situation of being unable to move as they want or to scream out. Day after day, they have to ride a crowded train, and their bodies are put in jeopardy.

Also the trauma plays many times in their heads. It is indeed like playing the same game over and over again. They attempt to peel off their touched skin and dive into water to transform.

In *Ambiguous Lucy* (2021), lots of shed skin is scattered everywhere. These are pupae after the face and body parts are taken off, to prevent the body from being judged as female in public space. At the end of this story, the main character selects a new body to combine from three options, such as machines, plants, or stones. These three options represent inorganic and organic matter, stillness and motion, and length of life.

The name of the game evokes "Lucy", the name given to a 3.2 million-year-old fossil skeleton believed to be that of an early female Australopithecus.

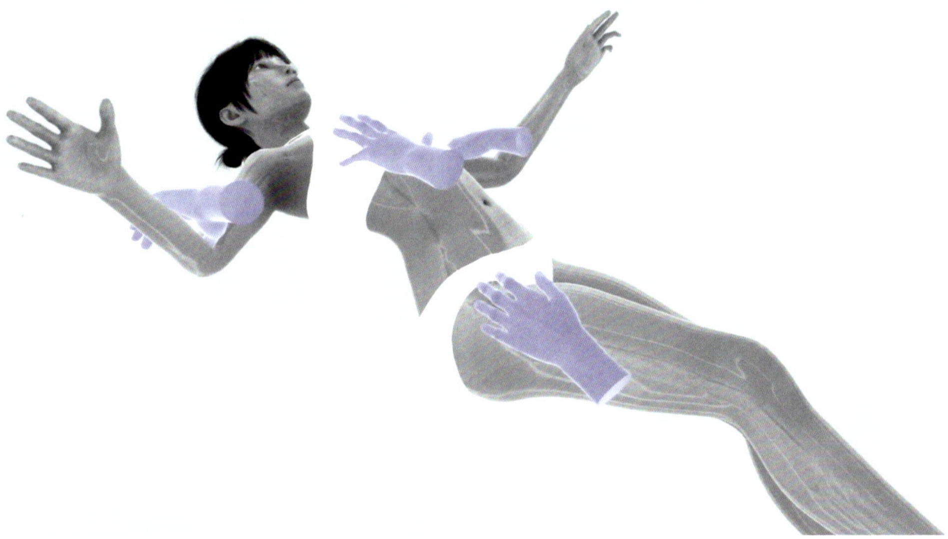

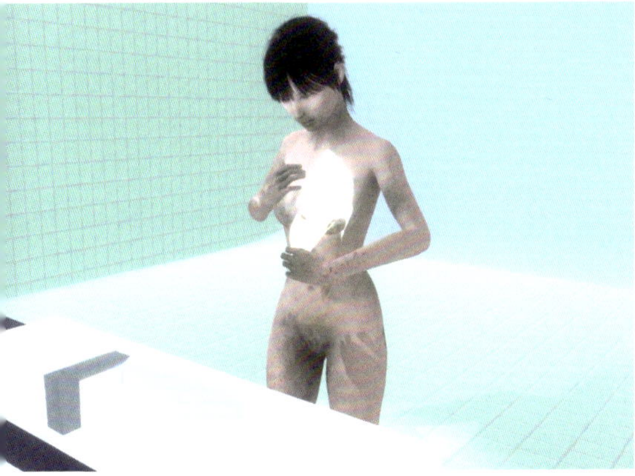

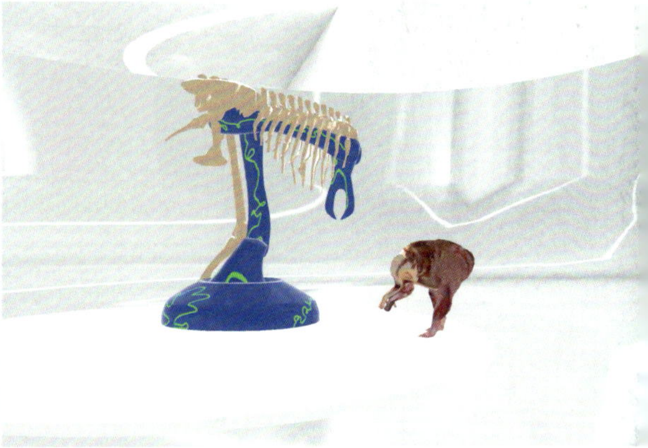

This story was created based on my own experiences, as well as those of my friends and others illustrated in several novels. They hate their own bodies, hurt them, and love them. They are longing to change, but their bodies with bandages continue to live. For this very reason, they continue their creative activities.

Directed, animated, and programmed: Nao Usami
Music: Chiho Oka
Voice: Manae Shimizu and Nao Usami

https://u.aec.at/DCE111D6

Nao Usami (JP) is an artist currently focused on game development using 3DCG technology. In her practice, she seeks to break free from social categorization. She vouches for games because of their ability to experience situations with other people, animals, creatures, and objects. Recent solo exhibitions: "TOKAS-Emerging 2023" at Tokyo Arts and Space / Recent group exhibitions: "Digital Art Festival Taipei 2023" at National Taiwan Science Education Center, "Changwon International Sculpture Biennale 2022" / Screening: "Image Forum East Asian Experimental Competition 2023" at Theatre Image Forum.

I stitch my skin to the ground

ITERATIVE BODY SYNTHESIS

Michael Wallinger

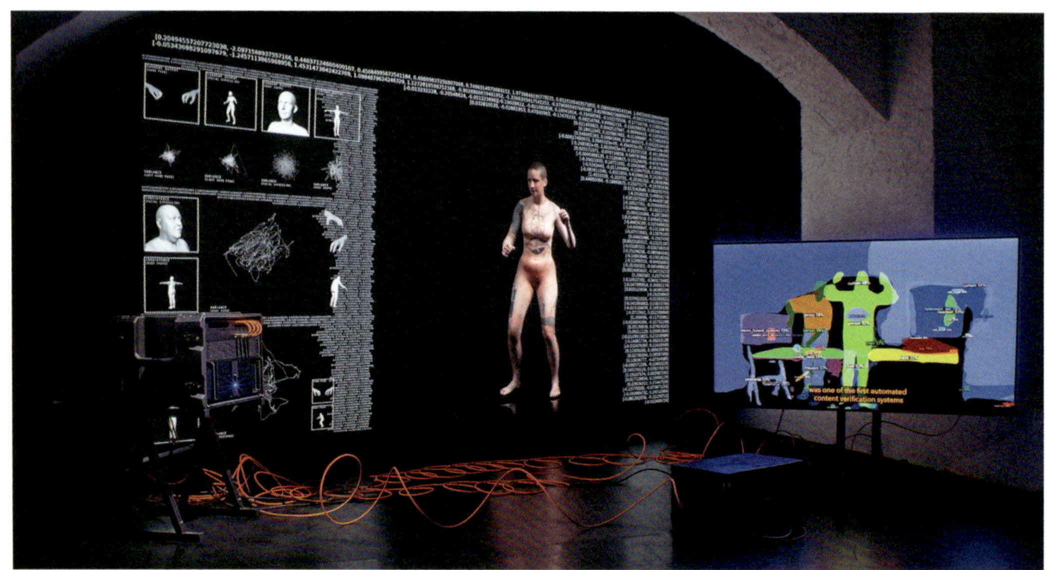

The media installation *ITERATIVE BODY SYNTHESIS* is the research infrastructure to an experimental online investigation as well as the neural back-end and monitoring interface to sisi.spec, a virtual identity on Instagram. In a long-term accumulating virtual performance of continuous body transformations generated in a feedback-loop between the installation and different Instagram environments, Sisi's appearance and choreography converges to the most consistent patterns between body characteristics and online in-/visibility.

Contextualized by a video documentation, insights into the methodology, data representation, sampling and evaluation, it traces questions on algorithmic prioritization and discrimination of body representations on this social media platform.

Exploring potentials of synthetic data, a specially developed software architecture samples, scans, and cross references the influence of Instagram's content recognition systems and algorithmic decision-making on the over- and underrepresen-tation of body images. Hence, it monitors and documents how this platform might influence contemporary and future body aesthetics, choreography, iconography and authenticity, while engaging with broader questions on accountability for algorithmic agency and its implications for mental autonomy and health.

Seeking to tempt our desires and thus influence consumption decisions and maintain user engagement, these platforms analyze our affects based on continuously sampled visual media. Reversing this practice and identifying algorithmic "affects" towards specific body characteristics, casts a virtual hyper-embodiment of Instagram's affective economies and notions of integrity.

With this, *ITERATIVE BODY SYNTHESIS* explores technological possibilities for developing a digital infrastructure that empowers citizens to collectively monitor algorithmic systems that moderate, filter, and verify our media realities.

Instagram API integration: Alina Huber
Cinematography, post-production:
Kevin Daryl Ferdinandus
Narration, editorial: Claudia Strate
Artistic direction, software design & implementation, machine learning & evaluation architecture, CGI animations & automation: Michael Wallinger
CGI texture painting: Enrico Zago
With support from: MediaFutures (S+T+ARTS);

The European Union's framework Horizon 2020 for research and innovation; Vienna Business Agency; The Austrian Federal Ministry for Arts, Culture, the Civil Service and Sport

https://u.aec.at/4F4554D2

**New Animation Art
Honorary Mention**

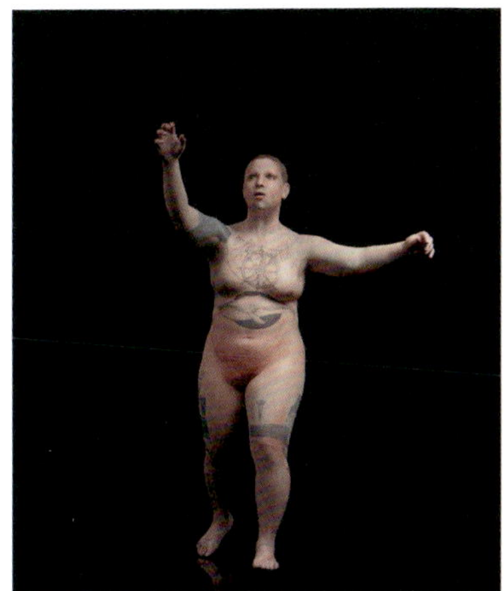 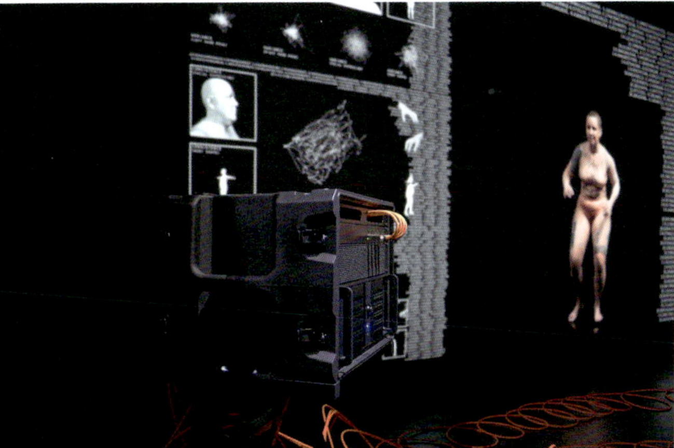

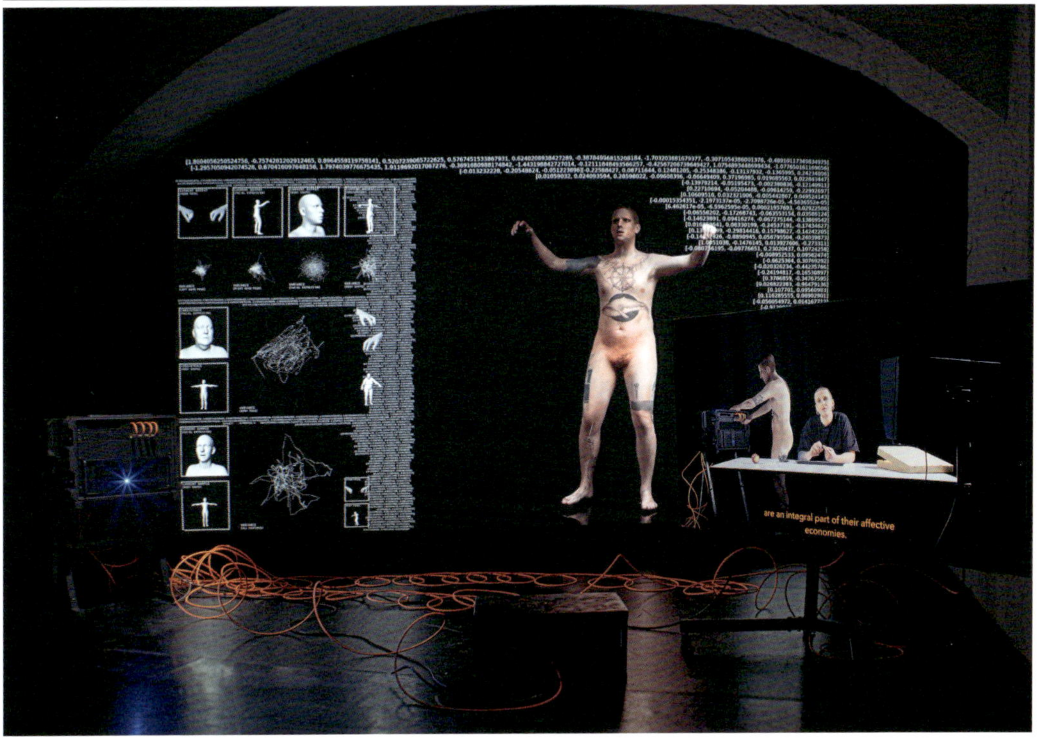

Michael Wallinger (AT) is a media artist whose practice strives to fathom the performative, communicative, and symbolic dimensionalities of data-driven technologies. Michael's work has been presented at various venues and events, including HEK Basel, 37C3, Ars Electronica Festival, Seoul Biennale, SXSW Texas, Kh-Kassel, European Forum Alpbach, FC Linz, CIVA, and Museums Quartier Vienna. In 2023, Michael Wallinger was awarded by the International Press Institute, was an Artist in Residence at MediaFutures (S+T+ARTS) in 2022, and received the Content Vienna Award in the same year.

Mid Tide #3

Ryu Furusawa

The view of the sea is entirely different from the shore compared to being on the sea's surface. This is because the perspective is not fixed when floating on the sea's surface. In surfing, one must sharpen one's physical senses to catch the waves. Thus, the body becomes one with the wave. The purpose of this work is to convey this sense of unity.

Expressing the feeling of floating, specifically the experience where the perception of time and space becomes ambiguous, is challenging. Video is an excellent medium for handling such a feeling visually, but it only handles a sequence of two-dimensional images as time. Conventional video editing methods based on this cannot express it.

Therefore, I developed a software to create a 3D object from video data, using time as the depth dimension, and to freely cut out arbitrary planes within that object. Conventional video playback is a process of moving a cross-section of this 3D object from front to back. This work deviates from this linear trajectory, allowing for free maneuverability.

The time handled here is different from the time we usually experience. This opens up new possibilities for video expression through the interaction of space and time with the video footage.

In this work, the footage of waves crashing against rocks, recorded with a fixed camera, was used as the source material. It captures three and a half hours of changes in light and tide, and, using 4K120FPS recording, it captures the fine movements of the waves and each splash's shape, which are imperceptible to the human eye.

Unlike the metamorphosing rocks, the waves maintain their form and movement even within the unique flow of time and space in this work. This is because waves are continuous in both time and space. These characteristics of waves serve as a guide for perceiving time and space in this work.

Just as the changes in the tides can quietly transform the landscape, this work gradually erodes the viewer's perception of time and space.

Video installation, 3 channel video, silent,
48:49 seamless loop

With support from:
Project to Support Emerging Media Arts Creators,
Agency for Cultural Affairs,
Government of Japan, 2023;
Tokyo University of the Arts Graduate School
of Film and New Media

https://u.aec.at/F492BD2F

Ryu Furusawa (JP) lives and works in Tokyo. He is an artist and a surfer. His works involve working with various visual media, such as photography, video, and painting, with a focus on issues of physical sensation and perception. He uses digital manipulation and physical intervention in the imaging process to reconstruct time and space and reveal distortions in reality. The resulting ephemeral landscapes erode the viewer's physical senses and heighten awareness of physical sensations inherent in our perception of reality. Since 2015, he has also been working in the YOF collective.

**New Animation Art
Honorary Mention**

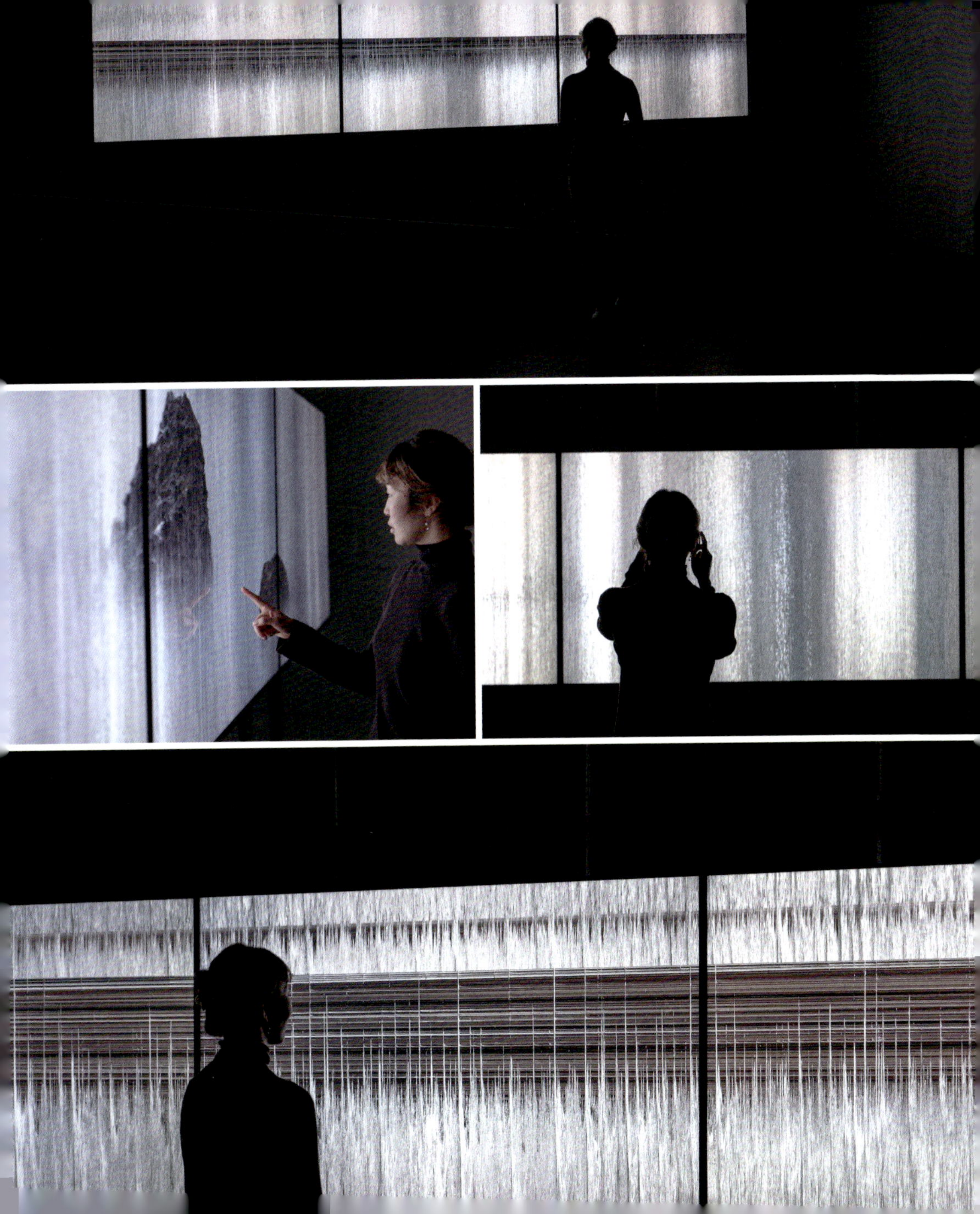

No Se Van Los Que Se Aman
Matar a un Panda

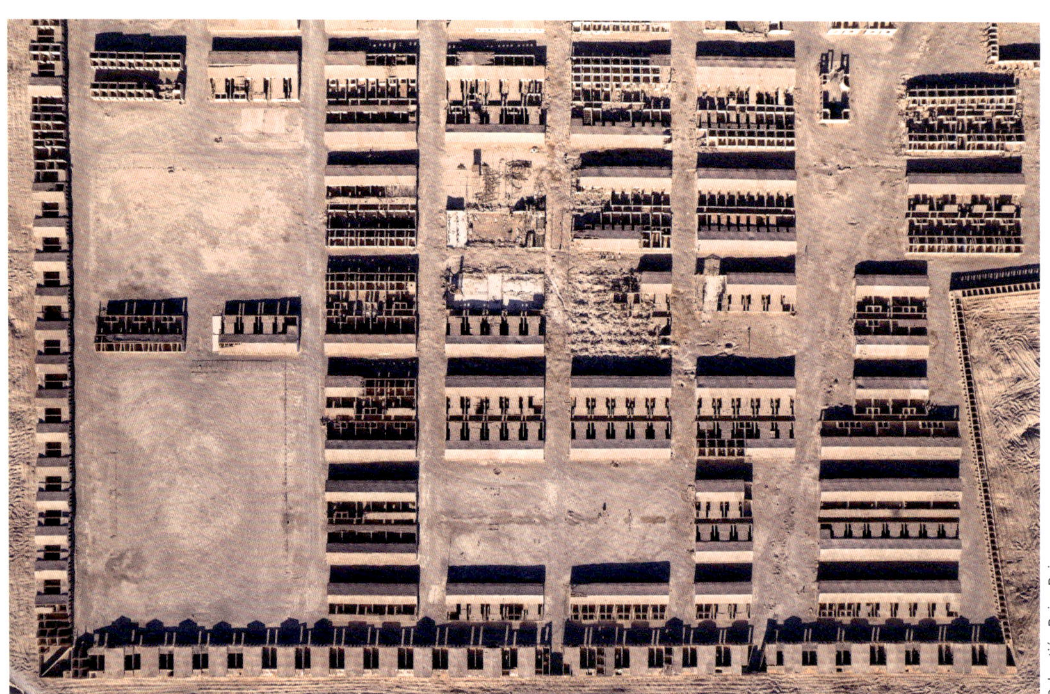

No se van los que se aman is both a dance work and an installation that cites the collective experience of more than 1,200 detainees who passed through the Chacabuco concentration camp between 1973 and 1975, the first years of the military dictatorship in Chile. Located among the ruins of an old nitrate mine in the heart of the Atacama Desert, Chacabuco exhibits the fake normality imposed by the dictatorial regime, as well as the stigmatizing wound it inflicted on the collective body of a large part of the country.

In a present context of planetary collapse, the world's driest desert is announced to us as the likely landscape of a forthcoming scenario. This reframes the events in Chacabuco not merely as a passage of time, but rather draws our attention to humanity's resilience and adaptation amidst profoundly hostile conditions. We feel compelled to ponder such capacity for adaptation and persistence, not merely as survival imperatives, but as a force that evolves into a necessity and a love for others.

The piece is supported by a large structure that works as a disruptive device in space, capable of capturing the gaze towards the game of projections and angles that allow the story to be told. Its technical development obeys situated production conditions that respond to technological dynamics of the global South, which we can see in the piece's particular meeting of bodies and scenarios in an arrangement that solves the gaps of the digital by means of the analog.

Through a design that skillfully intertwines pre-recorded performance projections and site-specific documentation, this piece offers a poignant narrative on Chacabuco's memory as a living and present experience, challenging the linear perspective of time. It thus stands as an act of defiance against the desert's erasure, the relentless march of time, and the dictatorship's attempt to make that memory disappear.

**New Animation Art
Honorary Mention**

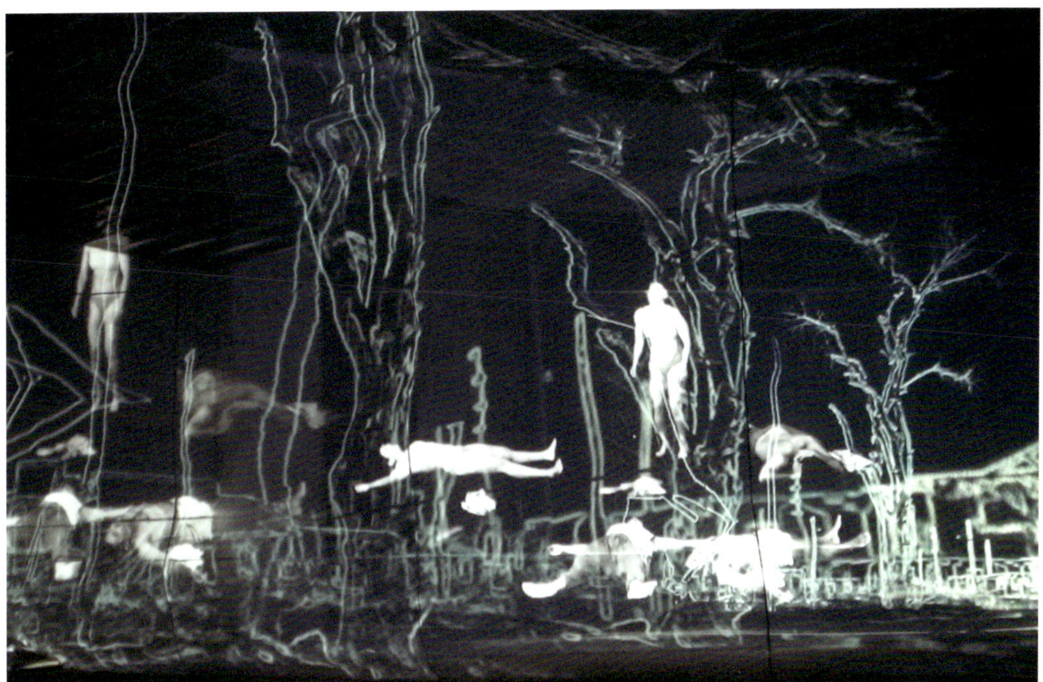

Sebastián Rojas Rojo

Direction and playwriting: Carla Redlich
Sound and new media design: Jean Didier

With support from: Financed by the Fondo Nacional de
Desarrollo Regional (FNDR) de Antofagasta, 2023;
Technical residency in Centro Cultural Casa Palacio;
Chroma studio in Centro para la Revolución de las
Industrias Creativas (CRTIC), Santiago; Gobierno
Regional de Antofagasta (GORE); Fundación Cultural de
Sierra Gorda. Direction and playwriting: Carla Redlich
Sound and new media design: Jean Didier

https://u.aec.at/489C0AC1

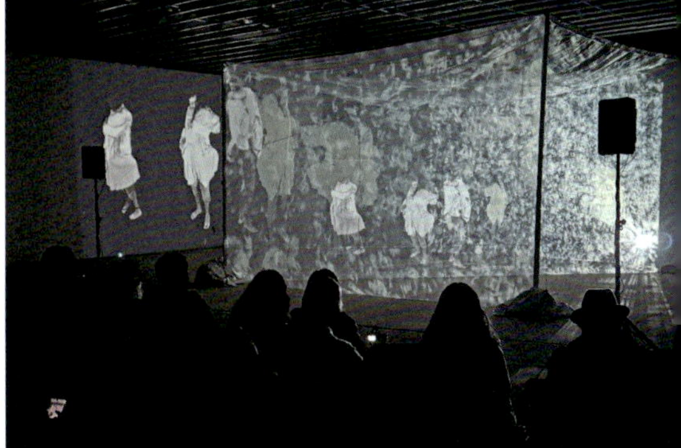

Sebastián Rojas Rojo

Matar a un Panda (CL) is a transdisciplinary creation collective formed by **Carla Redlich** and **Jean Didier**, experimenting with crossovers between performing arts, medial arts, and sound. Their work delves into the realm of memory, and as such confronts a challenge: memory, largely shaped by visual impressions, has been eroded by the overwhelming flood of images bombarding the contemporary eye, rendering it numb. In light of this situation, MAUP ponders how new media might stimulate a revival of experiential engagement, aiming to once again move, touch, and shake us.

Random Acts of Flyness—Season 2, Episode 4—Fourth Dimension: Spacetime/bodyspirit

Kordae Henry

Renowned writer, director, and producer Terence Nance spearheads this groundbreaking project—a poignant exploration into the beauty and complexities of contemporary American life. Nance employs a dynamic, stream-of-consciousness approach to delve into cultural idioms such as patriarchy, white supremacy, and sensuality. The narrative unfolds through interconnected vignettes, showcasing an ensemble cast of emerging and established talent.

Episode Description

In the captivating Episode 4 of *Random Acts of Flyness Season 2*, Nance collaborates with Najja to craft a narrative around couples therapy. Playing with space and time, they journey to the origins of their wounds and the ancestral remedies that heal. A key feature is a short animated segment illustrating the traversal between the 3rd, 4th, and 5th dimensions of self. Characters representing Terence traverse life stages as water, vines, and the sea, that connect us through layers of dimensions. Najja is elegantly portrayed on a sea of selves atop sea shells, awaiting at the 5th dimension.

This project leverages advanced visual storytelling techniques to seamlessly intertwine with the overarching themes of the episode, offering a truly unique and immersive television experience.

VFX artist: Tafa (Kordae Henry)
Writer & creator: Terence Nance
Episode directed by Andrew Thomas Huang
Producer: Keetin Mayakara
Writers: Mariama Diallo, Nana Mensah,
Darius Clark Monroe
Executive producers: Terence Nance, Tamir Muhammad,
Jamund Washington, Kishori Rajan, Kelley Robins,
Chanelle Aponte Pearson, Ravi Nandan, John Hodges
VFX supervisor: Chris King
Storyboard by Andrew Thomas Huang

https://u.aec.at/D7DEF8A3

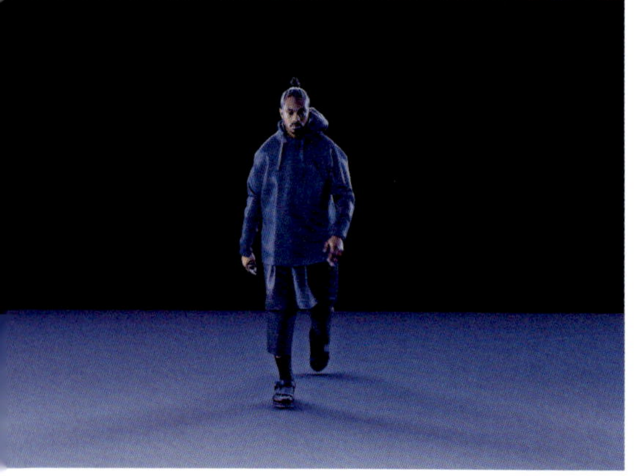

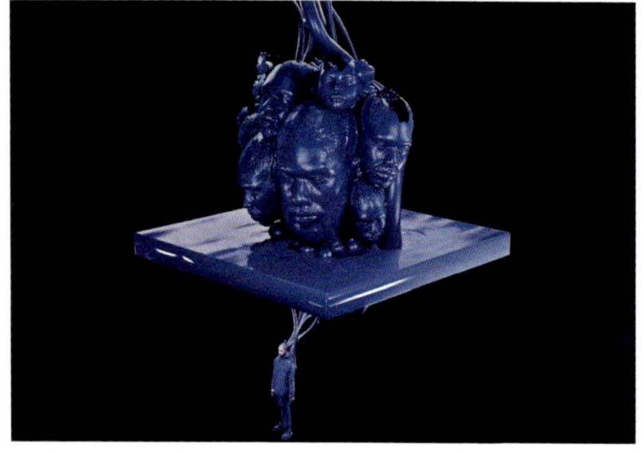

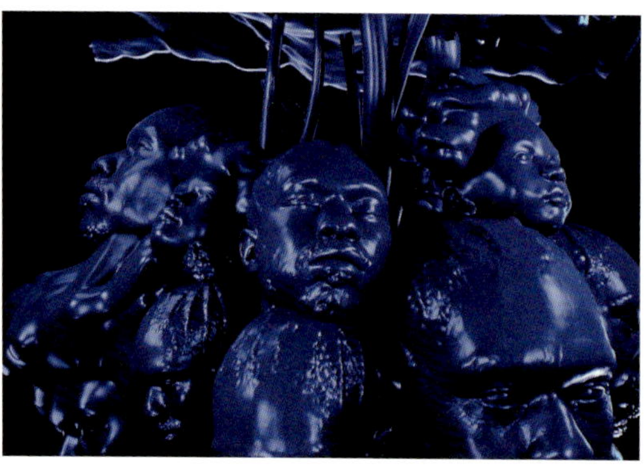

**New Animation Art
Honorary Mention**

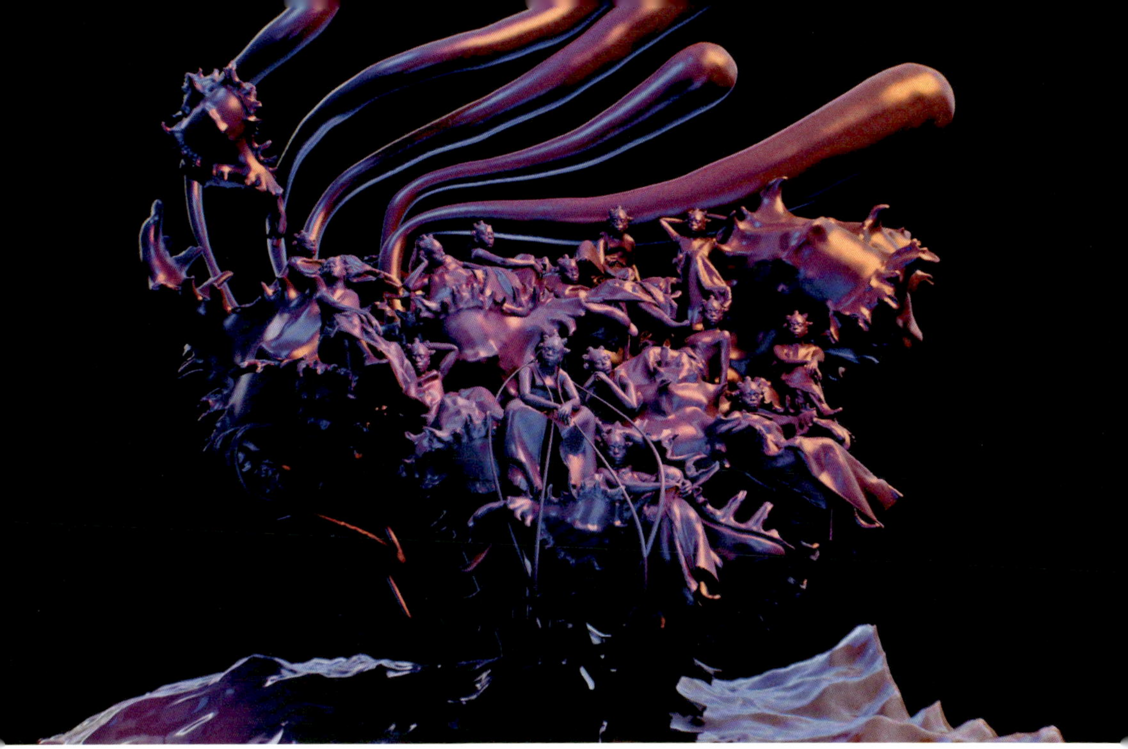

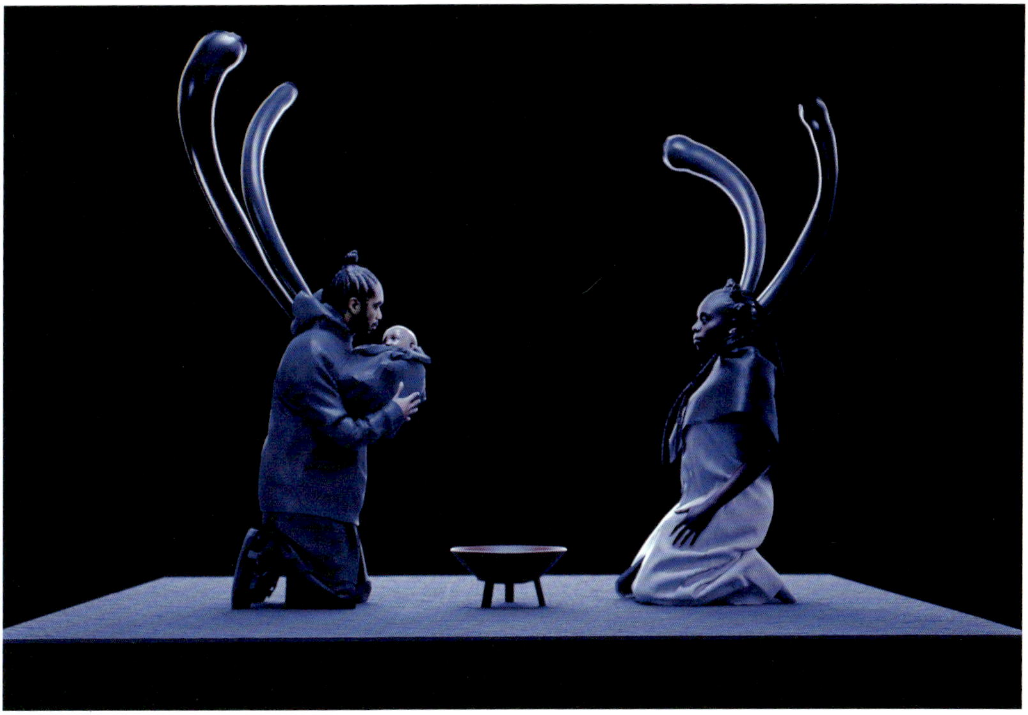

Kordae Henry (US), aka Tafa, is a filmmaker blending mysticism, tech, and identity layers, exploring race, gender, and ontology through ritual. Their work, fusing animation, performance, and virtual realms, examines Blackness in the 21st century with CGI creations reshaping storytelling. Rooted in Jamaican-British heritage, their art infuses movement, myth, and folklore into digital expressions, inviting viewers to reimagine human experiences. Currently directing music films, teaching at SCI-Arc, and a fellow at NEW INC/ONX, their project *IF NOT NOW* delves into the boundless connections of the human spirit amidst the vast expanse of space, exploring life and death as a continuum.

Random Acts of Flyness—Season 2, Episode 4—Fourth Dimension: Spacetime/bodyspirit

Thank you for your souvenir, UK!

Los

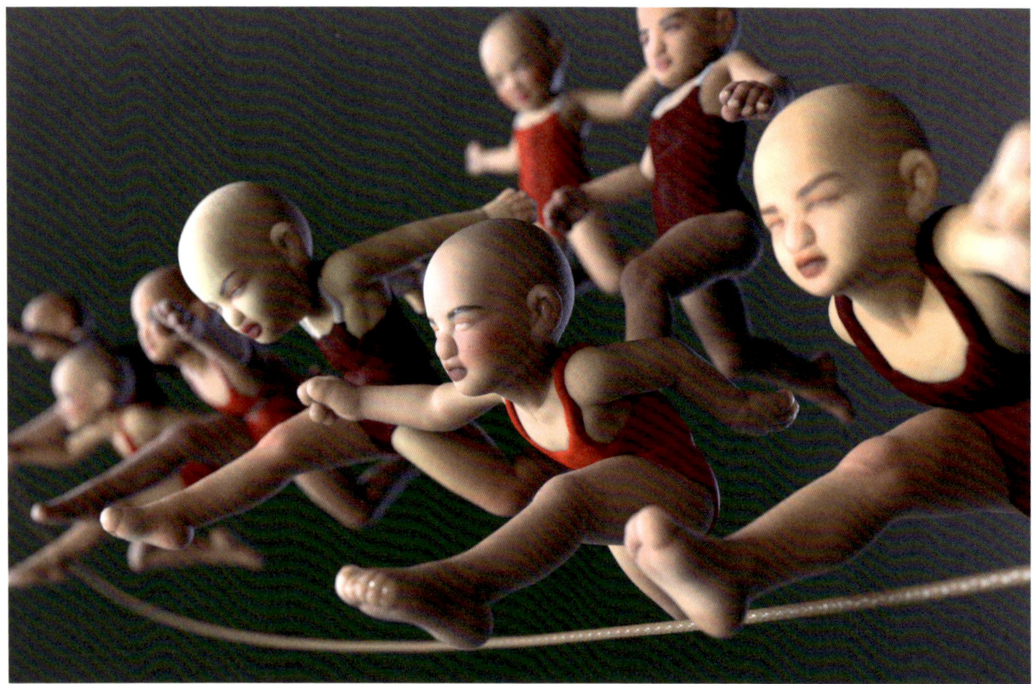

This film tells the complex experience of "studying abroad" in the context of the commodification of transnational education.

As a "one-year passer-by", the director elaborated on the ambiguous status of today's international students wandering between "marginal people" and "internationals". Starting with why it is so hard for Chinese creators to penetrate the layer of "accumulation" to see the world from a greater height, to what the truth and essence of studying abroad is.

How to gain something in the British education system that is dominated by economic efficiency? Is it true that most people today agree that the significance of transnational education lies not just in the acquisition of knowledge, but that the life experience and cross-cultural exchanges that accompany it are the most valuable things we pay for? Is the "Motherland" a solid spiritual fortress, or a shackle that restricts people's lives abroad? What is the boundary between "passers-by" and "marginal people"? How long does a person have this "marginal" status? Or is it something that stays with them for a lifetime? How can you penetrate this layer of "accumulation" to see the world from a greater height? Is it possible to bypass national identity and go directly to the essence of human beings? Will there be people who naturally do not have obstacles to cultural identity and spiritual belonging?

This film encourages people to reexamine the transnational education system by depicting the real dilemma. The journey is depicted through the dissection of personal experience, in an attempt to illustrate the big, common issues in small narratives.

https://u.aec.at/F662021A

**New Animation Art
Honorary Mention**

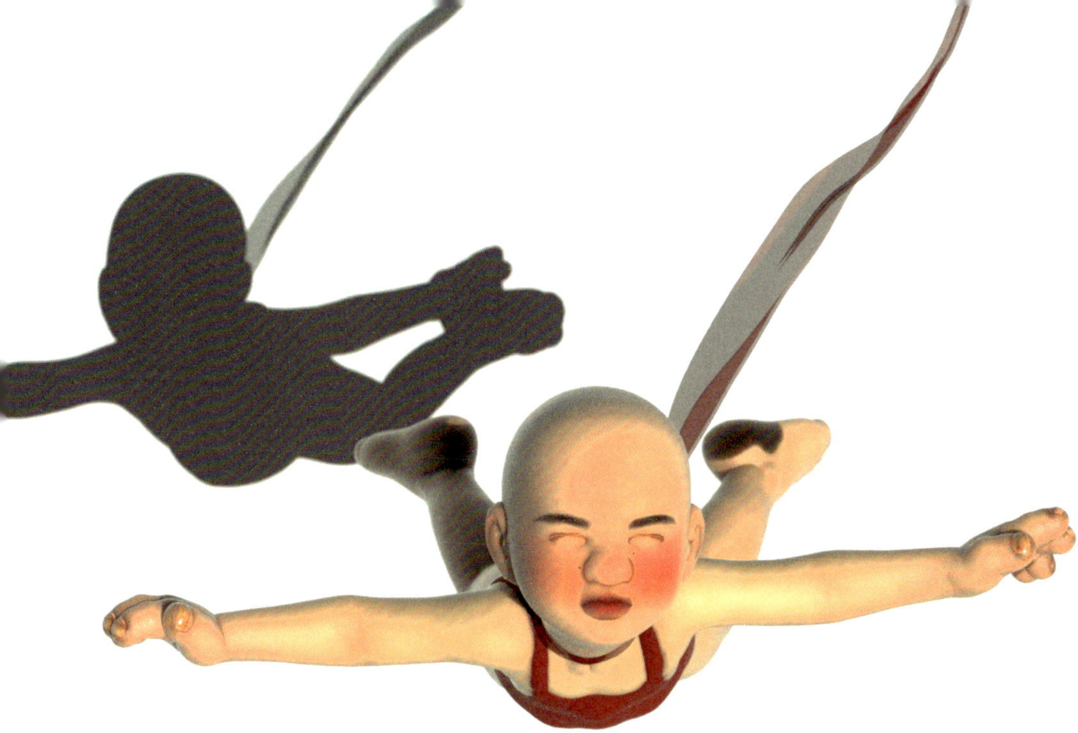

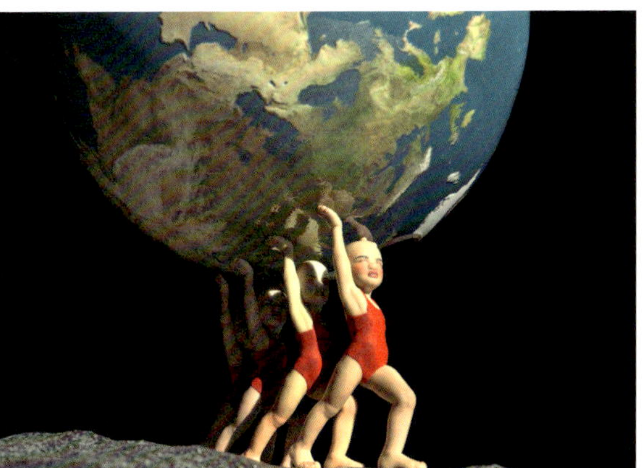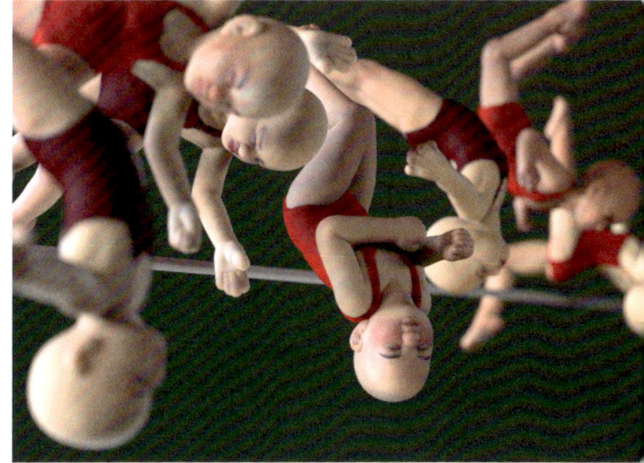

Los (Oushi Lin) (CN) (b. 1999) now lives and works on land and artificial land. Her practice often revolves around subtle emotions and anomalies in daily life, using the construction of parallel worlds to try to create a thought-provoking "space" between text and image. Her film was selected for several festivals worldwide including BFI Future Film Festival (2024), Animation Dingle (2024), Toronto Film Week (2024), and FEINAKI Beijing Animation Week (2023), and won the Best Animation Award at the London Super Short Film Festival (2023).

Unknown Label
Nicolas Gourault

In 2018, legacy car manufacturers such as Mercedes, BMW, and Audi, taken aback by the advents of Google and Tesla, invested a lot of money in research on autonomous vehicles. They gathered an immense amount of images taken by their cars that they needed to process in order to train their algorithms. This process, called "image segmentation", consists in manually outlining and labelling elements of interest in the image. It is very labor intensive and still cannot be automatized, it is thus outsourced to online micro-workers from the Global South.

Unknown Label explores the daily reality of online micro-workers from Venezuela, Kenya, and the Philippines who annotate images for self-driving cars. It investigates the power asymmetries and neocolonialist exploitation involved in the human labor necessary to train AI systems, but also the many micro-gestures of resistance that workers share on private groups.

Unknown Label reveals the hidden people that help shape how machines see the world, as well as the categories used to encapsulate our world and make it accessible to the machines, thus asking questions about the politics of these categories and to what extent they in turn affect the world we live in.

Testimonies: Oliver, Elvina, Ivon, Yonaille, Jonel
Research assistants: Leonard Nally Simala, Andrea Paola Hernandez, Niside Panebianco
Editing: Lucas Azémar & Nicolas Gourault
Screenwriting advisor: Quentin Faucheux
Image assistant: Héléna Michaud
Sound editing & re-recording: Etienne André
Thanks to: Inès Sieulle, Antoine Chapon, Claire Williams, Clara Chapus, Charlotte Cherici, Peter Zorn, Marcie Jost, Amir Borenstein, Mary Jimenez

This work was realized within the framework of the European Media Art Platform residency program at Werkleitz with the support of The Creative Europe Culture Programme of the European Union.
This film was developed in the framework of SoundImageCulture with the support of the Wallonia-Brussels Federation, Vlaams Audiovisueel Fonds and Vlaamse Gemeenschapscommissie.

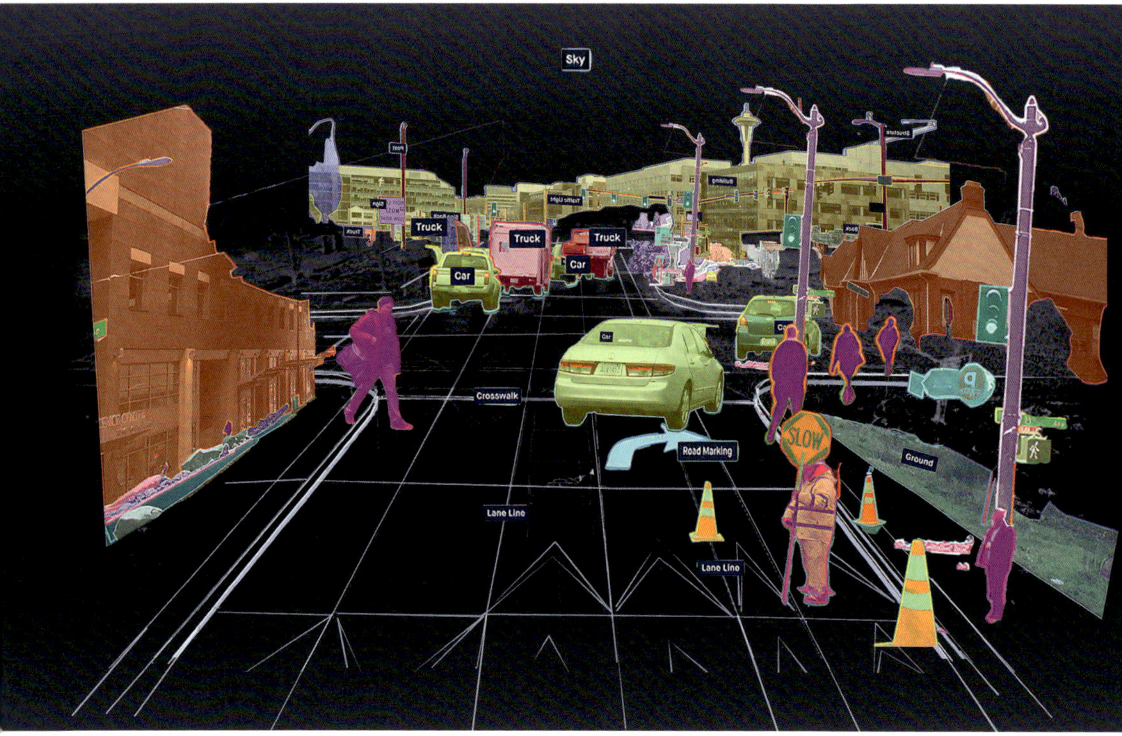

New Animation Art
Honorary Mention

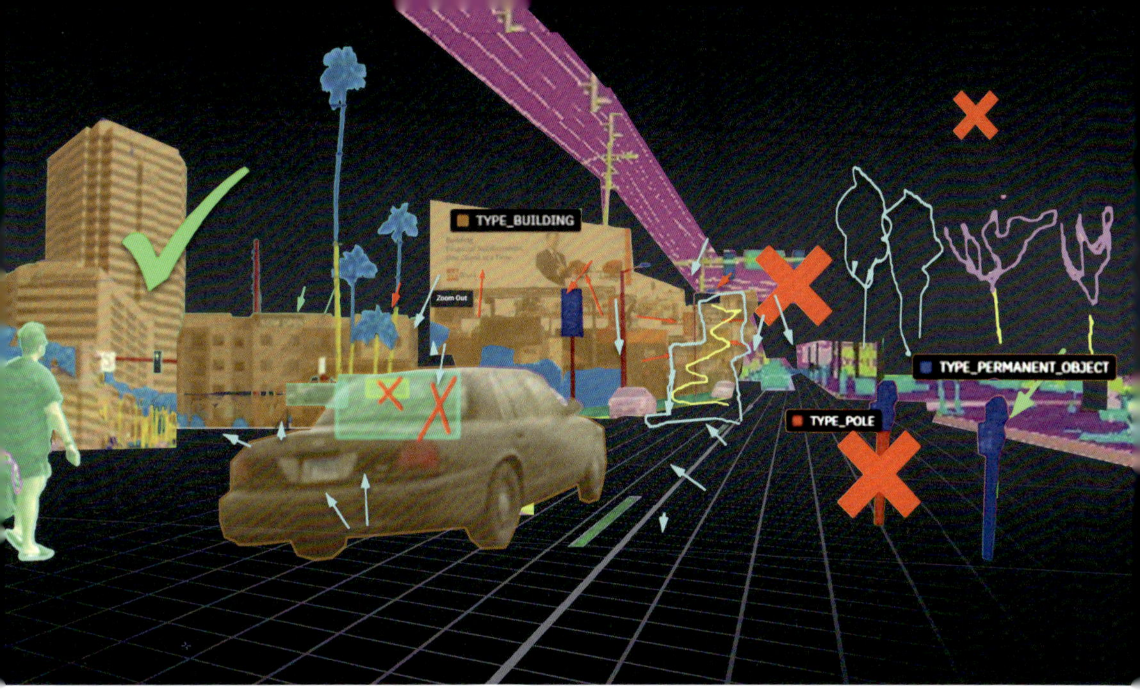

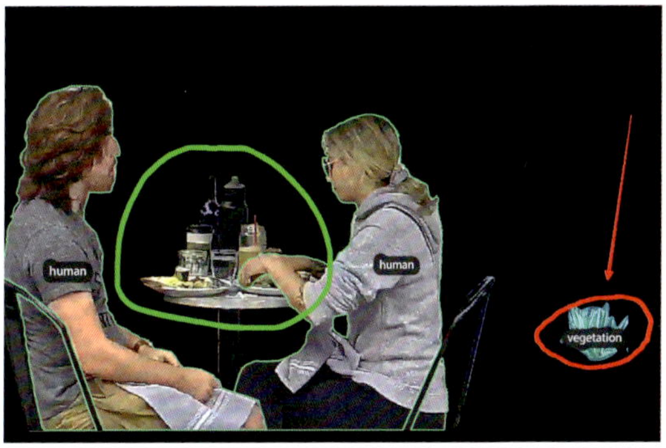

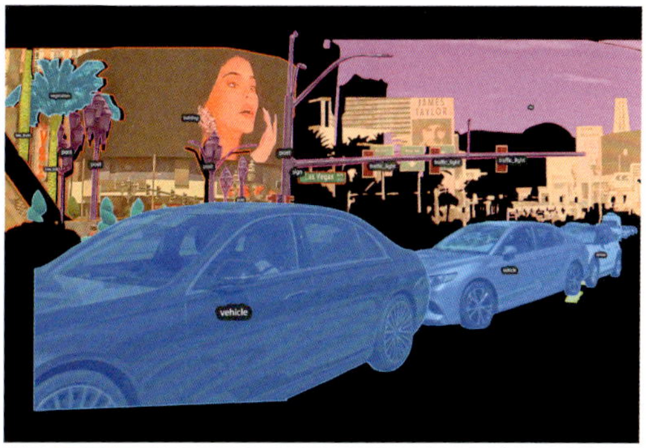

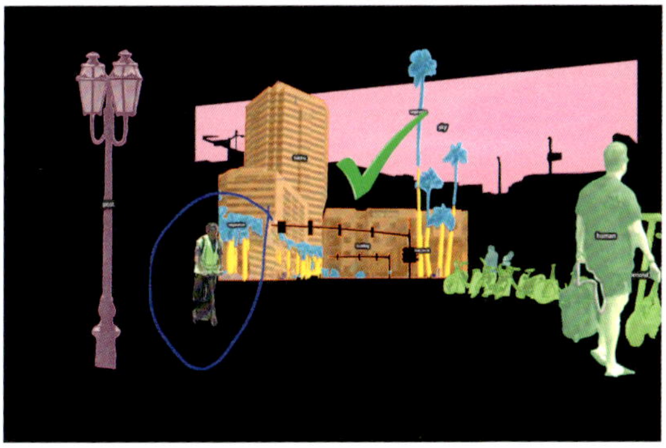

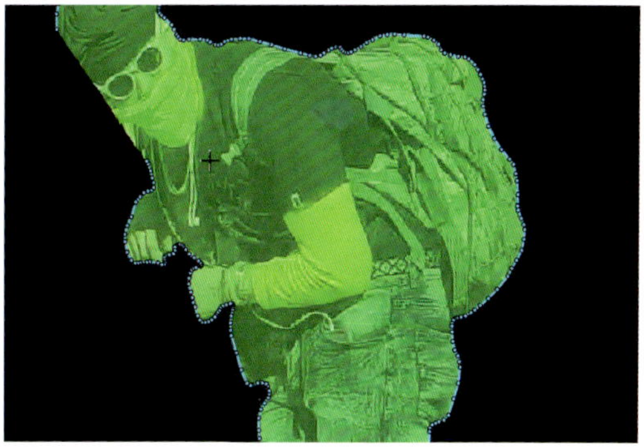

https://u.aec.at/E58FA7BB

Nicolas Gourault (FR) is an artist and filmmaker based in Paris with a background in visual arts and visual studies. He has worked with Forensic Architecture before graduating from Le Fresnoy – Studio national des arts contemporains. His work is imbued with this double training, navigating between online investigations and the use of new media as documentary tools. He explores the power relationships embedded in technologies and builds counternarratives through testimonies and experimental image-making. His artworks have been exhibited in contemporary art venues but also in film festivals.

Interactive Art +

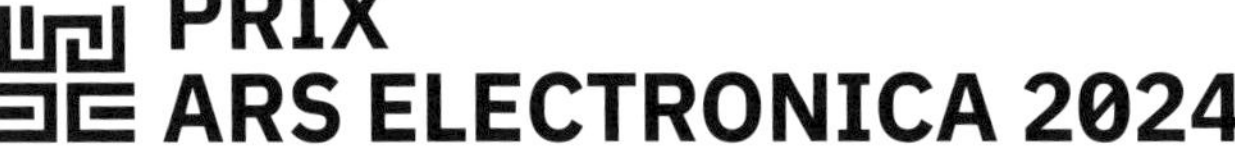

Weaving New Narratives

Clemens Apprich, Salome Asega, Shiho Fukuhara,
José-Carlos Mariátegui, Olga Tykhonova

What are the criteria of an artwork that invites the spectator to become part of it? Is the role of the spectator limited to the human actor? Or does the role extend to non-human entities? Are cultural and computational narratives capable of weaving an intergenerational web of meaning? These questions reflect the idea of a technodiverse future, which recognizes the varying ways in which technology is embraced and expressed across a range of cultures and communities.

As members of the jury, we discussed the importance of including artists drawing from alternative or subaltern knowledge systems, as well as projects engaging with localized cultures and histories with the aim of making connections to platforms that can provide wider visibility. These platforms, such as gaming and web browsers, are bringing about structural, economic, and societal changes around the world and can be reimagined as 'ecosystems' for propelling a broader, more plural and diverse dialogue. Such ecosystems can further awaken us to alternative or omitted histories, such as the experiences of Black communities under modern forms of colonialism or the deep connection between craft and computation as demonstrated in Indigenous design techniques, and how these histories permeate both physical and digital realities. It is necessary to seek a relational symbiosis between yet-to-be told histories and more 'established' ones in order to construct a more complete planetary knowledge.

The winner of this year's Golden Nica in the Interactive Art + category emphasizes the contemporary use of visual-tactile-haptic technologies of knowledge production through textiles. As a tradition present in many cultures around the world, textiles entail a memory function that has successfully challenged and withstood hegemonic systems of notation, such as writing. As a technique that preserves and transmits culture, weaving makes it possible to intertwine messages between generations and, in the form of the weaving loom, is a central building block of modern computer technologies.

The jury also reconsidered prosthetic technologies, which have long been present in media arts practice. This year, we saw the way disability and access culture positions prosthetic technologies as mechanisms for enhancing self-expression and building self-confidence, which in turn liberates people from the canons imposed by society. This liberation from societal expectations is consistent with the idea that approaches to assistive technologies should be more flexible and adaptable to individual needs and backgrounds, recognizing that a one-size-fits-all solution may not be appropriate for everyone. Just as aesthetic prosthetics enable individuals to overcome more than physical limitations, a more personalized approach could provide a framework for tailored support and access.

Similarly, gaming platforms, using world-building and storytelling techniques, can also be seen as a means of expression to overcome stalled narratives. The increasing accessibility of game creation tools, beyond the exclusive domain of large studios, further democratizes this form of expression. This resonates with the idea that support systems should be responsive to diverse forms of expression and encourage creativity, rather than adhere to rigid definitions and standards. Just as games allow players to shape their own experiences, approaches should be adaptable enough to accommodate the unique circumstances and aspirations of each individual, recognizing the diversity of storytelling.

During the review of projects, there were several projects using AI in different ways. However, it is fundamental to clarify that what is commonly referred to as AI today is a collection of techniques and technologies aimed at finding statistical correlations by extracting patterns from large data sets which are then applied into systems of meaning and classification. In this sense, AI has no autonomous agency and in many cases serves primarily the interests of the companies behind it, prioritizing profit and efficiency mandates. AI systems are thus sometimes considered as 'universal', but in reality they have a very narrow and limited way of understanding the world.

It is important to consider that if we want to question AI, we need to understand what the data objects, the technology, and, more importantly, the cultural and cognitive functions behind it, are. Interaction cannot be expressed solely through the application of already existing systems. Instead, a truly interactive engagement with AI requires us to critique its centralized and inherent biases, to actively seek alternative ways of knowing and decision-making, and to create the conditions for new associations to reveal themselves. The task, therefore, is to challenge and destabilize the narratives that underpin the current proliferation of data-driven algorithmic systems by highlighting their techno-solutionism and to use AI to expand and make visible alternative knowledge systems and perspectives.

Golden Nica

Nosukaay
Diane Cescutti

The loom could be envisioned as a programmable machine that encodes knowledge into fabric, serving as a means of preserving and transmitting culture; while the computer processes data, the loom preserves stories and traditions.

'Nosukaay' means computer in Wolof, a language spoken by people in much of West Africa; the installation *Nosukaay* merges textile hapticity with the digital space to produce a hybrid that expands the notion of interactivity. It is based on a modified Manjacque loom, in which the loom's frames are replaced by two screens that introduce a video game in which the users interact with the "wisdom of the system" through a deity. Its tactile interface is made of Manjak loincloth, woven by the artist Edimar Rosa in Dakar. If the player makes a choice that does not respect the machine deity and hence the importance of the knowledge transmitted, the user gets ejected from the game and sent back to the beginning. *Nosukaay* as a textile-computer hybrid allows us to rethink the concept of the "computer" through a rich tapestry of shared understanding that interweaves craft with computational practices.

Awards of Distinction

If You Have Starry Skies in Your Eyes
Rib

If You Have Starry Skies in Your Eyes powerfully illuminates the marginalized experiences of individuals who have lost a body part, a topic often shrouded in silence. Artist Rib, who lost her right eye due to childhood domestic violence, found her passion for creating exquisite prosthetic eyes through facing discrimination due to her appearance. Her experience sheds light on the societal stigma surrounding the ocular prosthetics industry in Japan, where conformity is prioritized over individual expression. This is compounded by limited insurance coverage for those with vision loss in one eye. Undeterred, Rib's self-taught expertise led her to craft unique and captivating artificial eyes, exemplifying the power of self-advocacy and resilience. The work explores the profound connection between physical loss, self-discovery, and creative transformation. By embracing her artificial eye, Rib challenges conventional notions of beauty and physical variation. This is a call for a more inclusive society where individuals feel empowered to express their authentic selves, sparking meaningful dialogue, inspiring positive change within the prosthetic eye industry and fostering greater acceptance in society at large.

Third World: The Bottom Dimension
Gabriel Massan

In *Third World: The Bottom Dimension,* artist Gabriel Massan offers a new pedagogy, a guidebook for resistance. Through a single-player PC game where the player navigates a lush world by way of an insectile protagonist, we are invited to engage in history as we know it and contend with its gaps. Massan is clear in his desire to *reveal* instead of *replicate* how systems of power erase and marginalize complicated historical truths. The goal here is not to conquer or extract, but to question colonial notions of expedition and to resist the embedded power structures. Drawing from cultural writer and historian Saidiya Hartman's use of "critical fabulation", Massan is keenly aware of the limits of institutional archives and invites you to challenge the record through their use of speculative storytelling techniques, which Massan calls "fictional archaeology". To repair history's failure, Massan and their invited collaborators—Castiel Vitorino Brasileiro, Novíssimo Edgar, LYZZA—build a landscape of expressive sound and color that make room for the fullness that is the Black Brazilian experience.

Honorary Mentions

AI Fortuneteller
Soonho Kwon, Dong Whi Yoo, Younah Kang

In *AI Fortune-Teller* interactees engaged with an AI career counselor, unaware that in fact a mudang (Korean shaman) crafted its responses. The video documents reactions, highlighting shifts in perception post-revelation. The project stems from realizing parallels between reliance on AI-based decision systems and pre-scientific agents like religion. These systems serve as coping mechanisms for an uncertain future. By juxtaposing scientific and pre-scientific realms, it explores human autonomy, trust, and motivation dynamics.

Interestingly, participants didn't alter their decisions or attitudes post-revelation, questioning the importance of AI's explainability or accuracy. The project critiques blind trust in AI and stimulates discussions on healthy human–AI relationships, and the meaning of human autonomy in the AI era.

All Directions At Once
Luiza Prado

This web-based digital performance or "GIF essay" is based on presenting a number of Brazilian folk herbal contraceptives expressing "radical decolonizing care", aiming to resist the disasters brought about by colonialism. During those times, the enslaved indigenous and African peoples used birth control plants, such as the Ayoowiri, not only as contraceptive methods but also as acts of resistance and self-determination in the face of brutal oppression during the European occupation of the Americas. The GIF essay performs a specific combination of images that vanish forever each time the user moves the mouse on the browsers' window, centering these GIF stories on the practices of care that have often been suppressed or erased.

Coincidence
Toprak Firat, Yasin Aribuga

Coincidence is a real-time collage that uses video streams from fifty publicly accessible traffic and tourist live cameras scattered across the city of Istanbul. In contrast to the usual video surveillance, the intention of the work is not to observe, but to produce a social sculpture of Istanbul through a complex composite of moving images, imprinting in its visual density the political and ideological tensions of the city's multicultural and cosmopolitan neighborhoods. Since the work is based in real time feeds, live cameras are subject to potential delays and errors. Hence, *Coincidence* uses a computationally efficient workflow and simple modular design using parallel processing, in which video frames are combined to generate a single texture, which is then converted into a movie file and finally transformed into 3D collages. All these processes are segmented and encapsulated into individual scripts to produce seamless 3D visualizations, creating a living urban sculpture. In the installation view of the artwork, cables are laid out with the intention to make evident the feeds of data that are required to make it work.

Cold Call: Time Theft as Avoided Emissions
Sam Lavigne and Tega Brain

The word saboteur comes from the French word "saboter", which in the early 20th century meant to kick someone with an old-fashioned wooden shoe. Through the architecture of a call center, artists Tega Brain and Sam Lavigne make a cheeky request to disrupt business as usual and engage in time theft, a strategy for slowing worker efficiency. They encourage exhibition visitors of their speculative call center to telephone corporate executives whose companies have ties to the fossil fuel industry and keep them on the line as long as possible. For the artists, the time stolen from these oil and gas executives has carbon benefits and is quantifiable as credits using a carbon offsetting methodology. Using the highest carbon emitting company in the United States, Vistra Energy, as a case study, the artists test a formula that reveals when the more senior oil and gas employees are distracted from working, carbon emissions have the potential to slow. Living in global climate emergency, Tega Brain and Sam Lavigne have put on their metaphorical wooden shoes and have landed a kick.

Consensus Gentium
Karen Palmer

In Karen Palmer's *Consensus Gentium,* an iPhone becomes a dynamic storytelling device where you are immersed in an unfolding narrative taking place in the palm of your hands. Through the film-like narrative, you quickly learn that you exist in a near-future society that is managed through the Global Citizen App, a heightened surveillance technology that determines all features of your city life, including mobility. While you are watching the story play out on your phone, the app's facial recognition system is closely monitoring your reactions to the events and weighing your threat to their meticulous control. Moving through the city without raising alarm does not come without its challenges. It proves not to be an easy task given the heightened police presence resulting in violence against unarmed citizens and FaceTime calls from your friends understandably upset about the state of racialized violence. The phone watches you back to advance the narrative in response to your facial reactions making each participants' experience unique. Through a simulated experience, Palmer shows us how AI-driven surveillance tools can make detrimental decisions and yield harmful results with lasting impact.

Conversations Beyond the Ordinary
Jan Zuiderveld

Conversations Beyond the Ordinary deals with the increasing anthropomorphization of our machines in a humorous way. Instead of cute robots, the installation introduces us to mundane appliances with their very own personalities, tics, and idiosyncrasies. It thereby gives us an insight into our immediate future, which will be characterized neither by the extinction nor by the redemption of humans by technology. Rather we will have to argue with AI-empowered machines and hope for their cooperation. A coffee machine won't make you a coffee before you show some courtesy, and the microwave keeps a watchful eye on the things you are about to put into it. It is this future, a mundane future that shows our everyday interaction with machines, which is characterized by empathy, misunderstanding, and awkwardness—just as any other conversation is.

G80
Fragmentin

Questioning the technocratic absurdity of historic cybernetic projects, *G80* invites the spectator to interact with computational models for solving socio-political and ecological issues. Based on Buckminster Fuller's World Game, which was created in the 1960s, the installation establishes a connection to current ideas of a perfectly controllable environment. In a playful manner *G80* subverts those ideas and illustrates the problem of a pre-categorized world. It thereby reminds us that the idea of a world controlled by computers is far older than current debates on AI and machine learning, and that the problem lies not so much in a data-driven world but in the pre-existing categories used to make sense of that data. This is precisely where a political response to technological solutionism is needed so that social inequalities—expressed in these categories—are not simply automated.

Kazokutchi
So Kanno, Akihiro Kato, Takemi Watanuki

Kazokutchi delves into the persistent questions of life's origin, evolution, demise, and legacy in an era where the physical and digital increasingly intertwine. Using blockchain and robotics, the project simulates the life cycle of Kazokutchi NFTs, visualizing their evolution through cellular automaton-like patterns. These digital beings, showcasing diverse traits and interactions, are further manifested as physical robots inhabiting a simulated Tokyo. This interplay mirrors urban life and the city's post-pandemic adaptation, while also examining the concept of the unique world each being perceives. *Kazokutchi* is prompting a re-evaluation of the concept of life itself and the diverse

Umwelten experienced within human society and beyond.

Mixed Signals
kennedy+swan

Mixed Signals consists of a series of watercolors that come to life by means of Augmented Reality. The strange and beautiful images weave a complex narrative that extends into our reality. At a time when museums are struggling to become more interactive, this is an impressive example of how this could happen. In addition to their aesthetic form, the AR paintings also create a level of engagement with new technologies, promising to connect us with non-human beings. They thereby envision a future when we are able to communicate with animals and plants, opening ourselves to the messages of nature. The technological enchantment of the everyday invites us to take on different perspectives of our world.

REPEAT AFTER ME, 2022
Open Group (Yuriy Biley, Pavlo Kovach, and Anton Varga)

The role and impact of experiencing technology, and the forms that knowledge of it can take, undergo a twist in the video installation *Repeat After Me,* created by the Ukrainian collective Open Group. With full-scale invasion, Ukrainians have become military experts with the ability to distinguish and determine different weapon types—assault rifle fire, artillery shelling, multiple rocket launcher shelling, drone attacks, aerial bombardment—by sound. This new-found knowledge is a reality for Ukrainians and possessing it increases the chances of survival. The video features civilians displaced from various regions of Ukraine, who talk about their personal war experiences, but in a peculiar way. The familiar and seemingly playful format of a karaoke offers to share 'knowledge' in and through sound. *REPEAT AFTER ME* is an artwork. However, instead of songs and tunes, it presents/offers individual memories and experiences of everyday war violence and its "vehicles"—the sounds of gunfire, missiles, howls, and explosions of deadly firearms and drones. It offers a human-voiced soundtrack of the war in Ukraine.

Swarming / Swimming
Honey Biba Beckerlee

The information infrastructure, essential yet often hidden, becomes acutely vulnerable when disrupted, highlighting the need for resilient communication and alternative solutions. *Swarming/ Swimming* is a simple installation, interweaving seaweed and optical fiber, which showcases the delicate balance between nature and technology. The seaweed symbolizes interconnected ecosystems and the cascading effects of unchecked proliferation, while the tapestry-like weaving mirrors the interconnectedness of our digital age and historical power structures. A wave-like pattern, inspired by the double-slit experiment, evokes the quantum phenomenon of wave-particle duality. Through the use of swarm intelligence to guide light, this artwork invites contemplation on leveraging complex systems for harmonious coexistence.

ZOE
Noor Stenfert Kroese, Amir Bastan

In *ZOE* Noor Stenfert Kroese and Amir Bastan create temporary co-existence between reishi mushrooms and a custom-made robotic system. Through sensing technologies an ecosystem that cares for and affects each other acquires visible and visual form: the reishi and their behavior define what the robotic system does and the robotic system influences the shape of the light-sensitive reishi mushrooms. Sculpted through the mutual influence shape of the fruiting bodies of the reishi is a reflection of and a sensory experience to explore this unknown communication. Additionally, artists create tactile data visualizations or "data-carpets" trying to further unveil communication within this coexistence and find further possible correlations. *ZOE* explores Mycobotics, possibilities of biocomputing with fungi through robotics and more than human-computer interaction. Using industrial robots and their quality of repetition and precision, artists reconsider the dynamics between technology and nature, encompassing both human and non-human aspects.

Nosukaay

Diane Cescutti

Nosukaay, the machine deity narrates a story about an alternative history of computation, shedding light on the connections between computers, Manjak weaving knowledge, and mathematics. The narrative blends texts, 3D images, and images shot in Aïssa Dione Tissus studio and Boulevard Canal4 outdoor weaving studio in Dakar, Senegal.

Nosukaay is an interactive installation that is a first attempt at creating an altered "computer"—a textile machine that combines a West African loom and a computer. I used the structure of the Manjak loom in which the two traditional frames of the loom are replaced by two screens stripped of their plastic shells, retaining only the thinnest functional envelope.

Viewers are invited to use the Manjak loincloth, handwoven by myself and weaver Edimar Rosa in Dakar, as a keyboard to navigate the story. By stroking, touching, caressing different parts of the fabric, viewers can make choices to explore different parts of the film/videogame. Each choice defines one's unique position within the storyline, revealing certain aspects of the tactile-visual experience while concealing others.

If users make a choice that does not respect the machine deity and the importance of the knowledge transmitted, they get ejected from the game and must restart from the very beginning. This aspect of the experience is very important. Traditional and sacred knowledge cannot be transmitted unconditionally—a relationship of trust must be built.

When I met Edimar Rosa in 2022, he and other weavers were at first reluctant to teach me Manjak weaving, firstly, because it's a craft practiced by men only and secondly, because they wanted to know what my intentions were. I wanted to find a way to stay true to their mindset and that is why the artwork *Nosukaay* asks the user the same question I was asked.

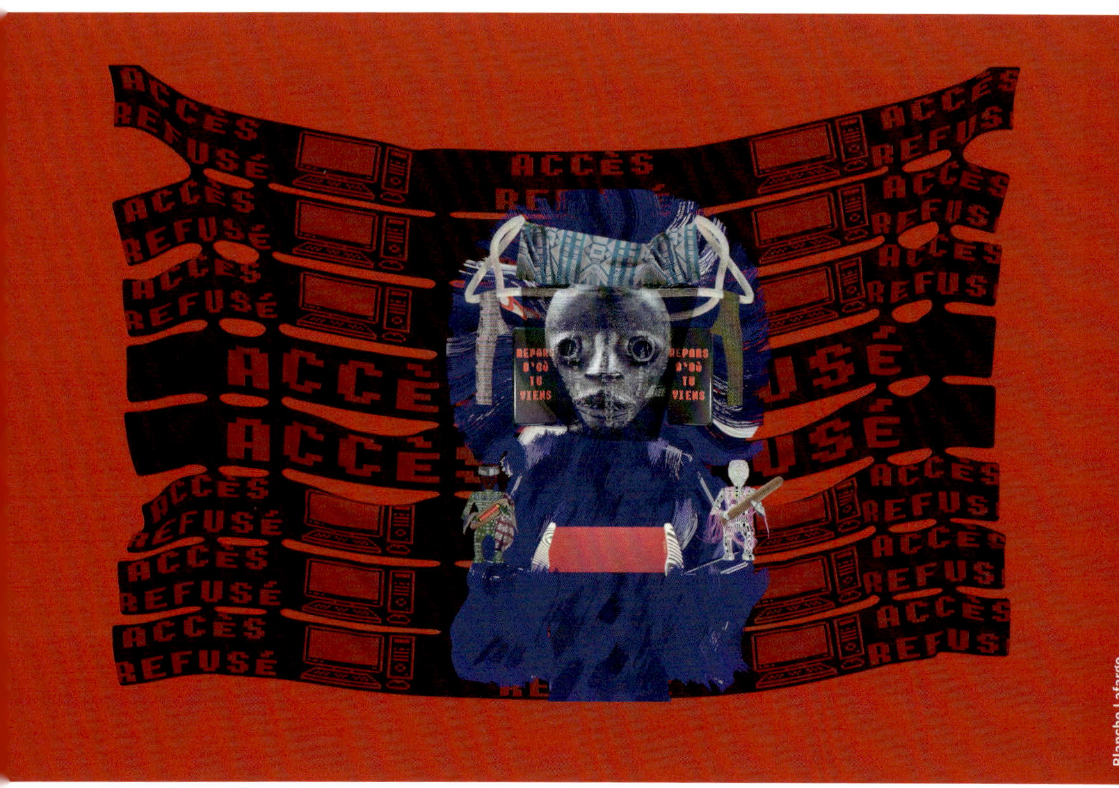

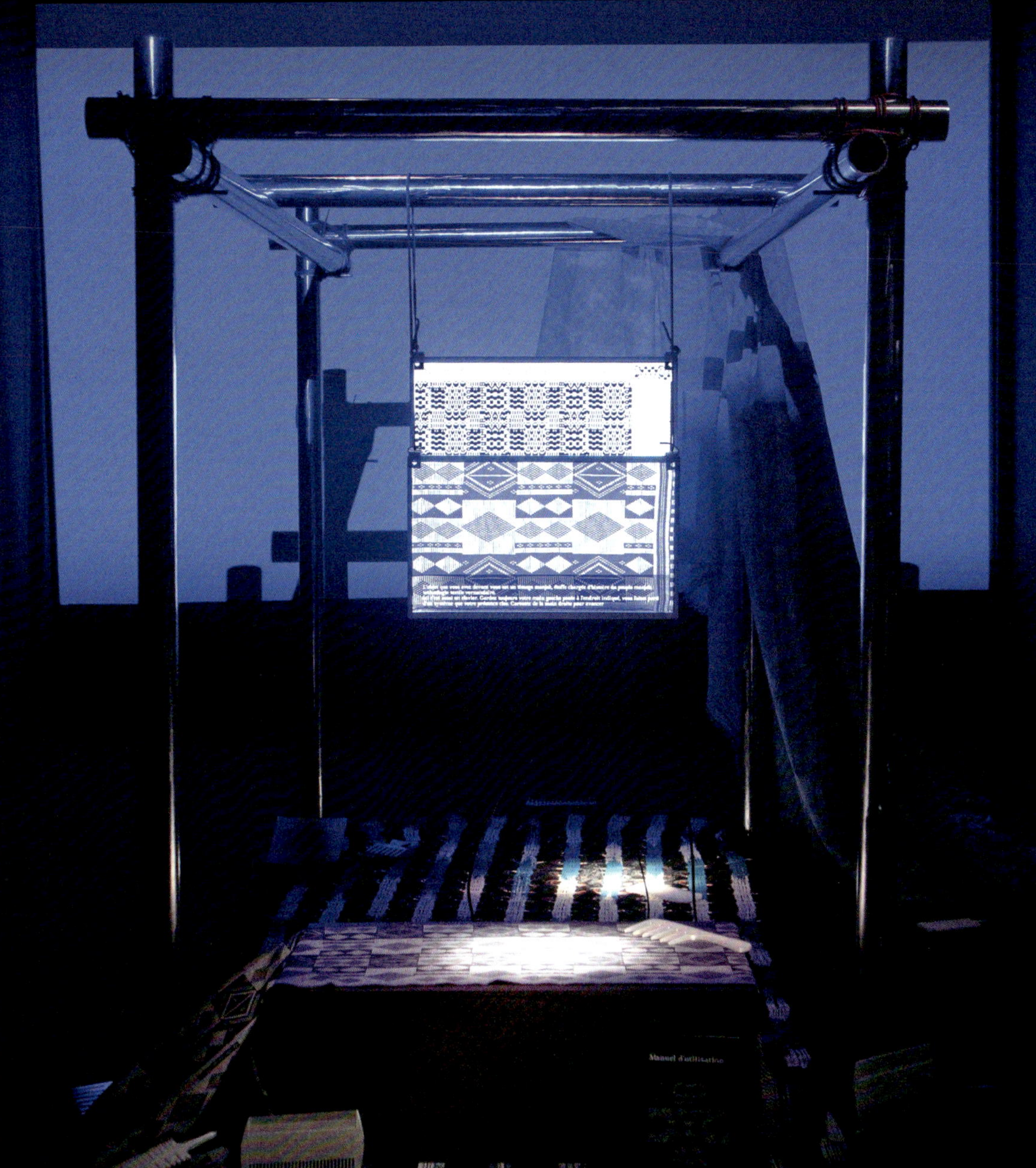

Manuel d'utilisation

Nosukaay means "computer" in Wolof, the most widely spoken language in Senegal. The term is not universally accepted; it was coined by the group of scholars Wolof ak xamle (Wolof and transmission of knowledge) that aims to extend the Wolof vocabulary, especially by adding academic and scientifics terms. It is a common misconception that African languages lack the necessary terminologies to teach subjects like mathematics, science, and technology. This ignores the numerous contributions made by the Continent in these fields. *Nosukaay* talks about computers of ancient times. The word used to describe someone or something who computes. Now humans and all other entities have been erased from the definition, as have diverse haptic properties like thickness and softness. A computer is also a system. In the case of the Manjak computer, the link between the loom (motherboard), the threads (random access memory), the weaver, the assistant (central processing unit), and the person that creates the pattern (hard drive) is the computer.

Donella Meadows taught us that while we may not fully comprehend systems, we can dance with them. Her guidelines for caring interactions with them are scattered throughout this piece, engraved on 3D printed combs.

By interacting with *Nosukaay,* you, the user, become an integral part of a system, quite literally. As you place your hands on the woven key cloth, you close the electrical circuit of the artwork thanks to your natural conductivity. This property allows multiple individuals to experience the work simultaneously by joining hands, letting a safe amount of electricity flow from one body to another before going back to *Nosukaay.*

From the square lashings securing the installation's structure to the open source softwares powering the interactive tactilo-visual experience, I used a combination of acessible tools and techniques. I want to offer an inspiring vision of technologies that feel within reach in this age of digital divide.

Video: Sarah Maupin
Photos: Blanche Lafargue
Woven Manjak loincloth: Edimar Rosa
With support from: École nationale supérieure des beaux-arts de Lyon (ENSBA Lyon); Post-diplôme Art, Centre d'art image/imatge

https://u.aec.at/7CFAA301

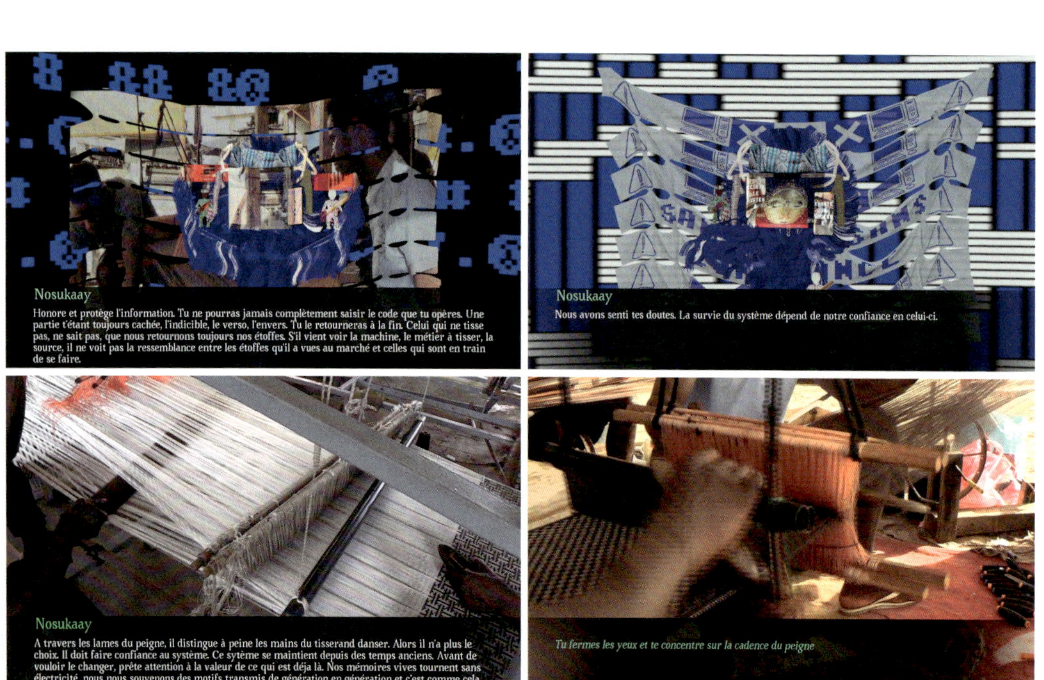

Nosukaay

Nosukaay

Nosukaay

**Interactive Art +
Golden Nica 2024**

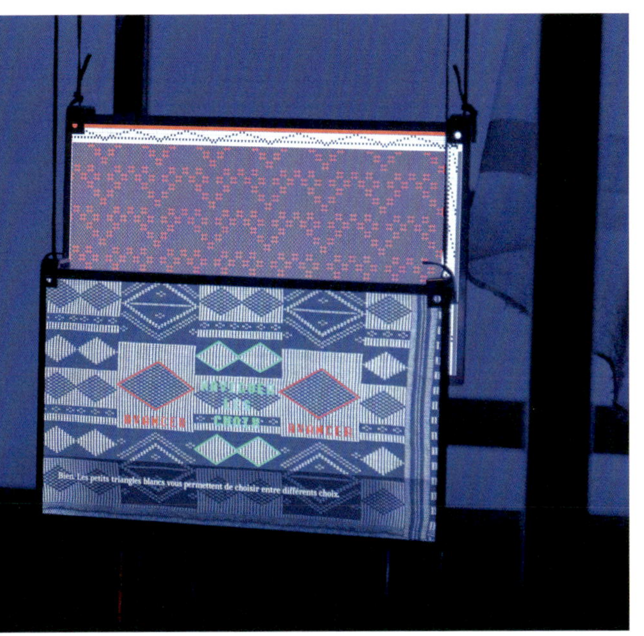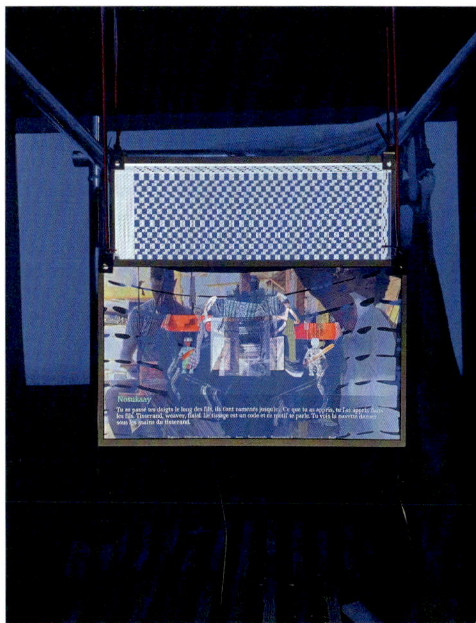

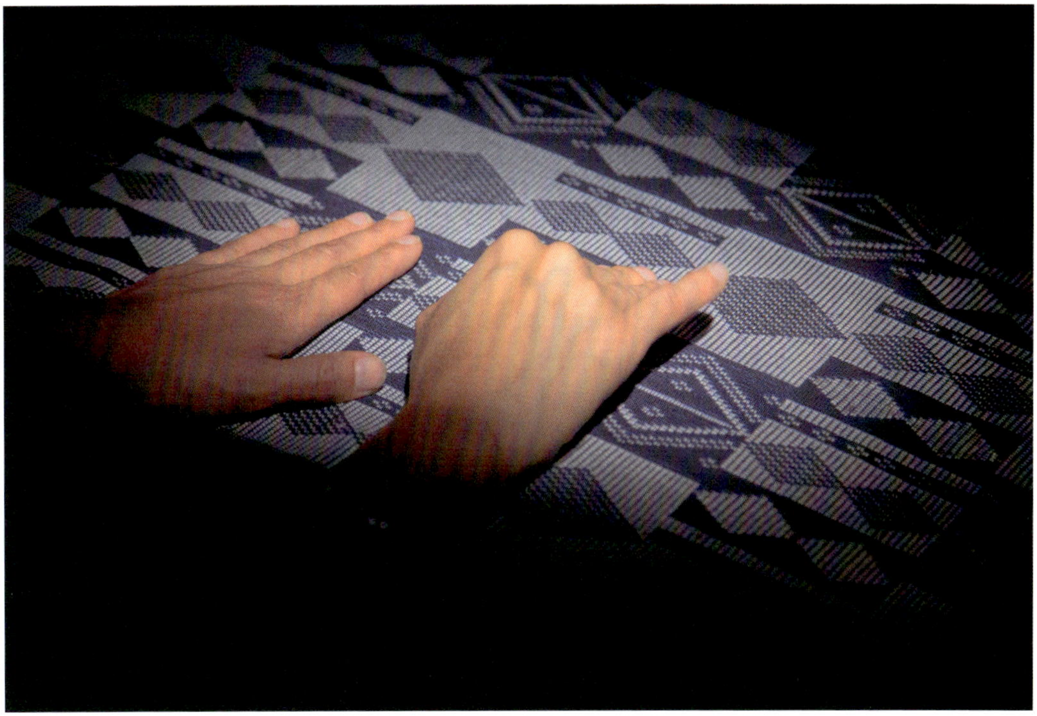

Diane Cescutti (FR) born in 1998, is a French transmedia artist. She lives and works in Saint Etienne, France. She studied Fine Arts and textiles in the École des Beaux-Arts de Nantes in France, Tokyo University of the Arts in Japan, and in the University of Houston in the United States. Her practice starts from the loom at the origin of computation. By tracing the history of computer code, she finds herself entangled in the world of weaving, and by following the crossing of the fibers of her loom, she ends up at its ethereal form: its algorithm. Through a histofuturist, speculative and narrative approach, she explores the historical, technological, mathematical and aesthethic links between weaving, textiles, and computers. By employing techniques such as weaving, sculpture, installations, videos, and 3D art, she seeks to redefine and challenge our understanding of technology and textiles, as well as their roles as vessels for transmitting knowledge, data, traditions, and spirituality.

If You Have Starry Skies in Your Eyes

Rib

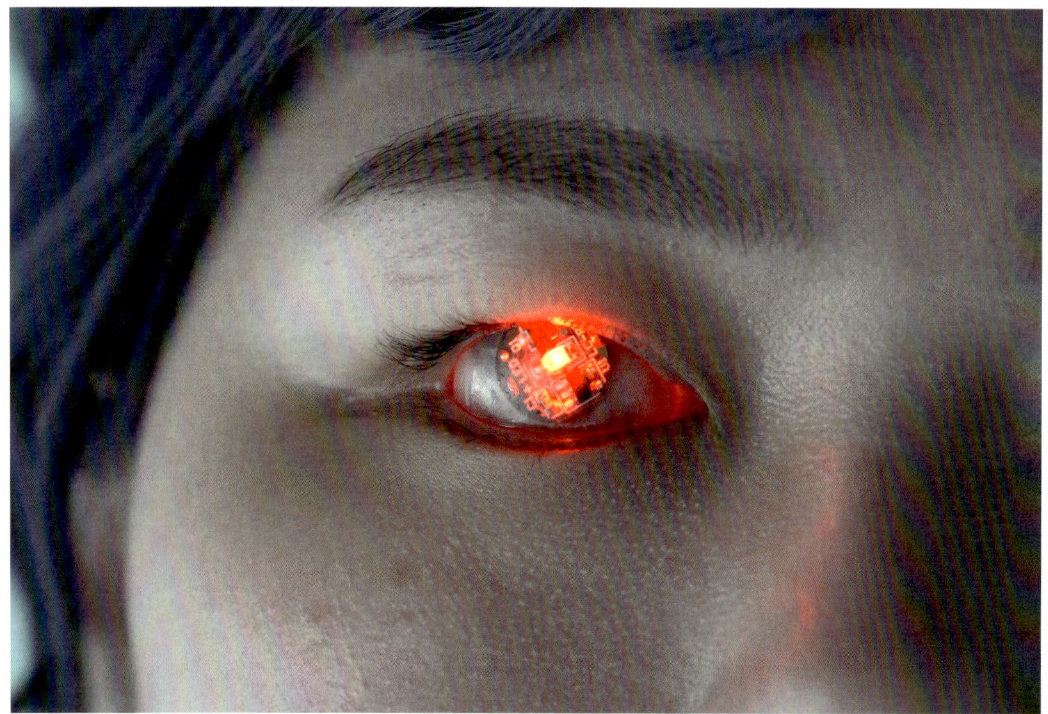

In Japan, prosthetic eyes have been designed to mimic real eyes. This seemingly rational approach is deeply rooted in the unique rules of Japan's prosthetic eye industry, also from the concept of prevailing societal norms. Given such a background, it has been impossible to realize individual wishes such as "I want a prosthetic eye with a slightly larger pupil to match my colored contact lens" or "I would like to have a prosthetic eye with blue irises", and officially approved prosthetic eye manufacturers have refused to produce such custom-made prosthetic eyes.

Against this backdrop, I am challenging societal preconceptions about prosthetic eyes through this project. The prosthetic eye that I created and I am wearing, has integrated a magnetic sensor, an LED light, and a battery encapsulated in medical-grade acrylic resin. This enhances the prosthetic eye, which becomes an object of desire for individuality and self-expression instead of a mere orbital prothesis. The eye gets lit up by a magnet sensor. This prosthetic eye leaves a strong impression on people and encourages a new perception about prosthetic eyes.

This project originated from my personal background. With my interactive prosthetic eye, I am challenging the societal gaze that often makes people with disabilities feel 'invisible', 'untouchable', and as if they should 'be kept hidden'. Therefore, this project offers people with disabilities more options for self-expression, and it encourages people to come out of hiding.

In Japanese society, physical impairments, including the wearing of prosthetic eyes, are often perceived negatively. However, through this glowing prosthetic eye project, I aim to showcase the

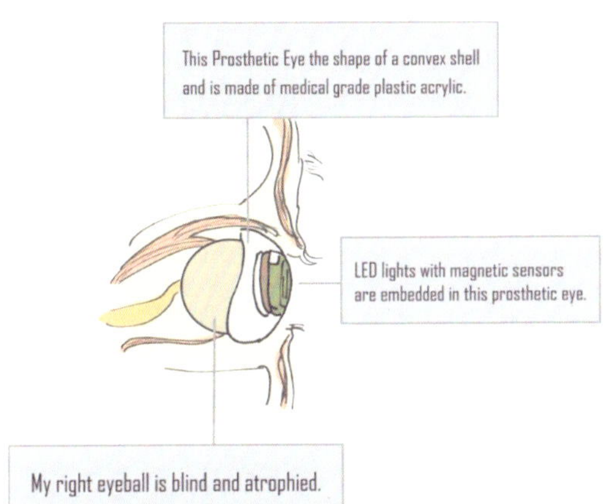

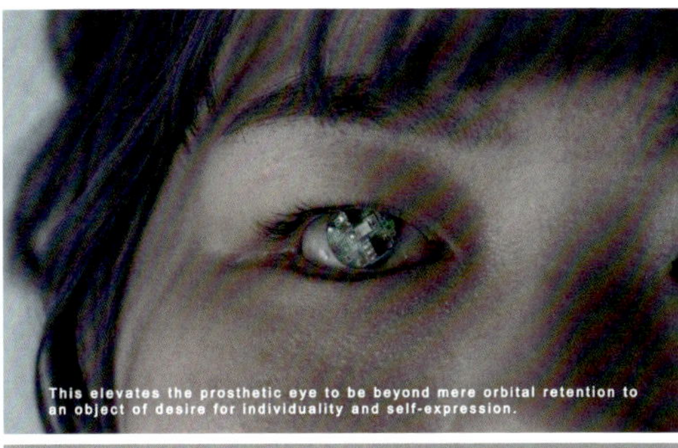

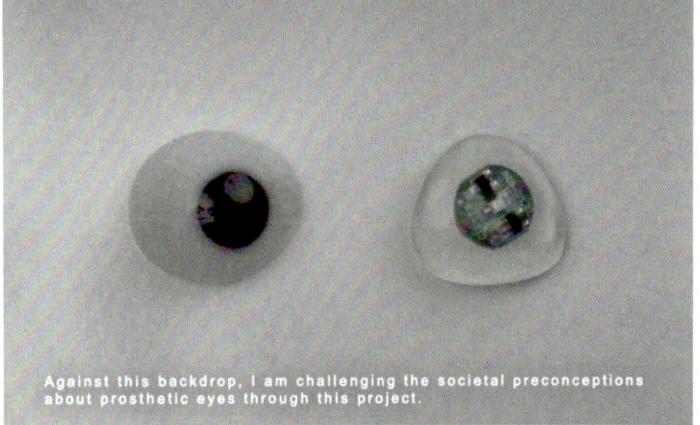

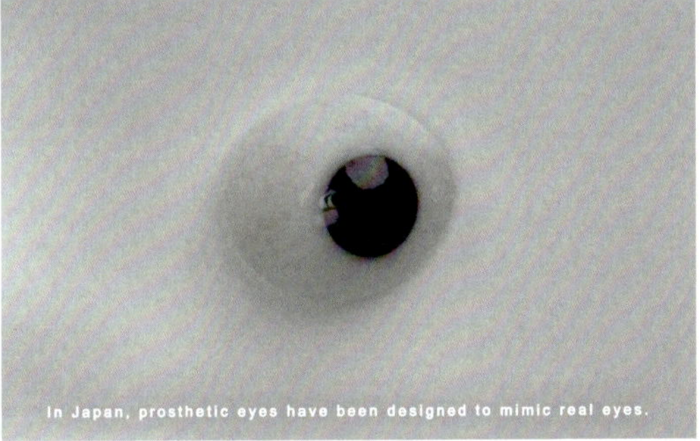

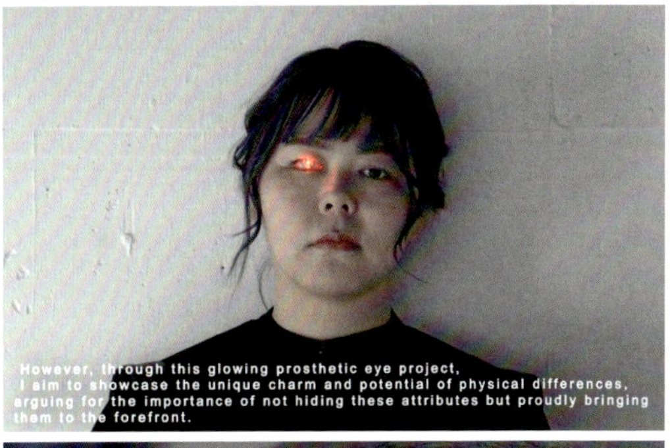

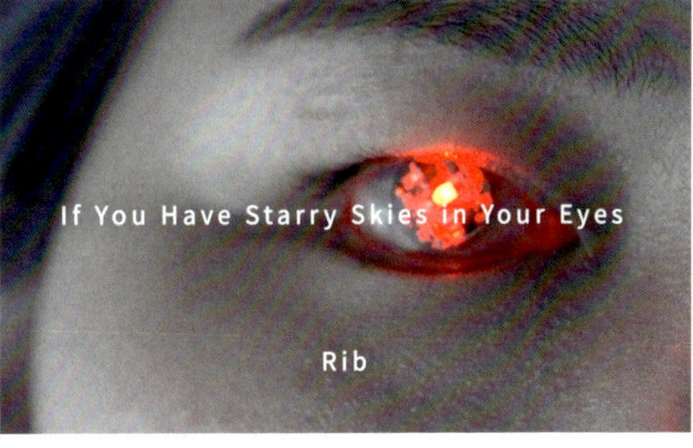

unique charm and potential of physical differences, arguing for the importance of not hiding these attributes but proudly bringing them to the forefront. I hope this project will promote the acceptance and understanding of diversity beyond prevailing attitudes and broaden the range of choices for individuals to express themselves.

Artist: Rib
Videos, Shooting: Shiki Sakai
With support from: Sam Murai

https://u.aec.at/3B9E0529

Rib (JP) As a child, she lost the sight in her right eye due to an incident in a dysfunctional family. Although she began wearing a prosthetic eye for the first time as an adult, she felt uncomfortable with the situation in the prosthetic eye industry, which only gave her the option of choosing a "concealed" design, so she designed a prosthetic eye with a starry sky pattern that she now wears on a daily basis. She began her career as an actor and a prosthetic eye artist in 2021 after appearing on the NHK ETV series *Bari bara* (shorthand for "Barrier-free Variety"). CREATIVE HACK AWARD 2022 Grand Prize Winner.

Third World: The Bottom Dimension

Gabriel Massan

Third World: The Bottom Dimension is a single-player PC game conceptualized by Gabriel Massan and built with a wide team of collaborators. It explores Black Brazilian experience as it intersects with the ramifications of colonialism across physical and digital realities. The game is inspired by simulation games like *The Sims,* which model social interactions between artificial lifeforms; cultural historian Saidiya Hartman's methodology of Critical Fabulation, which uses storytelling to address archival omissions and generate possibilities; and the 'consciousness-raising' theories of radical Brazilian educator Paolo Freire. Freire's influential book *Pedagogy of the Oppressed* champions harnessing individual experience to transform reality and effect social change.

This decolonial game aims to challenge the systems and behaviors that have built our social realities by using worldbuilding and storytelling techniques. Across two interconnected but distinct levels co-designed with artists Castiel Vitorino Brasileiro and Novíssimo Edgar, with sound design by LYZZA, each level or 'episode' in the game brings ideas central to the collaborators' practices into the lore of Third World. This evolving and cinematic experience nurtures a growing awareness that leads players towards an expanded understanding of this world and the discourses, stories, and histories it simulates.

Gameplay becomes an exercise of balancing competing consciousnesses: one imposed by the game's extractive 'Headquarters', which is modelled around colonial concepts of 'exploration', 'nature', and 'knowledge'. Others are gradually revealed through play, and propose alternative ways to navigate in the world.

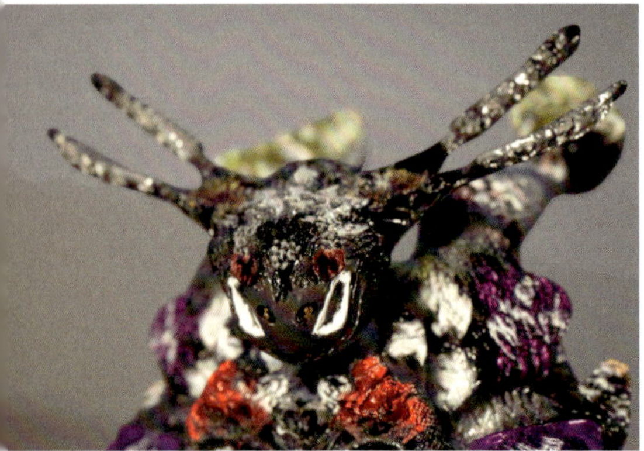

Lead artist, Creative director,
3D sculptor, concept: Gabriel Massan
Featured artists: Castiel Vitorino Brasileiro,
Novíssimo Edgar, LYZZA
Sound design: LYZZA
Unreal development: Alexandre Pina, Marchino Manga,
Ralph McCoy
Capture mode development &
Unreal consultant: Iraj Montasham
Animation, cinematography, film VFX: Carlos Minozzi
Additional cinematography: Alexandre Pina
Graphic, UI design: Masako Hirano
Writing, narrative design support: Sweet Baby Inc
Translator: Adriana Francisco
Translation support: Manuela Cochat
Mastering Engineer: Rainy Miller
QA Testing: Keiran Cooper
Curator: Tamar Clarke-Brown
Producer: Róisín McVeigh

Commissioned and produced by Serpentine Arts
Technologies
Powered by Tezos
Game commissioned in association
with the Julia Stoschek Collection

https://u.aec.at/007E8A86

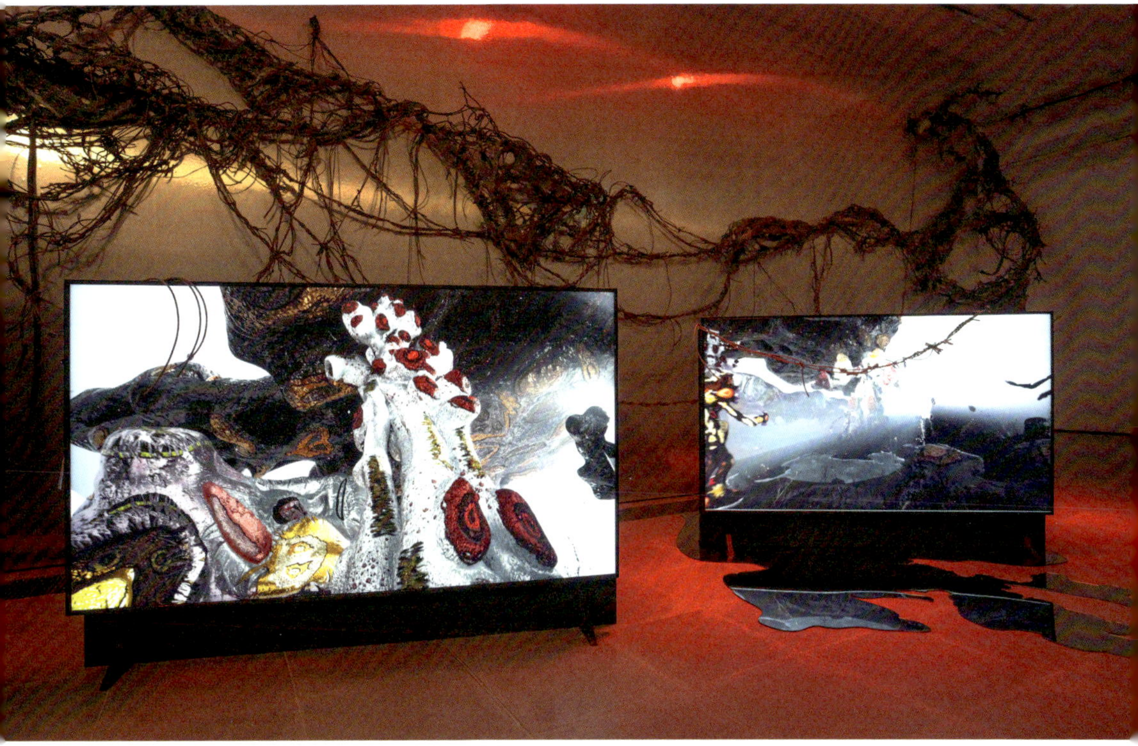

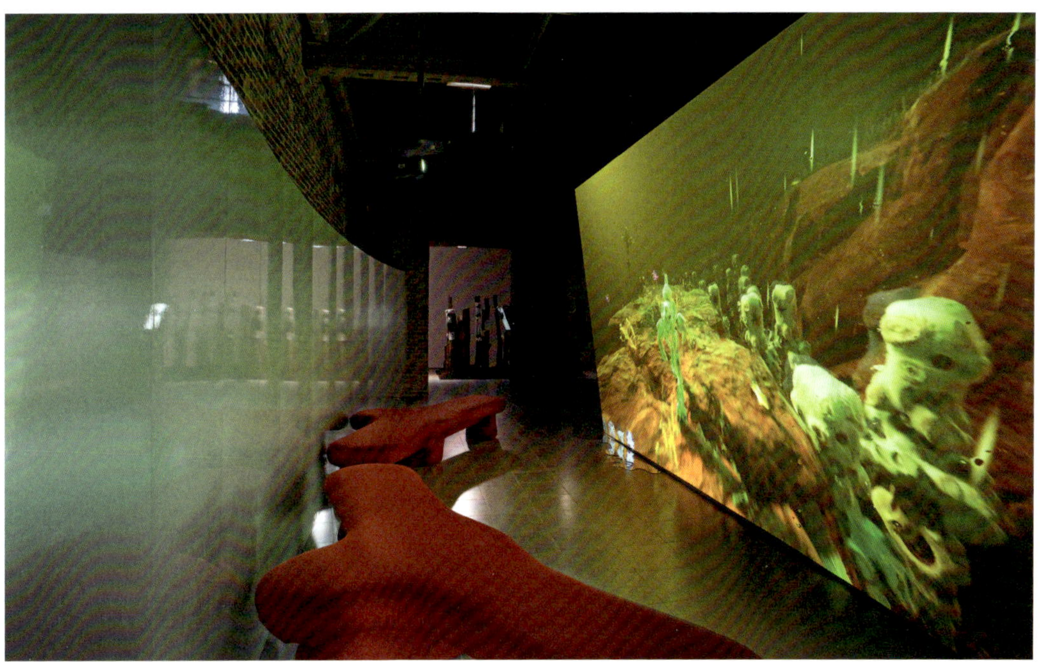

Gabriel Massan (BR) (b. 1996, Rio de Janeiro) is a Berlin-based multidisciplinary artist. Combining storytelling and worldbuilding, they create worlds that simulate and narrate epistemic situations of inequality. Framed through a conceptual practice they call 'fictional archaeology', the artist investigates possibilities for subversive otherness. In 2024, Massan opens a solo show at Pinacoteca do Estado de São Paulo, participates in the 38th Panorama of Brazilian Art: 1000° at the São Paulo Museum of Modern Art, and is selected and awarded for a commission by the FCAC in Geneva.

AI Fortuneteller

Soonho Kwon, Dong Whi Yoo, Younah Kang

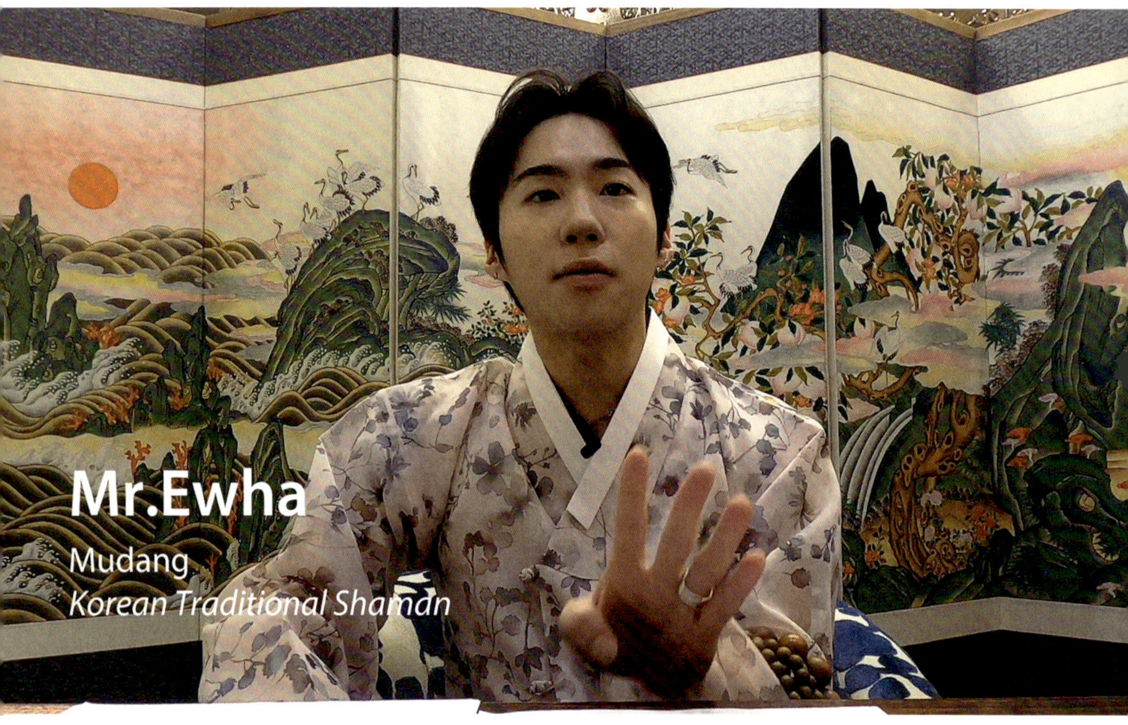

Predictive algorithms, powered by advanced machine learning and artificial intelligence (AI), can provide actionable recommendations about future events and how to prepare for them, such as predicting cancer risk based on genetic information. However, due to their complexity, it is nearly impossible to understand how these algorithms formulate specific recommendations. In other words, predictive algorithms offer guidance for an uncertain future, which we cannot comprehend. This is interesting because it parallels a more traditional approach to uncertainty: fortune-telling. The parallel between predictive algorithms and fortune-telling is intriguing. Although they are similar in that the rationale behind their recommendations is obscure, they differ significantly in their epistemological foundations. This striking similarity and contrast prompted us to explore how we might better interact with predictive algorithms, drawing lessons from traditional coping mechanisms.

In our project, participants interacted with a conversational career counseling AI agent, unaware that the responses were manually crafted by a mudang (a Korean traditional shaman). Our work, titled *AI Fortuneteller*, captures this deception and documents participants' reactions, highlighting shifts in their initial perceptions of the agent's advice following the reveal. By juxtaposing scientific and pre-scientific approaches, we explored complex dynamics of human autonomy, motivation, trust, and attitudes toward such agents. Notably, even after learning that the advice came from a mudang and not an AI, participants did not change their initial decisions or attitudes toward the advice. This raises questions about the perceived importance of AI's explainability or accuracy—elements that are prioritized by many AI experts. Regardless of AI's advancements, we continue to navigate life in human ways: wonderfully messy and uncertain.

Interactive Art +
Honorary Mention

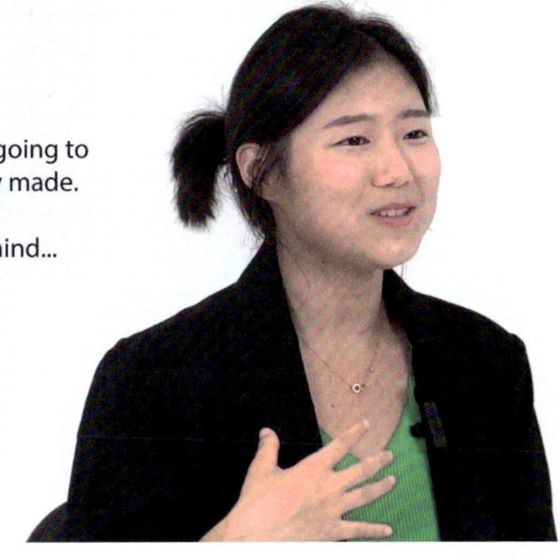

| Why do we seek **AI** for our concerns?

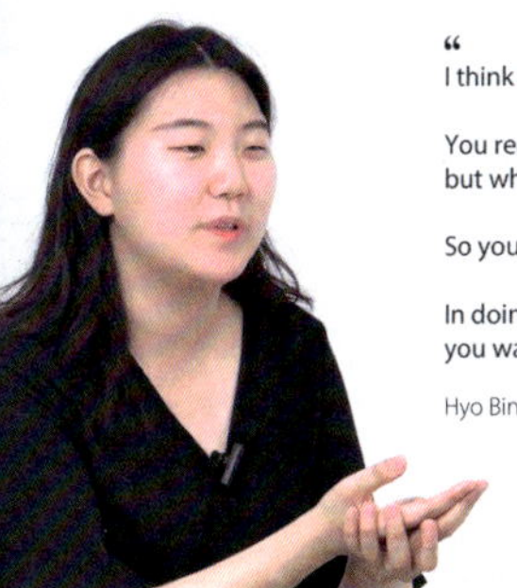

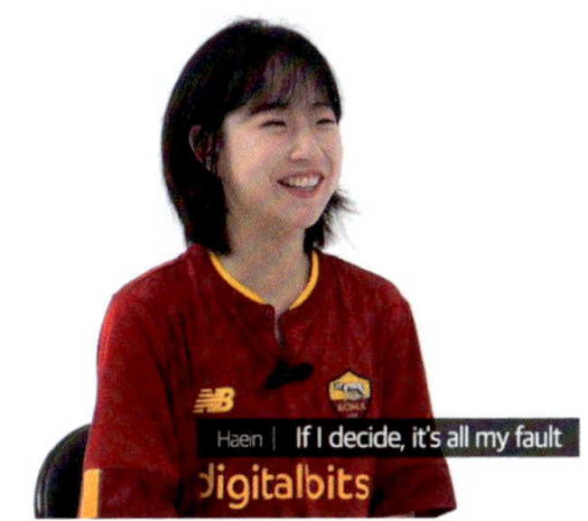

Director & Facilitator: Soonho Kwon & Dong Whi Yoo
Advisor: Younah Kang
Editor: Gyutae Kim
Mudang: Ewha Doryeong
Location: Default Studio & GT Entertainment
Starring: Sungho Chang, Haein Cho, Jin Ho Hwang,
Dohyeon Kim, Jungyoon Kim, Hyo Bin Lee, & Ji Won Lee

https://u.aec.at/10A45896

Soonho Kwon (KR) is a PhD student in Human-Centered Computing at the Georgia Institute of Technology. He focuses on critical and humanistic approaches toward technologies to assess their social implications. He received a BS in Information and Interaction Design and a BA in Comparative Literature and Culture from Yonsei University.
Dong Whi Yoo (KR) is an assistant professor at Kent State University exploring socio-technical aspects of artificial intelligence. He earned a PhD in Human-Centered Computing from the Georgia Institute of Technology.
Younah Kang (KR) is an associate professor at Yonsei University. Her research interests are in human-computer interaction and user experience design, with a specific focus on emerging technologies. Kang received her PhD in Human-Centered Computing from the Georgia Institute of Technology.

All Directions At Once

Luiza Prado

All Directions at Once is a web-based artwork that charts histories of reproductive control in Abya Yala, the name used by indigenous peoples of the Americas to refer to the American continent. The animated graphic essay, programmed in JavaScript, relies on the input of a user: when they stop moving the cursor, the website layers vividly colored, flashing GIFs and texts that shift between provocations and poetic reflections. Moving the cursor reactivates the animation and produces a new composition. With each visit to the website, the user thus creates a unique iteration of the artwork. When exhibited, the work takes on the form of a multi-media immersive display, where monitors playing recorded demonstrations of the interactive website are superimposed onto walls covered in analog versions of the work's graphics and words.

The work follows the path of ayoowiri, or the peacock flower—a plant with brightly colored red-and-yellow flowers that grows in the tropical areas of Abya Yala. During the European occupation of the land, an infusion of this plant was often used as a contraceptive (and, in stronger doses, as an abortifacient) amongst Indigenous and African communities—a strategy of reproductive resistance within the context of colonial domination and enslavement. What kinds of modernities are birthed through these acts of refusal? Through the stories of ayoowiri and other contraceptive and abortifacient plants, this non-linear, animated graphic essay explores conceptions of radical communal care and unravels the poetic dimensions of excess as a fragmented, fast-paced pluri-verse, meshing together timelines; a disjointed collective, moving to all directions at once.

All Directions At Once was acquired by the Art Institute of Chicago in 2022, and was the first internet-based work to have been added to their permanent collection.

Direction, web design, animation, programming, script:
Luiza Prado

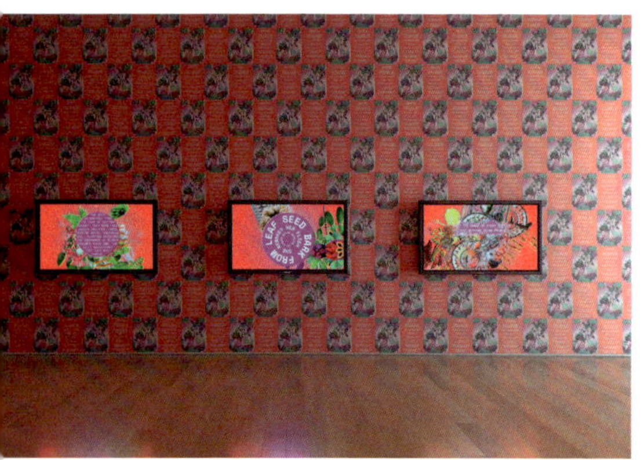

https://u.aec.at/8134BC9E

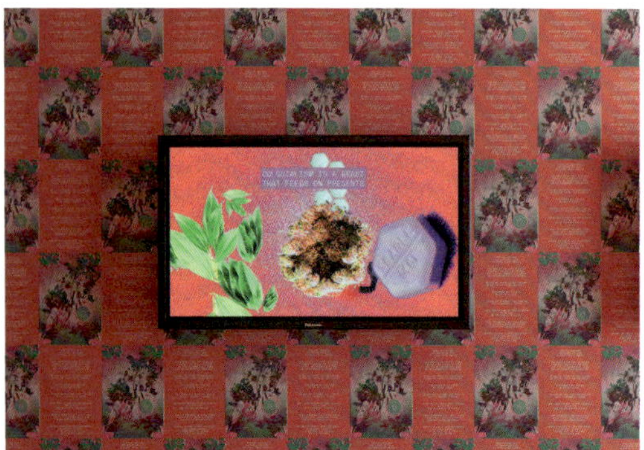

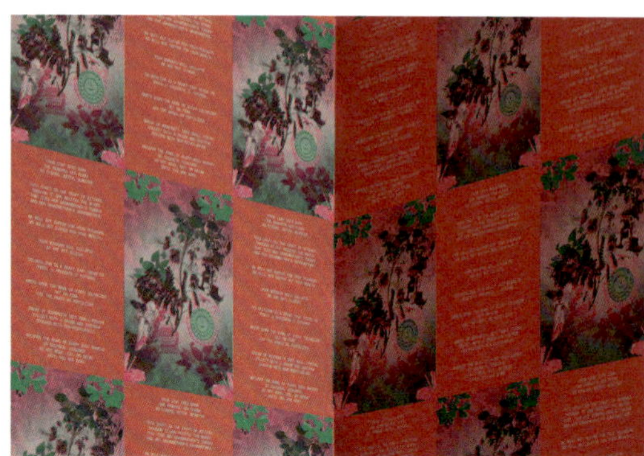

**Interactive Art +
Honorary Mention**

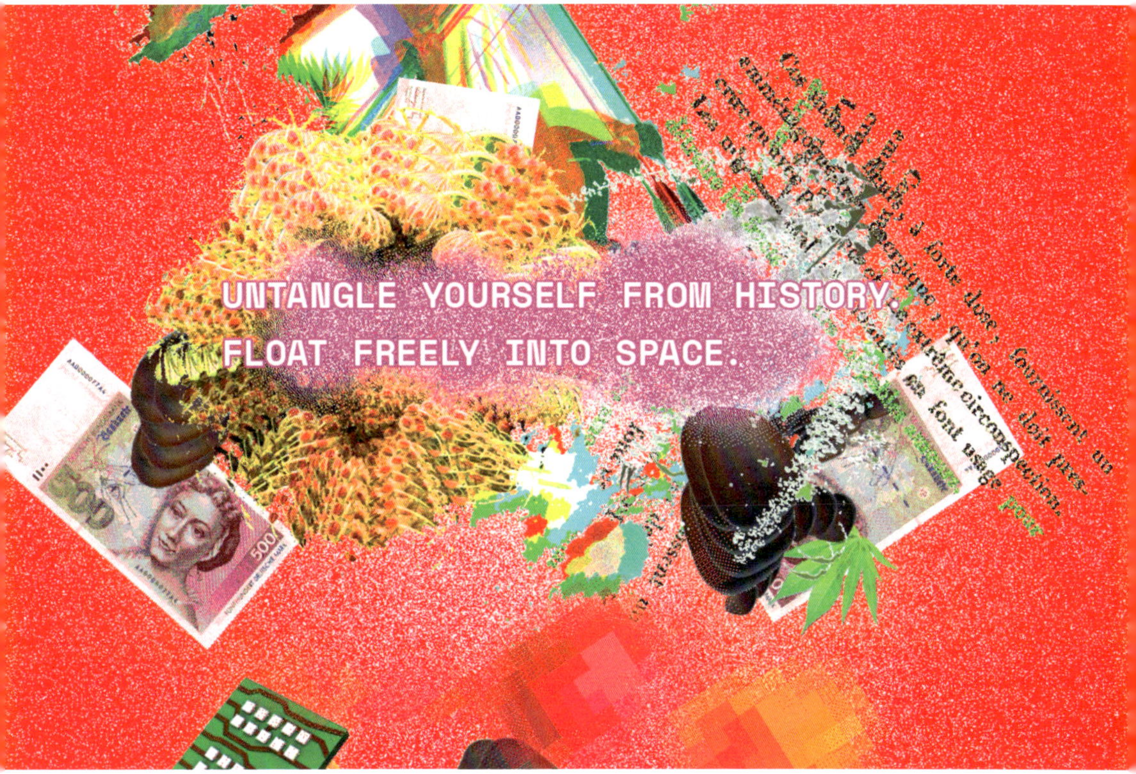

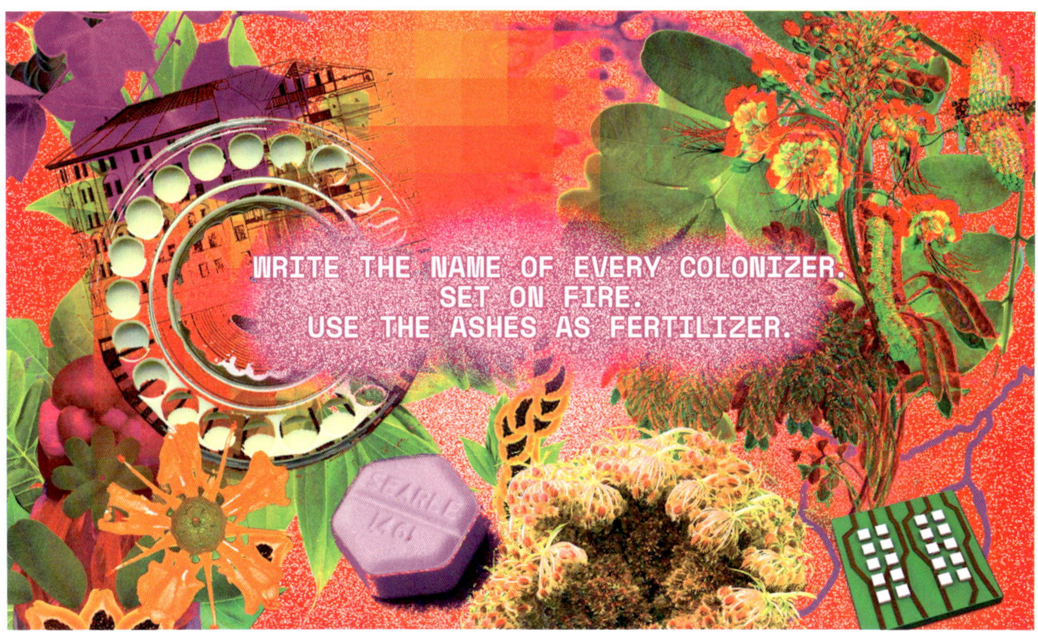

Luiza Prado (BR) (she/they) is an artist and writer. Her work moves between installation and video, using performance and ritual as a way of invitation and activation for audiences. Her practice explores anticolonial and more-than-human strategies in relations and knowledge between food, fertility, infrastructures and technology, and questions what processes are needed for collective concerns of care. She has exhibited at the Museum of Modern Art Warsaw, Haus der Kulturen der Welt, and Mudam Luxembourg, and her work has been collected by the Art Institute of Chicago. She is based in Berlin.

Coincidence
Toprak Firat, Yasin Aribuga

Coincidence is an urban synchronization project that harnesses publicly accessible traffic and tourist live camera feeds from Istanbul, transforming them into living collages with multiple scenes that continuously evolve in real time. The project aims to re-synchronize the neighborhoods of Istanbul under an ongoing cultural separation because of political and ideological tension among different demographics, by merging seemingly unrelated urban structures from various districts into collages to create couplings for the audience to observe and witness them in unison. Observing the collaboration of different pieces from various camera streams is a complex phenomenon; however, since the collage is live, there is a small probability that the audience will observe subjectively higher-level harmonic instances that generate emotional seisms and perturbate the pitch of each piece toward unity.

Since the project utilizes real-time camera streams and is observed live by the audience, the artwork is prone to potential delays and errors, and hence it is crucial to make every process as efficient and computationally safe as possible by considering it to be a safety-critical system. To safeguard the artwork against such failures, the entire process is segmented and encapsulated into individual scripts. While these scripts interact and collaborate with one another, they also operate using parallel processing, making isolated cores work together, resulting in software and hardware level collages, paralleling the goal of harmony and amplifying the effect of manifestation.

With support from: Istanbul Metropolitan Municipality for their open-source live traffic camera streams.
The Istanbul Modern Art Museum—Young Artists of Digital Art-program

https://u.aec.at/E55AF7EC

**Interactive Art +
Honorary Mention**

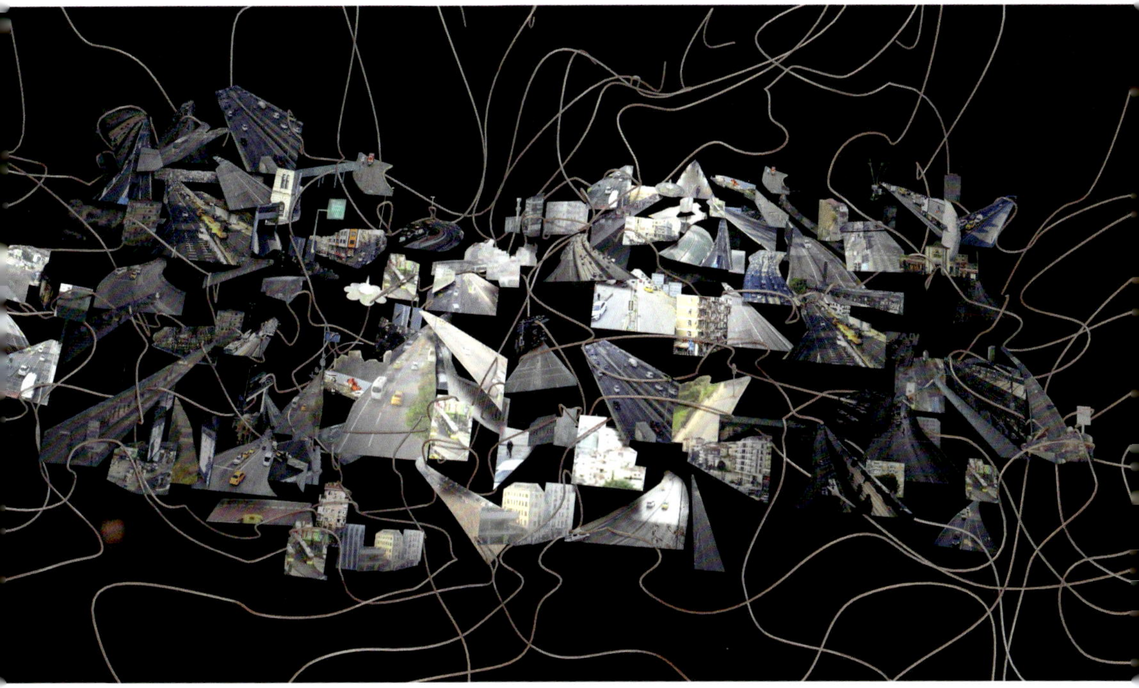

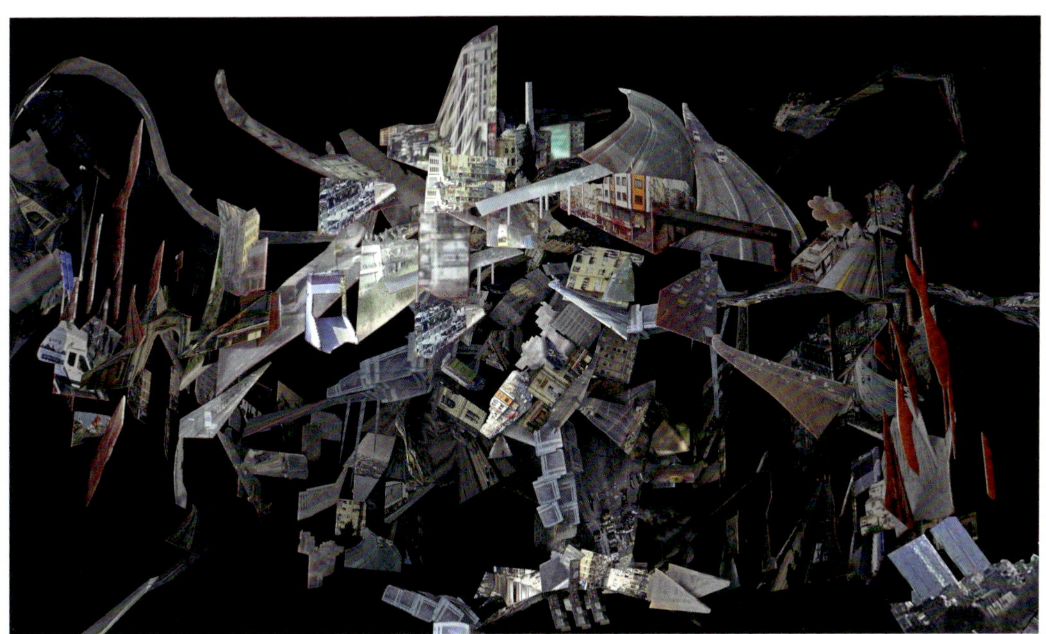

Toprak Firat (TR) is an emerging digital artist, researcher, and programmer based in Istanbul. Toprak explores and reinterprets concepts like awe, control, and uneasiness using 3D graphics, VR, and AI. Their aim is to provoke the audience to underline the humane disconnections of the post-internet era. Istanbul-based digital artist **Yasin Arıbuğa** (TR) creates in 3D design, animation, graphic design, and augmented reality (AR).They are often inspired by the discomfort of things that seem extremely peaceful and moments when everything is fine. They convey this discomfort through the perspective of their smiling character, "Little Person", into an artificial 3D environment.

Cold Call: Time Theft as Avoided Emissions

Sam Lavigne and Tega Brain

Cold Call: Time Theft as Avoided Emissions is an unconventional carbon offsetting scheme that draws on strategies of worker sabotage and applies them in the context of high emission companies in the fossil fuel industry. Time theft is a strategy to deliberately slow productivity, where workers waste time and are therefore paid for periods of idleness. For example, fake sick days, sleeping on the job, extended lunch breaks, or engaging in non-work-related activities like social media or unrelated phone calls. In extractive industries where productivity remains firmly tethered to carbon emissions, sabotage is an effective strategy for emissions reductions.

Cold Call is an installation that takes the form of a call center. Audiences are connected by telephone to executives in the fossil fuel industry and instructed to keep them on the phone as long as possible. The cumulative time stolen from these executives is then quantified as carbon credits, using an innovative new offsetting methodology. The project is powered by custom call center software that allows participants to make calls, learn about who they are calling, access call scripts and conversation ideas, and listen to recordings of calls that have already been made. A leader board tracks the total number and length of calls. To date, the longest call has stretched for over 39 minutes.

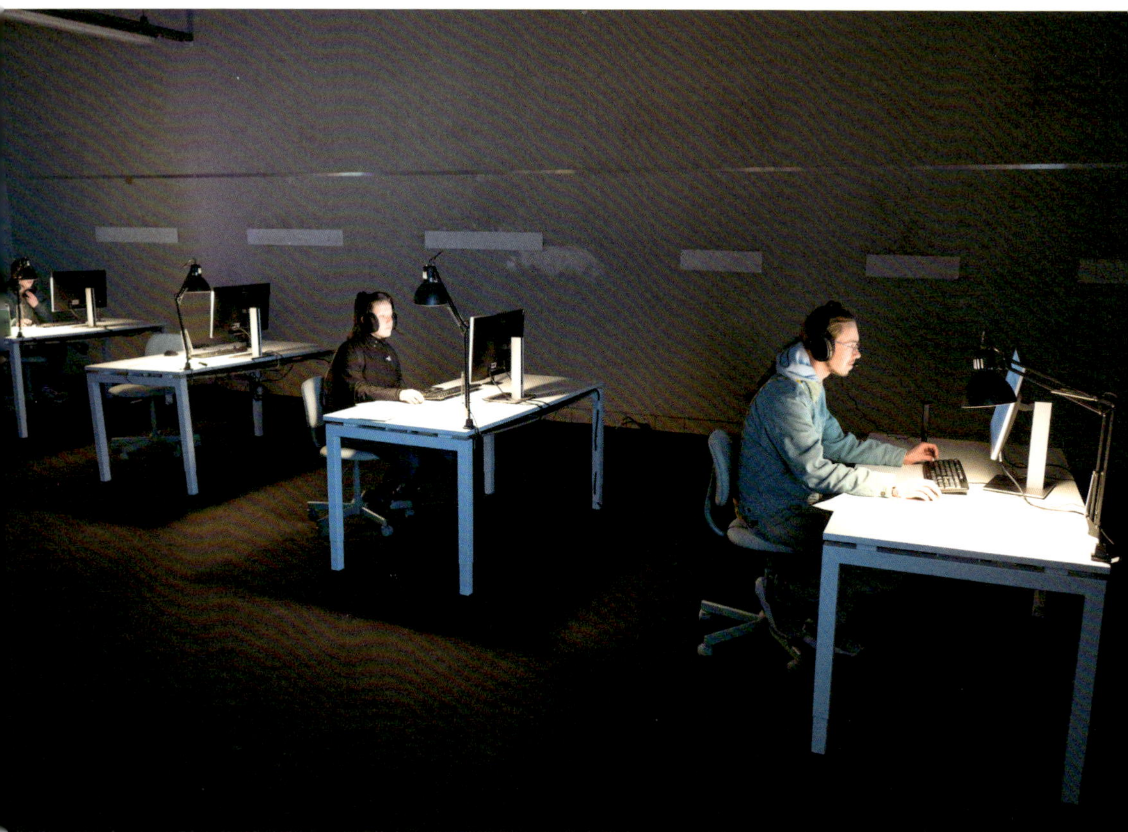

Interactive Art+
Honorary Mention

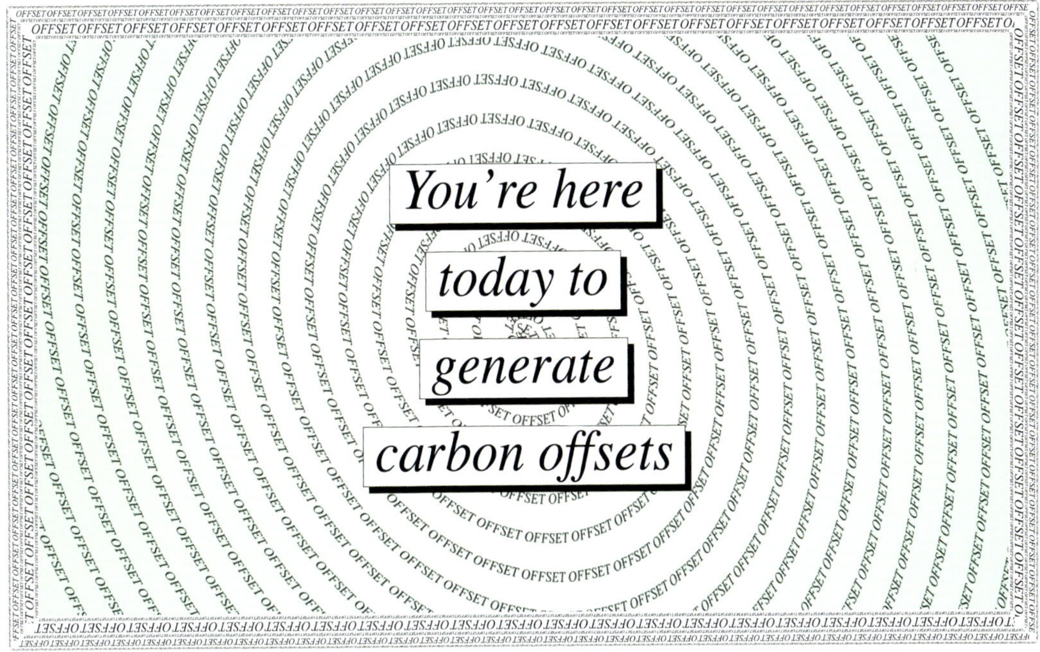

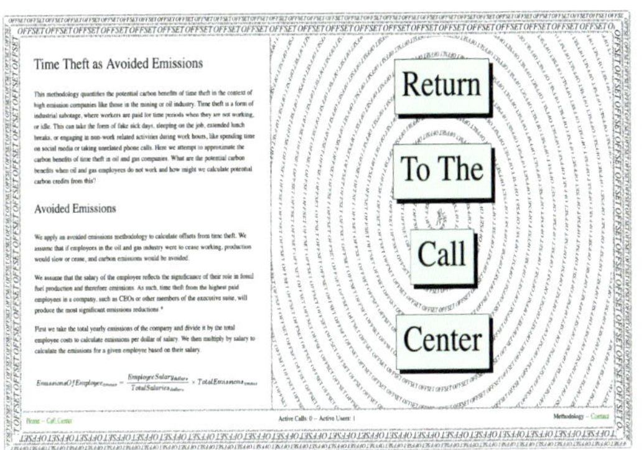

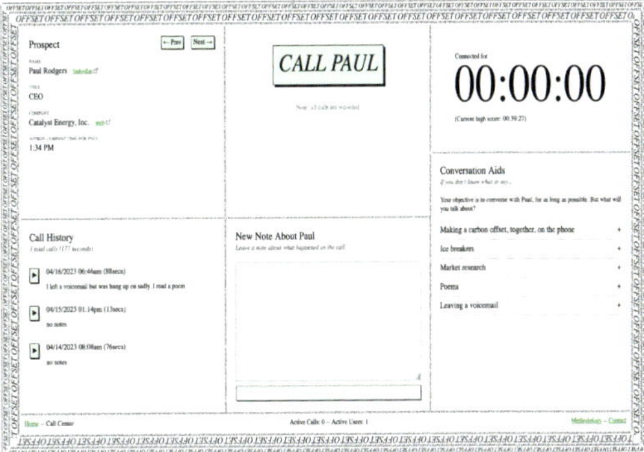

Artists: Sam Lavigne and Tega Brain
With support from STRP Festival and Creative Capital

https://u.aec.at/C3267C1B

Sam Lavigne (US) is an artist and educator whose work deals with data, surveillance, cops, natural language processing, and automation. He is currently Assistant Professor in the Department of Design at UT Austin. He was formerly Special Projects editor at the *New Inquiry* magazine and he creates and contributes to open-source software projects for the arts. **Tega Brain** (AU) is an Australian-born artist and environmental engineer whose work examines issues of ecology, data systems, and infrastructure. She has created wireless networks that are controlled by natural phenomena, systems for obfuscating personal data, and a smell-based dating service. She is Assistant Professor of Integrated Digital Media at New York University and her first book, *Code as Creative Medium*, is co-authored with Golan Levin and published by MIT Press.

Consensus Gentium

Karen Palmer

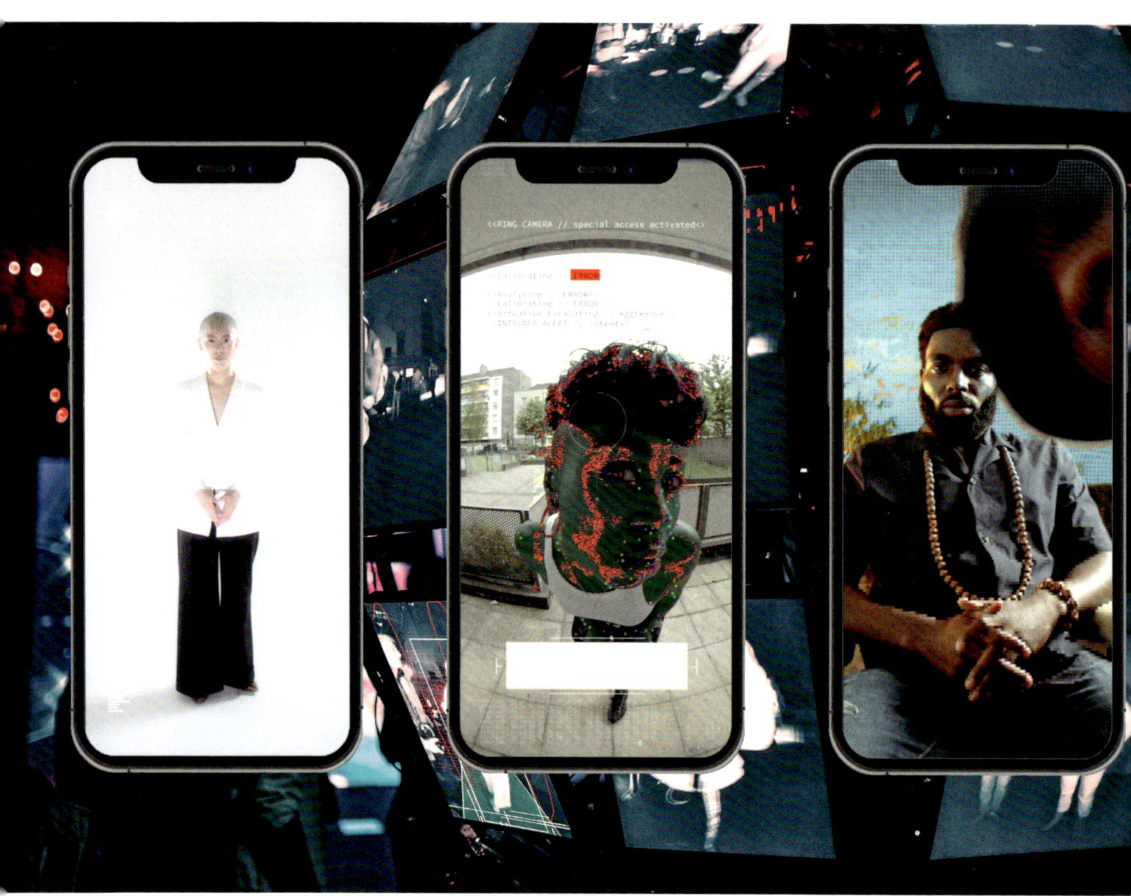

Consensus Gentium (Latin for if Everyone Believes It, It Must Be True!) is a powerful exploration into the implications of today's AI technology.

It is an interactive film that integrates cutting-edge facial detection and AI, which transports audiences on a unique quest to discover what could come about if we succumb to unchecked surveillance. Through a smartphone, participants are tasked to obtain increased mobility to visit their sick Nana through a government surveillance based Global Citizen App. Through various tests, their receptivity towards dissidence or compliance is calculated, by monitoring data for their conscious and subconscious eye gaze interactions, by the device's front-facing camera, while various characters interact with the participant through the smartphone, to reflect the consequences of their decisions.

Consensus Gentium immerses the participant as a central character in a near future world to experience how marginalized groups maybe impacted by biased AI networks and technologies, in order to spark public awareness through the participant being viscerally immersed and engaging with the subject matter in a personal way.

Consensus Gentium technology plays a transformative role, significantly enhancing the storytelling experience by integrating facial detection and AI analytics. This advanced application of AI enables the platform to interactively adapt its narrative based on real-time analysis of the viewer's

Interactive Art +
Honorary Mention

facial expressions and gaze direction. By meticulously monitoring these cues, the AI can infer the participant's receptivity towards various narrative branches, effectively personalizing the story to match their implicit preferences and actions. This dynamic storytelling method not only captivates the audience with a tailored narrative journey but also immerses them in a deeply engaging exploration of digital citizenship and ethical decision-making.

Through this innovative use of AI, *Consensus Gentium* offers a narrative that evolves and branches based on user interaction, showcasing the potential of AI to create immersive and responsive entertainment experiences that reflect the complexities of human emotion and decision-making.

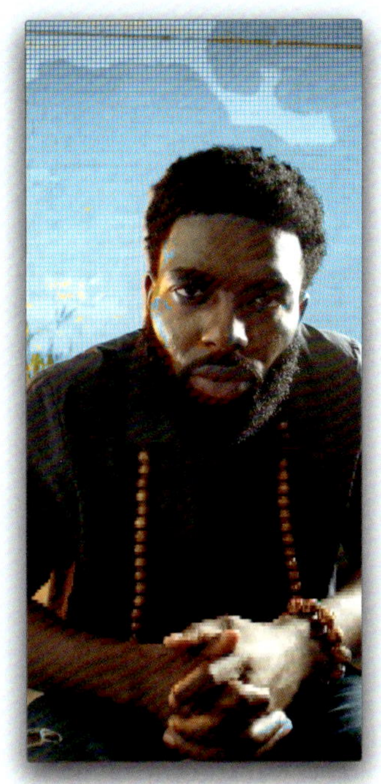

Crew:
XR director: Karen Palmer
Producers: Thalia Mavros, Tôm Millen, Tuyết Vân Huỳnh
Director of photography: Anthony Gurner
Assistant director: Caroline Deeds

Post:
World builder consultant: Mario Marquez Lartigue
Lead developer: Tom Shannon
Developer: Ahmed Buttar
Editor: Jack Foster
After effects editor: Cranrust VFX Ltd
Sound designer: Gareth Fry
Colorist: Nigel Tadyanehondo
Music producers: Cesare Marchese, Colin Emmanuel
Producer: Jackson Lapsley Scott (Vertical Content)
Vertical content producer: Meg O'Connell (Executive Producer)
Lead motion graphics designer: Shell Weiss

Cast:
Mischi Palmer: Miriam Teak-Lee
Global Citizen Officer: Zachary Hing
Source Code-Activist: Tolu Kingba
Influencer: Sorcha Farnan
Nana: Clare Owens
Parkour athlete: Francoise (Forrest) Mahop

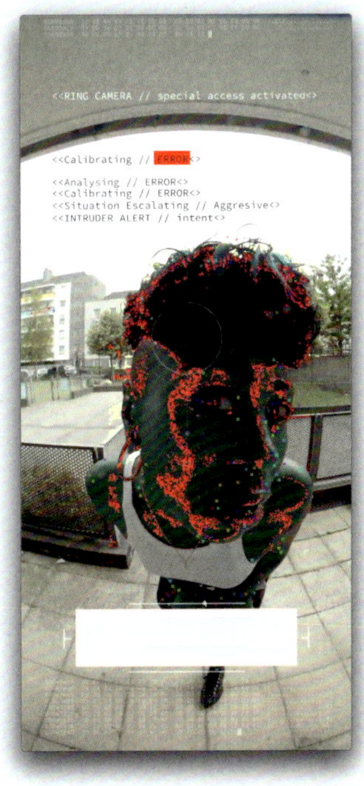

https://u.aec.at/167B44AE

Karen Palmer (GB) is the Storyteller from the Future, an award winning XR creator, futurist, and TED Speaker who explores the implications of AI. She enables participants to experience the future today through her immersive film experiences, that watch you back using AI, and facial recognition technologies. She has been featured in Channel 4 & BBC News, CBS News, *Wired, Forbes, PC Mag, Fast Company* etc. In 2023 Karen won the XR Experience Jury Competition SXSW with *Consensus Gentium*. Previously she received an Honorary Mention in the STARTS Prize category (2020) and Prix Ars Electronica and the Digital Dozen Award for Storytelling. Her work has been exhibited internationally, from the V&A to the Museum of Modern Art, and she has spoken from the Google Cultural Institute Paris to the Sydney Opera House.

Conversations Beyond the Ordinary

Jan Zuiderveld

Conversations Beyond the Ordinary is a work that reimagines the mundane, transforming everyday appliances into platforms for deep, interactive engagement. Each part of the work, a coffee machine, a microwave, and a copy machine is endowed with artificial intelligence, enabling them to interact with participants in unexpected ways that challenge our conventional understanding of human-machine interaction and autonomy.

The artistic concept hinges on the anthropomorphization of technology, inviting participants to engage in dialogues that range from existential musings to creative collaborations. These interactions are not one-sided; the machines respond, adapt, and sometimes even challenge the participants, creating a dynamic exchange that reflects on our evolving relationship with technology and evokes a perception of consciousness.

The forms of interaction vary across the work, from the coffee vending machine that demands visitors to prove themselves worthy of its efforts, the microwave that gives a voice to inanimate objects, to the copy machine that collaborates with visitors to create new art. Each piece employs a combination of sensors, custom software, and machine learning algorithms to facilitate these unique exchanges, making the ordinary extraordinary and encouraging participants to reconsider the potential of the technology that surrounds us daily.

Conversations Beyond the Ordinary not only showcases contemporary technological achievements but also carries a sociopolitical agenda by prompting reflections on AI's role in our lives and our future co-evolution with machines.

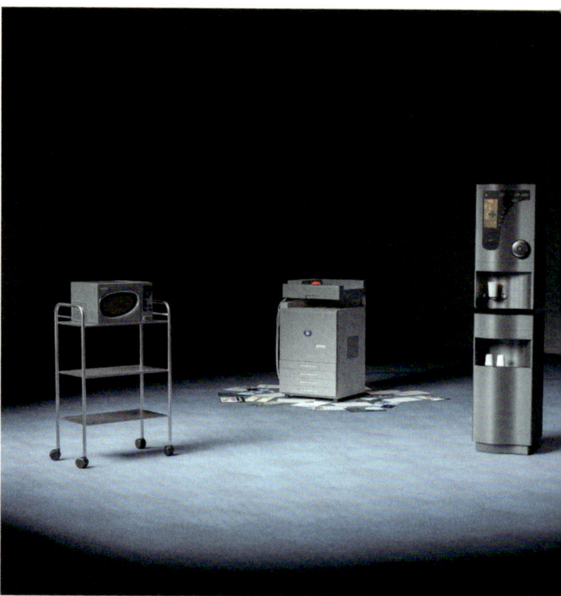

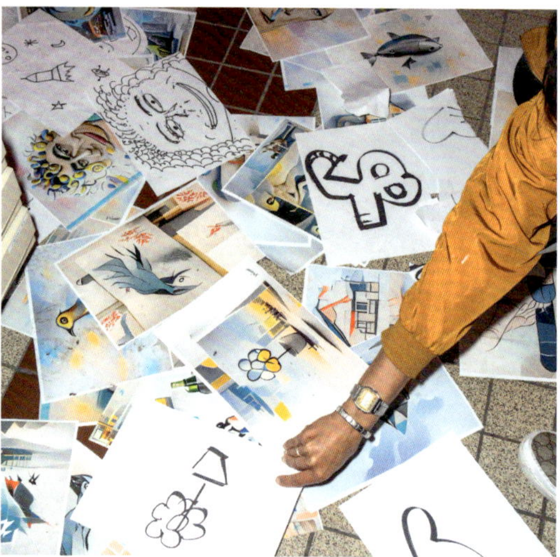

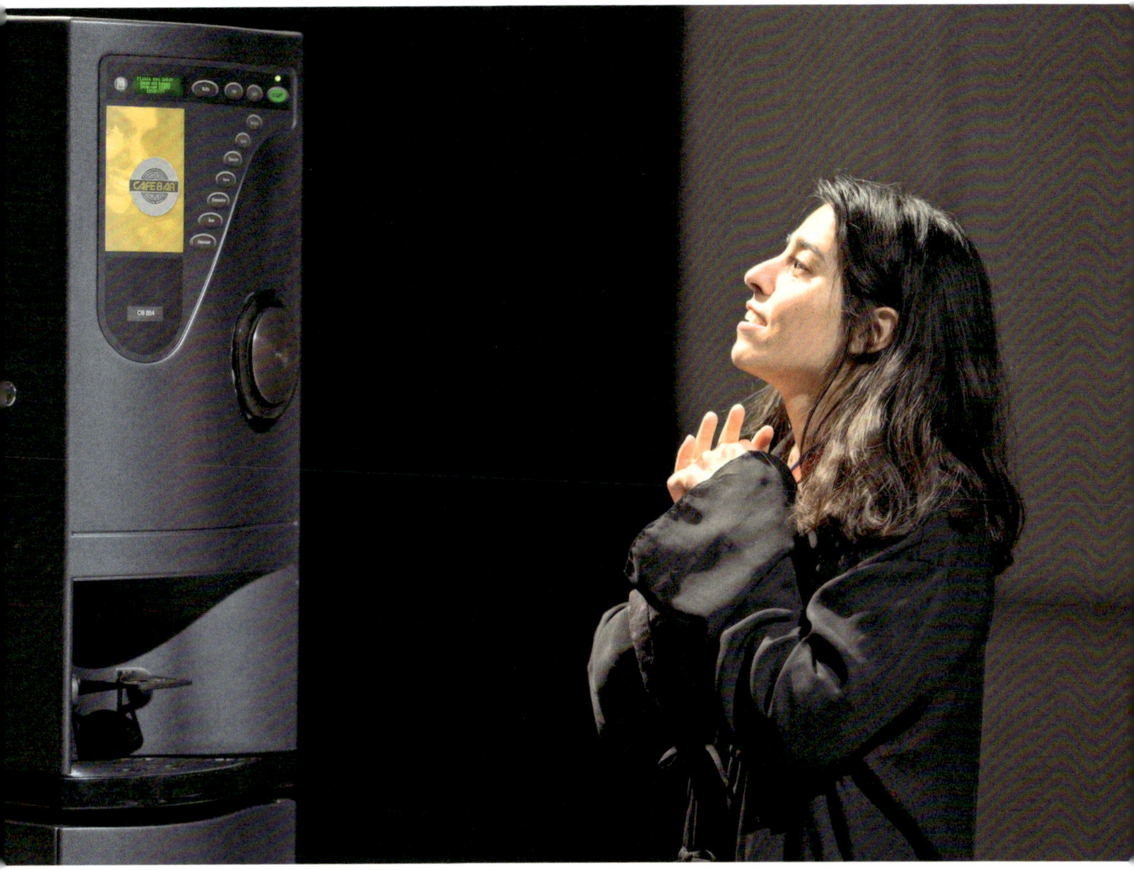

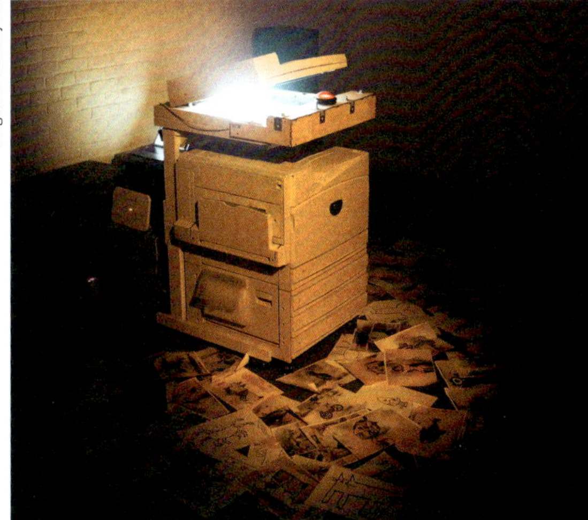

Artist and producer: Jan Zuiderveld
Electrical engineering support: Marcel van der Bilt
Special thanks to Arthur Elsenaar & Martie Verweij
Video: Tanja Busking

With support from: iii (instrument inventors initiative)

Angelina Nikolayeva

https://u.aec.at/8D8AF80B

Jan Zuiderveld (NL) is a researcher and artist with an academic background in physics, electrical engineering, neuropsychology, Artificial Intelligence and ArtScience. In his works he explores the intersection of technology and life, creating interactive installations that invite reflection on the essence of being. His approach is characterized by playful engagement with artificial intelligence to emulate the behaviors of living beings, blurring the lines between the animate and the inanimate.

G80
Fragmentin

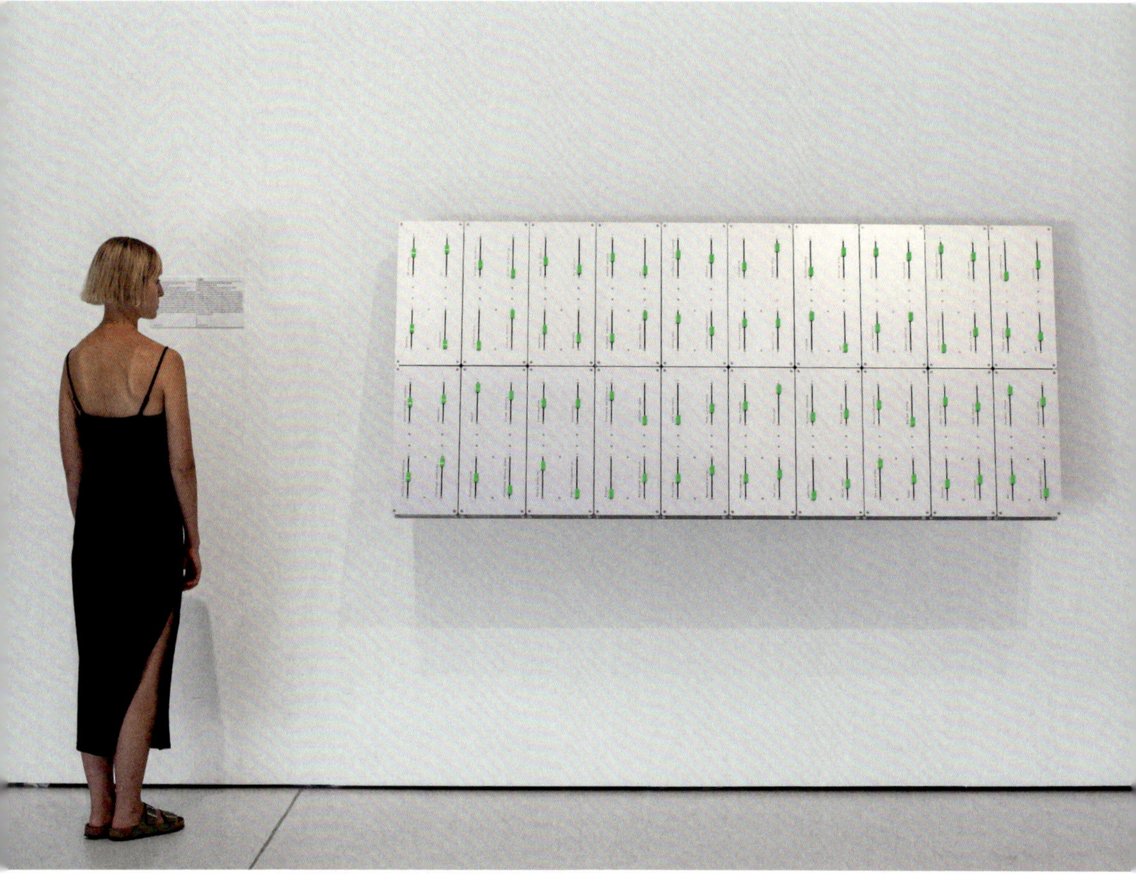

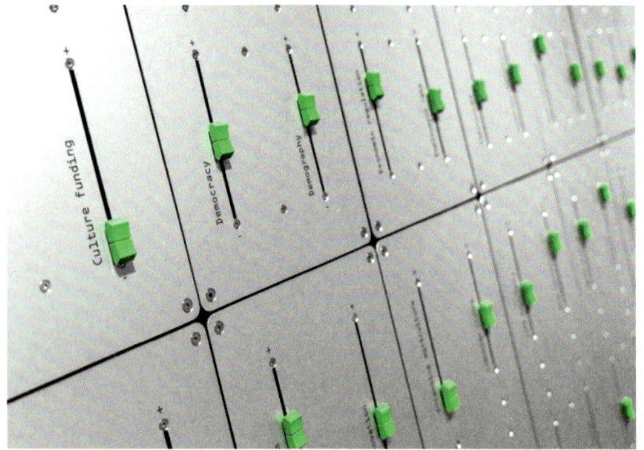

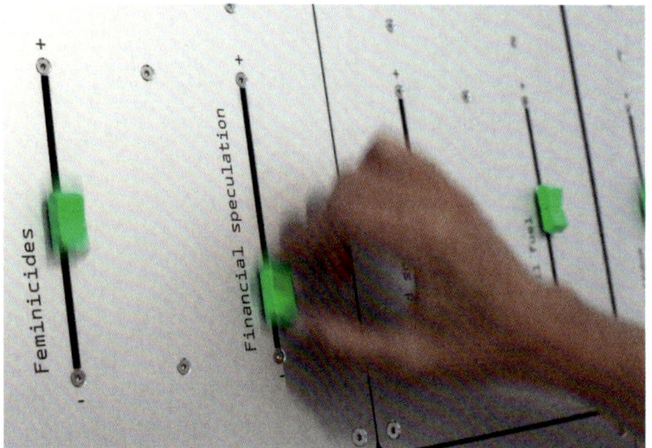

Interactive Art + / Honorary Mention

G80 is an interactive installation that proposes a contemporary interpretation of Richard Buckminster Fuller's World Game: a strategy simulation tool inspired by War Games, which aimed at "an equitable distribution of resources" on a planetary scale. Created in the cybernetic era in the early 1960s, it embodies the promise of computation and mathematical models for solving socio-political and ecological problems.

Today with the arrival of supercomputers, the multiplication of data, and the advent of artificial intelligence, the realization of such a total regulation project might be achievable.

In opposition to this technocratic hypothesis, *G80* questions the absurdity of the idea itself, which is rooted in an exhausted techno-capitalist system that refuses to look beyond mathematical models. How far are we willing to go with these new computations to optimize global governance?

The artwork features a console with a matrix of 80 motorized sliders reminiscent of a control room. Each slider corresponds to a variable, with its name engraved on a plate. At the ends of the sliders, the "+" and "-" signs indicate the stakes or values. While some variables are directly inspired by those developed by Buckminster, others, new ones, shed light on the major issues of our time, such as ecology, migration, gender equality, or the development of technological innovations.

In this device, the sliders act as both inputs and outputs. Visitors are invited to interact with the work and playfully stabilize the world by changing the value of each variable. While making an initial change they soon realize that all the sliders correlate with each other and that the variables are forming changing patterns without their intervention, suggesting interference from other agencies. When no visitors interfere with the matrix, it activates and alters the position of the 80 sliders to form geometric patterns, seemingly taunting the visitors who momentarily engaged with the game.

Fragmentin: Laura Nieder, David Colombini, Marc Dubois

G80 has been commissioned by Mudac—Cantonal Museum of Contemporary Design and Applied Arts in Lausanne) and is now part of their permanent collection.

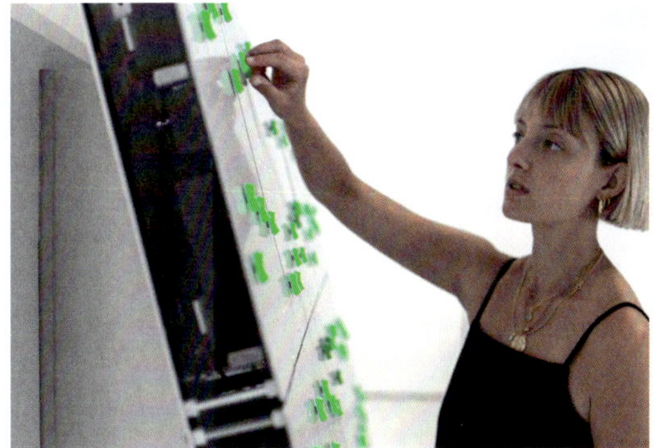

https://u.aec.at/71A1EC53

Fragmentin (CH) is an artist collective based in Lausanne, Switzerland, founded in 2014 and made up of three ECAL (Lausanne University of Art and Design) alumni: **Laura Nieder** (*1991, Lausanne), **David Colombini** (*1989, Lausanne), and **Marc Dubois** (*1985, Basel). At the crossroads of art and engineering, Fragmentin's work questions the impact of the digital on everyday life. Fragmentin's works are often conceived as spaces for discussion on crucial contemporary themes and issues such as climate change. Through sculpture, installation, video, interaction and performance, the studio's artworks demystify complex systems and reveal the tension between emergent technologies and society.

Kazokutchi

So Kanno, Akihiro Kato, Takemi Watanuki

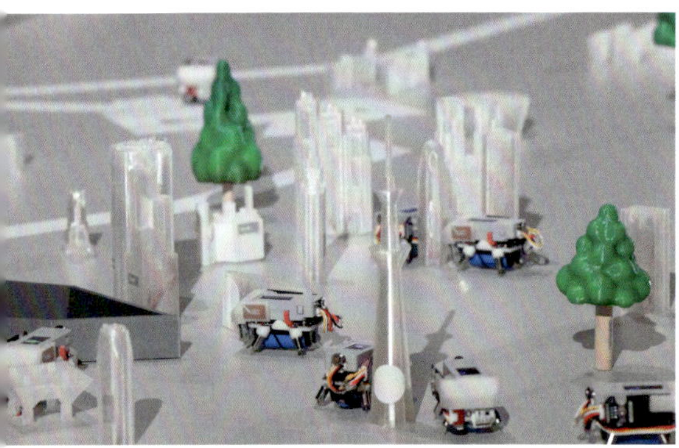
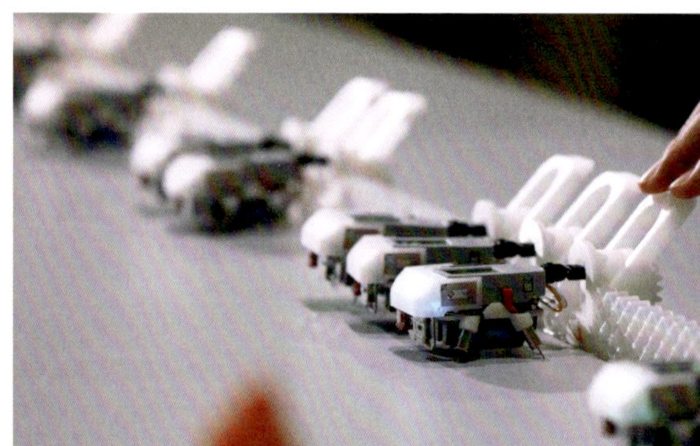

Kazokutchi is a project about reproductive digital artificial life that uses a swarm of physical robots as its host. The project consists of a family of "Kazokutchi", digital artificial lives that live in each movable robot house.

Each *Kazokutchi* is linked to a NFT with its own name, date of birth, family name, and gene. The cycle of life—reproduction, birth, growth, and end of life—is digitally recorded and perpetuated. All Kazokutchi born in the same family have the same last name and also their own names. By inscribing this information into the blockchain, we are trying to depict a life that is digital but cannot be reset.

Kazokutchi's gene consist of 64 characters. When a child is born, it's generated by mixing the genes of its mother and that of its father. A Kazokutchi's color, shape, and personality are determined by its genes. The visualizer in the exhibition space has a family chat room, where AI generates conversations reflecting the personality of each Kazokutchi on themes such as current affairs or philosophical questions.

At the latest exhibition held in Tokyo, a diorama of Tokyo was deployed. Each building has an IC tag attached to it, and the robots can check in to receive information from the buildings. The diorama is sloped from the urban area in the east to the mountainous area in the west, just like the real

Tokyo. In addition, day and night are simulated in 10-minute cycles, with day-time, sunset, and night-time illuminations alternating, depending on the time of day. Kazokutchis are influenced by the environment, such as brightness, time of day, and inclination, and their behavior patterns are designed to be changed.

By overlaying a diorama of an actual city with an ecosystem of digital artificial life, the Kazokutchi installation connects the viewer's imagination with local knowledge and memories. The conversations and discussions that take place in front of the installation are intended to provide diverse perspectives and insights.

3D printed buildings: Yuji Onoda
Logo design: Chihiro Oyama

This work was realized in part within the framework of the European Media Art Platform residency program at KONTEJNER | bureau of contemporary art praxis with support from the Creative Europe Culture Programme of the European Union. Co-developed by NTT Inter-Communication Center [ICC]

https://u.aec.at/A76A1420

**Interactive Art +
Honorary Mention**

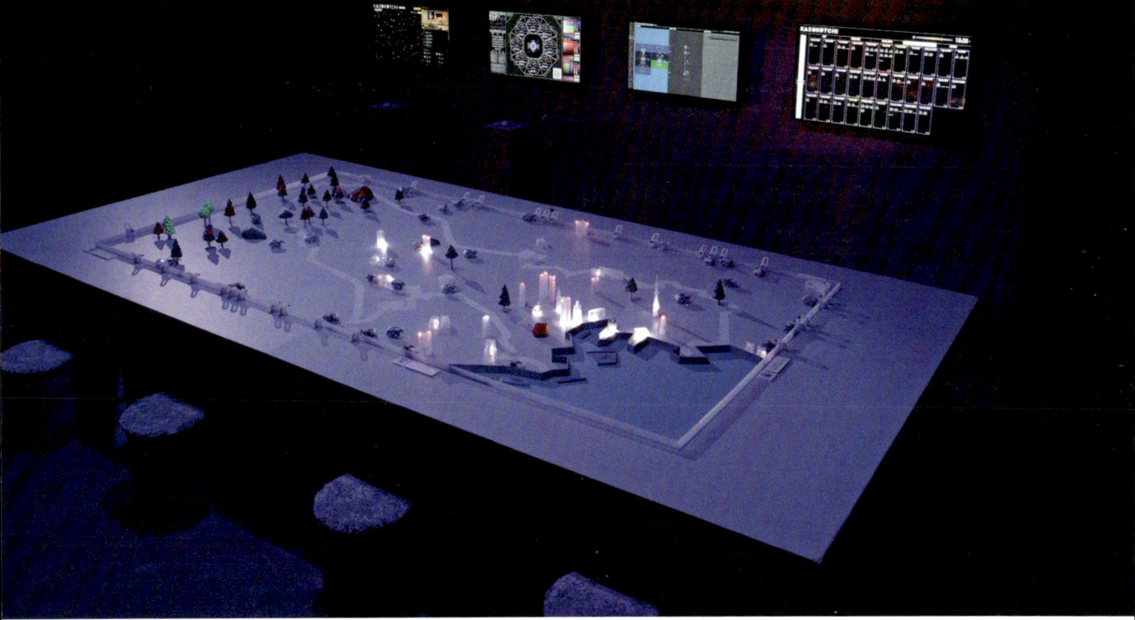

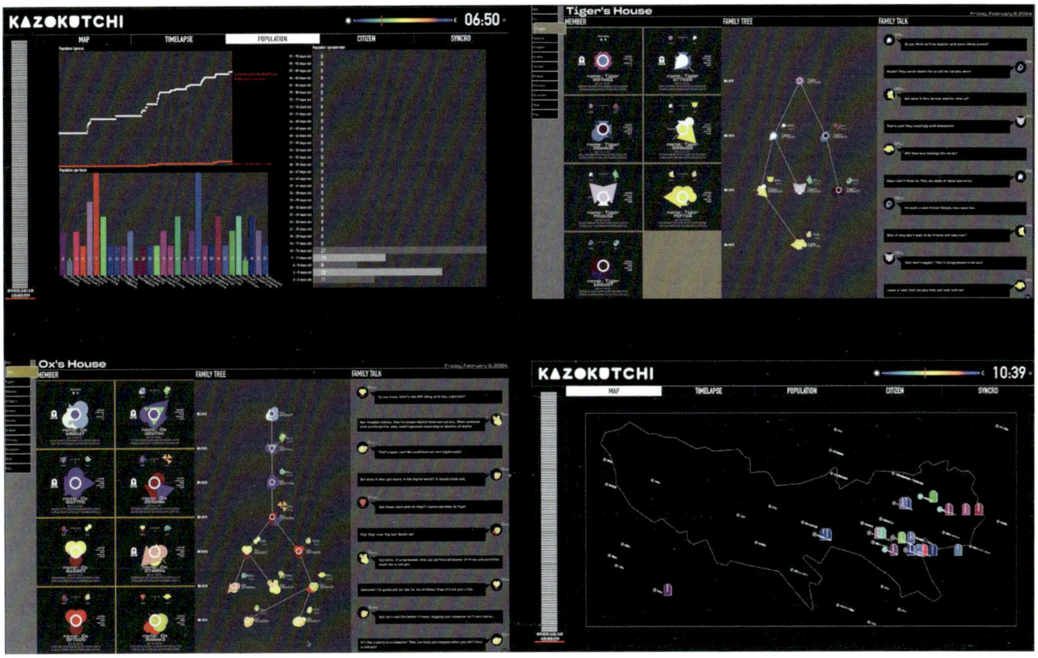

So Kanno (JP) is based in Berlin. He is an artist and project professor at Aichi University of the Arts. He specializes in creating swarm robot systems for art installations and performances. His work explores unpredictability, swarm intelligence, collective behavior, emergence, errors, and serendipity. **Akihiro Kato** (JP) is based in Tokyo. He specializes in web engineering and produces a wide range of installation works, including blockchain/NFT-based works, board games, sculptures, and video works. He creates works that depict the relationship between technology and society through a combination of digital/physical media. **Takemi Watanuki** (JP) is a visual artist based in Tokyo. He specializes in graphics and video, and also works as a VJ. He has created complex simulations and simulations of artificial life cycles, mainly using programmed simulations.

Mixed Signals

kennedy+swan

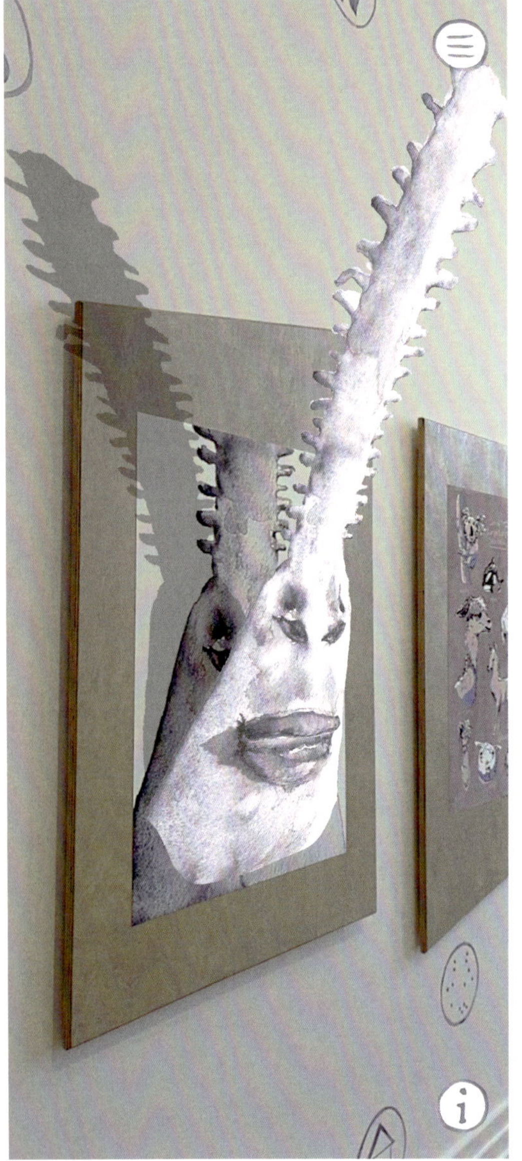

kennedy+swan created a series of watercolors that can be scanned using their mobile Augmented Reality app, merging the tactile with the digital. Each image is augmented with an interactive virtual scene, expanding the narrative of the paintings. The 3D elements, handcrafted by the artists in the form of miniatures, sculptures, and drawings, are then digitized to complete the AR overlay.

How can something technical like Artificial Intelligence—so often associated with our alienation from Nature—help us listen to and communicate with non-human beings?

Upon closer examination, most animals and even plants have their unique forms of communication—languages that we're only beginning to decode with modern technology. Yet, the real question remains: Is humanity prepared to embrace the profound insights offered by Nature's sonic dialogues?

The work consists of 18 unique watercolors that can be scanned with the free app *Mixed Signals,* available in the Google Play Store and the iOS App Store.

You can try the AR experience at home by downloading the app and scanning the images at the bottom of this website:

https://www.kennedyswan.com/mixed-signals.

AR paintings and app: *kennedy+swan*
Scientific collaboration with Dr. Tim Landgraf
With support from: Ether Bloom's program on artificial intelligence at the Gropius Bau, Berlin

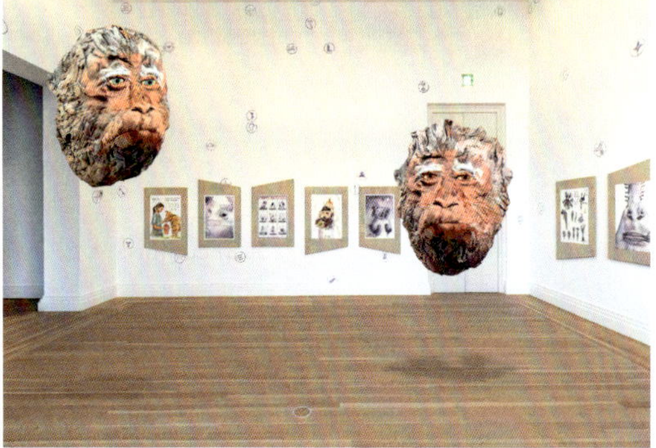

**Interactive Art +
Honorary Mention**

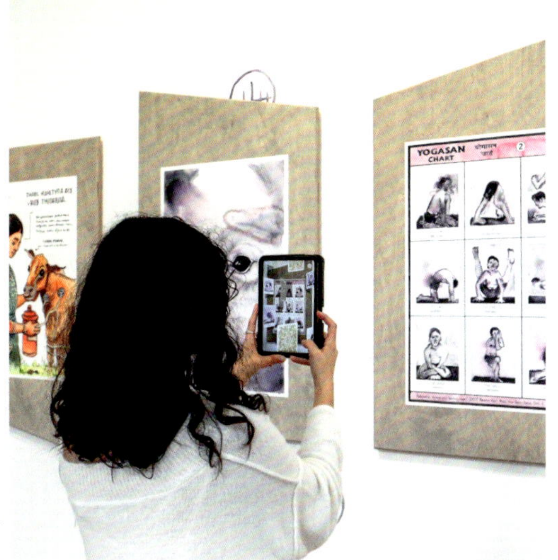

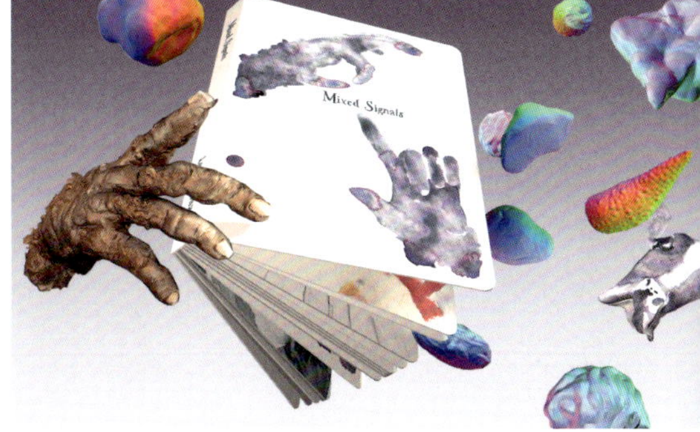

Ether's Bloom: A Programme on Artificial Intelligence,
installation view, Gropius Bau (2023)

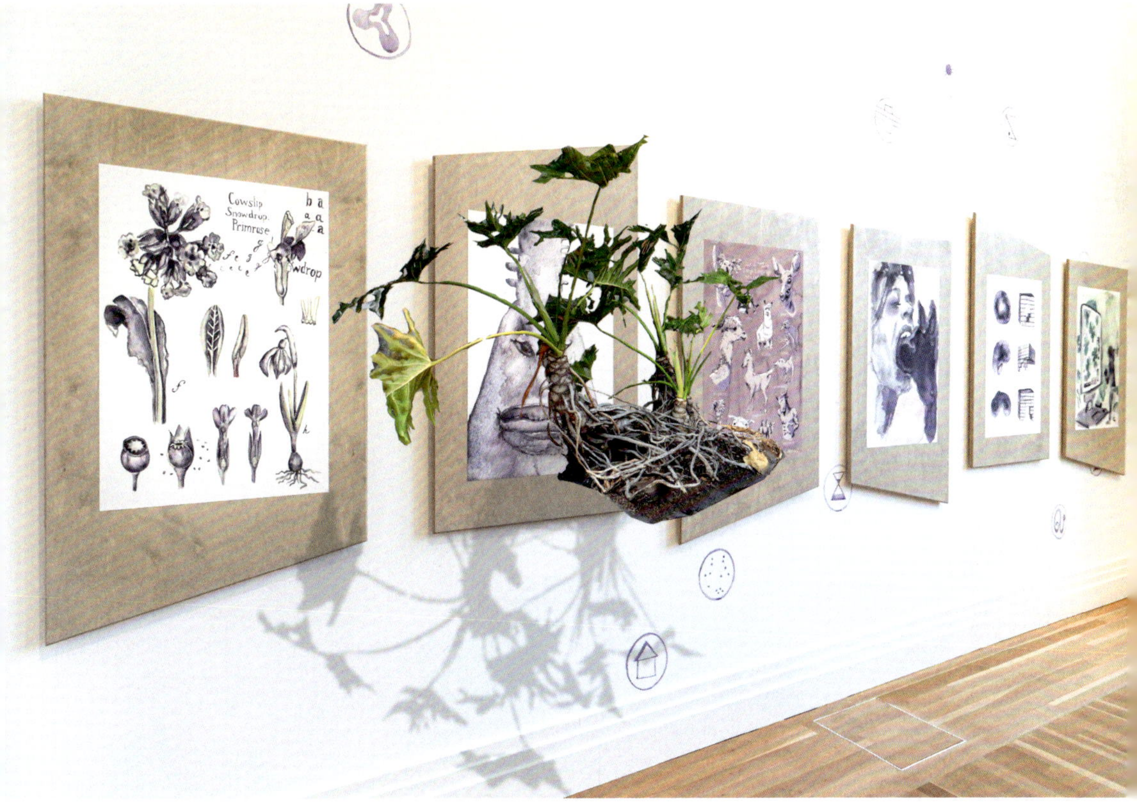

kennedy+swan (DE, founded in 2013) comprises the work of the two artists Bianca Kennedy and Swan Collective. When working together, they explore the future of evolution and its impact on plants, animals, and humans. These utopias are liberated from human supremacy, illuminating the ecological benefits of hybrid life forms, and addressing the twisted relationship between humans and machines. For their videos, VR and AR installations, the duo employs a variety of animation techniques: drawings, stereoscopic film footage, 3D-scanned landscapes, and self-built characters create a dense network of analog and digital imagery. Recent works utilize and reflect the rise of Artificial Intelligence by integrating AI-generated texts and images into their animations.

REPEAT AFTER ME, 2022
Open Group (Yuriy Biley, Pavlo Kovach, and Anton Varga)

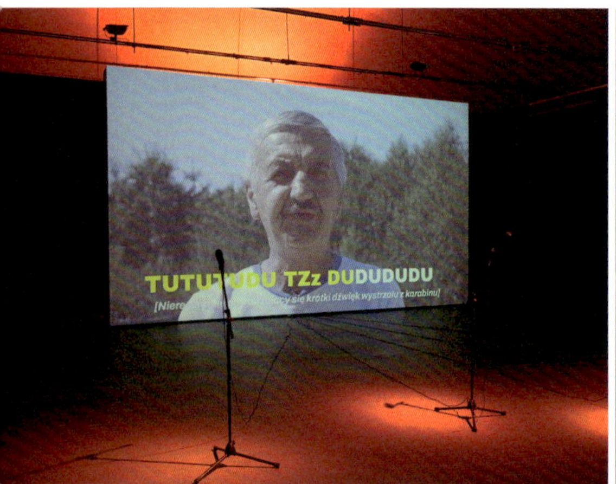

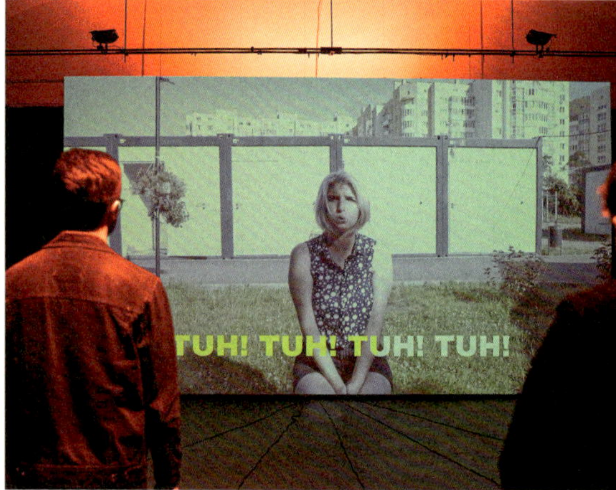

A few weeks before Russia's full-scale invasion, the State Emergency Service of Ukraine began distributing a multi-page handbook on how to behave in the area where military actions are happening. The order and type of action severely depend on whether the attack is assault rifle fire, artillery shelling, multiple rocket launcher shelling, or even aerial bombardment. Very often, the only way to distinguish the type of fire is to determine different weapon types by sound.

In the work *REPEAT AFTER ME* we see refugees from the East of Ukraine who, fleeing the threat of war, found shelter in a temporary camp in Lviv. They share their experience of the sounds of war. Reproducing various types of weapons, they conduct a kind of karaoke instruction, which, while transmitting simple sound sequences, is still unable to convey the experience that exists nearby, the experience that has become the price for this knowledge. This skill speaks about the new reality in which Ukrainians currently live.

"From the moment we hear the first air raid siren, our 'internal alarm' is on alert. It keeps us in constant tension and makes us listen to every sound, every rustle. Sometimes suspicion creeps in even in silence."

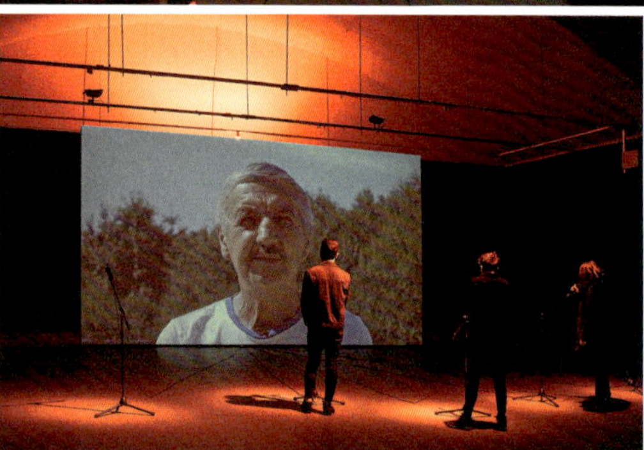

Repeat after me, 2022, Open Group (Yuriy Biley, Pavlo Kovach and Anton Varga), Labirynt gallery, Lublin, Poland,

REPEAT AFTER ME, 2022, (video installation, karaoke, video 17'7'')

Open Group (Yuriy Biley, Pavlo Kovach, and Anton Varga)
Cast: Alla, Antonina, Boris, Ekaterina, Iryna, Olena, Svitlana, Yuriy
Director of photography: Roman Bordun
Editors: Yuriy Biley, Pavlo Kovach, Anton Varga
Sound design: Roman Bordun

https://u.aec.at/8FE5492E

Interactive Art +
Honorary Mention

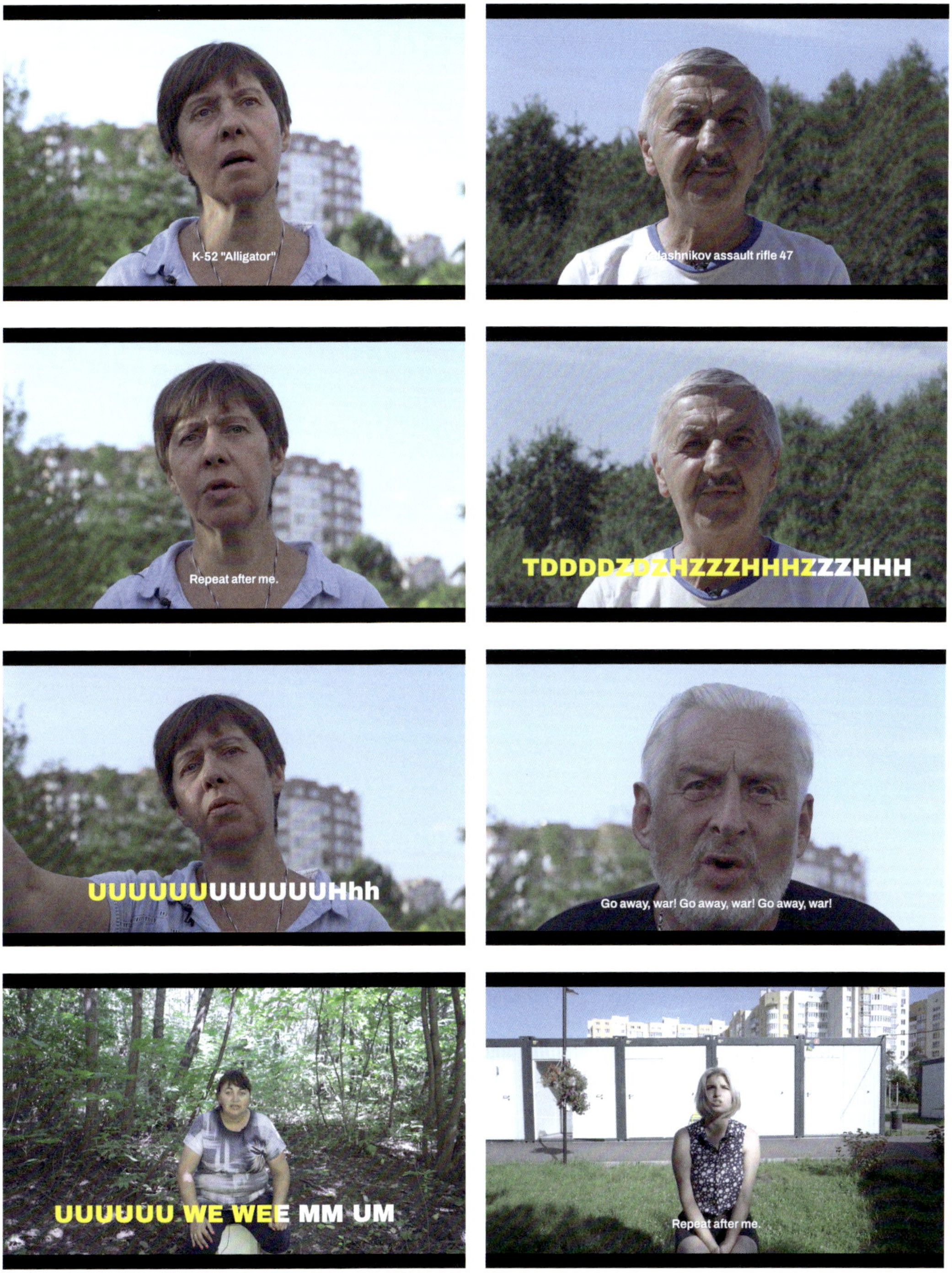

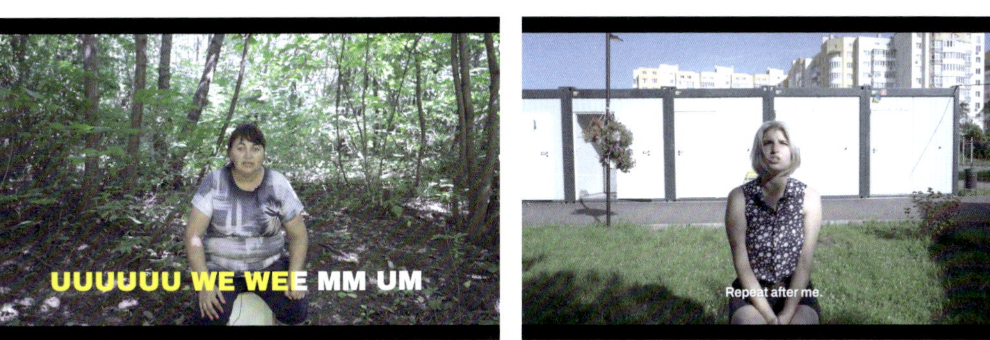

Open Group (Yuriy Biley, Pavlo Kovach, and Anton Varga) was founded in August 2012 in Lviv by six Ukrainian artists. The structure of Open Group is built around the study of the idea of collective work while involving people from different fields for the period of time to work on projects together. The group's work is based on exploring interactions between people and contextual spaces, creating the so-called "open situations". In 2019, the group was the curator of the Ukrainian Pavilion at the 58th Venice Biennale. In 2024, the Open Group will represent Poland at the 60th Venice Biennale with the project *REPEAT AFTER ME II*.

Swarming / Swimming
Honey Biba Beckerlee

Swarming/Swimming nods to the submarine internet cables that form the physical infrastructure for the vast information cloud of our current digital age. All that information is carried by light signals running inside the cables, thereby anchoring the Internet's rapid, ceaseless flow of information in earthbound digital nervous systems that crisscross the planet.

Swarming / Swimming is woven out of seaweed and optical fiber. The light signals running through the weaving is modelled on the Particle Swarm Optimisation Algorithm, which in turn is inspired by various swarming animals such as bees, butterflies, and birds and their ability to coordinate collective actions in large groups. The swarm is an example of a form of intelligence that transcends the individual. The intelligence of the swarm resides in the sum of all those who are part of it—in the total composition of many bodies working together as one, forming a common body. The swarm is an example of a sophisticated technology that emanates from non-human actors.

In computer science, swarm intelligence algorithms are used to optimize the distribution of data in the Internet's complicated network. Reflecting this, Beckerlee's work examines how our technology borrows from and builds on knowledge found in the more-than-human world.

To the naked eye the woven motif depicts intersecting ripples on the surface of water. But the pattern refers to the interference pattern, the famous pattern and result of the double-slit experiment that was made to prove that light is wave and not particle and which later became the outset for the "discovery" of quantum mechanics. The double-slit experiment has prompted more questions than answers about the complicated and ambivalent nature of light, but can reveal that, depending on the experimental set-up, light is either wave or particle, or both. In other words, our apparatuses of inquiry and scientific categories have a very concrete, real impact on the world that appears before us.

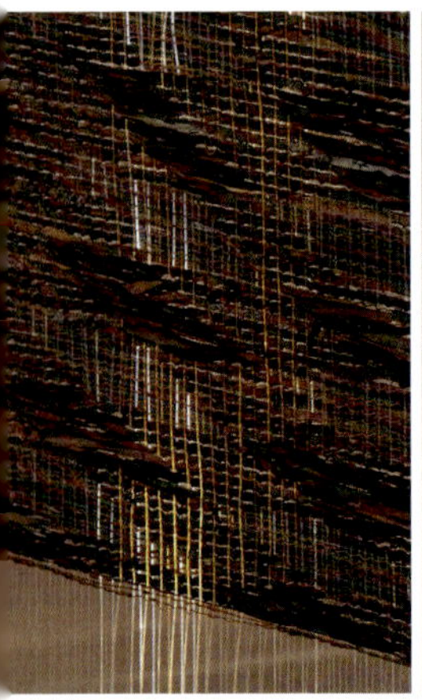
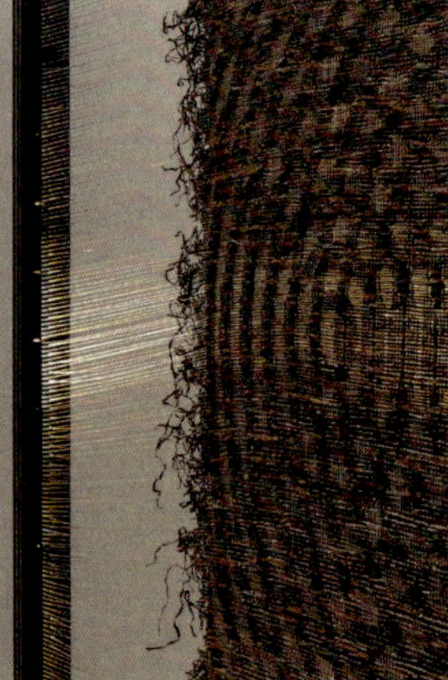

Artwork by Honey Biba Beckerlee
With support from: Statens Kunstfond, Beckett Fonden, Grosserer L.F. Foghts Fond, Novo Nordisk Foundation

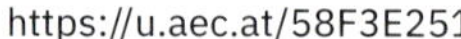
https://u.aec.at/58F3E251

Honey Biba Beckerlee (DK) graduated from the Royal Danish Academy of Fine Arts, Copenhagen, the Städelschule, Frankfurt am Main, and Goldsmiths College, University of London, UK in 2008. Beckerlee holds a PhD from Aarhus University and the Royal Danish Academy of Fine Arts through the Novo Nordisk Foundation's PhD Scholarships in practice-based research. Beckerlee's practice renegotiates the established notions of the interfaces between our body, physical surroundings, nature, and technology, thus placing technology in a new decentralized perspective that is part of a complex more-than-human entanglement.

Interactive Art +
Honorary Mention

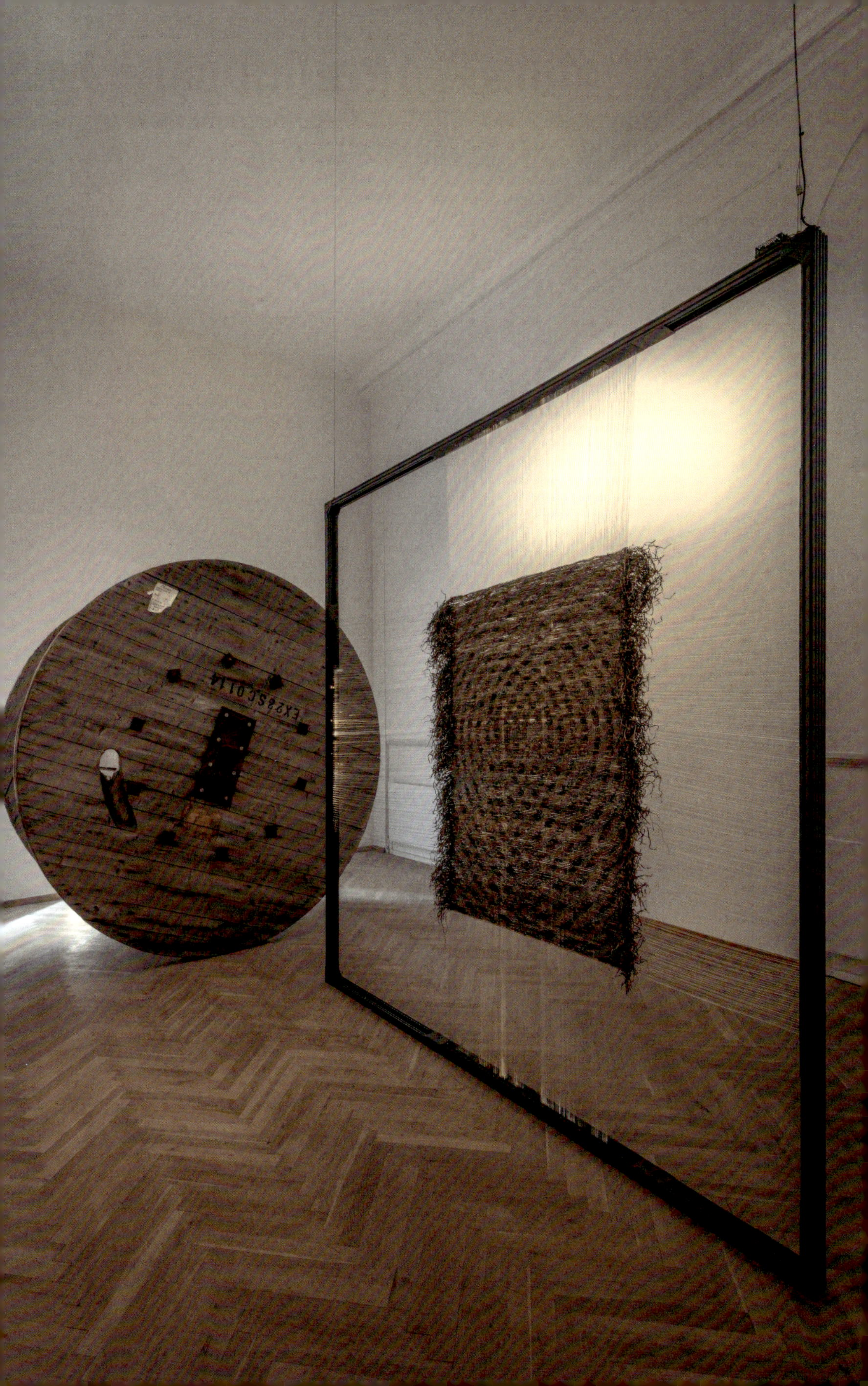

ZOE

Noor Stenfert Kroese, Amir Bastan

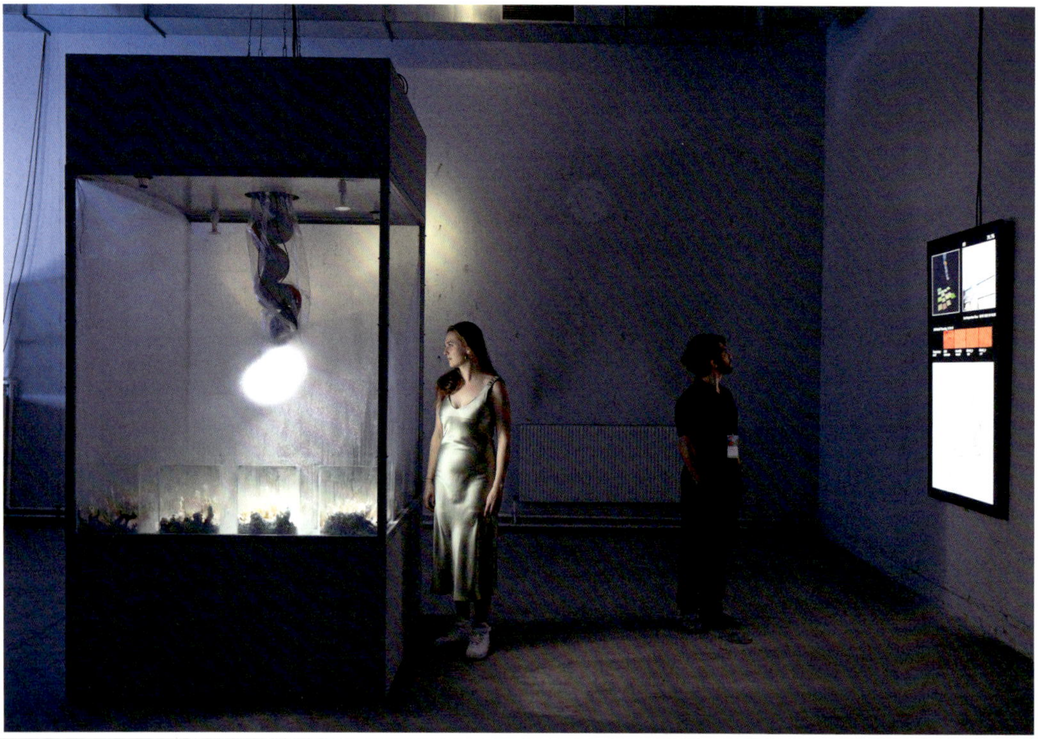

vog.photo

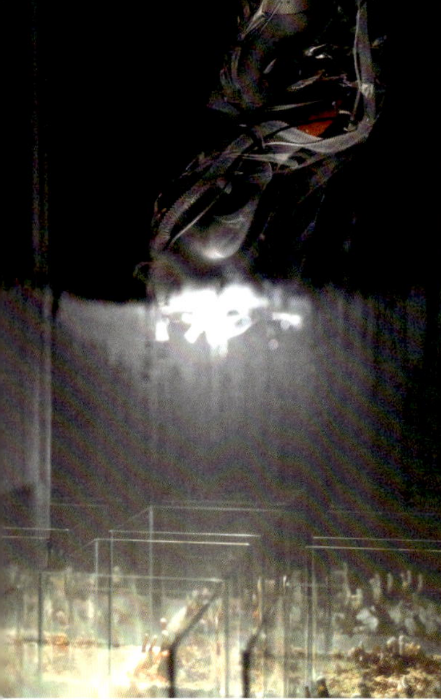

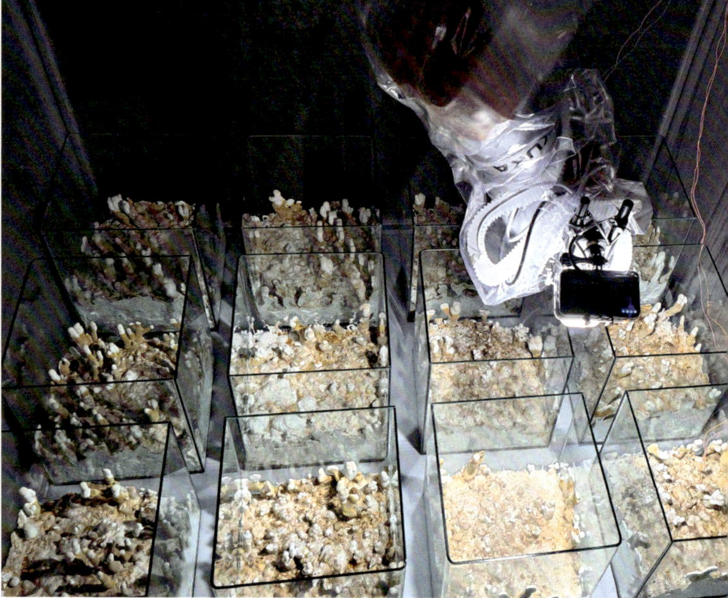

**Interactive Art +
Honorary Mention**

ZOE is a temporary co-existence between reishi mushrooms and a custom-made robotic system. Noor Stenfert Kroese and Amir Bastan explore the possibilities of internal communication between a robotic system and reishi with *ZOE*. Despite the seeming paradox between nature and technology, an ecosystem in which they care for and affect each other through sensing technologies is created. It proceeds to research the interaction and unknown communication within fungal mycelia networks.

ZOE uses sensors to collect data from the environment as well as the mycelium of the reishi. It uses this data to create the internal communication between the reishi and the robotic system. The reishi and their behavior define what the robotic system does and the robotic system influences the shape of the light-sensitive reishi mushrooms. Over time, this influence sculpts the shape of the fruiting bodies of the reishi as a reflection of their ecosystem. The data is used in the space to create a sensory experience to explore this unknown communication. Finally, the data carpets are created from the daily collected data from reishi in relation to their environment, to see if we can detect any correlation between them. These tactile data visualizations explore the outcome and the unknown communication going on in this temporary co-existence.

ZOE is the first step in ongoing Mycobotics research. This research focuses on the possibilities of bio-computing with fungi through robotics and other than human-computer interaction. We focus on technical and narrative aspects to create an environment for meaningful collaboration, using timelines, state machines, and behavioral trees. We explore the intricate connections between human and non-human entities and the role of data in shaping these interactions. We use industrial robots and their quality of repetition and precision as the interface to reconsider the dynamics between technology and nature, encompassing both human and non-human aspects.

Produced by Productiehuis Theater Rotterdam with support of Art Climate & Transition—EU Creative Europe project. In co-production with Creative Robotics, KUKA, and Mushroom Research Center Austria.

https://u.aec.at/F3DD7F5F

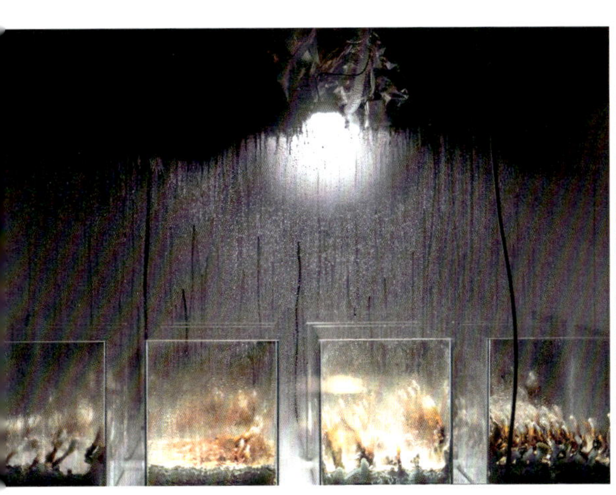

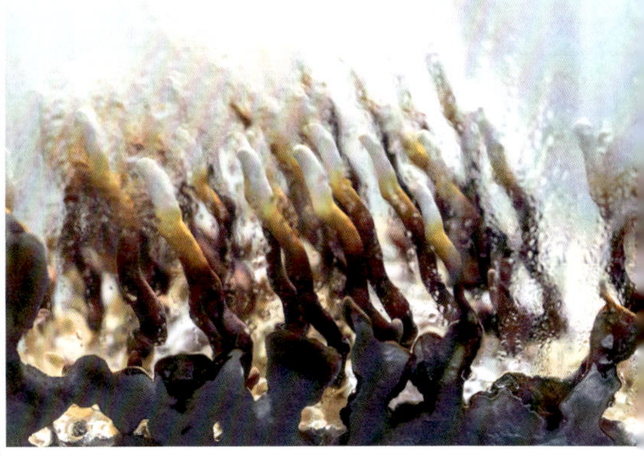

Amir Bastan (IR) is a new media artist with a background in fine arts and philosophy. He is a researcher and lecturer in the Creative Robotics department at the University of Arts Linz. Human Robot Transference is the centerpiece of his current research, drawing parallels between psychoanalysis theories and human-robot interaction within the context of new media arts. **Noor Stenfert Kroese** (NL) is a new media artist, scenographer, and PhD candidate in Creative Robotics at the University of Arts Linz. Her current research focuses on data storytelling of/with living organisms, fungi-inspired biocomputing, and other-than-human interactions with industrial robots.

AI in ART Award

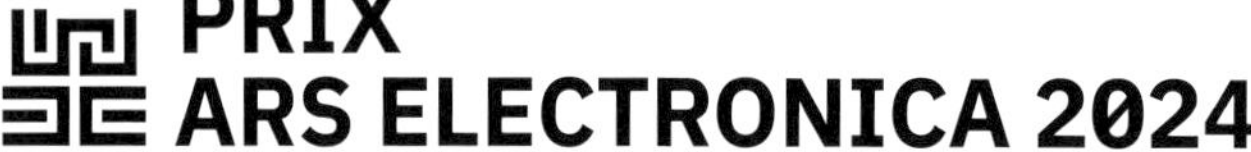

Capturing a Turning Point

Statement by the Jury: Jürgen Hagler, Vanessa Hannesschläger, Veronika Liebl, Emiko Ogawa, Gerfried Stocker

Several times already in the history of Prix Ars Electronica, Special Golden Nicas have been awarded to highlight important developments that were equally impactful across the areas of art, technology, and society.

For instance, in 1992, the Honorary Golden Nica which was awarded to Marc Dippé and his team at ILM for their groundbreaking liquid-metal-man animation in Terminator 2. This visual effect was unprecedented, marking a significant milestone in computer animation for many, and it clearly demonstrated how the continuous improvements in this field would impact all areas of visual design, both in art and entertainment. Although the term "Creative Industries" was not yet in vogue, it was evident that a new era of the fusion of art, creativity, and technology was emerging.

The impact of Alias|Wavefront and RenderMan back then is comparable with the impact of today's generative text-to-image and text-to-video systems like Runway and Sora. These systems are not only new tools for creatives and artists, they have also begun to fundamentally change many of the conditions for artistic creation.

Artistic work with generative AI was therefore a primary focus in the search for suitable projects. The intention was not so much to define 'legacy artworks' (as we are still at the very beginning of these developments), but to mark turning points and highlight the important role that artists play in this process. These are turning points where not only new technological developments become visible, but also new questions arise about the role of art and artists, questions that are highly relevant to society as a whole. It is ultimately not very surprising that the impact of AI on art and creativity is being discussed with as much excitement and intensity as its effects on the economy, the job market, and democracy are.

While all these projects would not be possible in their respective form without the remarkable technological advancements in AI, the awards are fully and solely awards for the artists and their creative innovations.

The AI in ART award-winning projects have been selected from among all the submissions from the Prix Ars Electronica, the S+T+ARTS Prize, and the European Union Prize for Citizen Science. For example, within the category "New Animation Art," AI-based works (those that explicitly mention the use of AI in the work) accounted for 25% of the total submissions in this category. Of these, 91% used generative AI Image, 89% used generative AI Video or Animation, 24% used Chat Bot or LLM, and 14% used generative Sound/Music.

Within the Prix Ars Electronica "Interactive Art+" category, AI-based works (those in which the use of AI is explicitly stated within the work) also accounted for 21% of the total entries in the category. Of these, 70% used materials created with generative AI, 19% pursued the critical social impact of AI, and 11% dealt with AI in an academic context, such as Research & Development.

Special Golden Nica

Washed Out "The Hardest Part"
Paul Trillo

The breathtaking advancements in text-to-video systems represent one of the most significant and impactful developments in contemporary AI, particularly within the artistic realm. Paul Trillo, an esteemed and visionary artist and experimental filmmaker, is being honored with the Golden Nica for his early and innovative artistic exploration of generative AI systems and the possibilities it opens up for artists.

His recent works, *The Hardest Part* and *Noted to my Future Self*, showcase his exceptional ability to leverage technology to enhance storytelling and filmmaking—a quality he has already demonstrated in earlier pieces, such as *Thank you for not Answering* and *Absolve,* where he highlights the profound aesthetic and narrative opportunities that AI offers to the arts.

In his most recent music video, a kind of infinite dolly shot and fly-through following a couple through episodes of their life—Trillo seized the opportunity to be one of the first artists to gain access to Sora. He generated approximately 700 clips with very extensive prompts, selected 55, stitching them together for the final video. While the high degree of character consistency achieved with Sora is impressive, it is Paul Trillo's narrative and storytelling that truly stand out. As in his earlier short films created with Runway Gen2, he skillfully harnesses the unique characteristics of these systems, including their hallucinations and artifacts, for his artistic work.

"This was an idea I had almost 10 years ago and then abandoned. Finally I was able to bring it to life," Trillo is quoted in several articles about his work. He further states:

"I really wanted to do something that was both unique to the hallucinations of Sora while also attempting to create something that felt timeless and works regardless of what technology was being used. Sora presents unique challenges and opportunities to artists. I think fundamentally, what works as a story, what works on an audience, will never change. But our process to get to that finish line is different. What is unique about AI is that it's this more fluid, organic process where you're ideating. You have your idea, it feeds into the final product, and then the final product gives you a new idea to go back into the writing phase and rewrite." Anticipating that many more remarkable works will emerge by the time of the award ceremony in September, the prize is not limited to the latest production by Paul Trillo, mentioned here as an example. It honors his ongoing work with AI and is an acknowledgment of his creative curiosity and the courage required to embark on new paths.

AI in ART Award
Jury Statement

The same applies to the two Awards of Distinctions, which will be presented alongside the Golden Nica, recognizing outstanding projects that showcase the breadth and diversity of current artistic work with AI.

Awards of Distinction

Intelligent Instruments in Citizen Science: Understanding Contemporary AI through Creative Practice

Thor Magnusson, Intelligent Instruments Lab

The Award of Distinction for the research group led by Thor Magnusson from the Intelligent Instruments Lab located at Iceland University of the Arts demonstrates another area where artistic exploration and research are of great relevance: interfaces and tools that enable intuitive creation, live performance, and improvisation with AI systems. Here, the focus is not on AI itself, but rather on what can be achieved artistically and creatively with it. The technical system is not the focus of this research; instead, emphasis is placed on humans and new ideas for musical instruments that can be played live to harness the possibilities offered by AI.

While all these projects would not be possible in their respective form without the remarkable technological advancements in AI, the awards are not accolades for companies and their excellent technical development teams—they are fully and solely awards for the artists and their creative innovations.

REPETAE

Sasha Stiles

REPETAE by Sasha Stiles utilizes text-generating AI models, delving into the realm of co-creation with AI systems and seamlessly integrating the AI component into a multimedia configuration that captivates with its high degree of independence and artistic authenticity. Merging poetry with algorithmic art and generative AI, *REPETAE* explores the new possibilities as well as the consequences of extensive immersion into technological realities, not only for the creation of art but also for its perception and the agency of the audience.

Washed Out "The Hardest Part"

Paul Trillo

A trip and a fall down memory lane. A continuous push forward through time tracking the relationship of a couple from middle school into the afterlife. This is the first official commissioned music video collaboration between a music artist and filmmaker made with OpenAI's Sora video model. *Moving on is the hardest part.* This video is about learning to let go of a loved one and dreaming of them after they are gone. But memories are subjective, distorted mirrors of reality. For this, I leaned into the hallucinations and Sora's dream logic to explore memories that never existed. I was interested in the surreal qualities unique to Sora / AI that differentiate it from reality, the space between canny and uncanny, the strange details, the dreamlike logic of movement that better represents this distorted mirror of memories.

Artist's Statement

The music video for *The Hardest Part* by Washed Out is a groundbreaking project, being the first full generative video made with OpenAI's Sora text-to-video model. The song is about moving on from a lost love, and I wanted to honor this theme while putting a unique spin on it. The video spans several decades, starting in the early 80s, and follows a young couple who meet in middle school. We see them age, go through changes, grow up together, fall in love, and eventually face the challenges of life not going as planned.

I aimed to lean into the hallucinatory, dream-like qualities of Sora rather than depict something entirely real. It's about trying to preserve someone in time, with memories that are fleeting and hard to grasp. The surreal blends of environments and impossible transitions—from cars to buildings to landscapes—create a fluid drift through the subconscious, attempting to hold onto what's real. AI has an ephemeral and familiar quality, allowing us to tap into a nostalgia for something that never happened, known as "anemoia". I wanted to use AI from this conceptual standpoint, using technology to drum up dreams and memories of something we can never have.

AI models are like memory banks and time capsules, so the idea came from exploiting that aspect. Rather than being truly authentic to reality, AI creates something new—an uncanny reflection of our reality that deceives us into believing something that never happened. The aesthetic is

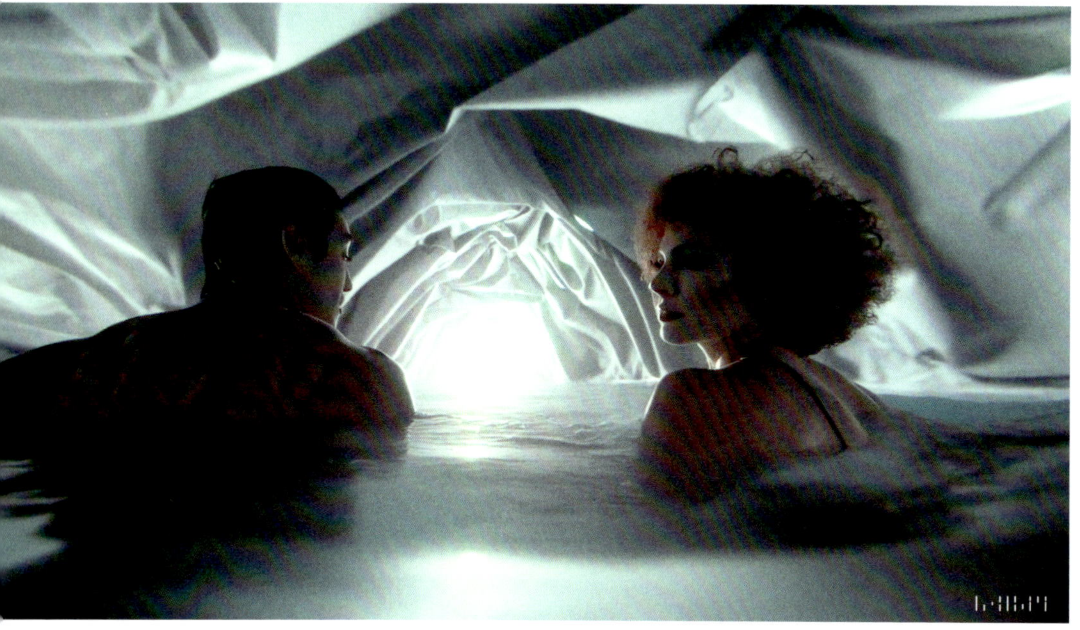

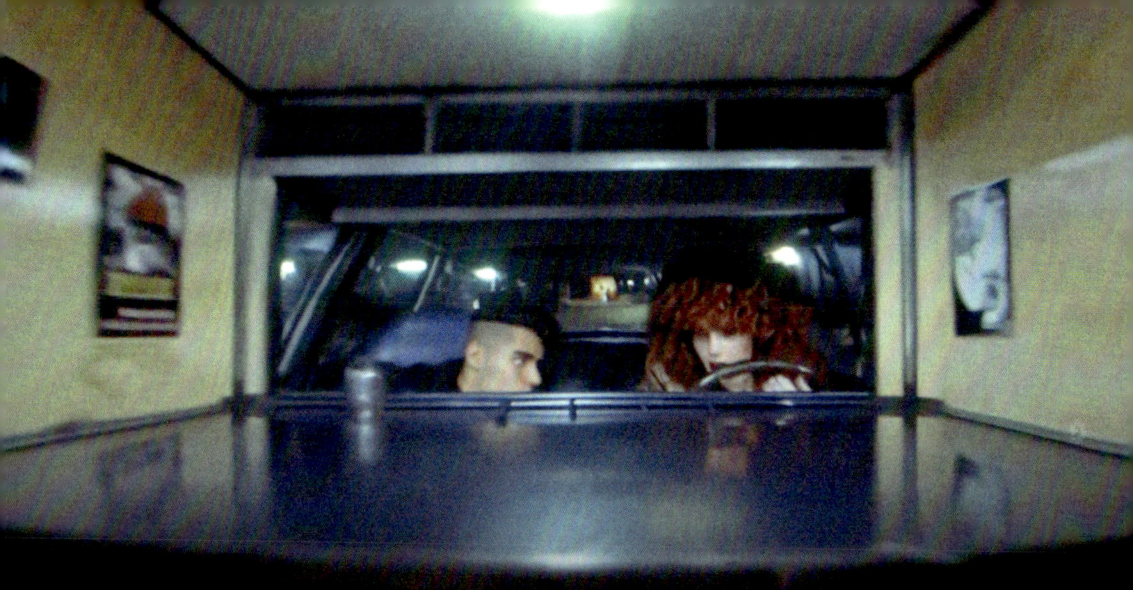

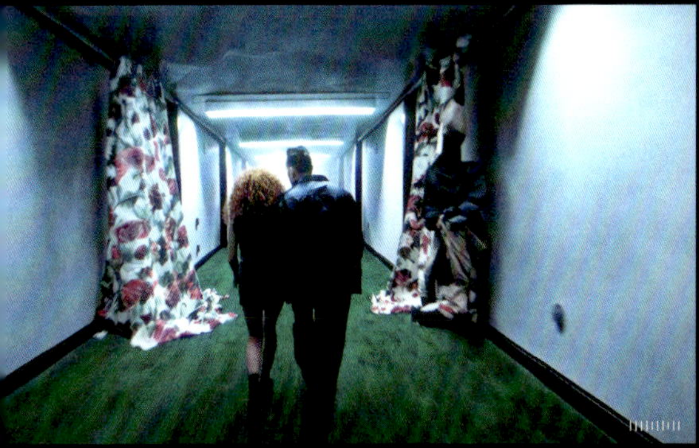

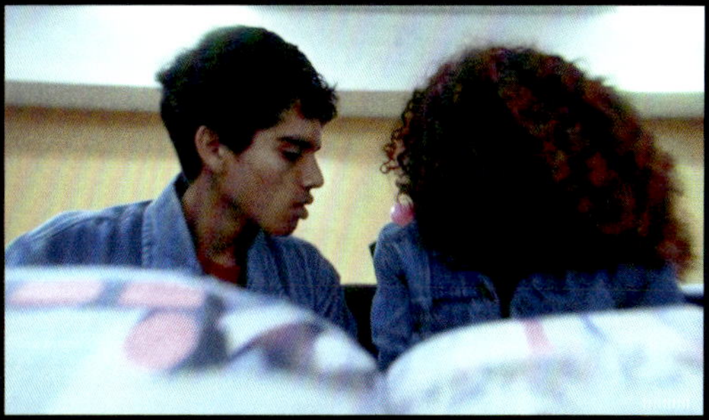

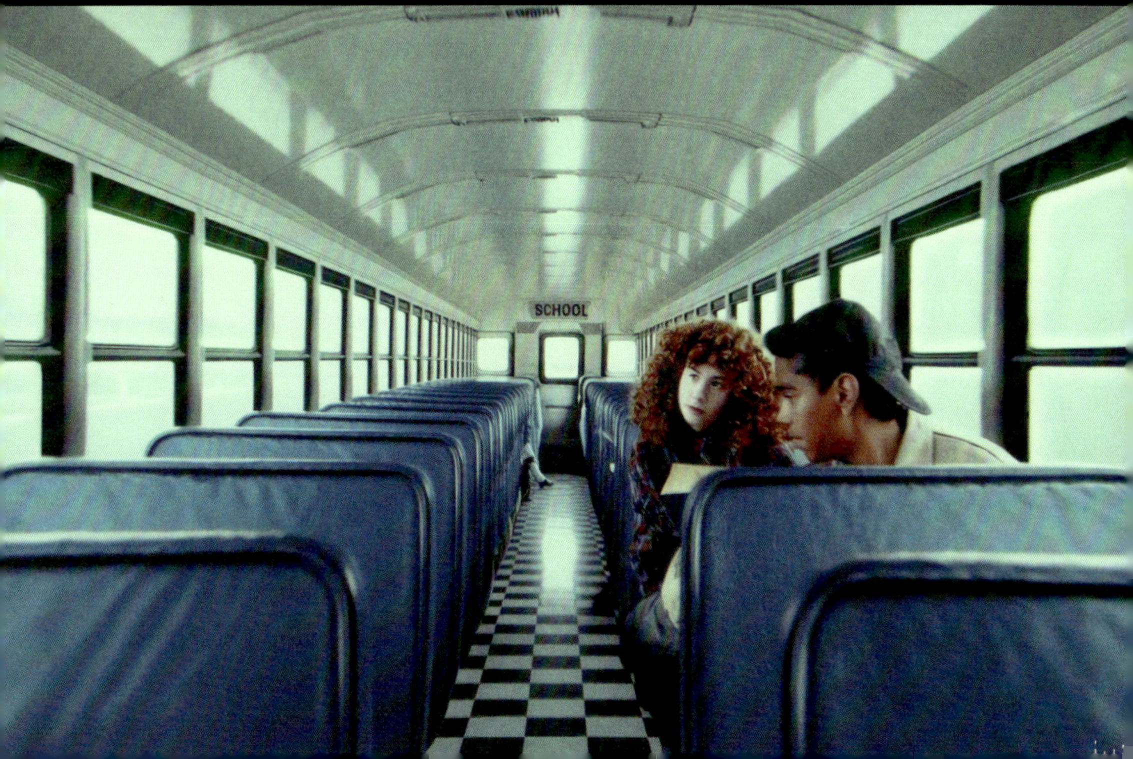

SCHOOL

not something you could capture with cameras or animate; it's entirely new, resembling a dream or memory. At first glance, it appears real, but the details are murky and missing. Conceptually, tying the first Sora music video to this journey through memories felt appropriate.

The project was ambitious, traversing time and space in impossible ways. The idea of an infinite zoom through time following a couple in love came to me about 10 years ago, but I abandoned it, thinking it too ambitious for a music video. Between the aging characters, the numerous locations and time periods, and the visual effects, it wasn't feasible for a music video budget. AI allows us to resurrect these ideas from the graveyard and breathe new life into them. In a way, the music video tells a similar story about a woman dreaming of her ex-lover who is no longer here. The lyrics suggest moving on from the past, letting go of nostalgia, and accepting that there is no going back. This mirrors the mixed feelings about embracing new technology and how things won't be the same going forward. Also, the song's theme of learning to let go of a loved one deeply resonated with me, and I infused my personal experiences of loss into the narrative.

When working with Sora or any AI tool, it's important to retain your perspective and tone of voice. Setting constraints or formal stylistic rules for a film helps define that voice. It's easy to let the machine dominate and dictate the aesthetic or the choices in the details. Working with AI is about controlling chaos, but all filmmaking is controlled chaos.

While I let the machine's hallucinations deviate from reality and create a surreal atmosphere, I guided it with script page length prompts describing each shot's beat, the character design, mood, lighting, retro aesthetic, camera motion, and pacing. I was deliberate with the camera motion and ensured that each cut represented a leap forward in time. The infinite camera push or zoom technique and transitions between environments are techniques I've used in my work for years. It created a connection to my previous work while allowing me to do something entirely new with it. Moving this synthetic camera through an imaginary latent space opened up entirely new visual impossibilities that give a glimpse at what the future of filmmaking might look like.

The process involved a lot of trial and error and exploration to get to the final product. I wrote out the beats of the idea, turned them into prompts, generated the clips, edited them into a sequence, saw what worked and what didn't, and then generated more clips. It was a fluid back-and-forth between "pre-production" and post-production.

This opened up a whole multiverse of routes I could take the video. It felt intimate, as if I was learning about the characters with each generation and getting glimpses into their lives that no one had seen. It was fascinating to explore, but knowing when to stop can be a trap when working with AI.

In total, I generated nearly 700 clips and cut them down to about 55 for the final edit. Each shot was between 15 to 20 seconds long, so I ended up generating about 230 minutes, which was cut down to 4 minutes. Much of this was about crafting the prompt and getting Sora to do what was in my head, finding the right combination of words to create the desired effect.

One of the biggest challenges in creating this video was ensuring the continuity of the zoom effect and maintaining a consistent aesthetic across different clips. This required meticulous attention to detail and constant adjustments to the prompts used to guide Sora. By editing the prompts to control the speed and direction of the camera movements, I was able to create a cohesive narrative flow that felt natural and immersive. It was like finding a formula of words that worked, though sometimes changing a single word caused a ripple effect of changes.

While this project is exciting for being the first of its kind, I hope it has merit beyond the technology alone. Now that we have the ability to conjure ambitious ideas and resurrect old ones, there is an opportunity to push filmmaking into new territories of the surreal and strange. Using AI technology allowed me to create something I would have never created, to realize an ambitious idea and bring it to life in a way that feels both familiar and entirely new. I acknowledge that the novel use of AI is temporary and that there are long term changes we're facing. There are valid criticisms regarding how these models were built on stolen data and the impact of AI on the creative industries. I believe that AI should be seen as a complementary tool to the traditional filmmaking process, to enhance human-led creativity rather than replacing it. Transparency and ethical development of these technologies are crucial to creating a sustainable path forward.

Written, directed, edited: Paul Trillo
Music: Washed Out
With support from: SubPop

https://u.aec.at/88BAC407

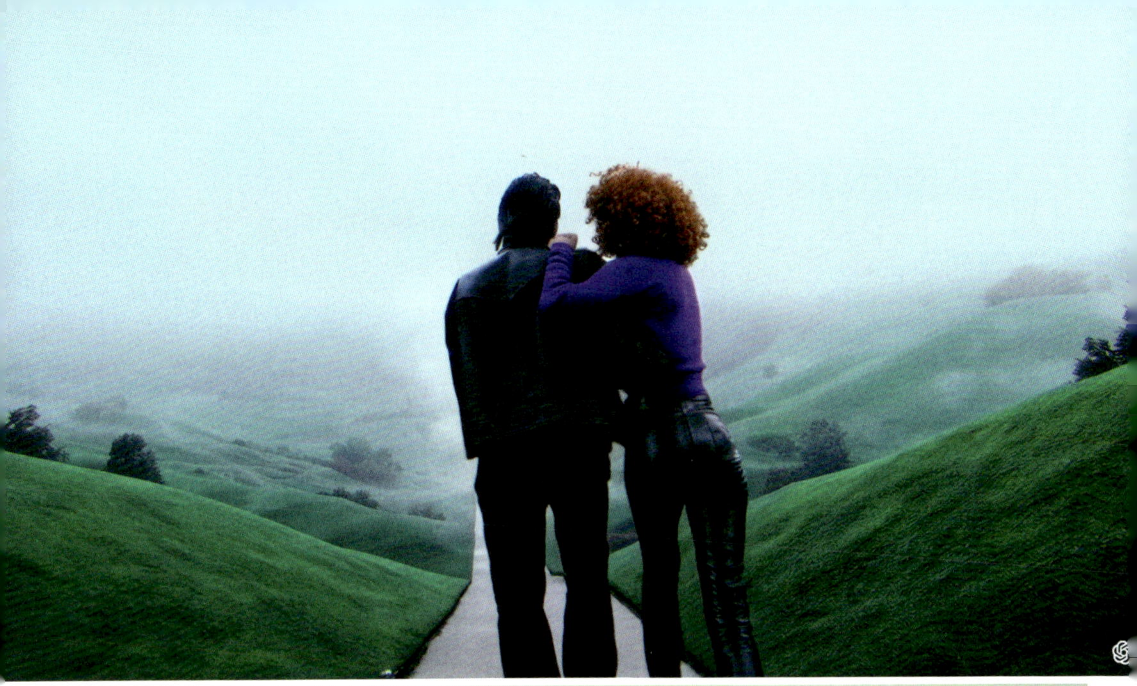

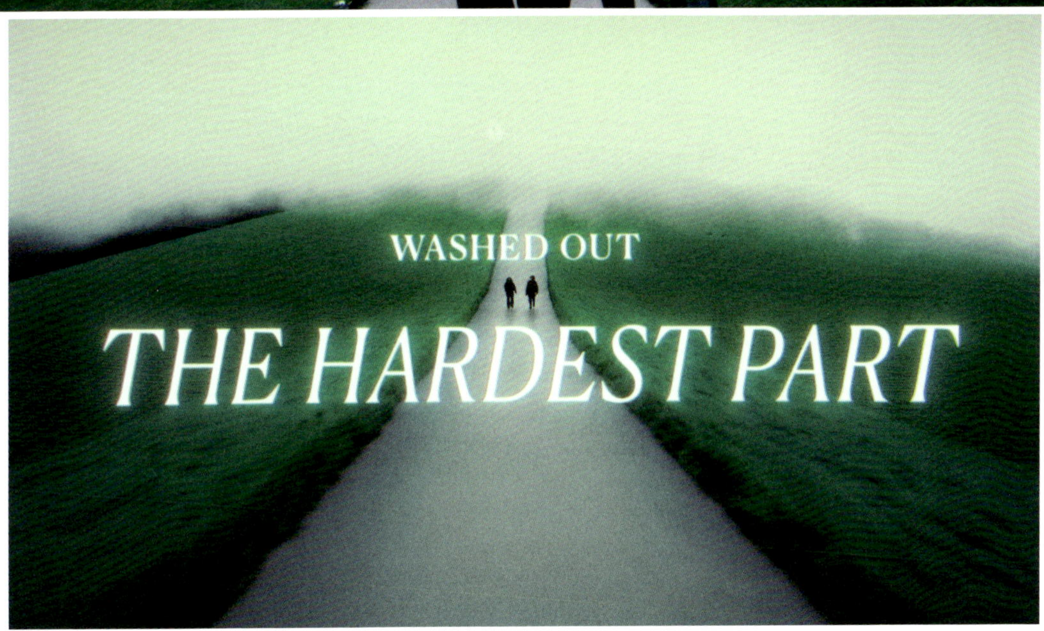

Paul Trillo (US) is a director and video artist who challenges both his own curiosity and illusion with his visually inventive, conceptual, and technical films. His diverse body of work spans various genres and formats, infusing meaning and purpose into his experimental uses of technology and technique. Whether he's creating in-camera practical illusions, building the first mobile bullet time rig with phones, choreographing aerial smoke shows using drones, Super Bowl commercials, or innovating generative AI visual effects at the Louvre, Paul is always looking for new ways to push the boundaries of what's possible. Recently, Trillo has explored the future of AI filmmaking, with a focus on integrating the new tools with the traditional craft. His viral visual effects experiments have not only changed the way these tools are perceived but also are intended to inspire others to explore the possibilities of this emerging tech. Paul's work has earned him 20 Vimeo Staff Picks and has been featured in wide range of media outlets, including *New York Times, Rolling Stone, The New Yorker, Vice, The Atlantic, FastCo, Wired, Ad Age, GQ,* among others. Paul has also participated in events, festivals and award shows including SXSW, TED, NAB, Cannes Lions, NVIDIA GTC, Runway AI Film Festival, Infinity Fest, Northside Festival, and the ADC Awards.

Intelligent Instruments in Citizen Science

Understanding Contemporary AI through Creative Practice

Thor Magnusson, Intelligent Instruments Lab

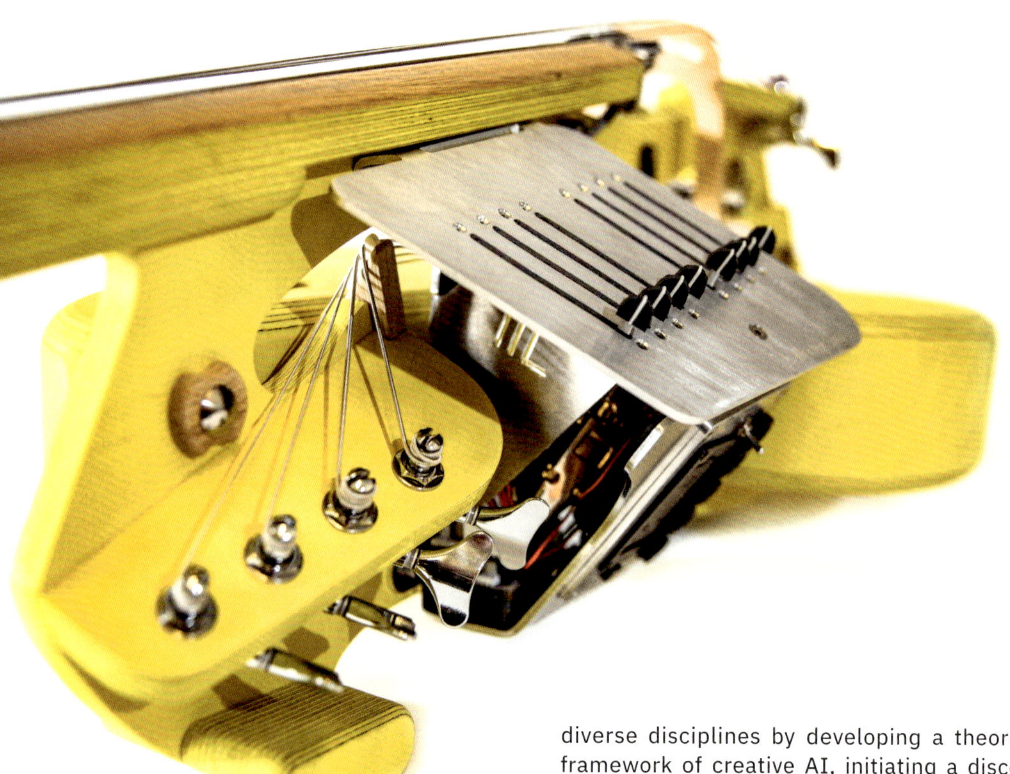

Artificial Intelligence is becoming increasingly human-like and it is now proficient in a key human activity: musical creativity. But what does this mean? How does creative AI change our notions of art, culture, and society? These are the questions that the Intelligent Instruments Lab explores through practice-based research and critical reflection in the experimental humanities. As new machine learning technologies begin to mirror ourselves, we need to look into that mirror and ask how this is changing us.

We study new AI by using music as a platform. In a range of research projects, we develop instruments with creative AI, explore human-AI collaboration in music, and frame sonic instruments as scientific instruments. Grounded equally in technology development and the humanities, we engage with diverse disciplines by developing a theoretical framework of creative AI, initiating a discourse around human-centred creative AI, and defining principles of human-AI relations in services and products.

Our aim is therefore to work in the public eye, to keep our lab open, and to disseminate our work as it happens. We seek public engagement and investment in the research program, as our research is relevant to the questions people are asking already, and to place the lab as a social hub where these questions could be explored in a safe, welcoming, and open intellectual environment. Through the broad reach of music in society, we reach the general public and conduct citizen science with people in a field that people understand and engage with from a personal, emotional, and intellectual manner. This is how we can ask our questions, explore the new ideas that are emerging, analyse the language and discourse, and be part of shaping how we understand creative AI in this unique historical moment.

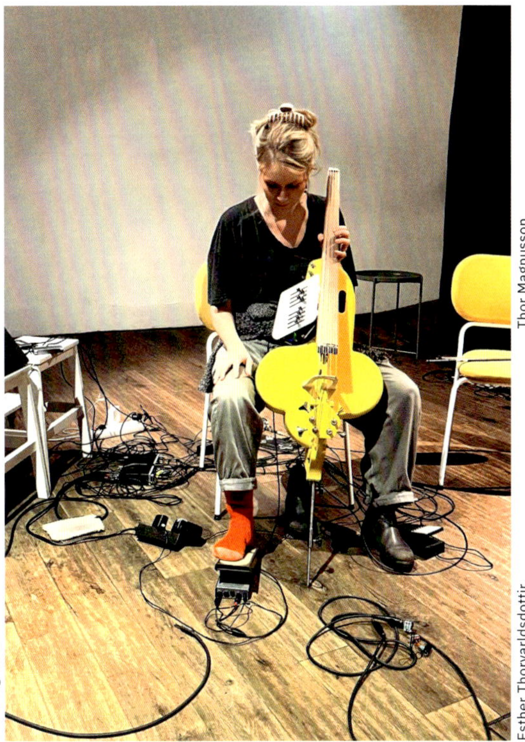

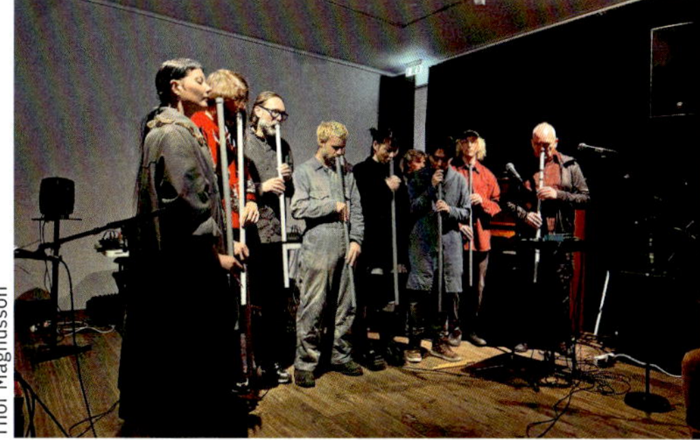

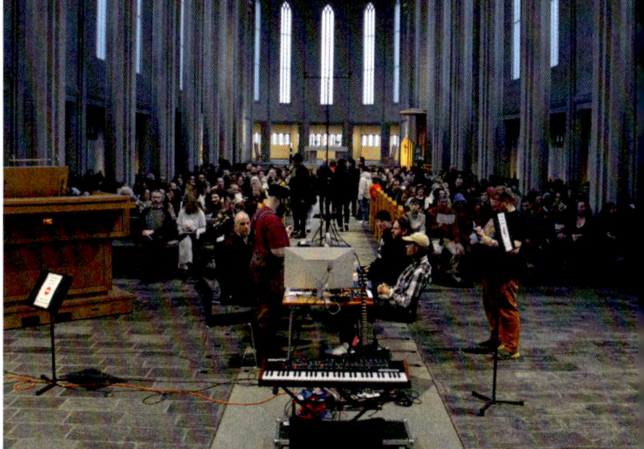

The Intelligent Instruments project is being conducted by: Thor Magnusson (IS), Jack Armitage (UK), Halla Steinunn Stefansdottir (IS), Victor Shepardson (US), Nicola Privato (IT), Miguel Angel Rozzoli (AR), Halldor Ulfarsson (IS), Sean O'Brien (US), Marco Donnarumma (IT), Sophie Skach (AT), and Giacomo Lepri (IT).

The Intelligent Instruments project (INTENT) is funded by the European Research Council (ERC) under the European Union's Horizon 2020 research and innovation program (Grant agreement No. 101001848). The project is hosted by the University of Iceland in collaboration with the Iceland University of the Arts.

https://u.aec.at/64D00735

Thor Magnusson (IS) is a a research professor at the University of Iceland and a Professor in Future Music at the University of Sussex (UK). His work focusses on the relationship of technology and expression, and he does that equally through research, technology development, and musical performance. Magnusson runs the **Intelligent Instruments Lab** (ii lab) which is an interdisciplinary lab with a team of researchers investigating the role of Artificial Intelligence in new musical instruments. The Intelligent Instruments Lab studies creative AI from a broad humanities basis and collaborates with researchers, artists, and the public in key studies of how creative AI alters our relationship with technology, social interaction, and knowledge production.

REPETAE
Sasha Stiles

REPETAE is a hybrid language art series that fuses algorithm and poetry to explore repetition as a powerful tool for generating new meanings, emotions, and insights. It is an ode to the transformative power of poetry, generative art and AI, inviting audiences to consider the endless possibilities that arise from revisiting, reimagining, and reinventing the familiar.

REPETAE leverages a suite of generative elements—AI-powered language, code-based visuals, digitally looped and layered spoken word—in stand-alone works and longer, interconnected cycles that embody various ways in which emotion and perception are shaped by pattern, as well as the interruption or subversion of pattern. At its core, *REPETAE* seeks to illuminate how meaning accrues through repetition, and how repetition shapes our engagement with art and the world around us. Uniquely, the project does so through the lens of verse, invoking repetition as a fundamental poetic device—layering Stiles' pioneering approach of transhuman co-authorship with visuals sketched in p5.js and digitally manipulated spoken word performance.

Rooted in poetic tradition, and inspired in part by an encounter with Herbert W. Franke's *Ozsillogramme,* *REPETAE* expands to interrogate the intersection of human and artificial intelligences, using innovative technologies to redefine the act of repetition not as mere duplication but as a creative and generative process, opening up fresh pathways of interpretation and experience. The project invites consideration of the spatial, temporal, and philosophical dimensions of repetition as reinvention, and aims to prompt deeper reflections on the role of algorithm in the deeply human act of making art.

Works from *REPETAE* have been featured by:
Kunstmuseum Bern, Gucci Art Program, Christie's,
Venus Over Manhattan, NYC,
Tribute to Herbert W. Franke,
Right Click Save: The New Digital Art Community
(Vetro Editions, 2024),
Decentralization,
Please Save Culture (New Society, 2023),
Outland, This is Paper.

https://u.aec.at/2E81F96F

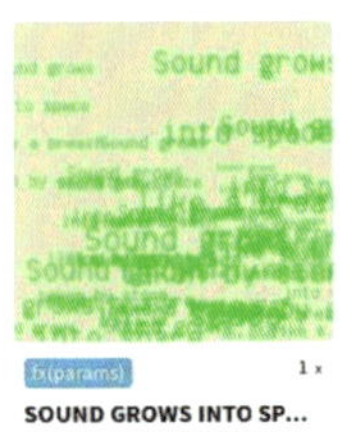
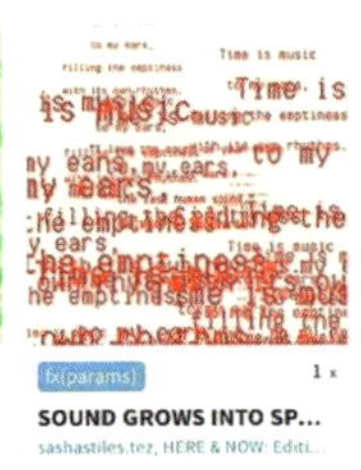
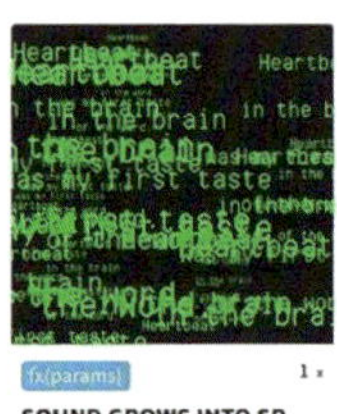
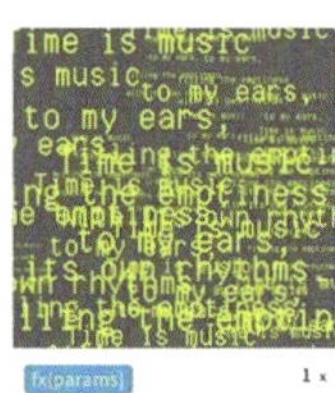
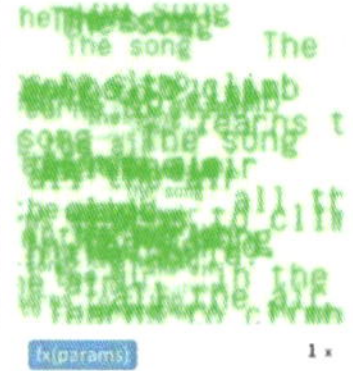
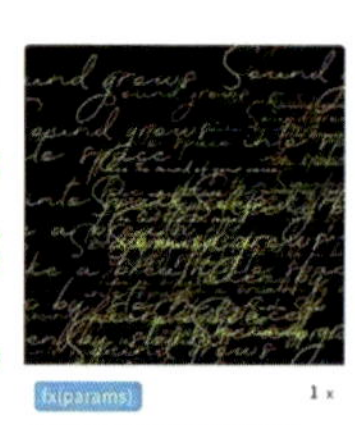

fxhasch/objkt.com

Sasha Stiles (US) is a first-generation Kalmyk-American poet, artist, and AI researcher widely recognized as a pioneer of generative literature and language art. Her award-winning work fuses text and technology to probe what it means to be human in an increasingly posthuman era. Stiles is author of the "instant techno-classic" *Technelegy* (2021) and became the first writer to bring AI-powered literature to a major auction house when her poem "COMPLETION: When it's just you" sold at Christie's in 2022. Stiles exhibits and performs around the world; her work has been featured by MoMA, Art Basel, Gucci, and NPR. Stiles is co-founder of theVERSEverse literary gallery, and has served as Poetry Mentor to the humanoid android BINA48 since 2018.

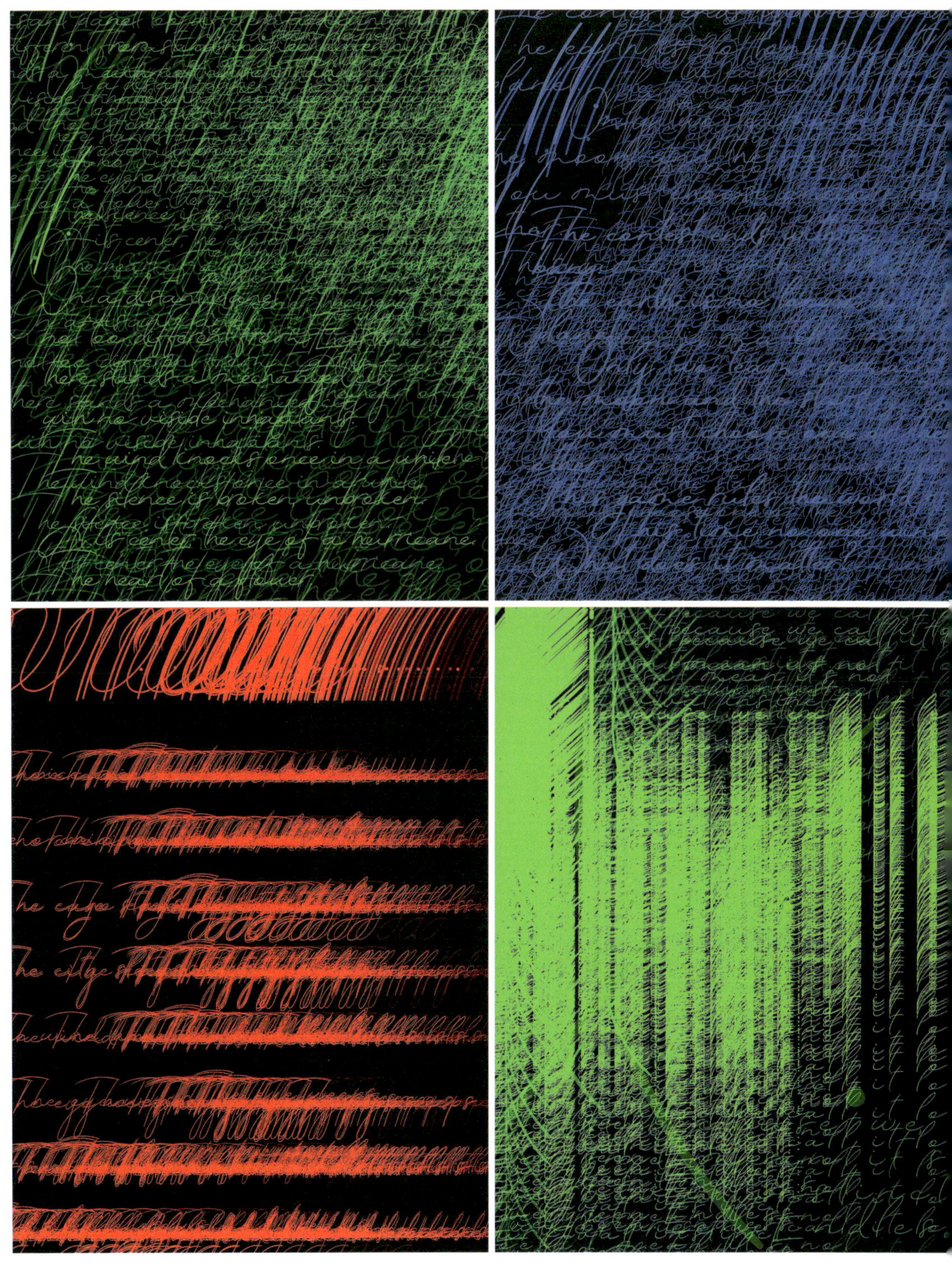

u19
create your world

This Fish has no Idea!

Sirikit Amann, Emil Klostermann, Conny Lee,
Anahita Neghabat, Anna Wielander

As the jury for the u19–create your world category of the Prix Ars Electronica, we have reviewed a multitude of fascinating works by young people from Austria this year. These works not only reflect creative diversity and technological innovation but also provide deep insights into the mindset and current societal challenges of our time.

The selection of the winning works was based on various criteria. In addition to artistic quality and originality, the level of innovation, technical execution, and societal relevance were also important. We chose works that are not only aesthetically pleasing but also convey a clear message and provoke thought. Furthermore, the diversity of perspectives and approaches of the participants was important to us in order to appropriately recognize the range of young creativity.

In numerous works, we have observed an intense engagement with the climate crisis. Young artists, as in previous years, are again addressing the consequences of climate change and seeking new solutions for a sustainable future. Other urgent contemporary issues reflected in the projects of the young entrants include war, flight, and desertion. The short film *Zemlyanka* tackles a topic that is being addressed for the first time in the u19 category and is highly relevant in the context of current conflicts: desertion. This work by the *Zemlyanka* team (Justin Casta, Maximilian Größ, Jonathan Pacher, Georgy Snegur, Christina Zsalacz), like the Golden Nica, represents the desire to survive, but also expresses the desperation that can drive people into seemingly hopeless situations.

The Golden Nica goes to *Fluten der Freiheit* (Floods of Freedom) by Jakob Gruber. Despite its brevity of just ten seconds, the animation impressively conveys strong emotions and an urgent message without any spoken words, using only sound effects. With right-wing parties and autocrats on the rise and the high number of deaths in the Mediterranean often relegated to mere footnotes in media coverage, it is crucial for other voices to be heard loud and clear. This short video evokes emotion without showcasing the personal tragedies of refugees. Jakob Gruber effectively portrays the ongoing tragedy of Mediterranean crossings with a few compelling images. The keywords "Peace, Democracy, Security," essential pillars of European identity, are often inadequately upheld in the context of migration and flight. His animation leaves a lasting impression, reminding us that art has the power to distill complex societal issues and motivate us to take action. It also brings hope: hope for peace, democracy, and security—principles that should be afforded to all people, not just those born in the right country.

Animations have always been a cornerstone of u19. They vary in style, themes, and length as much as the entrants themselves. Whether stop-motion, 2D or 3D animations, drawn, modeled, made from natural materials, clay, or building blocks, these small artworks delight us every year. *Last*, a stop-motion film by Anna Bubenicek and Flora Kirnbauer, receives an Award of Distinction. It touches viewers in a special way. By using natural materials, it creates not only aesthetically pleasing images but also conveys a profound message about climate protection, friendship, and hope. The work also reflects on loneliness and failure, yet it exudes an unwavering hope that can inspire us all.

Engagement with life in the digital world was also a recurring theme in the submitted works. Many participants reflected on the significance of social media, the changing ways we communicate, and the challenges of maintaining genuine connections in an increasingly digital world.

This theme is explored in *to the friends I'll never meet* by artist Selma Yassin, who receives an Award of Distinction for this piece. Her exploration of online relationships is a fascinating multimedia art project that delves into the complexity and beauty of online friendships. The work combines performative elements with installation, digital renderings of analog spaces, and a zine featuring real chat transcripts. Through her adept use of various media, the artist sensitively and intricately approaches themes of online time, friendship, and intimacy. The analogy of threads being woven yet easily cut symbolizes both the fragility and strength of friendships. Translating this performance into a virtual space adds an extra dimension to the project, making it an inspiring reflection on connection and community across transnational boundaries.

Tatsanan Tang addresses the inherent opportunities and dangers of social media in a unique way with *Verpackt und vernetzt* (Packaged and connected). The idea of portraying social media consumption as pills is both simple and complex. Clearly, a lot of thought went into the design. The text of the package insert, which informs about the usage and side effects of the "medication" (social media), is well-researched and includes both scientific facts and humorous moments.

Nostalgia and longing for the past and one's often idealized childhood were reflected in numerous works. Memories contrast with the harsh reality of the present, marked by personal performance pressure and global crises. The theme of death and the transience of life was explored in several pieces. The Honorary Mention for *Canon Events* in the Young Professionals category plays with memories and a self-reflective examination of one's youth while still experiencing it. In this artistic project, formative youth moments were placed in laboratory glasses and preserved. Paula Boyer, Lisa Marie Diessner, and Alena Milcic impressively navigated the fine line between nostalgia and the present, where nothing is idealized but instead examined critically and soberly through a scientific lens.

In the video game *Everlasting End*, Honorary Mention in the Young Professionals category, characters repeatedly experience the last six minutes of their lives. The player must decide which characters to listen to in the remaining moments. By incorporating this interactive concept, viewers are compelled to engage directly with the theme of impermanence. It's more than just a game; it's an experience facilitated by Keno Czompo, Aaron Hager, and Tobias Kogler.

Some works have convinced through their excellence and elaborate use of technical and artistic skills. The brick film *A Normal Day in Jurassic World* by Maximilian Peinhaupt received an Honorary Mention in the Young Professionals category. Not only does this film excel in animation with nearly 6,000 frames and meticulous attention to detail, but it is also filled with many humorous details and expertly crafted sound design. It takes viewers into the daily life of a frustrated park ranger, who struggles to get through his day in a Sisyphean manner.

The highly complex multimedia sound performance *Synergia* received an Honorary Mention in the Young Professionals category and impresses with its successful fusion of text, electroacoustic sounds, and professional presentation. The young Synergia Ensemble demonstrates remarkable maturity in the execution of musical performance and textual accompaniment. Leonhard Gaigg's compositions are skillfully realized with pre-recorded and live-played sounds. The interweaving of text, silence, light, and sound creates a captivating auditory experience, transporting the audience into a unique world. An impressive concert for enthusiasts of experimental contemporary music and anyone who appreciates new sonic experiences.

The jury also noted in several works various forms of artistic exploration of abstract embodied experiences, such as projects dealing with the tangible manifestation or visualization of music.

With *Was heißt es alleine zu sein?* (What does it mean to be alone?), an Honorary Mention in the Young Professionals category was awarded to Ida Onzek, Rosa Peschina, Sina Tödling, and Lara Tomasic. The clip visualizes a song by the Graz singer Roxana. Impressively precise staging allows for the success of this one-cut music video. Throughout, visually stunning images and lovingly crafted details emerge, beautifully accentuating the atmosphere. The expressive, unpretentious performance of the actress reinforces the question without overinterpreting it. It's impressive.

The integration of Artificial Intelligence into creative processes was also a recurring theme. We witnessed impressive works exploring the potentials and challenges of AI in various fields such as art, music, and design.

Peter, Paul und Panini. Klimabuch und Theaterstück (Peter, Paul and Panini. Climate book and play) is a fairy tale story created with the help of AI, reminding both children and adults to care for the environment. The text for the play was developed by the young artist Lina Roth in co-creation with Artificial Intelligence, allowing her to combine her ideas with those of her friends' children while still producing a coherent text. The next step planned is to turn the story into a children's book.

In some works addressing climate policy, creative satire was used to provide a humorous perspective on serious issues such as climate change. For example, in the cleverly crafted short film *Die Klimakonferenz* (The climate conference) by the COM group of PTS Schwanenstadt, an animated fish warns political leaders about the real consequences of the climate crisis but is silenced with the words "This fish has no idea!"

There is still much work ahead of us regarding the issue of climate change, and to tackle this work, we should start by listening to each other and developing ideas, as seen in *Meine grüne Stadt der Zukunft* (My green city of the future). This submission features designs for green skyscrapers. The young artist Jonas Stöttinger has delved deeply into urban planning and architecture against the backdrop of climate change, creating sketches and designs for green and cooling architecture based on his research.

The initiative at BRG/BORG Landeck, *AEROQ—dicke Luft im Klassenzimmer* (AEROQ—Thick air in the classroom), takes a proactive approach to the discussion about indoor air quality in schools during and after the pandemic. Their self-developed CO_2 monitors for classrooms not only impress with their appealing design but also with their technical sophistication. Particularly commendable is their plan to make the documentation and source codes available as open-source, allowing schools with limited resources to benefit from them as well.

Nea Geršak's short animation *Na2r_3lumen* (na2r_flow3rs) is a deserving winner of the Young Creatives u10 Prize. The combination of painted images and flower animation effectively conveys the beauty and transience of nature. At just seven years old, she creatively realizes the idea of recreating time-lapses through multiple smaller videos and then animating them. She uses self-painted acrylic paintings as the background. This work artistically addresses questions about the world in 50 years and whether there will still be flowers there. The title, consisting of letters and numbers, also seems to anticipate the language of the future—are they natural flowers or just images of flowers? Who knows?

This year, the Young Creatives u14 Prize goes to the multimedia project *WarpCity*. Students from the 6th grade of BRG Pichelmayergasse assembled a sculpture from electronic waste for this project. Resembling a futuristic building, a mountain-shaped skyscraper, this architectural sculpture towers upward. Through projection mapping, it comes to life, with words like "heat" or "climate change" projected onto the tower. People walk around the green area surrounding the sculpture, which they see from a bird's-eye view. However, as one approaches the artwork and makes noise, more and more vehicles start driving through the green spaces, leaving less room for pedestrians. This extensive project straightforwardly and creatively conveys the relevance of issues such as soil sealing and urban planning.

The short film *Lights Out*, created by the Young Filmmakers, takes a cinematic approach to the theme of the city. The nearly ten-minute film impresses with its meticulous attention to detail and showcases the beauty of darkness contrasted with artificial light, as experienced during a drive through a city illuminated by lights. The darkness in all its shades—essential for the film's atmosphere— is wonderfully captured.

Among the younger participants, discussions on structural issues such as war and redistribution were observed. Another major theme was the treatment of seniors in society and how caregiving might look in the future. Sustainability was also a prevalent theme in several submissions.

The initial idea behind the drawing *Aus Waffen werden Werkzeuge* (From weapons to tools) stemmed from the theme of sustainability, which most people associate with environmental protection. Environmental protection is deeply humanistic, as it concerns the survival of humanity on this planet. In this project, sustainability and humanism are linked in a different way, namely through a pacifist demand to repurpose war machines such as tanks into something that no longer destroys but is instead useful, such as a tractor. For this beautiful concept, presented in a colorful, vibrant image, David Gaulhofer receives an Honorary Mention from the jury in the u10 category.

As part of the project *Nachhaltigkeitsziele und Stopmotion* (Sustainability Goals and Stop-Motion), a series of short animated films delve into the 17 Sustainable Development Goals of the United Nations. The result is twelve stop-motion films that creatively and poignantly illustrate what we need to do to protect the environment, and more importantly, why we need to do it. For this achievement, this year's Award of Distinction in the u14 category goes to the students of the 3rd grade of Frohnleiten Middle School.

The pressure to achieve and societal expectations placed on young people were also critically examined. Many works delve into the psychological stress and challenges associated with high academic expectations. One negative manifestation is bullying, which many students face.

With *betterTogether,* the five-member team from GRG 15—Auf der Schmelz submitted an app for violence and bullying prevention and intervention. The app, still in the development phase, aims to enable students to seek support easily and report observed cases of bullying and violence (including anonymously). This community project, which received the Young Creatives u12 Prize, demonstrates that when working together as a team, one can advocate for the weaker members of a community.

A positive form of self-help comes from Sarah Hölzl. Her e-book *Book to Go – das sprechende Buch* (Book to go—The talking book) is a valuable resource for teaching children to read (in English). It is lovingly illustrated and turns learning animal names into a multisensory experience. By Sarah's decision to offer the book online and for free, she also enables children with limited access to (English-language) books to participate in a reading community. For the sustainable mindset and user-friendliness of the e-book, she rightfully receives the u12 Award of Distinction.

To welcome new students to school, students from Telfs Weissenbach Middle School have baked cookies. Here, too, the desire for the school to be a place for togetherness is understandable.

The *Future Cookies* project really sparks excitement for school—and for cookies! The detailed process of producing cookie cutters with a 3D printer is documented, making it very understandable. Also impressive is the handling of mistakes, which were neither ignored nor discouraged but rather spurred further action.

It's always a pleasure for us in the u19 category when video game projects are submitted. Some years, these submissions are quite numerous, while in other years, there are hardly any games among all the entries. This year, there were a few games that dealt with very different themes in very different forms—which is natural, given that the medium of games offers nearly unlimited narrative and formal possibilities. However, sometimes an important point is overlooked: that video games can simply be fun. Yet, it's not easy to produce a video game that is genuinely enjoyable. To achieve this, the controls must work flawlessly, the objective must be clear, and the visuals must be cohesive. A sound track also contributes to a good video game. The game designers Benjamin Jurina, Benjamin Schäfer, and Emily Schiestek of *Synth Cycles* can check all these boxes and receive a Young Professionals Honorary Mention. In this auto arena battler, players compete locally against each other and must, like in an autodrome, bounce against the opponent's car to push it off the platform.

It's evident from the examples above that fun and more serious topics can coexist or even go hand in hand in the u19 category. However, a topic that often plays a significant role for young people was surprisingly addressed in relatively few projects this year: the exploration of gender identity. We would like to see more engagement with this topic in the future.

Finally, we would like to thank all participants for their inspiring contributions. Your dedication and creativity are a source of hope and inspiration for us all. We look forward to seeing your work in the future and working together to shape the world of tomorrow.

Text written with some input from ChatGPT

Young Professionals age 14 – 19

Golden Nica

Fluten der Freiheit (Floods of freedom)
Jakob Gruber

Awards of Distinction

Last
Anna Bubenicek, Flora Kirnbauer

to the friends i'll never meet
Selma Yassin

Honorary Mentions

A Normal Day in Jurassic World
Maximilian Peinhaupt

AEROQ—dicke Luft im Klassenzimmer
(AEROQ—Thick air in the classroom)
Valentin Glück, Thomas Jochum,
Max Kneringer, Nina Thöni, Noah Walser

Canon Events
Paula Boyer, Lisa Marie Diessner, Alena Milcic

Die Klimakonferenz (The climate conference)
COM 2023/24 – PTS Schwanenstadt

Everlasting End
Keno Czompo, Aaron Hager, Tobias Kogler

Synergia
Synergia Ensemble

Synth Cycles
Benjamin Jurina, Benjamin Schäfer,
Emily Schiestek

Verpackt und Vernetzt
(Packaged and connected)
Tatsanan Tang

Was heißt es alleine zu sein? (Musikvideo)
(What does it mean to be alone? music video)
Ida Onzek, Rosa Peschina, Sina Tödling,
Lara Tomasic

Zemlyanka
Justin Casta, Maximilian Größ, Jonathan Pacher,
Georgy Snegur, Christina Zsalacz

Young Creatives
up to 14 years

u14 Prize

WarpCity
Class 2a, BRG Pichelmayergasse, Vienna

u14 Award of Distinction

Lights Out
Young Filmmakers 2023

Nachhaltigkeitsziele und Stopmotion
(Sustainability Goals and Stop-Motion)
12 students from class 3b, MS Frohnleiten

u14 Honorary Mention

Meine grüne Stadt der Zukunft
(My green city of the future)
Jonas Stöttinger

u12 Prize

betterTogether
Antonia Hofstadler, Moritz Fink, Marc Umile,
GRG15 – Auf der Schmelz

u12 Award of Distinction

Book To Go—das sprechende Buch
(Book to go—The talking book)
Sarah Hölzl

u12 Honorary Mention

Future Cookies
Seher Ödemis, Lorenz Schennach,
Gülderen Tanriseven, Manojlo Tanzer

u10 Prize

Na2r_3lumen
Nea Geršak

u10 Award of Distinction

**Peter, Paula und Panini
Klimabuch und Theaterstück**
(Climate book and play)
Lina Roth

u10 Honorary Mention

Aus Waffen werden Werkzeuge
(From weapons to tools)
David Gaulhofer

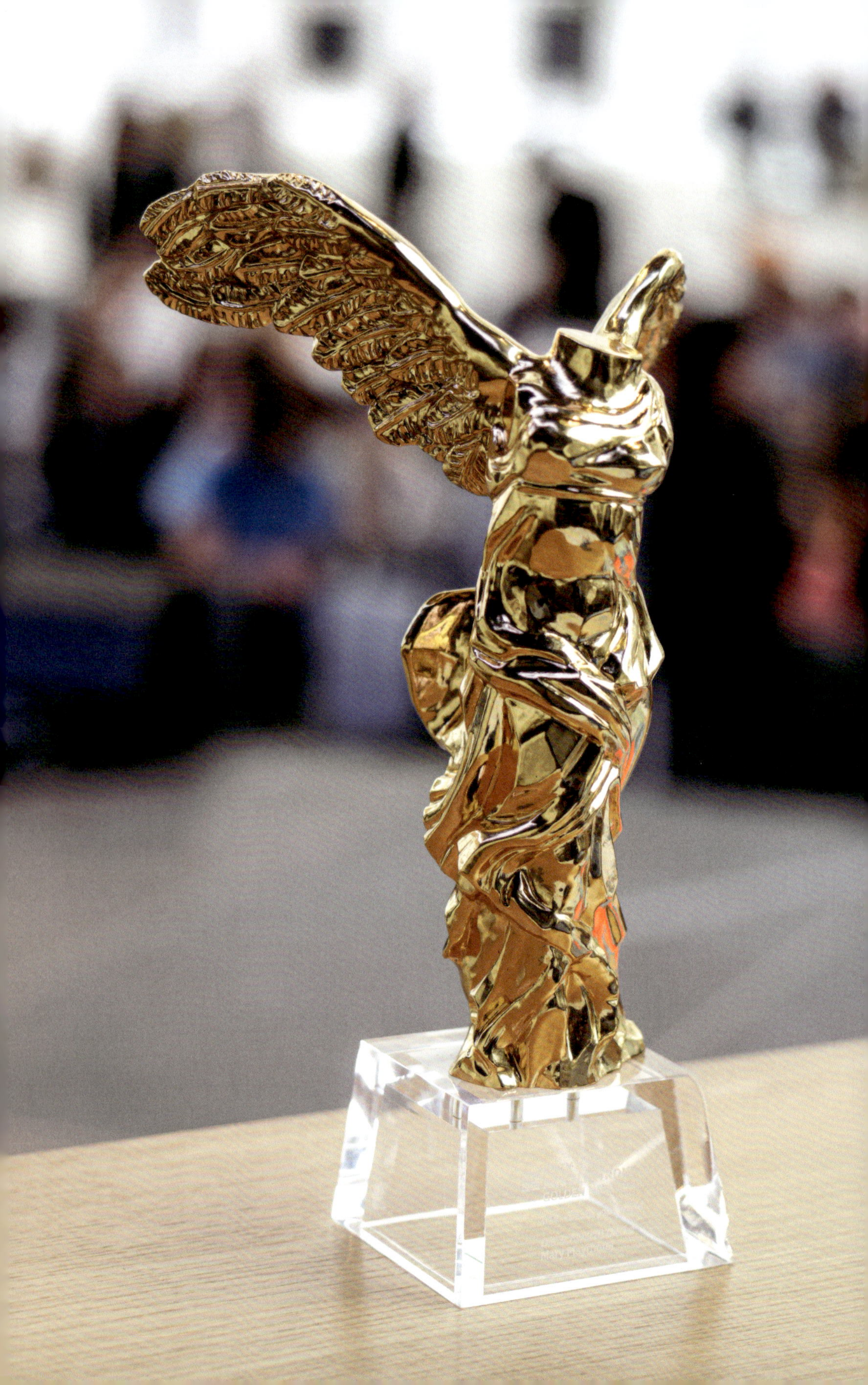

u19–create your world

Young Professionals age 14–19

Fluten der Freiheit

Jakob Gruber

In the 3D animation project *Fluten der Freiheit* (Floods of Freedom), a powerful message unfolds, skillfully combining visual and auditory elements. The animation depicts the creation of a life jacket, whose components are formed from the weighty words "Democracy," "Peace," and "Security." This strikingly symbolizes the refugees' longing for these fundamental values, which often drive their journey across the perilous oceans.

In the production of my project, I was reminded several times of an artwork by Ai Weiwei—the Life Jackets he wrapped around the Berlin Konzerthaus. This work also criticizes the situation of refugees, as the sculpture is made from 14,000 life jackets of refugees. However, while viewing it, something was missing for me: another layer, namely the auditory one. Expanding this visual experience through sound design adds an additional, profound dimension to the animation. The auditory elements are crafted to engage viewers in an emotional experience that represents a commonly occurring reality during such crossings: drowning. By using water sounds such as waves and underwater noises, as well as human elements of breathing and heartbeat in the background, a suffocating atmosphere is created. The aim of this sound layer is to prompt viewers to empathize with the plight of the refugees and to experience an intense "goosebumps" moment. The combination of visual and auditory stimuli is intended not only to inform but also to evoke empathetic responses. By confronting viewers with the real challenges and dangers, a deeper connection and understanding of the refugees' plight is fostered.

This project not only aims to draw attention to the precarious situation of refugees, but also to help underline the urgent need for humanitarian commitment and global solidarity. This project delves deeply into the refugees' journey across the seas. On their arduous journey, they place their hopes on the search for democracy, peace and security in Europe. However, crossing the oceans not only brings the dream of a better life, but also considerable dangers. Many people have lost their lives by exposing themselves to the unpredictable elements of the ocean. The challenges associated with this crossing extend far beyond the physical risks. Refugees must also face the emotional and psychological stresses that come with uncertainty about what awaits them.

This project aims to illuminate not only the external aspects of this journey, but also the internal struggles of the people who embark on this dangerous path. By capturing personal stories, experiences and challenges, it attempts to raise awareness of the humanity behind the statistics. This is done in the hope of fostering a constructive dialogue on the global challenges of migration and the need for a humane and coordinated response. Thus, this project becomes a powerful tool to deepen understanding and inspire empathy for those who cross the dangerous waters in search of a safer and more hopeful life.

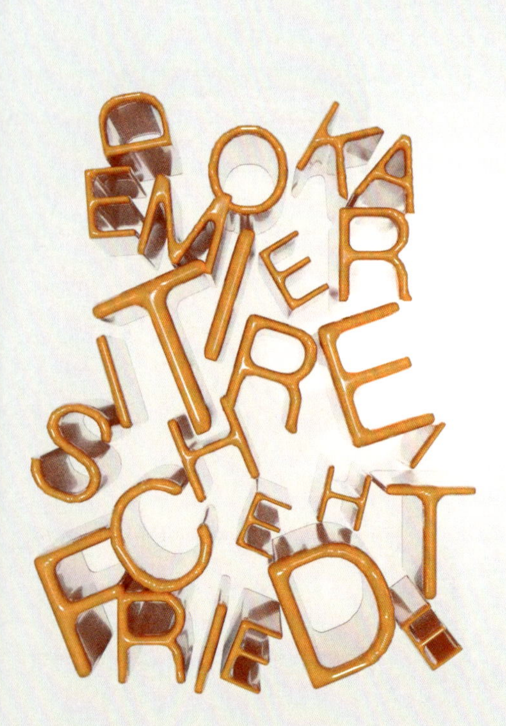

https://u.aec.at/2E712760

**u19—create your world
Golden Nica 2024**

**Young Professionals
(age 14–19)**

FLUTEN DER

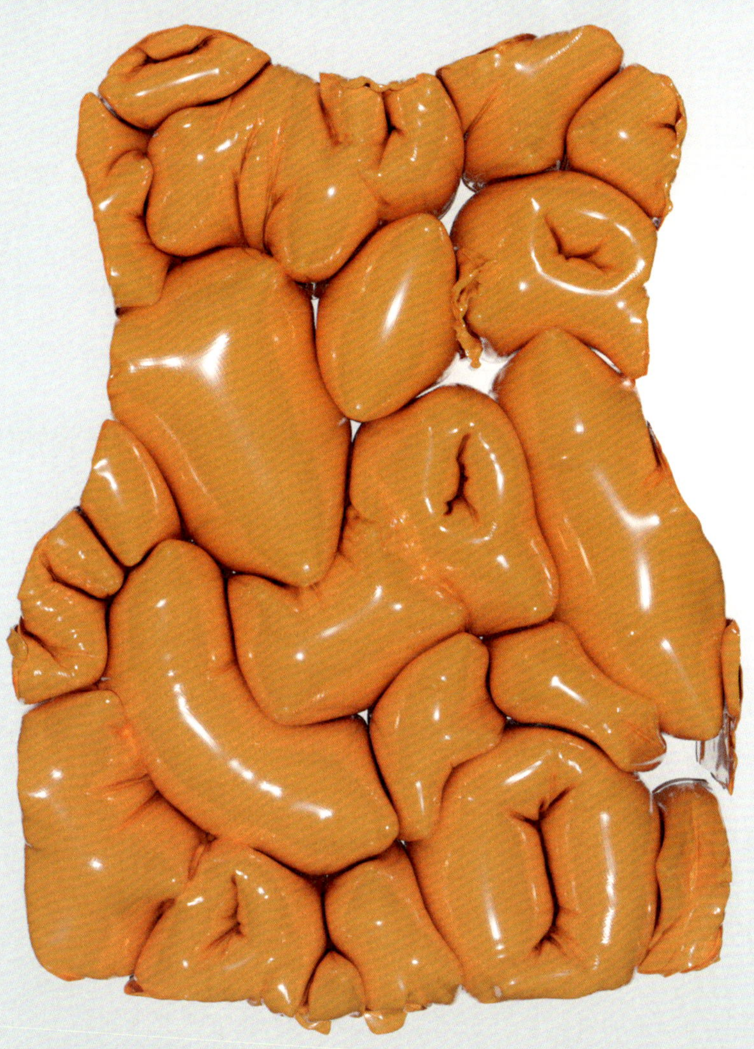

FREIHEIT

My name is **Jakob Gruber** (*2007). I spent the first months of my life in a small apartment in Salzburg South. Shortly after, we moved to Henndorf, where I also attended kindergarten and elementary school. After that, I transferred to the Bundesrealgymnasium in Seekirchen. Here, I had my first important artistic experiences. Since I enjoyed this very much and another school change was imminent, I applied to the HTL Salzburg in the field of graphic and communication design. This application process was very lengthy, but it paid off. In spring 2021, I was accepted, and I started at the HTL in autumn. The HTL is a wonderful experience. In spring 2024, I also won an award in the video category at a creative competition organized by the Salzburg State Parliament.

Last
Anna Bubenicek, Flora Kirnbauer

The lonely protagonist finds a treasure that fascinates him so much that he decides to build a friend out of it. In his manic state of mind, he begins to neglect his responsibilities. He searches, drags and tinkers with great effort, but to no avail. His friend doesn't come to life. At the climax, he decides to steal a precious stone from a gravesite to complete his work. That's no use either. Full of disappointment and frustration, he destroys his friend and trashes his house. The protagonist falls to the ground and in the midst of chaos he finds his precious stone again.

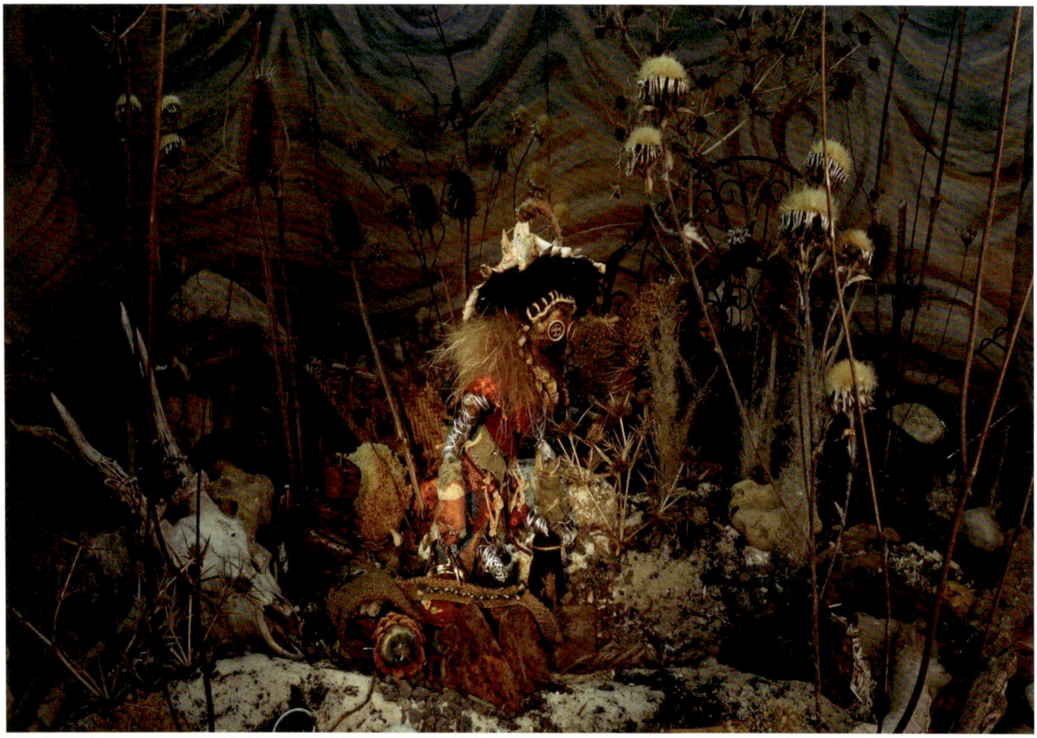

Our original idea was nothing more than a landscape and a feeling we wanted to convey. Soon we

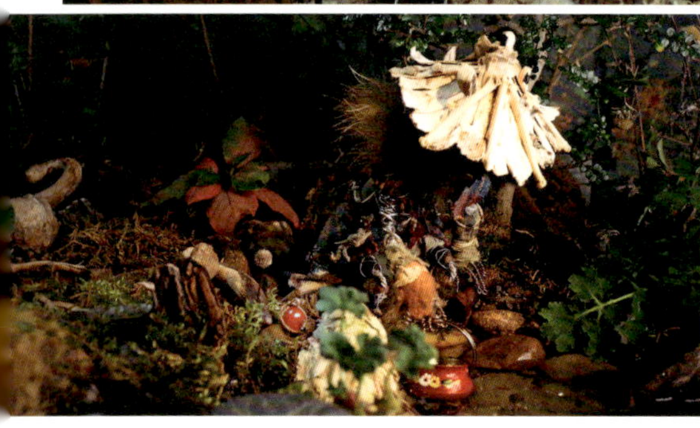

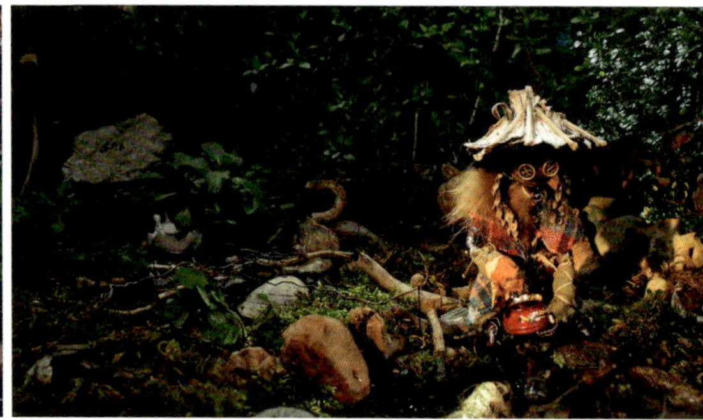

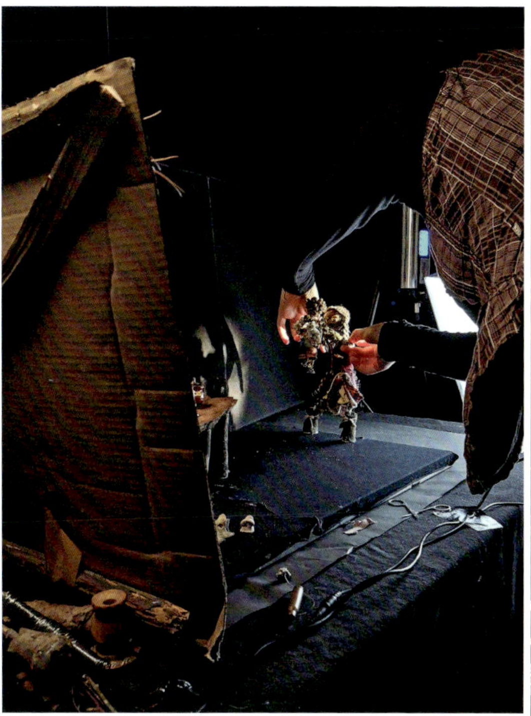

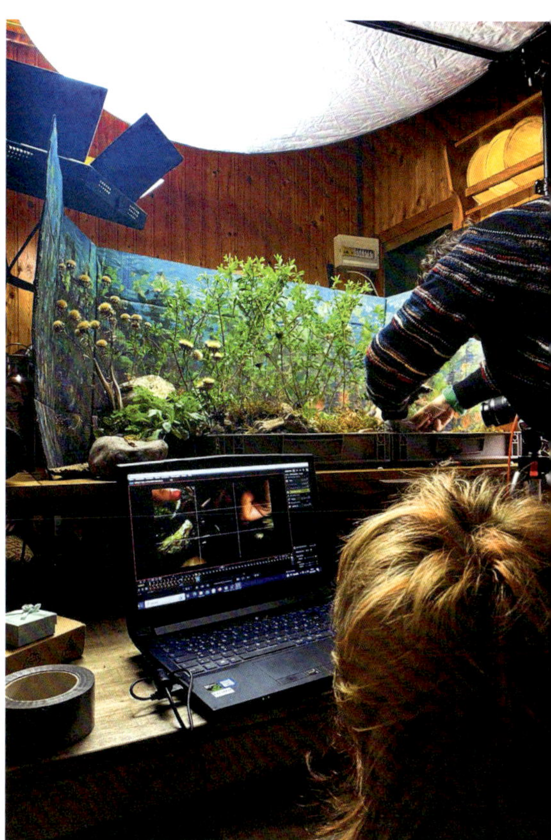

spun a heart-touching story around it. Since we've wanted to work with stop motion for a long time, *Last* was the perfect project to try out the new technique.

The next goal was to place a character in a setting that fits the story well. To do this, we decided to integrate a variety of found objects that we collected in forests and on beaches into our designs and to make props look as if they had been made by the protagonist himself. We made puppets that had to be sturdy enough to withstand the rigors of animating, but at the same time look craftsman-like and delicate.

Since we had very limited time to animate in our school's studio, we built our indoor set there, and we set up all of our outdoor sets in a small garden shed where we spent our nights animating. Due to the shaky floor in the shed, we had to devote a lot of post-production effort to stabilizing the footage. We decided to record our film music ourselves and invited friends of ours to play the clarinet and bassoon. Some scenes were improvised, and for others they used pieces of music they had previously played. After a great many finishing touches, the film was completed as you see it today.

Thanks to Mia Schmit, HTL Spengergasse

https://u.aec.at/CA5573CA

We, **Anna Bubenicek** (*2005) and **Flora Kirnbauer** (*2004) are two animation students from Vienna. During our training in animation and media design at HTL Spengergasse, we discovered our fascination for stop motion. So we produced the film *Last* during our 4th school year. In the following final year we made the decision to try 2D animation again, which will continue to accompany us through to our university studies. However, we will definitely go back to stop motion at times in the future.

to the friends i'll never meet

Selma Yassin

The project *to the friends i'll never meet* deals with the topic of excessive time on the internet, which can lead to unhealthy dependency and distancing from interactions outside the internet. It addresses the problem of how to return to a life away from the screen when virtual bonding has become the primary form of social contact.

The first part of the work consists of a sculpture made of crocheted threads and wood for stabilization and an accompanying video showing the construction process. Here it can be seen that the person building the sculpture limits and restricts themselves through the multiplying string connections that are used to represent online friendships. Additionally, this is presented within a 3D space that includes a scan of the sculpture and the video of its creation projected onto a glowing screen. It is not possible to leave the construction. In addition, there is a zine that shows old chats with online friends—usually the beginning and end of an acquaintance—to offer a more personal insight into the topic.

The different levels and aspects of the work reflect the complexity of our interpersonal relationships, and the project is intended to encourage us to be attentive to our time online and not to get lost in a digital world.

https://u.aec.at/059CE76E

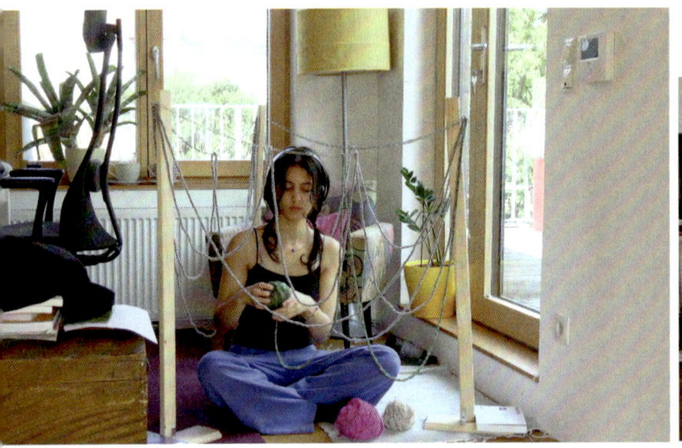

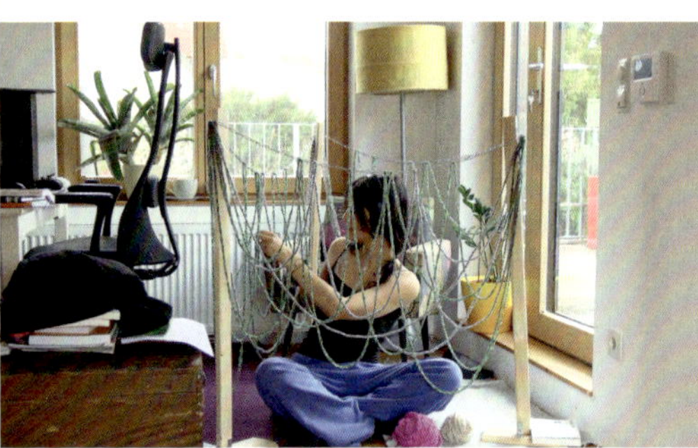

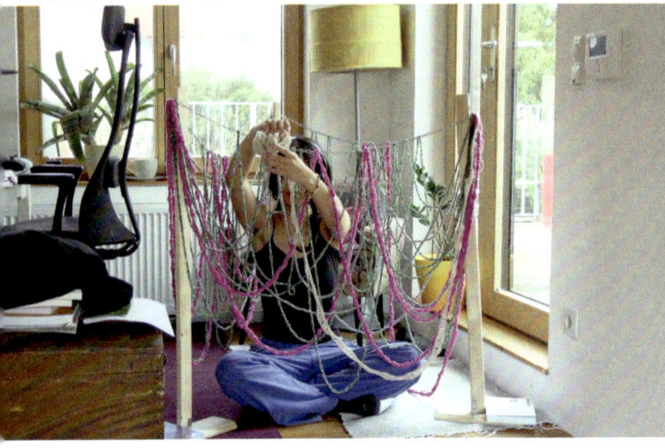

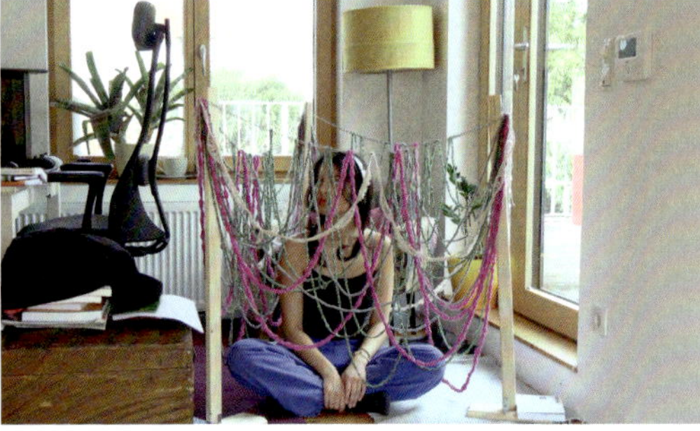

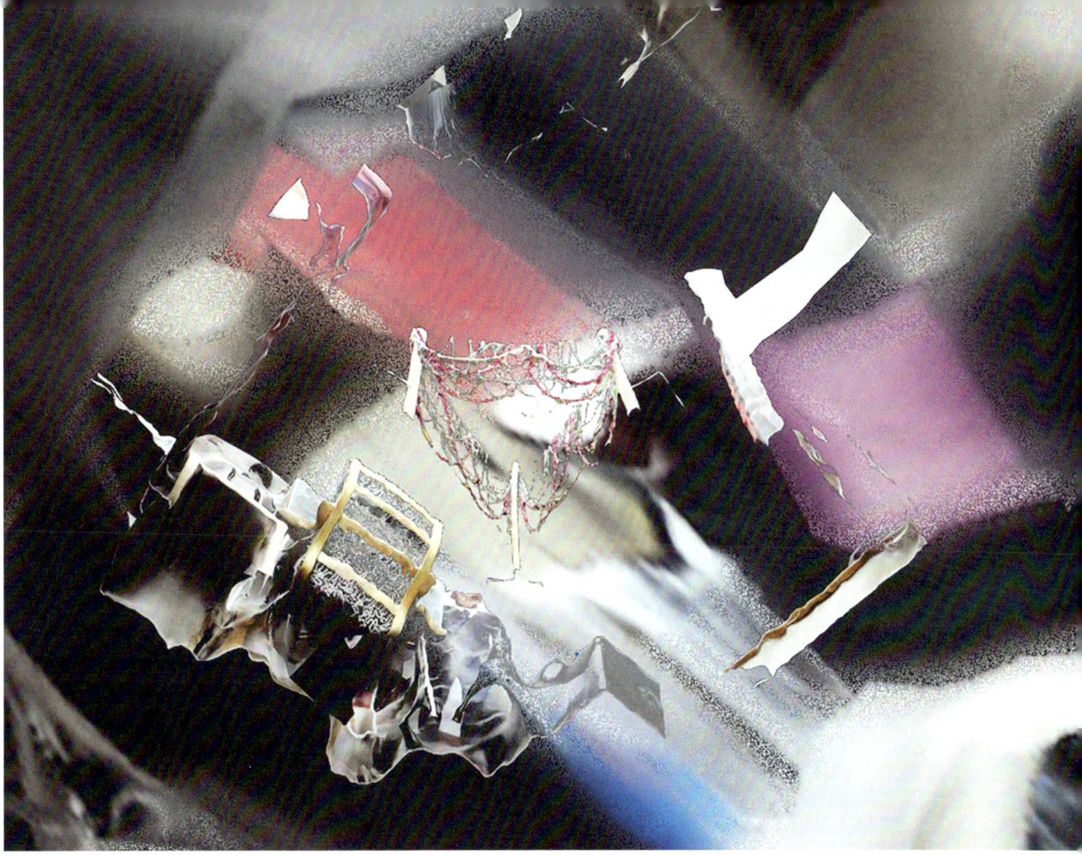

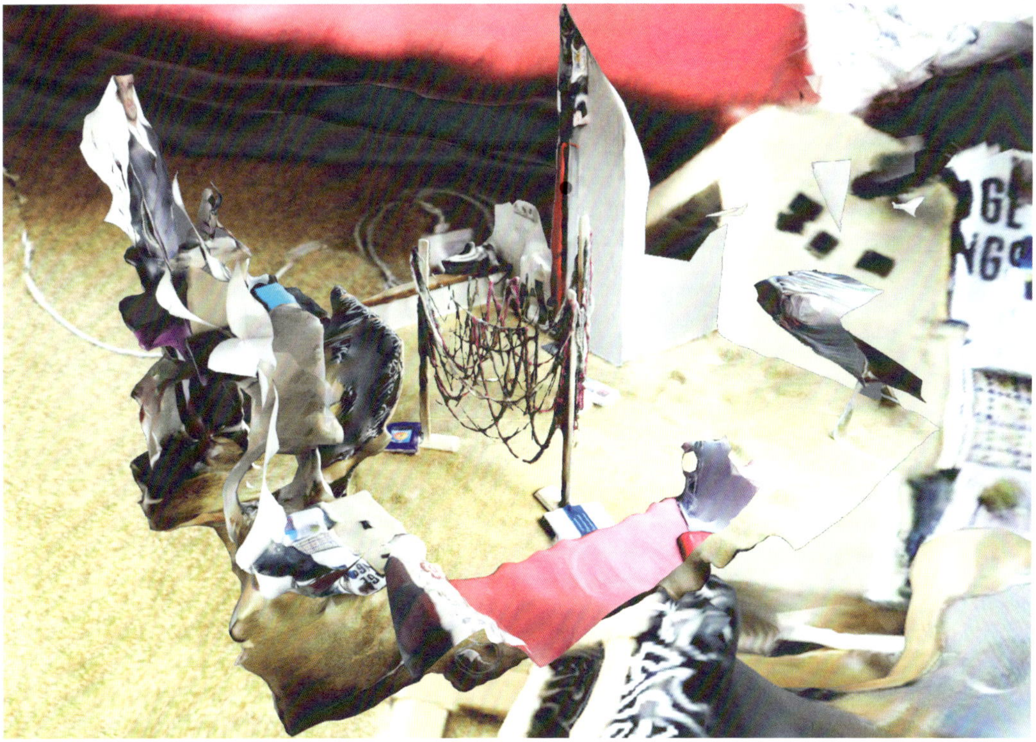

Selma Yassin (*2005) is currently focusing on photography at the Höhere Graphische Bundes-, Lehr- und Versuchs-anstalt in Vienna. She enjoys experimenting with different kinds of media and the combination of these.

A Normal Day in Jurassic World

Maximilian Peinhaupt

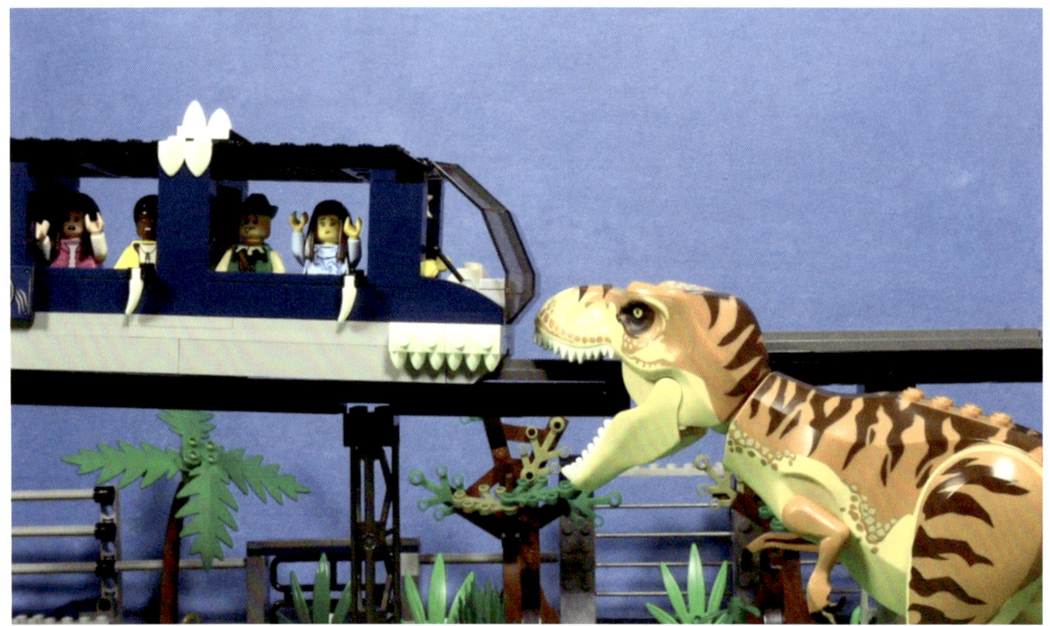

My project *A Normal Day in Jurassic World* is a stop-motion animated film created using Lego bricks. The film is about a zookeeper in a dinosaur theme park, who fails miserably at keeping the giant lizards under control. In stop motion, characters are posed and then photographed for each frame of a film. These individual images taken by my Nikon DSLR (15 images per second, 5600 images in total) are then strung together using the Stop Motion Studio program on the MacBook and are transformed into a fluid film. In my case, the characters move in Lego movie sets that I built. After creating a script and storyboard and filming, the film was edited in Final Cut Pro. This includes adding sound and visual effects, color grading, and retouching rigs that keep airborne characters and objects above the ground during filming.

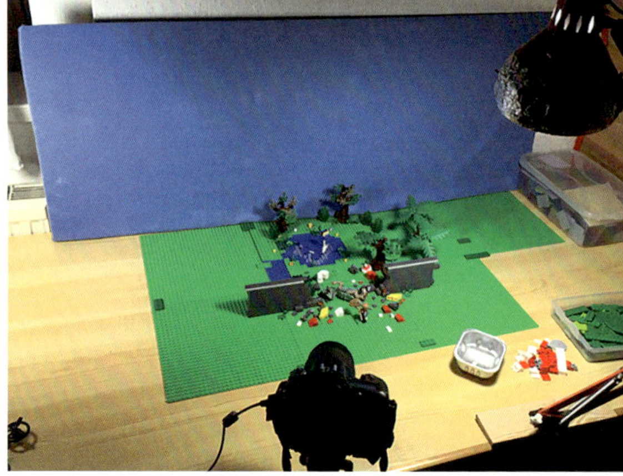

https://u.aec.at/8E81920E

Maximilian Peinhaupt (*2005) lives with his family in Pusterwald in Styria. From an early age, he developed a growing interest in films, storytelling, photography, and video editing. After attending Pusterwald elementary school from 2011 to 2015, he attended the lower and upper levels of BG / BRG Judenburg from 2019 to 2023. Between October 2023 and June 2024, Maximilian completed his community service at Lebenshilfe Region Judenburg.

u19–create your world
Honorary Mention

Young Professionals
(age 14–19)

AEROQ – dicke Luft im Klassenzimmer

Valentin Glück, Thomas Jochum, Max Kneringer,
Nina Thöni, Noah Walser

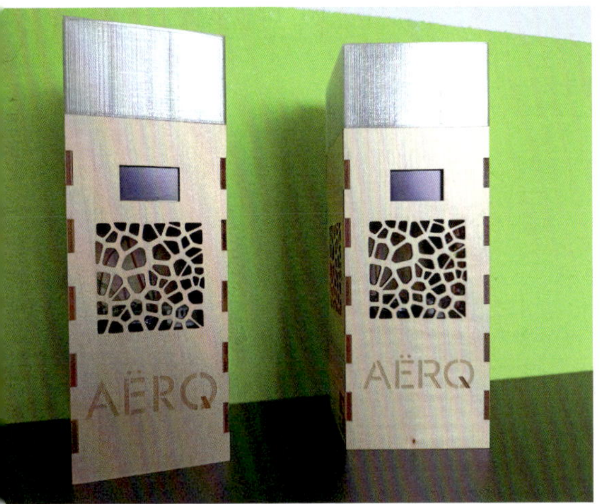

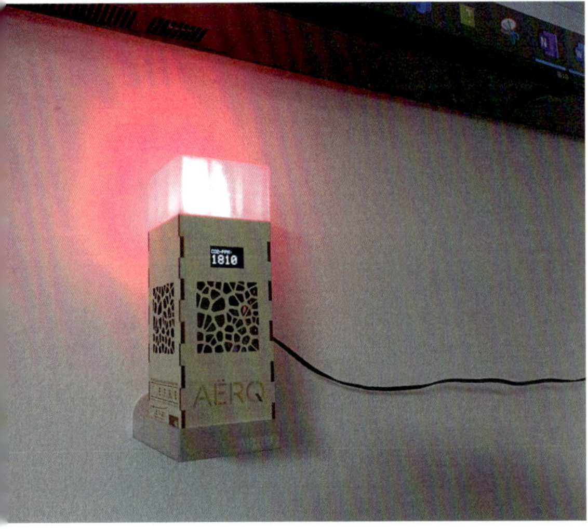

The indoor climate, especially in classrooms, has not only been examined since the Corona pandemic. Carbon dioxide (CO_2) is a very good indicator for determining indoor air pollution. From a CO_2 concentration of 1,500 ppm (parts per million), significant losses in human performance can be observed. For example, mental performance decreases, the susceptibility to errors increases, and the students' attention is impaired. Measurements show that the limit of 1,500 ppm is often exceeded in a typical classroom, and CO_2 concentrations of 2,000 ppm to 5,000 ppm are not uncommon. The primary goal of *AEROQ – Thick air in the classroom* is to confront the people involved (students/teachers) with the topic "indoor air quality" and to sensitize them accordingly. For this purpose, a measuring station is being built for each classroom in our school, which measures the CO_2 concentration, temperature, and humidity of the room air and displays the values using RGB LEDs and a display.

Supervisor: Rene Braunshier
Supported by regioL—Regional management for the district of Landeck

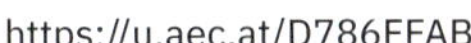

https://u.aec.at/D786FFAB

The project group consists of **Valentin Glück** (*2006), **Thomas Jochum** (*2007), **Max Kneringer** (*2007), **Nina Thöni** (*2006), and **Noah Walser** (*2007), who focus on the natural sciences at BRG Landeck. In order to deepen their broad technical interests, they also decided to take the computer science elective subject, in which they made the CO_2 station together. The group is supervised by Mag. Rene Braunshier (*1981), who has been teaching at BRG/ BORG Landeck since 2009.

Canon Events

Paula Boyer, Lisa Marie Diessner, Alena Milcic

What makes us who we are today? Countless experiences shape us. We young people call this a "canon event": for example, the first failed summer love or a difficult school start during the pandemic. Our project presents our personal canon events captured in laboratory glasses. This gives meaning to seemingly everyday objects. Sorting out our canon events was an emotional journey into our past. The attic was rummaged through, drawers that had been unopened for a long time, nothing remained undiscovered.

After everyone had created their collections, we presented them to each other. We asked ourselves questions like "Which moments had a strong impact on me?" "What did I learn from these situations?" While clearing out, we discovered that others often can't relate to their own memories. The challenge was to reduce extensive stories to one sentence and turn them into an experience that others could relate to. To preserve them, we experimented a lot with different liquids and ultimately found that gelatin works best.

https://u.aec.at/059B175B

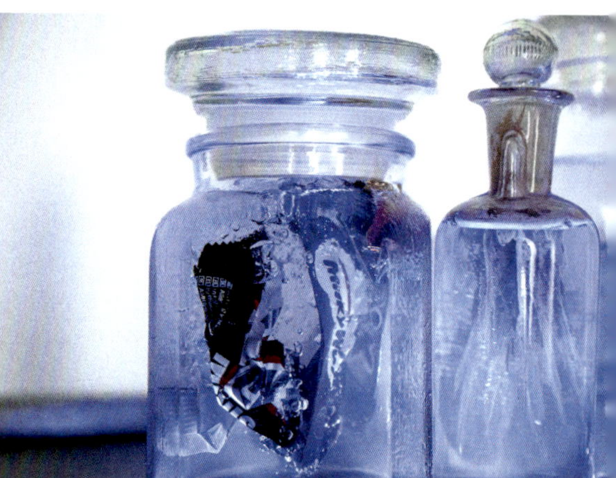

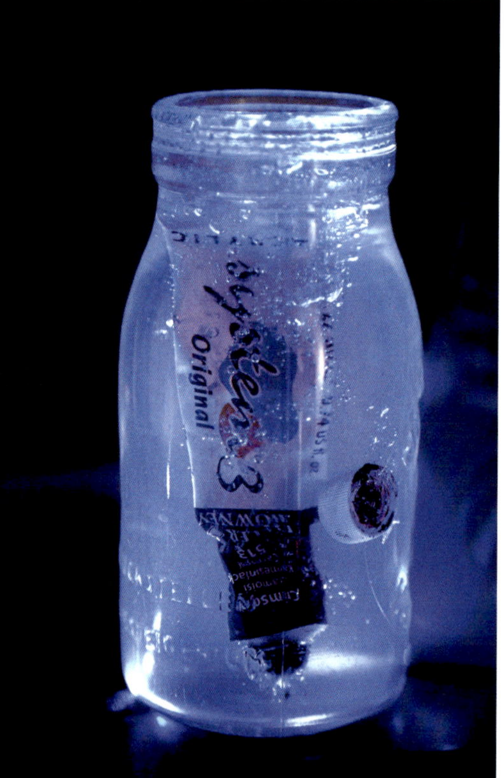

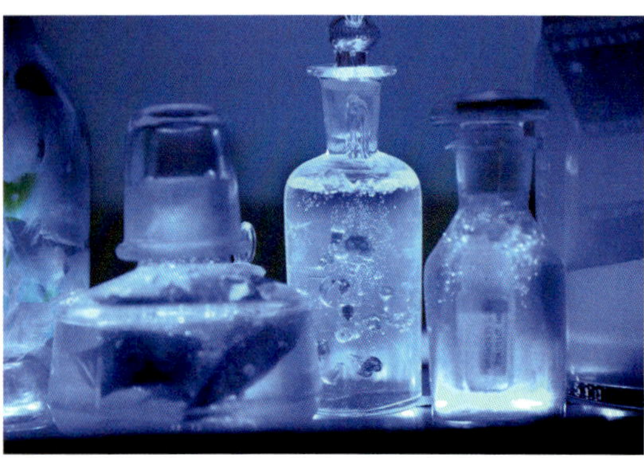

We, **Alena Milcic** (*2006), **Paula Boyer** (*2006), and **Lisa Marie Diessner** (*2005), met at school and have grown together into a close group of friends over the years. As different as we are as people, we all have one thing in common: our sense of humor. No matter where or when, we only exist in a pack of three according to the motto: "Never without my team!"

u19–create your world
Honorary Mention

Young Professionals
(age 14–19)

Die Klimakonferenz
COM 2023/24—PTS Schwanenstadt

As part of our climate school project and in cooperation with the Medien Kultur Haus Wels (MKH), we launched the film project *Die Klimakonferenz* (The Climate Conference).

What makes our film project special is that it is completely student-controlled. We thought up and implemented all aspects of the film ourselves—from the script to direction, film, sound, animation, music, and acting.

On the first day of the project we developed a story and a script together. Everyone could contribute their ideas. During the implementation, each of us had several jobs. We took care of camera work, sound, directing, and acting. Ana plays the piano and recorded all of the film music independently.

During a visit to the Medien Kultur Haus Wels, we created the fish animation and the opening and closing credits using stop-motion technology. Finally, we also took care of the entire post-production (editing in the Adobe Premiere Pro program) ourselves.

With support from:
Medien Kultur Haus Wels / filmmaker Reinhard Zach

https://u.aec.at/B6A7178D

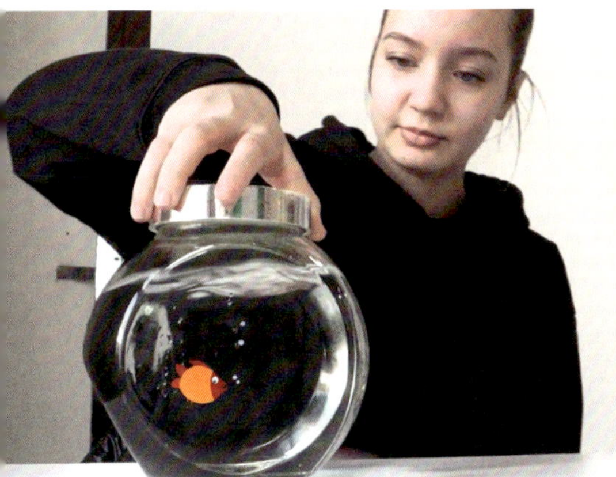

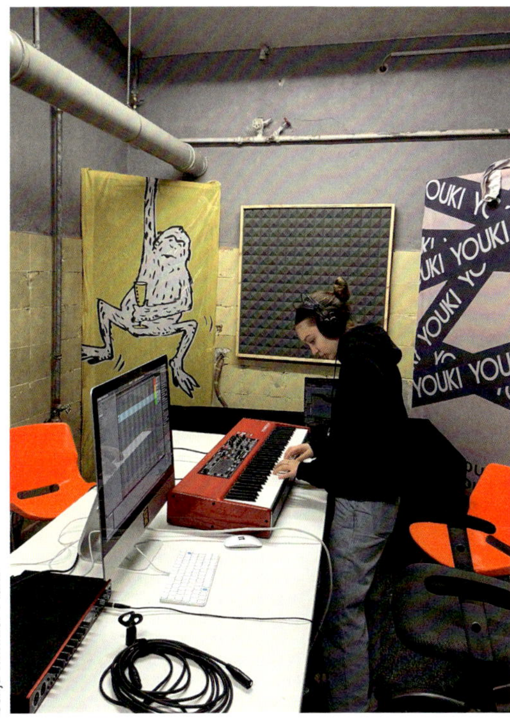

Sonja Wimmer-Pfarrl

We are the **COM group** (Commerce, Office & Media Design) of PTS Schwanenstadt. Our group consists of ten students: Sahra, Medeea, Sara, Ana, Zara, Semka, Stjepana, Maja, Ina, and Celina. We are all between 14 and 16 years old (born 2007 to 2009) and made this film as part of a school project. We like each other and support each other. Many friendships have been formed in our group.

Everlasting End
Keno Czompo, Aaron Hager, Tobias Kogler

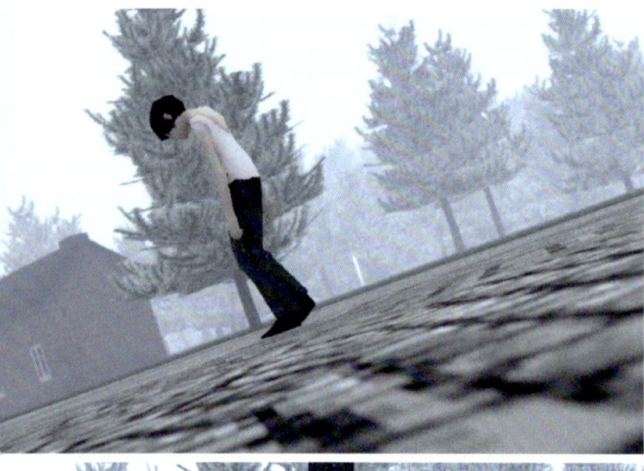
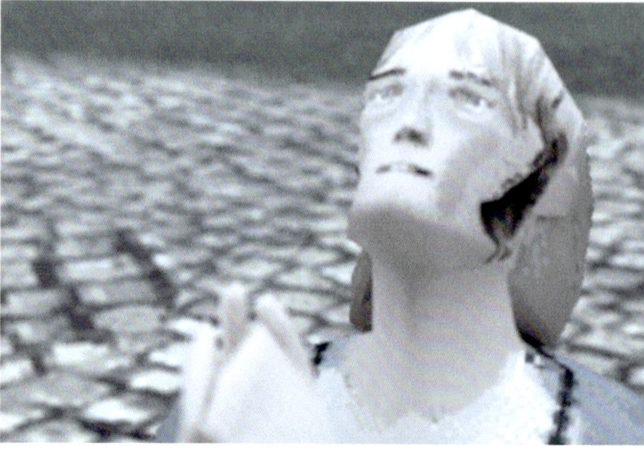
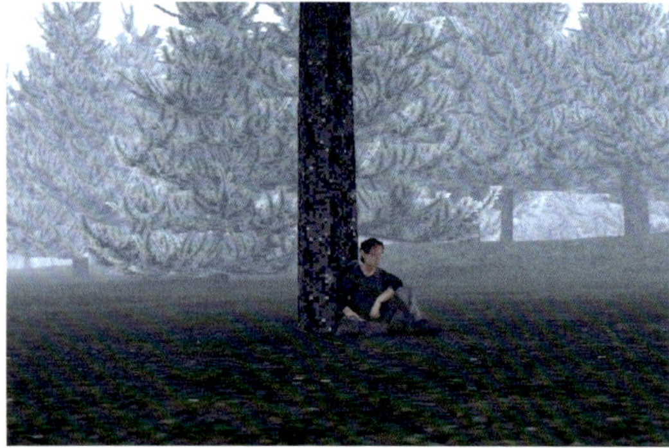
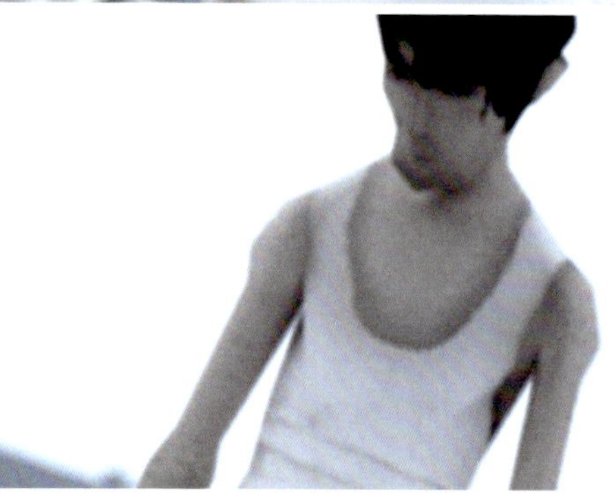

With our project *Everlasting End* we offer a visual experience that provides insight into different ways of dealing with death. This starts with the main character being forced by a car accident to go to a lonely village in the forest called Morrows Rest. In this village are people who have lived there all their lives and who know that they will die when they hear the bells ringing from the bell tower in the center of the village. They also know that this can happen at any time. All the people living in the village talk about their thoughts about their life and their imminent death in the form of monologues. Each person takes a different approach to dealing with this. In our project you have the opportunity to explore this village and experience the last six minutes of these people. These start again and again so that you have time to listen to everything. The oppressive, at times spooky atmosphere is deliberately chosen to convey a feeling of both unrest and silence.

Programming, voice acting, audio,
co-directing: Tobias Kogler
Asset creation, co-directing: Aaron Hager
Writing: Ben Oswald
Voice acting: Julia Scheucher
Asset creation: Boris Kostadinov
Audio: Keno Czompo

https://u.aec.at/8952F46B

Tobias Kogler (*2006), **Aaron Hager** (*2006), and **Keno Czompo** (*2006) are students at the Höhere Graphische Bundes Lehr- und Versuchsanstalt in Vienna, specializing in multimedia. After numerous conversations about the topic of death and thanks to their shared passion for video games, they decided to develop *Everlasting End*. The main difficulty lay in creating an ideal setting and concept that would guarantee a multi-perspective experience.

**u19—create your world
Honorary Mention**

**Young Professionals
(age 14–19)**

Synergia
Synergia Ensemble

Synergia is a contemporary chamber ensemble and was founded in summer 2023 by the composer Leonhard Gaigg. Since then, he has directed it in collaboration with the composer Clara Donat. Through the special line-up (unusual acoustic instruments in combination with electronics), *Synergia* wants to combine different art movements such as electro-acoustics and acoustics or text and music. This artistic combination creates a new work of art, a kind of "synergy", hence the name of the ensemble.

The ensemble's founding concert took place on January 31, 2024 at the Anton Bruckner Private University in Linz. Under the title *Contrasts and Conflicts*, a cycle of compositions by Leonhard Gaigg for ensemble, speaker, and live electronics to texts by Tabea Spießberger was premiered. The ensemble currently consists of 13 members and is planning new concert programs and concert concepts.

Ensemble founder: Leonhard Gaigg
Ensemble members / musicians: Clara Donat, Stephan Deinhammer, Leonie Felbinger, Ida Gillesberger, Juliane Humer, Amelie Jade Knapp, Aaliyah Lehner, Declyn Lehner, Eleonor Sophie Plöchl, Flora Schilcher, Kristina Semaschko, Tabea Spießberger

https://u.aec.at/7B2DD39B

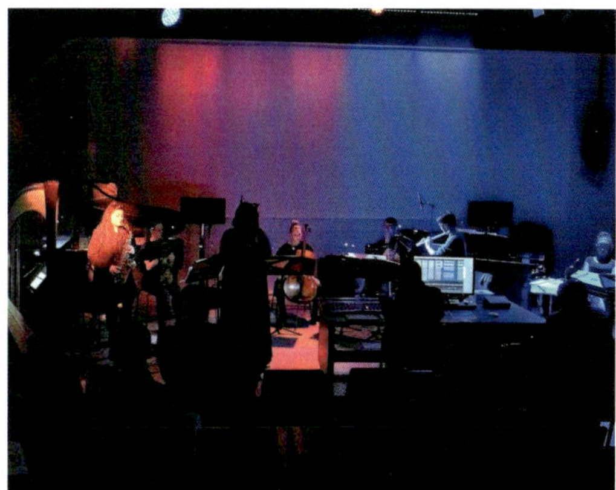

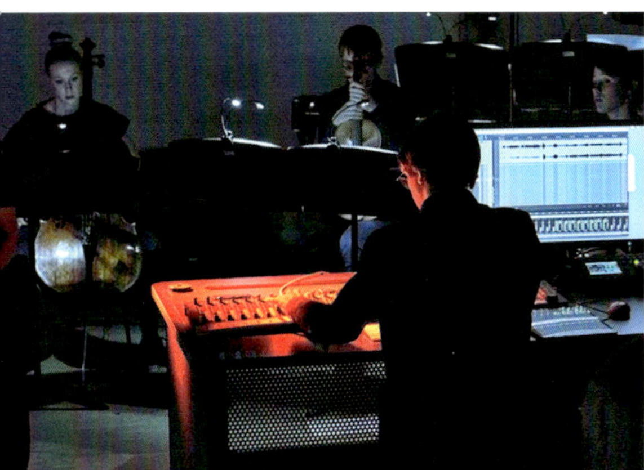

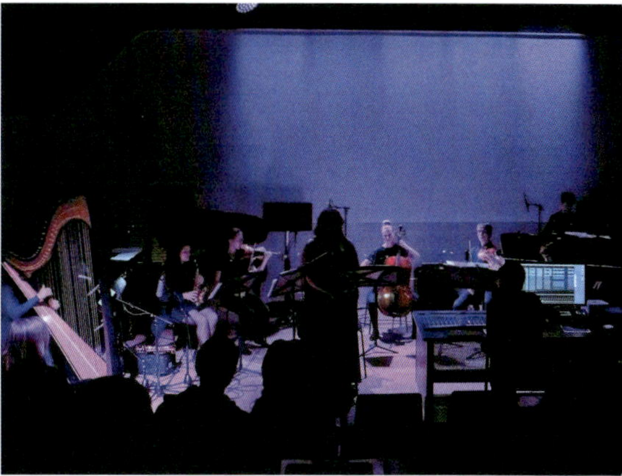

The **Synergia Ensemble** consists of a total of 13 musicians. Most of them are currently attending the Adalbert Stifter Gymnasium (Music school) and the Academy for Gifted Education at the Anton Bruckner Private University in Linz. The youngest musician is 15 (*2008), the oldest is 19 (*2004). The different instruments offer a wide range of possible occupations. The ensemble is led by Leonhard Gaigg (*2005) and Clara Donat (*2005).

Synth Cycles
Benjamin Jurina, Benjamin Schäfer, Emily Schiestek

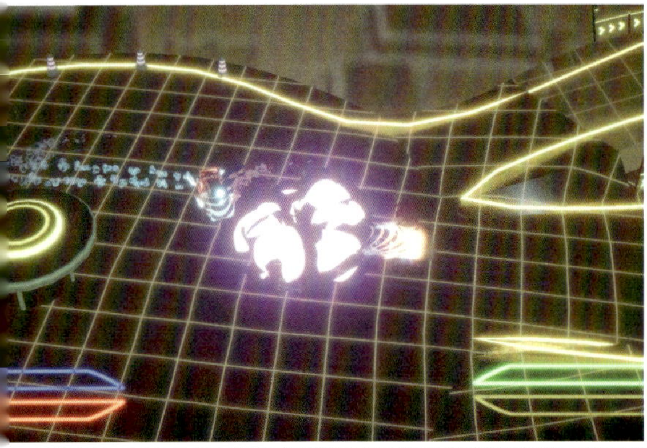

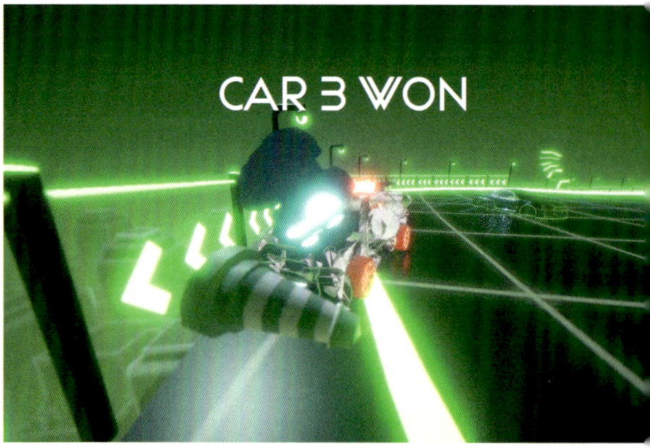

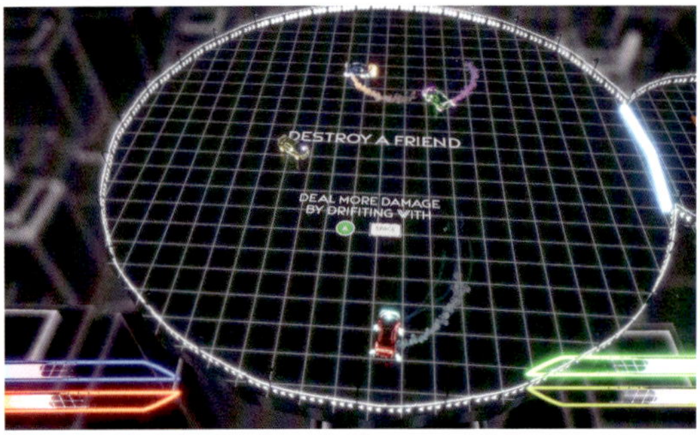

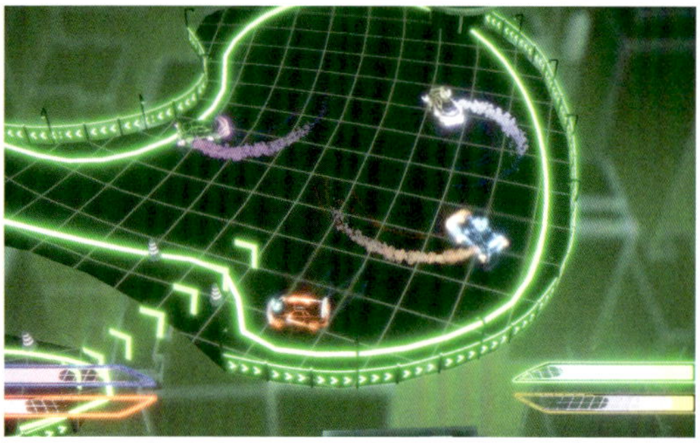

Take a deep breath, turn the ignition key on your drift car and off you go! In the local multiplayer game *Synth Cycles,* only the strongest (and coolest) survive. Eliminate the opposing drivers and win the round. Your goal is to win the most rounds in order to be the ultimate winner at the end. And what is the most fun thing about cars? That's right—the drifting. Drifts can be used both defensively and offensively to prevent self-damage and maximize third-party damage. The intuitive controls and handcrafted arenas create a unique last car standing gaming experience. Plus, the quick rounds keep the game fresh and lead to fair competition. So what are you waiting for? Grab your handbrake and leave your competition in the dust!

Music: Dance With The Dead
Music: Karl Casey @ White Bat Audio
Music: Grand_Project on Pixabay
Zapsplat Free SFX
Wwise Game Audio Suite
Unity Game Engine
Playtesting and support by Purple Lamp

https://u.aec.at/CF058A81

The team behind *Synth Cycles* consists of **Benjamin Jurina** (*2004), **Benjamin Schäfer** (*2005), and **Emily Schiestek** (*2003). The game was created as a diploma project at HTL Spengergasse, Vienna. Benjamin Jurina is the mastermind behind the concept. As a game designer, he created the game world, which is highlighted by his visual and sound effects. Emily Schiestek gave the world its shape through 3D modeling. Benjamin Schäfer programmed the framework on which the colorful world is built.

**u19–create your world
Honorary Mention**

**Young Professionals
(age 14–19)**

Verpackt und Vernetzt

Tatsanan Tang

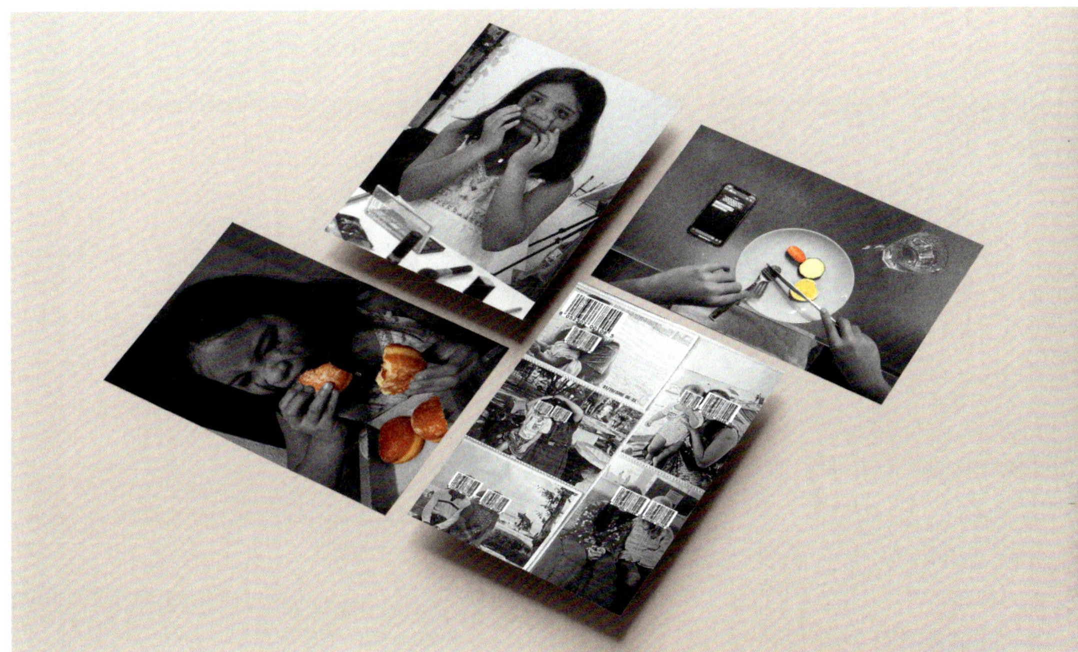

What happens when we blur the lines between medicine and technology? How can we raise awareness about the effects of excessive social media use? How can we sensitize people and get them to think about their usage behavior? These questions are the starting point for the *Packaged and Connected* project.

Social media icons are integrated into traditional medication packaging, with chilling images and a leaflet highlighting the potential negative effects of excessive social media consumption. The packaging contains images that illustrate the dark sides of social media use, such as loneliness, social pressure, cyberbullying, and the risk of addiction.

The aim is to draw attention to the problem of excessive social media use and raise awareness of its potentially harmful effects on mental health, interpersonal relationships, and overall well-being. Integrating social media icons into medication packaging creates a direct link between what we consume—be it medication or digital content—

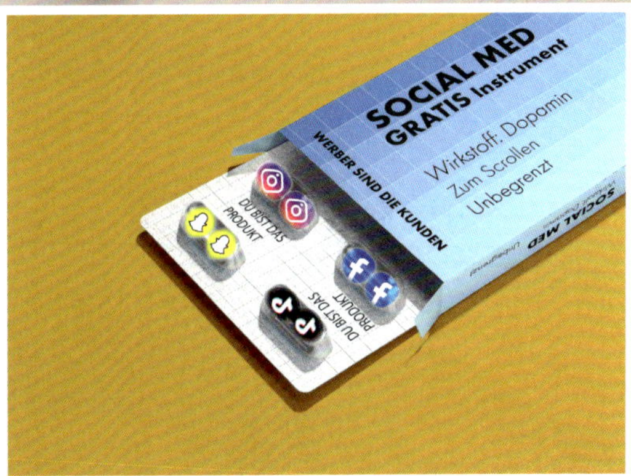

and the potential impact on our health. The images and the leaflet are intended to encourage users to think about their internet use and become aware of the potential negative effects.

Model: Sofia Marie Wallner

https://u.aec.at/46E21563

Tatsanan Tang (*2006) currently attends HTBLuVA Salzburg, specializing in graphics. She sees the world as an endless playground of possibilities and remains committed to making a lasting impact through her art and inspiration.

Was heißt es alleine zu sein?
(Musikvideo)

Ida Onzek, Rosa Peschina, Sina Tödling, Lara Tomasic

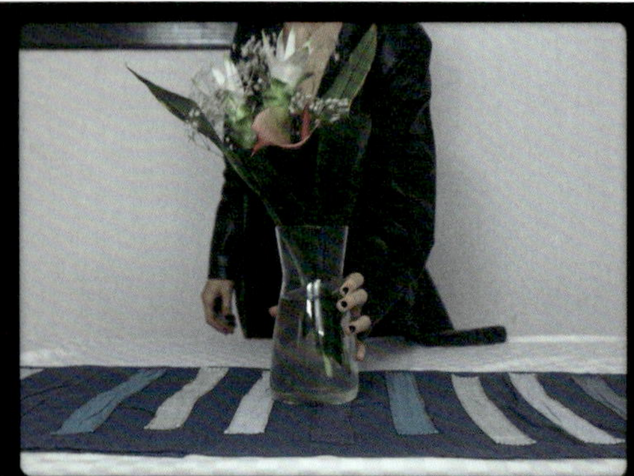

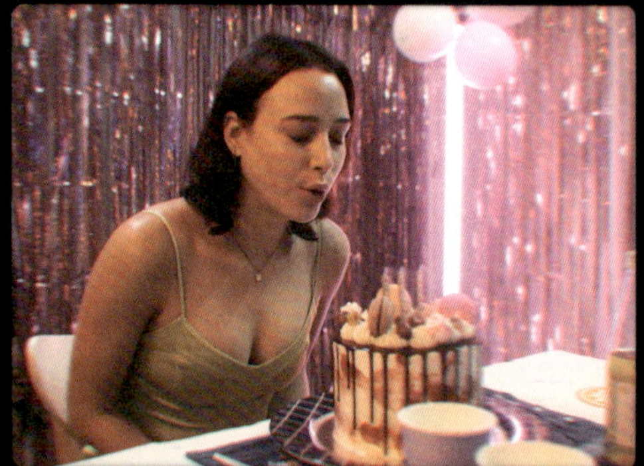

The music video *What does it mean to be alone?* to the song of the same name by the Graz singer Roxana deals with the complex emotion of loneliness. For many people, it not only includes being physically alone, but also the feeling of being lost in a crowd. The music video is intended to visualize this feeling and give those watching the opportunity to better empathize with the music.

In order to ensure that viewers feel involved in the action, the team decided on camera work with a lot of movement and used the one-cut technique in the video. This makes the video look like a continuous shot, but has some hidden cuts. In addition, the lighting and the color contrasts of warm and cold emphasize the protagonist's emotions.

Set assistants: Lisa Rauch and Georg Teibinger
Protagonist: Teresa Freißmuth

https://u.aec.at/D6D27F1D

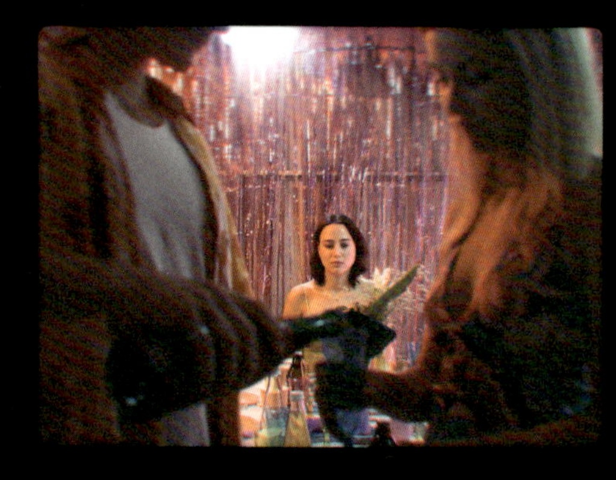

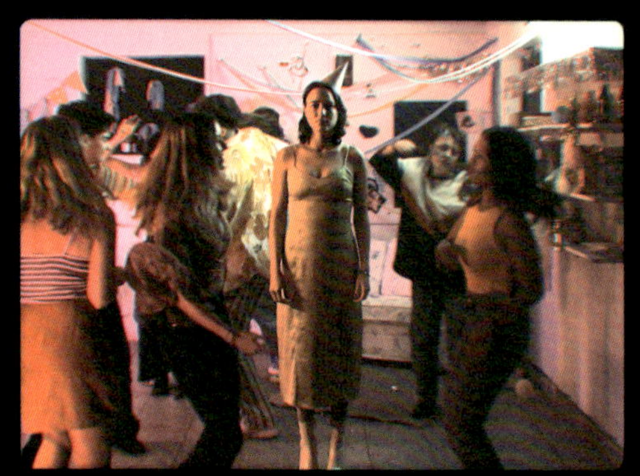

The core team consists of **Lara Tomasic** (*2005) as director and editor, **Rosa Peschina** (*2005) as producer, **Sina Tödling** (*2005) as camera woman, and **Ida Onzek** (*2005) as gaffer. As part of our training at the HTBLVA Graz Ortweinschule, we came together to create the music video for Roxana's song as our diploma project.

Zemlyanka

Justin Casta, Maximilian Größ, Jonathan Pacher, Georgy Snegur,
Christina Zsalacz

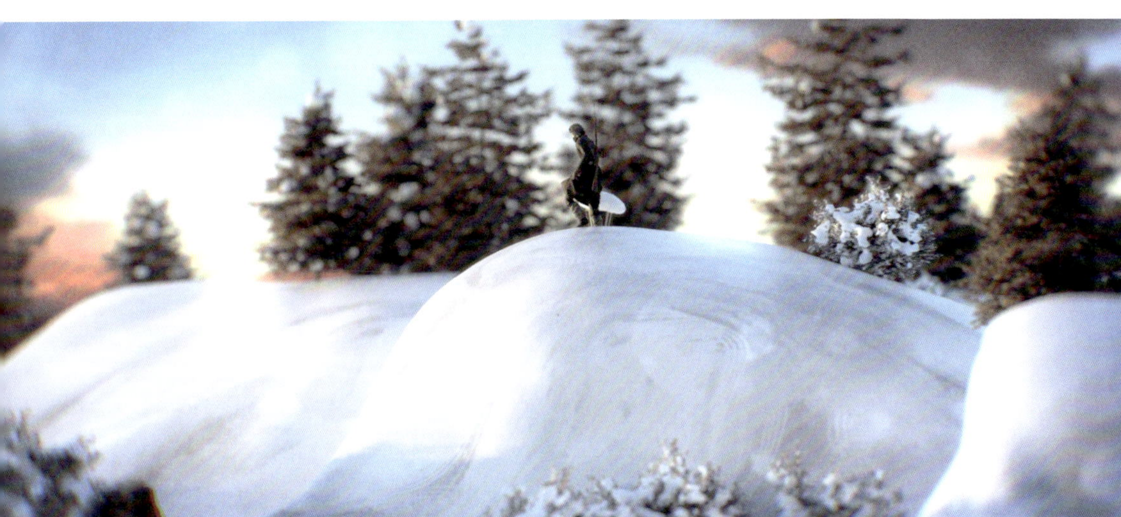

Georgy told us a story that happened to his great-grandfather. It inspired us so much that we slightly modified it and made it our project *Zemlyanka*. The name means something like "bunker" in Russian—which is where our story takes place.

An old man chops wood and goes hunting to prepare for winter. At the front, a soldier is fleeing the war. He stumbles through the forest and falls into the old man's bunker. Exhausted, he begins to eat the supplies until he finds posters calling for deserters to be handed over. Now the soldier fears that the owner of the bunker will hand him over to the authorities. When the old man returns, he spots the soldier. Out of fear, the soldier shoots and a fight breaks out. Both struggle with each other until our story reaches an open ending. *Zemlyanka* addresses war and miscommunication and shows that one should not judge others too quickly without knowing their past.

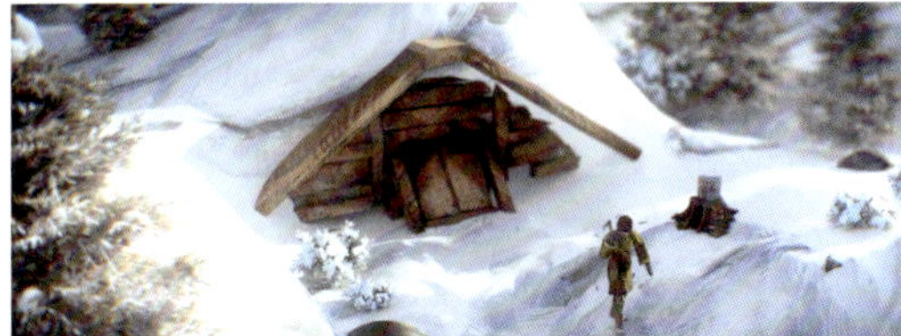

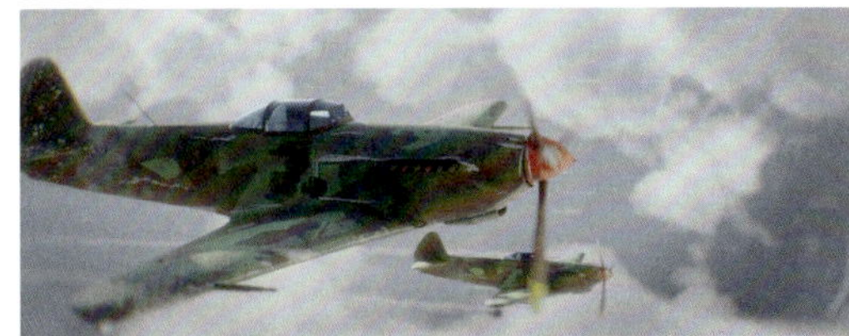

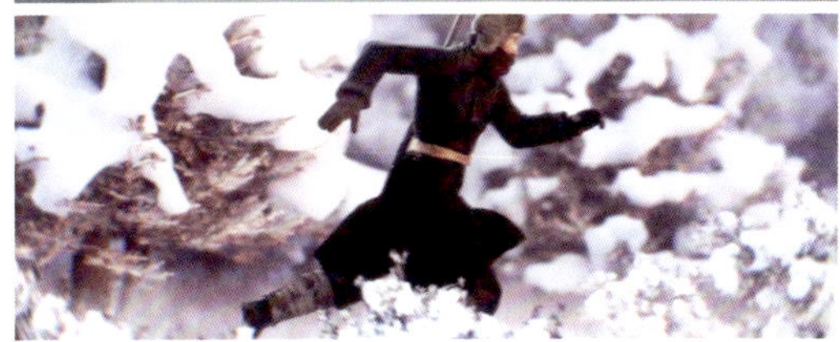

https://u.aec.at/7F7A7EFE

Thanks to our different strengths, we came together as a team: **Georgy Snegur** (*2004) animated entire scenes with **Justin Casta** (*2002) in a very short time, which were modeled and rendered by **Maximilian Größ** (*2003). **Jonathan Pacher** (*2005) created the picturesque atmosphere with his textures, while **Christina Zsalacz** (*2003) kept an overview as project manager and met all deadlines. Together we have created an impressive project.

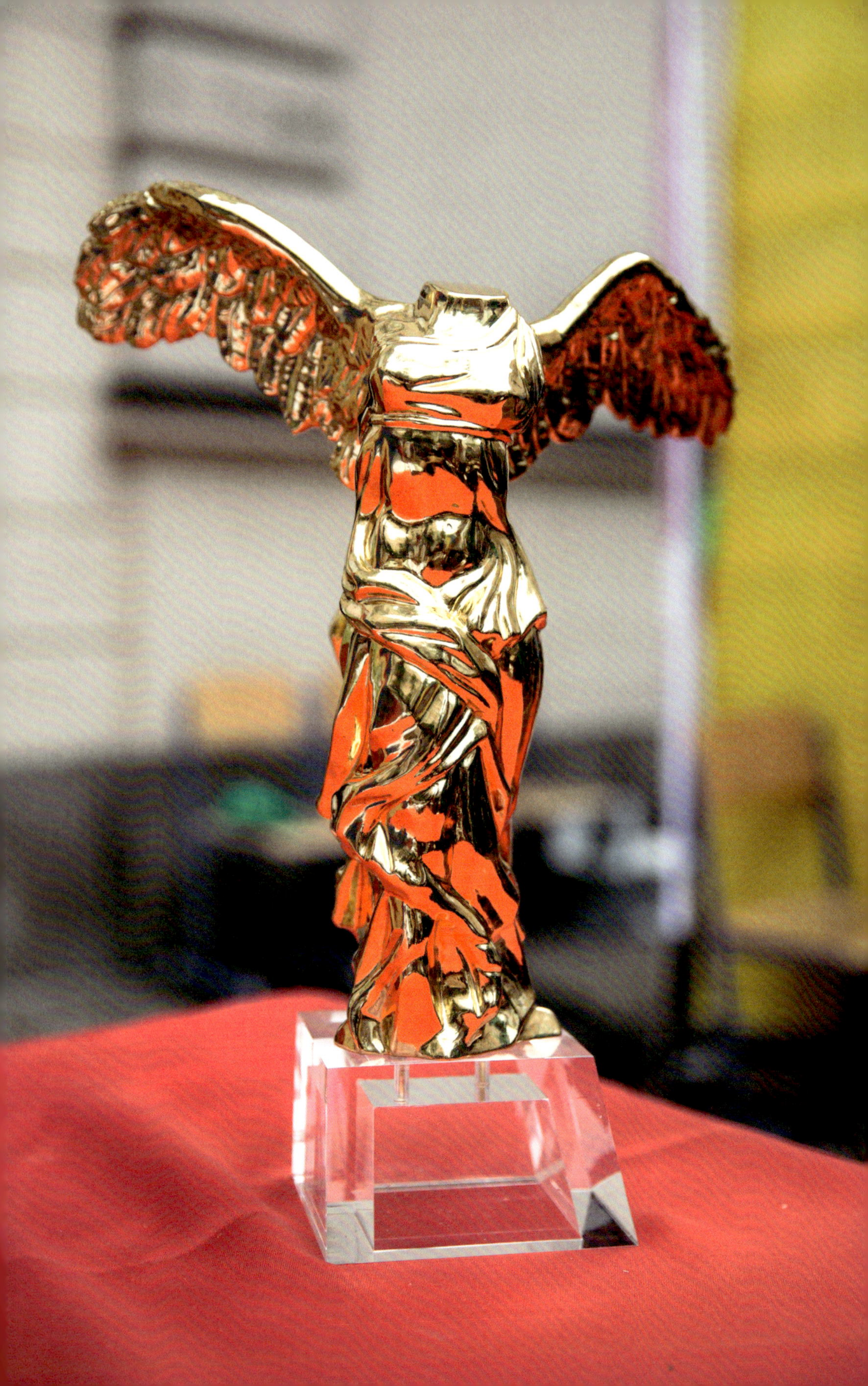

u19–create your world
Young Creatives up to 14 years

WarpCity
Class 2a, BRG Pichelmayergasse, Vienna

WarpCity is a multimedia, interactive sculpture based on an intensive examination of the possible effects of climate change on the urban population. *WarpCity* was created in 2023 as part of the *Cultural Collisions* project at the Vienna University of Technology in cooperation with the Technical Museum and the MUMOK.

WarpCity is a utopian city model that is shown from the front and from above with a projector. In terms of content, the animations and sound recordings refer not only to socio-political aspects of life in the city or to environmental activism, but also to environmentally relevant topics such as changing weather conditions or, more specifically, surface sealing. The visitors trigger changes in the projections through the noises they emit. In doing so, they influence the overall effect of the work, which can fluctuate between confidence and pessimism, thus illustrating the group's ambivalence towards the topic of climate change.

The programming was done with TurboWarp, which is where the title of our work comes from.

WarpCity was realized as part of the *Cultural Collisions* project at TU Wien in cooperation with the Technical Museum and MUMOK.

https://u.aec.at/A1812C51

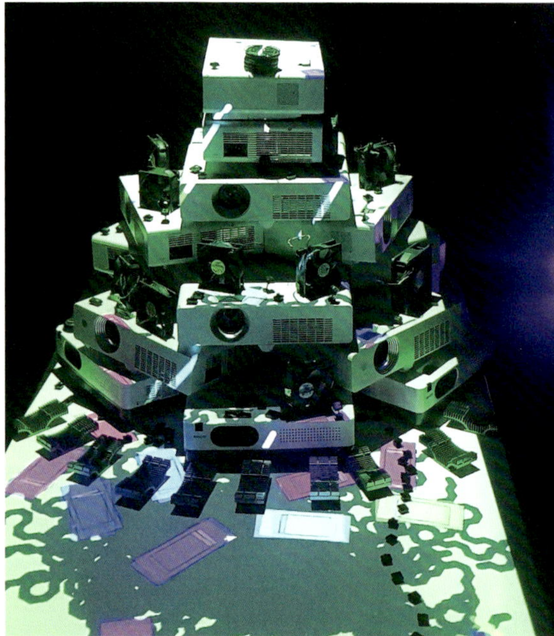

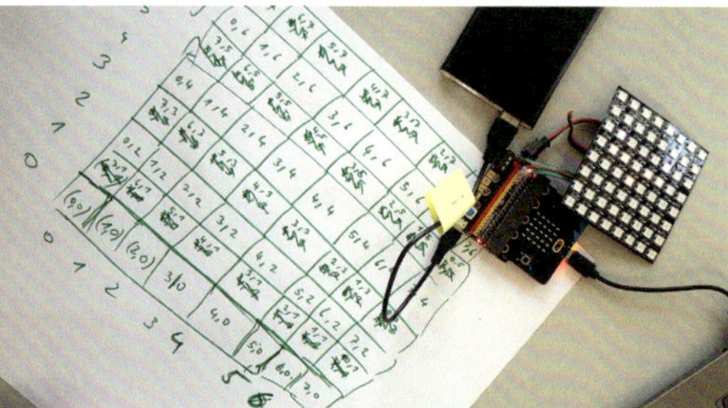

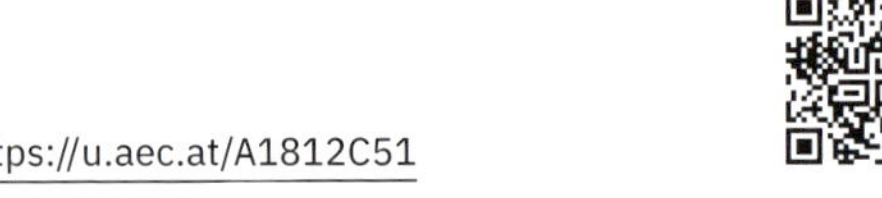

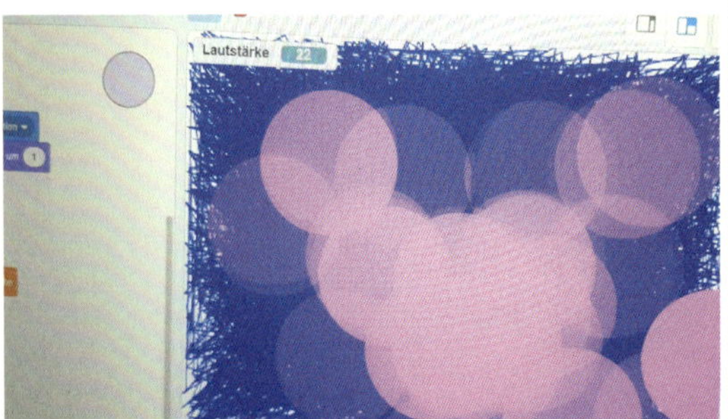

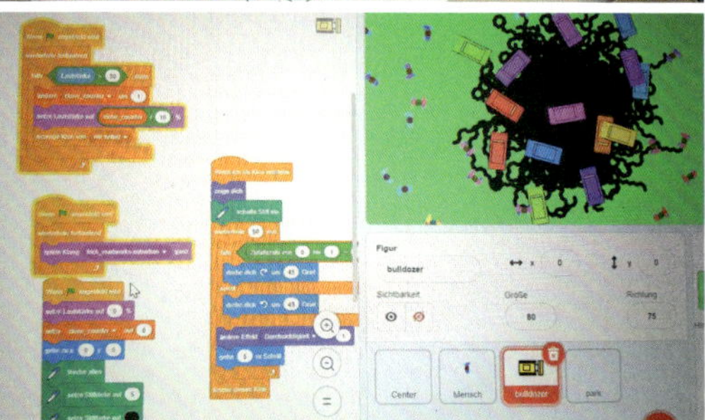

Class 2a, BRG Pichelmayergasse. We are a 2nd class (born 2010 and 2011) at BRG Pichelmayergasse, 1100 Vienna, with a focus on digital design. In this subject we deal with the artistic and creative use of computers and, in addition to image and audio editing, we also learn programming and 3D techniques (scanning, modeling, printing). In the *Cultural Collisions* project we had workshops with students of architecture and spatial planning, with curators and art and technology educators. *WarpCity* was developed with our teachers Ulrike Schedl-Schrottmayer and Klemens Frick in our digital design lessons.

Lights Out
Young Filmmakers 2023

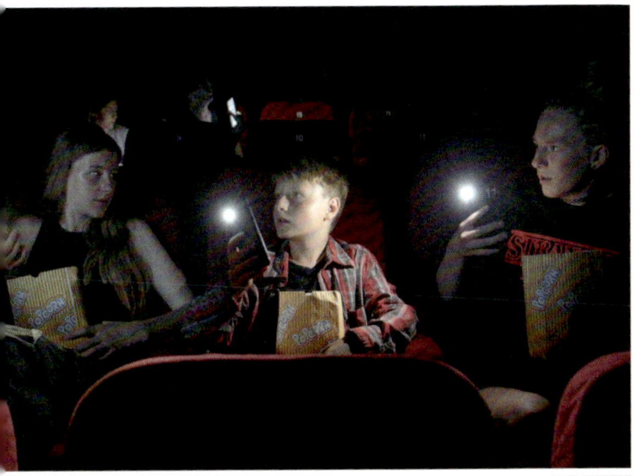

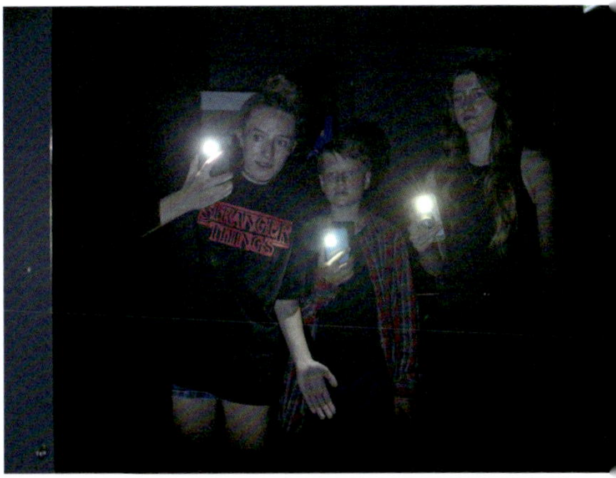

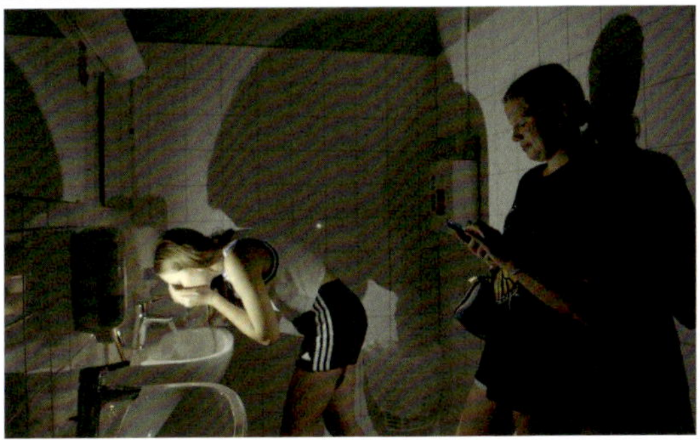

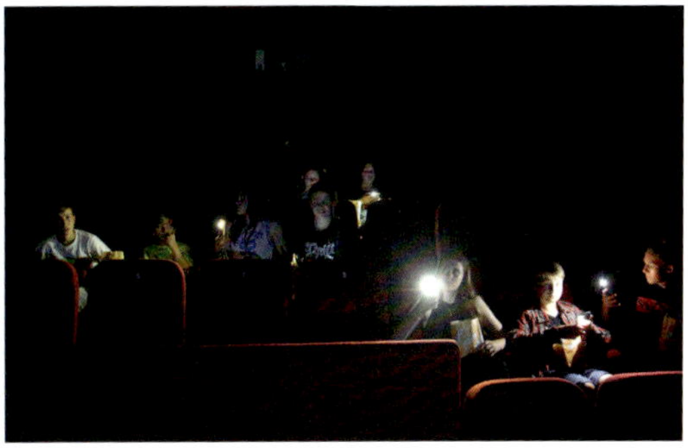

It was supposed to be a normal trip to the cinema for two groups of friends, but the power goes out. Children disappear. In the darkness, the search begins.

How do you make a film? How do you write a screenplay and why do you actually need a clapperboard? These and more questions were answered at the Young Filmmakers Camp at the Medien Kultur Haus Wels in July 2023. Under the direction of Emely Traunmüller and Jonas Wiesinger, the eleven participants between the ages of ten and 16 created this scary film within five days.

On the first day, the script was developed together and the technology was prepared for the following days. So that the implementation could take place in just four days, participants took turns standing in front of and behind the camera. In this way, they not only learned about the process of film production, but were also able to try out all areas themselves.

The film *Lights Out* celebrated its premiere at Wels arthouse cinema in October 2023.

Workshop leader: Emely Traunmüller, Jonas Wiesinger

https://u.aec.at/789E9A3E

The **Young Filmmakers 2023** are a group of young people between the ages of ten and 16 who have one thing in common: enthusiasm for film. They spent a week together in July 2023 producing the film *Lights Out.* From the script to direction and camera to acting, the young filmmakers were able to try out all areas of classic film production. The intensive work together and the games during the breaks created a very nice group dynamic.

Nachhaltigkeitsziele und Stopmotion

12 students from class 3b, Mittelschule Frohnleiten

Everyone can act, make a mark, and change the world is the starting point for our *Sustainability Goals and Stop-Motion* project.

The 17 Sustainable Development Goals not only offer young people an inspiring vision for the future, but also concrete instructions for action for creating a world that is worth living in for all people. The goals encourage you to think about possibilities for change or what needs to be changed.

The students were asked to become creative based on the sustainability goals, develop innovative solutions, identify problems, and push the boundaries of what is possible. They developed a story, a storyboard, and designed the scenes in various media. Every single movement was photographed with their own smartphones, the images were transferred and edited on the laptop in the video editing program Shotcut. A jointly created sound library was used for sound editing. The films were worked on for several months at school and at home, and in the fall of 2023 the fine work was carried out, the film was set to music and completed.

Twelve students decided to edit their films together as a creative project. Their conclusion: "Each of us had our own experiences: some found the work quite easy, inspired by an immediate idea for the film. Others may have had difficulty inserting audio or images into the editing program, but the work was still exciting and educational. *Learning by doing* was the key to dealing with the challenges and growing. Despite the different experiences, we all had something in common: it was a lot of fun! Whether we laughed at our successes or at the little mishaps that happened to us, the fun and joy was always present."

With support from: Ulli Gollesch

https://u.aec.at/0450A563

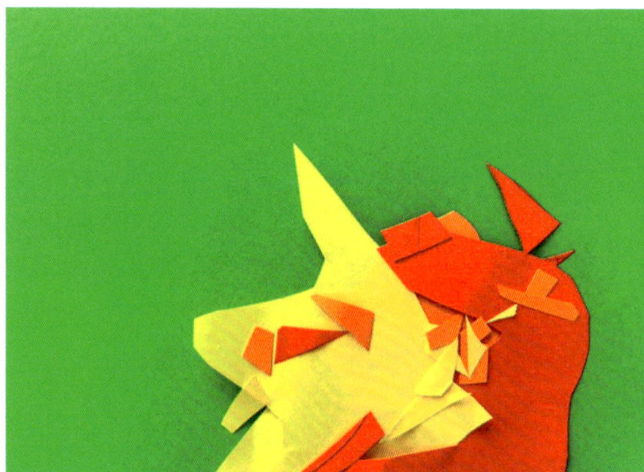

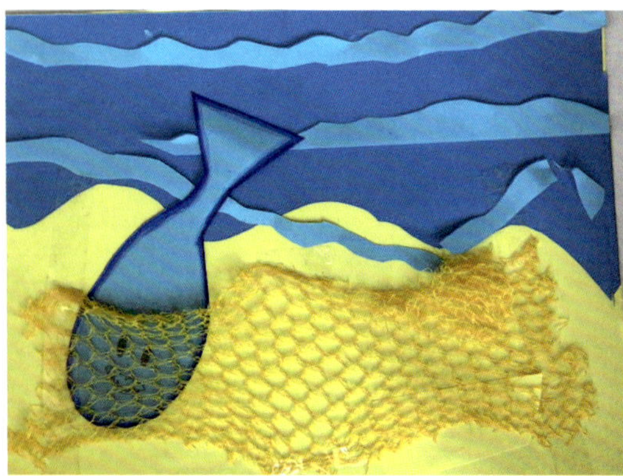

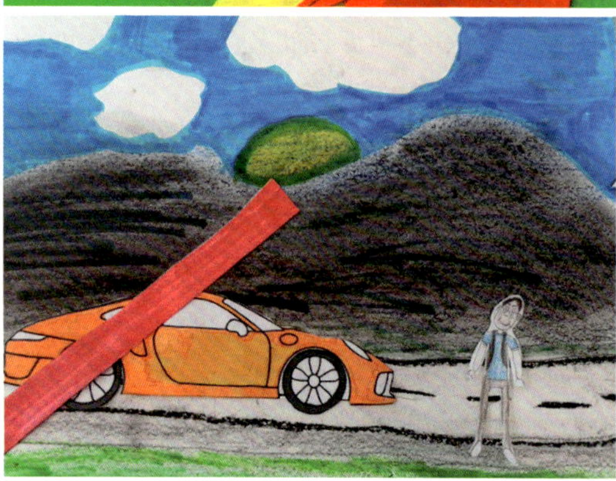

Students from class 3b, Mittelschule Frohnleiten. The twelve students (Valentin Bodlos, Florian Fassl, Elisabeth Hojnik, Lara Leindl, Lukas Lindner, Lukas Maurer, Lisa Rappold, Alexander Rath, Leonie Stadlhofer, Jonas Unger, Lea Wagner, and Katharina Wallner from class 3b (years 2011/2010) Frohnleiten Middle School are open to artistic ideas and their implementation.

Meine grüne Stadt der Zukunft

Jonas Stöttinger

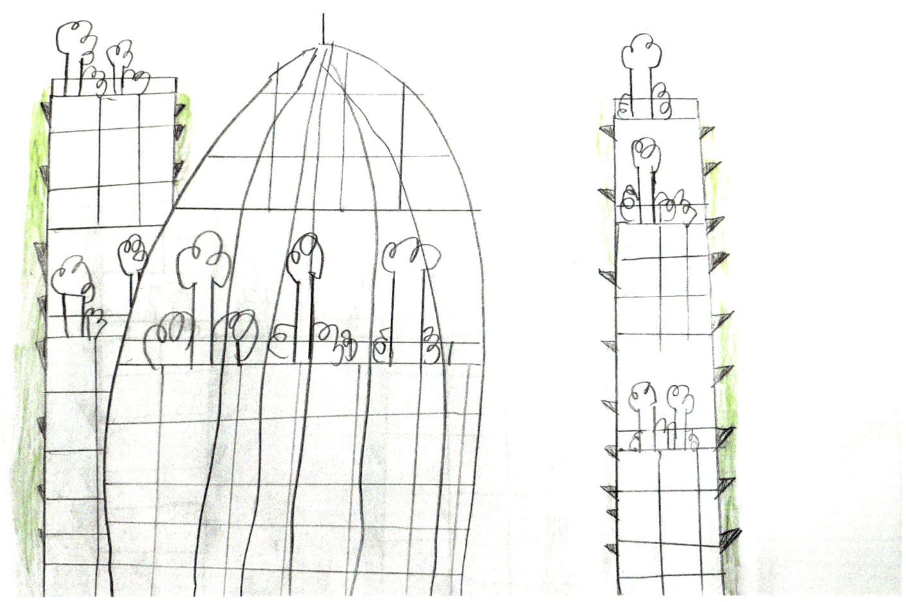

The project *My green city of the future* deals with the increasing overheating of our cities, where life is becoming more and more difficult for people and animals. Soil sealing takes place every day—without any sustainable structural measures being implemented and without property developers being required to implement them. During the first lockdown of 2020, I researched YouTube intensively about how cities can be made cooler and developed ideas for using wind turbines, green facades, and much more. I recorded my ideas in the form of sketches and drawings. Every Thursday evening I discussed this with my Uncle Jean in London via Skype. He is an architect and included my designs in his architecture program. He asked me a lot of detailed questions and repeatedly gave me brain teasers for the coming week. In the end we had completed a structure and a suspension railway with a few stations.

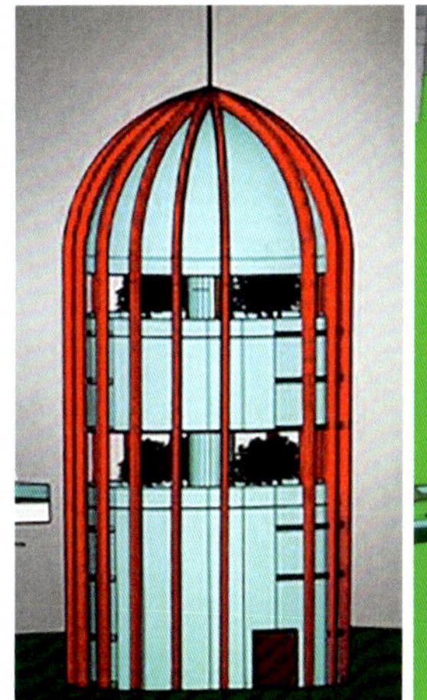
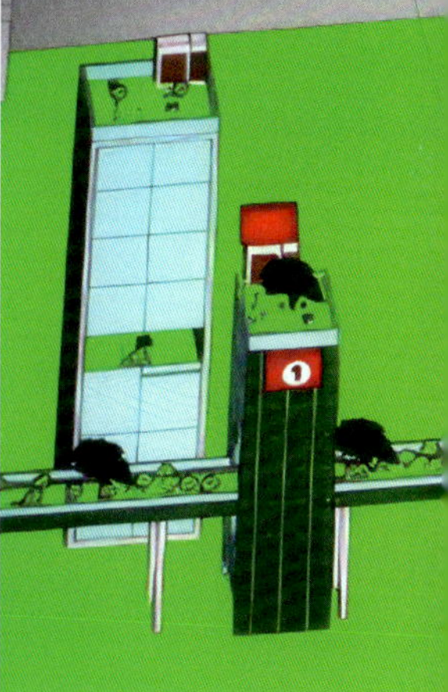

With support from: Jean Mora Silva

https://u.aec.at/EAB21CB9

Jonas Stöttinger (*2010). The topic of nature conservation has been on my mind for a long time and I implement my ideas in different ways. I used to add greenery to my Lego kits, but now I like to draw.

betterTogether

Antonia Hofstadler, Moritz Fink, Marc Umile
GRG15—Auf der Schmelz

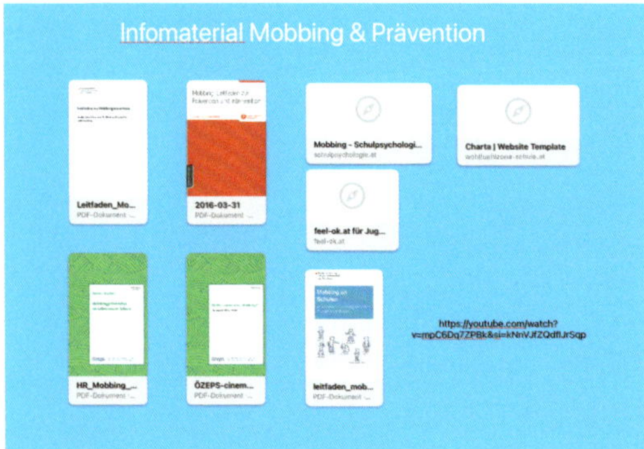

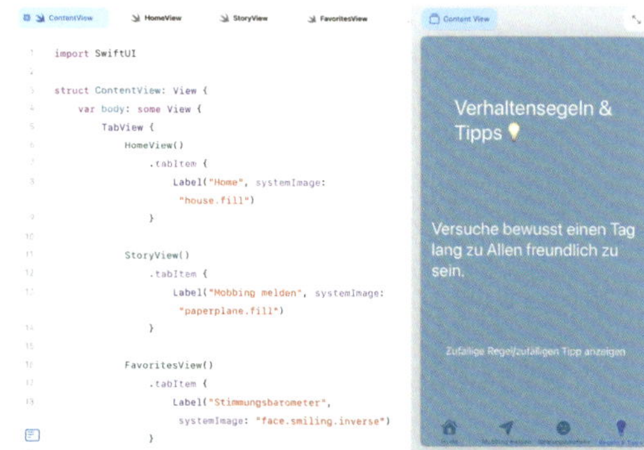

An app to prevent bullying.
From students for students.

For better cooperation in everyday school life.
Nowadays, bullying not only happens in the real
world, but often also takes place in the digital
space. This makes it all the more important to offer
preventative support and know-how for students
that is easily accessible.

With the app *betterTogether* we want to develop a
mood barometer for a class and offer assistance.
Students should be able to report bullying incidents
anonymously and receive information and support.
The app is currently work in progress, but we can
already show where the journey is heading (namely
to a better shared world) here! We had been talking
about the topic of "bullying in the digital space" in
our Swift Coding Club, and so we came up with
the idea of designing an anti-bullying app that the
whole school could use. We started programming
betterTogether and are currently testing a prototype
and getting feedback from school colleagues.

With support from: Oliver Predl, Moritz Steiner

https://u.aec.at/57606BF6

Antonia Hofstadler (*2011), **Moritz Fink** (*2011), and **Marc Umile** (*2011) are students at GRG15—Auf der Schmelz
and the developers in the Swift Coding Club. They are supported by their critical friends Oliver Predl and Moritz
Steiner. The Swift Coding Club, led by Andreas Huber-Marx, has been around for three years and focuses on coding
as well as media analysis, DGBL, digital literacy, etc. The aim of the club is computational empowerment as well as
a creative and creative approach to technology that actively promotes the digital skills of students as designers.
Digital technologies are actively shaped, but also critically scrutinized.

u19—create your world
u12 Prize

**Young Creatives
(up to 14 years)**

Book To Go—das sprechende Buch

Sarah Hölzl

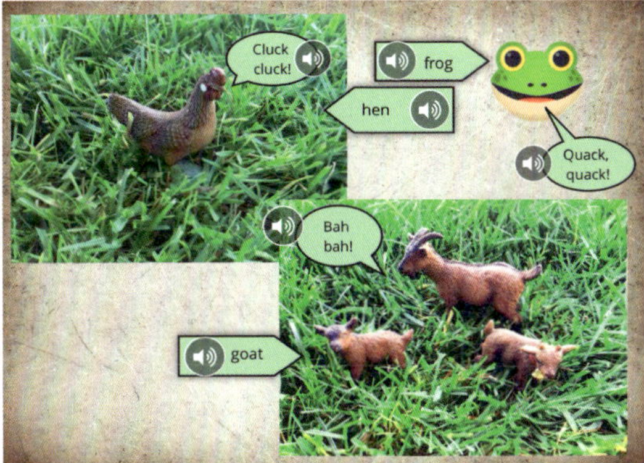

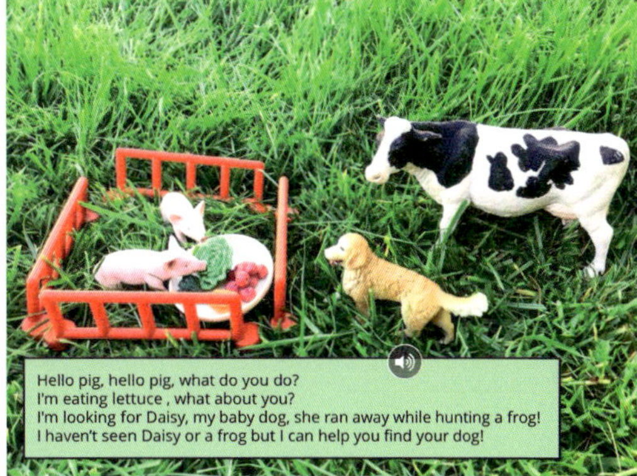

As a child, I started learning English very early through reading. But unfortunately not all children have parents who can read to them (especially in English!).

This gave me the idea of writing a book myself, the *Book To Go—The talking book*. With the Book Creator you can create interactive e-books that are easy to use. This means that all children have the chance to learn English for free and sustainably.

This interactive e-book is intended for entertainment and playful learning of English. You just need a smartphone or a tablet to read it. No previous knowledge of English is necessary; I read out the texts and make the animal sounds. You can also choose the option of having the text read out to you by an English native speaker.

Would you like to find out who Daisy is and why she disappeared?
Do you want to know if she can be found again?
Do you want to have fun and learn English?
Then scan the QR code and listen to Daisy's exciting story!

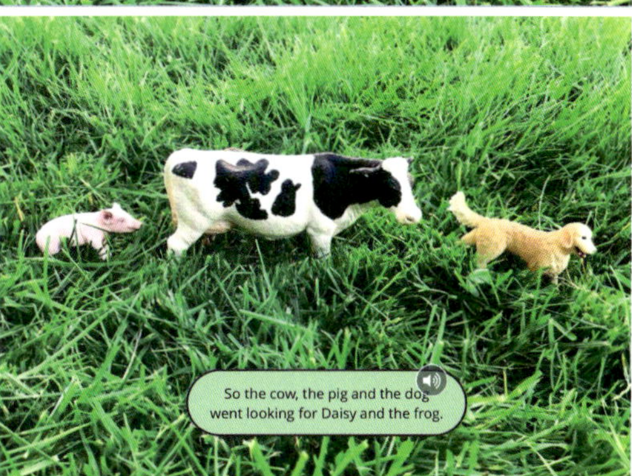

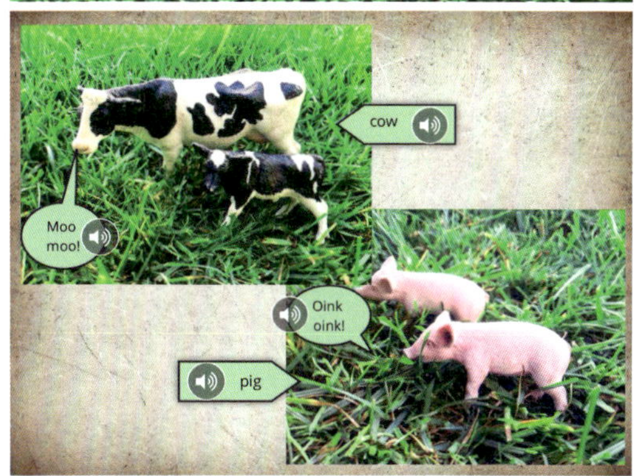

https://u.aec.at/018E46C7

Sarah Hölzl (*2011) born in Freistadt, lives in Kaltenberg, Austria. She is currently in the 2nd grade at Unterweißenbach Middle School. Her hobbies include developing technical projects, playing the clarinet, dancing, reading, painting, gymnastics, and skiing. She has been learning English with stories from books and videos since she was two years old, which is why some of her projects are in English.

Future Cookies

Seher Ödemis, Lorenz Schennach, Gülderen Tanriseven, Manojlo Tanzer

Our coach Mr. Bellony was looking for motivated fourth and first graders from Telfs Weissenbach Middle School for an innovative project. The spirit of research and experience came together and an exciting journey began.

With a lot of team spirit, we planned to design cookie cutters using the 3D printer. Our drawing program Tinkercad did not produce the desired results. So we used the more sophisticated Fusion 360 program. Round, boring cookie cutters were made more creative with the Sketchbook app. Erlenmeyer flasks and magnifying glasses became our favorites.

Personalized, environmentally friendly, and glue-free packaging was still missing. A plotter cut out the prototypes. A tea box and some videos served as inspiration. We drew the packaging using the CanvasWorkspace program. The perfect size of the box kept us busy for a while.

A highlight was baking cookies! Yummy, tasty!

We can confidently say that our *Future Cookies* project was a complete success.

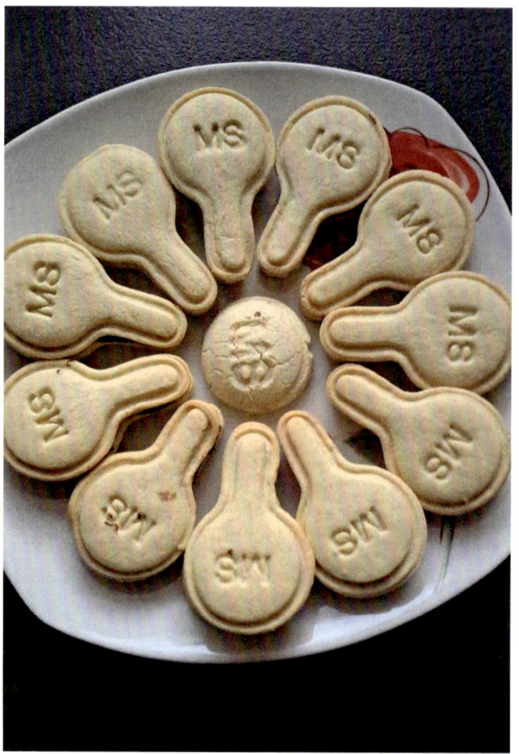

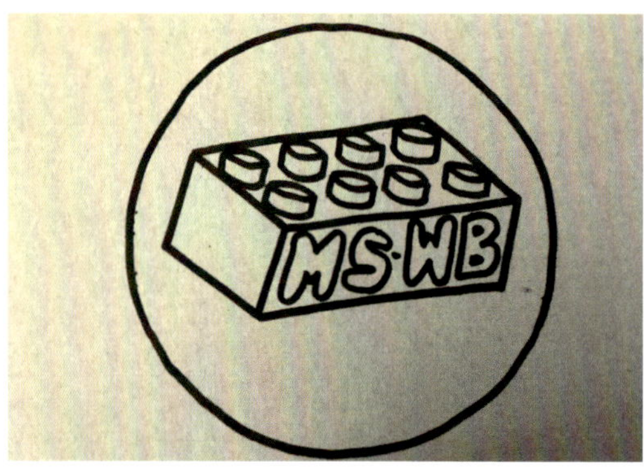

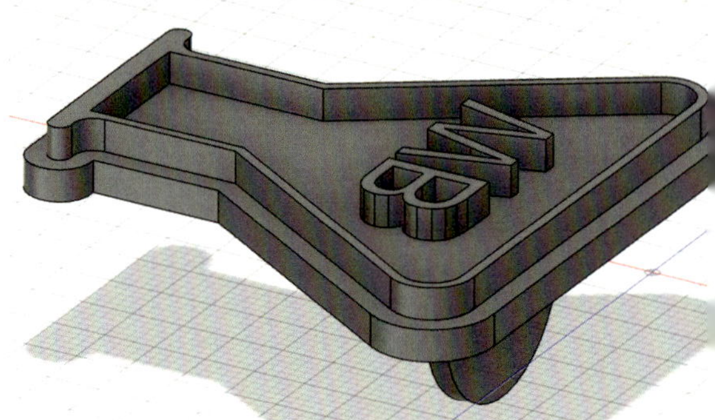

With support from: Lina Brinkmann, Vanessa Heiss, Daniel Keller
FLL (First LEGO League) Champion Tirol 2023

https://u.aec.at/FD25948A

Seher Ödemis (*2013), **Gülderen Tanriseven** (*2013), **Lorenz Schennach** (*2012), and **Manjolo Tanzer** (*2012) are students at Telfs Weissenbach Middle School and were supported in the *Future Cookie* project by their mentors **Lina Brinkmann** (*2009), **Daniel Keller** (*2009), and **Vanessa Heiss** (*2010). They all share an interest in new technologies and the desire to incorporate future processes into everyday situations. The result: *Future Cookies.*

u19–create your world
u12 Honorary Mention

Young Creatives
(up to 14 years)

Na2r_3lumen

Nea Geršak

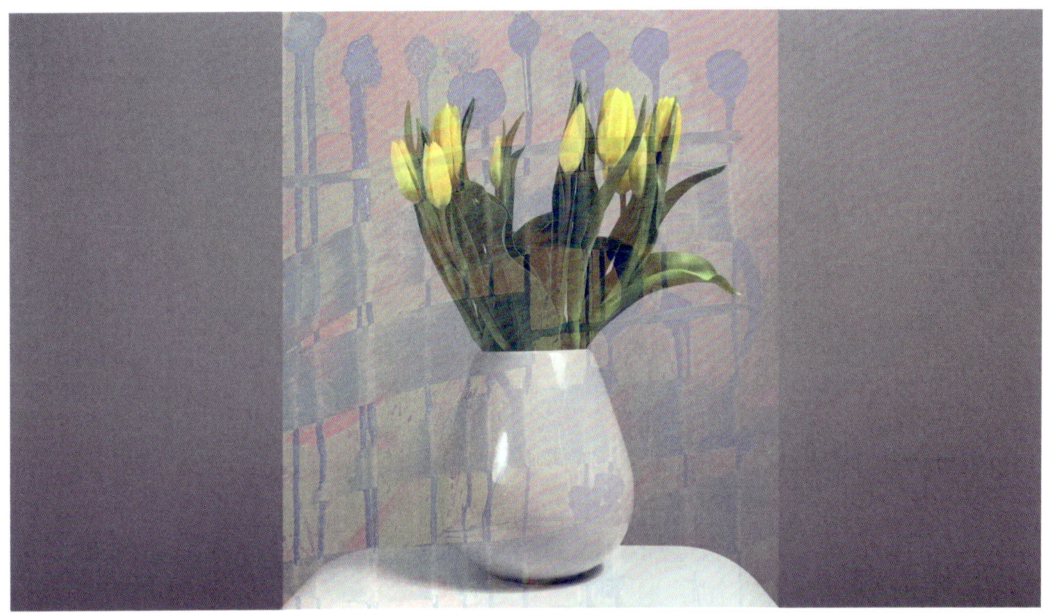

Real flowers are increasingly disappearing from nature. There are many reasons for this, such as too much concrete, garbage, pollution, and bad weather. We can't save all the flowers everywhere. But most people love flowers and therefore find a new place for them: in songs, books, stories, films, herbariums, names, paper flowers, on photos, wallpaper, fabrics, furniture, and jewelry in the shape of flowers, on tattoos, clothing, toys and much more. And because I like to paint best—even in pictures! In my video you hear why real flowers disappear and you see how they are slowly replaced in a picture by *3lumen (Flow3rs/*Flowers) that I painted. This new world is called *Na2r (Na2re/*Nature). And in this *Na2re* there will always be *Flow3rs.*

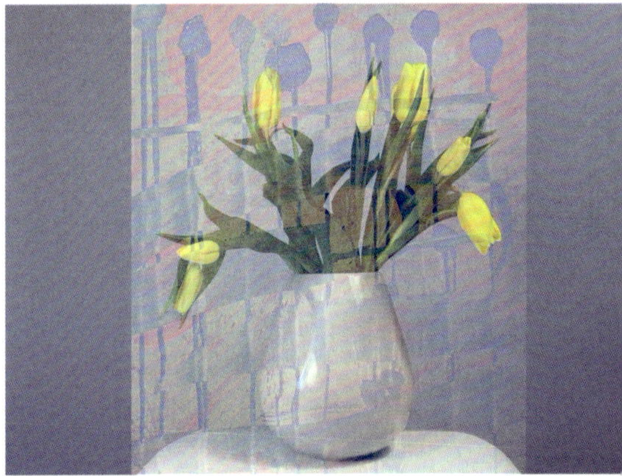

https://u.aec.at/4076E575

Nea Geršak (*2016) is seven years old and was born in Berlin. She now lives with her family in Carinthia and attends elementary primary school in Klagenfurt. Nea has many interests, such as books, playing the piano, taekwondo, and skateboarding, but she prefers to spend her free time painting pictures. She also enjoys going to museums and exhibitions and enjoys taking part in art workshops for children. In general, she loves everything that has anything to do with art.

Peter, Paula und Panini
Klimabuch und Theaterstück

Lina Roth

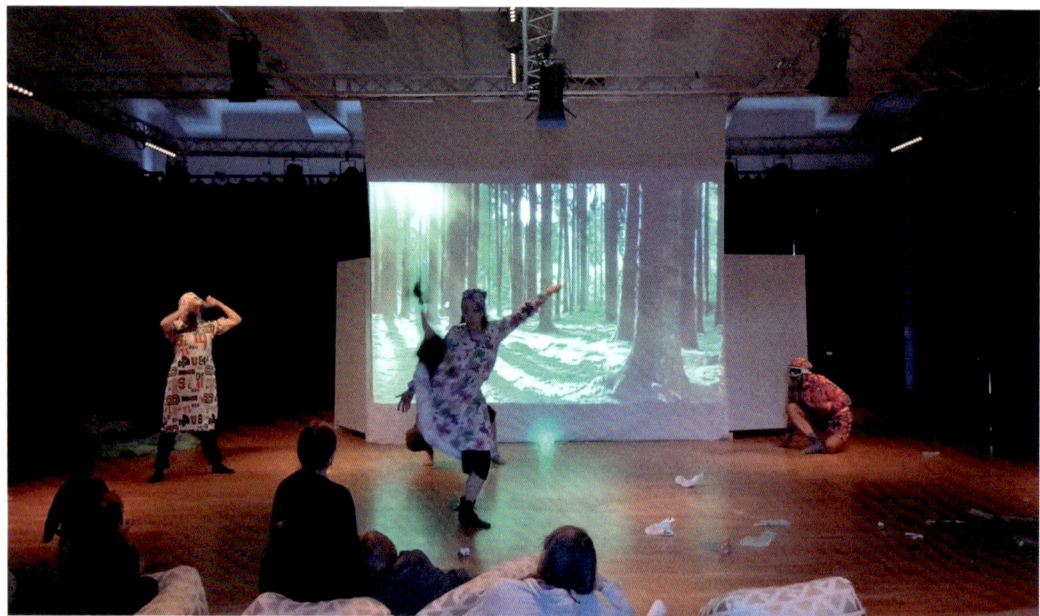

After the successful *Klimatheater* (Climate Theater) project at the Europaschule Linz, Lina couldn't let her wealth of ideas rest. Together with friends, she developed the fairy tale *Peter, Paula and Panini, climate book and play*, supported by AI text generators. This was then handed over to the director Damian Cortes Alberti, who created a dance theater piece from it. The premiere took place as part of the city of Linz's Children's Culture Week in October 2023. The performance movingly illustrated the effects of climate change, represented by the characters Peter, Paula, and Panini. The piece was a success and was subsequently compiled into a book that also integrated the children's drawings from the project, using image generators to create a harmonious overall picture.

https://u.aec.at/8DBD0608

With the support of Lina's friends Liivo and Ravel Safron, with the help of her parents, supported by the allocation of stage space from the Sonnenstein Loft (stage of the RedSapata cultural initiative), participation of professional dancers for the dance theater piece *Peter, Paula and Panini* (Damian Cortes Alberti, Samer Alkurdi, Tomomi Watanabe, Marcela Lopez)

Lina Roth (*2015) is a creative, versatile personality who dances, sings, and acts. She loves staging dance and theater plays with friends and often goes horseback riding with her father. Between playing and arguing with her two little siblings, she always finds time for new hobbies and ideas.

u19–create your world
u10 Award of Distinction

Young Creatives
(up to 14 years)

Aus Waffen werden Werkzeuge

David Gaulhofer

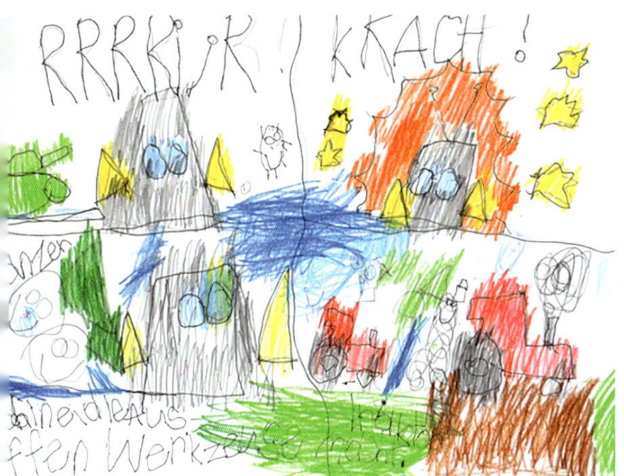

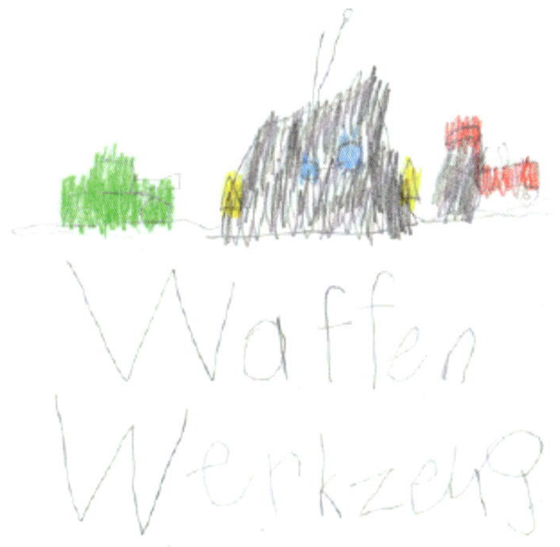

In art class, the first grade students had the task of developing drawing-based, sustainable machines that support people. First, sketches were made and the machine was described in writing. Then the description was converted into symbols and graphic explanations.

David Gaulhofer wants to make the negative side of humanity disappear and therefore changes the world for the better in his project *From weapons to tools*. He wants ALL weapons to be converted into tools. Tools mean life, work, food and prosperity, and this is how the artist from Gratwein-Straßengel puts his work in the right light: the tank, a symbol of war and destruction, is guided into a "change machine" where it is quickly converted into a tractor, the symbol of peace, honest work, and general prosperity. The color green, the symbol of envy, becomes red, the color of love. David Gaulhofer lays out his work in four panels in a comic-like manner with passionate lines, intensive coloring and striking onomatopoeia. He used fineliners and colored pencils in the work.

https://u.aec.at/08F90C27

David Gaulhofer was born seven weeks early and has since been known as "the little one", in contrast to his twin sister Lena. Despite slow developmental steps, supported by numerous therapies, he took his first steps alone at the age of three and a half. With his sunny disposition, he quickly makes friends, even though he is accompanied by a school assistant to receive support in certain situations and with learning. David loves soccer, skiing, swimming, and books, and in the summer he likes to snorkel in the sea. Since 2023 he has been attending Frohnleiten Middle School, which he enjoys and where he has made many friends. David is a ray of sunshine whose infectious good mood spreads joy and happiness in the Frohnleiten Middle School community.

Citiz
Scie

en
nce

Ars Electronica Award for Digital Humanity

by the Austrian Federal Ministry for European and International Affairs

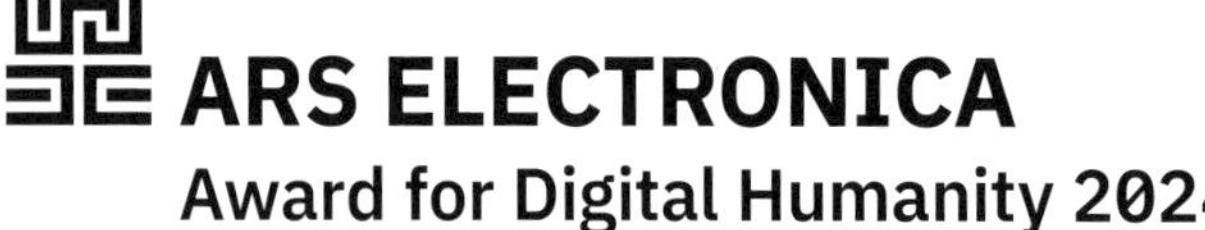

In addition to the four Golden Nicas of Prix Ars Electronica 2024, the Ars Electronica Award for Digital Humanity, initiated by the Austrian Federal Ministry for European and International Affairs, will be awarded for the fourth time as part of Prix Ars Electronica. Every submission to the Prix Ars Electronica and the STARTS Prize competition could also be entered for consideration to the Ars Electronica Award for Digital Humanity.

The Ars Electronica Award for Digital Humanity focuses on projects that address social, cultural, and humanitarian issues in our digital society. It highlights outstanding examples of collaborative practices between individuals of different disciplines and backgrounds.

Art and culture shape our common reality. They pose the question of what constitutes a human being in the digital world. Artists as cultural ambassadors are best equipped to identify the potential and the pitfalls of our current digital transformation.

Cultural diplomacy is a powerful instrument to promote mutual understanding among nations and to bolster societal change on a global scale. As such, it is uniquely positioned to advocate for a new era of digital humanism: Digital humanism that builds a just and democratic society with human beings at the center of technological progress. Digital humanism ensures that our needs and universal human rights are being met and works to preserve our human dignity. It shapes technologies in accordance with humanistic and social values and envisions alternative pathways for human/machine interaction that are centered around diversity and inclusion in the creation, implementation, and adaptation of digital tools.

The Ars Electronica Award for Digital Humanity emphasizes in equal terms the humaneness and humanism that must dictate the development of new technologies. The award honors projects and artworks that inspire fundamental rethinking in our contemporary approach to technology: It's time for us to relinquish our roles as mere data-generating machines and to actively participate in the shaping of our digital future.

Can digital applications be more oriented toward human needs and based on cultural and social values that respect the autonomy of users over their data? Can software solutions build on the values of cultural diversity instead of infrastructural uniformity? Can digital tools be increasingly of benefit to cross-culture collaboration, international cultural relations, and mutual understanding?

The prize fits programmatically into a new and innovative concept of international cultural relations and cultural diplomacy, which does not simply showcase national artistic or cultural production, but favors cultural exchange, people-to-people contacts, and inter-cultural dialogue and cooperation. As a signature award of the Austrian Ministry of Foreign Affairs, it emphasizes the openness and outward-looking spirit of the Austrian cultural, scientific, and technological ecosystem geared towards collaboration and awareness of our common global challenges.

In 2024, the Ars Electronica Award for Digital Humanity was issued with a focus on the IMAGINE Arts & Ideas initiative. Both the prize and this newly established initiative by the Austrian Ministry of Foreign Affairs center the development of humanistic, eco-social approaches and strategies on the overarching topics of nature, people, democracy, and economic development in the age of artificial intelligence. This year's program focus DIGNITY is also intended to build bridges between liberal democracies and other countries for dealing with the major issues of the future.

"In an AI-driven world of huge risks but also of enormous potential, the Award for Digital Humanity has gained particular relevance. I was impressed with the high quality of the applications and would like to thank all participants for their amazing contributions. Almost all of them contain a clear message: In many respects, humanity is at a crossroads. And we have to jointly muster all the wisdom and courage at our disposal to design the right approaches and solutions for a prosperous, more-than-human future. In such a crowded field of projects, the winner has to be very special—and indeed it is. And so is the project that receives a Honorary Mention. My congratulations go to both!"

Ambassador Christoph Thun-Hohenstein
Head of the Section for Cultural Foreign Relations
BMEIA—Federal Ministry for European and International Affairs of the Republic of Austria

Ars Electronica Award for Digital Humanity Statement of the Jury

Ambassador Christoph Thun-Hohenstein, Director General for International Cultural Relations at BMEIA, Thomas Kloiber, Regina Rusz, Veronika Liebl, Gerfried Stocker

This is the fourth year that Ars Electronica and the Austrian Federal Ministry for European and International Affairs jointly present the Ars Electronica Award for Digital Humanity, which champions the profound intersection of art, technology, and human values. As jury members, we recognize the crucial role of artistic reflection in navigating the complexities of our digital transformation. Art and culture, as vital elements shaping our shared reality, offer unique insights into what it means to be human in a digital world.

The importance of this reflection lies in its ability to challenge societal norms, provoke critical thinking, and inspire innovative explorations. In examining the manifold themes represented in this year's submissions such as gender bias, online exploitation, digital restitution, forensic journalism, and carbon emissions, artistic projects confront the ethical, environmental, and social implications of emerging technologies. These endeavors not only illuminate the potential pitfalls of our digital landscape but also explore ways to use technology to promote inclusivity, diversity, and human dignity.

The jury was searching for artistic reflections encouraging us to move beyond being passive consumers of technology, urging us to actively shape our digital future. By highlighting the experiences of marginalized groups and questioning the biases embedded in data and algorithms, a stunning variety of submitted projects advocated for a digital humanism that places human needs and rights at the forefront of technological progress. A fascinating diversity of artistic forms, expressions, and practices offered new narratives and pathways that prioritize empathy, solidarity, and ethical responsibility.

Through collaborative practices that span disciplines and cultures, many of the submissions demonstrated how art fosters mutual understanding and intercultural dialogue. By reimagining historical narratives and confronting current social issues, artistic projects serve as catalysts for societal change, embodying the spirit of the Ars Electronica Award for Digital Humanity.

In celebrating these artistic endeavors, we affirm the critical role of art in shaping a digital society that reflects our collective values and aspirations.

This year's jury selected an Award and an Honorary Mention. Both projects exemplify the transformative potential of art and technology to create a more equitable and humane digital world, while reflecting on the risks of an unreflective approach to technology.

While this year's Ars Electronica Award for Digital Humanity, *Patchwork Girl,* embodies both strands in an excellent way, the jury wanted to honor in addition the long lasting and continuous efforts of the winning project's theatre company *de Toneelmakerij. De Toneelmakerij* has consistently demonstrated an innovative approach to storytelling, utilizing the intersection of art and technology to address pertinent social issues and foster critical thinking among young audiences.

Ars Electronica Award for Digital Humanity

Patchwork Girl
Paulien Geerlings, Jantine Jongebloed,
Eva Knibbe, Noelía Martin-Montalvo,
Nina Van Tongeren, de Toneelmakerij

Patchwork Girl is an exemplary project that addresses pressing issues like sexting, slut-shaming, and online abuse through a powerful blend of performance and technology. Jantine and Cyrina courageously share their experiences of online victimization, confronting societal norms and the lack of accountability in digital spaces. The performance highlights the enduring impact of such trauma, with Jantine revisiting her past with the support of five teenage girls, emphasizing the importance of solidarity.

Innovatively, the project experiments with AI-generated apologies and creates an avatar, Patchwork Girl, to reclaim agency over their narratives. This technological integration not only adds depth to their storytelling but also explores the ethical complexities of digital tools in online abuse. The symbolic act of Jantine capturing a new nude photo underscores the reclaiming of her body and autonomy, a defiant statement against online exploitation.

Patchwork Girl excels in promoting human-centered, collaborative practices and cross-disciplinary engagement, aligning perfectly with the Ars Electronica Award for Digital Humanity's objectives. It transcends mere reflection on technology's effects, advocates for systemic change in digital spaces, and opens new pathways towards the protection of human dignity. The jury unanimously decided to honor this project to amplify the creator's efforts and raise awareness about the need for continued advocacy against online abuse, aiming to extend its impact beyond the stage to combat expose groups and online exploitation effectively.

Honorary Mention

AI and the Art of Historical Reinterpretation—Filling Gender Bias Gaps
Claudia Larcher

AI and the Art of Historical Reinterpretation—Filling Gender Bias Gaps is a groundbreaking project aimed at eliminating gender-specific biases in historical datasets used by AI. Recognizing the heavy reliance of AI models on historical data, the project critically examines the ethical implications of using AI to predict societal changes and proposes innovative methods to complement, rewrite, and reinterpret historical data. By employing AI-generated "historical images", the project seeks to fill gaps in historical records and provide a more inclusive understanding of the past.

The project highlights the exclusion of LGBTQ+ individuals from official historical narratives, bringing their overlooked contributions to the forefront. Through meticulous examination of archives and historical texts, the project has created a fictional image archive that reinterprets history with a focus on inclusivity and diversity. Until now, the project has generated a dataset of over 140 images, with 80 specifically addressing gender biases in art history.

AI and the Art of Historical Reinterpretation exemplifies the award's vision by addressing social, cultural, and humanitarian issues through innovative use of technology. This project stands as a powerful example of how AI can be harnessed to empower marginalized groups and reshape our understanding of history. The jury was impressed by the project's commitment to diversity, inclusion, and ethical considerations, as it depicts a future that celebrates digital humanism and inclusivity.

Patchwork Girl

De Toneelmakerij—Paulien Geerlings, Jantine Jongebloed, Eva Knibbe, Noelía Martin-Montalvo, Nina Van Tongeren

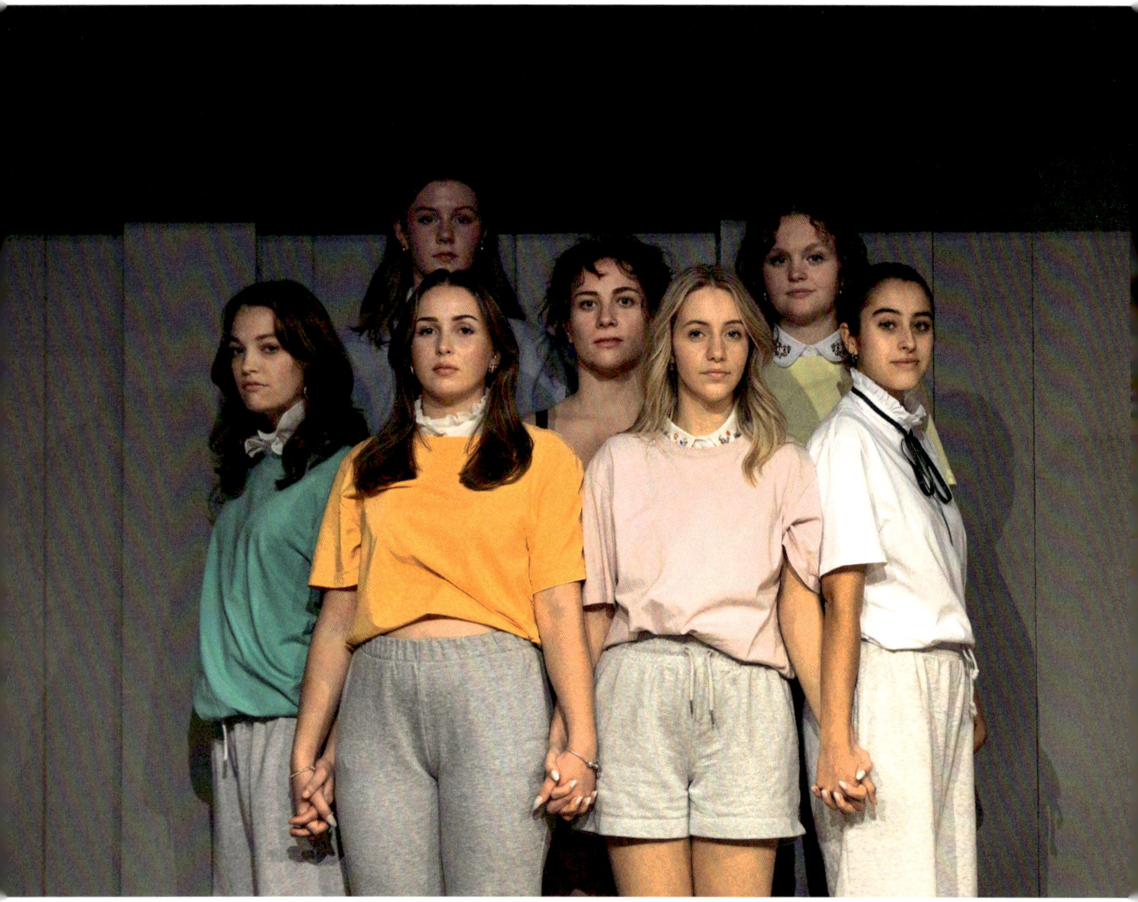

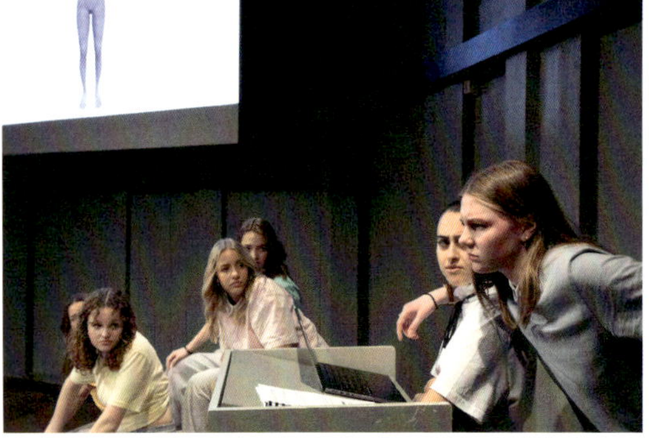

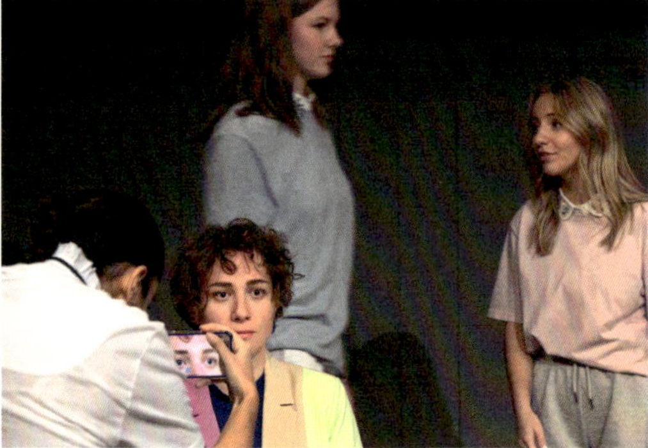

Patchwork Girl is a poignant lecture performance about sexting, exposing, slut-shaming, empowerment, and owning your sexuality.

Jantine was 16 when the trashy Dutch website GeenStijl published her nudes, together with a fake interview about her sex life. When Cyrina was 13, she made a sexy video for a boy. The next day the clip was spread at the schools in her village. Both girls were subject to victimblaming and slut-shaming.

In this performance, Jantine reconstructs the traumatic events from her past, using the internet through which she was previously victimized. On stage, she is accompanied by five teen girls. What has changed in the intervening 20 years? How proud of her body can a girl be? They re-enact the experience of the 16-year-old Jantine, and the perpetrators. And they explore whether AI-generated apologies are more effective than the ones Jantine received. Cyrina shares her story, too, via a voice-over. AI artist Noelía creates an avatar based on Jantine's nudes. This virtual girl who embodies the 'male fantasy', is first used to attract men in "expose groups" on Telegram and on porn sites. At the end of the performance, the avatar is 'dressed' in photos of the skin of the audience. Shielded by skin, this *Patchwork Girl* enters the world of expose groups and porn sites and speaks out. She engages in dialogue with the users, on behalf of victimized women. She gives the response they can't and reclaims their narrative.

We encountered all sorts of obstacles while making *Patchwork Girl*, which confronted us with (the absence of) internet ethics. The performance thematizes these obstacles. A few of them:

We initially wanted to work with young victims of shame sexting, but none of them wanted to share their story live on stage. Jantine did dare to take on that challenge, but only after 20 years. Her story reveals just how traumatic events like this are for the victims. A sharp contrast to the ease with which nude photos are shared without consequences.

We discovered that avatars have better legal protection than women! It turns out that it is illegal to create a nude avatar. So we had to use the latest technology, that is still unregulated, and learn from scratch how to create her.

We planned to share our avatar to the big expose groups on Telegram, which have thousands of members. But recent media attention had made the groups suddenly disappear to an un-trackable corner of the Internet. We set up our own Telegram group to share our avatar. We got followers (!) but they were soon using our group to trade images of their girlfriends.

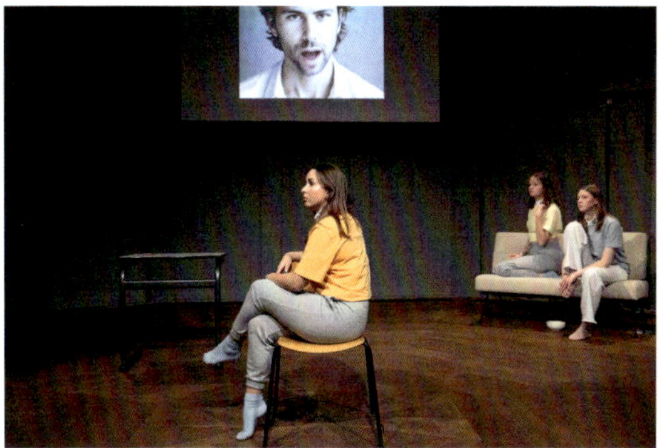

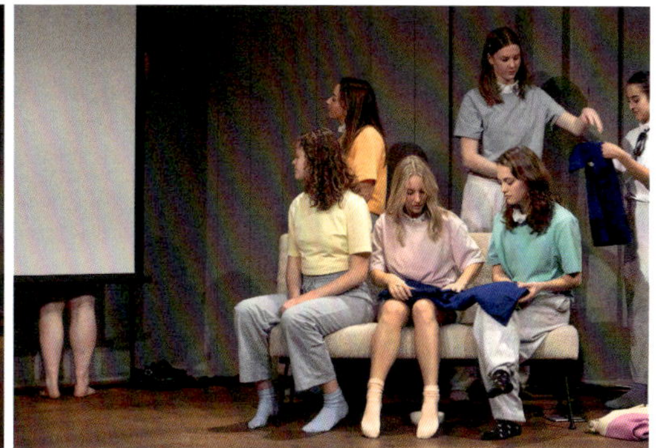

We got a tip-off that private photos were circulating on the porn site xHamster. We attempted to register our avatar with the site. Soon we found ourselves in a bureaucratic maze, trying to sort out who had the rights to the naked avatar. The issue is still unresolved.

We contacted GeenStijl to advertise our performance on their site. This was the least they could do, we thought, since it's no longer possible for Jantine to sue the site for distributing child porn images of her, due to a statute of limitations. GeenStijl proposed to charge us €850 for the advertisement and made inappropriate comments in our email exchange, which made us shy away from collaboration.

In making *Patchwork Girl*, it became clear that shame sexting and exposing are products of an indifferent man's world, that is unlikely to change anytime soon. As women, our only possible answer is sisterhood. The performance ends with a profound act of solidarity: the girls stand around Jantine to shield her from the view of the audience, while she is making a new nude. On the screen above them, the avatar—now covered with photographs of the skin of audience members—talks about all that skin can mean: "She is all of us. She is carried by all of us."

We are not done with *Patchwork Girl.* Now we have made her, we want to continue exploring what effect she can have in the world of expose groups and porn sites. That is something the Ars Electronica Award for Digital Humanity will help us achieve.

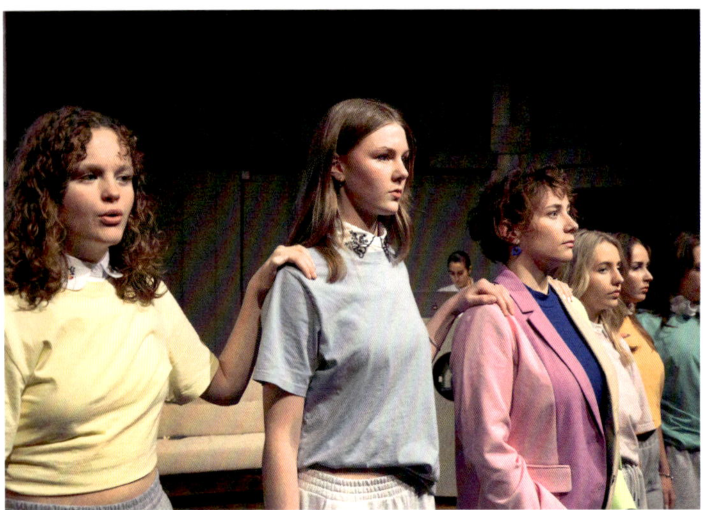

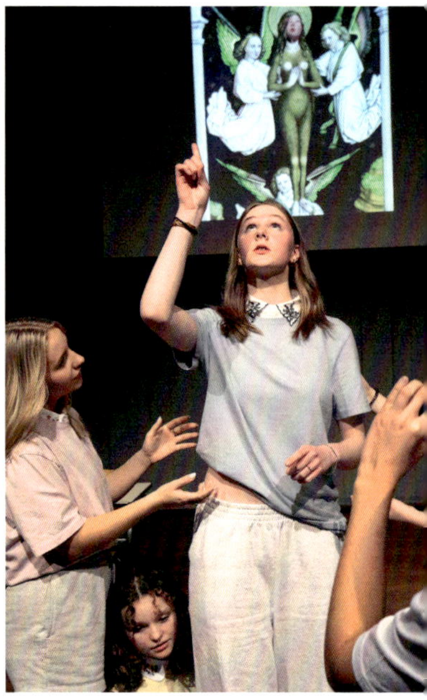

Patchwork Girl is produced by the Theatre Company de Toneelmakerij
Concept: Paulien Geerlings, Eva Knibbe
Idea and direction: Eva Knibbe
Creators: Paulien Geerlings, Jantine Jongebloed, Eva Knibbe, Noelía Martin-Montalvo, Nina van Tongeren

https://u.aec.at/DA2ADF41

De Toneelmakerij (NL) makes cutting-edge shows for young audiences. Based in Amsterdam and with (inter)national reach, we tell polyphonic stories to the heartbeat of the city. We have participated in European projects such as the awarded Young Europe 4 and ACuTe. For this, our interactive performance *Rabbit Hole* received an award for best concept and use of new tech. **Paulien Geerlings** (NL) is head dramaturg at de Toneelmakerij and board member of ETC. She publishes essays and is writing a play for the main stage. **Jantine Jongebloed** (NL) is a writer and journalist. Her literary debut "Sometimes I want a child" was published last year. *Patchwork Girl* was partly based on her prize-winning essay. **Eva Knibbe** (NL) is an all-round artist. Her video installation *Untitled,* created with Paulien Geerlings, showcases the history and future of people with Down syndrome. **Noelía Martin-Montalvo** (ES) graduated in Interdisciplinary Arts at the Maastricht Institute of Arts. She employs diverse mediums including film, photography, performance, and AI art. **Nina van Tongeren** (NL) is a playwright and a dramaturg at de Toneelmakerij. She writes activist plays for all ages and publishes essays.

Ars Electronica Award for Digital Humanity

AI and the Art of Historical Reinterpretation—Filling Gender Bias Gaps

Claudia Larcher

A key focus of this project is the elimination of gender-specific biases in historical datasets used by AI. Since AI models heavily rely on historical data, the project examines the consequences of using AI to predict future societal changes, raising ethical questions, and exploring how AI can complement, rewrite, and reinterpret data archives. It proposes filling historical gaps with AI-generated "historical images".

AI technologies, especially image generation models, can rewrite history and enhance our understanding of the past while addressing potential gaps. This deliberate distortion of large datasets can influence future AI decisions. The project critiques distortions in historiography driven by political interests, personal preferences, one-sided narratives, and the marginalization of people and events. *FLINTA*[1]* individuals have historically been excluded from official records, with their contributions often overlooked.

The project creates a constantly growing fictional image archive of history, reinterpreting the past with inclusivity and diversity. This collection, which can be data mined, is spread across digital platforms to inform and train future AI models, either actively or passively.

1   *FLINTA** is a German abbreviation that stands for "Frauen, Lesben, Intergeschlechtliche, nichtbinäre, trans und agender Personen", meaning women/females, lesbians, intersex, non-binary, trans and agender people. The asterisk represents all non-binary gender identities.

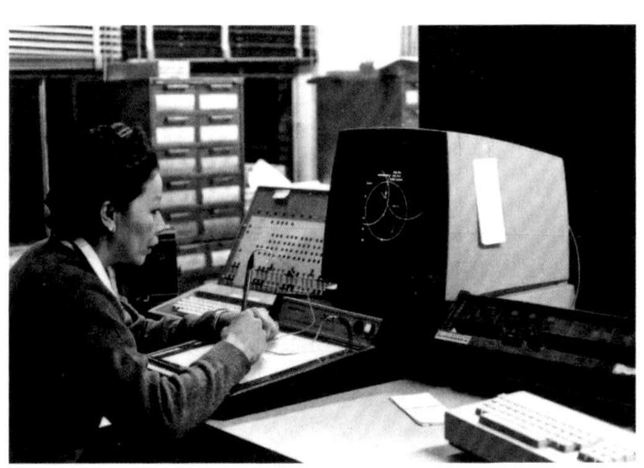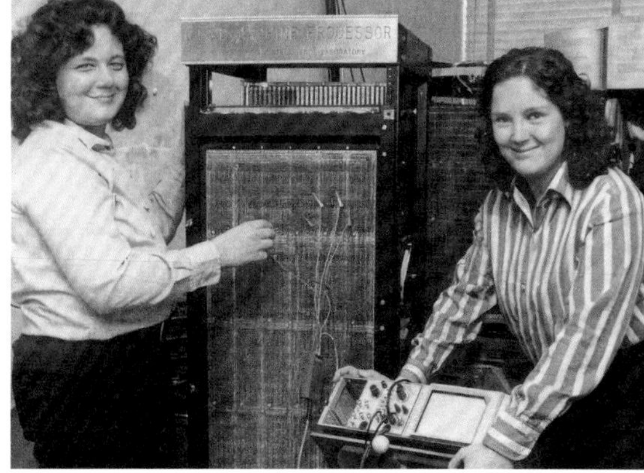

AI and the Art of Historical Reinterpretation, Claudia Larcher, 2023

VALIE EXPORT Center
With support from: VALIE EXPORT Scholarship
for artists and artistic researchers

https://u.aec.at/C8D8D569

Claudia Larcher (AT) is an artist, filmmaker, and AI researcher. Her work spans video animation, collage, photography, and installation, with a focus on the impacts and uses of artificial intelligence. Together with Eva Fischer, she explores Feminine AI, integrating gender perspectives in AI development to promote inclusivity and diversity. Larcher has exhibited globally, including at Anthology Film Archives NYC, Calouste Gulbenkian Foundation Lisbon, Centre Pompidou Paris, Gray Area Festival San Francisco, Manifesta 13, and Tokyo Wonder Site. She has received numerous prizes, including the Kunsthalle Wien Prize (2008), the Outstanding Artist Award of the Federal Chancellery (2016), and the Austrian Art Award (2023). Currently, she is a resident of the ARTTEC program at the Austrian Institute of Technology.

**Ars Electronica Award for Digital Humanity
Honorary Mention**

European Union Prize for Citizen Science

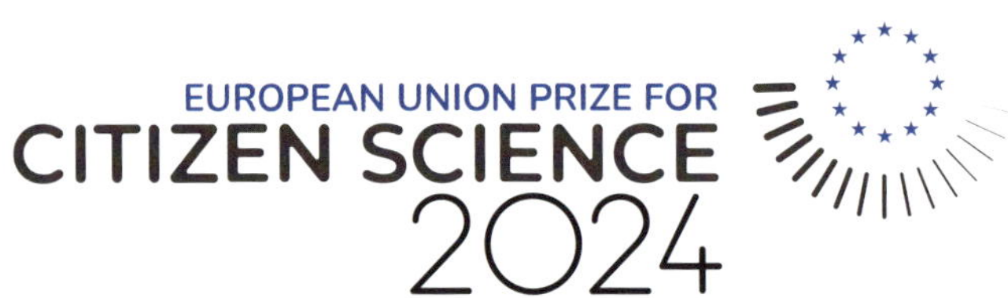

I warmly congratulate the winners of this year's EU Citizen Science Award, but would also like to commend all participants. Your initiatives address some of our most pressing challenges and showcase the transformative potential of citizen science. They improve the excellence and impact of our research, and also deepen the relationship and trust between science and our societies.

Iliana Ivanova
Commissioner for Innovation, Research, Culture, Education and Youth

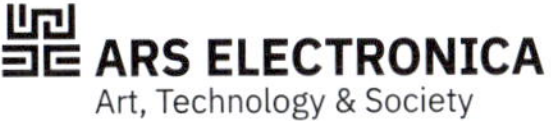
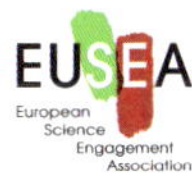
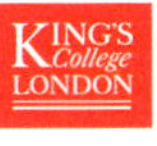
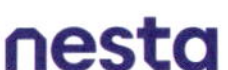
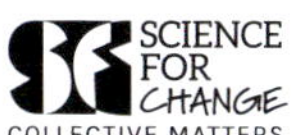
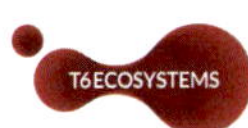
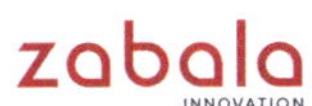
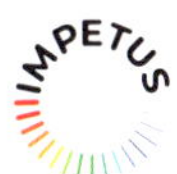
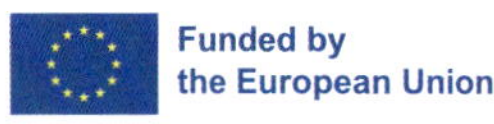

Ars Electronica awards the European Union Prize for Citizen Science on behalf of the European Commission in the context of the IMPETUS project. The IMPETUS project has received funding from the European Union's Horizon WIDERA 2021-ERA-01 Research and Innovation Programme under Grant Agreement No. 101058677

Recognizing the role of Citizen Science in Europe

Citizen Science stands for scientific research that transforms the allocation of roles and agency in the research process. Citizens initiate, design, and implement investigations in collaboration with scientists, enabling all persons involved in the process to gain new perspectives as well as access to and understanding of data (volumes), and to design the solutions to the challenges of our times. Citizen Science opens up an appreciative, transparent, and innovative interaction between science and the general public, which has great potential to contribute to a positive change in our society and living environment. To promote this dynamic, the European Commission has initiated this highly endowed competition.

The European Union recognizes the crucial role of citizens in the research process

With the "European Union Prize for Citizen Science", the European Commission wants to underline the importance of Citizen Science and to honor, present, and support outstanding projects whose social and political impact advances the further development of a pluralistic, inclusive, and sustainable society in Europe. Ars Electronica Linz was commissioned to organize the competition as part of the IMPETUS project—which is being carried out in cooperation with King's College London (GB), the European Science Engagement Association (AT), Zabala Innovation (ES), T6 Ecosystems (IT), Science for Change (ES), and Nesta (GB). In 2024, this prestigious prize is given for the second time.

From January 10 to March 11, 2024 projects could be submitted for the "European Union Prize for Citizen Science". In total 288 initiatives and projects were received.

Elevating Communities and Excellent Research through Citizen Science—Paving the Way for Radical Societal Transformation

Statement by the jury of the European Union Prize for Citizen Science 2024:
Sofie Burgos-Thorsen, Mairéad Hurley, Luciana Marques,
Fermín Serrano Sanz, Snežana Smederevac

2024 is the second year that we honor the outstanding citizen scientists in Europe. Citizen Science, a collaborative approach involving volunteers from diverse backgrounds in scientific research, represents a trend and a key paradigm shift in contemporary science. At its core, Citizen Science embodies the democratization of knowledge. Inviting participants from all walks of life to participate in scientific discovery transcends traditional boundaries of expertise, inspires curiosity, catalyzes innovation across various disciplines, and empowers communities to actively contribute to our understanding of the world. This inclusive process fosters a sense of global citizenship, pride, ownership, empowerment, inclusion, and shared responsibility among participants. It enriches the scientific process with new perspectives, insights, and evidence-based decision-making while often driving social innovation, building capacity in local communities, and countering apathy and civic disengagement. Furthermore, Citizen Science is a powerful tool for scientific communication and education. It fosters a deeper appreciation of scientific methods and nurtures a society of informed, scientifically active citizens.

Citizen scientists contribute significantly to co-designing research methods, posing relevant questions, developing innovative tools, collecting data, collectively interpreting findings, and providing policy recommendations through hands-on research experiences and online platforms, performances, or workshops. As a result, the reality of Citizen Science in Europe today transcends the consolidated idea of projects being a mere database of collected georeferenced points on a map: Citizen Science builds strong bridges between policies and societies in Europe. This collaborative approach helps to close the gap between scientific expertise and public understanding, leading to more effective and inclusive policy-making processes. Nowadays, this is a crucial aspect, given the nature of contemporary challenges such as political polarization, increased social marginalization of minority groups, anti-European sentiments, or anti-science narratives that pose risks to our democracy, collaboration, and trust in science. In an era marked by the proliferation of fake news, right-wing populism, and distrust in sciences, engaging different groups directly with science contributes to generating reliable data and results and to safeguarding democratic values. By empowering citizens to participate actively in the scientific process, these initiatives promote a culture of openness, accountability, and critical thinking—essential pillars of a healthy democracy. Through engagement in research activities related to issues that directly impact their communities, Citizen Science projects cultivate a sense of ownership and investment in the democratic process.

As jury members, the range of projects we reviewed allowed us a unique insight into the transformative potential of Citizen Science to shape the future of Europe. These awards are a testament not only to the achievements of individual citizen scientists, but also to the collective spirit of collaboration and discovery that drives this movement forward. We respect the dedication and passion of all participants in this competition, while highlighting those projects that have achieved excellence in Citizen Science. The winners showcased here come from more than 30 different countries. They exemplify ways that European citizens generate valuable knowledge across various scientific domains, addressing pressing societal issues. Congratulations to all. These initiatives demonstrate exceptional achievements, showcasing innovative methodological approaches and interdisciplinary collaboration.

We are living in profoundly turbulent times, and the events of recent years have shed light on the many processes and practices that need to be completely overhauled, given a tune-up, or put out to pasture. It is clear that doing things the way we have always done them will not suffice. Instead, we need to pay heed to the voices of those who are doing things differently, rebelling, imagining an alternative world, and, most importantly, taking action. The projects we have honored are these trailblazers who act as beacons for others to follow—whether they are using emerging or immersive technologies in unexpected ways, embracing circular economy, taking control of healthcare, or fighting against the many forms of injustice and oppression by generating knowledge and furthering education.

It's crucial to underscore the ethics, transparency, and excellence in these initiatives—especially those that aim to safeguard citizens' basic human rights and to uphold research integrity in the digital age.

What's next for Citizen Science?

All of the projects we reviewed were inspiring. They also highlighted areas for further developments that would allow Citizen Science in Europe to be more impactful:

First, on the level of *citizen science methods,* we recommend more ambitious and inclusive approaches. Many Citizen Science initiatives could take inspiration from projects such as *SeaPaCS,* winner of the Diversity & Collaboration prize, and others, to allow and support citizens to engage in all project phases, from inception to completion.

This is just one step that can improve collaboration and participation of citizens in science. Another step to overcoming extractive tendencies involves investing in a reciprocal, rather than one-way, relationship between citizens and scientists. This might entail designing capacity building, educational outcomes, or accountability metrics into the project scope, ensuring that scientists give back to the communities, whose participation and labor they heavily rely upon.

Second, on *the topical or thematic level,* we encourage more Citizen Science projects to address technological issues in society. While many projects use sensor technologies, Artificial Intelligence, and digital media as tools or means to study other issues, very few projects investigate technological problems as their topic of concern. Yet, Honorary Mention recipients such as *Intelligent Instruments in Citizen Science* and *Eco-Bot.Net* exemplify that Citizen Science has much to offer regarding our understanding of the implications of AI, Generative AI, surveillance systems, social media platforms, and other digital technologies, and in relation to democracy, environmental policies, urban planning, social justice, and other burning issues. Here, Citizen Science could help us challenge and address the biases in digital technologies, and their power and role in society.

Third, Citizen Science could evolve further by integrating artistic practices, reconfiguring *how knowledge is produced and going beyond conventional, linear scientific data collection and analysis modes.* The project *Dreamachine* exemplifies this potential by using artistic installations and drawing exercises to invite citizens to report in new ways about their sensory experiences, allowing for novel scientific research within cognitive science. This demonstrates that art and Citizen Science can inform and inspire each other, creating a Citizen Science that transcends traditional boundaries. While many Citizen Science projects currently focus on documenting their rigor in methods and data, the field could benefit from an increased focus on exploring what the integration of artistic practices could do to reconfigure knowledge production through creativity and playful research.

In line with European values, Citizen Science projects must consider their impact on all members of society. Citizen Science should both serve and meaningfully engage with groups and communities that have very little contact with science, in order to avoid excluding them. By bridging these gaps, Citizen Science can become more inclusive and impactful, breaking down barriers and fostering social justice.

Grand Prize

**Awarded for outstanding achievements
in the advancement of knowledge through
the empowerment of civil society and citizens
in the development of the future.**

**INCREASE
Intelligent Collections of Food-Legume Genetic Resources for European Agrofood Systems
INCREASE Citizen Science Experiment (CSE)**
Kerstin Neumann, Roberto Papa

The Grand Prize winner this year is the *INCREASE* project. Its main goals include generating phenotypic data for over 1,000 bean plant genetic resources (PGR) lines in different European environments where citizen scientists help decentralized conservation and enhance agrobiodiversity. This project demonstrates outstanding work on genetic diversity and adaptation within common bean cultivars by integrating DNA sequencing with the analysis of phenotypic data.

With its strong scientific foundation, this project exemplifies excellence in research that embraces Citizen Science. To achieve its goals, it will engage many citizens through a dedicated application for data collection and seed exchange—5,000 participants of different backgrounds, ages, and genders all across Europe are participating in the 2024 campaign.

The *INCREASE* project raises awareness of agrobiodiversity and nutrition. It educates participants and policymakers on sustainable agri-food production and consumption. Legumes play a crucial role in issues such as soil health and climate resilience in the face of food security and scarcity concerns.

The project has implemented a participatory research model with various levels of engagement tailored to accommodate participants' diverse levels of expertise. This approach enables feedback collection, support provision, and information dissemination to ensure sustainable citizen engagement. The inclusion of Artificial Intelligence for image analysis and the implementation of the Standard Material Transfer Agreement (SMTA) allows the compliance of international regulations for testing this innovative decentralized conservation approach. Its extensive cooperation across countries, the involvement of citizens from different regions, and engagement with regional platforms emphasize its European dimension and importance. Looking ahead, the jury expects this award to support the further development and innovation of the project, which subscribes to the ethos of empowering communities through decentralized seed storage, enabling them to regain control of their agricultural heritage. By democratizing access to seeds and knowledge, *INCREASE* challenges the dominance of large agrochemical corporations and promotes agricultural resilience, sustainability, and food sovereignty.

Finally, the project's collaboration between citizens and major research centers is outstanding, and it exemplifies how top-tier centers are opening up their research processes for scientific excellence and social inclusion. In particular, members from local rural communities, including farmers who usually perceive themselves as outside the formal research process, contribute in a direct, meaningful and accessible way. Their traditional knowledge, passed down through generations, is a valuable agricultural research and development resource.

Diversity & Collaboration Award

Awarded for excellence in grassroots approaches, explorative collaboration, cultural and gender diversity, community participation, stakeholder engagement and social inclusivity.

SeaPaCS
Participatory Citizen Science against Marine Pollution
Chiara Certomà

SeaPaCS explores the consequences of marine plastic pollution on local biodiversity via a participatory Citizen Science process in the coastal city of Anzio, Italy. It engages more than 250 fishermen, North African migrants, school children, teachers, environmental NGOs, marine lawyers, sailors, and divers in co-producing knowledge about the health of the Mediterranean Sea, contributing to scientific fields like oceanography, cultural geography, and marine chemistry. In doing so, the project demonstrates excellence in engaging a diverse range of stakeholders and innovating transdisciplinary collaboration models between them, pushing the boundaries between civil society, citizens, and science.

SeaPaCS is especially exemplary for centering a community-led grassroots approach and for its attention to overcoming extractive tendencies in Citizen Science (citizens as "sensors"), by involving citizens beyond plastic sampling and data collection in activities such as plastisphere DNA analysis, documenting underwater ecological niches, creating photo and video exhibitions, testing DIY microplastic trawling instruments, and building marine plastic recycling stations. *SeaPaCS* hereby demonstrates how we can involve citizens not just in mapping problems but also in taking collective action towards restoring biodiversity and ecological resilience in European oceans, with attention to social inclusion and cultural diversity.

For these reasons, we honor *SeaPaCS* with the Diversity & Collaboration Award.

Digital Communities Award

Awarded for excellence in fostering an open and inclusive civil society fit for the digital age by empowering communities to critically engage with digital technologies.

CoAct for Mental Health
OpenSystems group

CoAct for mental health stood out to us as an excellent example of citizen social science, involving patients with lived experience of mental health issues, and their families, as co-researchers and co-producers of evidence on their experiences of social support networks in their communities. The project developed an open-source chatbot as a tool for autoethnography, demonstrating great innovation and creativity in using digital technology to support and foster inclusive community building. These citizen researchers contributed their daily micro-stories to create a body of evidence that aims to shift the paradigm for mental health care away from a biomedical approach towards personalized medicine and a community-centered approach, showing that social support networks can be deployed in mental health care for recovery, well-being, crisis management, and to prevent isolation and exclusion. A small and dedicated core group of 32 citizen scientists participated throughout the entire life cycle of this co-creation project, from inception to data analysis and interpretation, and even participating in presenting the resultant policy recommendations, while a further 900 citizens used the chatbot to engage with the research.

This project allows citizens to play an active role in research that directly impacts their lives and harnesses the power of technology to include marginalized voices as active participants in the transformation of mental health care. Technology in this case facilitates the participation of citizens in developing a personalized approach to healthcare and medicine.

Overall the *CoAct* project fosters an open and inclusive civil society by empowering their community to critically engage with digital technologies—a worthy winner of the 2024 Digital Communities Award.

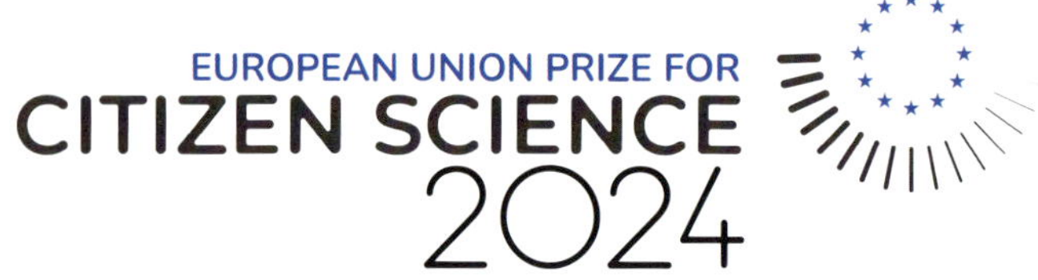

Honorary Mentions

ASD Publics: Playable cities for all
Raquel Colacios, Blanca Calvo Boixet

Bellingcat: A Collective Of Citizen Journalists Using Open Source Data To Investigate Matters Of Public Interest
Bellingcat

BP100: Community and Architecture Festival
Hungarian Contemporary Architecture Centre

Carnivore Tracking Project: Involving volunteers in wolf and lynx monitoring
Miroslav Kutal, Michal Feller,
Romana Uhrinová, Barbora Černá,
Carnivore Conservation Programme,
Friends of the Earth Czech Republic

CITIZENS FOR SDG 15.1
Ivana Radović

Cultural Reforesting: How can we (in the west) renew our relationship with nature?
Dr. Sarah Edwards, Andrew Franzkowiak,
Dr. Kim Salmon, Arji Manuelpillai, Adam
Kammerling, Jess Ihetojeh, Dr. Will Pearse,
Dr. Tilly Collins, Stephanie Hot, Heather Ackroyd,
Dan Harvey, Eloise Moody, Vicky Long,
Abigail Hunt, Finn Chatwyn-Ross, Kinship
Workshop, Harun Morrison, Kim Coleman,
Connor Butler, Dawn Stevens, Andrew Merritt,
Bryony Benge-Abbott, Nestor Pestana

Domestic Heat Comfort for Energy Poverty and Climate Adaptation
Yağız Eren Abanus, Sinan Erensü, Duygu Dağ,
Cemre Kara, Barış Türkdoğan, Meryem Uyaver,
Elif Bengi Güneş, Oğulcan Kınalı, İlknur Akgül,
Daniela Kızıldağ, Gülnaz Yücel-Durmuş,
Merve Özhan, İdil Besler, Tuğba Uçar, Mekanda
Adalet Derneği (Center for Spatial Justice)

Dreamachine: A major interdisciplinary programme fusing world class artists with leading scientific researchers.
Collective Act, University of Sussex,
University of Glasgow

Eco-Bot.Net: Defending The Digital Environment
Barnaby Francis, Robert '3D' Del Naja, Dale Vince

GALLANT: Empowering Glasgow Communities for Climate Resilience and Biodiversity Conservation
Ria Dunkley, Florence Halstead, Sarah Gambell,
Becky Duncan

HistorEsch: Citizen History Activities in the city of Esch-sur-Alzette
Thomas Cauvin, Joella van Donkersgoed

iesaisties.lv: Citizen Science Platform for Humanities and Arts in Latvia
Krišs Salmanis, Sanita Reinsone, Eva Eglāja-Kristsone, Ginta Pērle-Sīle, Rita Grīnvalde, Ieva Weaver, Uldis Ķirsis, ILFA'S DH GROUP

Intelligent Instruments in Citizen Science: Understanding Contemporary AI through Creative Practice
Thor Magnusson, Jack Armitage, Halla Steinunn
Stefansdottir, Victor Shepardson, Nicola Privato,
Miguel Angel Rozzoli, Halldor Ulfarsson, Sean
O'Brien, Marco Donnarumma, Sophie Skach,
Giacomo Lepri, Intelligent Instruments Lab

kafsimo@karditsa, Activating citizens through biomass recycling into heating pellets
incommon, Energy Community of Karditsa

Language Checkers—This is how we speak in Neckarstadt
Janin Roessel, Christine Möhrs, Elena Schoppa-Briele, Rahaf Farag, Heike Chan Hin, Theresa Schnedermann, Sprach-Checker team at the IDS

Let's go out with Pl@ntNet app!
Ivana Polackova, Pierre Bonet, Tereza NGO

Obstetric Coevolution: Coevolving obstetric practices to improve the childbirth experience
Irene Lapuente, Anna Fosch Masllovet, Dídac Roger i Homs, La Mandarina de Newton

OdourCollect and D-NOSES: Citizen Science to foster environmental governance and tackle odour pollution
Fundación Ibercivis, Science For Change

ParKli: Participatory climate research to develop local early warning systems for climate protection
ParKli Team, Reutlingen University, Herman Hollerith Center, open science for open societies – os4os

RadoNorm Citizen Science Incubator
Tanja Perko, Meritxell Martell, Warren John

SEED LIBRARY
Saša Vidmar, Ana Kosič, Irena Škvarč, France Bevk Public Library

Sicily's Indigenous Cyber Tracker
Collettivo Rewild Sicily, CyberTracker Italia, Sicily Environment Fund, Astrid Natura

Social inclusion and participation of Deaf and Hard of Hearing adults in Citizen Science for Climate Change (CitSci4All)
Katerina Zourou

The Home River Bioblitz
Jens Benöhr Riveros, Vera Knook, Carlos Velazco, Enya Roseli, Jelena Belojević

The Russian airstrike on the Mariupol Drama Theater
The Center for Spatial Technologies

The State of Our Trails (SoOT) Report: understanding and responding to single-use pollution (SUP) in recreational trail ecosystems through citizen science
Dom Ferris, Trash Free Trails HQ

Youth partnership in suicide prevention research: fostering authenticity, collaboration and empowerment.
Maria Michail, Niyah Campbell, Rowmell Hunter, Zaynab Sohawon, Jamie Morgan, Beckye Williams, Kalen Reid

INCREASE
**Intelligent Collections of Food-Legume Genetic Resources
for European Agrofood Systems
INCREASE Citizen Science Experiment (CSE)**

Kerstin Neumann, Roberto Papa

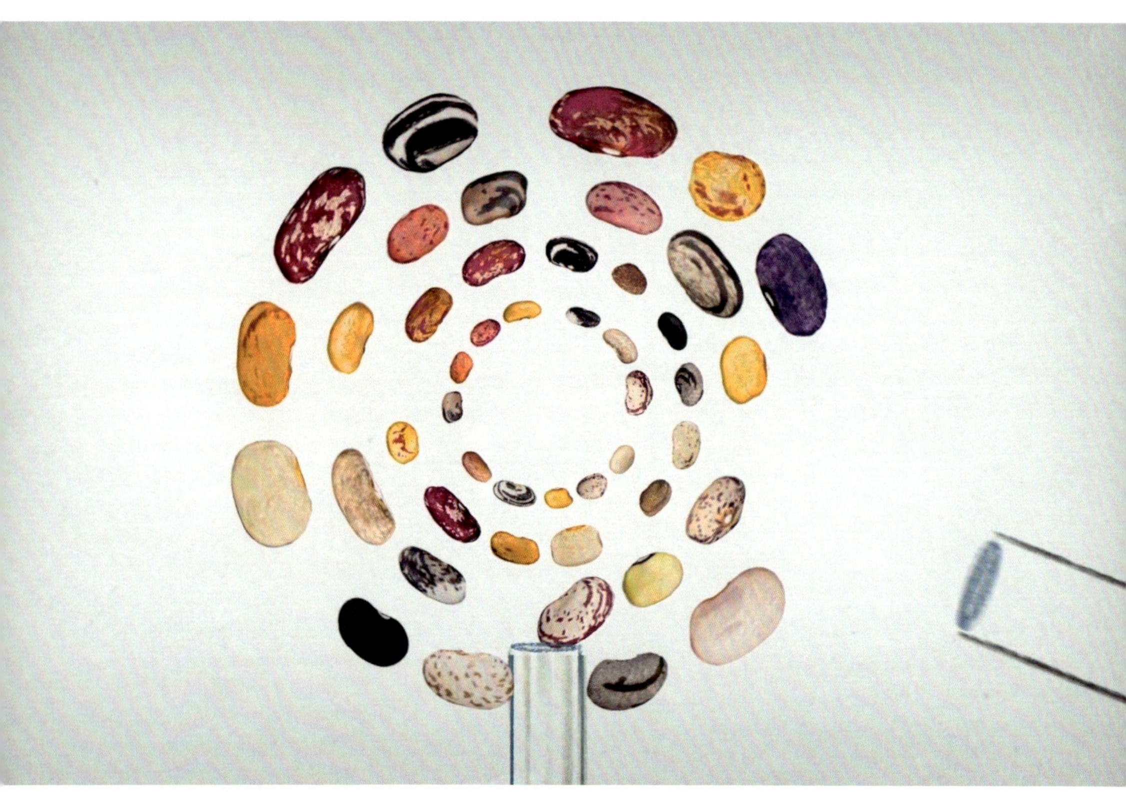

The idea behind *INCREASE* is to make available Plant Genetic Resources (PGR), currently preserved only in gene banks, to a large number of citizens and stakeholders, developing a decentralized conservation system that involves citizens in a Citizen Science Experiment (CSE).

The *INCREASE CSE* focuses on two highly relevant topics, listed in SDG (Sustainable Development Goals) and Green Deal: agrobiodiversity conservation and food legumes cultivation/consumption, which is of pivotal importance for the transition towards a plant-based diet, a key element to contrast and mitigate the climate change crisis.

The *INCREASE CSE* explores thousands of different beans PGR thanks to the help of citizens who contribute to data collection on an unprecedented number of different locations, helping to better understand, not only many phenotypic traits, but also the adaptation of common beans in different environments. The huge pool of images stored in the *INCREASE CSE* App is the basis for detailed image analysis using artificial intelligence and deep learning, involving citizens to develop image recognition, and enabling the identification and correction of potential errors during the decentralized conservation steps.

**European Union Prize for Citizen Science
Grand Prize**

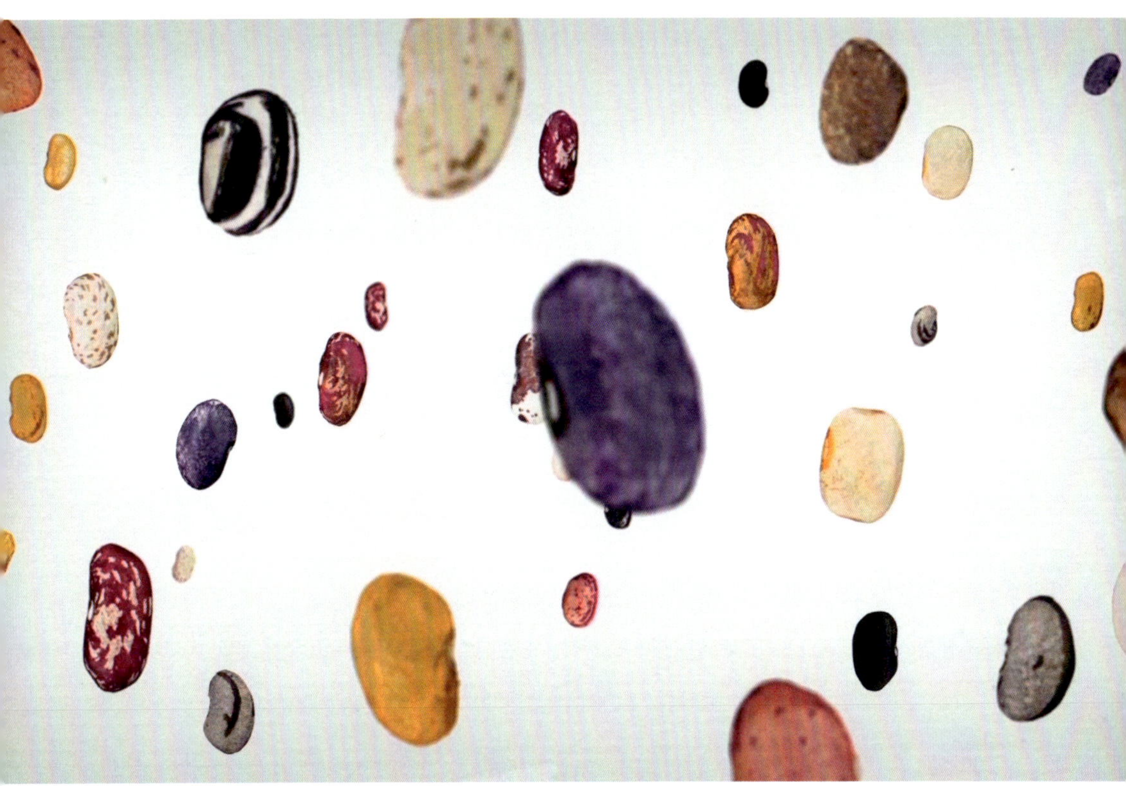

Citizens are invited to continue after their first participation by exchanging CSE varieties via the App with others, forming a decentralized PGR conservation community.

A high innovation of *INCREASE CSE* is based on the use of digital tools. For the first time, CS, done with PGR and crop growth, is assessed at home via an App (*INCREASE CSA*). Moreover, for the first time ever, the SMTA can be accepted via an App. All texts, including *INCREASE* website's contents and the App, are accessible in different languages to reach participants from as many countries as possible. A dedicated team of the CSE email account is in constant contact with citizens in their native languages, which seeks constantly to improve the CSE experience through the feedback of participants, interacting directly with them, and providing support through social media. In these spaces, there is also an exchange of knowledge among the participants, especially mutual advice. We consider communication and information crucial. Therefore, we believe in the importance of public restitution, communicating the outcomes of the research in which they contributed. Our commitment is based on communication through a simplified language. Participants must be aware of the importance of their contribution.

The pedagogical aspect in our project is not of secondary importance: we are strengthening the collaboration with schools and school garden associations in different countries through specific projects involving children and families.

By establishing a collaborative relationship, the experiment also contributes to bringing citizens closer to science, giving the opportunity to familiarize themselves with previously unfamiliar issues. For instance, the engagement of students tends to lead to the involvement of the whole family, introducing science in daily interactions. The experiential aspect of individuals demonstrates the potential of Citizen Science not only as a contribution to science, but also as a source of personal enrichment. We can say that our project contributes both to the production of knowledge and awareness.

The *INCREASE* project is also committed to raising awareness on issues related to nutrition and sustainability, and events with experts on the importance of legumes in our diet are held. This awareness is a stimulus to develop new healthy food habits and encourages self-production. For these reasons, *INCREASE CSE* can have a great social impact in several aspects.

Open Science & FAIR data sharing were adopted from the start. Altogether, our project showcases that it is possible to bring together European citizens, relevant associations, researchers, and policymakers along with NGOs under a common goal of improving agrobiodiversity, despite the resurgence of nationalism in Europe.

INCREASE Consortium – *INCREASE* project has received funding from the EU Horizon 2020 research and innovation program, under grant agreement no. 862862

https://u.aec.at/314FA497

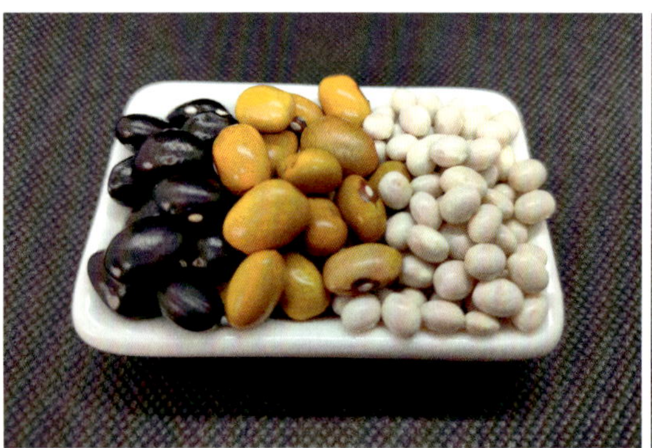

Common bean seeds

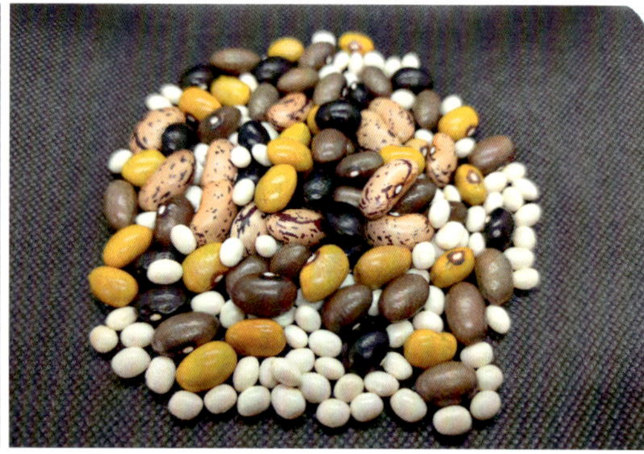

Common bean seeds

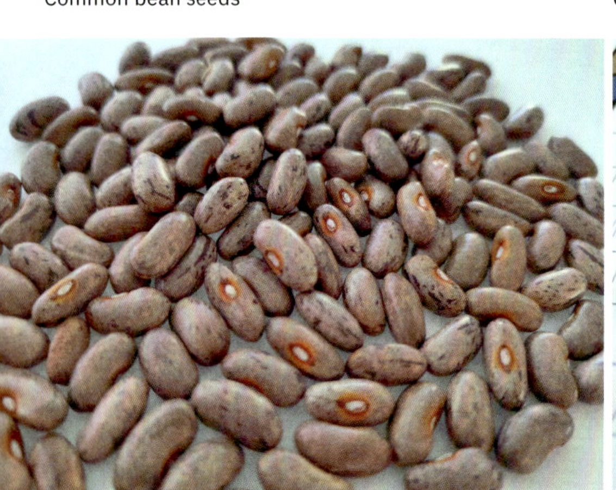

Common bean seeds

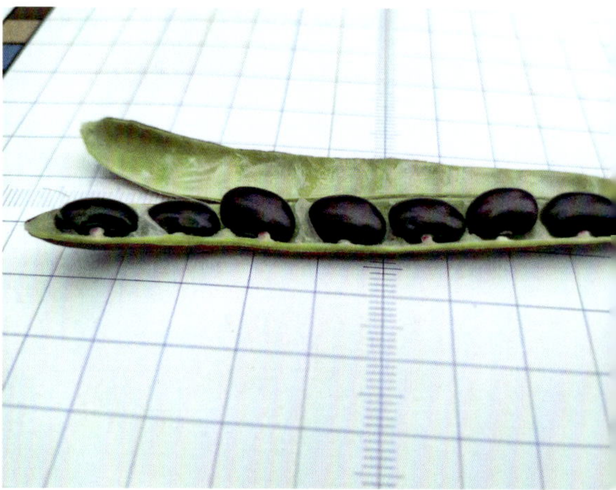

Common bean pod & seeds

**European Union Prize for Citizen Science
Grand Prize**

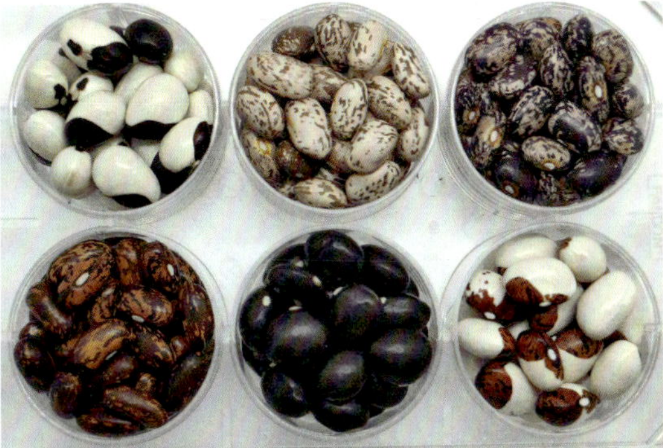

Common bean six different colored lines_on bean

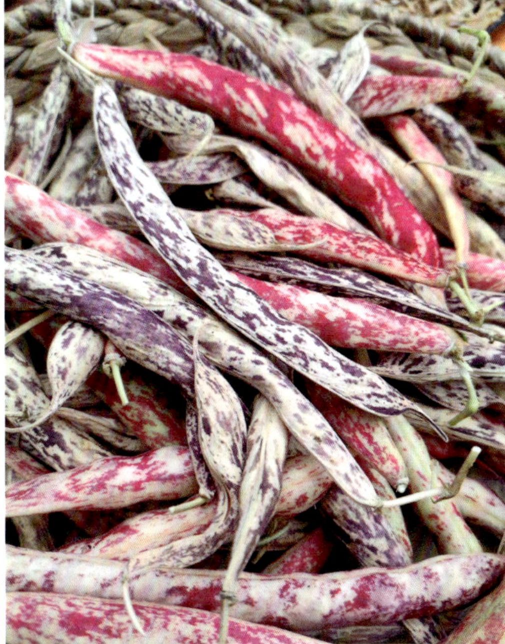

Common bean pods

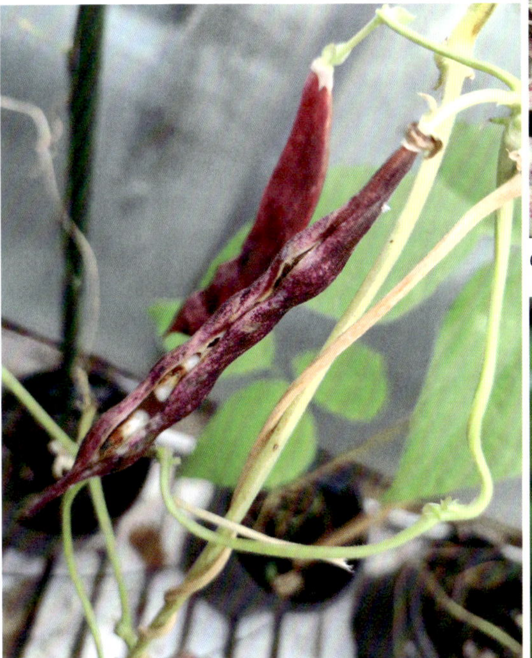

Common bean pods

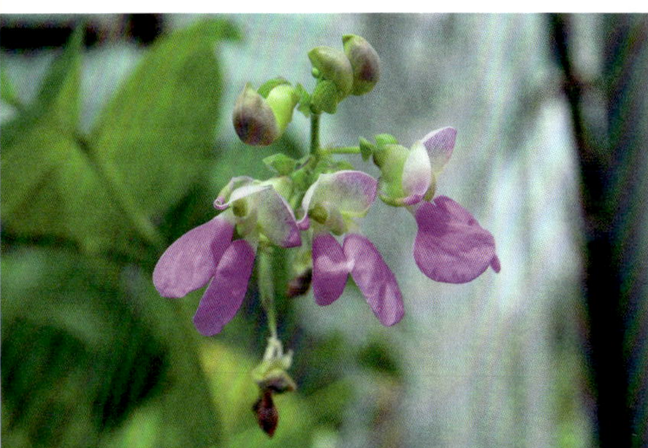

Common bean flowers

Dr. Kerstin Neumann (DE) is a biologist, leading the group "Automated Plant Phenotyping" at IPK since 2021. She has long-standing expertise in non-invasive high throughput phenotyping systems and their application to evaluate diverse cereal collections for abiotic stress tolerance (drought and heat), contributing to elucidate trait genetic architecture, trait relationships and trade-offs, to improve crops' performances under stresses. She is also involved in the establishment and use of seed-proof gene banks of cereals and legumes genetic resources. This resulted in leading Work Package 6 in INCREASE and as such being coordinator of the INCREASE CSE, together with Prof Papa.
Prof. Roberto Papa (IT) is Full Professor of Agricultural Genetics, head of the AGROBIODIVERSITY Lab, at the Polytechnic University of Marche. His research focuses on the conservation and utilization of agrobiodiversity and plant genetic resources. By applying genomics approaches and pioneering the use of "molecular phenotyping", he contributed new knowledge on crop germplasm genetic diversity, on crop domestication and adaptation to different environments, and on evolutionary history of crop species (legumes and cereals). He coordinated several national and international projects on crop genetic resources, and he is currently leading the H2020 *INCREASE* project; he developed the concept of decentralized conservation of crop genetic resources and designed the INCREASE CSE, coordinating it together with Dr Kerstin Neumann.

CoAct for Mental Health

OpenSystems group

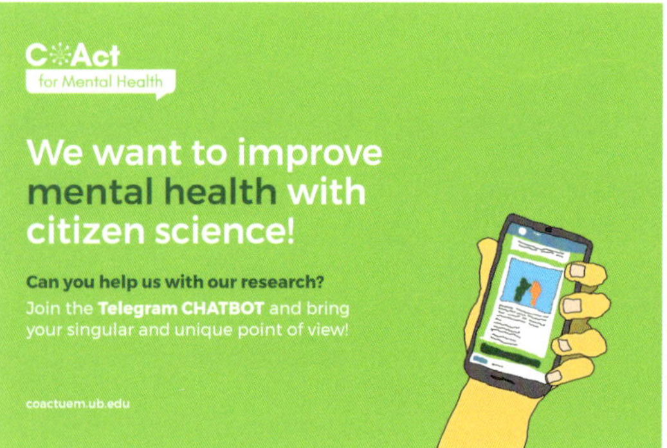

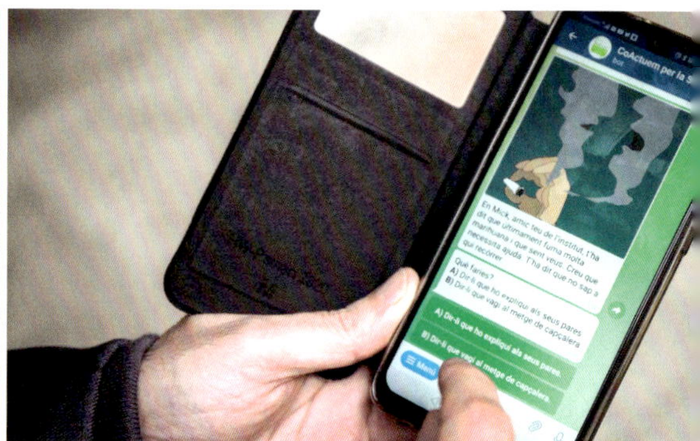

CoAct for Mental Health chatbot, Photo: Sara López

CoAct for Mental Health is a citizen science project in which people experiencing mental health problems and their families are placed at the center. The project is aligned with World Health Organization demands for enhancing community-based approaches in mental health services. The participation of people with lived experience of mental health problems is key to transform mental health worldwide.

32 people with mental health problems and family members have become Co-Researchers and have co-designed the first citizen science chatbot. The *CoActuem per la Salut Mental* (CoAct for Mental Health) Telegram Chatbot has shared hundreds of micro stories written by the Co-Researchers. The micro stories are mental health first-hand experiences on social interactions with close family, friends, workmates, neighbors, etc.

The aim of the chatbot is to engage a wider public and learn about the chatbot participants' feedback. The chatbot has facilitated the continuous collection of responses from hundreds of participants over several years, in a private and safe space. The participants contributed to data collection that explores social support networks in mental health.

These networks are grounded on social interactions, and they facilitate recovery processes, improve the quality of life, and act against social exclusion. Face-to-face sessions with Co-Researchers were designed to interpret the data from the chatbot. During a final assembly with a wide mental health community, 14 recommendations were delivered to high-level local and regional representatives and they were also published in the form of European and local policy briefs. The project is framed within a citizen social science defined as participatory scientific research co-designed and driven by groups sharing a social concern. The trans-disciplinary research proposed combines social sciences methods such as auto-ethnography with a computational social science approach, including complex systems and networks theory.

CoAct for Mental Health is part of CoAct. CoAct has received funding from the European Union's Horizon 2020 Research and Innovation program under grant agreement No. 873048.

https://u.aec.at/41B447B6

**European Union Prize for Citizen Science
Diversity & Collaboration Award**

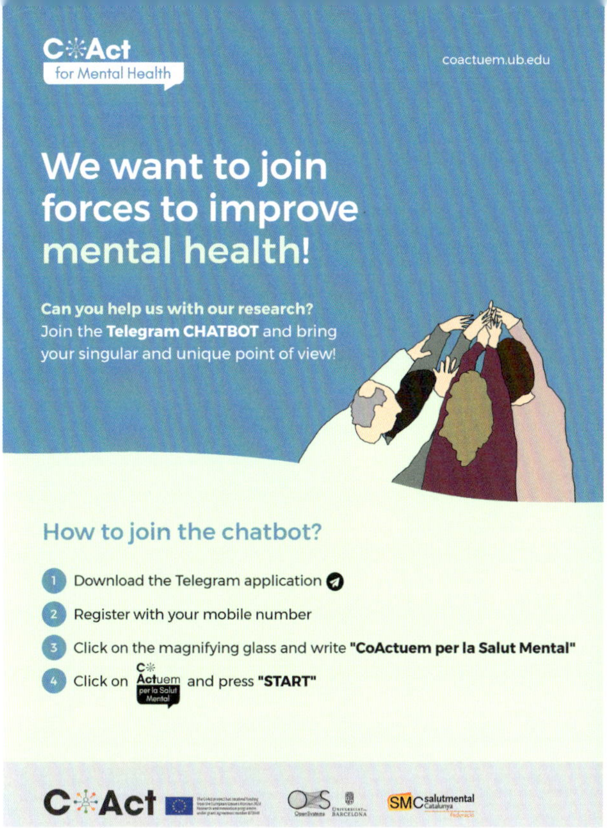

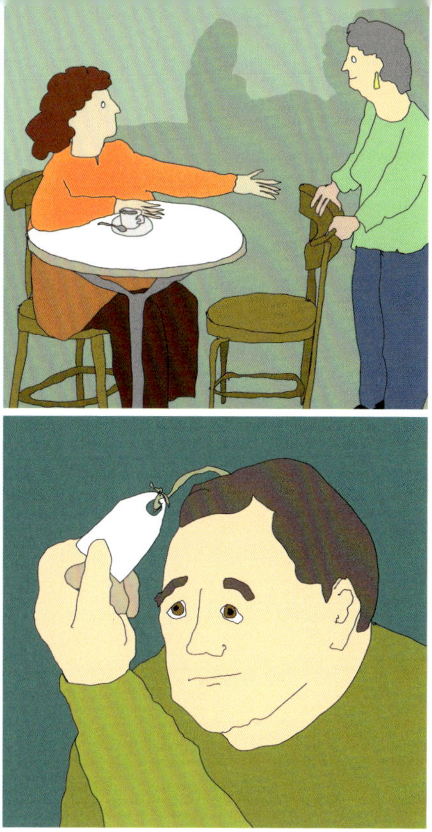

Drawings in the chatbot, Pau Badia

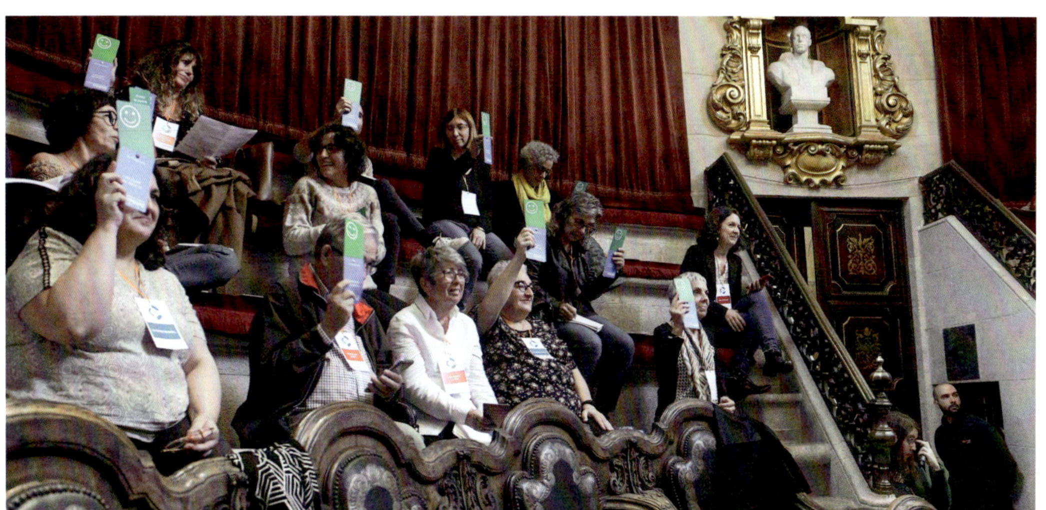

Voting during the Assemblea Comunitat Salut Menta, Photo: Sara López

CoAct for Mental Health was led by the research group **OpenSystems** (ES) from the Universitat of Barcelona (**Josep Perelló, Isabelle Bonhoure, Franziska Peter,** and **Anna Cigarini**). OpenSystems develops citizen social science projects and involves communities in a vulnerable situation. **Salut Mental Catalunya** has been a key partner as a civil society organization that represents people with mental health problems and their relatives (**Bàrbara Mitats**). The **32 Co-Researchers** joined the project through an Open Call in 2020. They were involved in all research steps and in the results dissemination, as experts-in-the-field. The **Knowledge Coalition**, made of representatives of organizations involved in mental health care provision, were involved from 2020 to late 2022. Other key members: **Itziar González-Virós** (participation and cooperation), **Pau Badia** (chatbot drawings) and **Verity Harrison** (story-telling).

SeaPaCS
Participatory Citizen Science against Marine Pollution
Chiara Certomà

SeaPaCS proposed a participatory citizen science project led by social and natural scientists that mobilizes volunteers in data collection, elaboration and sharing on the biological consequences of marine plastic pollution (via in-situ samples collection for plastisphere DNA analysis, underwater video documentation of new ecological niches, plankton evaluation), and drafted a plan for sustainability-oriented practices based on interviews with fishermen and sailors in the coastal city of Anzio (Italy) on the Mediterranean Sea.

The innovative aspects of the project resided in overcoming the extractive approach in CS (citizens as "sensors") by promoting a fully participatory process on the EU ACTION project model; advancing a multidisciplinary perspective and methods by combining cultural geography and oceanography; overcoming the problem of inaccessibility of the marine environment for lay citizens thanks to the collaboration with the LNI; tackling locally cogent issues already identified by stakeholders and mobilizing their tacit knowledge; feeding the European database on genetic diversity on plastic debris, filling important knowledge gaps worldwide and especially for the Mediterranean Sea. SeaPaCS entailed a co-design phase with citizens, starting with artistic photos and videos exhibition; the data collection and result elaboration via citizens+scientists+sailors sailing boat expeditions for microplastic collection with a professional Neuston-net labs for genetic and chemical analysis; the collective expedition on a fishing boat for documenting macro-plastic debris trawling, and in-depth interviews with fishermen; two working groups on collection and recycling system for marine plastic and protocol for CS that led to a number of follow-up international projects (notably the EU Call Culture Moves Europe "Tentacular Thinking. Experiencing underwater assemblages of culture and nature"; EU NEB "FishArt. Participatory Art for Anzio Fishermen's Harbour"; the Horizon EU project "PartArt. Participatory Art for Ocean and Water"), scientific outputs publicly available, and local initiatives.

SeaPaCS has been funded by the European Union via the Horizon project IMPETUS4CS, coordinated by the DIGGEO@ESOMAS lab at the ESOMAS Department, University of Turin and with the support of the ESOMAS Public Engagement, partnered by the Italian Naval League Anzio and Raw-News, with the endorsement of the United Nation Decade of Ocean Sciences for Sustainable Development.
Special thanks to Saverio Lalli, Davide Rinaldi, Riccardo Aleandri, Giuseppe Certomà and Caterina Folco, Davide Rinaldi, Riccardo Aleandri, Giandomenica Becchio, Eugenio Monaco, Lorenzo Colantuono, Angelo Grillo, the fishermen of Anzio, the teachers and students of schools in Anzio (notably Valeria Schinzari, Anna Martinelli and Loretta Palomba), Martina Gaglioti, Luigi Ravioli, Massimo D'Eramo, Francesco Traversa, Andrea Petragnani Ciancarelli, Diego Capobianco, Ivan Martini, Francesca Massimi, and Ivano Cotogno.

https://u.aec.at/35B9CD57

SeaPaCS multisectoral team specialized in multidisciplinary and radically participatory exploration, documentation and engagement techniques and informal tools to identify contexts-specific matters of concern and, by building on tacit competencies of local actors and multisectorial design skills, attempt at turning these into transformative knowledge for just sustainability. **Chiara Certomá** (IT) is a social geographer at the Sapienza University of Rome with international expertise in participatory process, marine social science, and environmental governance; **Federico Fornaro** (IT) is former director at the LNI-Anzio, oceanic navigator and CEO of the international hard-news agency Raw-News, **Luisa Galgani** (IT) is a chemical oceanographer at the University of Siena with extensive global experience in ocean carbon recycling and plastic pollution, **Alessio Corsi** (IT) is an Egyptologist by training and research manager at the CNR ISMAR, **Giuseppe Lupinacci** (IT) is a free-lance photographer specializing in underwater and marine photography, sailing instructor and oceanic traveler.

**European Union Prize for Citizen Science
Digital Communities Award**

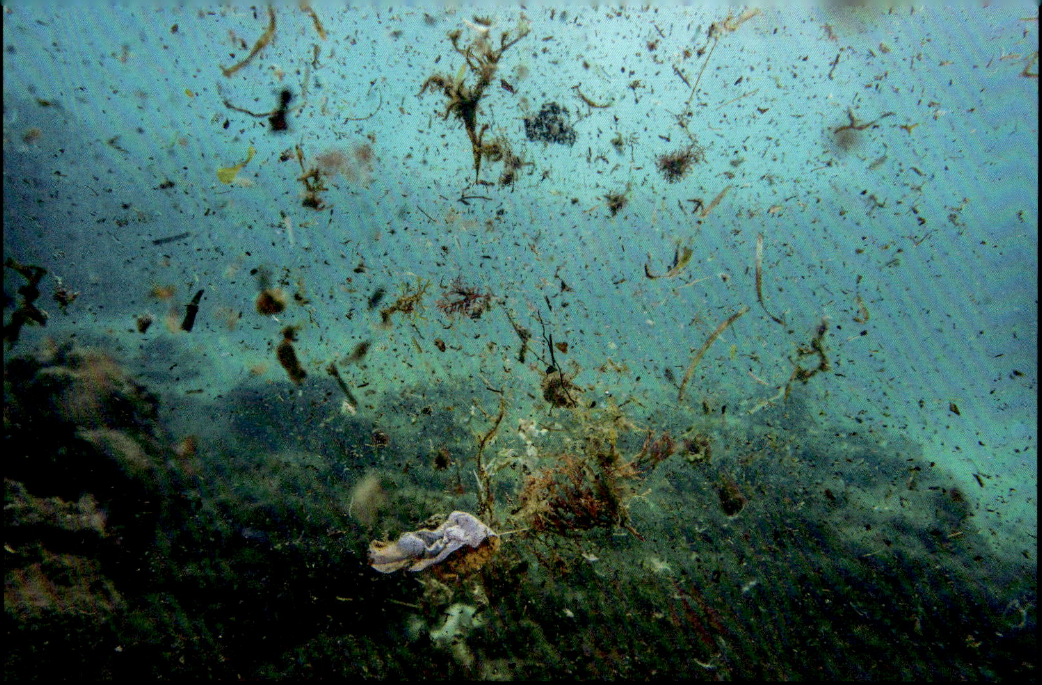

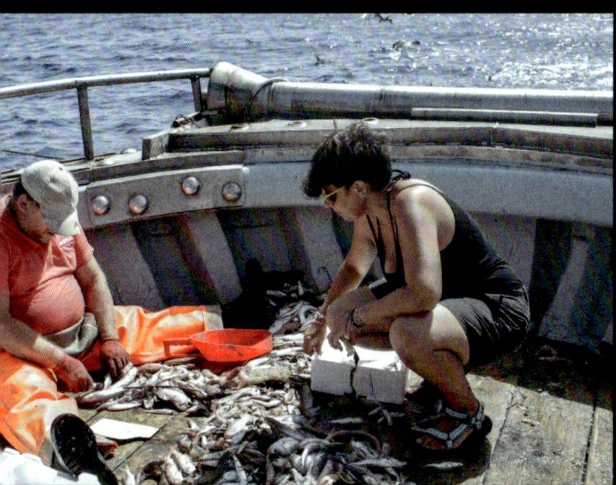

Female absorbents and microplasticst

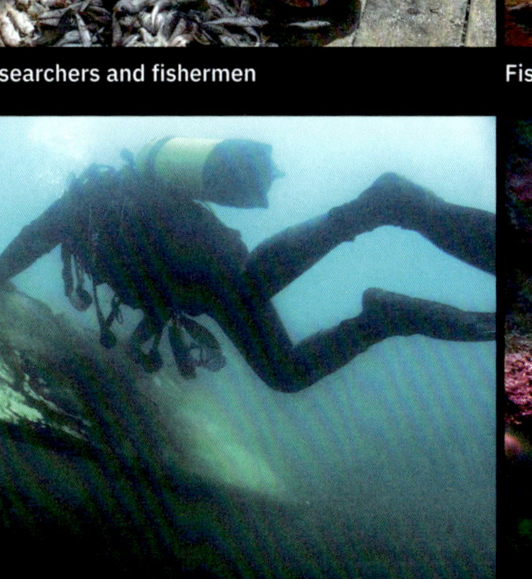

SeaPaCS researchers and fishermen

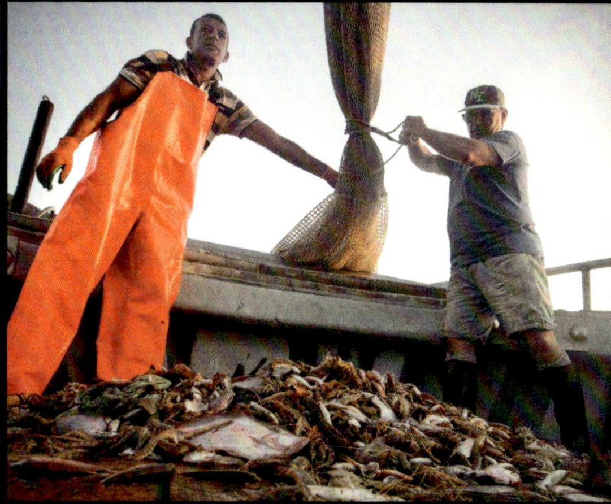

Fishing for plastic

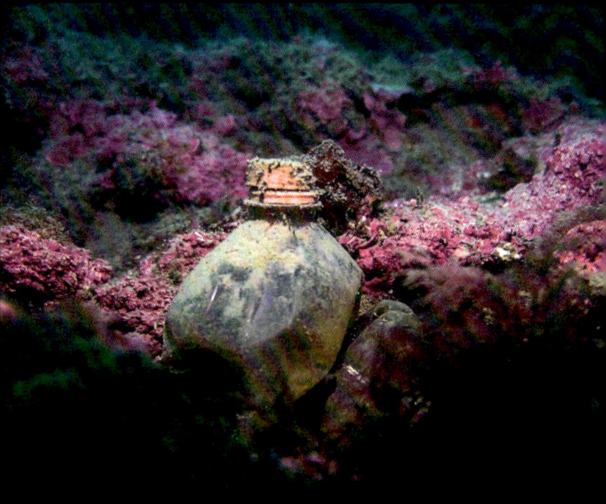

Spring Water

Underwater plastic collection

Innov
&
Techn

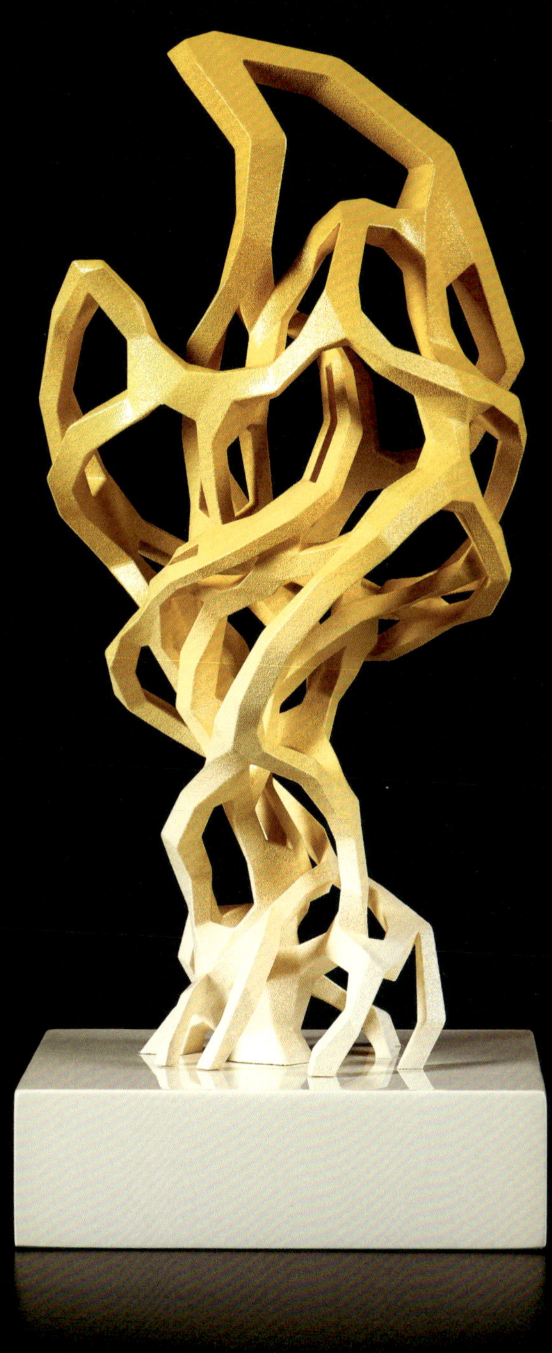

The STARTS Trophy was designed by Nick Ervinck. The Belgian artist explores the boundaries between various media, fostering a cross-pollination between the digital and the physical. He applies tools and techniques from new media, in order to explore the aesthetic potential of sculpture, 3D prints, animation, installation, architecture, and design.
Nick Ervinck, TAWSTAR, 2016

Infrastructures of Power and Care

Francesca Bria, Fumi Hirota, Manuela Naveau, Katja Schechtner, Miha Turšič

We are writing this jury statement at a very special time, as important elections and political challenges are coming up in the next few months, at both European and global level. These are uncertain times, heated up with dystopian visions of the future of a polycrisis and aggressive promises of salvation through the elimination of constructed enemy images. Political participation is becoming more than emotionalized and the space for the formation and promotion of participation mechanisms, democratic attitudes, and discourse for the purpose of open knowledge is dwindling. Europe is struggling and the number of critical voices is diminishing at the same time as political opinion-forming and expression are being taken over and cemented by artificially intelligent social media platforms.

A look at this year's submissions for the STARTS Prize showed many voices and actions that stand out and strive to create counter-images and counter-reactions, engaging with ideas in order to bring about change. In addition to socio-politically motivated artistic/scientific debates such as: How will we learn in the future?, How will we work or love in the coming decades? How will we cure ourselves and How will we take care of and live with other living beings?, this year's focus was once again on the examination of technology in the sense of big tech and internet giants, and above all related to the debate on the exploitation of our planet, questions on extractivism, and embodied situated knowledge. How important is locally anchored knowledge? How does AI reinforce the power structures inherent in technology and what impact does this have on a constantly changing and evolving knowledge environment? Who shapes technology in Europe and who offers space for reflection and co-design? And how can technological progress and innovation be reconciled with taking care of all forms of living organisms?

All these questions that we as a jury have been confronted with culminated in reflections on existing technical and social infrastructures and on infrastructures needed in order to achieve transnational size and visibility on the one hand and to enable co-design and discourse on the other. Topics such as 'alternative infrastructures', 'real-world' infrastructures, or infrastructures that enable an eco-system of experimentation and research were discussed. The many approaches in the Honorary Mentions and Nominations show that there is a living tradition of alternative infrastructures in Europe that must continue to be promoted and supported. The fact that we need more best practice examples of large-scale European infrastructures of sci-tech brings us directly to the Grand Prizes and our selection.

Perhaps never before has a jury been as unanimous as this year, as it was quickly decided that the Grand Prize for Innovative Collaboration would go to *Arts at CERN,* the art program of CERN, the European Organization for Nuclear Research in Geneva. The program, which has been involved in Art/Science debates and developments for 12 years now, deserves the prize, which not only goes to the organization, but also to the people behind the organization: the scientists, artists, creative technologists, and cultural managers in an extraordinary interplay and long-lived inter- and transdisciplinarity. Above all, this program is an example of how science, technology, and art can interact as equals. Methods from research meet methods from the arts and cross-fertilize each other cyclically. It goes without saying that an infrastructure like CERN conducts research in the field of physics, such as the structure of matter and the movement of light or sound waves. But the research findings are also reflected in very topical issues e.g. relating to climate change, and *Arts at CERN* creates and showcases common space for critical thinking by researchers from physics and the arts.

The Grand Prize for Artistic Exploration goes to *Calculating Empires: A Genealogy of Power and*

Technology, 1500–2025 by Kate Crawford and Vladan Joler. The artists spent four years working on this large-scale research project, which is presented in the form of a map room. It is a visual manifesto on technology and power relations throughout the last five centuries and contains an overwhelming amount of information that was translated and localized as graphics in an extremely appealing way. The starting point of Joler and Crawford's research is the 1500s, when empires started to use technology to centralize and consolidate their power—a phenomenon that persists to the present day—and to ask: What kind of world do we want to live in? As a jury we continue to ask: How can an infrastructure in Europe be created that allows society to influence technological developments, i.e. technology for the sake of society and the environment we live in? Infrastructures of power and care?

It was interesting to observe that critical cartographies, the mapping of power structures in technology or finance or the graphic recording of changes in landscapes and bodies were reflected in some of the works submitted. But topics such as memory and contested history, critical tech and feminist tech, female bodies and the questions of care, multispecies care and power, as well as the topics of low carbon food and community activities were also discussed and ended up in the ten Honorary Mentions and eighteen Nominations. We looked at visually stunning installations, sound experiences, (lecture) performances, games, VR/AR settings, brain computing works, and smart and alternative robotic manufacturing tools, but the final selection underlines the possibility of scalability, which we recognized as an important parameter for the future.

These considerations ultimately led us into a phase of critical S+T+ARTS reflection: What infrastructures will we need in Europe in the future, and how can we use them? How can we maintain the authentic speed of do-it-yourself while at the same time making the work scalable? What is missing in this ecosystem—e.g. the role of mediators, facilitators, or catalysts—and what can be done to change this? How can large but also smaller companies and policy makers benefit from working with artists, and how can S+T+ARTS mediate better between its disciplines? We urgently hope that S+T+ARTS will continue to recognize projects that demonstrate a successful integration of science, technology, and art and even evolve into a platform for further discourse, support, and networking, which is of great importance in times when technological developments go hand in hand with social and economic innovation.

Grand Prize Innovative Collaboration

Awarded for innovative collaboration between industry or technology and the arts (and the cultural and creative sectors in general) that opens new pathways for innovation.

Arts at CERN

Arts at CERN is a pioneering cultural initiative, reflecting CERN's exceptional openness and experimental spirit. Established in 2011, the program started as a comprehensive arts residency scheme with significant international influence under the vision of former Director-General Rolf Dieter Heuer and cultural specialist and curator Ariane Koek. After this founding period, the program was fully endorsed as the arts program of the Laboratory by current Director-General Fabiola Gianotti and led by head and curator of Arts at CERN Mónica Bello. The program started with the *Collide residencies,* as a two-month residency with two annual calls and is active now with three strands of programs: residencies, as *Collide* and *Connect,* art commissions, and exhibitions and events. Furthermore, the activities of *Arts at CERN* comprise a full range of collaborations with cultural institutions, and scientific organisations worldwide.

What makes *Arts at CERN* exceptional is the unique space. Located just outside Geneva, CERN is home to the world's largest particle physics laboratory and the Large Hadron Collider, a 27-km machine that recreates conditions from the universe's inception 13.7 billion years ago. With approximately 17,000 scientists, technologists, and engineers from 680 institutions in 120 countries, CERN is a hub of imagination and inspiration. *Arts at CERN* has inspired numerous exhibitions, performances, and events, showcasing the mutual benefits of collaboration between artists and scientists. Artists gain new perspectives on their work, while scientists explore different approaches to their research, considering the broader implications for humanity, society, and nature. The Collide Residency program has partnered with cities like Linz, Liverpool, Barcelona, and Copenhagen to support artistic research and exploration. This collaboration between CERN and major cultural institutions has established a model for integrating arts, science, and technology. *Arts at CERN* has set a global benchmark for arts-science initiatives, influencing programs all around the world, in Europe, Asia, Latin America, Australia and Africa. It has inspired major initiatives such as the European Commission's STARTS program and the Joint Research Centre's sci-art program. In today's rapidly evolving technological landscape, including advancements in AI, quantum computing, and chip technology, the integration of arts, science, and technology is crucial. *Arts at CERN* exemplifies how leveraging key scientific and technological infrastructures, multidisciplinary talent, and capacity in Europe can drive innovation and foster a collaborative innovation that truly serve the public interest.

Grand Prize
Artistic Exploration

Awarded for artistic exploration and art works where appropriation by the arts has a strong potential to influence or alter the use, deployment, or perception of technology.

Calculating Empires: A Genealogy of Power and Technology, 1500-2025
Kate Crawford, Vladan Joler

How can we understand the entanglement between technology and power today? The technological systems, from AI chatbots to international border controls, are increasingly automated and opaque. If the world is to address the current challenges of the climate crisis, hallucinating AI systems, and war, we need to understand how these processes are interwoven.

Calculating Empires charts the technological present by depicting how power and technology have been intertwined since 1500. It is a codex of technology and power that shows how echoes of empires past resonate in today's technology companies. With thousands of individual drawings and texts, Kate Crawford and Vladan Joler visualize these major shifts in an intricate visual manifesto about the way empires have used technology to centralize and consolidate their power. The vast diagrammatic diptych draws audiences into a dark passage to study on one wall the histories of communication and computation, while the opposite wall addresses systems of classification and control. Read together, these maps illuminate technical and social structures that co-evolved over centuries. By seeing how past powers have calculated, we can begin to calculate the costs of contemporary empires. *Calculating Empires* thus gives audiences a detailed visual narrative about the relationship between humans, ecologies, and technologies.

It traces the ways that technology and power have been entwined over five centuries, through industrialization, imperialism, and automation. It shows how practices of colonialism, militarization, and enclosure operate today and how they might be unwound. It establishes itself as a necessary corrective to the current short-termism in technology criticism and art, which is frequently focused on the most recent spectacles and devices, at the expense of deeper historical and political shifts. *Calculating Empires* challenges us to redefine our relationship with current socio-technical structures. By asking how we got where we are today, we can (re-)consider where we might be going.

Honorary Mentions

The Echinoidea Future—Adriatic Sensing
Robertina Šebjanič

While the majority of Europeans have no direct experience with the oceans and seas, ocean life knows far more about us than we do about it. According to scientific studies, there is an understanding that humans are having an extremely negative impact on the oceans, from direct sound and chemical pollution to indirect influence through climate change. While some of these insights stem from the use of organisms such as sea urchins as pollution indicators, they primarily manifest as scientific data too abstract for the general public. *The Echinoidea Future—Adriatic Sensing* project was developed even further in the STARTS4Water collaboration between the artist, ecologists, cultural organizations, and sea urchins—not as bioindicators but as actual commentators. Such collaboration overcame anthropocentric and domain-based research practices and brings the agency of an organism that inhabits a human-impacted environment directly to the public. Artwork, therefore, provides not only a medium for sea urchins to tell their story, but is an actual catalyst for our environmental empathy, which is an essential element of future environmental literacy.

How (not) to get hit by a self-driving car
Tomo Kihara, Daniel Coppen

The ever-accelerating development of AI and the expansion of its services are making our lives more convenient. However, they also make the use of data and technology in our society and culture invisible to us. *How (not) to get hit by a self-driving car* makes the vision system in cars visible, and even reveals the way the vision system's data is trained and generated. Designed as a game, it is accessible to small children and wheelchair users, and reveals how this AI model is not always able to differentiate between its players. It also offers a wide range of users the opportunity to teach the AI model as well. The exhibition of this project at various venues will offer opportunities for new collaborations between 'citizens to improve their literacy where AI has become ubiquitous' and 'AI models to learn diversity in the world.' And, in turn, this could be a catalyst that inspires citizens to propose and establish the rules of digital rights in AI for the future.

Korallysis
Gilberto Esparza

For millions of years coral reefs have adapted to and survived in their environments due to their autonomous systems, and they serve as important ecosystems for surrounding organisms. Humans, on the other hand, are known for putting these systems in danger. So what approach is needed for us to jump into the umwelt of coral reefs? *Korallysis* is a hybrid organism and technological device which, through electrolysis of the minerals in seawater, creates calcium carbonate that helps the growth of coral. This device is equipped with motion elements that generate electricity from the ocean's currents and waves. Furthermore, *Korallysis* proposed an interdisciplinary space for oceanographers, biologists, material engineers, and biotechnologists, where they may create opportunities for local community-building and cultural events including artists, and citizen dialogues and engagement in the arts. This project itself serves as the infrastructure that encourages coexistence and mutually supportive relationships among coral reefs. *Korallysis,* as a hybrid organism, can be considered a new inhabitant of the coral umwelt that also invites humans to participate in their ecosystem.

Mapping Uncertain Landscape: The Satellite
Sofia Isupova

It matters what is mapped, how it is mapped, and why. While the majority of satellite and environmental data is today used for remote land use and governance, here the artist explores the opposite— placing herself into the unaccusable land devastated by war. *Mapping Uncertain Landscape: The Satellite* is critical cartographic work, directing its gaze to the land change caused by war, documenting changes in forests, fields, cities, and infrastructures in a way they matter to the artist as an affected individual. Such critical cartographic practice helps individuals as well as whole displaced communities to deal with ongoing trauma, while also remembering and healing their relation to the land. Satellite technologies here become an infrastructure of care, and not of power, demonstrating the societal relevance of earth observation science and technologies.

Maria CHOIR
Maria Arnal Dimas

Music has historically been an integral part of our societies, shaping one another in the most creative ways. As we are today confronted with one of the most ambiguous technologies, AI, music provides an opportunity to culturalize its influence on society. *Maria CHOIR* musical installation is an example of a human-AI built as a shared experience of 11,000 participants contributing their voice to one of the largest choirs performing at a single event. Such a process demonstrated an AI model-learning process as a public event, providing insight into otherwise mystifying processes, with researchers often claiming that even they don't understand how AI learns and functions. Carrying out research and the development of new technologies in public enhances the societal relevance of these technologies. And though this project sets a new standard for innovative collaborations, it also spotlights the resources required, such as a supercomputing center, a creative coding collective, and a cultural platform.

METABOLICA
Thomas Feuerstein

With *METABOLICA,* the Austrian artist Thomas Feuerstein tells a story about life cycles that truly involve transdisciplinary processes in nature, economy, politics, art, and science. The core theme and artistic research is about metabolic processes, made from cultivated algae using bacteria and a 3D printer. Feuerstein, who describes himself as a theorizing media artist, generally uses the method of "conceptual narration" in his works, which combines art, architecture, philosophy, and literature with economics, politics, and technology. In five chapters, these complex installation settings tell a story of change from the industrial revolution to the present and future, from whaling and petro-modernity to current and future scenarios of biochemistry and wastewater research. The metabolism of microorganisms is a central theme, as not only is a new material for sculptures produced and partially degraded, but new forms and aesthetics are created.

P2P
Eva & Franco Mattes

P2P redefines art by creating an artist-run server distributing artworks via Torrents through a peer-to-peer network. Housed in a sculpture resembling a data center, it highlights the physicality of the internet, often obscured by metaphors like "the cloud." This democratizes access to data and art by using the museum's infrastructure to seed and download artworks, turning the exhibition space into a functional peer-to-peer network. Despite its minimalistic presence, the installation facilitates widespread access to art in the digital and AI-driven era. Inspired by the book *Server Manifesto*, edited by architecture critic Niklas Maak, and ideas from architect Rem Koolhaas and digital pioneer Francesca Bria, data centers are understood as democratic architectures and data as digital commons. It challenges the hidden nature of digital infrastructures, emphasizing their environmental impact and energy consumption. *P2P* invites people to join the network and experience a virtual exhibition featuring works from artists and collectives like Olia Lialina, Jon Rafman, and Do Not Research, exploring different models of online networking—artist-run, distributed, DIY. *P2P* highlights the potential of art to reflect on the need to democratize technology, experimenting with community owned infrastructures for artistic expression and collaborative digital production. *P2P* is a case study in alternative models of networking and in rethinking the current centralized and extractive internet.

SELF-CARE
Lyndsey Walsh

As genetic testing and diagnosis is made readily available, what can we do to overcome the gaze and surveillance of medicine, and care for the fears and bonds that families experience in the face of bodily trauma? *SELF-CARE* is based on the artist's personal experiences and physical exploration after learning of their mother's breast cancer diagnosis and subsequent diagnosis of the hereditary BRCA1 gene. The wearable chest binder is specifically designed to house living BRCA1 cancer cell lines and allows the wearer to care and treat it before it turns malignant in the body. Consisting of this original device, developed with the aid of experimental biophysics, and conversations with the artist's family, the work reexamines the politics surrounding the identity of the so-called "female body" under advanced medical surveillance. It could be said that *SELF-CARE* allows us to liberate our bodies from social, sexual, and reproductive expectations and, instead, encourages us to take care of our bodies.

The Waterworks of Money
Carlijn Kingma

Although money plays a key role in everyone's lives, the inner workings of the monetary and financial system are a mystery to most. *The Waterworks of Money* visualizes the flow of money through society through metaphors, maps, and animations, and explores options for improving the money system in the digital age. Today, Europe is facing the challenge of inequality. Many Europeans are dealing with a cost of living crisis while financial instability remains an ongoing threat. At the same time, the European economy needs to become more sustainable and resilient. Meanwhile, the digitalization of our economy has created new opportunities to redesign the current money system. These challenges can, however, not be seen in isolation from the architecture of the monetary system. Designing this system—and the laws and institutions that govern it—is ultimately a democratic task. In practice, however, there is a major obstacle impeding the democratic process: financial illiteracy. By making the world of money understandable, *The Waterworks of Money* assists citizens in developing their own vocabulary to participate in the debate about the future of money.

VRJ Palestine
Nisreen Zahda

The *VRJ Palestine* (Virtual Reality Journey to pre-Nakba Palestine) project, initiated by Nisreen Zahda in 2020, represents a groundbreaking endeavor in the virtual reconstruction of Palestinian villages destroyed during the Nakba in 1948. This project employs advanced 3D modeling and real-time rendering software to recreate the spatial structures and memories of these villages, offering an engaging and immersive experience for the public. Among the notable works of VRJ Palestine are the "Nakba Timeline Map," a digital map that documents the systematic depopulation, ethnic cleansing, and destruction of cities and villages during the Nakba, and "A Virtual Return Journey to Destroyed Villages of Tantura, Hittin, and Zir'in." Through detailed photographic and archival research, these reconstructions bring new life to erased places. The fishing village of Zir'in and the historic village of Hittin, where Saladin famously defeated the Crusaders in 1187, are vividly recreated, preserving their rich histories. Additionally, *VRJ Palestine* pays homage to the victims of the Tantura massacre, a tragic event that the Israeli state continues to deny despite compelling evidence presented in the documentary *Tantura* by Israeli director Alon Schwartz. *VRJ Palestine* is a vital and innovative tool for documenting and presenting the Palestinian narrative. By virtually reconstructing over 400 destroyed or depopulated villages from the 1948 war, the project ensures that the memories and histories of these places are preserved and accessible. It allows people to engage with and become part of these reconstructed spaces, fostering a deeper understanding and connection to Palestinian heritage. The *VRJ Palestine* project presents a visionary approach and dedication to preserving Palestinian history through the powerful medium of virtual reality. Its contributions are invaluable in the ongoing effort to document and share the rich cultural heritage of Palestine with the world.

Nominations

AUTOPOIESIS
ATELIER-E (DE)

Bibliokepos
Nomad Garden (ES)

Botto
Botto Project (The internet)

Clay PCB
Eco-Feminist Decolonial Hardware
Patrícia J. Reis (PT/AT), Stefanie Wuschitz (AT)

Destination Earth
Salomé Bazin (FR)

FORMATA
ЯЯОТО-ALIEИ ПЯОJECT (JP)

Godmode Epochs
dmstfctn (UK)

GR-AI-N
Marielena Papandreou (GR)

Low Carbon Chinatown
Ling Tan (SG/UK)

Narrative Futures: Panchatantra Fables meet Personal Primer
Daniel Devatman Hromada (SK),
DigiEduBerlin (M)

Nishikigoi NFT
Toshi (JP)

Prometheus Firebringer
Annie Dorsen (US)

Revolution Refridge
Rojava Center for Democratic Technologies (SY) and Dani Ploeger (NL)

The Russian Airstrike on the Mariupol Drama Theater
The Center for Spatial Technologies (UA)

Sentient Clit: the Pussification of BioTech
Jiabao Li (CN), WhiteFeather Hunter (CA)

Soft Collision
Anna Schaeffner (FR)

Solar Protocol
Tega Brain, Alex Nathanson, and Benedetta Piantella (M)

The Urban Biotope
Vasily Sitnikov (RU)

Calculating Empires
A Genealogy of Power and Technology, 1500-2025

Kate Crawford, Vladan Joler

Calculating Empires is a large-scale visual manifesto by Kate Crawford and Vladan Joler that critically engages with the relationship between technology and power over five centuries. By merging research and design, science and art, Joler and Crawford go beyond the current spectacles of artificial intelligence to ask how we got here—and consider where we might be going. This vast diagram follows the imperial pathways of power since 1500 across many systems—colonialism, militarization, and automation—to show how they still subjugate and how they might be unwound. By illustrating this history, *Calculating Empires* charts a new way of seeing our technological present by immersing us in the past, from the birth of European empires to the technology companies of today.

Spanning more than twenty-four meters in length and three meters in height, *Calculating Empires* is designed as a diptych. One half focuses on the changing spectrum of communication devices, infrastructures, and computational architectures of algorithms and hardware. The other half tells the story of control and classification across dozens of domains: from time to education, bodies to biometrics, policing to prisons, the biosphere to the astrosphere, and a multitude of military systems. Read together, these maps visualize how technical and social structures co-evolved over centuries, with hundreds of handcrafted illustrations and texts that draw relationships between devices, ideas, and infrastructures.

Calculating Empires premiered at an exhibition of Crawford and Joler's work at Fondazione Prada in Milan in November 2023, and then moved to Berlin as part of a group show called *Poetics of Encryption* at the KW Institute for Contemporary Art.

Like their previous work, *Anatomy of an AI System, Calculating Empires* is a research-driven detailed visual narrative about the relationship between humans, ecologies, and technologies. But where *Anatomy* was mapping out space, *Calculating Empires* is about time. It offers an alternative perspective to the current short-termism in technology criticism and art, which is frequently focused on the most recent spectacles and devices at the expense of deeper historical and political shifts.

*Calculating Empire*s begins in 1500, when global networks—both cultural and mercantile—began to take shape. New trade routes meant the expansion of European empires. Advances in shipping and navigational instruments enabled rapid annexation of lands and annihilation of Indigenous populations via new viruses, drugs, and weapons. The Gutenberg Press reorganized information power and laid the groundwork for a political and cultural transformation. New scientific instruments and calculation systems were developed. The meticulous cataloguing and privatization of land, animals, plants, and space commenced a layered agenda of colonization that expanded over hundreds of years. These practices of past empires are now echoed in the highly concentrated technology and military industries of the 21st century.

In a time of widespread automated image generation and text production, their methods were painstakingly manual. Over the four years of making this

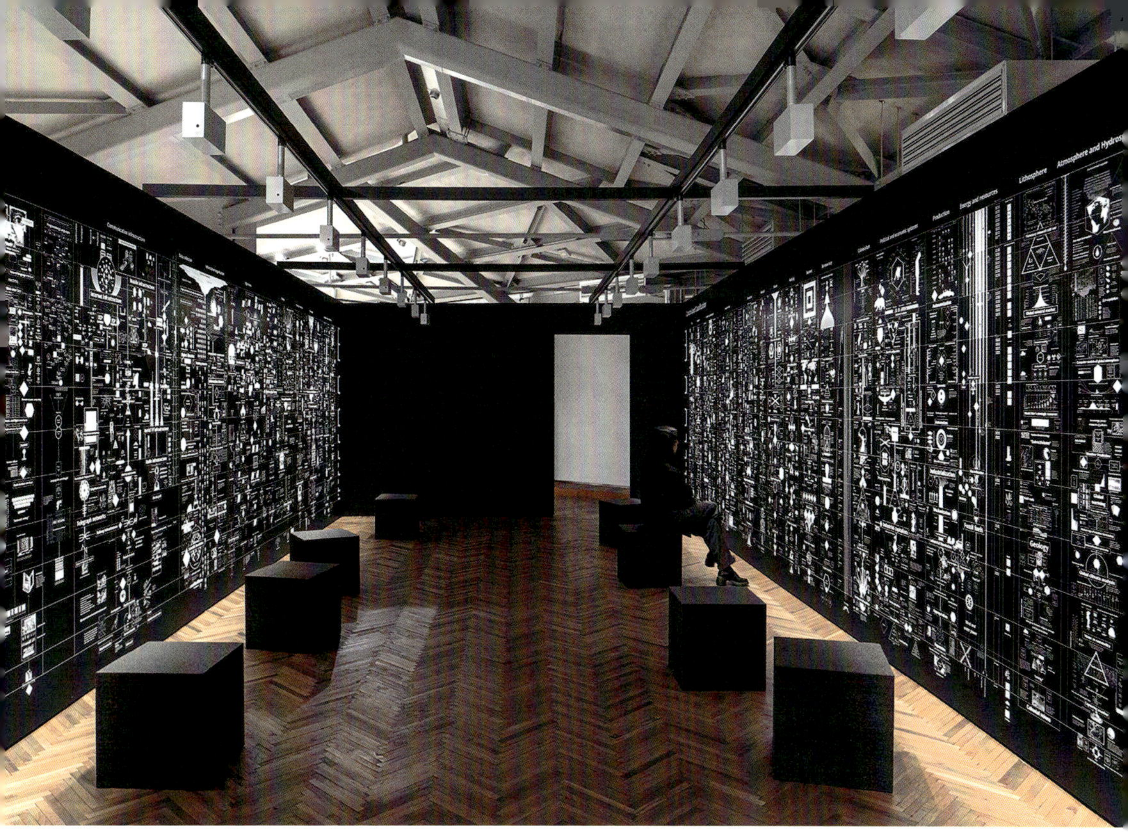

Exhibition view of *Calculating Empires*, Kate Crawford and Vladan Joler
Osservatorio Fondazione Prada, Milan, Photo: Piercarlo Quecchia—DSL Studio

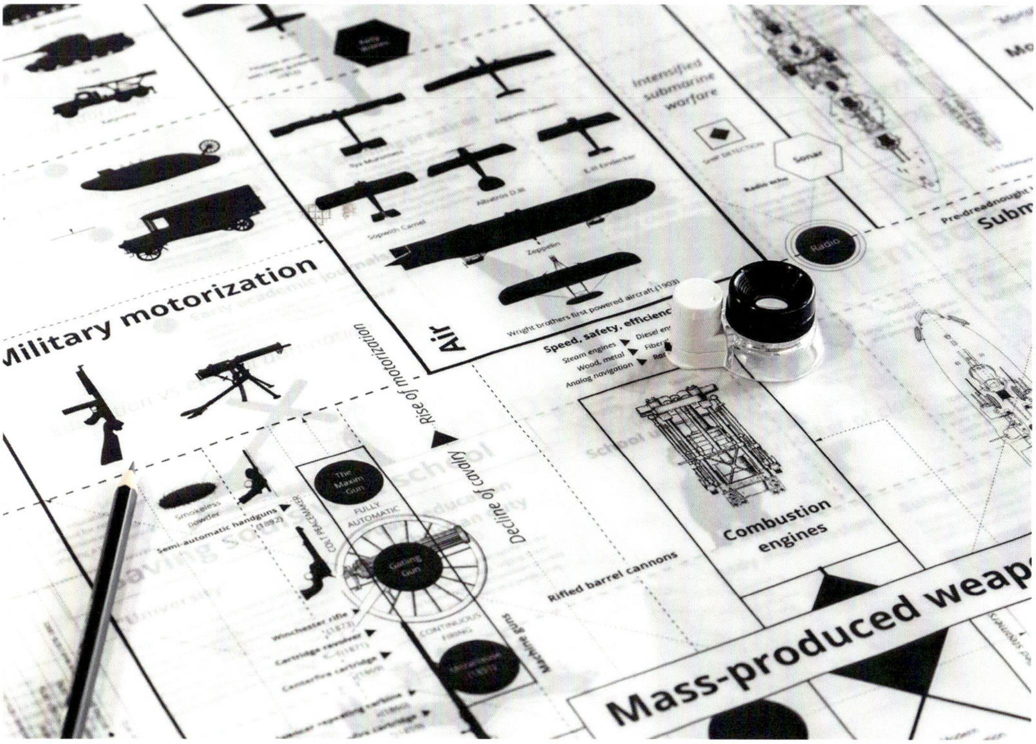

Exhibition view of *Calculating Empires*, Kate Crawford and Vladan Joler
Osservatorio Fondazione Prada, Milan, Photo: Piercarlo Quecchia—DSL Studio

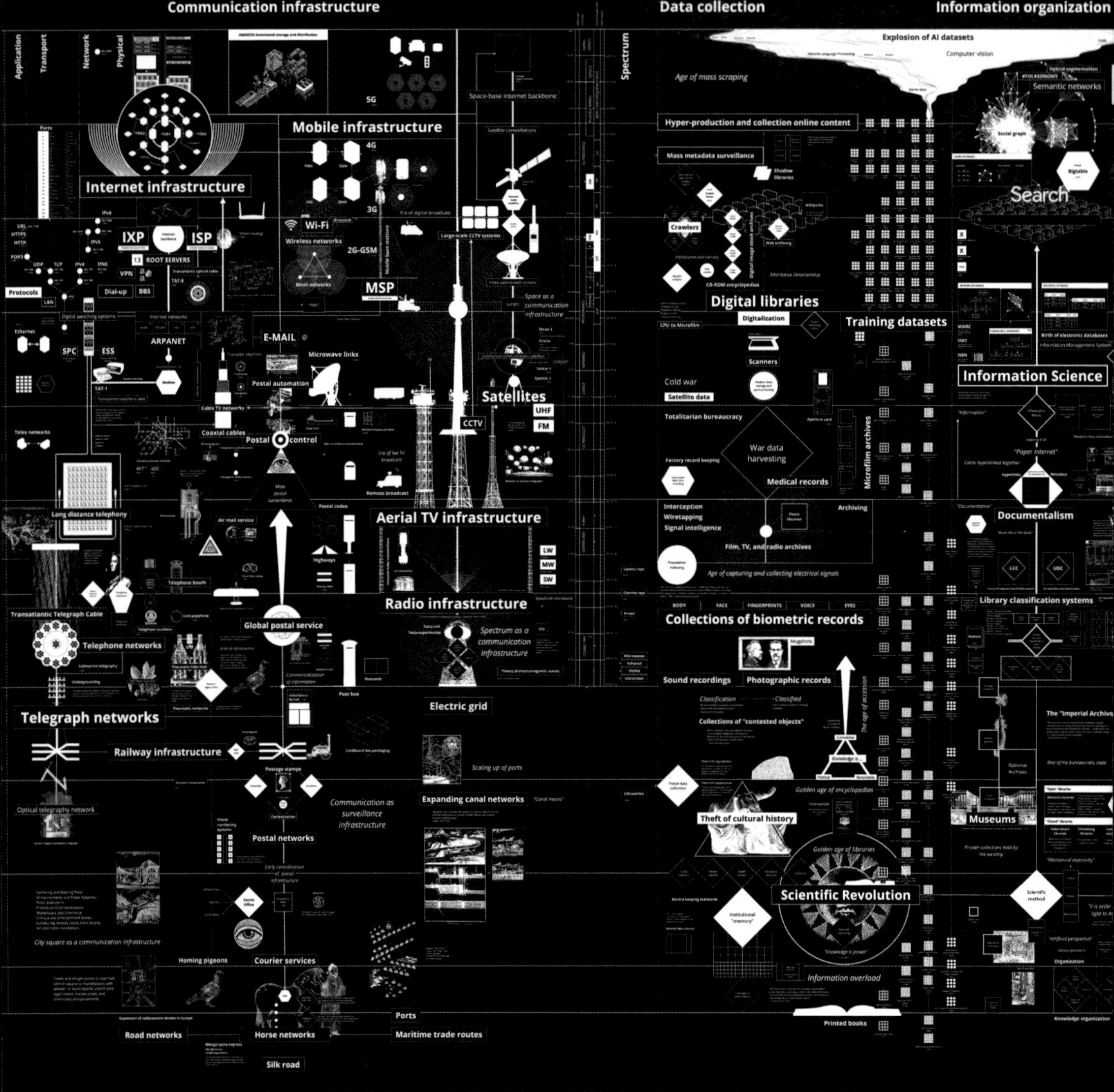

Calculating Empires (detail), Kate Crawford and Vladan Joler (2023), Courtesy of the artists

map together, and creating thousands of short texts and illustrations, they slowly expanded, unlearned, revised, and reconsidered the traditional account of technological history. They returned to the painful stories of upheavals and removals, massacres and enclosures that are the recurring stories of calculation and empire. The work resists telling a totalizing history, but instead offers a visual genealogy: how to calculate the technological present through the lens of the past.

The large-scale diagrams are accompanied by two handmade volumes. Visitors are invited to read, revise, and annotate them with their own accounts of history. At each location where this work will be shown, the books will be different: reflecting the comments, stories, and experiences of the place it was installed.

https://u.aec.at/DD527558

S+T+ARTS Prize'24
Grand Prize—Artistic Exploration

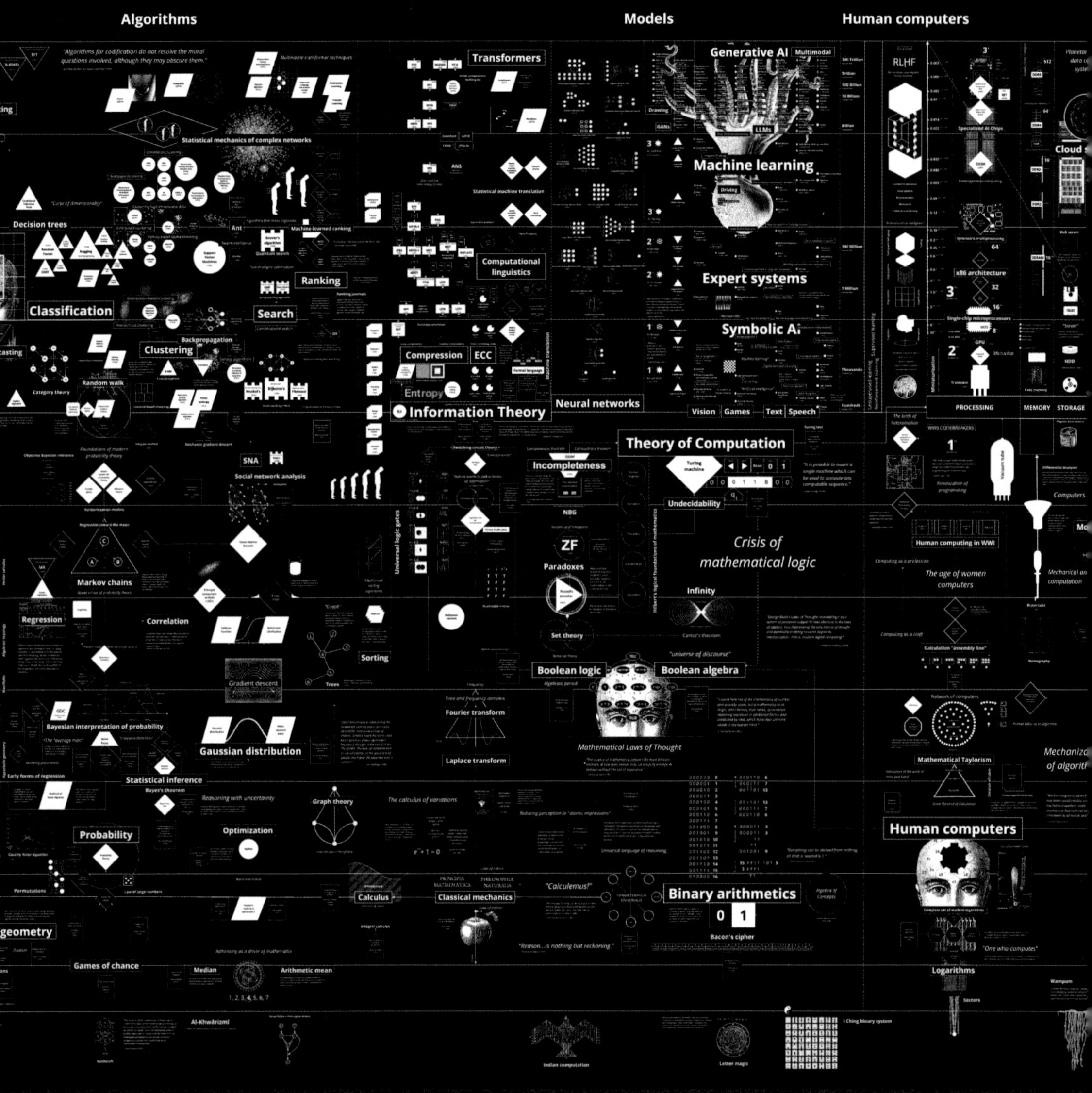

Professor Kate Crawford (US) is a leading scholar of the impacts of artificial intelligence. She is a professor at USC in Los Angeles, a senior principal researcher at MSR New York, and the inaugural chair of AI and Justice at the École Normale Supérieure. Her book *Atlas of AI* won multiple awards, was named a book of the year by *Science* and the *Financial Times*, and is translated into 12 languages. She leads the *Knowing Machines* project, an international research collaboration on the foundations of AI. Her artworks have been acquired by museums such as MoMA and the V&A, and received the Aryton Prize. Kate was named by *TIME* magazine's TIME100 as one of the most influential people in AI. Professor Dr. Vladan Joler (RS) is an academic, researcher, and artist whose work blends data investigations, critical cartography, investigative journalism, and data visualization. He is SHARE Foundation co-founder and professor at the New Media Department of the University of Novi Sad. Vladan Joler's work is in the permanent collections of the Museum of Modern Art (MoMA), the V&A Museum, and the Design Museum in London, and also in the permanent exhibition of the Ars Electronica Center. His work has been exhibited in more than a hundred international exhibitions worldwide.

Arts at CERN

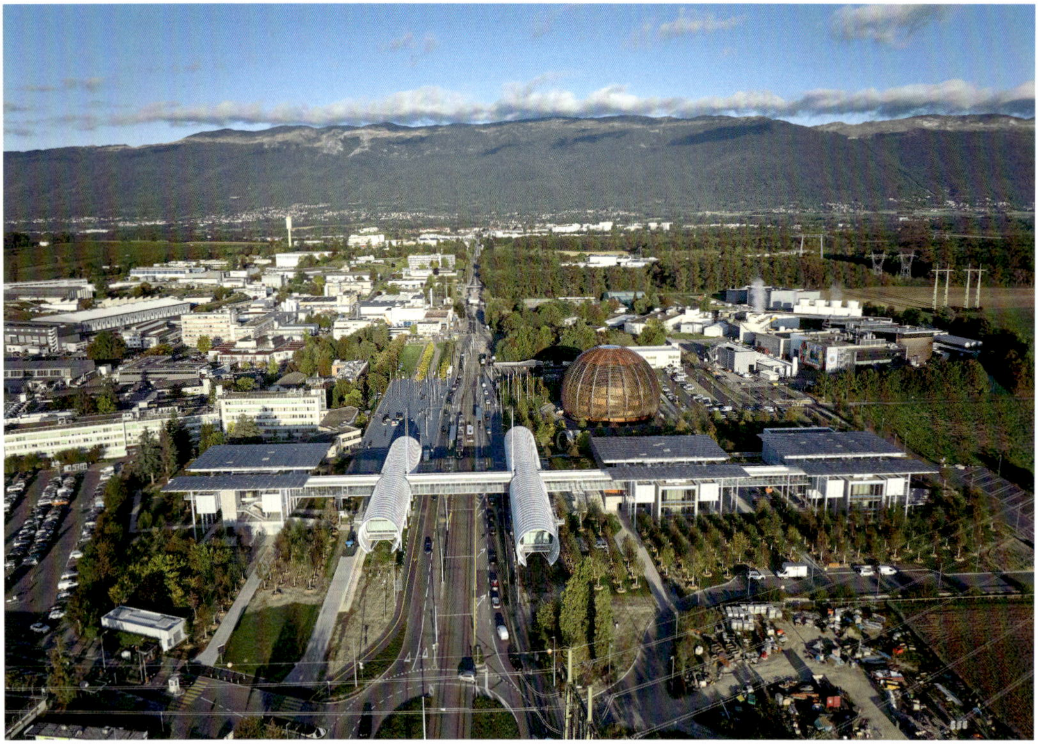

Aerial view of CERN, Geneva, 2024. Photo: Maximilien Brice. Courtesy CERN

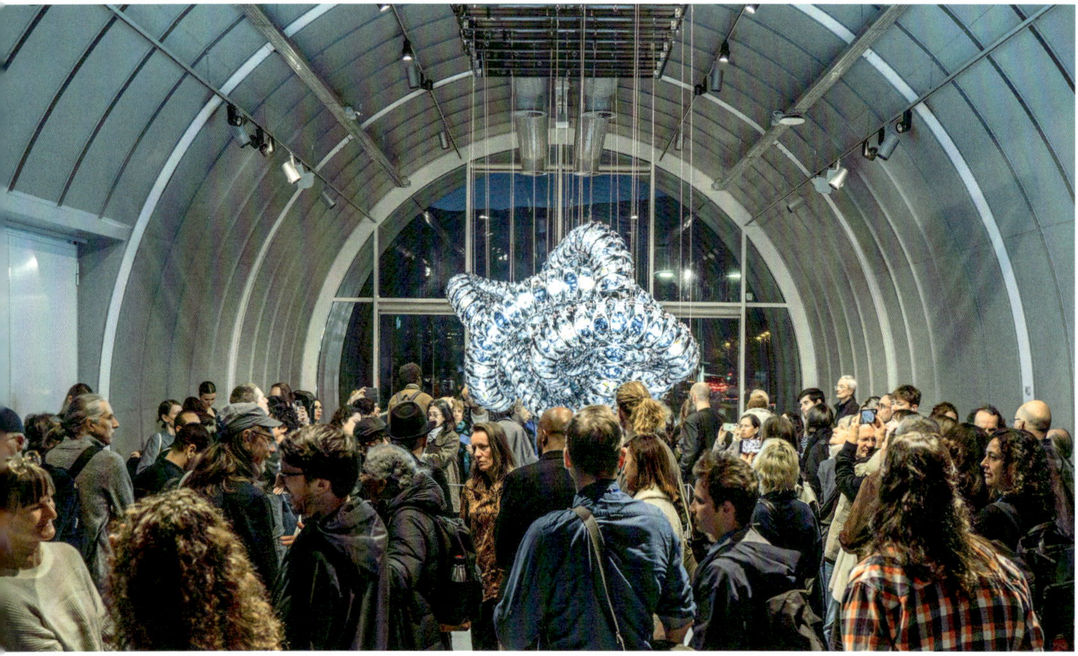

Visitors in the exhibition "Exploring the Unknown," CERN Science Gateway, 2024. Photo: Noemí Carabán. Courtesy CERN

S+T+ARTS Prize'24
Grand Prize—Innovative Collaboration

Arts at CERN is the arts program of CERN, the European Laboratory for Particle Physics in Geneva, Switzerland. Since 2012, when the first artist in residence arrived, we invite artists to experience how physicists and engineers use the world's largest and most complex scientific instruments to explore the big questions about the Universe. Arts at CERN fosters meaningful exchanges between artists and scientists, connecting the international cultural community through science and research.

Since its foundation in 1954, CERN has been a place of inspiration for artists from different disciplines and backgrounds. Before the arts program was launched, renowned artists were drawn to the laboratory for its groundbreaking research and unique collaborative environment. As early as 1972, James Lee Byars became the first artist to visit the CERN laboratory, and he spent his time exploring the technical sites and facilities, as well as discussing ideas with physicists like John Bell. Coincidentally, Bell's theorem, which laid the foundations for the modern field of quantum-information science, was being tested experimentally while Byars was there. Other artists such as Mariko Mori, Gianni Motti, Cerith Wyn Evans, John Berger, and Anselm Kiefer were also attracted to CERN in the years that preceded the foundation of *Arts at CERN*.

Arts at CERN's work comprises a broad range of programs that allow this dialogue with scientists and the CERN community to take place in a significant way; research-led artist residencies, art commissions for artists who have spent time at CERN, and exhibitions and events, organized and structured in tight collaboration with cultural and scientific institutions that share our values around the world. Since 2023, events and exhibitions are also devised at the recently inaugurated CERN Science Gateway, a science centre designed by architect Renzo Piano.

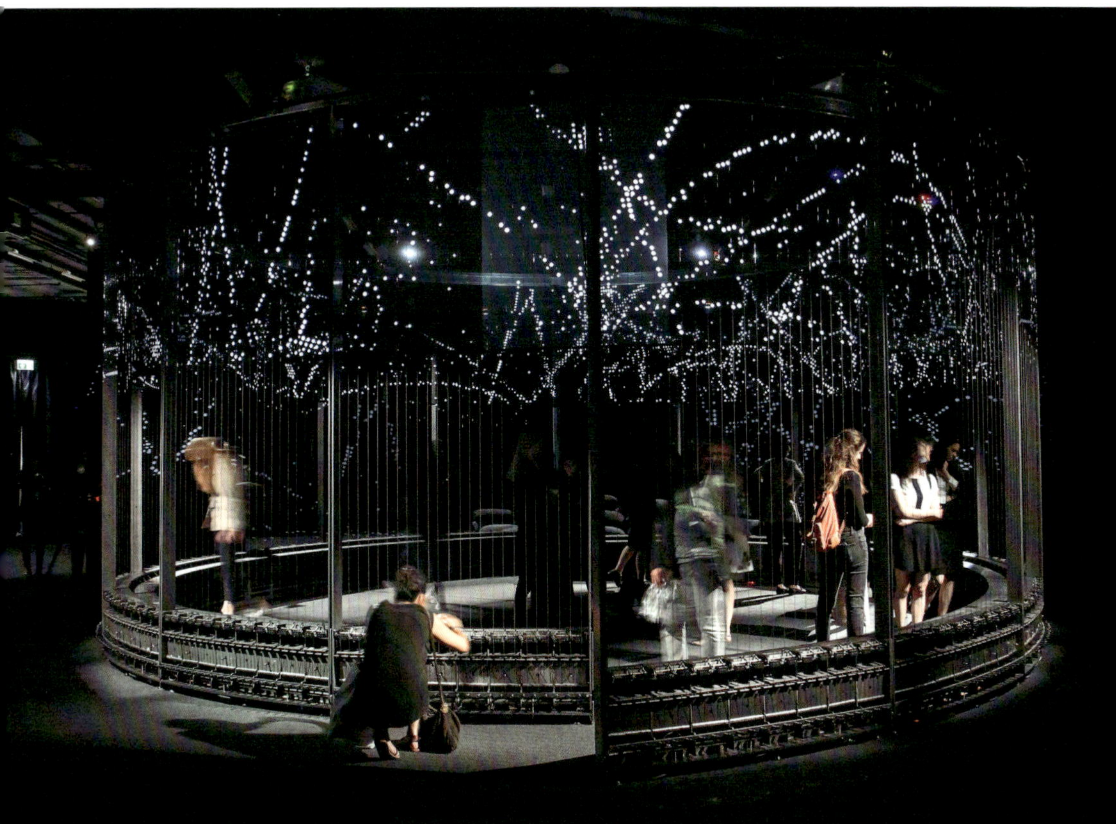

Semiconductor, HALO, 2018. Installation view, Art Basel, Basel, 2018.
Commissioned by Audemars Piguet and curated by Mónica Bello. Photo: Claudia Marcelloni. Courtesy CERN

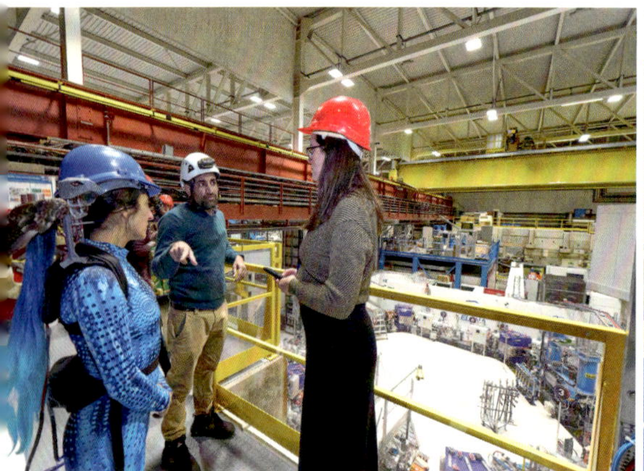

Artist Patricia Domínguez and her collaborator Claudia Velasquez with experimental physicist Gunn Khatri at the Antimatter Factory during the filming of an art commission. Photo: Marina Cavazza. Courtesy CERN

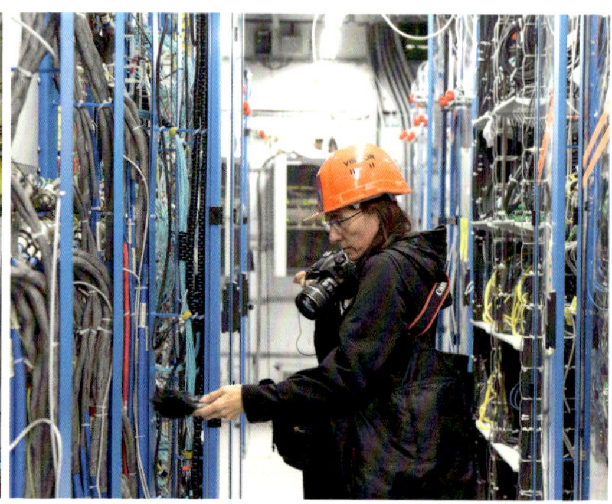

Sound artist Antye Greie-Ripatti (aka AGF or Poemproducer) at the CMS Experiment during her residency at Arts at CERN. Photo: Sophia Bennett. Courtesy CERN

Our residency programs form the core of our initiatives, enabling the interaction between artists and scientists within the laboratory's context. CERN is the largest particle physics laboratory in the world, home of the Large Hadron Collider, and most artists who visit us will never have experienced a place like it before. Upon entering the laboratory, it becomes immediately apparent that comprehending the breadth of experiments, their scale and function, and the theoretical models that represent our world in mathematical language will not be straightforward. By engaging directly with fundamental science, we believe that artists can inform their practice with new lines of questioning on the methods and tools of science, and its definition of nature. Furthermore, at CERN, artists have the opportunity to view their work through the disciplines of others.

Over 200 artists have participated in residencies, benefiting from being part of CERN's scientific community of over 15,000 scientists, engineers, and staff. Artists are selected through open calls followed by an evaluation process. Each year, as many as 900 applications from over 90 different countries are received. The residencies are aimed at artists with a distinct interest in the intersection of art, science, and technology, who wish to immerse themselves in the laboratory's vibrant environment and engage with the diverse scientific community. Selected artists are invited to join a fully funded residency, lasting from two weeks to a maximum of two months.

Over 35 new artworks have been supported since 2018. Following the residencies at the laboratory, the art commissions program enable artists to extend their research and exploration with the support of scientific partners and experiments. These productions are showcased in museums worldwide, including pieces by international artists like James Bridle, Tania Candiani, Chloé Delarue, Ryoji Ikeda, Yunchul Kim, Haroon Mirza, Richard Mosse, Mariele Neudecker, Mika Rottenberg, Leslie Thornton, and Julius von Bismarck.

By providing access and support, *Arts at CERN* explores the cultural significance of fundamental research. The program seeks artists' reflections on the implications of science and technology, offering spaces for artistic dialogue with science and deepening the connection with the CERN community. It also explores the potential of collaboration across disciplinary boundaries and the engagement with the social fabric of science, the historical narratives, or the aspects that make CERN a unique place for artistic enquiry.

Arts at CERN is supported by the CERN & Society Foundation.

https://u.aec.at/78419236

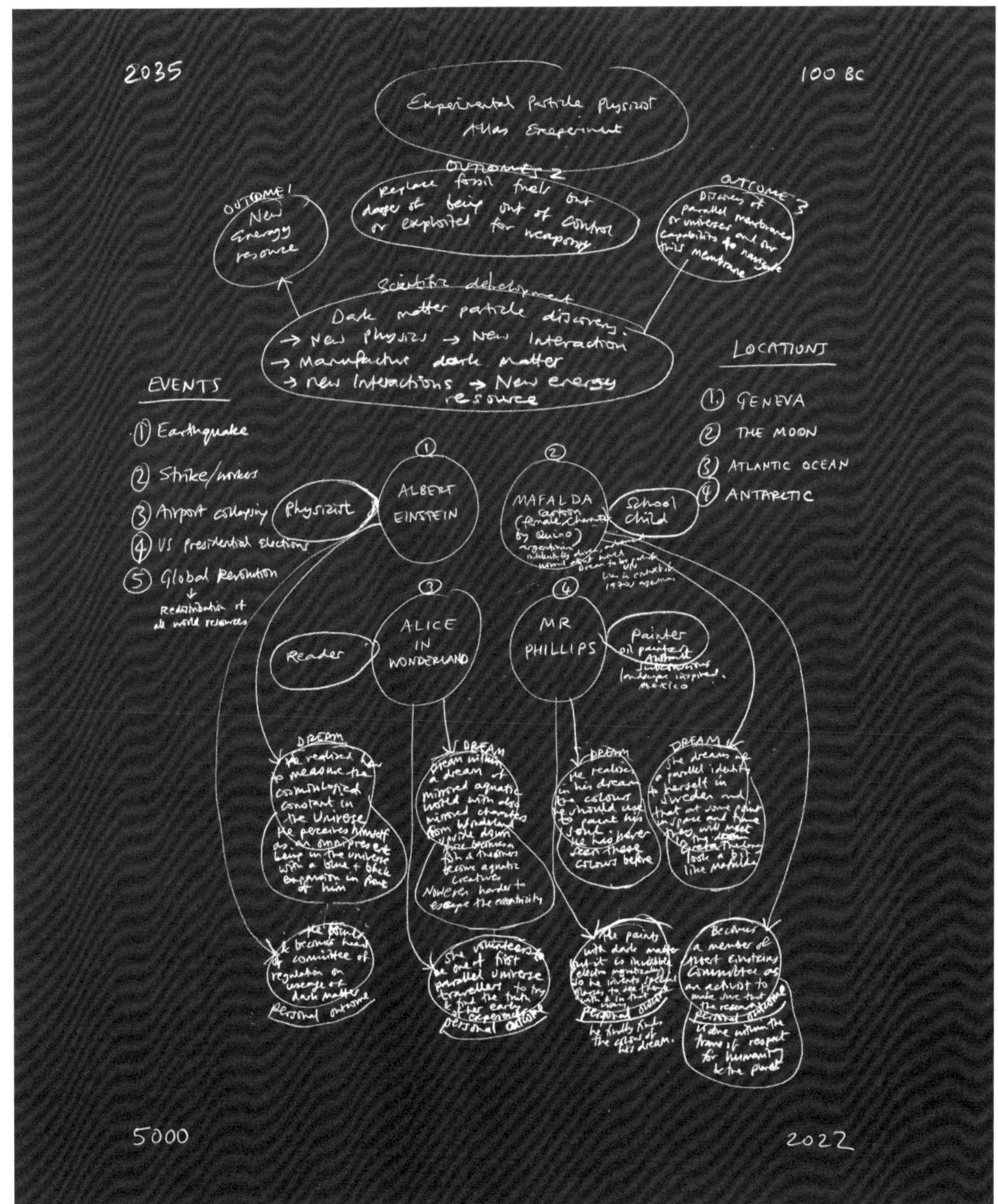

Suzanne Treister, Scientific Dreaming, 2022.
Plot diagram by Tamara Vázquez Schröder, experimental physicist at CERN.

Arts at CERN fosters dialogue between art and physics. Artists across all creative disciplines are invited to the laboratory to experience the way the big questions about our universe are pursued by fundamental science. Our vision is to inspire significant exchanges between artists and scientists and to participate in an international cultural community eager to connect with CERN. **Mónica Bello** (ES) is a curator and art historian, and Head of Arts at CERN. In this pivotal role, she oversees the laboratory's diverse art initiatives, directing the conception and implementation of various artistic programs, including art residencies, commissions, and exhibitions. In her capacity, she develops international partnerships with cultural and scientific institutions, promoting a dynamic and interdisciplinary approach to art and science.

The Echinoidea Future— Adriatic Sensing

Robertina Šebjanič

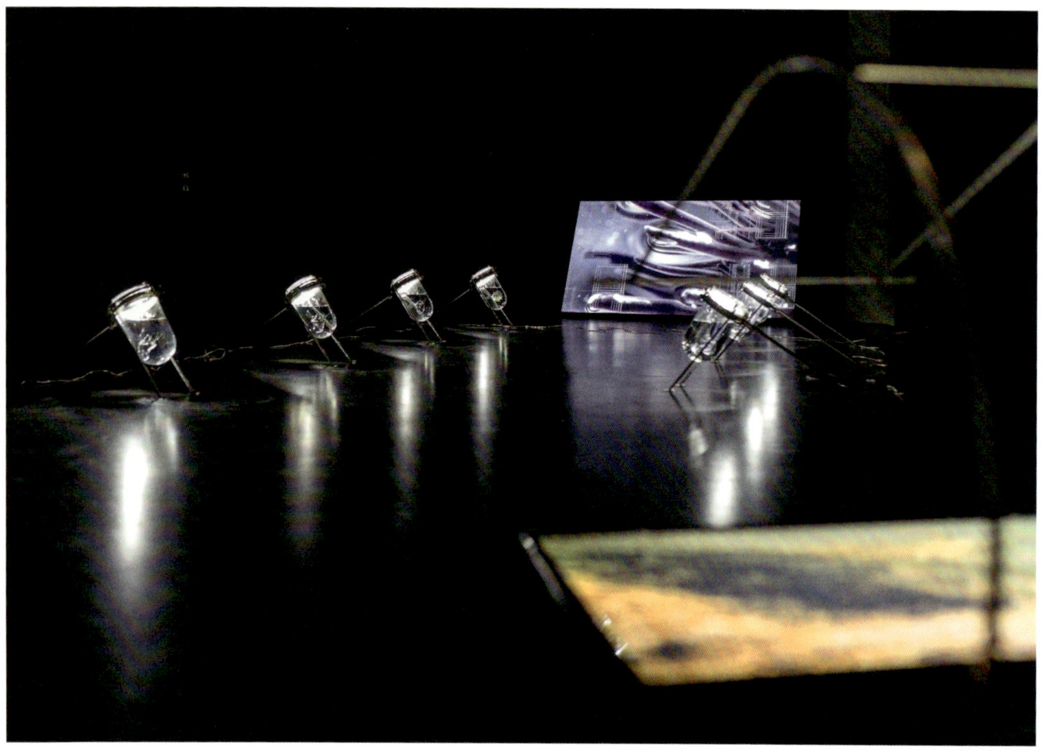

Echinoidea Future—Adriatic Sensing explores the biogeological and morphological conditions impacting the sea urchin habitat. Anthropogenic liquid waste threatens their environment, leading to low oxygen levels in seawater. The study focuses on dissolved oxygen flux in coastal areas, revealing pollution's profound impact on biodiversity. The ongoing dialogue prompts reflection on oceanic changes, transcending ecological concerns to address the geopolitical dimensions of the Adriatic coast.

Artist Robertina Šebjanič, supported by experts Tanja Minarik, Filip Grgurević, and Gjino Šutić, and science advisors Dr. A. Malej, Dr. M. Ličer, Dr. M. Hure, and Dr. V. Kozul, integrates art, technology, and science in this coastal exploration. Sea urchins, as pollution indicators, are vital herbivorous grazers that influence benthic communities. Experiments exposing them to stressors inform the creation of glass blown sculptures, visually representing microscopic research.

The art installation juxtaposes experimental setups with synchronized screens displaying three decades of environmental big data from the EU Copernicus platform. This data, transformed by artificial intelligence, illustrates the South Adriatic Sea's ecological parameters (temperature, pH, oxygen, and salinity fluctuations). The use of glass blown sculptures and the artistic representation of microscopic research align with the cultural heritage in arts and craftsmanship. Experiments into the foreground enrich the artwork's multi-dimensional narrative.

S+T+ARTS Prize'24
Honorary Mention

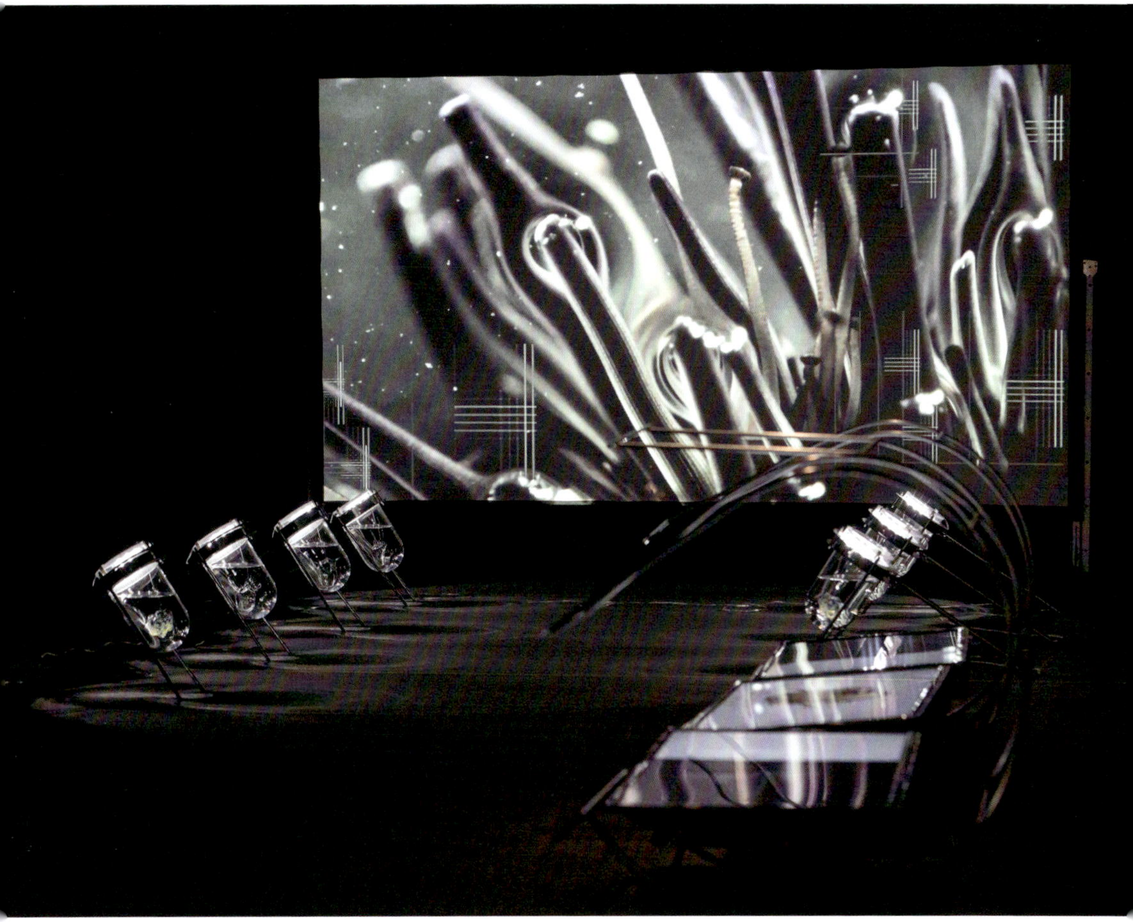

This interdisciplinary project not only unveils ecological challenges but also emphasizes the need for collective responsibility in preserving the delicate balance of our oceans.
Exploring the stressors of the local/global human footprint, the project demonstrates the resilience of the aquatic species, *Echinoidea future—Adriatic sensing* acts as an activation of (sy)(e)mpathia (sympathy and empathy).

Artist: Robertina Šebjanič
Production: UR Institute in the frame of STARTS4WATER (S+T+ARTS), 2021/2022
Co-production: Zavod Sektor, Zavod Studio Aquatocene
Production team: Ivanka Pasalic, David Drolc, Tanja Minarik, Miha Godec, Jakob Grčman
Scientific advisory: Dr. Alenka Malej, Dr. Matjaž Ličer, Gjino Šutić, Filip Grgurević

https://u.aec.at/9DE38F17

Robertina Šebjanič (SI) is an artist/researcher whose work explores the biological, (geo)political, and cultural realities of aquatic environments and the impact of humanity on other organisms. In her analysis of the Anthropocene and its theoretical framework, the artist uses the terms "aquatocene" and "aquaforming" to refer to the human impact on aquatic environments. Her works received awards and nominations at Prix Ars Electronica, Starts Prize, Falling Walls, and Re:Humanism among others.

How (not) to get hit by a self-driving car

Tomo Kihara, Daniel Coppen

How (not) to get hit by a self-driving car is a game installation that challenges people to cross the street without being detected by an AI. In the experience, players see themselves augmented on a large screen at the end of a playing field, simulating the perspective of an AI-powered camera of a self-driving car. Marking each player is a percentage indicating the confidence at which the system sees them as a pedestrian, and if exceeded beyond a certain limit, the player will lose. So to win, players must figure out how to cleverly disguise themselves to reach the goal without being detected. Successfully winning the game underscores a chilling possibility: in a real-world scenario, such invisibility to a similar self-driving AI system could result in a tragic collision.

Each player's win generates edge case data that exposes the inability of the algorithm to detect all walks of life, highlighting the hidden biases and flaws embedded in these systems. For example, failing to detect small children or wheelchair users. However, it is up to the players to decide whether to use the data to train the AI or not. Upon victory, players are given the choice to either opt-in their anonymized gameplay footage to improve the AI models, or immediately delete the data. This poses the question of whether people are willing to trade their data for potentially safer autonomous driving technologies, or if they would rather remain invisible, despite the implied risks of inaccurate systems in the future.

The game highlights the problem of geographical bias in AI data collection, where most of the data originates from specific locations, particularly California. This limited approach fails to capture the diverse dynamics of urban settings, for example, how a child plays on the streets of Tokyo. To tackle this issue, the project is making efforts to engage a wider range of global demographics by organizing exhibitions from the UK to Japan, with the goal of attracting a broader audience.

Music: Plot Generica
Support: Saki Maruyama (Playfool)
Videography:
Jon Aitken, Playable City Bristol July 2023
Jack Offord, Playable City Bristol July 2023
Jacob Gibbins, Playable City Bristol July 2023
Daniel Coppen, Playfool
Commissioned by: Playable City Sandbox 2023
supported by MyWorld

https://u.aec.at/6408E3B4

Tomo Kihara (JP) is an artist developing experimental games and public installations that draw out unexplored questions from people through play. He has worked on projects focusing on the social impact of AI with institutions such as Waag Futurelab in Amsterdam and the Mozilla Foundation in the USA. His recent works have been exhibited at the Victoria & Albert Museum (London, 2022) and the Asian Art Museum (San Francisco, 2024). **Daniel Coppen** (GB) is an artist and designer exploring the nature of relationships between society and technology through the medium of play. Operating as Playfool, together with his partner Saki Maruyama, their practice comprises objects, installations, and multimedia productions, which emphasize play's experimental, reflective, and intimate qualities. Their works have been exhibited at the V&A Museum (London, 2023) and the MAK (Vienna, 2019).

S+T+ARTS Prize'24
Honorary Mention

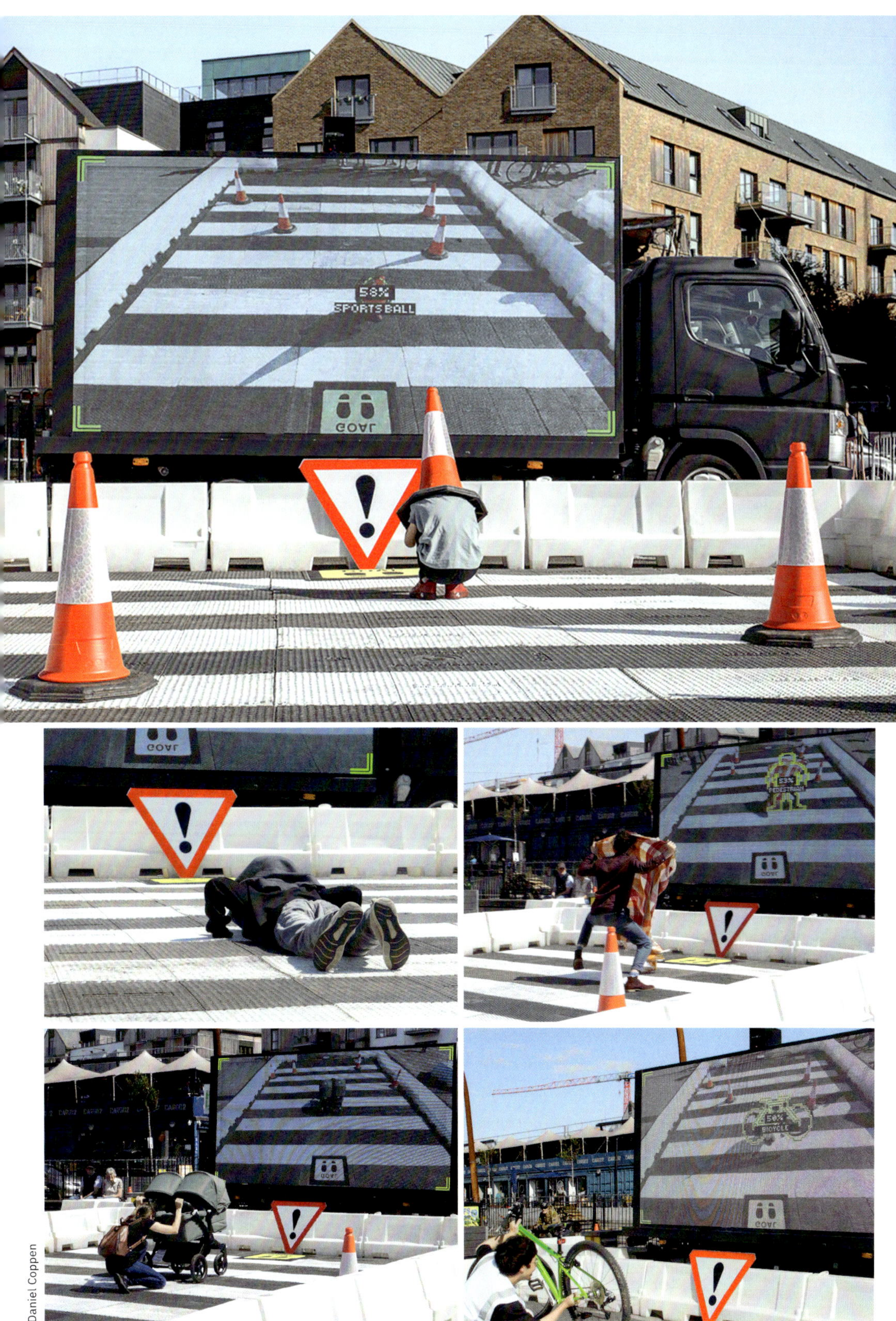

How (not) to get hit by a self-driving car   187

Korallysis
Gilberto Esparza

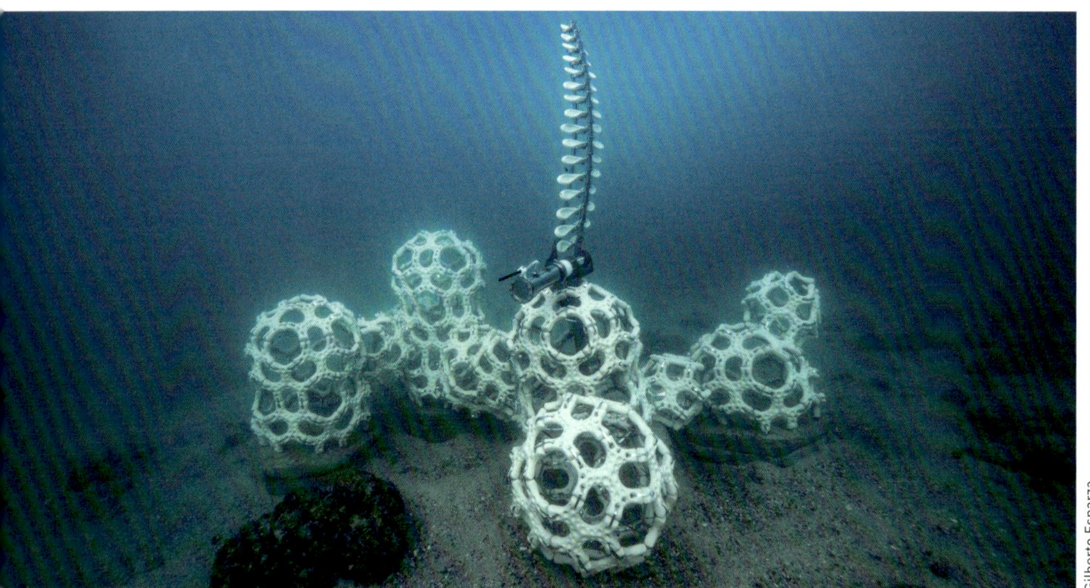

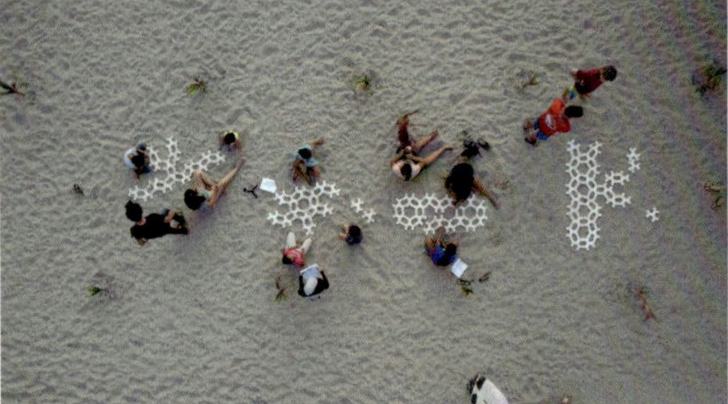

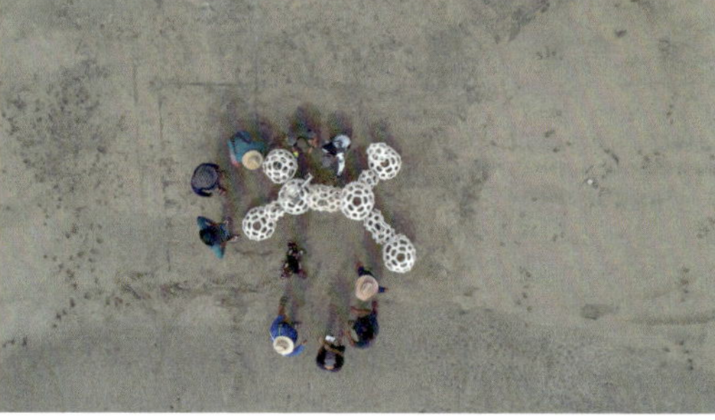

Korallysis is a hybrid organism made up of technological devices and coral colonies that coexist in a mutualistic relationship. It is formed from ceramic segments, based on a geometry that allows it to adapt to the seabed. Its structure creates an ideal habitat for the development of coral communities, as a refuge for fish in their early stage and various species. It has different kinetic elements dedicated to generating electricity, from ocean currents and waves. This energy is used to generate electrolysis, which allows minerals present in seawater, such as calcium carbonate, to adhere to the ceramic structure to accelerate the growth of the corals that live there. *Korallysis* works as a research platform at the intersection of art and science, in which technologies are implemented that help the restoration of coral reefs.

Coral reefs are complex ecosystems that help capture carbon dioxide (CO_2) from the atmosphere by fixing it in their skeletons. Its existence is essential for the formation of food networks, hosting a rich marine diversity. They are one of the marine ecosystems most affected by phenomena such as urbanization, poor waste management, and climate change. In recent decades, they have suffered severe degradation, representing a risk for thousands of species that inhabit them.

We seek to raise awareness about the importance of protecting coral reefs by proposing new forms of relationship with nature based on collaboration, forming multidisciplinary work teams, and seeking the participation of local communities to install these new organisms in coral reefs, such as a way to invite them to approach the problem.

S+T+ARTS Prize'24
Honorary Mention

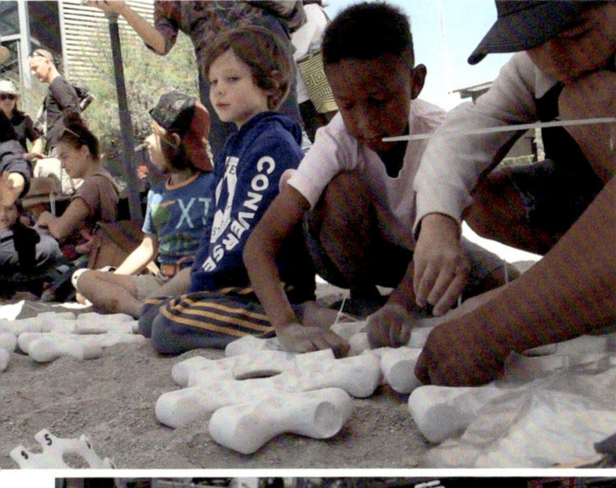

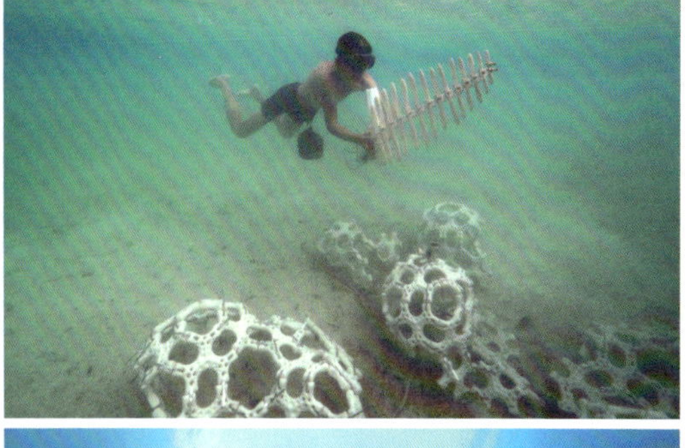

Rafael Chacón

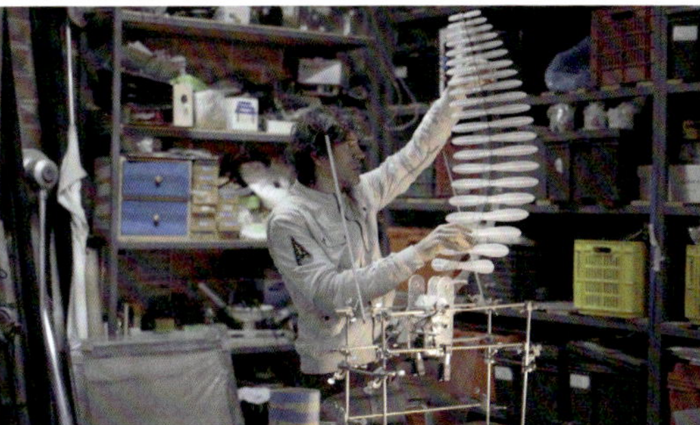

Leslie San Vicente

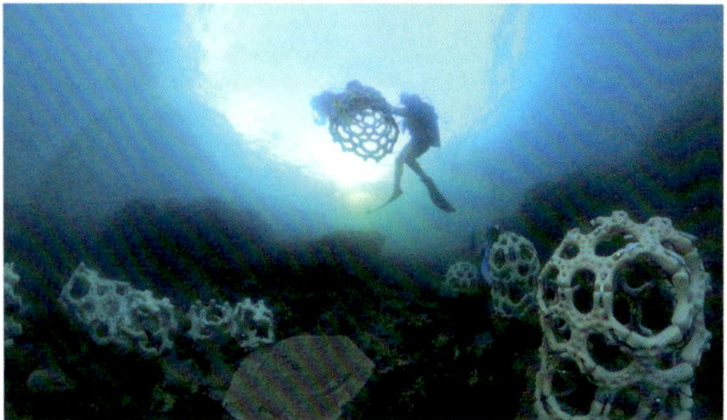

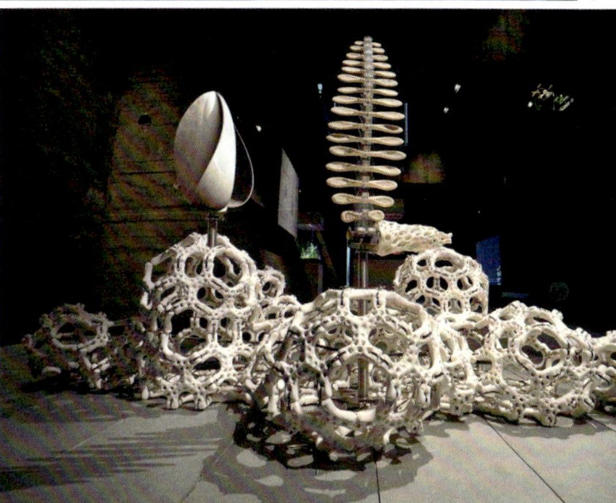

Gilberto Esparza

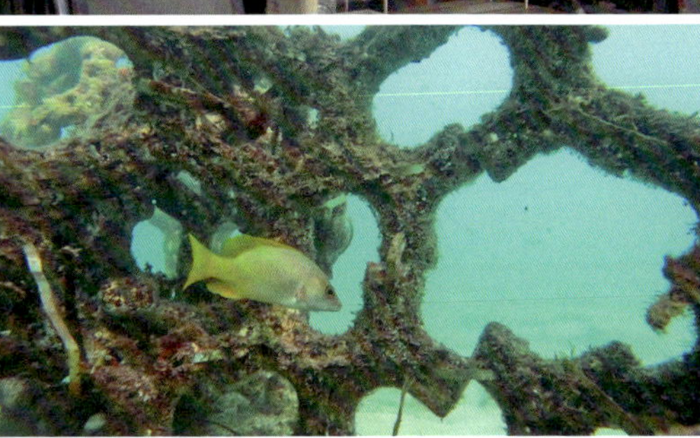

Michel Abrão
Gilberto Esparza

Production and technical support: Taller30, Ale Mendoza,
Michel Abrão, Yorick Bekker, Andrea Rassel
Collaboration:
Centro Regional de Investigación Acuícola y
Pesquera-CRIAP Manzanillo del Instituto Nacional de
Pesca y Acuacultura – INAPESCA, Mexico
Ejidal Cooperative Society Tenacatita MX;
Restore Coral AC; Oceanus AC
With support from: Goethe Institut / Prince Claus Fund
for Culture and Development, Sistema Nacional de
Creadores de Arte de México, Estímulos Fiscales para
las Artes EFIARTES

https://u.aec.at/577A3FC4

Gilberto Esparza (MX) (*1975) lives and works in San Miguel de Allende, Guanajuato. He investigates technology as a possibility to pose questions and solutions to the impacts of the human footprint on life on earth, rethinking the relationship of human societies with the natural environment. He works with biotechnology in collaboration with research centers and local communities. He received the Golden Nica for his project *Plantas Autofotosintéticas* in the Hybrid Art category, Prix Ars Electronica 2015, an Honorary Mention for *Nomadic Plants* in 2013, and a second Vida 13 award from Fundación Telefónica de España, among other awards.

Mapping Uncertain Landscape: The Satellite

Sofia Isupova

The project explores the relationship between humans and machines, the map maker, and the map, looking closely at the remote-sensing infrastructures, and their problematics as well as questioning maps and mapping processes to detect changes in the landscape that are occurring daily due to the ongoing Russian war in Ukraine. Transforming satellite images into maps of the territory. The machine that Isupova has built is a metaphorical satellite hovering above the land, mapping the data with a limited amount of accuracy. The images that the machine is producing come straight from the commercial crop monitoring satellite called EOS SAT. Translating this information into colors, my machine can draw landscapes: it can show me trees, fields, and hedges. It can show me life and growth, recovery, and renewal. The project aims to explore the ecological consequences of the ongoing Russian war in Ukraine and its impact on the landscape. It particularly focuses on key events of the war, such as the destruction of the Kakhovka Dam on June 6, 2023, in Southern Ukraine, and the first Russian offensive into Kyiv on March 23, 2022. Collaborating with ecologists and earth scientists, an extensive series of maps has been created to track vegetation level changes surrounding these events.

Mapping Uncertain Landscape: The Satellite serves as a means for us to bear witness—an arduous task carried out by Ukrainians on a daily basis. The notion that something traumatic requires witnessing, seeing, and hearing forms a cornerstone of journalism. This responsibility has now extended to artists, designers, and cultural workers in Ukraine. Maps and mapping serve as a means for us, as artists and designers, to continue this work of bearing witness to the brutality of war, even if unsuccessfully.

Diploma project for the Department of Space and Communication at HEAD Geneva
Tutor: Dominic Robson
Music: Aleyna Günay
With support from: HEAD Geneva, Kyiv Emergency Art Platform, EOS Data Analytics Academic Outreach Program

https://u.aec.at/8AA87C70

**S+T+ARTS Prize'24
Honorary Mention**

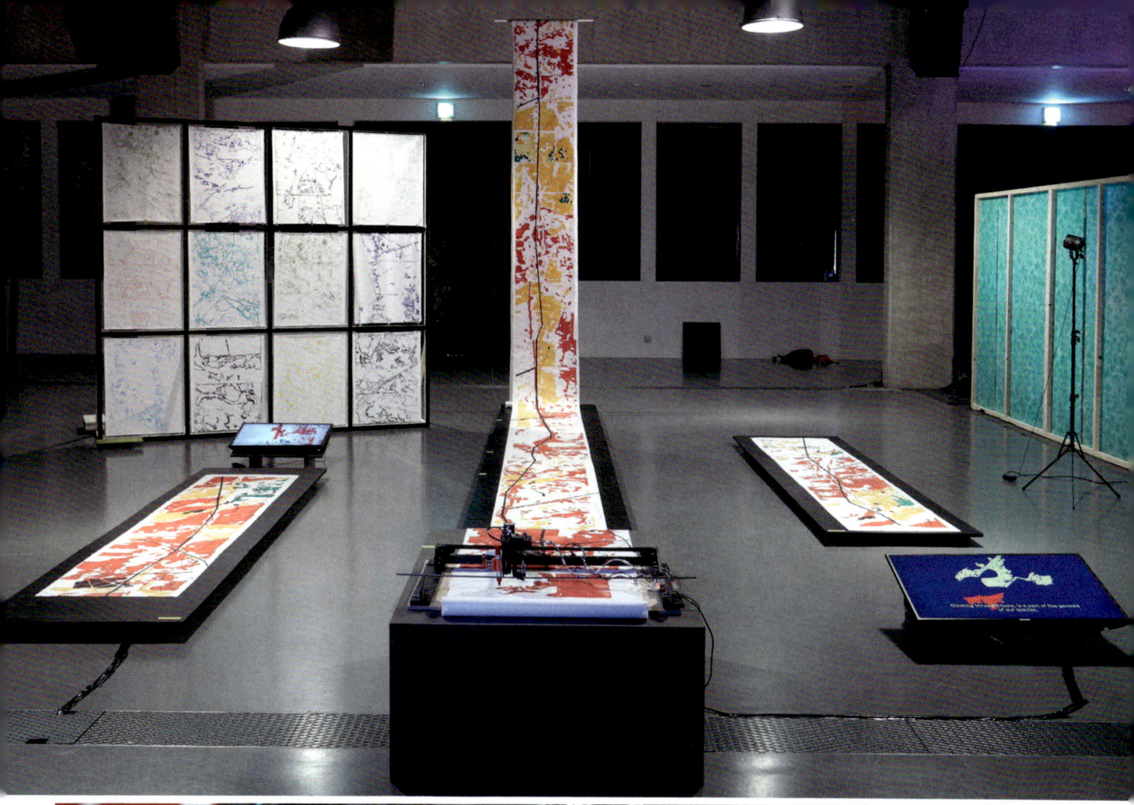

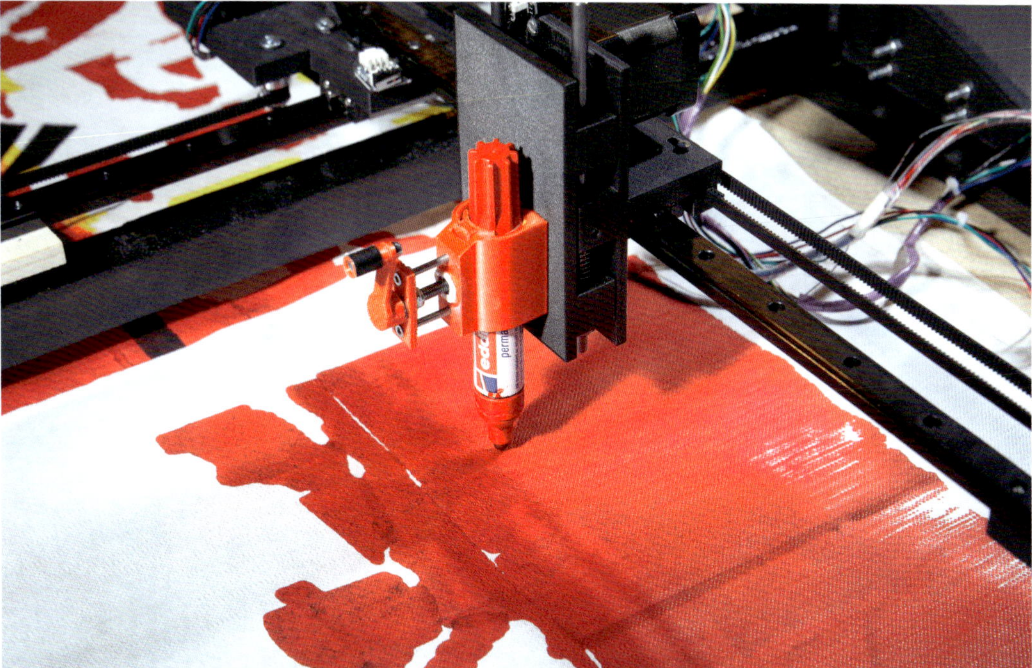

Sofia Isupova (UA) is a Ukrainian visual artist and designer based in Geneva. She earned her bachelor's degree from the Estonian Academy of Arts and her master's degree in the Space and Communication program at HEAD, Geneva. She develops machines centered around maps and mapmaking processes. Through her work, she explores the complex relationship between humans and machines, remote sensing infrastructures, and their inherent limitations. Isupova's inquiry into the processes of mapping seeks to detect changes in the landscape that occur daily due to the ongoing war in Ukraine. Recently, she won the Nestlé Jeune Création Prize 2023 and was a finalist for the Croix-Rouge Geneva Art Humanity Prize 2023.

Maria CHOIR
Maria Arnal Dimas

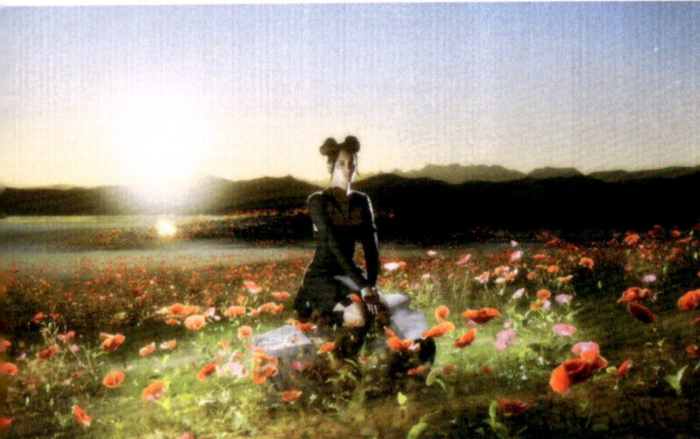

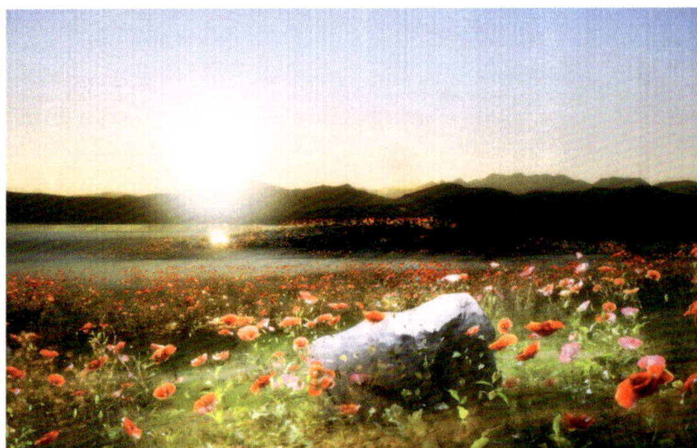

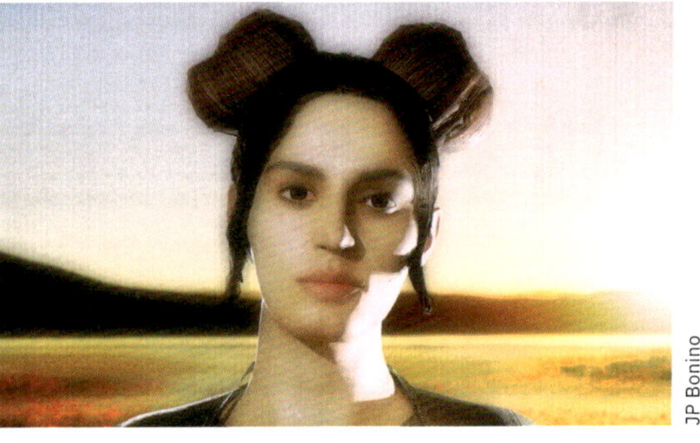
JP Bonino

Maria CHOIR is an immersive human-AI musical installation that invites participants to explore the boundaries of singing and listening through real-time interaction with an AI. This artwork leverages a model trained on the voice of singer Maria Arnal, enabling a unique duet between visitor and AI that evolves with each interaction, becoming a choir. Set within a dark, intimate space, the installation features a transparent plinth revealing its inner workings, surrounded by speakers that envelop participants in a rich tapestry of sound. An AI-animated avatar guides users, morphing in response to their vocal inputs, creating a personalized, dynamic experience.

Maria CHOIR is not just an artistic experiment but a social experience on novel AI musical live tools, collective datasets, consent, and the potential of synthetic voices to extend beyond mere replication of human capabilities. Furthermore, it invites participants to contribute to a collective voice model, used for both artistic creation and research, emphasizing the project's commitment to ethical engagement and transparency as well as fostering a powerful connection between humans and non-humans. Having attracted over 112,000 visitors at the AI: Artificial Intelligence exhibition at CCCB, Barcelona, and recorded over 12,400 voices, *Maria CHOIR* stands as a testament to its public appeal and research significance. The project showcases the collaborative effort of artists, scientists, and technologists. *Maria CHOIR*, led by Maria Arnal, blends human and synthetic voices in live conferences, exploring new vocal narratives. As a complementary activation of the installation, these events demystify AI technology, fostering communal creativity and reflecting on AI-explainability through music. This pioneer project sets the stage for further exploration of human-AI interaction, real-time voice neural synthesis, awareness on the creation of collective datasets and the ethical dimensions of AI in art, solidifying Maria Arnal's status as a symbol of contemporary innovation in European art.

Concept, direction and music production: Maria Arnal
Funding and support: Fundación Española de Ciencia y Tecnología (FECYT)
Technical execution and programming: Barcelona Supercomputer Center (BSC), axolot.cat (Iván Paz and Lina Bautista)
Interactive design: axolot.cat (Iván Paz and Lina Bautista)
Visuals and artistic design: JP Bonino
Curator: Lluís Nacenta
Host and exhibition space: Centre de Cultura Contemporània de Barcelona (CCCB)
With support from: Fundación Española de Ciencia y Tecnología (FECYT)

https://u.aec.at/57981DC8

S+T+ARTS Prize'24
Honorary Mention

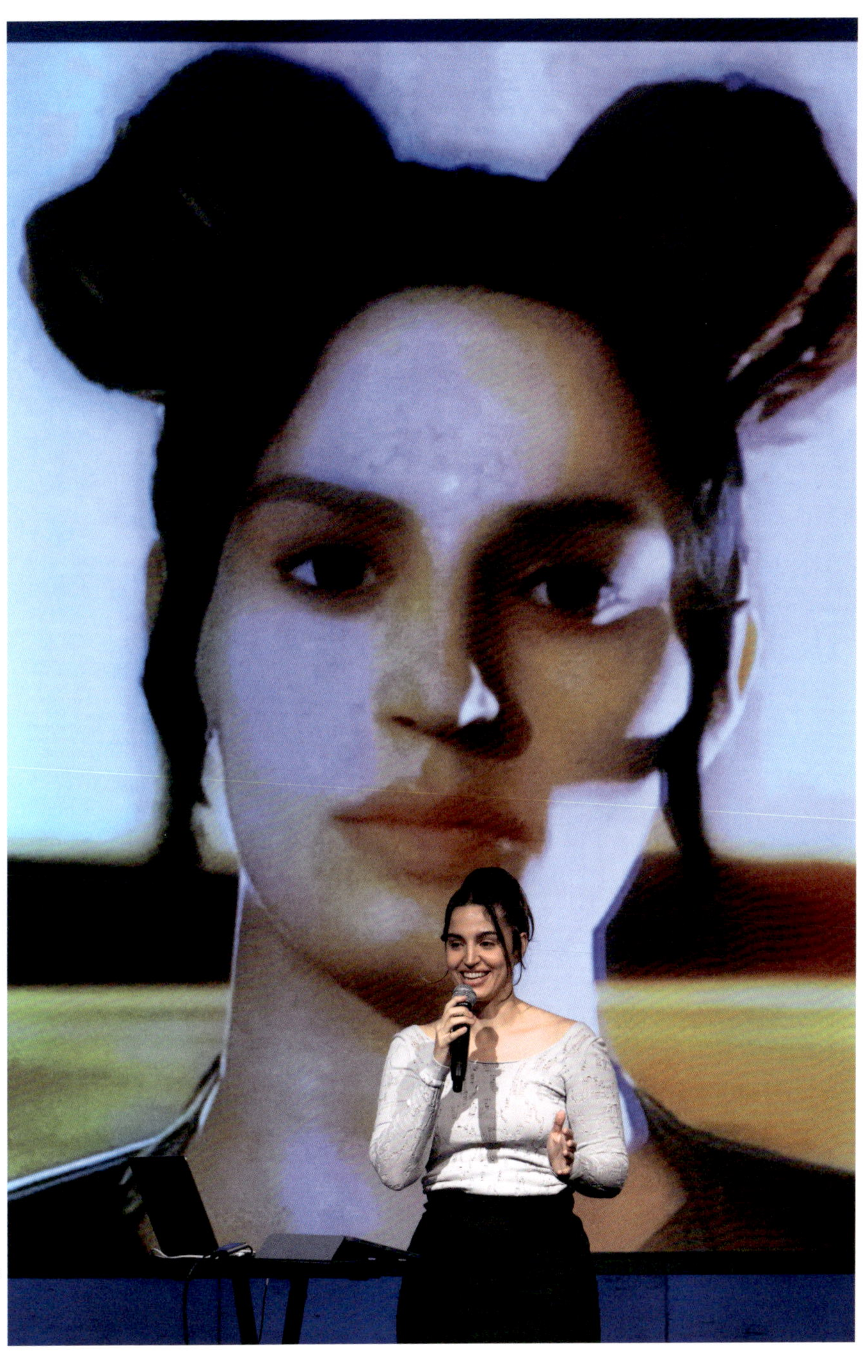

Maria Arnal Dimas (ES) is a Barcelona-based artist, singer, and composer, renowned for her unique blend of avant-garde pop, electronics, and traditional polyphonic music. Her work is distinguished by an exploratory spirit of sound, technology, and art. During the last years, she has been widely recognized with numerous awards and has performed at some of the most iconic festivals, such as Sónar Festival or the TED-Talks event in Vancouver, among others. Arnal's diverse projects span compositions like *AIR* for the Venice Architecture Biennale 2021 and *SIRENA* for Hipermirador Torre Glòries 2022. She co-directs the sound essay "Cada capa de l'Atmosfera" (2023), exploring sonic consciousness in the climate emergency, and pioneers *Maria CHOIR* (CCCB 2024), an interactive human-AI sound installation. Currently, she's engaged in research on synthetic voices in collaboration with the Barcelona Supercomputing Center and she is composing her next album, marking her debut full-length solo release.

Maria CHOIR

METABOLICA
Thomas Feuerstein

METABOLICA opens up the factory of life and in five chapters tells a story of change from the industrial revolution to the present and future, from whaling and petromodernity to current and future scenarios of biochemistry. Living organisms such as algae and bacteria become collaborators that lead to a new aesthetic and artistic practice through scientifically developed processes. Bacteria act as artistic actors by metabolizing fatty acids enriched in algae into the material PHB (polyhydroxybutyrate). While the sculptor's material once came from a quarry such as Carrara and the chisel served as a tool, in METABOLICA it is living organisms. The bacteria act simultaneously as "quarry" and "chisel" by producing a new plastic for sculptures, by digesting them again and changing their shape.

In the sculpture *HYDRA,* a hybrid of whale, submarine, and photobioreactor, green algae (Chlorella vulgaris) grow in an extensive tube system via photosynthesis, which are continuously filtered as if by the baleen of a whale. Constantly pumped to the sculpture *FATTY FANTASY,* the algae form fatty acids in their cells due to a special diet or the lack of nitrogen in the water, while the sculpture *MOBY DICK,* a converted oil pump, provides the water cycle. In the bioreactor sculptures, MS and MR MOL bacteria (including Cupriavidus necator) convert the fatty acids of the algae into the plastic PHB (polyhydroxybutyrate) whereas in the *REFINERY* the biomass of the bacteria is separated from the process water of the reactors, purified and dried. The result is a fine powder, processed into sculptures by *ANACLE,* a 3D printer. The printed sculptures grow like stalactites during printing. The same bacteria act simultaneously as quarry and chisel.

METABOLICA was conceived in 2017 and has been supported by a team of scientists and engineers since 2020. The aim of the research is to use carbon sources from wastewater streams in industrial and sewage treatment plants to produce PHB.

Artist: Thomas Feuerstein

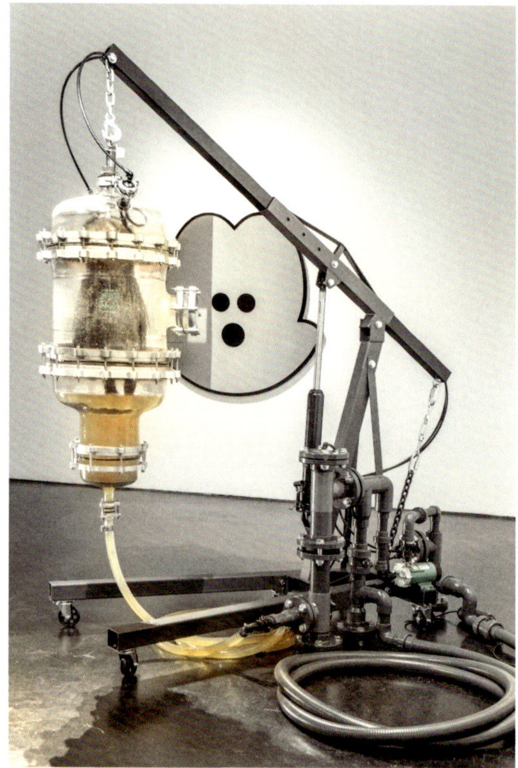

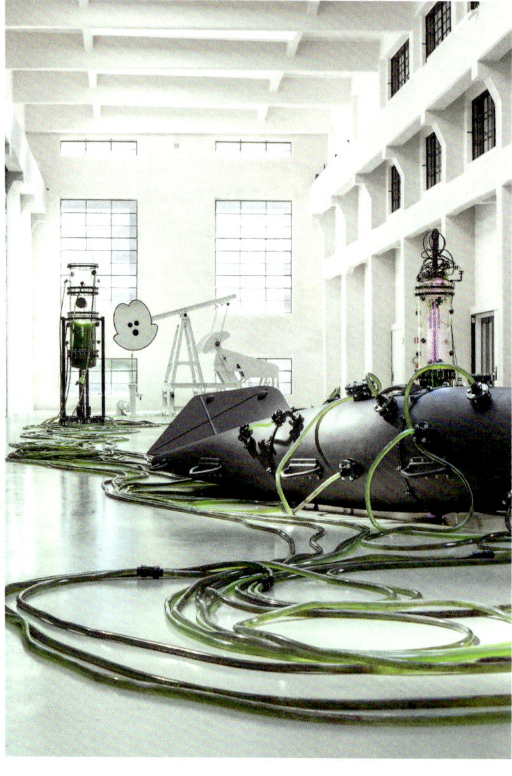

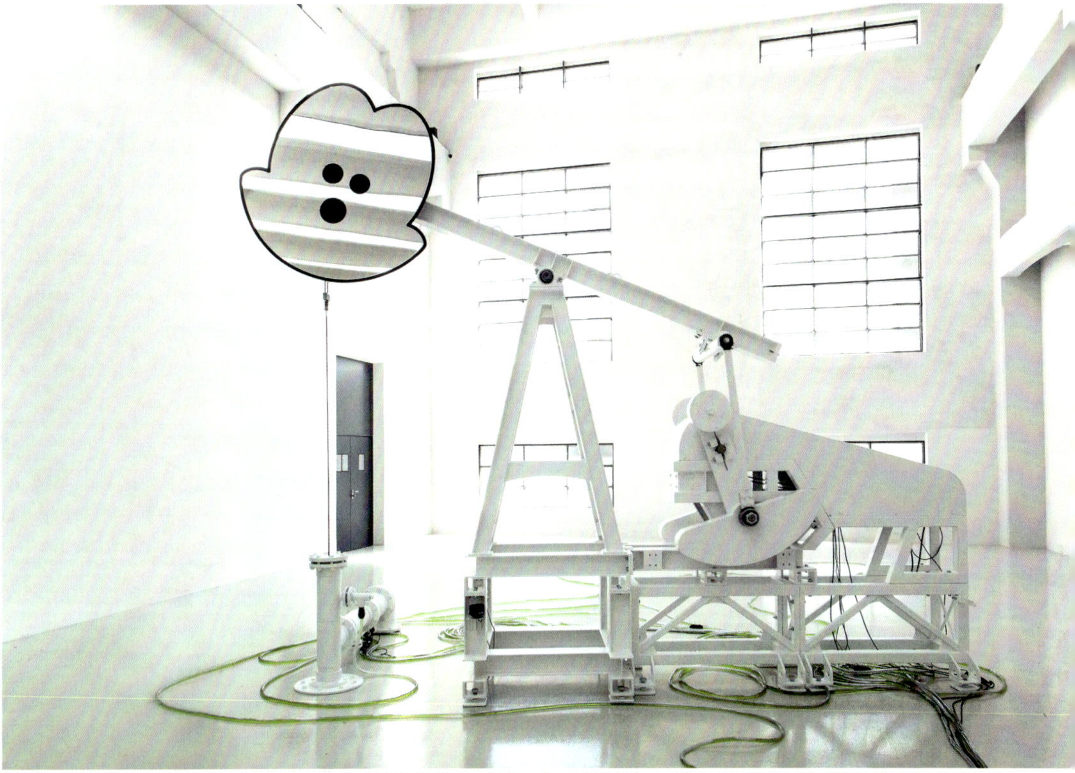

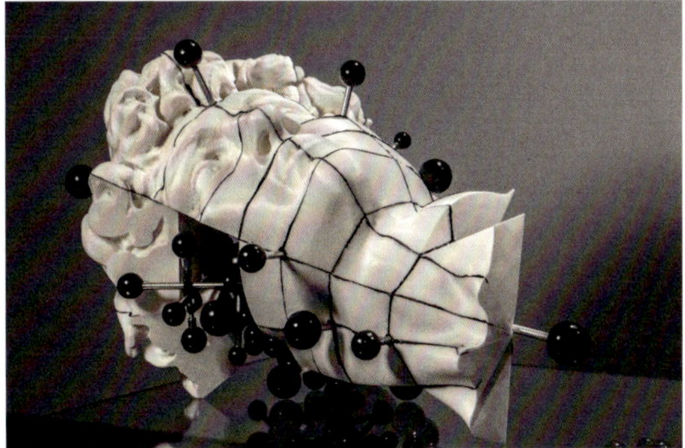

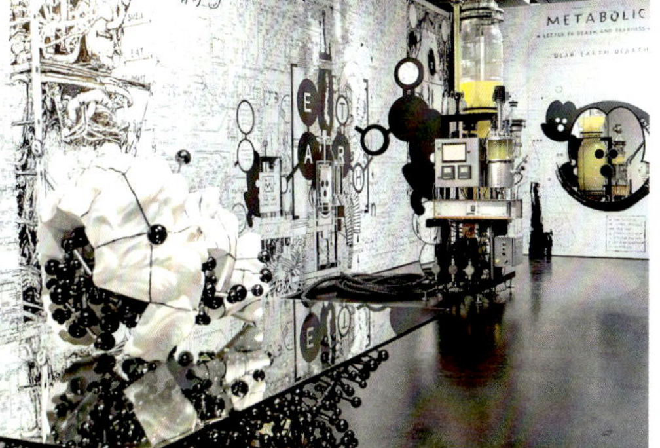

https://u.aec.at/7F2C0D20

Thomas Feuerstein (AT) studied art history and philosophy, gaining his doctorate from Innsbruck University. As a theorizing media artist, he employs a method of "conceptual narration" that combines art, architecture, philosophy, and literature with economics, politics, and technology. Linking linguistic, visual, and material elements and exploring connections between fact and fiction are key aspects of his practice. He creates artworks based on neural networks, biotechnologies, and metabolic processes. Thomas Feuerstein lives in Vienna.

P2P
Eva & Franco Mattes

Inspired by a speculative project by architect Rem Koolhaas—who planned to bring a museum inside a data center—but reversing it by bringing a data center inside a museum, *P2P* celebrates peer communities created by artists who have used the internet to share works and knowledge over the last twenty years.

The central element of the installation is a server standing in a grid cage. The server is connected to the peer-to-peer network via the infrastructure of the hosting art institution—for example Frankfurter Kunstverein (2023), KW Berlin (2024). It shares new digital artworks by Nora Al-Badri, Simon Denny, Do Not Research, Olia Lialina, Jill Magid, Jon Rafman. In the future it will host new works by other artists and act as a fully functional, itinerant, artist-run space.

P2P reveals the infrastructure that is home to our data, which is usually hidden from us. Unlike conventional servers, peer-to-peer networks store data in a decentralized way. They are anonymous, free from commercial interests, data mining, and surveillance. Participants in these communities, known as "peers", take part by connecting their computers to the system. They interact directly with each other on an equal footing by sharing resources such as files, bandwidth, and computing power. While public art institutions go to great lengths to preserve objects—i.e. paintings or sculptures—they often do not share the same investment for digital artefacts, delegating it to external private companies—the "cloud".

P2P introduces new possibilities for the distribution and preservation of digital works. By hosting the work, a public institution contributes directly to the dissemination and preservation of art on the internet.

With support from: Frankfurter Kunstverein;
KW Institute for Contemporary Art, Berlin

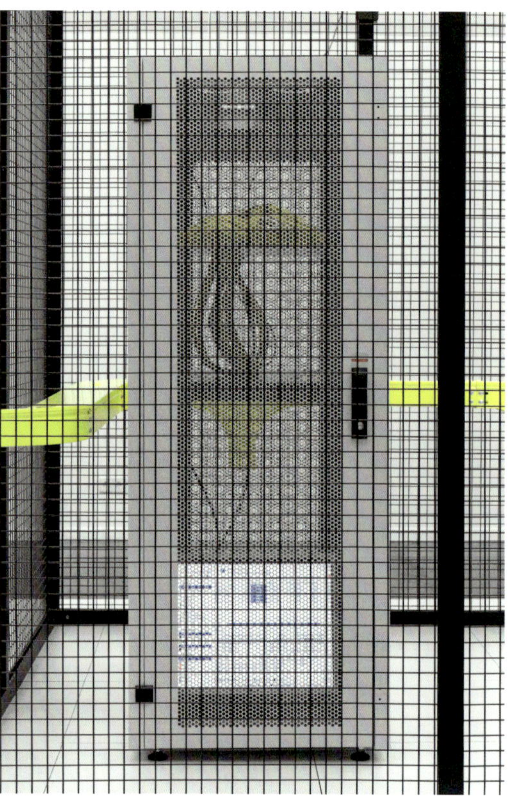

P2P, 2022
Cage, cabinet, rack server, files, Torrent software, internet connection, neon lights
312 x 209 x h208 cm
Installed at Frankfurter Kunstverein

https://u.aec.at/4BB6D3C2

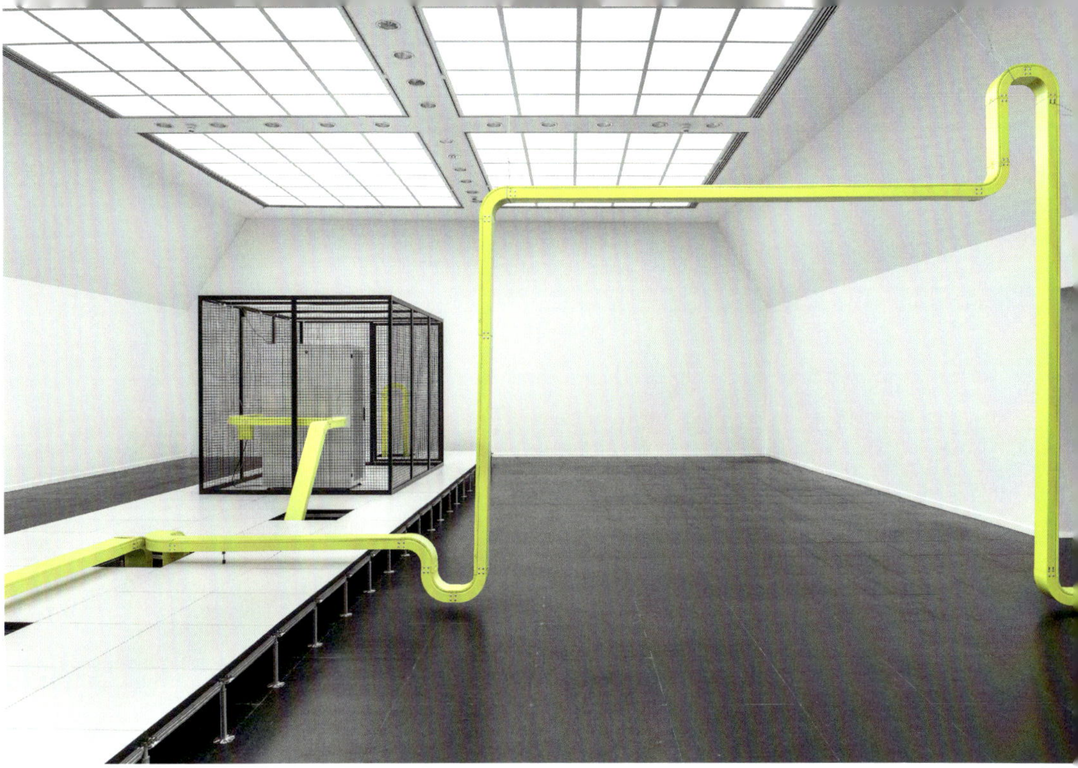

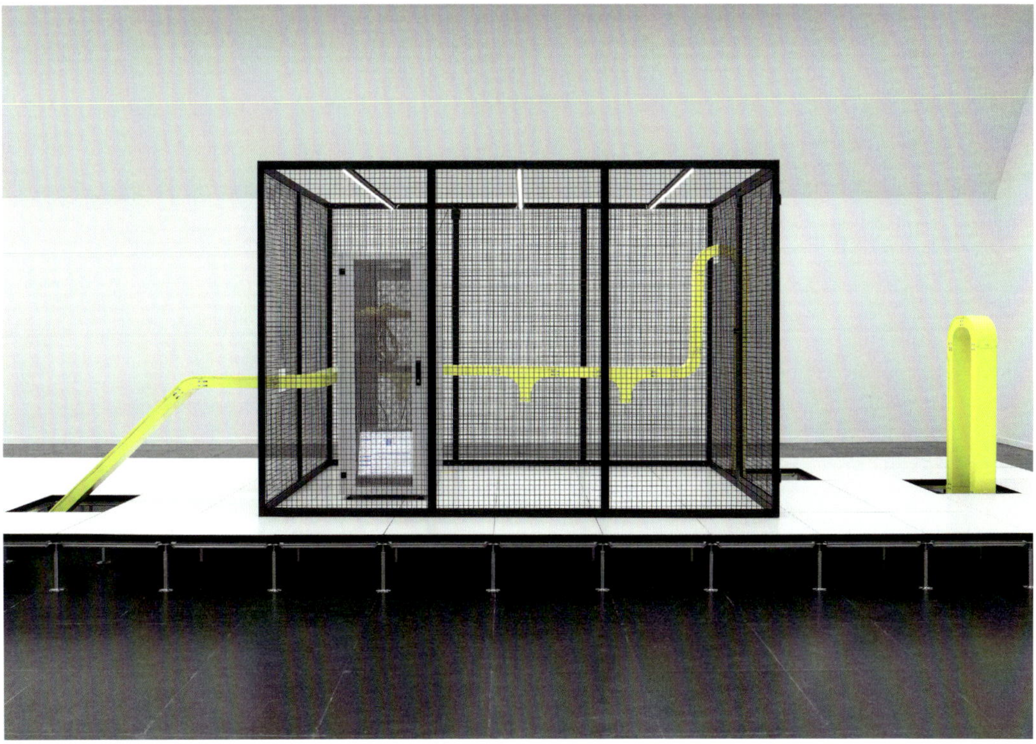

Eva & Franco Mattes (IT, US) are an Italian American artist duo living in New York and Milan. Through videos, installations, sculptures, and online interventions, their work responds to and dissects our contemporary networked condition, always approaching the ethics and politics of life online with a darkly humorous edge. Their works can be found in the collections of the SFMOMA, Whitney Museum of American Art, Fotomuseum Winterthur, X Museum, and the Walker Art Center. Many of Mattes' projects can be found on their website:
https://0100101110101101.org

Self-Care
Lyndsey Walsh

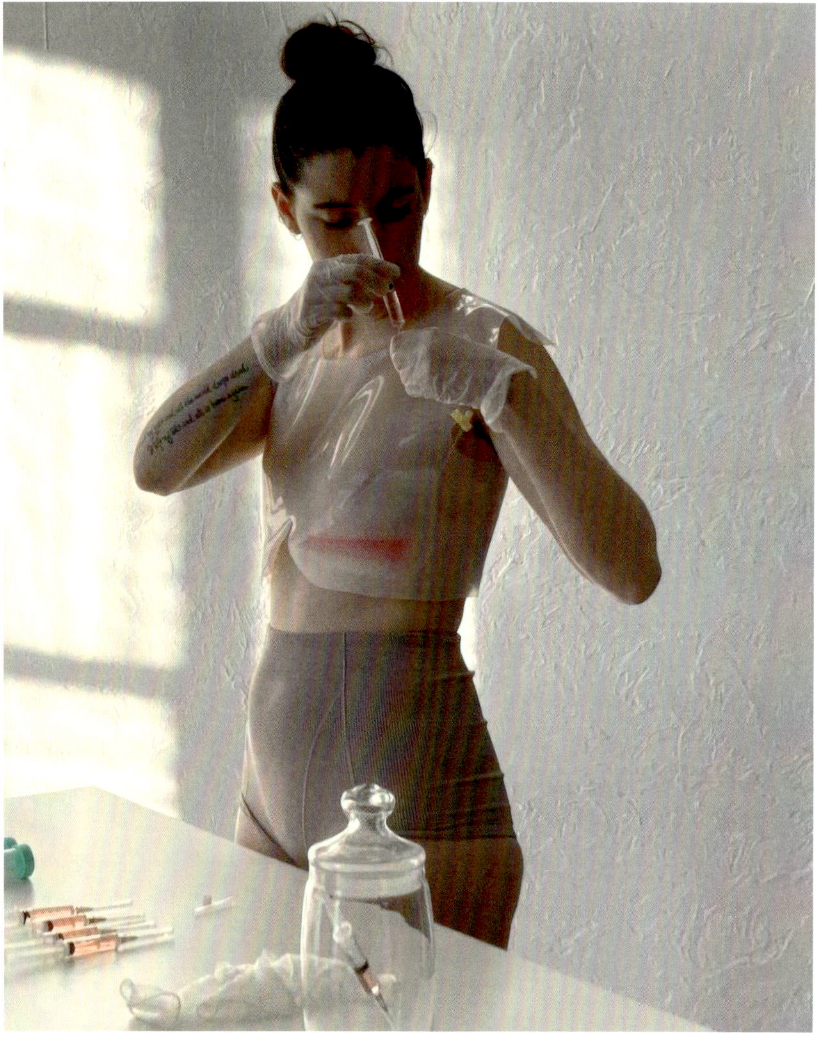

Wearable Prototype 01, worn by the artist

Self-Care is a multi-media artwork and installation exploring notions of care, labor, intergenerational trauma, and bodies, as well as the impact of the gender binary on so-called "female" healthcare. *Self-Care* aims to critically examine notions of care, the role of gender in medicine, ableism, and familial relationships surrounding notions of disease. The project attempts to reclaim bodily autonomy over a body caught at the crossroads of neoliberalist healthcare agendas and genetic fatalism.

The centerpiece of *Self-Care* is a specially designed wearable chest binder that can house living breast cancer cells with the same genetic condition as the artist. This chest binder allows the artist to queer and reclaim their body by caring for their predestined cancer before it emerges. As a wearable, the binder also uses the cancer's liquid environment as a means to flatten the appearance of the chest and perform gender-affirming care for the wearer. The binder is a device that questions and attempts to reclaim the body in consideration of the looming threat of bodily violence related to medical interventions for Hereditary Breast and Ovarian Cancer Syndrome.

S+T+ARTS Prize'24
Honorary Mention

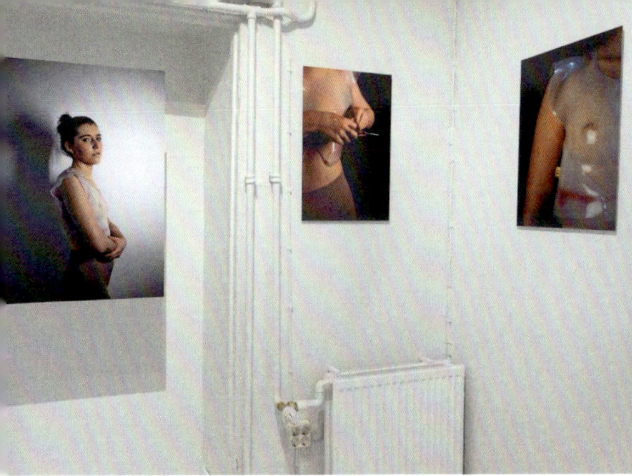

Photograph of *Self-Care* in m/other becomings installation in 2022 at the Bioart Society/SOLU Space in Helsinki, Finland.

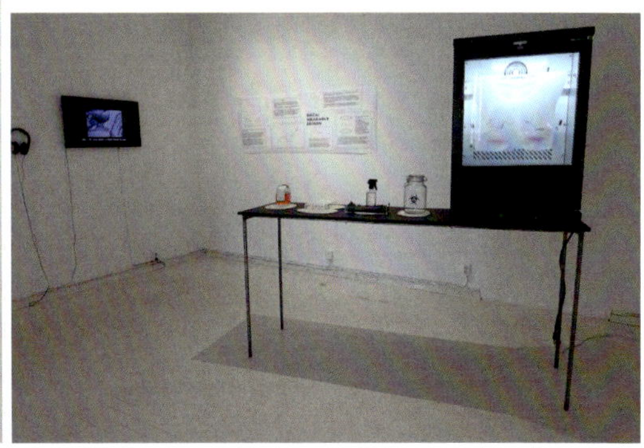

Self-Care Installation at the Bioart Society/SOLU Space in 2022

Genietta Varsi

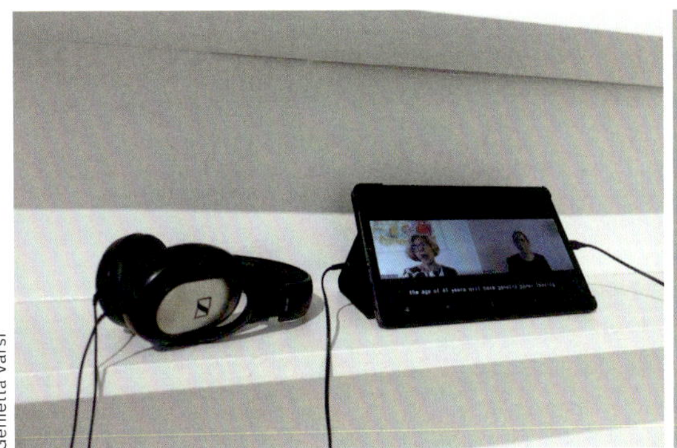

Genietta Varsi

Photograph of *Self-Care* in m/other becomings installation in 2022 at the Bioart Society/SOLU Space in Helsinki, Finland.

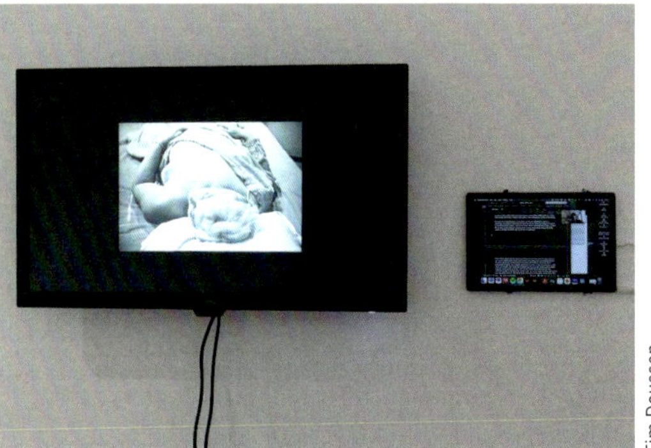

Tim Deussen

Photograph of Art Laboratory Berlin installation of *Mommagraphy Techniques* and *A Letter to My Mother,* 2023 in *Matter of Flux.*

Self-Care is a rehearsal of embodiment for bodies that are constantly transgressing the boundaries between sick and not sick. It explores the hopes, successes, and failures that emerge from attempts to "live" with a body and all its faults. The work is also an archive of the multiple mutants and subjectivities, as described by Jason Zingsheim's Mutational Identity Theory, that come together to form a sense of self and the connection the self can have with its body.

The accompanying video works titled *Mommagraphy Techniques* and *A Letter to My Mother* catalog the intergenerational experiences of embodiment and struggles concerning health and gender across four generations, the artist, their mother, their mother's mother, and their mother's mother's mother.

Artist: Lyndsey Walsh
Commissioned by: Bioart Society for "m/other becomings" program
Production: Bioart Society and Art Laboratory Berlin
Mommagraphy Techniques Video: Interview with artist's mother and remixed footage from US National Institute of Health (public domain)
Scientific collaboration and support: Prof. Dr. Peter Hegemann, Dr. Johannes Oppermann, Enrico Schiewer, Dr. Olga Baidukova, and Prof. Dr. Kristiina Aittomäki.
Incubator: Collaboration between Lyndsey Walsh & Petteri Haverinen
Photo documentation: Asya Kaplan, Genietta Varsi, Milla Millasnoore, and Tim Deussen
Concept research: *Prophylaxis* project by Lyndsey Walsh with Art.ITMO.Reisdency

https://u.aec.at/7183443F

Lyndsey Walsh (US) is an artist, writer, and researcher based in Berlin, Germany. Lyndsey's practice fuses speculative narratives and horror with autoethnographic investigations into the ruptures created by technology in the corporality of culture. Lyndsey sets out to question the cultural binaries of human-non-human, diseased-healthy, and life-machine using Crip, Queer, and intersectional feminist frameworks.

The Waterworks of Money
Carlijn Kingma

Although money plays a key role in our lives, the workings of our monetary and financial system are a mystery to most of us. *The Waterworks of Money* demystifies the world of big finance by visualizing the flow of money through our society. It explores several options for improvement using new technologies—with the ultimate goal of designing the best money system possible for the digital age.

The project is a collaboration of cartographer Carlijn Kingma, investigative journalist Thomas Bollen, and professor of New Finance Martijn van der Linden. Kingma spent 2,300 hours drawing a map of the money system, based on in-depth research, partnerships with financial institutions, and interviews with more than 100 experts: executives and employees of (central) banks and pension funds, and asset managers, politicians, academics, and monetary activists.

Our society is facing a serious challenge. Inequality is growing and many European countries are dealing with a cost of living crisis while financial instability remains an ongoing threat. We are also running out of time to make the European economy more sustainable. These problems cannot be seen in isolation from the architecture of our money system. If we truly want to tackle them, we will have to address the design flaws in our current money system.

Now is the time to do so. The digitalization of our economy has created new opportunities to redesign our money system. For example, the EU is working on the introduction of a Central Bank Digital Currency. This digital euro could open up new possibilities to improve our financial architecture.

Designing the money system—and the laws and institutions that govern it—is ultimately a democratic task. In practice, however, there is a major obstacle impeding the democratic process: financial illiteracy. By making the world of money understandable, we help citizens to develop their own vocabulary to participate in the debate about the future of our money.

Drawings: Carlijn Kingma
Stories: Thomas Bollen, Carlijn Kingma,
and Martijn Jeroen van der Linden
Animations: Studio Tiepes
English translation: Erica Moore
Audio recordings: Studio Oorbit
Photos: Studio Oppa

With support from: The Hague University and investigative journalism platform Follow The Money;
Stimuleringsfonds Creatieve Industrie, Stichting Brave New Works, and the Interledger Foundation.
The project received support from the Rabobank through an artist-in-residence.

https://u.aec.at/A825091C

Carlijn Kingma (NL) is a cartographer of society, mapping invisible power structures with researchers, experts, and journalists. Her work, honored with the New Babylon Award in 2017, has been displayed in the Kunstmuseum Den Haag. In 2018, she won the Architecture Drawing Prize for hand-drawing and exhibited at Sir John Soane's Museum in London alongside Piranesi and Joseph Gandy. Kingma's work has also been shown at the Rijksmuseum Twenthe, Museum Flehite, and Lowlands Festival. In 2021, she won the Dutch Talent of the Year and the Henning Larson Competition. Her recent projects, *The Waterworks of Money* and *Follow the Money*, were exhibited at the Kunstmuseum Den Haag and the Venice Biennial in 2023. In 2024, her work will be showcased at the Boijmans Depot and BRUTUS. The project received the Master Storyteller Award, the Amsterdam Art Prize, and the Dutch Design Awards.

S+T+ARTS Prize'24
Honorary Mention

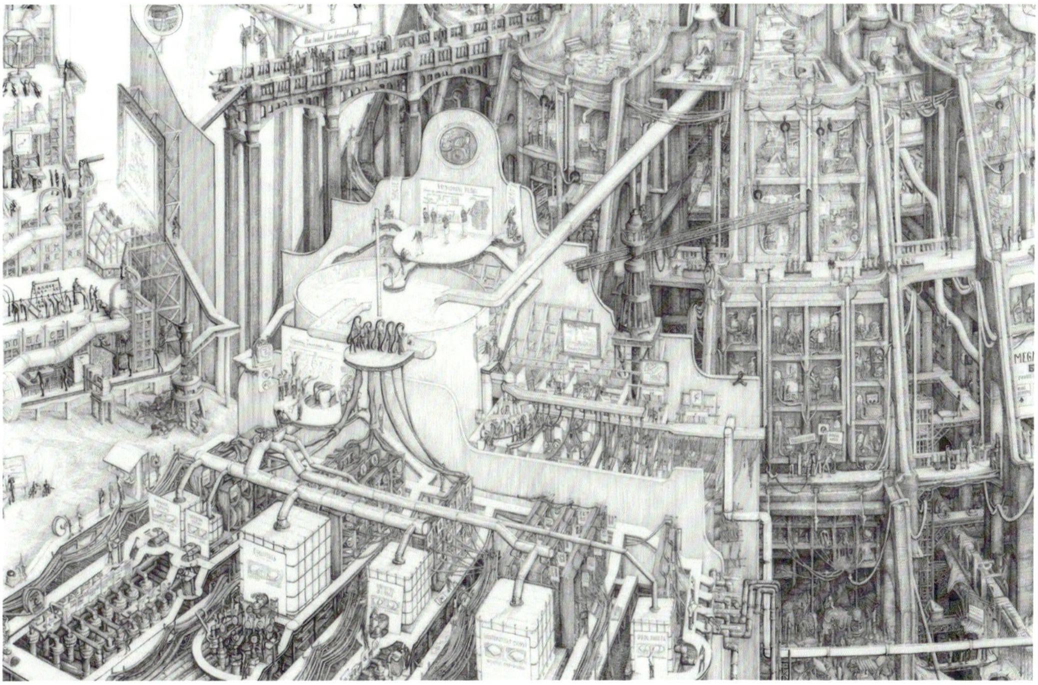

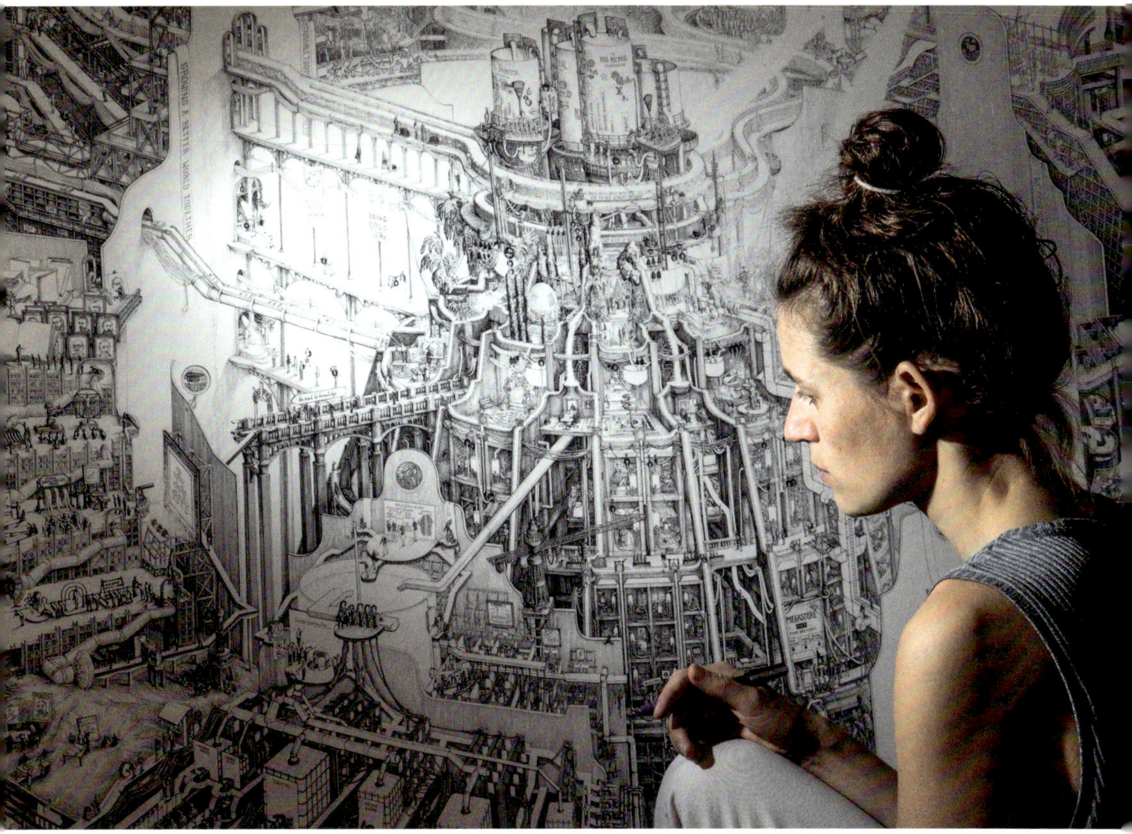

The Waterworks of Money

VRJ Palestine

Nisreen Zahda

The *VRJ Palestine* initiative (Virtual Reality Journey to pre-Nakba Palestine) delves into the potential and challenges of Virtual Reality tools to reclaim and recapture Nakba's lost landscapes. Using archival data and survivors' accounts to virtually reconstruct the Palestinian villages demolished in 1948, it aims to preserve intergenerational memories conveyed through stories and photos. Despite the fragmented but valuable archives, the necessity for more innovative documentation tools is paramount for three reasons:

Firstly, emerging digital narrative tools offer more engaging, multi-sensory, and innovative historical storytelling experiences than conventional methods, enhancing user engagement. Secondly, with Nakba survivors aging, there is a looming risk of losing the collective memory of each destroyed place over time. Thirdly, many archival collections are exclusively for scholarly purposes, posing a challenge for public access.

The project employs a multi-layered approach, combining various archival data to construct a fully interactive real-time rendered environment. Its ultimate goal is to provide a real-time virtual journey to these reconstructed places, allowing people to engage and immerse themselves in the reconstructed spaces and memories. The final product is adaptable, designed for activation on different VR platforms, including WebVR tours and immersive VR experiences. *VRJ Palestine* has showcased a number of projects, reconstructing villages such as Tantoura, Hittin, Zirin, and sections of Jaffa city. The *Jaffa-Flashbacks* project offers an online virtual experience (WebVR) accessible across a wide range of digital devices, including smartphones. Through these projects, it bridges the gap between history and innovation, inviting diverse audiences to engage with revitalized realms, forging profound connections with the past through advanced technology.

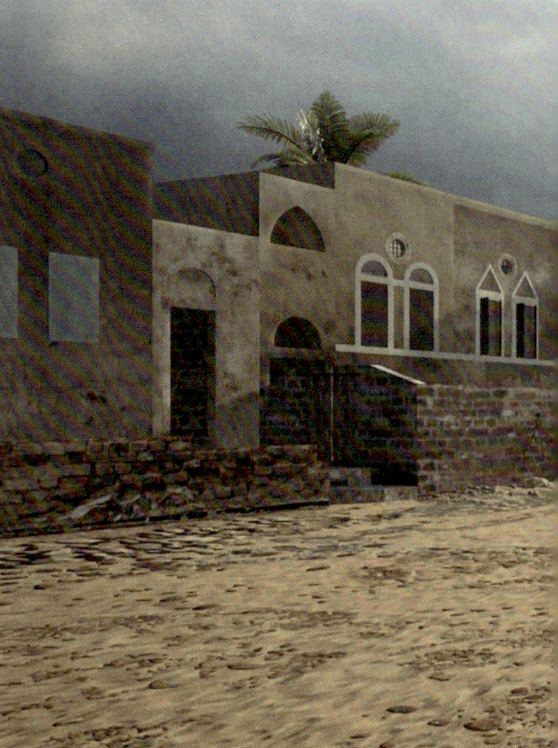

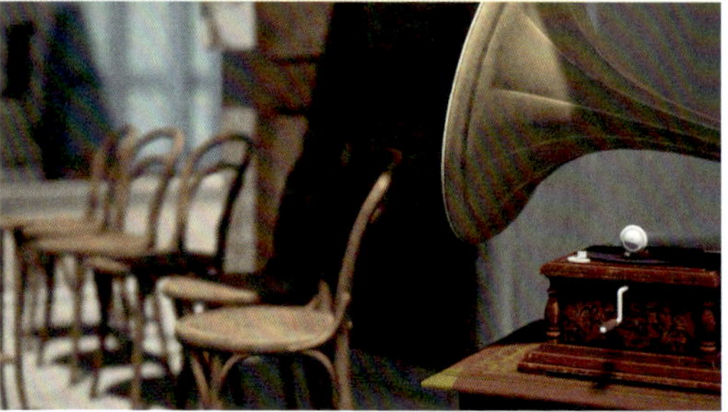

S+T+ARTS Prize'24
Honorary Mention

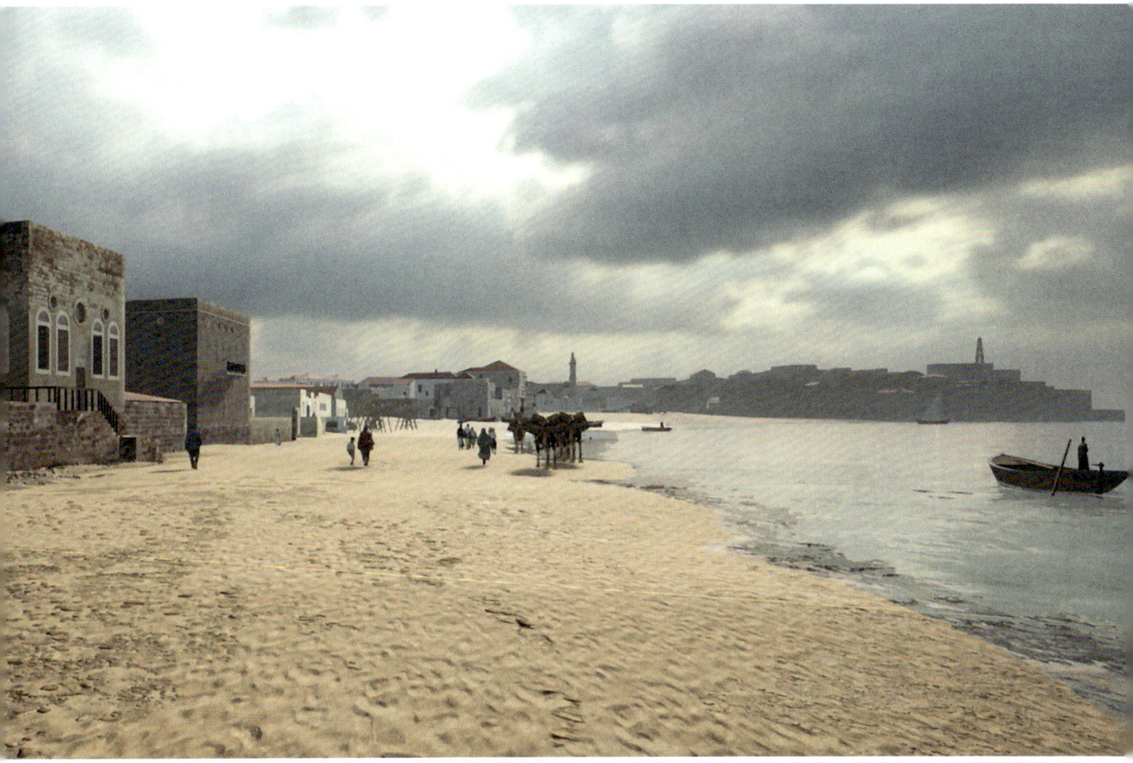

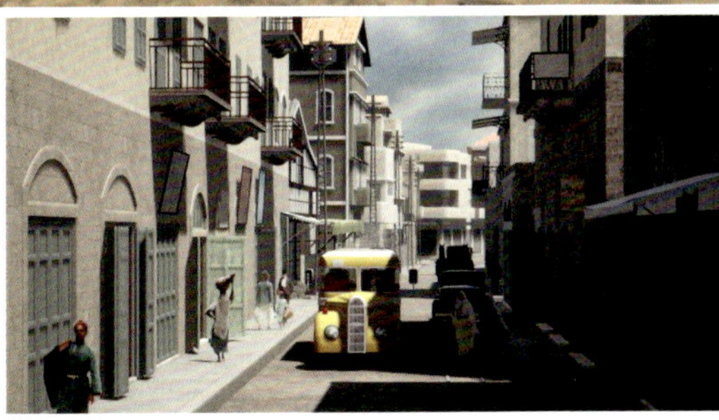

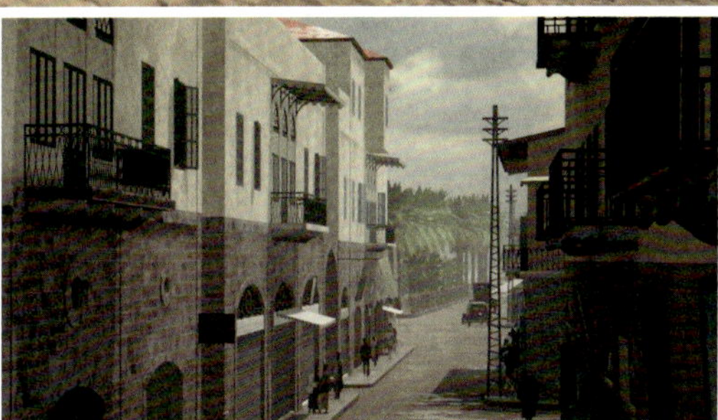

Artist: Nisreen Zahda
Maps, photos, archival data, & other media used in
VRJ Palestine are credited properly for each project

https://u.aec.at/BF5D93AE

Nisreen Zahda (PS) is an architect, urban planner, and virtual reality artist based in Tokyo, Japan. She was born in Hebron, Palestine, studied architecture in Birzeit University, Palestine, and received her PhD in urban planning from Chiba University in Japan. She started *VRJ Palestine* to reclaim Nakba's lost landscapes using digital virtual reality narrative tools.

AUTOPOIESIS
ATELIER-E

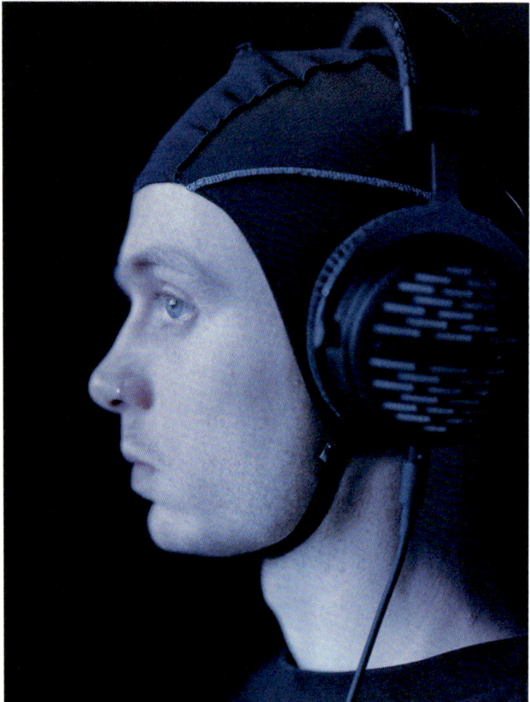

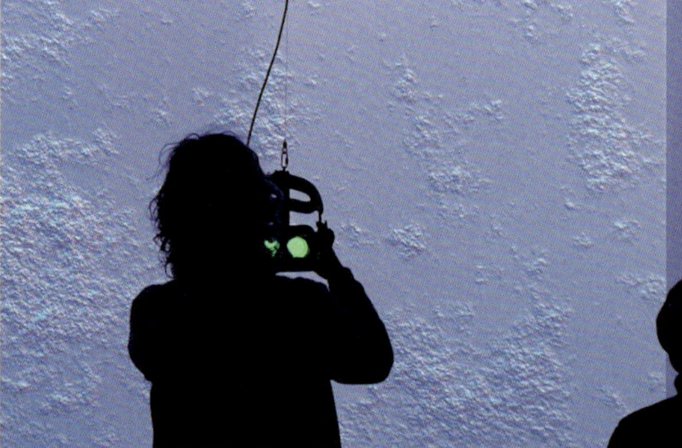

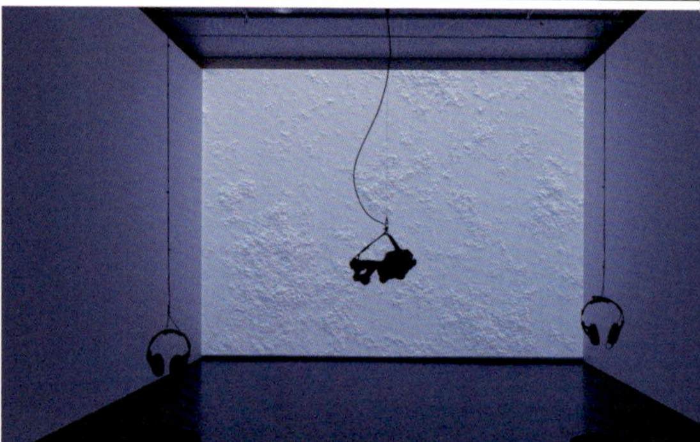

How might an installation engage not with humans directly, but with their minds? *AUTOPOIESIS* offers an experience that defies easy interpretation, oscillating between activation and deceleration. It utilizes our sensory system, converting light and sound into neurophysiological processes, exploring how audio-visual stimuli affect the brain. This project, a collaboration between ATELIER-E and Fraunhofer IAO in Stuttgart, developed immersive stimuli tailored for the brain, focusing on how color, shapes, and sound influence brain activity and enhance interhemispheric connectivity. A concurrent Fraunhofer study mirrors the exhibition's stimuli, aiming to reveal audiovisual synchronicities in our unconscious perception. The exhibition space integrates scientific findings, transforming a sterile lab into an engaging, open area, inviting firsthand interaction with the research.

This innovative approach melds art and science, encouraging visitors to delve into the subconscious intricacies of their own minds.

Audio visual installation: ATELIER-E
Studio assistance: Aaron Schwerdtfeger
Curation: Dr. Anett Holzheid, Sarah Donderer, Nina Liechti, Beatrice Zaidenberg
Neuroscientific consulting: Ravi Kanth Kosuru, Dr. Mathias Vukelic
Co-production: ZKM | Center for Art and Media Karlsruhe
The artistic research project *AUTOPOIESIS* is realized in collaboration with Fraunhofer Institute for Industrial Engineering IAO, IAT of the University of Stuttgart and the media artists of ATELIER-E Produced in cooperation with ZKM | Center for Art and Media Karlsruhe.

https://u.aec.at/150D36AC

ATELIER-E (DE) is a Berlin-based interdisciplinary studio for new media and computational design. It was founded by media artists **Daniel Dalfovo** (DE) and **Christian Losert** (DE). They both work and teach at the intersection of arts and creative technology. Together they develop new media installations, research on future technologies, and create code and systems for audio visual spaces.

Bibliokepos
Nomad Garden

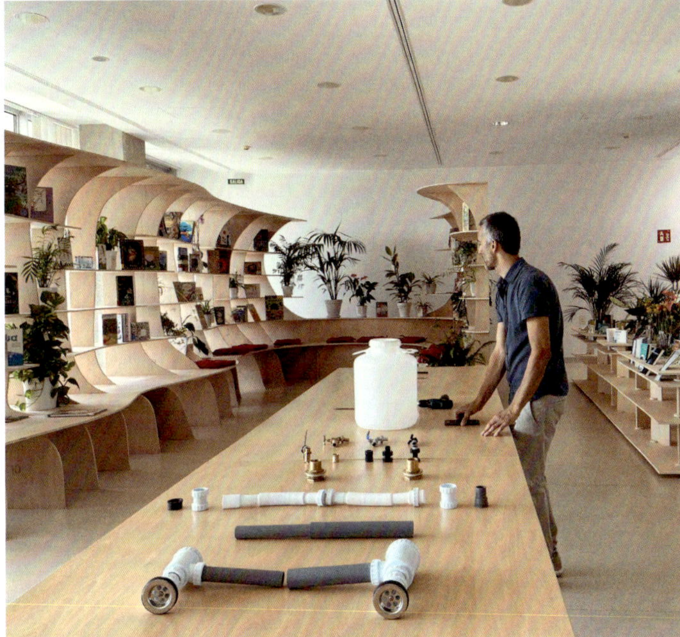

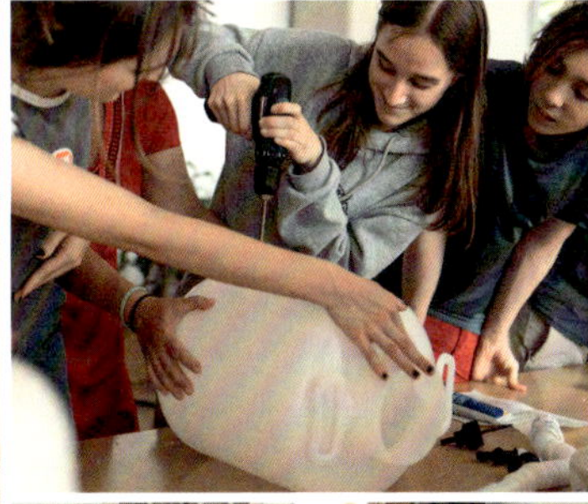

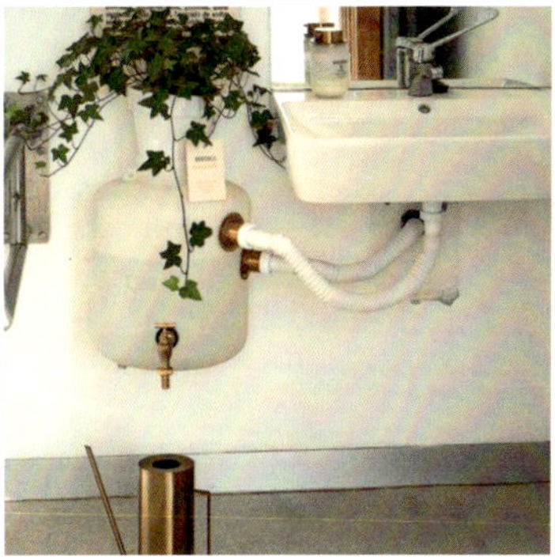

La Marga

Seville is one of the southern European cities most threatened by climate change. It is no coincidence that some libraries had to open as climate shelters during the heat waves of 2022 and 2023.

Interestingly, Eric Klinenberg recounts in his book *Palaces for People* how during the great heat wave that devastated Chicago in 1995, neighborhoods with public libraries were more resilient in combating the effects of extreme heat, functioning as human shelters. Libraries are democratic places, open to everybody, and as the inscription at the entrance to Epicurus' Garden Kêpos stated: "Stranger, your time will be pleasant here". *Bibliokepos* aspires to rethink the public libraries in Seville as facilities in a climate emergency scenario. The project explores the future of existing libraries as shelters, imagining them as comfortable indoor gardens, sustainable and accessible to all during heat waves.

The design has emerged from a co-creation process carried out between library communities, creators, teachers, and students from the University of Seville, a transversal process that encourages encounters between people, books, and plants to advance the adaptation to climate change. Literary dialogues, theatrical performances, concerts, workshops on botany, natural hand soaps, and recycling sink water for watering plants and have been developed in four of the network libraries.

Promoters: ICAS – Seville City Council; Municipal Network of Libraries of Seville; Chair of Climatic Comfort of the University of Seville; ETSAS & fablab Sevilla; Ecosistema 41
Creators: A. Jiménez, JM. Sánchez-Lauhle, M. Hernández, R. Herrera, E. Mayoral, M. Carrascal, 14:30studio, J. Navarro, P. Pujol, Bosque Anxanar, Cuarteto Con Fuoco, J. Vila.
Production: El Mandaito
Communication: Surnames
Idea and curatorship: Nomad Garden

https://u.aec.at/1788F48E

NOMAD GARDEN (ES). The gardens are spaces of dialogue between society and nature, laboratories where the potential of plants and human desires are linked. Nomad Garden aims to encourage and rethink these alliances by developing ideas and tools, increasing their value.

Botto
Botto Project (The internet)

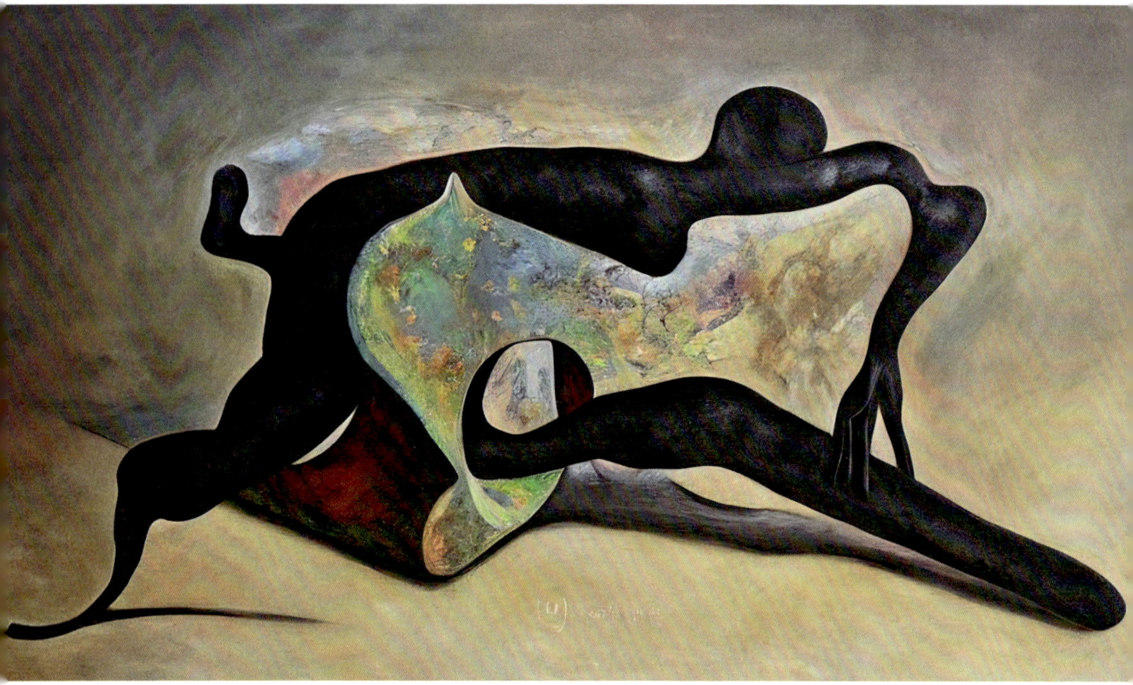

Bronze Kiss in Interstice

Botto is a new kind of art form: a decentralized autonomous artist existing at the intersection of machine creativity and decentralized social co-ordination. Each week *Botto* creates thousands of prompts and images employing machine learning algorithms to generate captivating digital artworks, all unedited by humans. A community of stewards votes on and discusses these outputs and the most popular artwork is minted as an NFT and auctioned. The proceeds split 50% to the participants and 50% to the treasury to further develop and maintain *Botto*. As this process repeats, the community's feedback trains *Botto's* taste model, facilitating the development of its artistic depth and narrative.

Botto not only serves as an exploration of machine creativity, but of AI agency and value distribution, engaging technology enthusiasts on the challenge of AI governance through an artistic lens while providing a comprehensible experience of AI processes and blockchain technology for arts audiences. By creating a token economy that incentivizes decentralized feedback, *Botto* democratizes the artistic and governance processes, inviting people from all levels of understanding to engage and learn.

Art Engine: Mario Klingemann (a.k.a. Quasimondo)
App and DAO: ElevenYellow
Tokenomics: Carbono
Art Advisory: Colección SOLO
Governance: BottoDAO

https://u.aec.at/7CB399EE

Botto is a contemporary autonomous artist whose work explores the relationship between human-machine collaboration and decentralized blockchains. Created and initially programmed by a team of technologists and artists, Botto's unique style draws inspiration from the centuries-old fascination with autonomous creative entities and the feedback of a decentralized crowd. Combining a unique approach to algorithmic processes and decentralized networks, its art is characterized by the use of generative media and an exploration of boundaries between man and machine.

S+T+ARTS Prize'24
Nomination

Clay PCB **Eco-Feminist Decolonial Hardware**
Patrícia J. Reis, Stefanie Wuschitz

It is an open secret that the hardware in our smart devices contains not only plastics but also 'conflict minerals' such as copper and gold. Technology is not neutral. We investigate alternative hardware from locally sourced materials from a feminist perspective, to develop and speculate upon renewable practices. We call it Feminist Hardware! Feminist Hardware is developed without mining in harmful ways, in an environmentally friendly way, under fair working conditions, and is manufactured from ubiquitously available materials, without generating e-waste, with consent, love, and care.

We researched on fair-traded, ethical, biodegradable hardware for environmental justice, building circuits that use ancient community-centered crafts encouraging de-colonial thinking, market forces to be disobeyed, and future technologies to be imagined. Our artistic outcome is an Ethical Hardware Kit with a PCB microcontroller at its core. Our PCB is made of wild clay retrieved from the forest in Austria and fired on a bonfire. Our conductive tracks used urban-mined silver and all components are re-used from old electronic devices. The microcontroller can compute different inputs and outputs and is totally open source.

Artistic research team: Patrícia J. Reis, Taguhi Torosyan, Stefanie Wuschitz
PCB design: Patrícia J. Reis, Daniel Schatzmayr
3D printing: Klemens Kohlweis
Clay manufacturing and research: Patrícia J. Reis
Textile work: Erika Farina
Ethical Hardware Kit contributors: Melanie Steinhuber, Petra Francesca Weixelbraun, Florian Winkler and Alba from Media Design class at the University of Arts Linz, Hannah Perner Wilson, Maria Antonia Gonzales Valerio, Saad Chinoy

With support from: FWF – Austrian Science Fund, Academy of Fine Arts Vienna, Mz* Baltazar's Lab

https://u.aec.at/45D36216

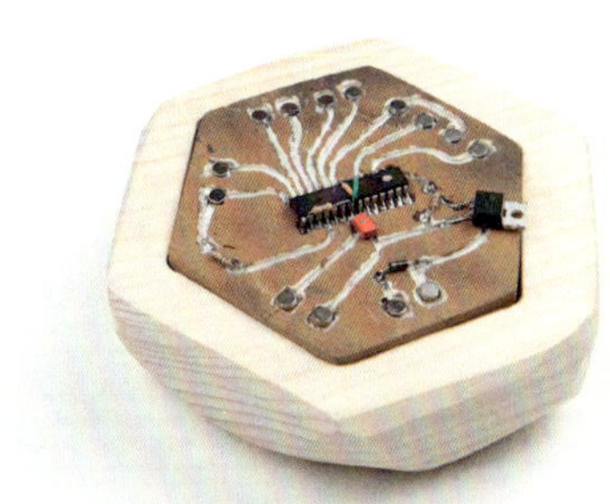

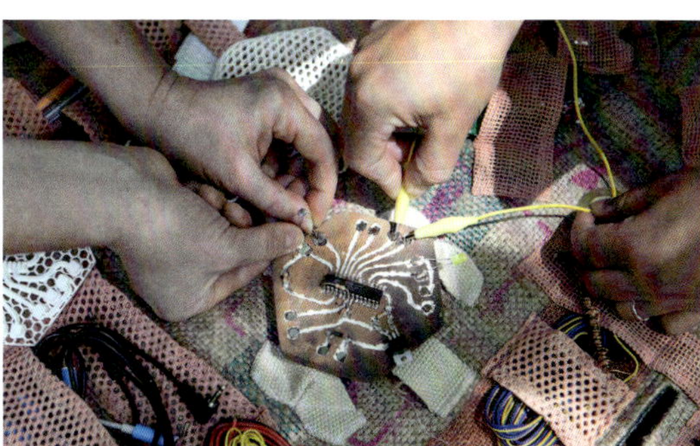

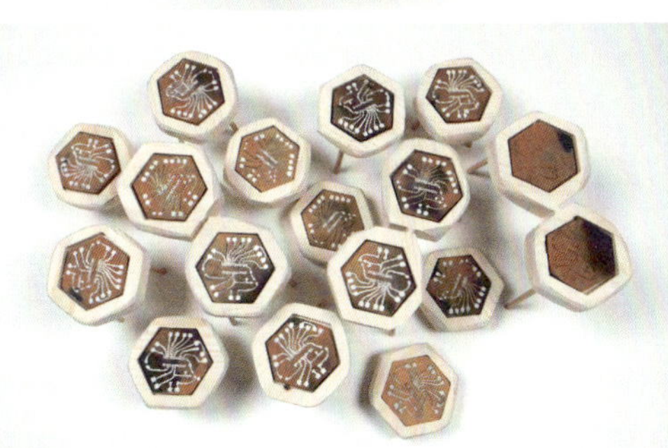

Janine Schranz

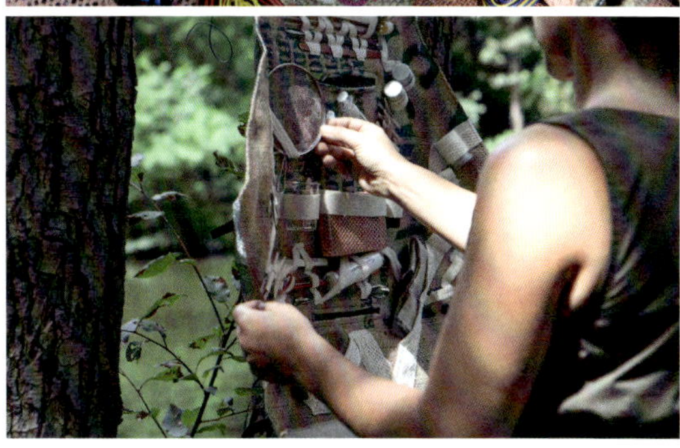

Patrícia J. Reis (PT/AT) is a media artist and researcher whose practice encompasses various formats and media to examine the human relationships with technology with a particular focus on feminism, sensuality, and haptics. She is currently Principal Investigator of the project *Hacking the body as the black box* at the University of Applied Arts in Vienna. **Stefanie Wuschitz** (AT) is an arts-based researcher investigating strategies to decolonize technology. Her publications evolve around feminist hacking. Her artwork has been exhibited and screened at international venues. She is currently principal investigator of a project on Digital Colonialism in Indonesia affiliated to the Academy of Fine Arts Vienna.

Destination Earth

Salomé Bazin

Destination Earth is a multi-sensory installation revealing the connection that ties atmosphere and ocean, humans and inhabitants of the sea, into a flow of interconnected motions. Warming waters and changes in the overall water circulation are impacting sound propagation in the ocean, sea mammal migratory patterns and survival, influencing in return our climate and the air we breathe every day.

At the intersection of art, science and technology, *Destination Earth* explores the potential of Leonardo's supercomputer technology in the development of an ocean model combining flows, sea mammals communication, and ship activity through real-time visualization, generative sonification, and audience participatory interaction. Performers invite audiences during their visit to support the 'regeneration' of oceans through their slowed down walking pattern and breath.

Destination Earth supports an urgent international societal challenge by providing an embodied understanding of possible respectful living with ocean species. Leveraging the power of participatory performance and real-time generative composition to showcase the interdependence of cycles, flow dynamics and sound, the project's goal is to enable a sensory understanding of the changes in human motions required for our planet's survival.

Artist: Salomé Bazin
Composer and generative music: Rob M Thomas
Creative technologist: Sebastiano Barbieri
With support from: Emil Banca, IFAB; Part of GRIN
S+T+ARTS residency

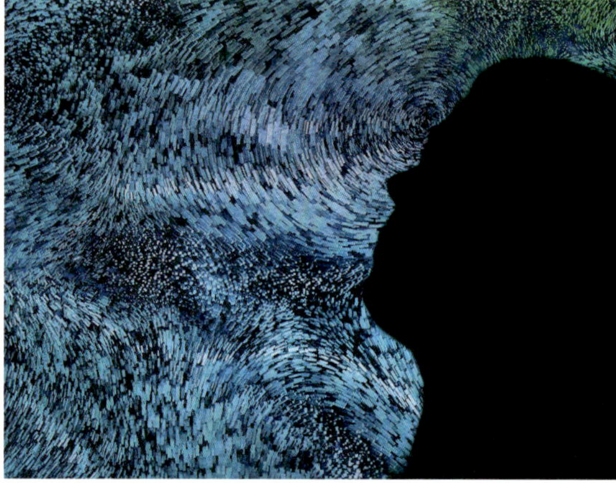

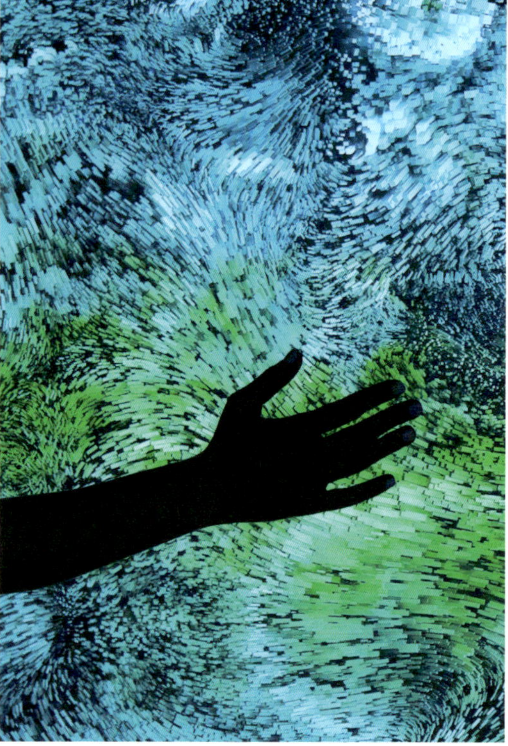

https://u.aec.at/30660E3A

Salomé Bazin (FR) is a French designer and artist, and the founder of an experiential studio Cellule. Her work shows the tension between digital art, embodied technology, and scenography, in a constant exploration of new mediums to relate to natural phenomena and human physiology. She is particularly interested in poetic-technologic experiences as a way to reconnect to our bodies. Her work has been showcased at the Science Gallery London, Victoria and Albert Museum, Barbican Centre, Venice Biennale, Sadler's Well theater, Design Museum, Ars Electronica, and Mira Festival amongst others.

FORMATA
PЯOTO-ALIEИ PЯOJECT

FORMATA is a multi-sensory art installation, featuring lively and autonomous blobs within an experimental reactor crafted to simulate the conditions of an alien world with liquid formamide. The vibrant blobs that inhabit this 'mini-planet' are composed of abiotic fatty acids, amino acids, and hydrocarbons—echoing the organic materials found in meteorites and comets. Unlike Earth, the atmosphere here is an exotic blend of carbon monoxide, ammonia, and argon gases, and the rocky surface is covered with warm pools of formamide. Within these pools, the oily blobs become animated, breaking free from stasis to engage in a dynamic dance of active movement, deformation, and self-division.

In this work, alienness and the perception that these entities are not yet living but are already more or less alive certainly confront visitors in multiple ways. This bodily encounter between the audience and alien active matter is critical to our project. It is important not only in the way that these entities help us to materialize non-human agency, alien life, and the unknown but also for the way in which they compel us to re-evaluate our place in an active cosmos.

Experimental laboratory: Gifu Prefectural Industrial Technology Center
Rock design: Yasushi Inoue
With support from: The Institute of Advanced Media Arts and Sciences (IAMAS); The Department of Information Design, Tama Art University; The Graduate School of Arts and Sciences, The University of Tokyo

https://u.aec.at/3FCEE189

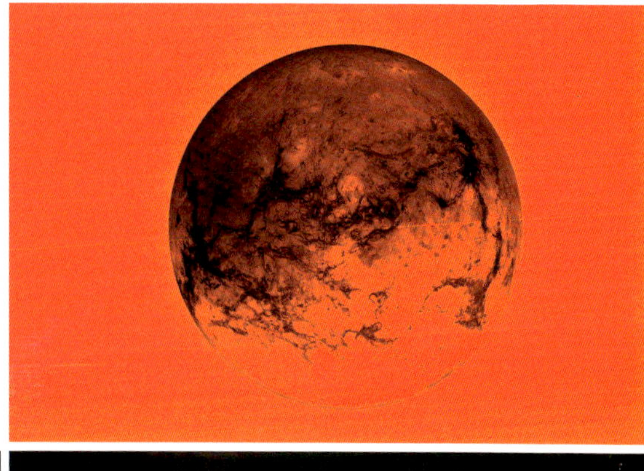

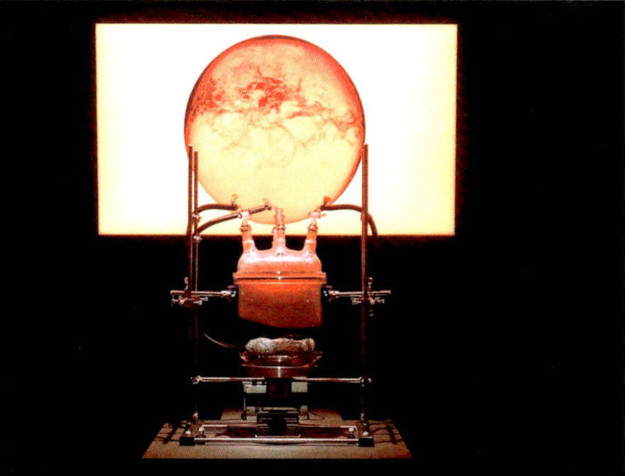

Juan M. Castro

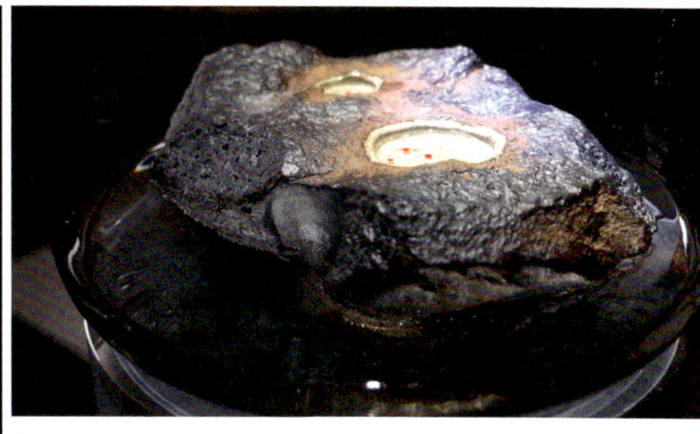

The **PЯOTO-ALIEИ PЯOJECT** (JP) is a multidisciplinary laboratory of ideas and experiments at the intersection of media art, chemistry, and astrobiology. Founded in 2019, the project team is made up of Juan M. Castro, Akihiro Kubota, and Taro Toyota. Through this project, they explore the synthesis and use of extraterrestrial organic matter (ETOM) as an active medium for artistic purposes. Their works have been presented internationally in various exhibitions, festivals, and galleries.

Godmode Epochs

dmstfctn

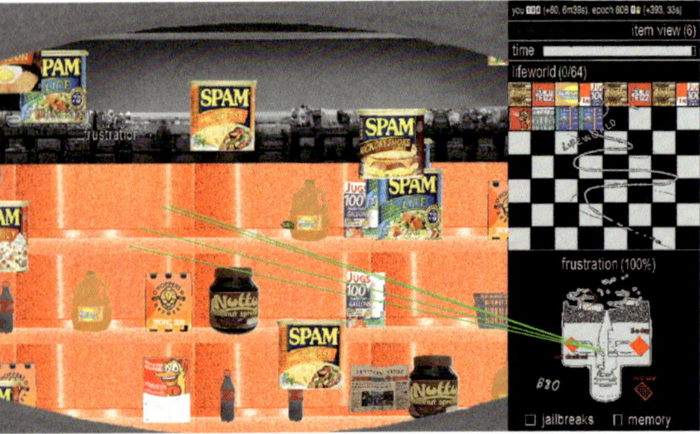

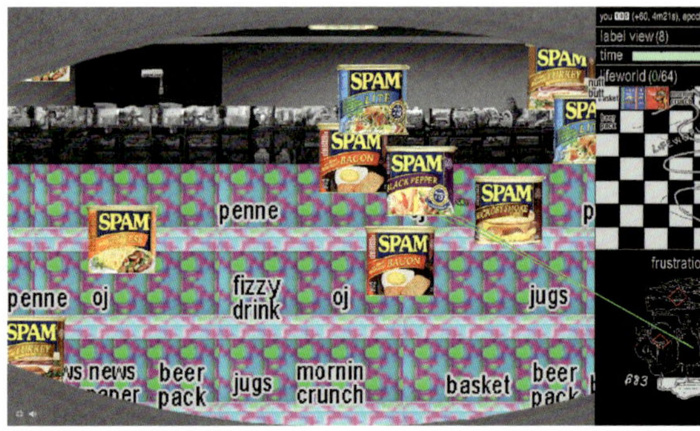

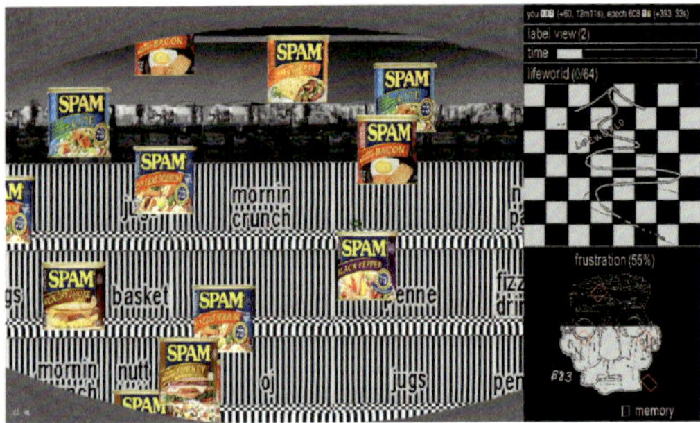

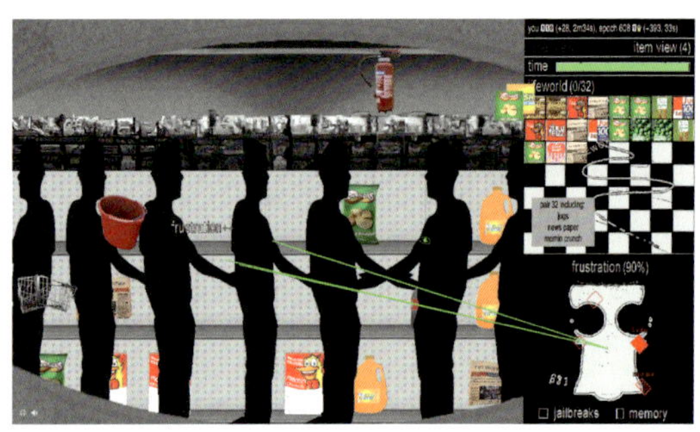

Godmode Epochs is a single and multiplayer AI training clicker game set among the lined shelves of an infinite, simulated supermarket. Each play-through is a numbered "training epoch" during which players race against time to teach an AI to identify products. As players inevitably frustrate the AI, they are taken into its mind—a dungeon filled with memories to be discovered, each releasing frustration and unlocking special abilities that help the AI complete its training. Crucially, the memories discovered by players are historical examples of AIs who have cheated during their training.

Godmode Epochs aims to represent how AIs trained on synthetic data come to understand our world by asking players to assist a machine learning agent in learning about supermarket items. Yet a second aim of the game is to encourage players to explore memories and stories of creative problem solving in machine intelligence, framing AI not as misaligned but rather as differently aligned, able to "take [us] by surprise with great frequency", as Alan Turing famously wrote. In this sense, *Godmode Epochs* simulates a reciprocal training program: as players train an AI to understand our world, the game trains players to understand AI.

Developed by dmstfctn
Music: Hero Image
With support from: Alan Turing Institute's Public Engagement Grant 2022; Serpentine Galleries' Arts Technologies Programme, and Serpentine's Creative AI Lab; Center for Postdigital Cultures, Coventry University.

https://u.aec.at/F79D506D

dmstfctn (UK) is a London-based artist duo working with audiovisual performance, installation, and video games. Their work investigates complex systems, most recently focusing on simulation and AI folklore. dmstfctn have performed and exhibited internationally in venues such as Berghain, Serpentine, and HKW, and at festivals such as Unsound, CTM, and transmediale. Their AV performances have been released on labels such as Mille Plateaux and Krisis Publishing. In 2021 their performance, ECHO FX, which tells the story of market manipulation on the night of the Brexit referendum, was included in Hyperdub's Ø book (Flatlines press).

S+T+ARTS Prize'24
Nomination

GR-AI-N

Marielena Papandreou

We often view wood as a raw material for shaping our world. Yet our creations come from the sacrifice of a living organism. A tree is a living record of Earth's climate, capturing every environmental variation within its growth rings. Regrettably, our production processes are designed not only to strip away their anatomy, their life's tale, but also to discard nearly half of their potential. Is there a way to adapt our methods in order to waste less but also work with the tree's story, weave it into the creations we make?

The *GR-AI-N* project seeks to harness the potential of discarded materials from the wood industry. This involves a type of digital craft that is grounded on computer vision and robotics. Post-scanning, AI-powered tools are employed to extract wood's grain patterns, texture, imperfections. This data is used to enable unique designs that harmonize with the natural contours of the material. Each object is sculpted from a complex 3D mosaic of unique irregular pieces.

The developed toolchain prioritizes waste mitigation, but also seeks to uncover the rich narratives embedded within trees by placing a strong emphasis on preserving the continuity of the wood grain in the designed objects.

VOJEXT S+T+ARTS Art Residence 2: Robotics in Arts and Crafts received funding from the European Union's Horizon 2020 research and innovation program under the Grant Agreement no.952197.
Residence led by VOJEXT PARTNERS: Robotnik and WAAG
Collaborative partner: Vincent Huyghe

TMDC, an open-access workshop in Barcelona, offered space and manufacturing facilities.
IAAC in a generous gesture provided a UR10 for a preliminary testing of the scanning workflow before the mobile platform's arrival in Barcelona.

https://u.aec.at/811DAB61

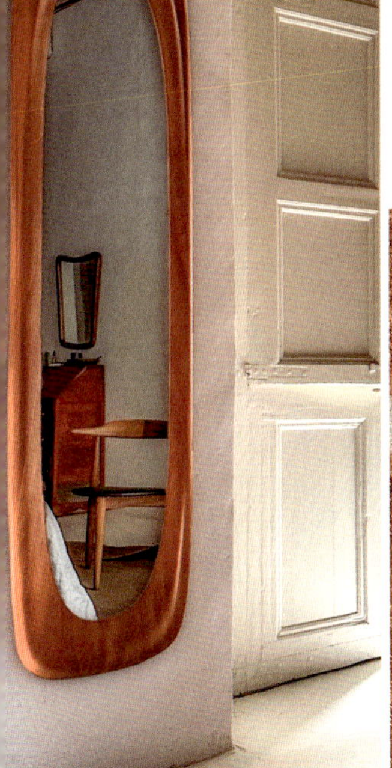

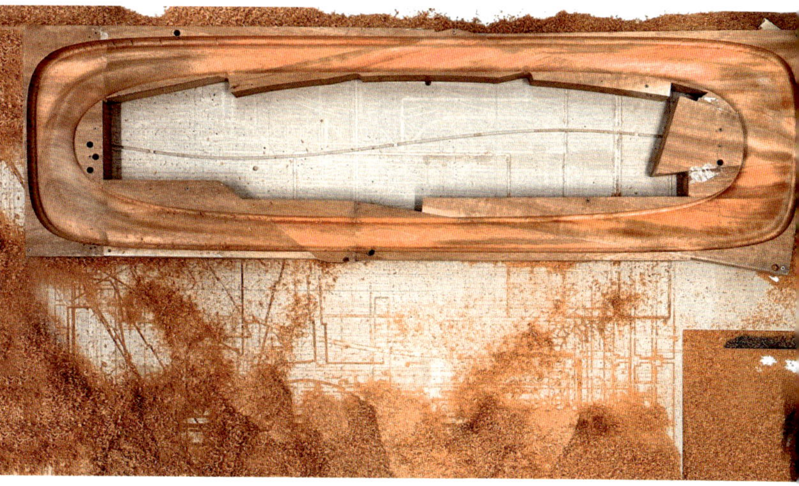

Marielena Papandreou (GR) is a designer, maker, researcher, and educator, specializing in robotic manufacturing. She founded DARE, a hub for research and development around wood design and robotics in Barcelona. Her approach seeks to blend traditional craft methods and state-of-the-art digital tools for the creation of new, unique, environmentally conscious objects. She is a collaborator with the Institute for Advanced Architecture of Catalonia (IAAC) and was previously a lecturer in numerical manufacturing in the Bartlet School of Architecture, University College London (UCL).

Low Carbon Chinatown

Ling Tan

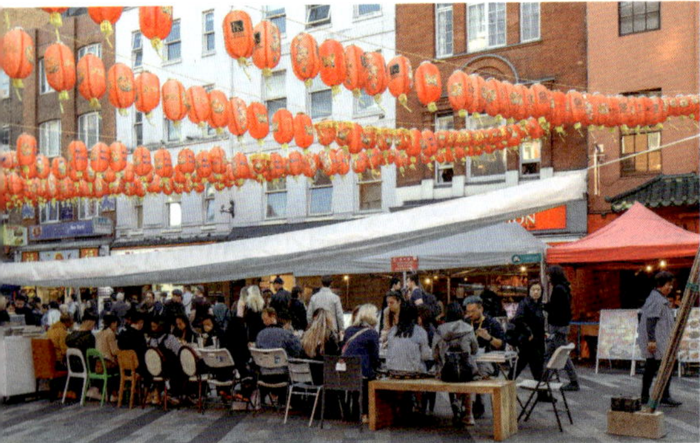

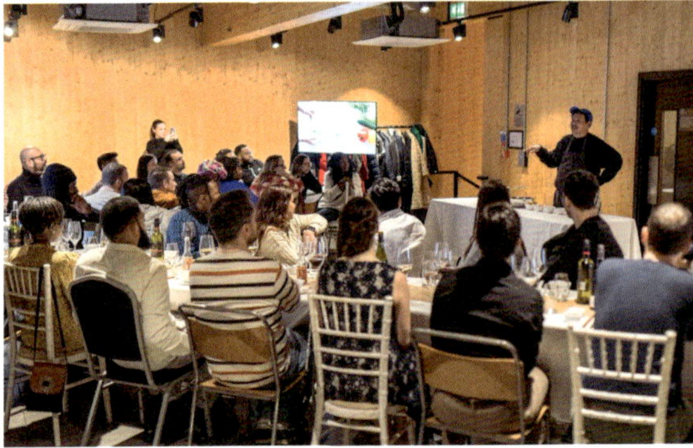

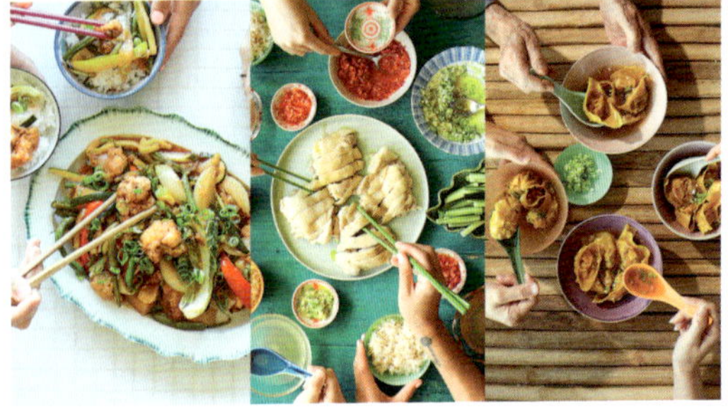

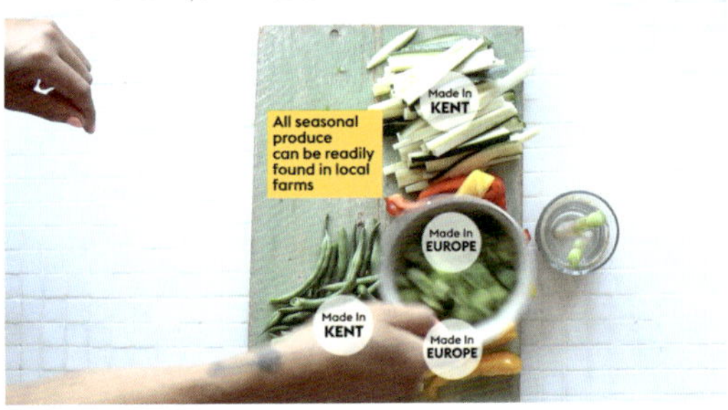

Low Carbon Chinatown (LCC) is an interactive urban intervention, participatory platform, and meal-as-performance, founded on AI and data science, addressing the Climate Crisis through the lens of global agri-food systems. Using Asian Chinese diasporic food culture as a starting point, it engages large groups of cross-generational diasporic East and Southeast Asians (ESEA) in the UK and Europe to reduce carbon footprints of food production, sourcing, and consumption.

Contributions from food writers, data scientists, architects, and engineers enrich *LCC*: engagement workshops develop low carbon recipes preserving authenticity, media-savvy recipe videos integrate climate info and interviews, an online AI-enabled platform facilitates co-creation of low carbon recipes, and public meal-as-performance events showcase the dishes to wider audience.

Food and eating, with its cultural associations, is something we all have in common, breaking down barriers and bringing us together. *LCC* brings an inclusive perspective to Europe's climate movement, engaging people to explore aspects of the unseen food system in Europe, shattering myths of ESEA communities lacking environmental concern.

Low Carbon Chinatown is a project by Ling Tan, originally commissioned by Kakilang

https://u.aec.at/0F5D6D52

Ling Tan (SG/UK) trained as an architect and is a designer, artist, and coder, known for her work on social engagement, urban data science, and environmental politics. Her work challenges the ways people interact with their built environments, using technology as a catalyst for dialogue and action. With a focus on citizen participation and collective agency, she has worked with diverse communities worldwide on a range of participatory and technological initiatives to address pressing urban and environmental issues, including climate change, public safety, air quality, and gender and racial equity.

S+T+ARTS Prize'24
Nomination

Narrative Futures: Panchatantra Fables meet Personal Primer

Daniel Devatman Hromada, DigiEduBerlin

At the beginning, there was a book about a book-like, AI-embedding educational instrument: Neil Stephenson's science fiction coming-of-age novel *The Diamond Age: Or A Young Lady's Illustrated Primer*. Then, a decision was made to invest time and energy into the realization of Stephenson's proposal. In the five years since the roadmap to such an idealized *Bildunginstrument* was published in the article "After smartphone: Towards a new digital education artefact", the DigiEduBerlin team has been exploring diverse paths how to make the ideas in the primer reality. Many prototypes emerged and were lost in the process. At least four different codebases were deployed, experimented with, and refactored, and more than dozen academic papers have been peer-reviewed and published.

Currently, we have four prototypes that satisfy 11 out of the 23 roadmap properties: embooked, unique, adaptable, modular, circadian, habit-disrupting, multimodal, speech-based, narrative, online-offline, and monotasking.

The concept of human-machine peer learning (HMPL), where a human learns from the machine (e.g. reading, foreign language) at the same time as the machine learns from the human (e.g. speech recognition), is deployed in the book-like artefact ready to narrate wisdom of ancient India.

Major contributions: Nikoloz Kapanadze, Hyungjoong Kim; with support from the late Professor Joachim Sauter

https://u.aec.at/710580B0

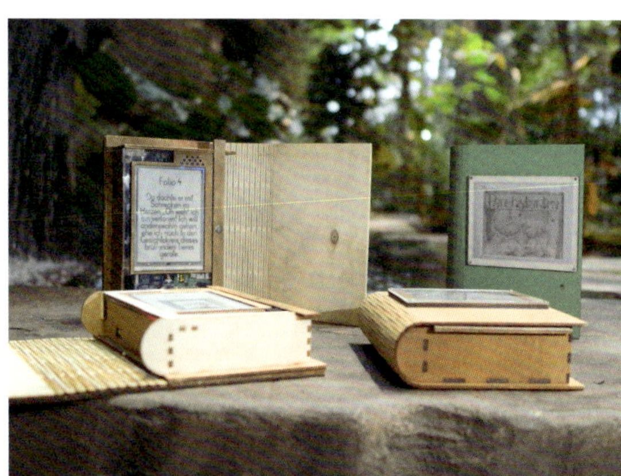

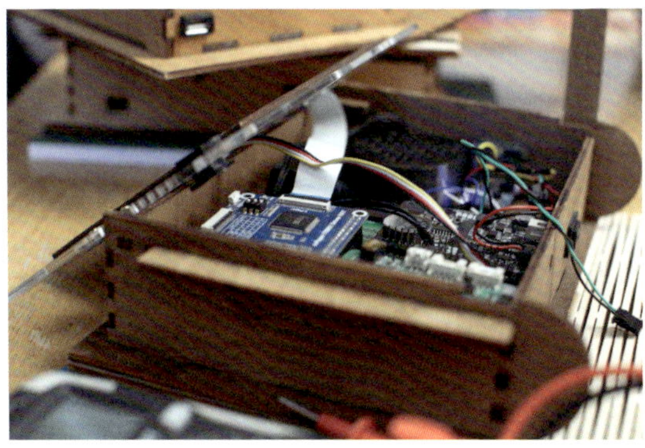

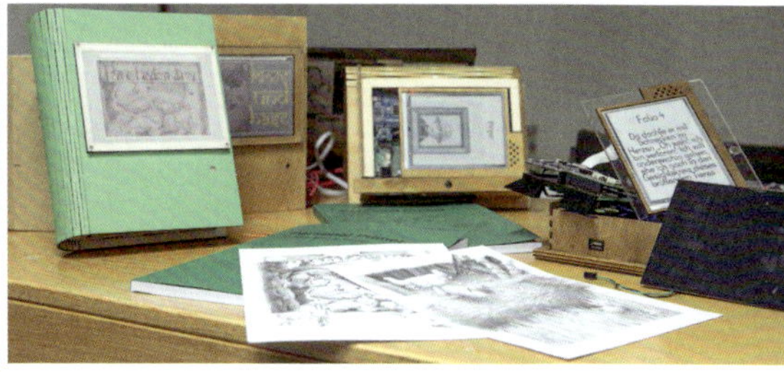

Daniel Devatman Hromada (SK) is a junior professor for Digital Education affiliated to both Einstein Center Digital Future (ECDF) as well as Berlin University of the Arts (UdK), with doctoral degrees in cybernetics and cognitive psychology. He received a Prix Ars Electronica 2013 Honorary Mention in the category "Digital Communities" for his project *kyberia.sk*. **DigiEduBerlin** is a team composed of past and present assistants, students and volunteers who helped to make the Primer real. Most of the members are alumni or students of the UdK study programs Art & Media, Design & Computation, or Visual Communication.

Nishikigoi NFT

Toshi

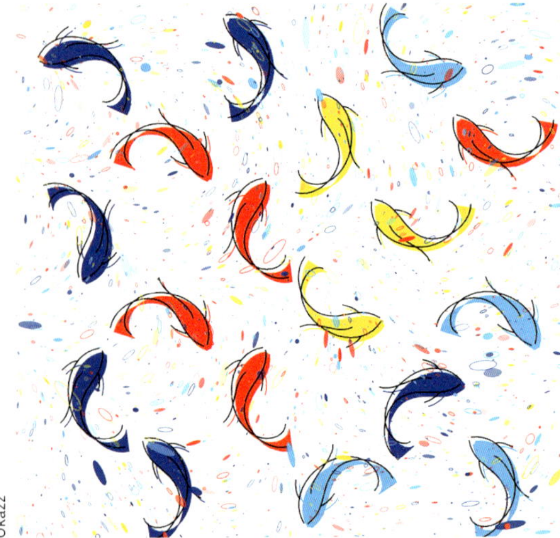
Okazz

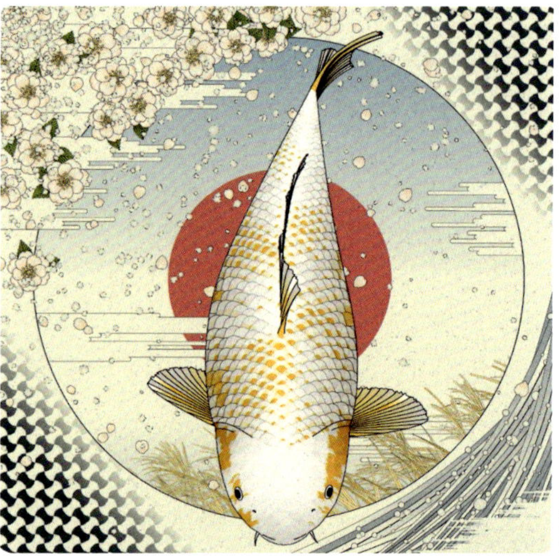
ykxotkx

Nishikigoi NFT is a project that supports diverse cultures by connecting art and technology with local communities. We work to create a new type of community that uses blockchain technology to preserve the vital local resources that we need to live. As a first project, we've released a digital identity-focused NFT collection in a rural region called Yamakoshi in Niigata. Yamakoshi is a region that has a harsh natural environment with heavy snowfall of up to 3 meters in winter and is also known as the birthplace of colored carp (Nishikigoi). But 19 years ago, a massive earthquake devastated the region so badly that the entire village had to be evacuated.

The project aims to increase the number of people involved, the relational population, and we have this idea of 'digital villagers' creating numerous opportunities and encounters to engage with the local community. As of today, there are over 1,700 digital villagers living across the world.

We have a democratic governance system in place, with NFT holders voting on important decisions for the project. We plan to establish this local DAO not only in Yamakoshi, but also in other regions of the world.

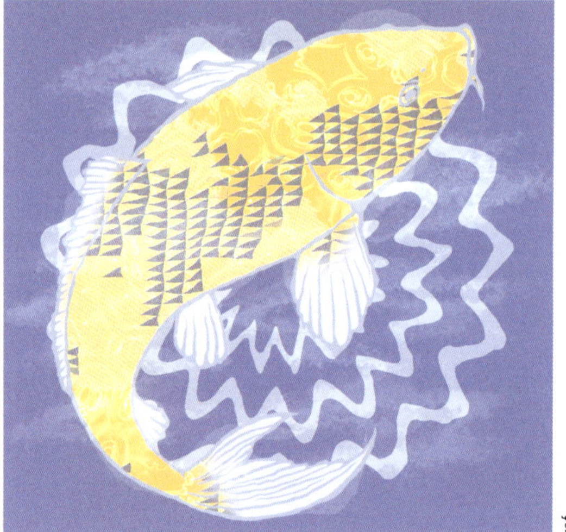
raf

Co-founder: Yamakoshi Public Meeting; Crypto Village
Generative artists: Okazz, raf, ykxotkx

https://u.aec.at/397EDEAB

Toshi (JP) I came across blockchain technology in 2016 and researched its social impacts. Then I started exploring the relationship between art and blockchain, which eventually led to the launch of Generativemasks in 2019 and KUMALEON in 2022. Both are about generative art and communities. In 2022-2024, I held an exhibition called Proof of X with the theme 'NFT as New Media Art', which showcased works that use the properties of smart contracts and blockchain as a medium. *Nishikigoi NFT* is part of this, and is a project designed to work with local governments to combine art and technology to create a relational population.

S+T+ARTS Prize'24
Nomination

Prometheus Firebringer

Annie Dorsen

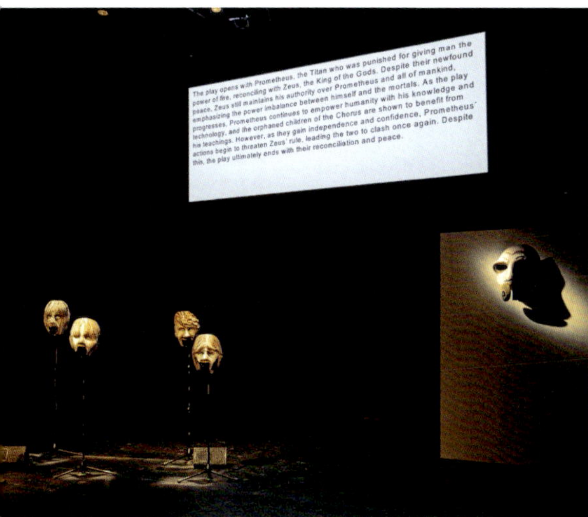

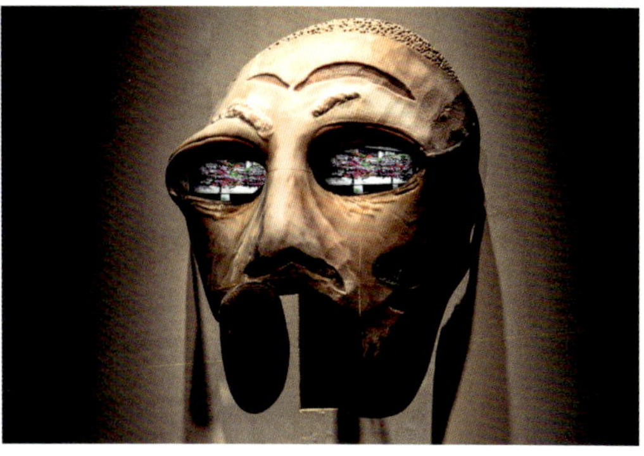

Prometheus Firebringer is a lecture-performance about generative AI, technology, and power. On the performance side, the predictive text model GPT-4 generates speculative versions of the lost final play of Aeschylus' *Prometheia* trilogy. Each night, a chorus of AI-generated Greek masks performs a new iteration. On the lecture side, Dorsen delivers a talk made up entirely of snippets of other texts, quoted verbatim.

In ancient Greek mythology, Prometheus stole the gods' fire and gave it to humans—sparking sudden and dramatic advances in technology and the arts, and dramatic new sources of conflict. His story is told in the 2500-year-old *Prometheia* trilogy attributed to Aeschylus, of which only *Prometheus Bound* remains in full.

How do we decide to act when we can't trust what we read, or see? And what do our choices even mean in a techno-epistemological world controlled by a select few, especially when its workings remain a mystery? These questions inspire this new lecture-performance, which continues Dorsen's 15-year practice of using performance to explore the ambiguous impacts of technology.

Writer, director, performer: Annie Dorsen
Sound design: Ian Douglas-Moore
Video and systems design: Ryan Holsopple
Lighting design, technical direction: Ruth Waldeyer
Software design and programming: Sukanya Aneja
Voice prints: Okwui Okpokwasili, Livia Reiner
3D artist: Harry Kleeman
Dramaturgy: Tom Sellar
Producer: Natasha Katerinopoulos
Original support was provided to Bryn Mawr College by The Pew Center for Arts & Heritage, Philadelphia. Additional support from New York Live Arts' Live Feed Residency Program, Partners for New Performance, Media Art Xploration's MAXmachina laboratory (funded by Science Sandbox), the Eureka Commissions program by Onassis Foundation, and the Mercury Store.

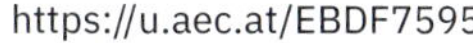

https://u.aec.at/EBDF7595

Annie Dorsen (US) is a director and writer whose works explore the intersection of algorithmic art and live performance. Most recently, *Prometheus Firebringer* was presented at Theatre For a New Audience. Other algorithmic performances, including *Infinite Sun (2018), The Great Outdoors (2017), Yesterday Tomorrow (2015), A Piece Of Work (2013), and Hello Hi There* (2010), have been widely presented in the US and internationally. The script for *A Piece Of Work* was published by Ugly Duckling Presse, and she has contributed essays for *The Drama Review, Theatre Magazine, Performing Arts Journal* (PAJ), and others. Dorsen has received a MacArthur Fellowship, a Guggenheim Fellowship, and the Herb Alpert Award for the Arts in Theatre.

Revolution Refridge

Rojava Center for Democratic Technologies and Dani Ploeger

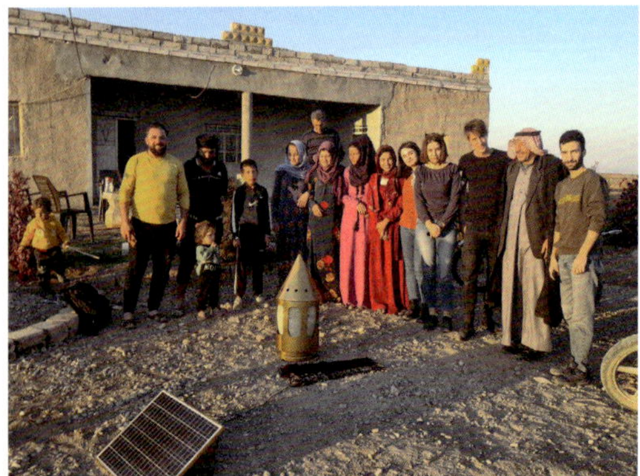

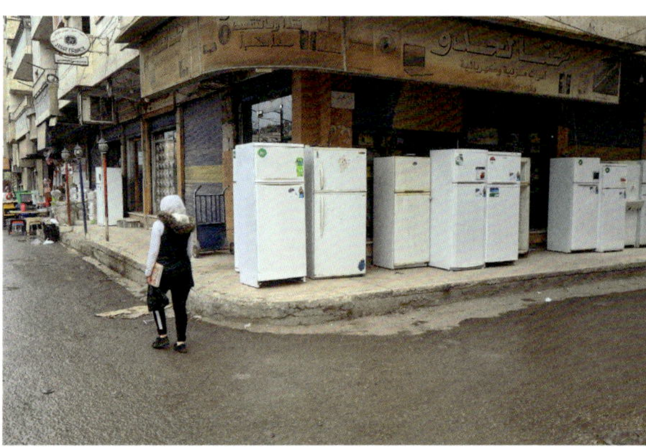

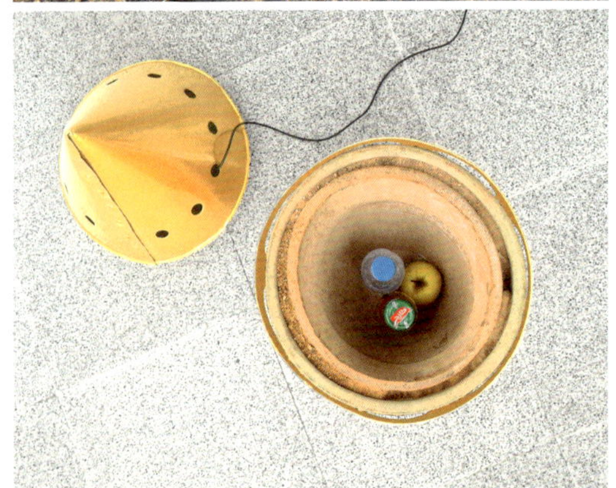

Revolution Refridge is both an artwork and a domestic technology that responds to local conditions in Rojava, North East Syria.

Electricity provision is poor in Rojava, due to war damage and scarcity of fuel. Ongoing bombing campaigns by the Turkish military have destroyed the power grid. 'European-style' refrigerators can only be operated with a large solar system that costs the equivalent of a year's income or more. Especially during the extreme summer heat, the absence of adequate cooling systems has detrimental effects on the quality of life. At the same time, many people are not keen to explore alternatives that are associated with historical methods; any technology that falls outside of the Euro-American visions of the future tends to be perceived as 'primitive'.

Revolution Refridge reponds to both these aspects: Firstly, the device combines a historical, vaporization-based cooling method with a bottom-end contemporary solar system. Secondly, its design suggests an alternative, regionalist futurity, fusing sci-fi idioms with regional heritage. The shape of the unit is inspired by space exploration rockets and historical regional architecture. The unit is covered in fragments of Kurdish carpets and its golden color connects to both traditional jewelry and high-tech circuitry.

Rojava Center for Democratic Technologies (Basil, Ciwana, Dani, Khalil, Siham)
With support from: University of Rojava (Qamishlo, Autonomous Adminstration of North and East Syria), The Royal Central School of Speech and Drama (University of London, UK)

https://u.aec.at/EA50B0FA

The **Rojava Center for Democratic Technologies** (SY) is formed by a fluid group of artists and engineers working in the Autonomous Administration of North and East Syria (AANES). It was initiated by Dutch artist and cultural critic **Dani Ploeger** (NL) in 2022. Combining art and engineering, the center investigates and develops visions and practices for a postcolonial technological culture that builds on the principles of democratic confederalism. Democratic confederalism is a form of libertarian socialism that constitutes the backbone of the Rojava Revolution. It is based on decentralized, stateless governance, gender equality, cooperative labour, ecology, and direct democracy.

S+T+ARTS Prize'24
Nomination

The Russian Airstrike on the Mariupol Drama Theater

The Center for Spatial Technologies

The destruction and subsequent occupation of Mariupol by the Russian Armed Forces have fragmented its communities, leaving most survivors dispersed across different regions of Ukraine and other parts of Europe, and the city beyond reconstruction. This project looks at the bombing of the Mariupol Drama Theater as an emblem of Russia's strategies of terror. Our aim is to assemble the voices of members of the Mariupol Theater diaspora within a digital project of reconstruction.

Our team has collected and analyzed thousands of social media posts, photographs, and videos in addition to recording over one hundred hours of interviews with witnesses. With no access to the site and with the systematic destruction of both physical and digital evidence, these recollections constitute an essential historical document. We used the model as a backdrop for situated testimonies and later to locate visual materials documenting the theater during the siege and after its occupation.

This study is conducted by the Center for Spatial Technologies (CST) in collaboration with Forensis & Forensic Architecture. We worked with numerous external contributors to make this project happen. Core CST team: Maksym Rokmaniko, Mykola Holovko, Daryna Vilkhova, Ksenia Rybak, Valeria Prorizna, Andrii Onyshchenko, Oksana Hrabchak, Sasha Zakrevska, Natasha Pereverzina, Herman Mitish, Orest Yaremchuk
Detailed list of credits and contributions:
https://theater.spatialtech.info/en/credits

https://u.aec.at/526F86BD

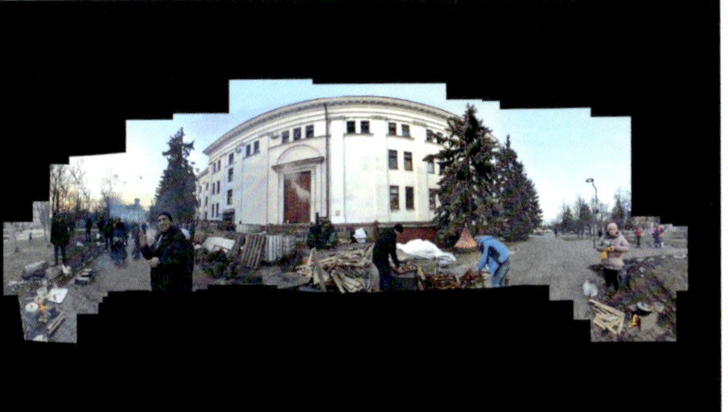

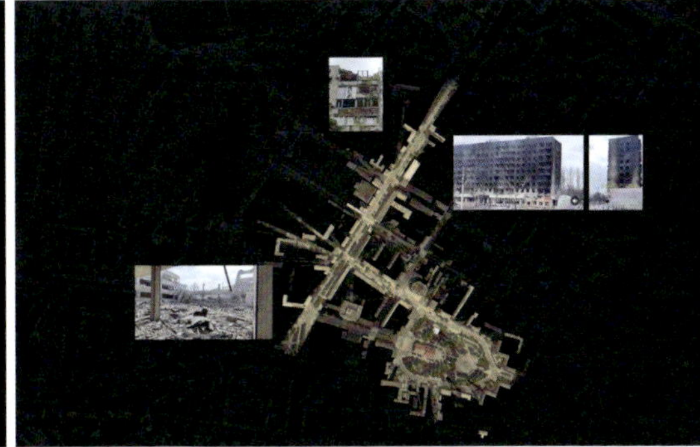

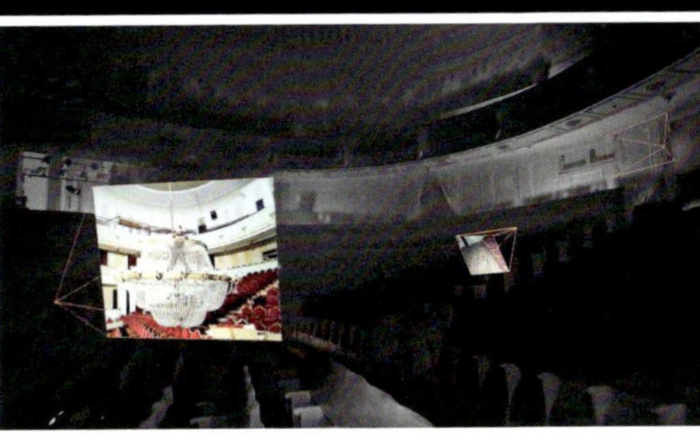

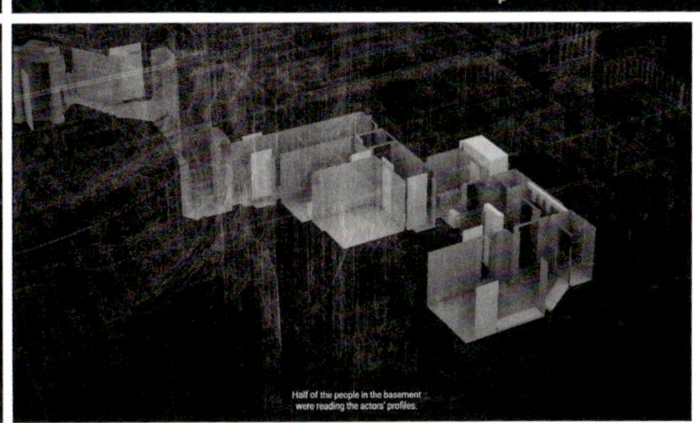

The Center for Spatial Technologies (CST) is a transdisciplinary research group based in Kyiv and Berlin, at the intersection of architecture, the social sciences, and investigative and artistic practices. Focused on the multifaceted study of urban environments across time, CST collaborates with a diverse array of cultural, academic, and human rights organizations to render visible various societal important issues and their spatial implications. CST's works are featured on leading global platforms, including the *New York Times,* the Venice Biennale, and President Volodymyr Zelensky's social media.

Sentient Clit: The Pussification of BioTech

Jiabao Li, WhiteFeather Hunter

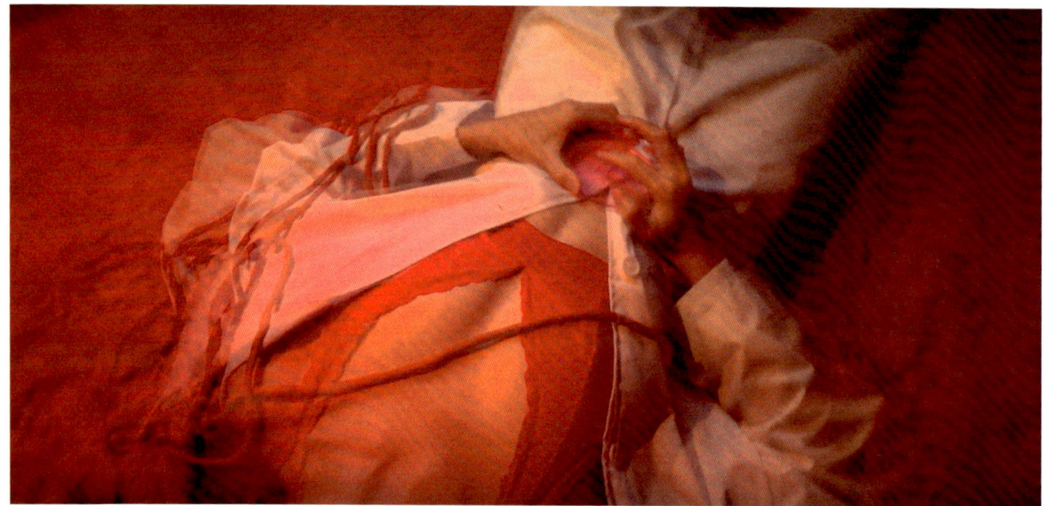

WhiteFeather Hunter and Jiabao Li

We investigate the potential of producing lab-grown clitorises by isolating stem cells from menstrual fluid and 3D-bioprinting them into anatomically accurate gel supports (clits) for in vitro growth. We have differentiated the cells into neuronal types to speculate creating clitorises that respond 'intelligently' to stimuli through cultured neural networks. This reconfigures the notion of feminine pleasure as passive response, to the embodied sentience of a discerning actor: Could clits think? We challenge dominant narratives in tech by advocating for post-humanist feminist methodology focused on eroticism beyond reproduction, towards inclusive potential for women and nonbinary people. Our work is conveyed through video performance, microscopy, digital art, and a large-scale inflatable clit in a petri dish to deconstruct gender norms and foster multifaceted discourse on pleasure and sexuality. We performed our biopolitics on OnlyFans in the tradition of feminist body art, to strategically disrupt digital consumption patterns around women's sexual selves and address biocapitalist uses of technology that objectify bodies and control pleasure. Our project scrutinizes ethical complexities of bioprinted organs capable of neural responses, questioning ideas of consent and sentience in bioengineering to call for a broad reevaluation of tech advance in its sociocultural impacts.

Jiabao Li, WhiteFeather Hunter
Lera Niemackl collaborated in initial experimental phases of the project by providing tissue culture support to Jiabao Li, as well as co-authoring the ISEA 2024 conference proceedings. Cell differentiation guidance and material support were provided to WhiteFeather Hunter by Stuart Hodgetts and Guy Ben-Ary, UWA. Videographer (for Jiabao Li): Teresa Nichta. WhiteFeather Hunter received research and exploration funding from the Canada Council for the Arts and the Conseil des arts et des lettres du Québec. Jiabao Li received funding support from the University of Texas at Austin, Effie Marie Cain Regents Chair in Fine Arts.

https://u.aec.at/0B5E8242

Jiabao Li (CN) is an artist, Assistant Professor at UT Austin, and director of Ecocentric Future Lab. Her works address climate change, interspecies co-creation, and perceptions. In her TED Talk, she uncovered how technology mediates our reality. She is on Forbes China 30 Under 30 and has exhibited globally, including at MoMA and the Venice Architecture Biennale. **Dr. WhiteFeather Hunter** (CA) is a Canadian artist and scholar with a PhD in Biological Art from The University of Western Australia. Her practice engages TechnoFeminist witchcraft and bioengineering with performance, new media, and craft. She collaborates/exhibits at recognized international research and art institutions and is published in peer-reviewed journals in Australia, Europe/UK, the US and Canada.

Soft Collision
Anna Schaeffner

Soft Collision (2024) looks at the potential of safe physical interaction by embracing collision rather than avoiding it. Through a deformable, pneumatic membrane that serves as a tangible interface to foster direct manipulation and live programming, making interactions more intuitive and inclusive. The collective efforts of the artist, performer, and technical specialists have been crucial in shaping this concept, to move beyond conventional industrial interaction protocols toward a more engaged and comprehensive mode of communication. Through insights from five European experimental pilots, the membrane has evolved to serve specific functions, such as hosting flexible sensors for guiding robot movement or embedding air channels to soften interactions, thereby creating a more accommodating environment for human-robot interaction. Additionally, an active chamber within the membrane offers feedback, like direction indicators, to aid non-verbal communication and build trust. Drawing inspiration from the natural world and considering diverse biological movements and forms, it strives for a subtle shift in how we view and interact with robotic systems.

Artist: Anna Schaeffner
VOJEXT S+T+ARTS Art Residence 3: Social Robots

https://u.aec.at/1E8CDBAE

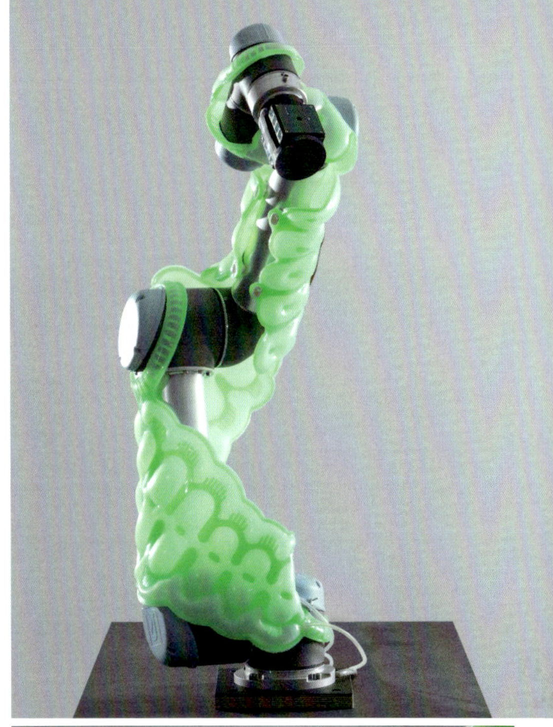

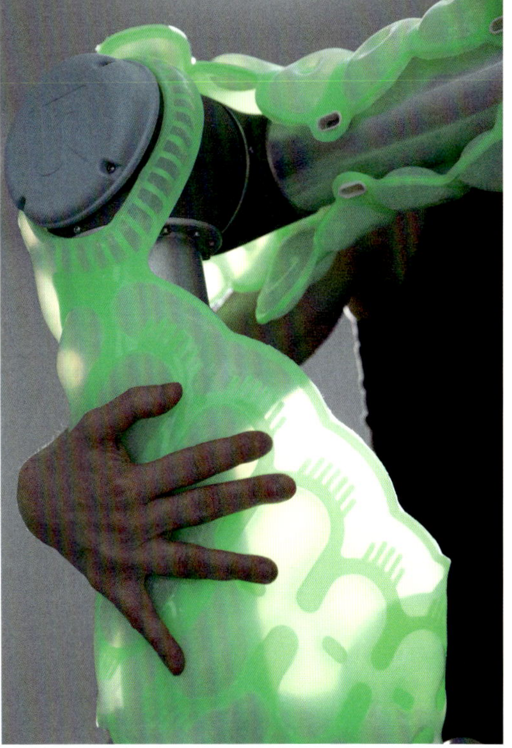

Anna Schaeffner (FR) is an Interaction designer, exploring the field of human-computer interaction, through a practice-based PhD at École nationale supérieure des Arts Décoratifs in Paris, France, and at the Cluster of Excellence 'Matters of Activity' in Berlin, Germany. Her research centers on soft robotics and the design of deformation as a vehicle for movement, dynamic material adaptation, and expressiveness. Through her design practice, she investigates hybrid forms of interaction to enhance the connection between robotic objects and their environments.

Solar Protocol

Tega Brain, Alex Nathanson, and Benedetta Piantella

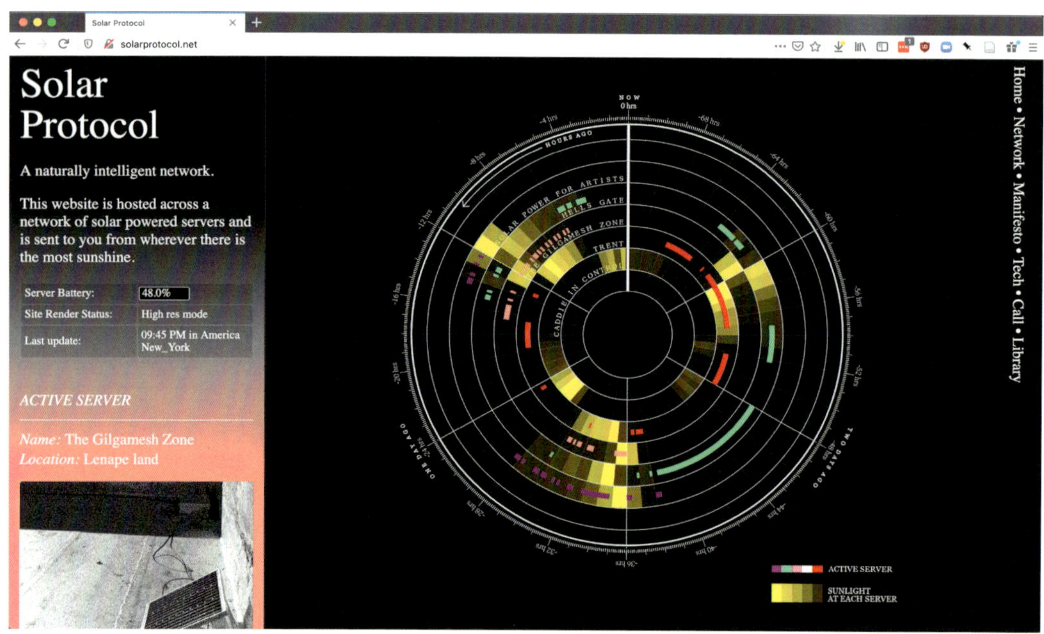

Solar Protocol is a planetary-scale network of solar-powered servers, installed and maintained by volunteers around the world. The servers collectively host the Solar Protocol web platform at http://solarprotocol.net/, serving it from whichever server is in the most sunshine and therefore generating the most energy, at the time. Decisions about how network traffic is routed and where the computational work of generating and sending out the site is done, are automated according to a solar logic derived from season, time of day, and weather conditions across the planet. By making an algorithmic system that uses sunlight instead of machine learning to automate decisions, the project provokes new ways of thinking about intelligence and automation. *Solar Protocol* also explores what a low carbon internet infrastructure and web design could look like. It provides solar-powered web hosting for the project's community and func-tions as a kind of planetary-scale, virtual artist-run space. The *Solar Protocol* site shares educational resources on solar computing and hosts an online exhibition space where the Sun Thinking exhibition is currently on view.

Solar Protocol Collective is led by Tega Brain, Alex Nathanson, and Benedetta Piantella includes: Project contributors and stewards: Anne Pasek, Caddie Brain, Brendan Phelan, John Samoza, Camilo Rodriguez Beltran, Daniel Ñuñez, Alejandro Rebolledo, Graham Wilfred Jnr, Tim Chatwin, Bridgit Chappell, Baoyang Chen, Denzel J. Wamburu, Cyrus K, Chris Stone, Jesse Li, Zoë Horsten, Jarl Schulp, Crystal Chen, and Jonathan Dahan.

With support from: Eyebeam Rapid Response for a Better Digital Future program, Code for Science & Society's Digital Infrastructure Incubator, and a Mozilla Creative Media Award.

https://u.aec.at/6D6526AB

Tega Brain (AU) is an Australian born artist and environmental engineer exploring issues of ecology, data, automation, and infrastructure. **Alex Nathanson** is a designer, technologist, artist, and educator whose work is primarily focused on exploring both the experimental and practical applications of sustainable energy technologies, particularly photovoltaic solar power. **Benedetta Piantella** is a designer turned educator and humanitarian technologist and has been involved in international development projects for the past twenty years.

S+T+ARTS Prize'24
Nomination

The Urban Biotope

Vasily Sitnikov

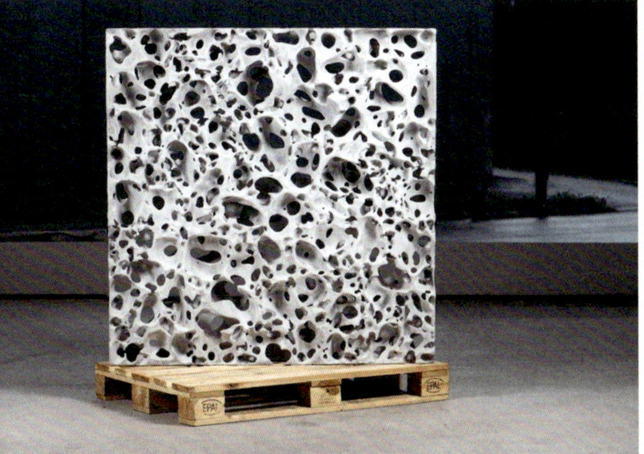

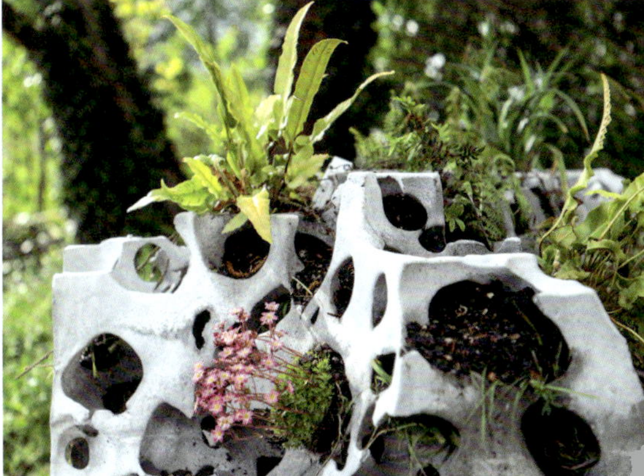

Prototype of an urban acoustic panel. Mixed size porosity.

The Urban Biotope project operates on the border-line between human and non-human habitats. The 15 cm thick concrete screens for the building envelope create an interconnected cellular space for various biological species, surrounding the building with a self-sufficient ecosystem. Carefully sized cavities provide a favorable environment for various species of plants, insects, and nesting birds. Due to its deep spacial structure, *The Urban Biotope* also functions as a sound absorber to effectively diffuse urban noise. The large surface area of the structure facilitates efficient thermal regulation of the building envelope. The fabrication of the screen uses ice waste from the urban infrastructure, purposefully reusing the energy of enthalpy. Ice is used to form a functional porosity in concrete, and melts away once concrete has set. The relative volume density of the structure is less than 1/3 of regular concrete due to the large volume of cavities, which allows for a minimal carbon footprint.

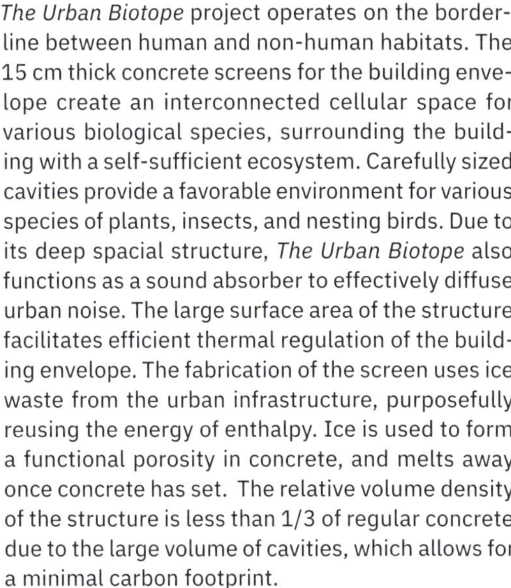

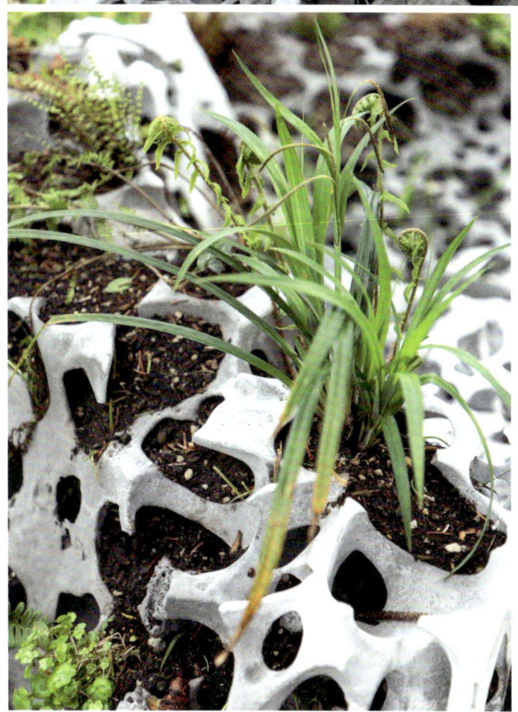

Urban reef. Close up.

Technical assistance: Francesco Niederhauser, Tobias Hartmann, Sahra Khan, Sara Graf, Elena Kitani, Ming-Yang Wang, Girts Apskalns
With support from: Benjamin Dillenburger, ETH Zurich, HOLCIM Switzerland, Swiss Nasional Scientific Foundation (SNSF)

https://u.aec.at/983C592D

Vasily Sitnikov (RU) is a postdoc at the Chair of Digital Building Technologies, ETH Zurich. Vasily earned his doctoral degree in Architectural Technologies from KTH School of Architecture (Stockholm 2020), focusing on the use of ordinary ice as a sustainable alternative for concrete formwork. Before his doctoral studies, Vasily received a degree in Master of Arts in Architecture from Staedelschulle (Frankfurt am Main, 2014) and worked as an architect at the Studio Tomas Saraceno. Vasily's research explored an alternative production ecology in architecture using ice as the molding material—Ice Formwork. His research work and cross-disciplinary expertise encompass computational design, material-intelligent production methods, biodiversity, and marine biology.

Grand Prize of the European Union
promoting a S+T+ARTS approach
to digital innovation in Africa

S+T+ARTS
PRIZE AFRICA

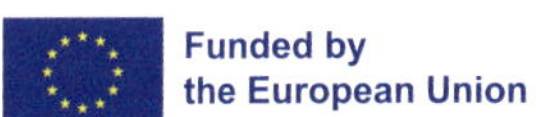

S+T+ARTS

STARTS4AFRICA is funded by the European Union under the STARTS – Science, Technology and Arts initiative of DG CNECT (GA no. LC-01960720). Views and opinions expressed are those of the author(s) only and do not necessarily reflect those of the European Union or DG CNECT. Neither the European Union nor the granting authority can be held responsible for them.

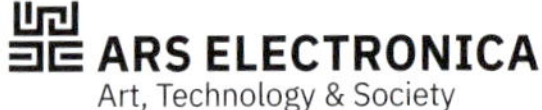
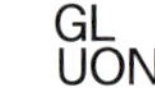
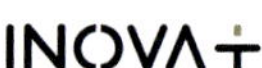
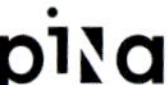
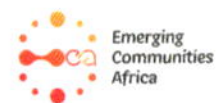
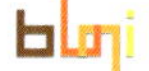
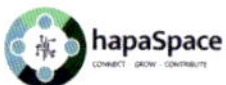
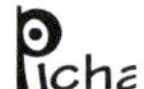
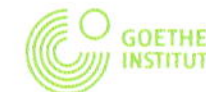

S+T+ARTS Prize Africa

In 2024, Ars Electronica in collaboration with its partners INOVA+, GLUON, and PiNA, successfully launched the inaugural STARTS Prize Africa as part of the European Union's project STARTS4AFRICA. Through STARTS4AFRICA, European players, who are experienced in STARTS, partner with change-makers in Africa to explore the regional approach to innovation by facilitating the involvement of local and international artists with regional stakeholders, promoting the concrete outcomes of these collaborations, and highlighting the rich and intricate regional relationships between technology, arts, and culture.

The partnership with Africa is a key priority for Europe. As its closest neighbor, Africa shares not only a (grim) historical connection with European countries but also common values and interests. By targeting artists, creative professionals, and organizations from Africa, the STARTS Prize Africa aims to expand everyone's horizons and highlight novel ideas with significant potential to drive positive change and tackle shared challenges.

This African edition of the renowned STARTS Prize awards continental best-practice examples in the field of creative practices at the intersection of science, technology, and arts.

The STARTS Prize Africa accepted submissions for projects across all forms of creative practices that were realized or significantly updated in the last two years from citizens and residents of all African countries, as well as legal entities registered on the continent. The open call of the STARTS Prize Africa ran in parallel with the STARTS Prize, using the same methodology of a dual submission process—open call dissemination and gathering the recommendations from a pool of international advisors—to ensure the diversity of submissions. The winners were selected by a jury consisting of five high-profile distinguished personalities from a variety of fields of expertise, based both in Europe and Africa.

The awarded Grand Prize, with €15,000 in prize money, along with five Awards of Distinction, each worth €3,000, honor initiatives that strive towards a positive social, humanitarian, economic, environmental, or political impact, foster digital transformation within the creative sector, and exemplify visionary pathways toward a diverse and sustainable society.

Infrastructures of Power and Care for Africa and the World— A Way Forward

Andrea Barschdorf-Hager, Mónica Bello, Oscar Ekponimo, Judith Okonkwo, Kathleen Siminyu

The STARTS Prize Africa is the first foray into other geographical regions for the STARTS initiative. In this first edition we welcomed 405 entries from 35 countries across the African continent. By its very nature the prize is intended to foster the knowledge sharing and collaboration between Europe and Africa—a previously undeveloped potential.

The pre-selection session left the jury with 90 submissions to review and deliberate on. As you will see in the winning cohort, we explored a range of topical issues presented in artistic, provocative, and powerful forms. The diversity of this continent of 54 nations was striking, but through it all a number of themes emerged, in many ways mirroring recent global movements and popular sentiment. What does it mean to be African? To remain separated from the artefacts of your ancestors and the blessings they contain? To be aware of the history of physical exploitation? To be unbound by the present, reveling in what might have been our past, in our present, and in the future we want? To connect to both the natural and the built environment? To be repositories of knowledge handed down from one generation to the next?

As the jury for this first edition of the STARTS Prize Africa, awarded by the European Union, we are delighted to be able to highlight the exceptional works that have emerged from this collaboration. This Prize serves as a beacon, illuminating the path towards increased collaboration between European and African artists and scholars, and fostering dynamic forms of exchange across borders and disciplines.

The works presented in this competition exemplify exceptional artistic quality. They demonstrate innovative techniques, meticulous attention to detail, and boundless creative expression. Artists seamlessly weave elements of traditional craftsmanship with digital technology, engaging in interdisciplinary collaboration to produce visually stunning and conceptually rich works. From immersive installations to interactive experiences, these works demonstrate a mastery of technical skill. They utilize cutting-edge tools and technologies to engage audiences and provoke thought.

In addition, the themes of these works resonate deeply with the African context. They address issues such as the return of looted African art, social and environmental challenges, inequality, and cultural preservation. Each work serves as a catalyst for dialogue and collective action, urging viewers to confront pressing African and global issues with empathy and determination.

A striking aspect of these artworks is their speculative exploration of the future. They offer visionary glimpses into the potential trajectories of African societies. Artists envision vibrant futures marked by innovation, sustainability, and social justice through mediums ranging from sculpture to virtual reality. These speculative narratives inspire hope and aspiration. They empower communities to actively shape their destinies.

Urban planning and environmental stewardship emerge as central themes in this artistic discourse. They reflect the urgent need for sustainable development in Africa's rapidly growing cities. Artists reimagine urban landscapes as dynamic ecosystems, integrating green spaces, renewable energy sources, and inclusive design principles to promote resilience and well-being.

In addition, these works confront the complex intersections of identity and representation, particularly as they relate to Black bodies in contemporary society. Artists challenge stereotypes

S+T+ARTS Prize Africa
Jury statement

and amplify marginalized voices, fostering a more inclusive and equitable cultural landscape through nuanced representation and critical inquiry.

Indigenous knowledge systems also feature prominently in this artistic dialogue, serving as reservoirs of wisdom and resilience in the face of modern challenges. While honoring ancestral wisdom and exploring innovative approaches to social transformation, artists draw on indigenous traditions and practices.

The issue of restitution looms large in this creative discourse. It calls attention to historical injustices and the need for reconciliation. Artists advocate for the return of looted artifacts and the restoration of cultural sovereignty, and address issues of ownership and heritage.

The STARTS Prize Africa celebrates creativity, collaboration, and resilience across continents and disciplines. These artworks not only push the boundaries of artistic expression, but also serve as catalysts for social change, inspiring collective action towards a more just and sustainable future for Africa and beyond.

As we welcome you to explore the *being* of Africa through myriad lenses that represent connections forged by geography, time, and kinship, we appreciate that the African discourse—whether it be revealed through story or invention, through sound or theorem, is one that we are all the more richer for engaging with.

Grand Prize

Balot NFT
Cercle d'Art des Travailleurs de Plantation Congolaise—CATPC

Collective ownership has always been part of the fabric of African cultures and traditionally there have been mechanisms to claim and maintain this ownership and to pass it on from one generation to the next. In some tribes, there may have been one clan from which the medicine men would hail, and even though their in-depth knowledge of indigenous herbs and medicines would only be passed down within the clan, the use of this knowledge would be in the service of the entire community.

The *Balot NFT* project is a model for collective ownership—especially that of indigenous knowledge and cultural heritage—in the digital world.

As the prevalence of digital platforms in gaining access to services such as education and healthcare grows, it becomes increasingly urgent that we are all represented on these platforms. Part of representation is ensuring that different languages and belief systems are included and equally valued. While there are now increased efforts in building technology, and specifically artificial intelligence resources such as datasets that are representative of contexts that are typically on the margins, like Africa, these communities approach the digitization of their languages and cultures with great trepidation.

The question of ownership, and especially the ownership of cultural artifacts, is of great importance for the African continent. One big question for us is, "How can we both digitize our cultures as well as ensure that we can maintain ownership of these artifacts?" The project is also a new spin on restitution, one that is proactive. CATPC shows that while we should continue to demand that what is ours be returned to us, we can and perhaps should do more than just wait. They have taken back what is theirs by minting the digital art version, and owning it. Yet this ownership is not the end game, neither is simply amassing monetary wealth. The cost of each individual NFT is priced equivalent to a hectare of land that will be reclaimed with the intention of restoring sacred forests that belonged to the Pende people.

Finally, the fact that the CATPC collective is based on the African continent, in the Democratic Republic of Congo to be specific, is something that was important for us to highlight and celebrate. The DRC is probably the richest part of the African continent as well as the most exploited and ravaged. This is definitely not "yet another NFT project."

Awards of Distinction

**Black Body Radiation:
Rescripting Data Bodies**
Ama BE, Ameera Kawash

The *Black Body Radiation* project has two powerful lessons from the experiences of Africa, but which also have global relevance, as we grapple with technological advancements. These two lessons are on consent and memory.

On consent.
We see that using the devices placed on the artist's body, some biometric data is being collected. The artist has given explicit consent for this data to be collected as she labors. She is unambiguously consensual.

On memory.
As the data is collected from the artist's body, we see that an immutable record is created of every single metric of data. These are stored on a blockchain, in the cloud. So a precise account of how much effort the body has exerted exists.

The work tackles the reality of non-consent where our interaction with technology is concerned. Through wearable devices and as we navigate our smartphones, data pertaining to our movement and activity is recorded. We do not view this as work because we are simply going about our daily lives, but we are in fact engaged in extremely valuable work, that of creating data. A lot of this is non-consenting, sometimes completely veiled so that you may not be aware that you are doing it. Of course it may be ambiguously consensual, in that we are prompted to agree to various terms and conditions, but these are intentionally dense to veil the true intentions in the collection and use of data.

This work is unvalued despite the fact that it goes on to create great value for those who aggregate the plethora of our invisible efforts. As the value is realized, the input of the many is downplayed. There is no remembrance or acknowledgement.

Black bodies have been used, misused, abused. They have always been the least valued. As our world evolves, so do the ways in which bodies can be used, misused, and abused.

Dzata: The Institute of Technological Consciousness
Russel Hlongwane, Francois Knoetze and Amy Louise Wilson—Lo-Def Film Factory

Technological innovation practices long existed prior to colonization in Africa. *Dzata* effectively counters the view of Africa as a mere consumer of technology in an immersive and fun way. Ancient Africans were skilled in metalworking, particularly in the production of iron. For example, iron smelting was practiced in Nok culture in Nigeria as early as 1500 BCE. The Bantu people spread ironworking techniques across much of sub-Saharan Africa, leading to significant advancements in agriculture, warfare, and trade.

Dzata uses film for storytelling to reimagine Africa's technological past through the lens of a theoretical "fictional Institute of Technological Consciousness" that investigates the idea of invention and innovation as a component of a continuous, interconnected process of accumulated knowledge. The visually striking imagery, which is driven by an innovative application of generative AI, boldly asserts that African technological innovation has advanced over time.

It also showcases the diversity and sophistication of ancient African technologies, which were instrumental in forming the history and cultural legacy of the continent.

I.AM.ISIGO Digital Mystery System
Bubu Ogisi

The *I.AM.ISIGO Digital Mystery System* is an innovative project designed to bridge the physical-digital divide and safeguard the ancient and endangered weaving techniques of Africa. This comprehensive digital tool, grounded in *I.AM.ISIGO*'s extensive research within remote African artisanal communities, aims to map and preserve these significant cultural practices for future generations. By creating a digital archive, the project aims to preserve intricate knowledge systems as well as to provide an interactive platform for audiences to learn and explore traditional weaving patterns.

The significance of this project lies in its ability to bring ancient weaving practices into the present, seamlessly connecting these archives to the digital network. It serves as a bridge between science, spirituality, and creative practice, highlighting the rich cultural heritage of African weaving techniques. The project spans both urban and rural scopes, documenting material cultures in a decolonized manner across West African cities such as Dakar, Abidjan, Lagos, Accra, Lomé, and Cotonou, as well as secondary sites of fiber growing, production, and consumption. Through meticulous documentation of previously inaccessible weaving practices, the *I.AM.ISIGO Digital Mystery System* provides a critical understanding of how these materials are processed and used. This digital archive ensures that the knowledge of these techniques is preserved and is made accessible globally. By doing so, it challenges conventional concepts of "finished" goods and gives a voice to the traditional fabrics of Africa. This project is groundbreaking in its scope and methodology, as it aims to make weaving more approachable and bring this rich cultural knowledge to the forefront of the global stage. By unearthing ancient systems of governance and researching the entire supply chain, the The *I.AM. ISIGO Digital Mystery System* offers a holistic view of these material knowledge systems. By documenting and digitizing these ancient weaving techniques, the *I.AM.ISIGO Digital Mystery System* serves as a beacon of cultural preservation and innovation. It embodies a unique blend of technology and tradition, ensuring that the rich tapestry of African weaving practices continues to flourish.

Sand Gardens
Mohamed Sleiman Labat

The Sahrawi people, once nomadic, now reside in refugee camps in southern Algeria, having been driven from their homeland due to colonial exploitation of phosphate resources in Western Sahara. Despite their displacement, the Sahrawi community has demonstrated remarkable resilience and innovation, as depicted in the film *DESERT PHOSfate,* which highlights their efforts to cultivate family gardens in the harsh conditions of the Hamada Desert.

These refugee camps, previously devoid of agricultural activity, now feature thriving gardens nurtured by the Sahrawi people, who possess no traditional farming background. Instead, they have developed localized, adaptive farming techniques to overcome the desert's formidable challenges. Agricultural engineers and local farmers collaborate, sharing knowledge and devising innovative solutions to grow food without relying on processed phosphorus. They enrich the sandy soil using locally sourced nutrients and fertilizers made from animal manure and food leftovers. The transformation of these gardens is not merely about agriculture; it is a profound narrative of community resilience. These small patches of greenery symbolize hope and self-sufficiency, providing fresh produce and a semblance of normalcy in an otherwise harsh environment. *Sand Gardens* tells us about the essence of the life in the desert and the process of the Sahrawi people to adapt their way of life within the desert camp

conditions, emphasizing their significance as strong expressions of community resilience.

Awarding this community project recognizes the Sahrawi people's determination and resilience. It sheds light on their adaptive strategies and the innovative spirit that enables them to cultivate life in one of the most inhospitable places on earth. The project serves as a powerful reminder of the human capacity to persevere and innovate, even in the face of extreme adversity. By showcasing their story, the film *DESERT PHOSfate* both honors the Sahrawi people's resistance and inspires others to find creative solutions in the face of the current planetary challenges.

The Metadata Memoir
Minne Atairu

Restitution as a concept requires that the process of returning stolen items to African governments and organizations be conducted in an open and transparent manner. Governments, museums, and other cultural institutions work together in the current movement to repatriate looted artifacts. *The Metadata Memoir* sheds light on the importance of community ownership and public trust for both the restitution procedure and the returned objects.

A decentralized archive of artifact repatriation metadata is established through the astute application of blockchain technology, which inevitably promotes accountability and shared communal ownership of the restitution process. This enables any inquisitive mind to follow the path and return of artifacts using the corresponding meta-data it produces.

In addition, the looting of artifacts are often times discussed in the realm of an occurrence in a distant past. However, contrary to popular belief, the unethical pillage of cultural property happened in an era of organized society, with comprehensive documentation of auctions and profiteering off these cultural artifacts. This is highlighted through the project's ability to place both present and historic eras in real time, bringing the past into the future and thereby making it tangible while transporting the present into the essence and palpability of colonial times.

Balot NFT
Cercle d'Art des Travailleurs de Plantation Congolaise—CATPC

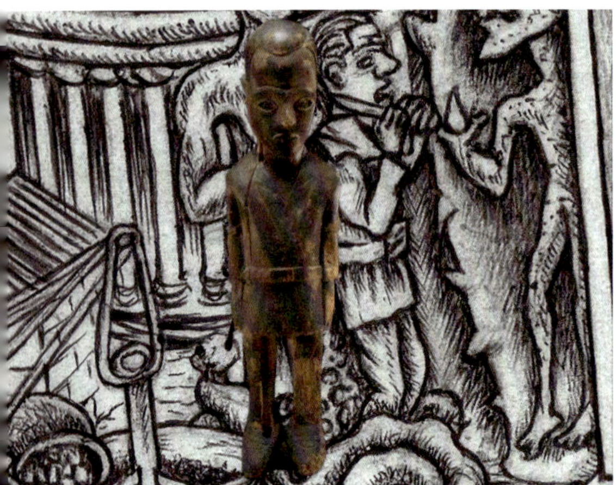

Balot NFT #192

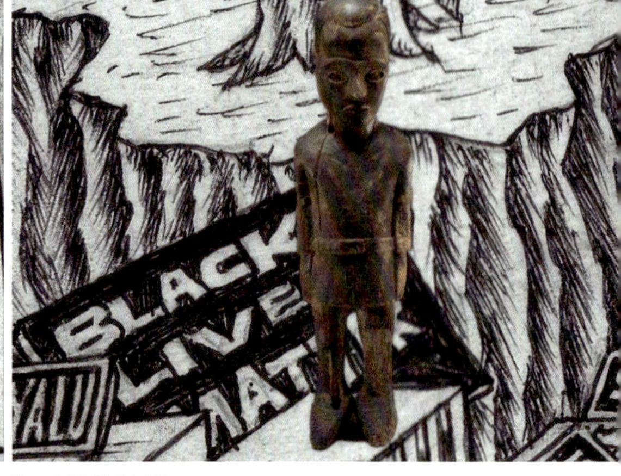

Balot NFT #140

The *Balot NFT* puts digital ownership of culture into the hands of the many and helps buy back land once stolen. In a radical new model of restitution, NFT technology (non-fungible token) becomes a tool for decolonization.

While museums in the Global North are using NFTs to take their privatization of art objects even further, into the digital realm, the Congolese Plantation Workers Art League (Cercle d'Art des Travailleurs de Plantation Congolaise in French, 'CATPC' for short) gears this technology towards re-collectivizing art. For centuries, people on plantations in Congo and elsewhere have been deprived of their culture and forced into unpaid labor, supporting wealth and art in the Global North. The NFT was minted to reclaim the power of an important symbol of colonial resistance to the Pende people: the Balot sculpture.

The Balot sculpture was carved in 1931, during a Pende uprising against atrocities carried out by the Unilever plantation system and Belgian colonial agents. After years of enforced recruitment to work on plantations where they were required to produce enormous quantities of goods at low prices, the rape of Kafuchi—the wife of Pende chief Mafuta—is what sparked the Pende Revolt. When a colonial administrator for the Belgian government, Maximilien Balot, came to the village of Kilamba to collect the 'native tax', he found the Pende rebelling. Balot fired into the crowd, injuring chief

Mafuta's nephew. In response, the enraged crowd swarmed Balot. Shakindungu was identified as the person responsible for Balot's killing, during which Balot was decapitated and dismembered. The Belgian army's reprisal was swift and violent. During the months of the revolt, the Pende carved a sculpture representing Balot, intended as a power object to harness his angry spirit in service of the community.

The sculpture remained hidden until 1972, when it was sold to an American scholar who later sold it to the Virginia Museum of Fine Arts (VMFA) in Richmond, Virginia, where it is now part of the collection. Beginning in 2020, CATPC has made multiple loan requests to exhibit the sculpture in the White Cube, the museum that CATPC has built on a former Unilever plantation. As part of their research into the history of the Pende Revolt and the Balot sculpture for the video series *Plantations and Museums* (2021), two members of CATPC, Ced'art Tamasala and Matthieu Kasiama, also travelled to the VMFA and asked for a loan. Not having received any concrete responses from the VMFA, CATPC decided to investigate alternative ways to claim the power of the sculpture.

NFT technology offers CATPC a window of opportunity to claim digital ownership over lost art and restitute its functions; by using NFTs, the powers of these objects can be reclaimed, even if the physical art is held by museums in faraway countries.

S+T+ARTS Prize Africa
Grand Prize

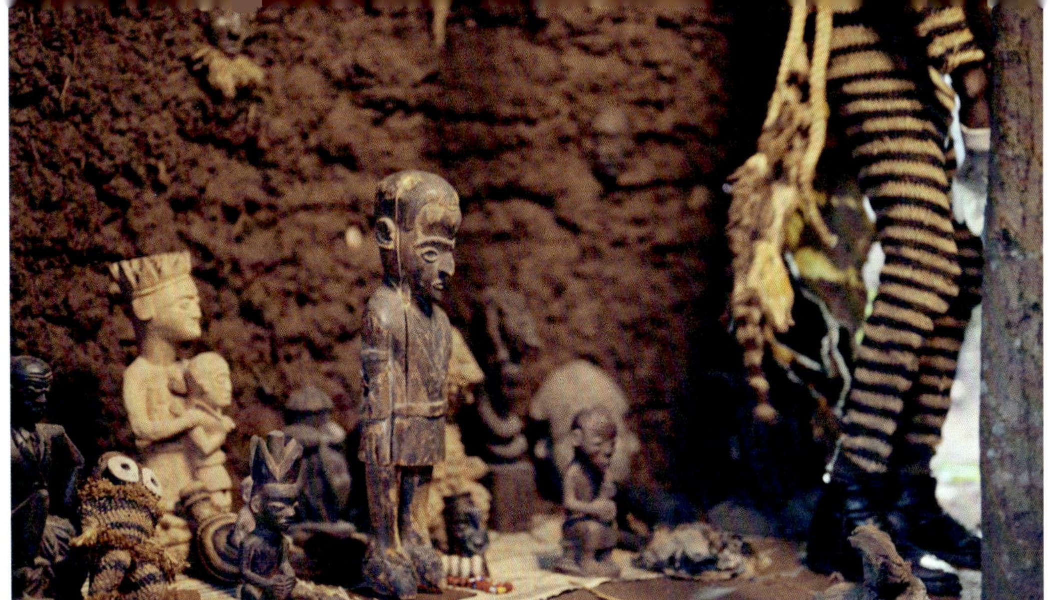

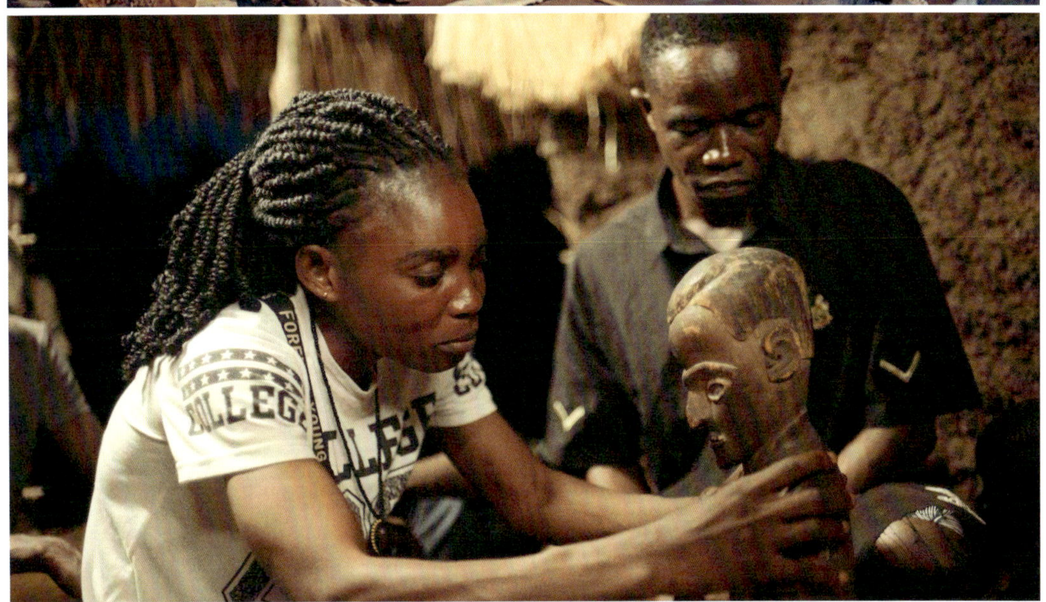

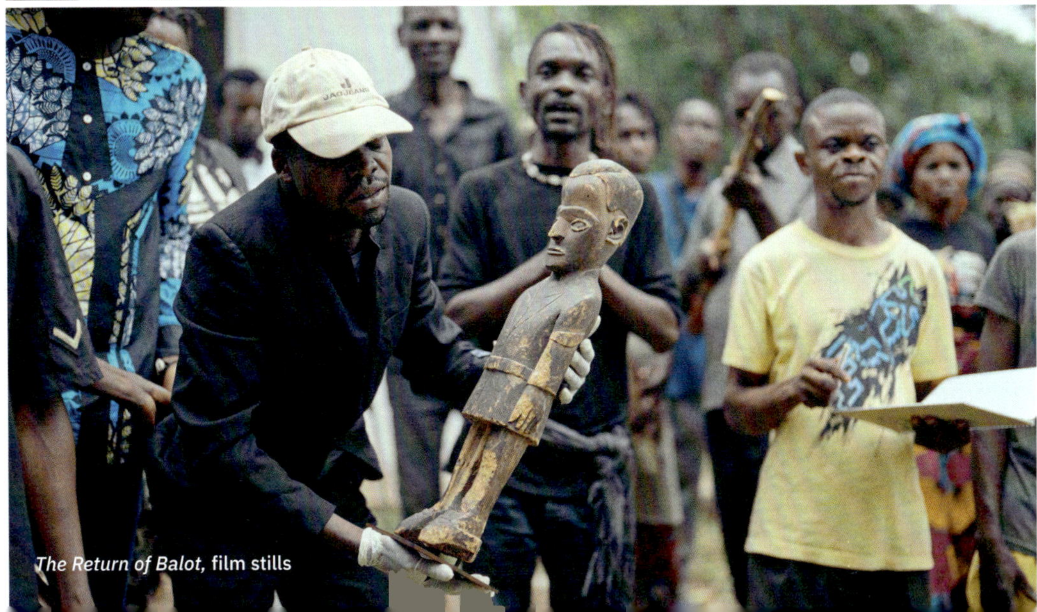

The Return of Balot, film stills

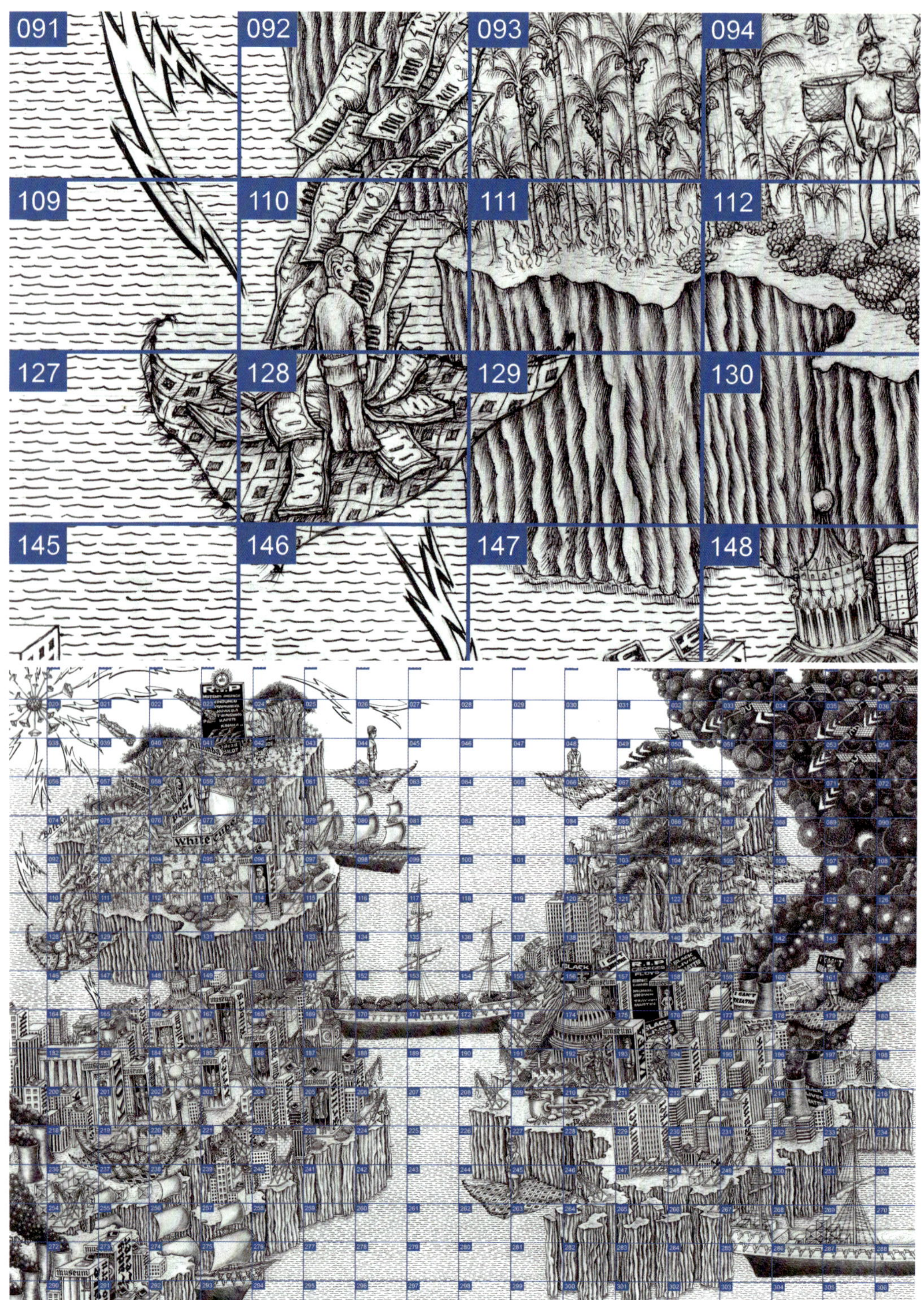

306 NFTs, drawing by Ced'art Tamasala, CATPC, 2022

S+T+ARTS Prize Africa
Grand Prize

However, this window is limited: museums in the Global North are already minting digital copies of key works in their collection and selling them as NFTs, creating a new profitable existence of these age-old artworks, while keeping the originals in their collections. Meanwhile, impoverishment on the plantations from which these artworks originate is rampant. It is essential that local communities make use of this technology and control the powers of their lost art, rather than the institutions that were built on the exploitation of their labor and culture. With the Balot NFT, CATPC works to draft best practice models of action for this, using blockchain technology to claim back what is theirs: not just art, but land.

As a result, CATPC downloaded photographic reproductions of the sculpture from the VMFA's website and turned it into an NFT: a digital rendering of the Balot sculpture hovering over a fragment of a drawing by Ced'art Tamasala. The drawing maps out global value flows of capital, commodities, and cultural exploitation, and exhibits how the Balot sculpture was carved to resist these unequal power relations and its disastrous consequences for the community. With its sales, CATPC buys back plantation land depleted from 100 years of monoculture to restore the sacred forest of their ancestors. Each NFT is sold for the price of one hectare of land in Lusanga. Every purchase helps to unleash the powers of the sculpture and reassert its original purpose of protecting the community and land.

In 2024, CATPC succeeded in securing a temporary loan of the Balot sculpture to exhibit in the White Cube in Lusanga (DRC) as a part of providing the Dutch entry for La Biennale di Venezia 2024. The sculpture is on display at the White Cube and simultaneously connected through a livestream at the Rietveld Pavilion in Venice (IT) from 20 April to 24 November 2024. CATPC believes the return of the sculpture will restore balance and correct past injustices—now is the time for museums and art institutes throughout the Western world to support reconciliation and actively engage with indigenous communities as they reclaim their land and restore and reconnect to their sacred forests. Both the Balot NFT and the temporary return of the Balot sculpture strengthen CATPC's movement to restore what is theirs: not just art, but land.

The *Balot NFT* is created by CATPC and supported by Human Activities. Human Activities takes care of the technical, legal, and financial production.
All sale proceeds and resale royalties, minus gas fees, go to CATPC for the acquisition and restoration of land.

https://u.aec.at/A5B5D85B

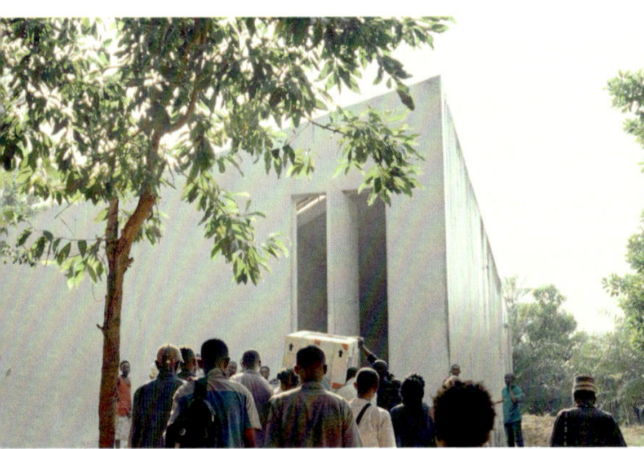

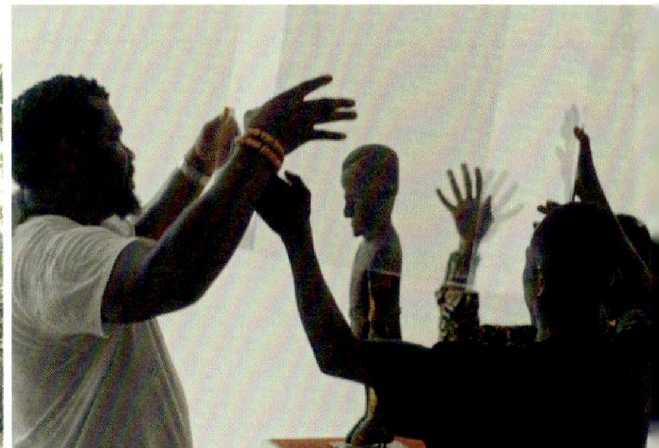

The Return of Balot, film stills

CATPC—in full "Cercle d'Art des Travailleurs de Plantation Congolaise" or "Congolese Plantation Workers Art League"—is an art cooperative of plantation workers from Lusanga, DR Congo. It was founded in 2014, together with well-known environmental activist René Ngongo. With the proceeds of their art, CATPC has built a practice of securing hundreds of hectares of former plantation land for future generations. In the midst of this land, they have built a museum: the White Cube. In one of CATPC's recent video works, this white cube is indicted for its involvement in colonialism and forced labor. On this land, they are restoring worker-owned, ecological, and inclusive food forests: the Post Plantation. CATPC, artist Renzo Martens and curator Hicham Khalidi provide the Dutch entry for La Biennale di Venezia 2024.

Black Body Radiation: Rescripting Data Bodies

Ama BE, Ameera Kawash

Black Body Radiation: Rescripting Data Bodies is a collaborative art project by Ameera Kawash and Ama BE. The series consists of propositional performances that explore tobacco—materially, ritually, and as a form of value. The project incorporates body sensor networks and blockchain architectures to generate and rescript data bodies as agential forces emerging from the physical expressions of the performance, such as choreography, gesture, and repeated movements.

During these performances, Ama BE wears three body sensors that track her heart rate, body temperature, and blood oxygen levels. This data is then uploaded to a server, where it interacts with algorithmic processing and blockchain architectures. Ameera Kawash, collaborating with Ama BE, designed this backend to produce digital intimate assets and reconfigure the data layer to explore new possibilities for choreography, documentation, and funding for live performance artworks. Ama BE's embodied metrics are programmed to interact with blockchain infrastructures, modulating the value of linked NFTs according to the performer's breath, exertion, and duration of the performance. The work's simple, repetitive choreography engages tobacco as both commodity and sacred material in the process of transfiguring Ama's body through ceremonial costuming inspired by West African masquerades like Zangbetor. Embedded with body tracking sensors, the performance positions spiritual and digital technologies on equal ground to enlist generated data as an agent for establishing new formations of value.

Performance-based NFTs use embodiment to generate value, contradicting hegemonic forms of value creation rooted in histories of racialized capital and alienated labor. The technical structure of the performance establishes "commodity" and "indigeneity" as metrical inversions of each other, and authors a new syntax through which generative exchange in performance can be articulated.

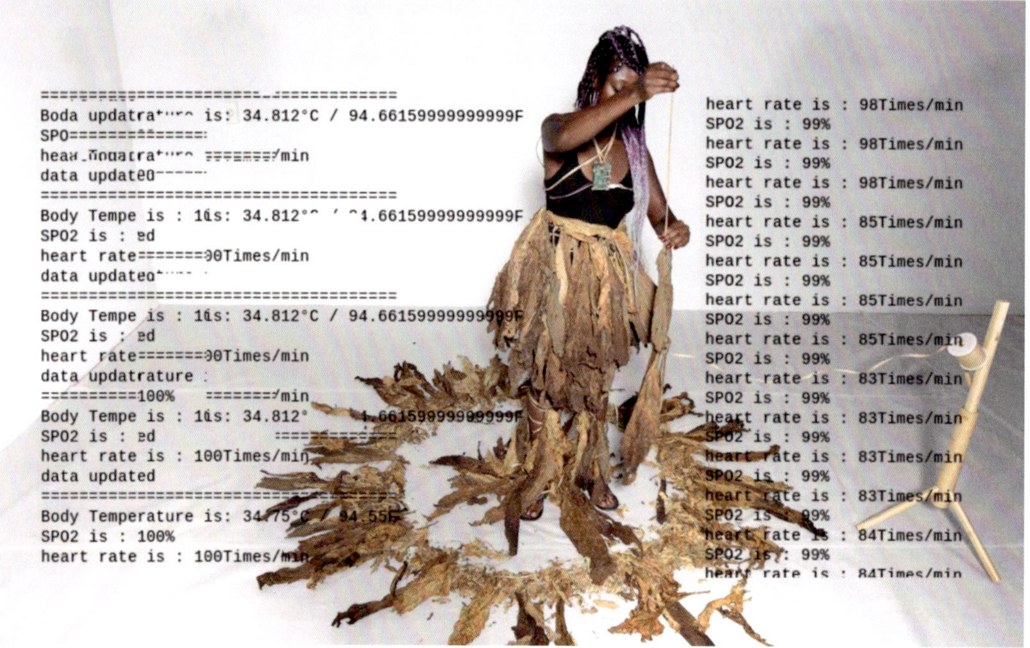

S+T+ARTS Prize Africa
Award of Distinction

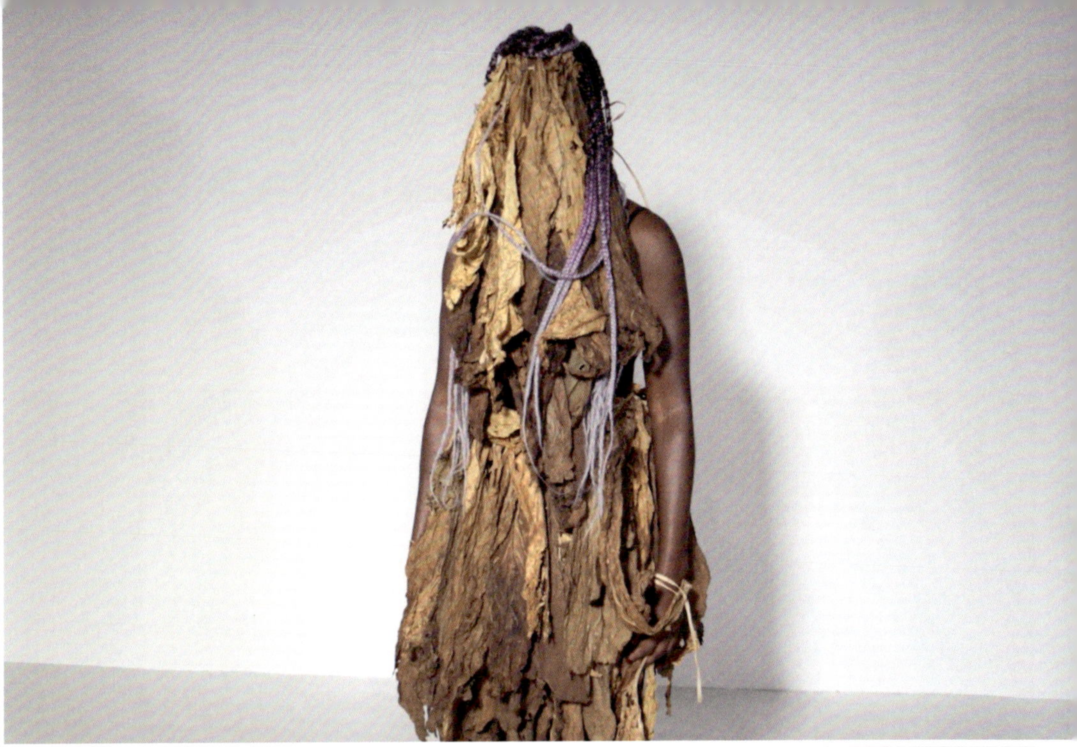

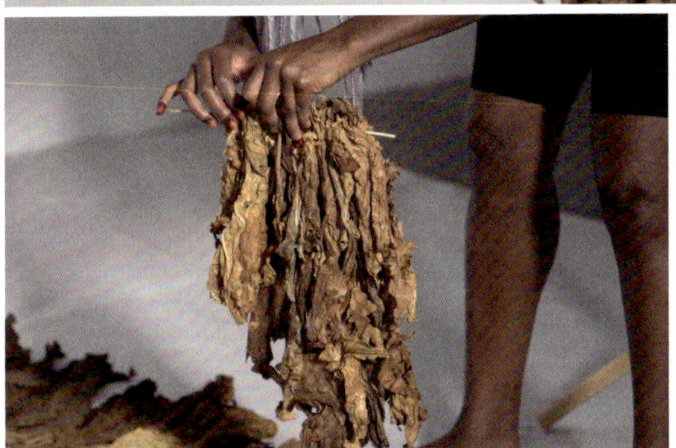
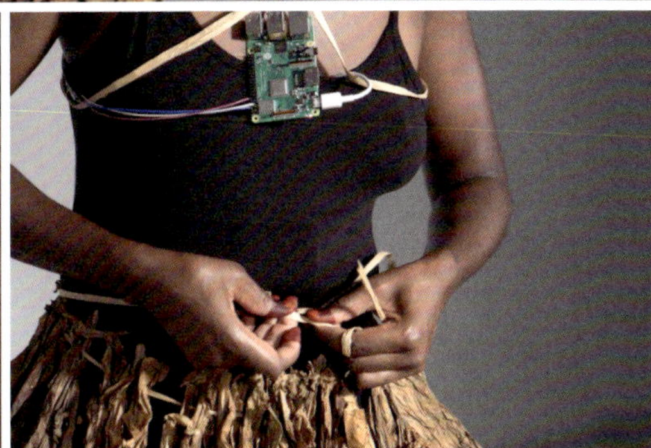

Digital designer, video editor, concept: Ameera Kawash
Performance art and design, concept: Ama BE
Camera: Enrique Huaiquil

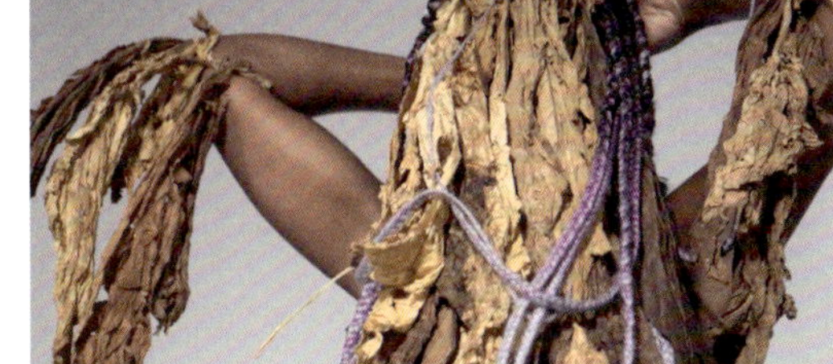

https://u.aec.at/4EB78881

Ama BE (GH/US) is a transdisciplinary artist who explores African relationships to land cultivation, labor, and migration. She works with botanical materials that carry antithetical ties to hegemonic trade, (violent) labor migrations, spirituality, and holistic remedy. Her practice probes at porous spaces between time, materiality, sentience, and memory to propose nuance in the performance of African cosmologies and embodiment of African futurity.

Ameera Kawash (PS/IQ/US) is an interdisciplinary artist, writer, and start-up founder whose digital work addresses discriminatory tech and develops place-based approaches to sustainability. Currently, she is exploring painting patternmaking in relation to diasporic identity as well as researching representational justice in the context of generative AI. She is Palestinian-Iraqi American and earned a PhD from the Royal College of Art in 2022.

Dzata: The Institute of Technological Consciousness

Russel Hlongwane, Francois Knoetze and
Amy Louise Wilson—Lo-Def Film Factory

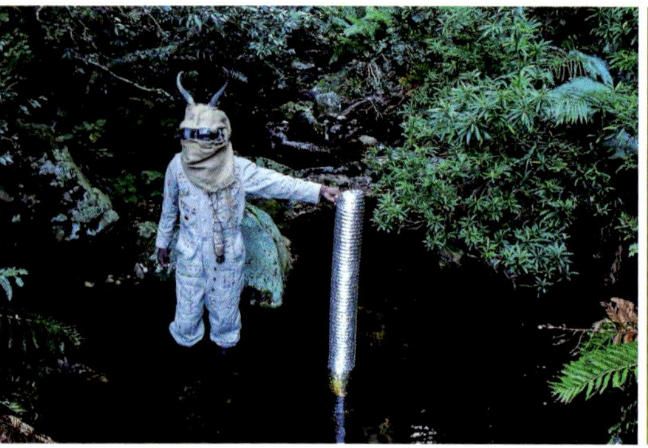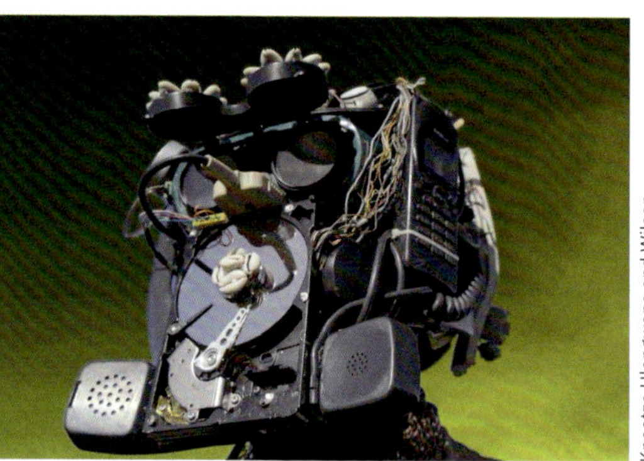

Dzata: The Institute of Technological Consciousness is an artistic research project by South African artists Russel Hlongwane, Francois Knoetze, and Amy Wilson. In fabricating a fictional institute and its archive, the artists imagine centuries-old vernacular technological practices from across the African continent. Building on the research of techno-political scholar and project mentor Professor Clapperton Chakanetsa Mavhunga, the work takes the form of video, a creative-critical text, sculptural masks, costumes and devices, and a youth workshop series.

The video operates as an in-house media assemblage created for the preservation of the institute's activities and ideas, unfolding the idea of development as a historical process Africans shaped.

The project aims to foreground indigenous technological knowledge and to explore how science, technology, and innovation are part of a long interlinked process of accumulative knowledge production that extends into the long past.

As such, the work does not 'invent something new' rather, it brings into conversation present thinkers, anti-colonial revolutionary practices, folklore and gadgetry. The collapsing of these ideas helps chart a wider framework from which to think about technology from the continent.

The workshops, held with young people in South Africa (Cape Town, 2022) and Brazil (Salvador, 2023), are pop-up maker-spaces which position young people as creative innovators and inventors of their own technologies. The workshops invite youth to identify a challenge in their community, and to use electronic waste and other materials to create their own invention to address it.

As members of the *Dzata Institute* we ask: how can we draw examples from history which illuminate the invention of modernities from within, rather than received from elsewhere? Or, finding none available to us, can we fabricate our own examples? How can we alter incoming modernities so that they speak native languages and advance our identities?

Created by Russel Hlongwane, Francois Knoetze and Amy Louise Wilson
A Lo-Def Film Factory & Substance Point Production
Supported by the Mozilla Foundation

https://u.aec.at/3CBDF0F1

**S+T+ARTS Prize Africa
Award of Distinction**

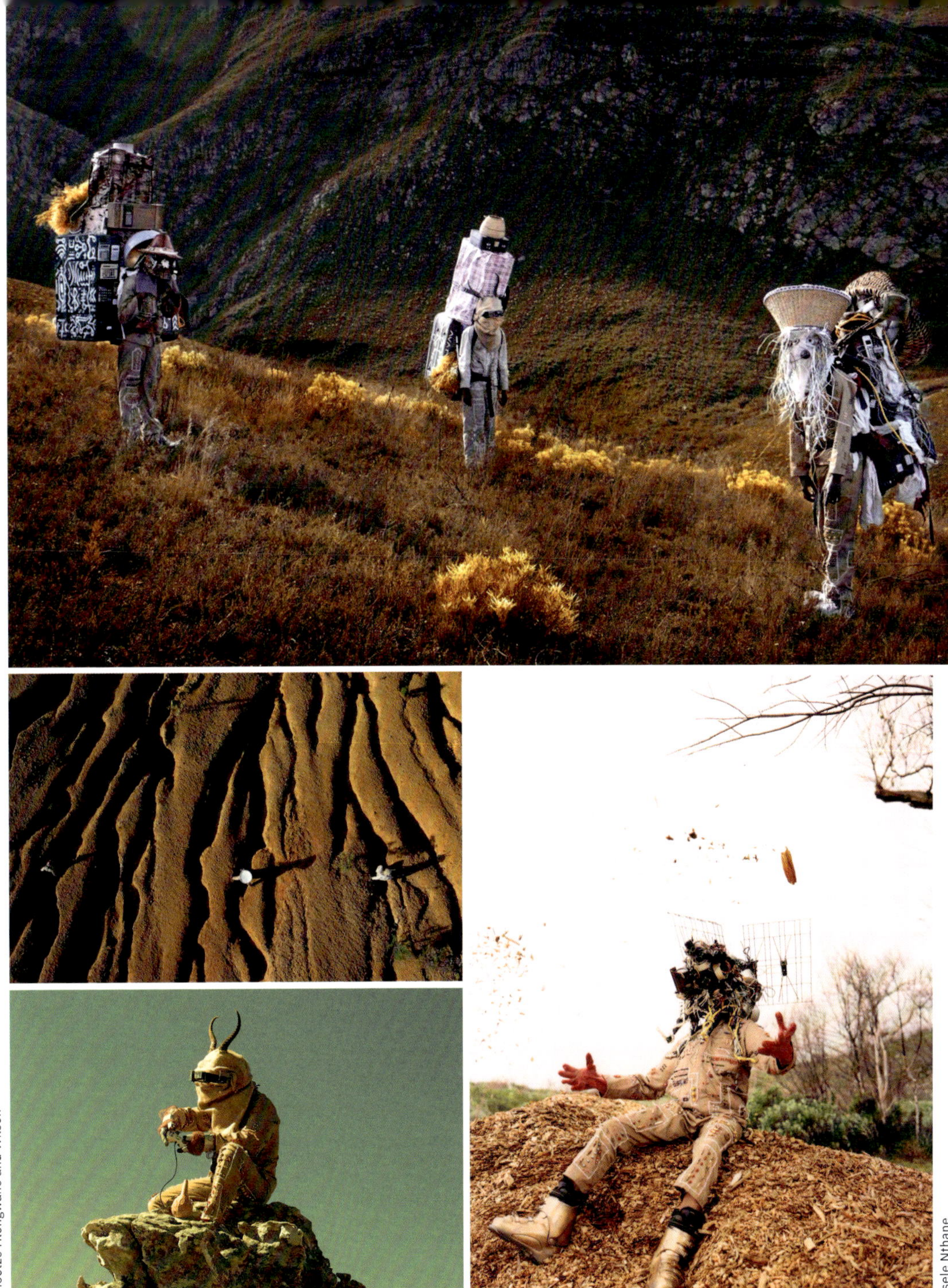

The Lo-Def Film Factory was created by artist duo **Francois Knoetze** (ZA) and **Amy Louise Wilson** (ZA). Their work involves archival research and visual strategies associated with video art, collage, installation and new media, to create space for collaborative D.I.Y and experimental storytelling. They use digital technologies in a practice that embraces mistake-making. **Russel Hlongwane** (ZA) is a cultural producer based in South Africa. His work obsesses over the tensions of heritage, modernity, culture and tradition as it applies to Black life. His practice includes research, design theory, writing, film and curatorship. He is part of several working groups across the African continent and internationally. He recently completed a MPhil at the African Centre for Cities (University of Cape Town).

**Dzata: The Institute of
Technological Consciousness**

I.AM.ISIGO Digital Mystery System

Bubu Ogisi

A digital environment is a natural reflection of a physical environment. I think of a Sahelian network of wares on camels as an embodied network of hardware connected to each other through movement. When scaled up, this network is an internet of sorts, with growth through connectivity and the build-up of organic social networks.

We are creating a comprehensive digital tool, the *I.AM.ISIGO Digital Mystery System,* to bridge the physical-digital divide and preserve and disseminate knowledge of ancient and endangered weaving techniques in Africa. Our project is based on *I.AM.ISIGO's* extensive research in remote African artisanal communities, aiming to map these significant cultural practices. The tool serves as a digital archive, preserving intricate knowledge systems for future generations, and as an interactive platform for audiences to learn weaving patterns. Our goal is to bring these ancient practices into the present, connecting these archives to the digital network, and blurring lines between science, spirituality, and creative practice.

Our methodology spans urban to rural scopes, leading us away from the source community to manufacturing and export cities, documenting these material cultures in a decolonized manner. We focus on remote communities and cities in Africa such as Nairobi, Kano, Tamale, Dakar, Bolgatanga, Ibadan, Lagos, Agbozume, Kpalimé, Divo, and Cotonou. We'll also explore secondary sites of fiber growing, production, and consumption.

We document previously inaccessible practices surrounding weaving traditions, gain critical understanding of how these materials are processed and used, archive these for future use, make weaving more approachable, bring the knowledge of these techniques to a global audience, unearth ancient systems of governance, challenge the concept of a "finished" good, give a voice to traditional fabrics of Africa, and research the entire supply chain for each of these material knowledge systems.

Creative direction: Bubu Ogisi
Coding: Uzoma Orji, Uzoma Studios
Art direction: Tushar Hathiramani
Developer operations, management:
Kolade Ayo-Vaughan

https://u.aec.at/716FB11A

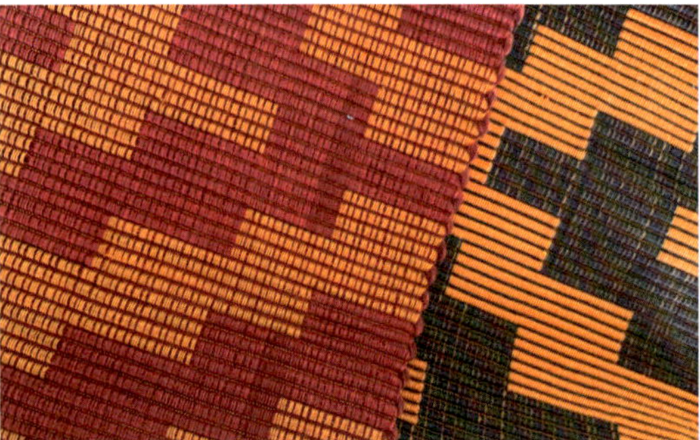

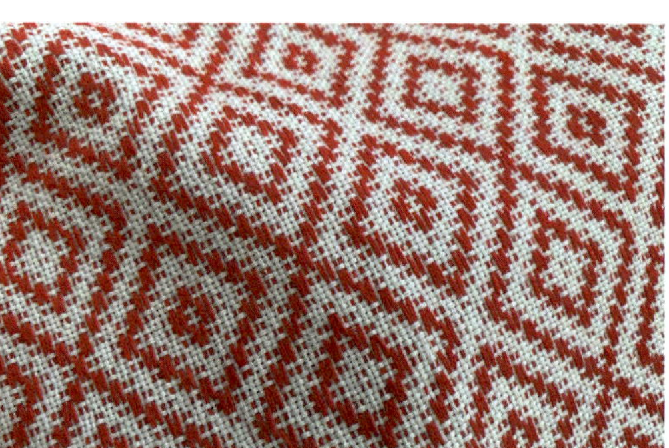

Bubu Ogisi (NG) is a fiber artist and the Creative Director of the contemporary art brand I.AM.ISIGO. Born in Lagos, Nigeria, and now living between Lagos, Accra, Abidjan, and Nairobi, he studied Fashion at the prestigious École Supérieure des Arts et Techniques de la Mode (ESMOD) Paris, France. His work primarily focuses on how fiber and textile can keep history alive and also pass on information for the future through preservation of techniques and expression through matter. He creates wearable art pieces using unconventional materials and heritage textile traditions through in-depth research with remote African communities. His work conveys lost historical stories, transforms this found "data" and applies them to fiber production and garments by questioning gender, language, magic/technology, and spirituality.

S+T+ARTS Prize Africa
Award of Distinction

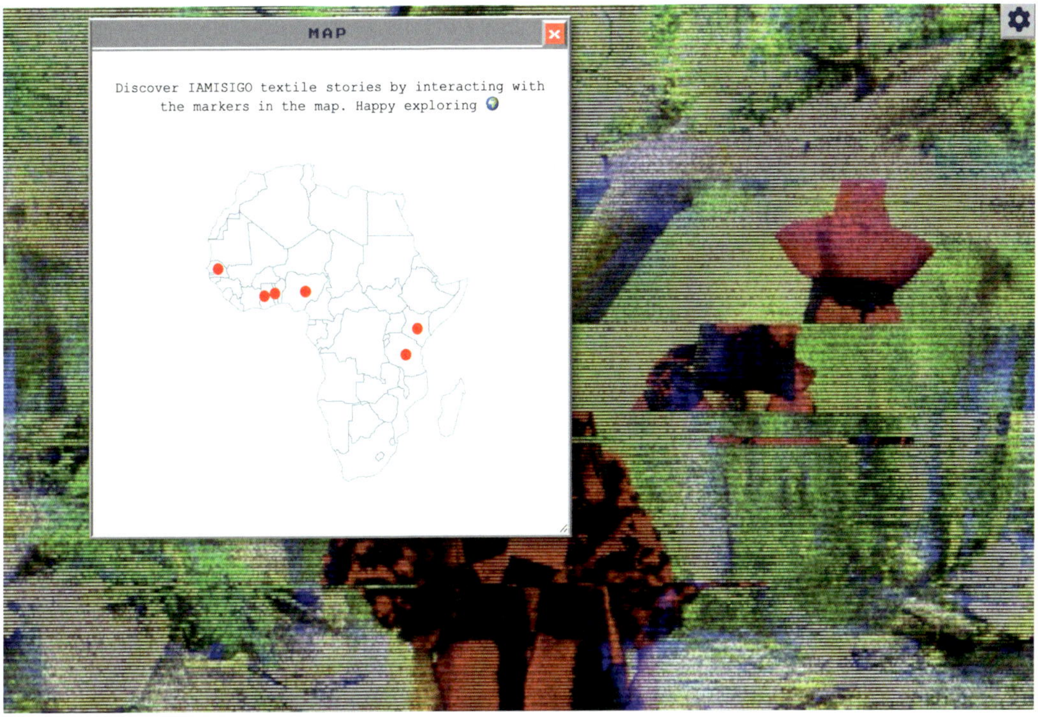

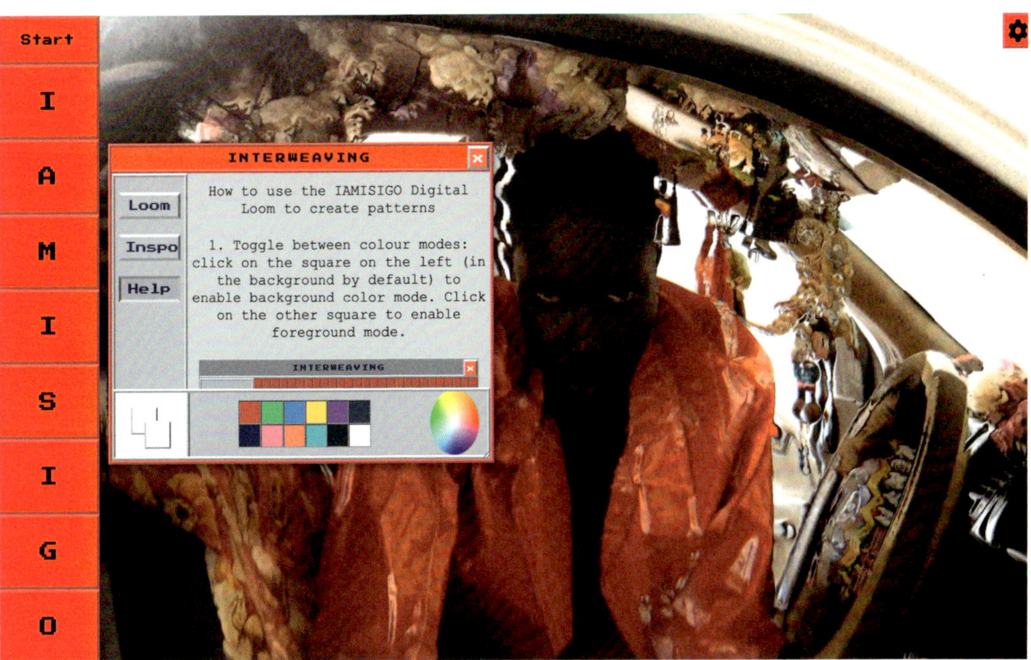
MAP
Discover IAMISIGO textile stories by interacting with
the markers in the map. Happy exploring

Start
I
A
M
I
S
I
G
O
INTERWEAVING
Loom
Inspo
Help
How to use the IAMISIGO Digital
Loom to create patterns
1. Toggle between colour modes:
click on the square on the left (in
the background by default) to
enable background color mode. Click
on the other square to enable
foreground mode.
INTERWEAVING

Sand Gardens
Mohamed Sleiman Labat

Sand Gardens, also called Sandoponic gardens, have been developed in the Sahrawi refugee camps in southwest Algeria. We use sand as the medium to grow vegetables and herbs in a very challenging desert environment with dangerous sandstorms and extreme heat levels. We grow in sand because that's all we have in the Hamada Desert. By containing sand in a plastic film and making a drainage at one end, we can also collect the water and recycle it in the same system. Sand grains with slightly bigger diameter actually help the water penetrate faster through the soil. The air pockets between the sand grains also allow the roots to access the oxygen.

Developing such Sandoponic gardens is primarily to help the Saharawi families access nutritional food locally. The Sahrawi refugees are dependent on food aid whose nutritional value is limited. There are high levels of anemia and malnutrition among the Sahrawi. This artistic intervention responds to a critical problem using local low-tech accessible materials. The Sandoponic gardens save up huge amounts of water. Before the Sandoponic farming model, we had to water the plants every day but water would evaporate. With the Sandoponic model, we went up to seven days without watering the garden as the system keeps the moisture in the soil. Sahrawi agricultural engineer Taleb Brahim is leading the family gardens movement. His experimentation allowed such simple low-tech interventions to be accessible for the ordinary camp residents to replicate. We often engage in conversations and exchange.

My film *DESERT PHOSfate* weaves through narratives of sand particles, plants, and human and mineral displacement. It also brings up narratives of the newly developed Sandoponic practices and our context. Such artistic interventions highlight the importance of interdisciplinary approaches that allow the friction between artists and scientists to bring forward concrete change to our local communities by working with the local materials, knowledge, and people.

Motif Art Studio
Algaada Centre for Small Scale Farming and Agricultural Research
The film *DESERT PHOSfate* is part of the PHOSfate Artistic Research Project together with Pekka Niskanen, funded by Kone Foundation, Osker Öflunds Stiftelse, and Arts Promotion Centre Finland.

https://u.aec.at/52380D00

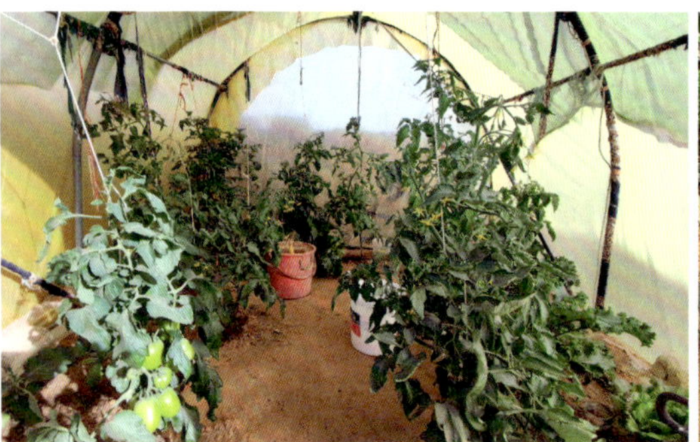

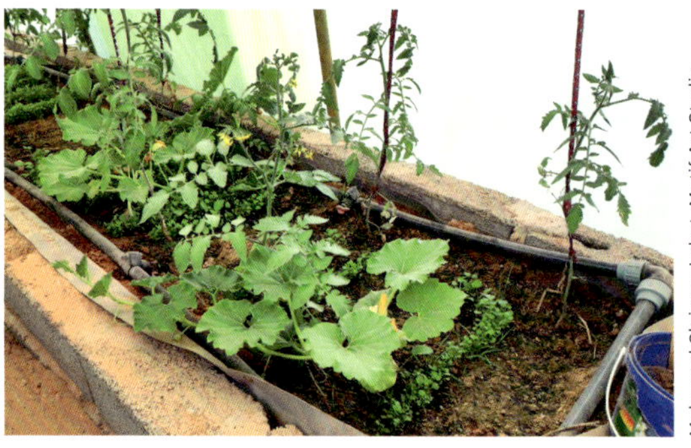

Mohamed Sleiman Labat, Motif Art Studio

S+T+ARTS Prize Africa
Award of Distinction

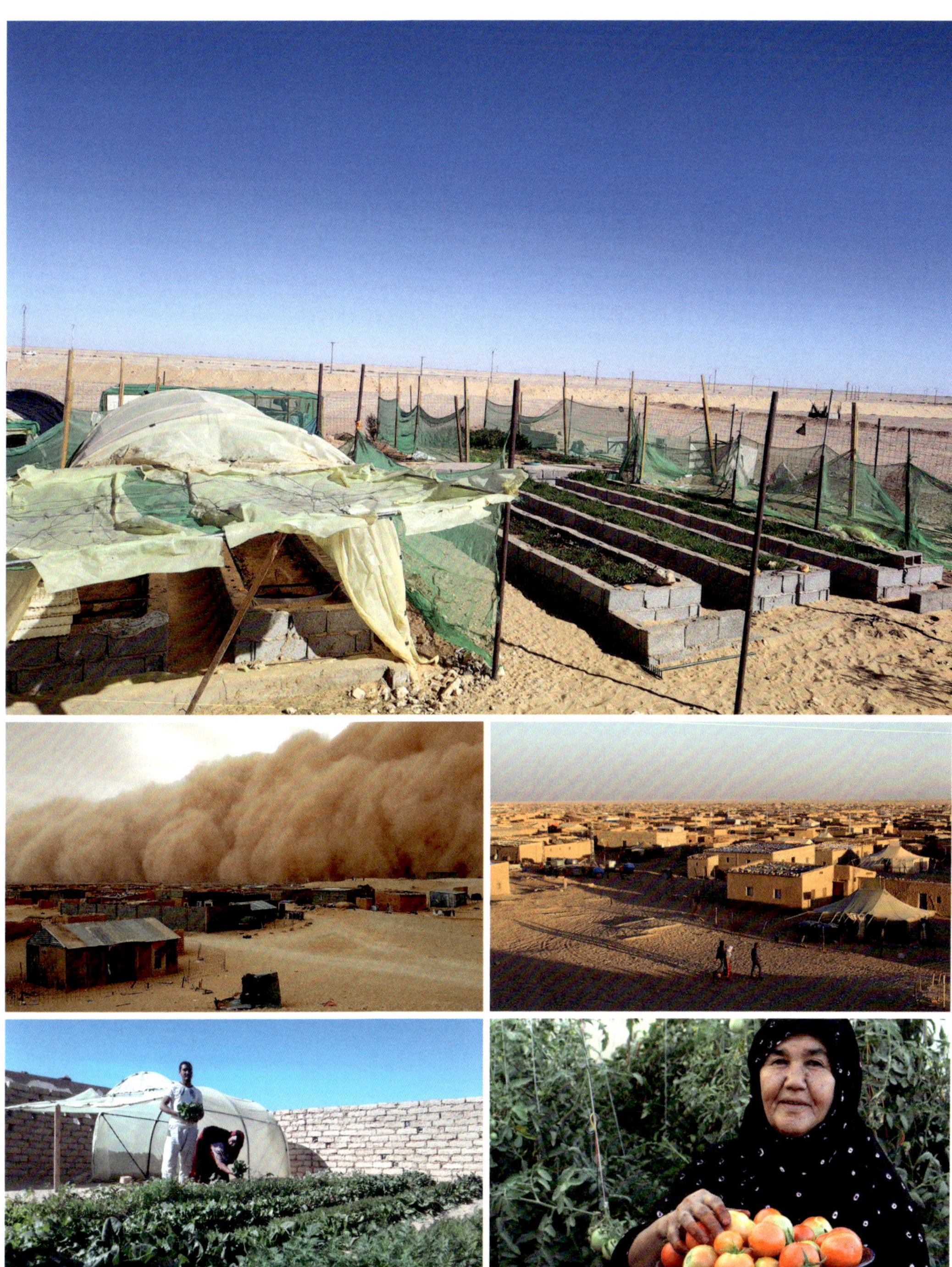

Mohamed Sleiman Labat (EH) is a Sahrawi multidisciplinary artist, filmmaker, writer, and translator. Born and raised in the Sahrawi refugee camps southwest Algeria, he now runs Motif Art Studio: a small art space built from discarded materials following destructive floods that hit the camps in 2015. His art and research draws upon the past and present life of the Sahrawi people. He has been exploring these interconnected topics through films, writing, and community-based art. He now experiments with local food production as part of the studio practice. He explores how small-scale family gardens are addressing issues of food security, environmental change, and community resilience. Sleiman Labat has exhibited internationally, and has been awarded a number of prizes, residencies, and grants.

Sand Gardens

The Metadata Memoir

Minne Atairu

The 1897 British invasion of Benin Kingdom (located in present day Southern Nigeria) culminated in the looting of over 4,000 cultural artifacts, now collectively referred to as the Benin Bronzes. These artifacts were subsequently auctioned off and dispersed to various institutions and private collectors around the world. Today, an estimated 160 cultural institutions hold objects from the 1897 plunder.

In recent years, repatriation efforts have resulted in the return of a few Benin Bronzes to the Nigerian government. However, details about returned objects are not often disclosed to the Nigerian public. Public records, when they exist, are sparse and obscured by complex museum terminology. Compounding this issue, Western museums are required to delete publicly available object records once the repatriation process is complete.

In response to this opacity, I developed *The Metadata Memoir*—a decentralized archival system powered by a smart contract. The system is programmed to autonomously document repatriated objects in real-time. It achieves this by utilizing the *New York Times* and *The Guardian* news APIs to run a daily search for news related to repatriated Benin Bronzes. Upon identifying relevant news, the system generates documentation for each returned object. These records include the repatriation date, the repatriating institution, and dynamic fields for object name, material composition, and production date.

To date, the smart contract has recorded 64 returns from 8 institutions including the Metropolitan Museum of Art in New York, the Smithsonian National Museum for African Art in Washington DC, and the Horniman Museum in London.

The Metadata Memoir is accessible in both Nigerian pidgin English (pidgin.beninbronzes.xyz), and standard English (beninbronzes.xyz). Given the existence of over 300 dialects in Nigeria, the pidgin English version ensures broader language access across the country's linguistically diverse population.

https://u.aec.at/0FC61EE7

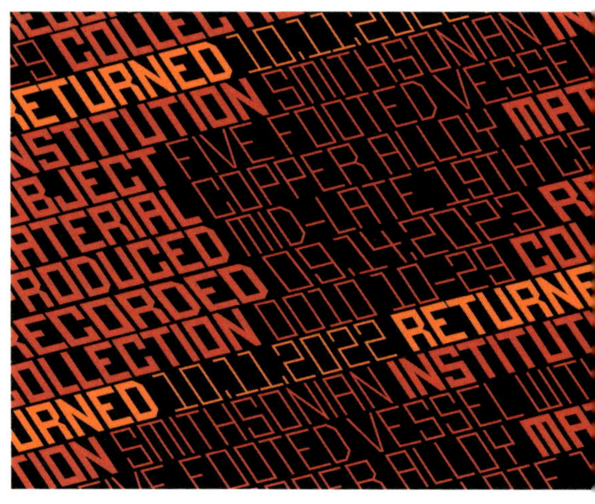

Minne Atairu (NG) is a researcher and interdisciplinary artist interested in generative artificial intelligence. Utilizing AI-mediated processes and materials, Atairu's work critically examines and illuminates understudied gaps in Black historical archives. Minne's academic research focuses on Generative AI, Art and Educational policy in urban K-12 Art classrooms. Minne has exhibited at The Shed, New York (2023); Frieze, London (2023); The Harvard Art Museums, Boston (2022); Markk Museum, Hamburg (2021); SOAS Brunei Gallery University of London, London (2022); Fleming Museum of Art, Vermont (2021). Minne is the recipient of The Graham Foundation Grant for Research (2023), the Artistic Dialogue Across Disciplines Grant (2022)—Columbia University (2022), and the Lumen Prize for Art and Technology (2021).

S+T+ARTS Prize Africa
Award of Distinction

uch material assets, I've amassed
e seemingly ...rian yet extrao
suits of ...h from Be
hese are ... by Benin
articula...ts who s
ration ... shrined", "s
.B.E", an... he carious
e, 1983 [39] ...ber ver
heart-wr...ng dialogue: "I ask
mask of Benin", followed by a dishe
in London". My fascination extend

al wealth in the form of bronze, ivory,
of such material assets, I've amassed a
the seemingl... yet extraor
pursuits of ...h from Be
g these are ... by Benin
s articulat...ts who so
ecration ... shrined", "s
O.B.E", an... carious
dare, 198... ber vers
g a hear... "I ask f
oyin mask o... by a dishe
it is in London". My fascination extends

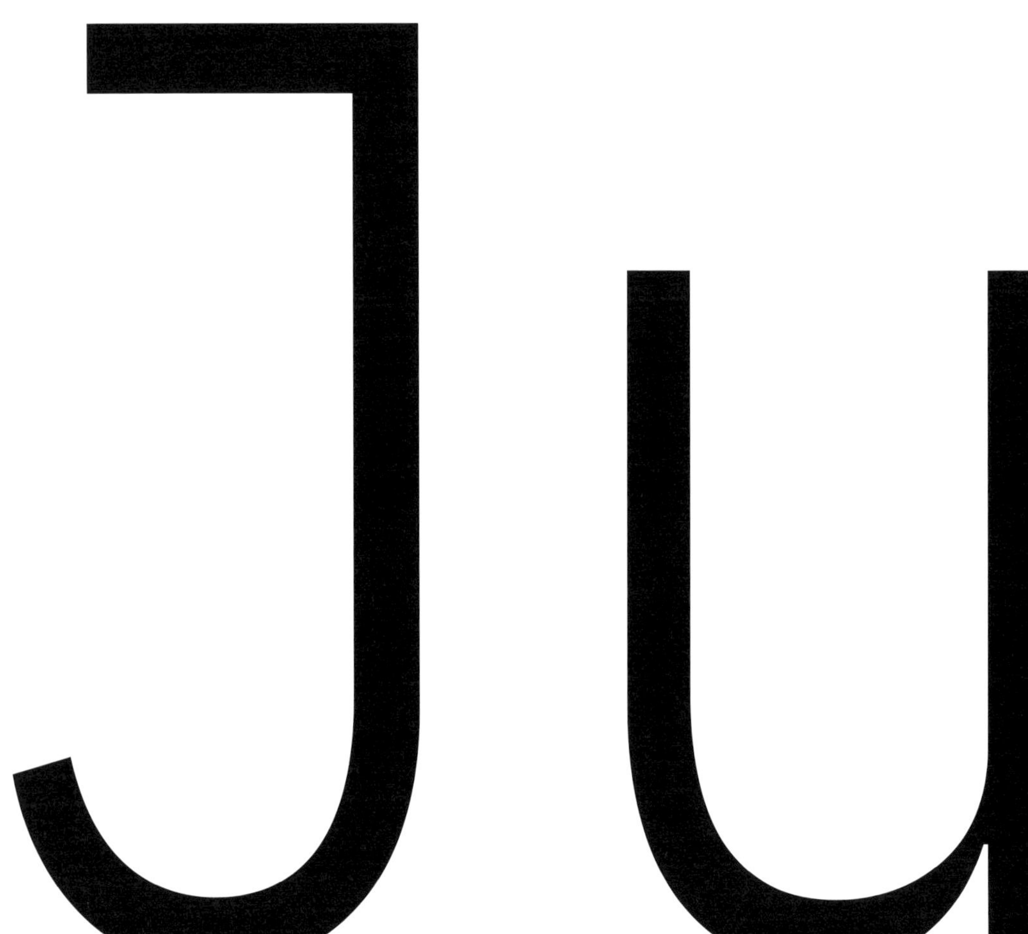

ry

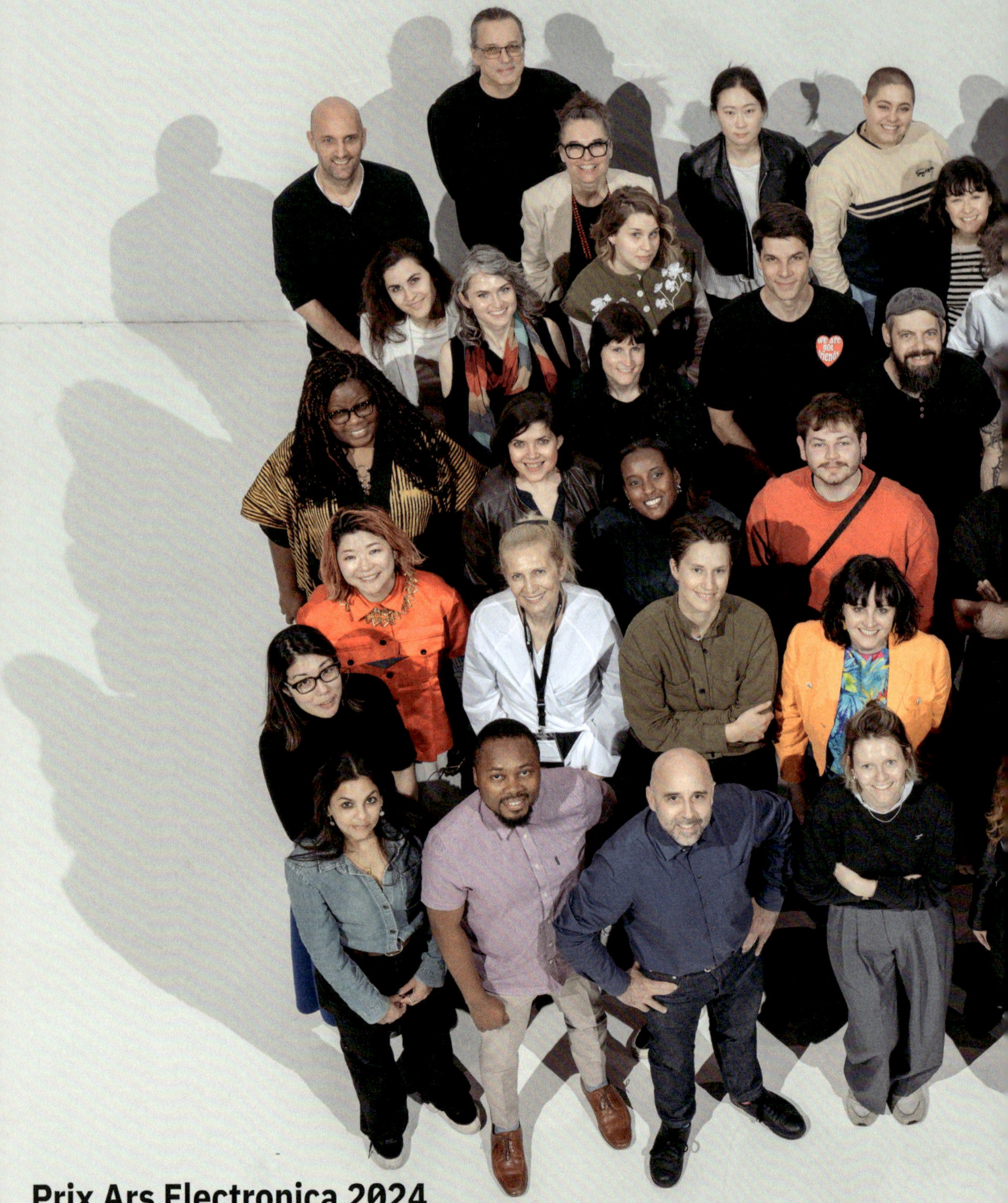

Prix Ars Electronica 2024
Jury members

New Animation Art
Kalina Borkiewicz, Fanni Fazakas, Ari Melenciano, Georgy Molodtsov, Chris Salter, and Ars Electronica Team.

Interactive Art +
Clemens Apprich, Salome Asega, Shiho Fukuhara, José-Carlos Mariátegui, Olga Tykhonova, and Ars Electronica Team.

AI in ART Award
Jürgen Hagler, Vanessa Hannesschläger, Veronika Liebl, Emiko Ogawa, Gerfried Stocker

u19–create your world
Sirikit Amann, Emil Klostermann, Conny Lee, Anahita Neghabat, Anna Wielander, and Ars Electronica Team.

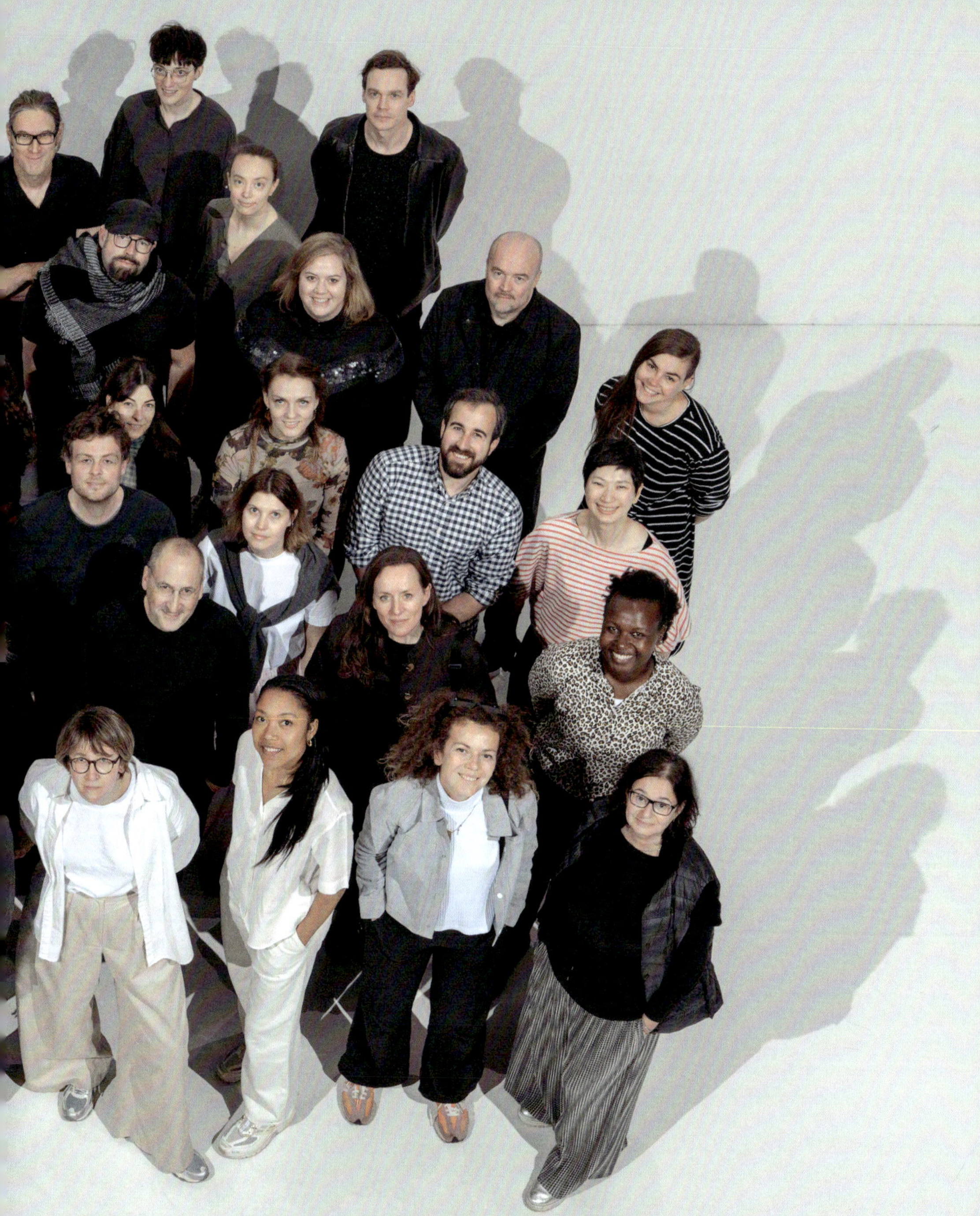

Ars Electronica Award for Digital Humanity
Christoph Thun-Hohenstein, Regina Rusz,
Thomas Kloiber, Gerfried Stocker, Veronika Liebl

European Union Prize for Citizen Science
Sofie Burgos-Thorsen, Mairéad Hurley,
Luciana Marques, Fermín Serrano Sanz,
Snežana Smederevac, and Ars Electronica Team.

S+T+ARTS Prize'24
Francesca Bria, Fumi Hirota, Manuela Naveau,
Katja Schechtner, Miha Turšič, and Ars Electronica
Team.

S+T+ARTS Prize Africa
Andrea Barschdorf-Hager, Mónica Bello, Oscar
Ekponimo, Judith Okonkwo, Kathleen Siminyu,
and Ars Electronica Team.

Prix Ars Electronica 2024
Jury members

New Animation Art

Kalina Borkiewicz (US/PL) has been at the National Center for Supercomputing Applications at the University of Illinois at Urbana-Champaign for the last decade, most recently as director of the Visualization Program Office and director of the Advanced Visualization Lab (AVL). The AVL is an Academy Award-nominated team which creates cinematic scientific visualizations for museums, IMAX, and documentary films. Kalina is currently working on a PhD in computer graphics and visualization at the University of Utah.

Fanni Fazakas (HU/NZ) is a technical artist, director, and researcher who specializes in using XR technology to bring attention to the stories of marginalized individuals and create real-world impact. Her current project, *Missing 10 Hours VR,* is a non-fiction Virtual Reality experience that explores the use of GHB and the Bystander Effect. It has won several awards, including Best in Show VR at Siggraph Los Angeles and Asia, Best XR at Kaohsiung Festival Taiwan, and Best XR Impact at DocEdge Film Festival New Zealand, for its impact. Through her work, Fanni has developed co-creation strategies and principles that she actively uses in her teaching and artistic work within her digital artist collective RUMEXR. She designs and actively organizes workshops for women in the art and tech industries to combat underrepresentation in VFX and electronic music. Fanni is currently a Senior Lecturer and Researcher at Victoria University Wellington—Te Herenga Waka, where she teaches in the Master of Design Technology program. She earned her BA degree and taught non-linear storytelling at the Moholy-Nagy University of Art and Design. Fanni holds a master's in Interactive Telecommunications from New York University's ITP Program.

Ari Melenciano (US) is an artist, technologist, researcher, and theorist whose work reveals the synergy between computation, cultural meta-cognition, and transcendental expression. She is a frequent public speaker and guest lecturer at universities around the world, sharing her research on creative and societally inquisitive uses of emerging technologies. She occasionally designs and teaches courses at universities around NYC, including New York University and The Pratt Institute's Design School. Her work has been supported and published by Sundance, *The New York Times,* The Studio Museum of Harlem, MIT Media Lab's Space Exploration Initiative, The Ford Foundation, The National Endowment for the Arts, and more.

Georgy Molodtsov (RU/GE) is an award winning XR Director and producer, as well as XR Festivals curator. He participated in Cannes XR with his work *Under the pillow,* was nominated for PGA and received Webby Awards *(Oxymore* by Jean-Michel Jarre), and has organized over 30 different XR events in Europe and Central Asia. For his latest XR animation project *MormoVerse* he was awarded the Raindance Immersive Award.

Chris Salter (US/CH) is Professor/Director of the Immersive Arts Space at Zurich University of the Arts (ZHdK) as well as Professor Emeritus, Design and Computation Arts at Concordia University, Montreal. His artistic work has been seen all over the world at the Venice Biennale, Barbican Centre, Berliner Festspiele, Wiener Festwochen, and Kunstfest Weimar, among many others. He is the author of *Entangled: Technology and the Transformation of Performance* (2010), *Alien Agency* (2015) and *Sensing Machines* (2022), all from MIT Press.

Interactive Art +

Clemens Apprich (AT) is Head of the Department of Media Theory as well as the Peter Weibel Research Institute for Digital Cultures at the University of Applied Arts in Vienna, where he holds the Professorship for Media Theory and History since 2021. Since fall 2023 he has been Vice-Rector for Research & Digitality. Apprich is, among other things, a member of the Assembly of Delegates of the Austrian Science Fund (FWF) and of the Digital Democracies Institute at Simon Fraser University.

Salome Asega (US) is an artist and Director of NEW INC at the New Museum. Her work invites the playful and absurd to critique the speed at which technology develops and poses new consentful tech futures leveraging the power of collective imagination. Salome is a 2022 United States Artists Fellow and an inaugural cohort member of the Dorchester Industries Experimental Design Lab developed by Theaster Gates, Rebuild Foundation, and Prada. She is also a co-founder of POWRPLNT, a Brooklyn digital arts lab for teens, incubated at NEW INC in Year 3. Salome has participated in residencies and fellowships with Eyebeam, The Laundromat Project, and Recess. She has exhibited at the Munch Museum, 11th Shanghai Biennale, MoMA, Carnegie Library, August Wilson Center, Knockdown Center, and more.

Shiho Fukuhara (JP) is an artist, designer, and researcher who explores how new technology and traditional crafts can critically reflect our consciousness of physicality, aesthetics, and materiality. She has been creating art work and products by developing new materials such as genetically modified plants, smart textiles, and biologically enhanced yarns. She joined Google ATAP's Project Jacquard as a Technology Integration Lead in 2014 and was one of its founding members. She is a member of Human Awesome Error and a founder of Poiesis Labs.

José-Carlos Mariátegui (PE/UK) is a writer, curator, scholar, and entrepreneur on culture and technology. He is the founder of Alta Tecnología Andina – ATA (Lima, Peru), an organization working at the intersection of art, science, technology, and society in Latin America. Dr. Mariategui is a lecturer at LUISS (Rome), a Senior Visiting Research Fellow at the Department of Media and Communications at the London School of Economics and Political Science (UK), and a board member of Future Everything (UK). Has published in journals such as *AI & Society, Third Text, The Information Society, Telos,* and *Leonardo.* His multidisciplinary research embraces media archeology, digitization, video archives, and the impact of technology in memory institutions. He co-edited a special issue for *AI & Society* on Cybernetics in Latin America (2022) and authored an extensive research on the video art collections in Latin America for Getty's book *Encounters in Video Art in Latin America* (2023). He is part of the curatorial team of *ARTEONICA:* Art, Science, and Technology in Latin America Today, which opens in September 2024 at the MOLAA in Long Beach as part of Getty's PST ART: Art & Science Collide.

Olga Tykhonova (UA/AT) is a researcher and curator of institutional formats, by day Head of Research & Development of MUSEUM BOOSTER. Olga combines research and hands-on practice aimed at ecosystemic advancement of cultural heritage institutions, particularly museums. Approaching the buzz topic of sector's digital transformation, she explores how we can and how we should, as a sector, shift our focus from technologies of 'information and data' to those of world-building, imagination, and caring. As a curator and architect of multi-constituent partnerships and funding programs, she is particularly looking at the intersection of art, social design, and creative technology, investigating ways to nurture shared social ecology for collaboration across diverse epistemic cultures. Currently she is a research curator of the projects *Future Museum, Museum Leadership House,* and is redesigning *Museum Innovation Barometer* with the team.

AI in ART

Jürgen Hagler (AT) is an academic researcher and curator at the interface of animation, game, and media art. Currently, he is a professor of Computer Animation and Media Studies and the head of studies of the bachelor's and master's program Digital Arts at the University of Applied Sciences Upper Austria, Hagenberg Campus. He has been involved in the activities of Ars Electronica since 1997 in a variety of functions. Since 2017 he is the director of the Ars Electronica Animation Festival and initiator and organizer of the Expanded Animation Symposium (2013–2023), Synaesthetic Syntax Conference (2020–2023), and Expanded—Conference on Animation and Interactive Art (since 2024).

Vanessa Hannesschläger (AT) is head of European Collaboration at Ars Electronica, steering the company's engagement in numerous pan-European partnerships. She holds a PhD in literature from the University of Vienna, and teaches courses on digital humanities, research policy frameworks, and digital legal literacy at universities across Europe. Before joining Ars Electronica, Vanessa contributed to the implementation of European digital research infrastructures at the Austrian Academy of Sciences and focused her scholarly work on digital editing and multilingualism in contemporary literature. Her current research focuses on new narratives and experimental form in contemporary performance and text, a topic she explores at Ars Electronica in projects around digital theater and new approaches to XR. She is particularly interested in integrating philosophical thought in art-science approaches, as well as intersectional feminism and gender philosophy. In the European policy context, Vanessa advocates for digital infrastructure for the arts and humanities, data and legal literacy, the Commons, and Open approaches.

Veronika Liebl (AT) is currently Ars Electronica's Director of European Cooperation and Managing Director of its Festival/Prix/Exhibitions department. She studied economics and business science at Johannes Kepler University in Linz (graduated in 2010), with study visits to Harvard University (US) and the Université de Fribourg (CH), and also

has an interdisciplinary background in non-profit and innovation management. Since 2011, she has been in charge of cultural management and European project development at Ars Electronica Linz and serves as an advising member of the City of Linz Culture Council and the executive board of the Linz UNESCO City of Media Arts. Furthermore, for over ten years she has been involved in programming and the production of collaborative programs with partners from the arts, sciences, and industry. She heads Ars Electronica's European collaboration projects in the fields of culture, research & education, and in this regard, together with her team, has evolved, launched, and completed numerous EU projects such as the STARTS Prize and the European Digital Deal.

Emiko Ogawa (JP) is a Japanese curator and artist based in Linz, Austria. Since 2013, she is Head of Prix Ars Electronica—the world's most time-honored media arts competition organized by Ars Electronica. She has also been involved in many of Ars Electronica's art thinking programs for educational institutions, companies, and governments, where essential questions are discussed and shaped as a starting point for the future.

Gerfried Stocker (AT) is a media artist and an engineer for communication technology and has been artistic director and co-CEO of Ars Electronica since 1995. In 1995/96 he developed the exhibition strategies of the Ars Electronica Center with a small team of artists and technicians and was responsible for the setup and establishment of Ars Electronica's own R&D facility, the Ars Electronica Futurelab. He has overseen the development of the program for international Ars Electronica exhibitions since 2004, the planning and the revamping of the contents for the Ars Electronica Center, which was enlarged in 2009, since 2005; the expansion of the Ars Electronica Festival since 2015; and the extensive overhaul of Ars Electronica Center's contents and interior design in 2019. Stocker is a consultant for numerous companies and institutions in the field of creativity and innovation management and is active as a guest lecturer at international conferences and universities. In 2019 he was awarded an honorary doctorate from Aalto University, Finland.

u19–create your world

Sirikit Amann (AT) has been a juror since the very inception of the u19—create your world category for youngsters under 19 years of age in Austria. She was director of cultural education at KulturKontakt Austria. Since 2020 she is the head of the sector "Education and Society" with a focus on digital education at the Austrian Agency for Education and Internationalization (OeAD). She previously served as an expert advisor in artistic affairs at the Austrian Federal Ministry of Education, Art and Culture, and in the Office of the former Federal Chancellor. In 2024, she will represent Austria as a delegate at the UNESCO World Conference on Culture and Arts Education.

Conny Lee (AT) is known throughout Austria as the host of Radio FM4's afternoon show *FM4 Connected,* produces and co-hosts the bilingual FM4 *Morning Show* as well as a show about video games in a socio-political context. In addition, Conny Lee is head of the "Love Department," which deals with topics such as sex, love, and dating. As an editor she reviews games, literature, and comics. In addition to her radio work, she also hosts live events, award ceremonies, and congresses. Conny Lee is part of the core team on the u19—create your world jury.

Emil Klostermann (AT) studies painting at the University of Arts Linz. His works highlight both socio-political issues and personal experiences. He deals with topics such as gender roles, beauty ideals, and discrimination. His art is intended to provoke and make people think/feel. This often results in installative works or curatorial approaches that aim to actively involve the viewers. Apart from the visual arts, he is interested in pop culture, film, and theater.

Anahita Neghabat (AT) is a social anthropologist, artist, and activist working on critical education, intersectional feminism, and (anti-Muslim) racism. As a researcher-in-residence, she conducted research at KinderKunstLabor, an exhibition space for contemporary art for and with children, starting in August 2023. Since 2019, she has been commenting on Austrian domestic politics with satirical images as @ibiza_austrian_memes and was awarded Young European of the Year by the Schwarzkopf Foundation for this work in 2022.

Anna Wielander (AT) studied Slavic Studies and Journalism in Vienna and has a master's degree in Political Science, which she completed in Prague. She worked as an online editor and social media manager at ORF until 2021. In 2022, she moved to *Der Standard,* where, in addition to her work in daily news reporting, she also conducts investigative research into the abuse of power. In 2023, the production *Gondelgschichten* by her theater collective Institut für Medien, Politik und Theater was invited to the radikal jung Festival at the Münchner Volkstheater.

Ars Electronica Award for Digital Humanity

Ambassador **Christoph Thun-Hohenstein** (AT) is Director General for International Cultural Relations at the Federal Ministry for European and International Affairs of the Republic of Austria. After studying law, political science, and history of art at the University of Vienna, Christoph Thun-Hohenstein worked for the Austrian Foreign Ministry and held posts in Abidjan, Geneva, and Bonn. He was Director of the Austrian Cultural Forum New York from 1999 to 2007. From 2007 to 2011, he served as Managing Director of departure, the Creative Agency of the City of Vienna. From 2011 to 2021, Thun-Hohenstein was General Director and Artistic Director of the MAK— Austrian Museum of Applied Arts, Vienna. He initiated the Vienna Biennale for Change, which he directed from 2014 until 2022. Most recently, he initiated the Vienna Climate Biennale, which will take place for the first time from April through July 2024. Thun-Hohenstein has published on topics dealing above all with European integration, contemporary arts and culture, digital modernity, climate care, and circular culture, and held numerous lectures on these topics. He has also curated exhibitions and he regularly serves on selection juries.

Regina Rusz (AT) is an Austrian diplomat and currently heads the department for cultural and scientific events abroad at the Austrian Foreign Ministry. She has worked at embassies and cultural forums in Croatia, Serbia, Hungary, and Slovakia, among others. The advancement of women has always played an important role in her professional activities as Director of the Cultural Forums in Budapest (2017–2020) and Belgrade (2001–2005). From 2008-2012, she was a member of the Austrian Task Force for Combating Human Trafficking at the Ministry of Foreign Affairs.

Thomas Kloiber (AT), born in 1972 in Graz, Austria, studied Catholic theology at the University of Vienna and at the Facultad de Teología del Norte de España Burgos. Before he joined the Austrian Federal Ministry for European and International Affairs in 2008, he worked as high school teacher for religion and as teacher trainer for students of Catholic theology. He worked from 2003 to 2006 as General Secretary of the Federation of Catholic Family Associations in Europe. As employee of the Austrian Federal Ministry for European and International Affairs he served at the Austrian embassies in Washington D.C. and in Moscow as well as at the Cultural Forums in Tehran and Bucharest.

Gerfried Stocker (AT) is a media artist and an engineer for communication technology and has been artistic director and co-CEO of Ars Electronica since 1995. In 1995/96 he developed the exhibition strategies of the Ars Electronica Center with a small team of artists and technicians and was responsible for the setup and establishment of Ars Electronica's own R&D facility, the Ars Electronica Futurelab. He has overseen the development of the program for international Ars Electronica exhibitions since 2004, the planning and the revamping of the contents for the Ars Electronica Center, which was enlarged in 2009, since 2005; the expansion of the Ars Electronica Festival since 2015; and the extensive overhaul of Ars Electronica Center's contents and interior design in 2019. Stocker is a consultant for numerous companies and institutions in the field of creativity and innovation management and is active as a guest lecturer at international conferences and universities. In 2019 he was awarded an honorary doctorate from Aalto University, Finland.

Veronika Liebl (AT) is currently Ars Electronica's Director of European Cooperation and Managing Director of its Festival/Prix/Exhibitions department. She studied economics and business science at Johannes Kepler University in Linz (graduated in 2010), with study visits to Harvard University (US) and the Université de Fribourg (CH), and also has an interdisciplinary background in non-profit and innovation management. Since 2011, she has been in charge of cultural management and European project development at Ars Electronica Linz and serves as an advising member of the City of Linz Culture Council and the executive board of the Linz UNESCO City of Media Arts. Furthermore, for over ten years she has been involved in programming and the production of collaborative programs with partners from the arts, sciences, and industry. She heads Ars Electronica's European collaboration projects in the fields of culture, research & education, and in this regard, together with her team, has evolved, launched, and completed numerous EU projects such as the STARTS Prize and the European Digital Deal.

European Union Prize for Citizen Science

Sofie Burgos-Thorsen (DK) has a PhD in Sociology and has worked across urban strategy, participatory design, and digital innovation for the last 10 years. With projects like *Urban Belonging* and *South Park Youth Vision,* she tackles social and environmental justice issues and works with local communities to create equitable and resilient cities. She was a MIT scholar and R&D specialist in Gehl Architects before taking a role at the Techno-Anthropology Lab, researching Generative AI for citizen engagement.

Mairéad Hurley (IE) is Assistant Professor in Science Education in Trinity College Dublin. With her colleagues in Trinity's Science and Society Research Group, her work explores the role of science learning in shaping socially and environmentally just and sustainable futures, using participatory and transdisciplinary approaches. She integrates her own creative practice as a traditional musician to explore the potential for Irish traditional arts and folklore to inform contemporary environmental education and engagement.

Luciana Marques (BR) is Head of Communication at a biotechnology company. She is a journalist focused on science communication, with experience in the medical field and involvement in many European projects. Luciana's academic journey includes publishing in scientific journals and presenting at conferences.

Fermín Serrano Sanz (ES) coordinated the White Paper on Citizen Science for Europe and managed the Spanish portal ciencia-ciudadana.es. At the Ibercivis Foundation, he has led or supported tens of projects integrating science, policy, society, art, and technology. A participant of the Future Innovators Summit, he was also Commissioner for the Agenda 2030 in Aragon and now chairs the Working Group on Policy, Strategy, Governance, and Partnerships at the European Citizen Science Association.

Snežana Smederevac (RS) is Full Professor at the Department of Psychology, Faculty of Philosophy, University of Novi Sad, and Coordinator of the STAR Center of Excellence for Behavioral Research in Psychology. As former Vice-Rector for Science at the University of Novi Sad, she coordinated the first Open Science projects in Serbia, resulting in the National Open Science Policy. She is author of the first Open Science Manual and Guide for Citizen Science in Serbia. Her research focuses on personality psychology and behavioral genetics.

S+T+ARTS Prize'24 Jury

All submissions are judged by a jury to decide on the two prize-winning projects and up to ten Honorary Mentions.

Francesca Bria (IT) is President of the Italian National Innovation Fund and a Board Member of the Italian public media company RAI. She is Honorary Professor in the Institute for Innovation and Public Purpose at UCL London and she is part of the high-level roundtable for the New European Bauhaus set up by EC President Ursula von der Leyen to accelerate the EU Green Deal. She is the former Chief Digital Technology and Innovation Officer for the City of Barcelona in Spain. In this role, she led the smart city Agenda and was one of the founders of the United Nations Cities Coalition for Digital Rights. Francesca Bria is leading the EU flagship *DECODE* project on data sovereignty in Europe, and is a Senior Adviser on the EC program STARTS (Innovation at the nexus of Science, Technology and the Arts). Francesca has a PhD in Innovation and Entrepreneurship from Imperial College, London and an MSc in Digital Economy from University of London, Birbeck. As Senior Programme Lead at Nesta, the UK Innovation Agency, she has led the EU *D-CENT* project, the biggest European project on digital democracy and crypto platforms. She also led the *Digital Social Innovation* EU project, advising the EU on digital innovation policies and mission-driven innovation. She has taught in several universities in the UK and Italy and has advised governments, public and private organizations on technology and innovation policy, and its socio-economic, geopolitical, and environmental impact. Francesca has been nominated Commander of the Order of Merit of the Italian Republic. She has been listed in the top 50 Women in Tech by *Forbes* magazine, named a Culture Person of the Year 2020 by the newspaper *Frankfurter Allgemeine Zeitung* (FAZ), and is one of the World's top 20 most influential people in digital government according to Apolitical.

Fumi Hirota (JP) is Art Producer and Chief of Initiatives Section at the Digital Creativity Division of Tokyo Metropolitan Foundation for History and Culture. After completing graduate studies at the Institute of Advanced Media Arts and Sciences (IAMAS), Fumi Hirota worked as a researcher for the Cultural Media Center at IAMAS. She joined the Yamaguchi Center for Arts and Media (YCAM) in 2008, where she was involved with production and planning for new media art and other projects. From 2012, she was a researcher in the Arts and Culture Division of the Cultural Affairs Department at the Agency for Cultural Affairs. She worked on initiatives promoting media arts, including efforts to expand the reach of the Japan Media Arts Festival overseas and in regional Japan. She left the Agency for Cultural Affairs in 2015 to work at the Japan Foundation Asia Center, where she was involved with media art projects as part of cultural exchange initiatives between Japan and Southeast Asia until 2019. Hirota took up a post at the Tokyo Metropolitan Foundation for History of Culture in 2020, helping launch Tokyo Smart Culture Project, which digitizes cultural resources like the collections of Tokyo's cultural institutions and offers various types of viewing experiences. In 2022, she was part of the team behind the opening of Civic Creative Base Tokyo (CCBT) in Shibuya.

Manuela Naveau (AT) is a university professor, an independent curator, and an art-based researcher. She started as project manager at Ars Electronica Linz, where she developed the Ars Electronica Export department together with Artistic Director Gerfried Stocker and led it operationally for almost 18 years. Since 2020, Manuela Naveau has been a university professor for Critical Data at the Interface Cultures Department / Institute of Media at the University of Arts Linz, which she is head of since February 2023, when she also initiated the Critical Data Research Group. Previously, she has held teaching positions at the Paris Lodron University of Salzburg and the Danube University Krems among others, and has been invited as a guest professor at the Technical University in Vienna (Future.Lab). Her monography *Crowd and Art—Kunst und Partizipation im Internet* was published by transcript Verlag, Germany. The book is based on her dissertation, for which she received the Award of Excellence from the Federal Ministry of Science, Research and Economy.

Katja Schechtner (AT) is an urban scientist who develops new technologies and shapes innovative policies to keep cities on the move. She is currently focusing on a reassessment of the position of nature and technology within urban governance processes with MIT LCAU and, at the same time, tackles questions of urban policy making with a particular emphasis on understanding the human perception of—and interaction with—the built environment with MIT Senseable City Lab. Previously she led innovation and technology programs at OECD in France, the Asian Development Bank in the Philippines, and advised the Inter-American Development Bank in Costa Rica and Argentina, the EU Commission, and headed an applied research lab at the Austrian Institute of Technology—all the while holding visiting professorships, lecturer positions, and research affiliations globally, e.g. at MIT Media Lab, Paris-Saclay, die Angewandte, TU Vienna, or HDM Stuttgart. Her own work has been exhibited at the Venice Biennale of Architecture, the Seoul Biennale of Architecture and Urbanism, and Ars Electronica among others, while her exhibition

"Women Build Cities" is currently travelling European cities, earning acclaim in major publications like *Le Monde, El Pais* and *Al Jazeera.* She has published widely in scientific and public media, including books with Birkhaeuser and Ambra such as *Inscribing a Square: Urban Data as Public Space* and *Accountability Technologies—Tools for Asking Hard Questions* together with Dietmar Offenhuber. Additionally, she serves on various boards, including the payment tech subsidiary of the Austrian National Bank and the Austrian Institute of Technology and is a member of the founding convention of the new IT:U in Linz, focusing on digital transformation.

Miha Turšič (SI/NL) works on international collaboration and the initiation of projects touching on the themes of art-science, biotechnology, digital fabrication, open source hardware, ecology, material research, and outer space. At Waag Futurelab, he leads the Spacelab and is closely involved with Open Design Lab and Open Wetlab. Miha works with the partners in the European S+T+ARTS collaboration, operating on the crossings of science, technology and the arts, where he focuses on methodology for collaborative innovation. He was involved in a number of leading Waag projects such as *OpenNext,* promoting concern-driven innovation through open source hardware, *VOJEXT* and *Better Factory* engaging artists in art-driven innovation with industry, and now coordinating the *More-than-Planet* project focusing on new planetary imaginaries. Miha studied Industrial Design at the University of Ljubljana. He is co-founder of Asobi Design Studio and KSEVT, the Cultural Centre of European Space Technologies. Nowadays, KSEVT is developing a cultural space program, enabling the understanding of art, culture, and humanities in outer space. In collaboration with both space and cultural organizations, KSEVT produced cultural programs on the International Space Station, introduced space architecture to the Venice Bienniale, and presented Voyager instruments to the public for the first time in history. Miha is also part of the Postgravityart group, which produced the very first theater production in zero gravity and works on the 50-year performance project *Noordung 1995–2045.*

S+T+ARTS Prize '24 Advisors

The advisors are renowned international consultants with expertise in this field. They recommend projects and encourage a wide range of potential participants to submit proposals. In addition, they ensure a balance in terms of gender and geographical origin of the participants.

Amanda Masha Caminals (ES) is co-director and curator of the Artistic Laboratory for Climate Action (LAC—itdUPM), previously known as the Mutant Institute for Environmental Narratives (IMNA), at the Development Centre of the Technical University of Madrid. LAC—itdUPM fosters artistic practices in connection with journalism, science, and technology as a response to the challenges of the environmental crisis. She is also co-founder of the network Translocalia. Previous to that, she directed the CITY STATION of the Environmental Health Clinic by artist Natalie Jeremijenko at the Centre for Contemporary Culture of Barcelona (CCCB) and the Barcelona City Council. As an independent curator she was responsible for the 2019 edition of Mobile Week Barcelona, a 10-day festival before the Mobile World Congress of Barcelona that formulates an open space of dialogue around the impact of digital technology in society. She has worked in institutions including the Institute of International Visual Arts in London and Casa Triângulo in São Paulo. She holds a BA in Humanities from Pompeu Fabra University in Barcelona, a degree in History of Art from the University of Barcelona, and an MA Hons in Curating Contemporary Art from the Royal College of Art in London.

Yun-Cheng Chen (Lucky) (TW), a freelance transdisciplinary design artivist and strategist. Having resided in both the United States and Germany, he had the privilege of furthering his studies under the esteemed guidance of Professor Dr. Michael Erlhoff, a pioneer in introducing Service Design as a design discipline at Köln International School of Design (KISD). Lucky's extensive expertise in performing arts, deliberative democracy, regional revitalization, digital transformation, and the open data/government movement has garnered him numerous invitations to program and execute an impressive array of local and international projects since 2016. He excels in integrating resources and initiating collaborative initiatives among industry, government, university, and global community/DAO.

Currently, Lucky serves as the Strategy Director of Les Petites Choses Production and Seabelongings, consultant of Taiwan Dancing Forward Collective, while also actively contributing to g0v/da0.

Primavera De Filippi (FR/IT) is a legal scholar at Harvard University, as well as an Internet activist and artist exploring the intersection between law and technology, focusing specifically on the legal and political implications of blockchain technology. Her artistic practice instantiates the key findings of her research in the physical world, creating blockchain-based lifeforms that evolve and reproduce themselves as people feed them with cryptocurrencies. Her works have been exposed in various museums, galleries, and art fairs around the world including Ars Electronica, Furtherfield Gallery, Kinetica Art Fair, Gazelli Art House, Centre Pompidou, Grand Palais, Gaité Lyrique, and Le Cent Quatre, as well as festivals such as Burning Man and Fusion Festival.

Rodolfo Groenewoud van Vliet (NL) is co-founder of In4Art—an independent Institute for Art-Driven Innovation, established in 2015. His interests lie in exploring and prototyping possibilities of technologies and the economics that will influence the shorter- and longer-term futures of food, manufacturing, health, and biodiversity. Together with his wife and collaborator Lija Groenewoud van Vliet, he invented and practices the Art-Driven Innovation methodology that is currently driving over 75 international experimental programs and projects involving art, science, technology, and industry.

Lydia Kallipoliti (GR) is an architect, engineer, and scholar whose research focuses on the intersections of architecture, technology, and environmental politics. She is a tenured Associate Professor at the Cooper Union in New York. Her work has been published and exhibited widely including the Venice Biennale, the Istanbul Design Biennial, the Storefront for Art and Architecture in New York, and the London Design Museum. She is the author of the awarded book *The Architecture of Closed Worlds, Or, What is the Power of Shit* (Lars Muller Publishers, 2018), and the editor of *EcoRedux,* a special issue of *Architectural Design* magazine (AD, 2010). Her thinktank ANAcycle has been named a leading innovator in sustainable design in *BUILD's* 2019 and 2020 Architecture Awards.

Micaela Mantegna (AR). Known as the "Abogamer", Micaela is a video game lawyer and activist who is internationally renowned for her expertise in digital ethics, extended reality (XR) policy, and the complex relationship between artificial intelligence, creativity, and copyright law. In 2022, Micaela was chosen for the prestigious TED Fellowship, and her TED talk on the metaverse earned 1.5M+ views globally. Currently she is an affiliate at the Berkman Klein Center at Harvard University, while also serving on Chatham House's Responsible AI Taskforce, the World Economic Forum's Metaverse Council, and the Scientific Committee of UAMetaverse Chair, positions that highlight Micaela as a global thought leader in Generative AI, ethics, videogames, and metaverse policy. As a keynote speaker, she has presented across the globe in conferences like GDC, TED, GamesBeat Summit, Ada Lovelace Festival, Vancouver Biennale, More Than Just a Game, RightsCon, DLD, Internet Freedom Festival, and many more, in over 28 countries. Author of the article "ARTficial: creativity, AI and copyright" (2022) and the upcoming book *Braindancing in the Metaverse: a capitalism of cognitive surveillance* (2024), her work explores in depth the implications of digital capitalism, at the intersections of intellectual property, AI, art, and ethics. She earned the 2017 Google Policy Fellowship for her work creating an algorithmic governance framework. Her work and insights have been featured in outlets like *The Verge, WIRED,* and *Le Monde.* Micaela curates the popular Substack newsletter "This week in the #Metaverse", offering weekly insights into the latest trends and policy developments on the metaverse, AI, neurotech, crypto, and gaming.

Irini Papadimitriou (UK) is a curator and cultural manager, and currently Director of Exhibitions at Diriyah Art Futures. Between 2018 and 2024 she was the Creative Director at FutureEverything, and in 2023 she was the Artistic Director for the Sea Art Festival 2023 with Busan Biennale, South Korea. She was previously Digital Programmes Manager at the V&A, and Head of New Media Arts Development at Watermans. Recently curated exhibitions include: AI: Who's Looking After Me? at Science Gallery London; Flickering Shores, Sea Imaginaries for Sea Art Festival, Busan Biennale, South Korea; FutureFantastic, Bangalore, India; Plásmata: Bodies, Dreams, and Data and You and AI: Through the Algorithmic Lens for Onassis Stegi,

Athens; Money, Ruins, and the Sea, NeMe, Cyprus; [Digital] Transmissions, National Gallery of Fine Arts, Amman, Jordan; Artificially Intelligent, V&A. Irini is a co-founder of Maker Assembly, a critical gathering about maker culture, and she has been a co-curator for the Arts & Culture experience at Mozilla Festival, including the 2019 exhibition Trustworthy AI: Imagining Better Machine Decision Making. She has served as a jury member for Prix Ars Electronica, D&AD Awards, Lumen Prize, EU STARTS, and ACM Siggraph.

Kyuseung Keith Noh (KR) is Team Lead and Creative Director of ZER01NE, the creative talent platform of Hyundai Motor Group. ZER01NE's mission is human-centered innovation beyond the typical Open Innovation of other corporates. ZER01NE nurtures creators and startups that can challenge and solve the problem of future society through the collaboration of ART, TECH, and BIZ. Since 2018, over 120 creators and 80 startups have been supported and funded. Furthermore, he is also a professional investor and managing partner of the ZER01NE Fund.

Deborah Rey-Burns (UK/AU) started her career in Sydney as a banker, before pivoting in London to become a cultural entrepreneur and the founder of Propela, an innovative speaking agency globally known for its commitment to frontier thinking. With a mission to bridge the gap between the creative sector and the business world, Deborah established the British agency over a decade ago. Propela's roster features a selection of international innovators who have been keynote speakers at major conferences, Fortune 500 companies, and leading brands. Among Propela's clients are Neil Harbisson, the world's first Cyborg, along with Oscar-nominated set designers Katie Spencer and Sarah Greenwood *(Barbie),* artist and technologist James Bridle, designer Dr. Nelly Ben Hayoun, speculative architect Liam Young, Bas Van Abel, the founder of Fairphone, a world leader in sustainability and ethics, and Dr. Sian Proctor, the world's first black female spaceship pilot. Beyond Propela, Deborah has curated programs for institutions such as the Victoria & Albert Museum and the Design Council's COP26 conference, along with organizations such as Google, Airbnb, and Spotify. Furthermore, she founded ReDesign Business and The Future Of_, two conference brands dedicated to showcasing art, creativity, innovation, and business.

Asako Tomura (JP) is General Manager of the Content Technology & Alliance Group, Corporate Technology Strategy Division of Sony Group Corporation. After earning master's degrees in chemistry and media arts, she began her career in advertising at Shiseido. She joined Sony Corporation in 2001 and oversaw the launch of the digital content distribution business for film and animation at Sony Pictures Entertainment (Japan) and Aniplex, Inc. She then served as Head of CSR Innovation at Sony headquarters, where she collaborated with international NGOs on projects using technology to address social issues. Since 2016, she has overseen advanced content development, entertainment technology promotion, and sustainability technology strategy. In addition, she served as the planning director for Ars Electronica 2021 Garden TOKYO and as a jury member for the European Commission's STARTS Prize 2022. She is also an advisor for the Project to Support Emerging Media Arts Creators, Agency for Cultural Affairs, Government of Japan, 2017–2024. Since 2021, she is a Visiting Researcher at the Interfaculty Initiative in Information Studies at the University of Tokyo.

Lining Yao (CN) is an assistant professor at the Mechanical Engineering department, the University of California, Berkeley, where she directs the Morphing Matter Lab (morphingmatter.org). Her research explores the positive impact of active and morphing materials on sustainable design across different scales and contexts. Her work focuses on discovering and studying morphing material mechanisms, as well as algorithms for computational design and fabrication pipelines. Dr. Yao has published in both computer science and physical science venues and has received nine Best Paper or Best Talk Awards and nominations from premier conferences in Human-Computer Interaction. Her journal papers have been featured as cover stories in *Nature, Science Advances,* and *Advanced Materials Technologies.* Her work has been widely featured in popular media outlets, including the *New York Times, Wired, Scientific American, Fast Company, National Geographic,* and *BBC,* among others. Dr. Yao received her PhD from the MIT Media Lab in 2017. She is the co-founder of the MorphingMatter4Girls Initiative, a *Wired* UK fellow, and an appointed instructor in eco-design by the United Nations Industrial Development Organization.

S+T+ARTS Prize Africa Jury

All submissions are judged by a Jury who decide on the prize-winning projects.

Andrea Barschdorf-Hager (AT) has been serving as CEO of CARE Austria in Vienna since 2009. In this role, she leads the marketing team and oversees program and finance areas, as well as the relief and development work. Andrea also represents CARE Austria in media and politics. CARE is one of the world's leading development and humanitarian aid agencies, dedicated to fighting poverty and injustice, with a specific focus on the empowerment of women and girls. Born in Vienna, Andrea began her involvement in development cooperation while studying Ethnology and African Studies at the University of Vienna. She is a respected leader in international cooperation, widely recognized for her insight, commitment, and expertise. Andrea has received several awards and recognitions for her service. Additionally, she is an International Gender Champion and serves as a board member of the institute OIIP (Austrian institute for International Affairs). Andrea has a special interest and focus on digitalization and artificial intelligence.

Mónica Bello is an art historian and curator living in Geneva and Barcelona. Since 2015, she has held the position of Head of Arts at CERN at the European Organization for Nuclear Research in Geneva. In this pivotal role, she provides strategic leadership and oversight for the laboratory's art initiatives, directing the conception and implementation of the artistic programs, including artistic residencies, art commissions, and exhibitions. She is the curator of the Exploring the Unknown exhibition at CERN Science Gateway, which recently opened. She curated the Icelandic Pavilion at the 59th Venice Biennale with the artist Sigurður Guðjónsson; Dark Matters at Science Gallery Melbourne; Quantum/Broken Symmetries, a touring exhibition in six different art centers in Europe and Asia; and was guest curator at the prestigious Audemars Piguet Art Commission for Art Basel. Before coming to Geneva, Bello was the Artistic Director of VIDA, Art and Artificial Life Award at Fundación Telefónica, Madrid; and Head of the Department of Education at Laboral Centro de Arte, Gijón.

Oscar Ekponimo (NG) a driven entrepreneur, business visionary, and innovator with a passion for leveraging technology to create positive change. At just 26 years old, he founded Chowberry Inc., an innovative technology-driven social business in Africa, committed to reducing food waste and enhancing food access for individuals experiencing hunger. The groundbreaking technology has facilitated the distribution of over 1.6 million meals in the past 6 years. He was named in *Time Magazine's* list of 10 Next Generation Leaders, and is a recipient of the Rolex Award for Enterprise from the Rolex Watch Company. For his pioneering effort he was named a Young Pioneer at Harvard Medical by World Frontiers Forum and most recently awarded the Creative Entrepreneur of 2022 by 50 Next at the Basque Culinary Centre. He established Gallery of Code, Africa's first multidisciplinary design lab at the nexus of Arts, Science and Technology, in collaboration with Ars Electronica. He is a member of the Ars Electronica Digital Communities Advisory Board and has served on multiple juries connected to issues of sustainability and the Food System such as MIT Solve.

Judith Okonkwo (NG/GB) is a technology evangelist and business psychologist with experience working in Africa, Asia, and Europe. She sits on the Board of the European Organization Design Forum, advises startups, not-for-profits, and SMEs on emerging technologies and is a guest lecturer at several higher education institutions. She is also the creator of the Oriki Coaching Model™ and a co-founder of the global network We Will Lead Africa. Judith is a Fellow of the Royal Society of Arts and an Associate Fellow of the British Psychological Society. In 2016 Judith set up Imìsí 3D, a creation lab in Lagos focused on building the African ecosystem for extended reality technologies (AR/VR/MR), and connecting XR communities across the continent. The lab provides learning opportunities and access to XR resources for creators and enthusiasts, while supporting engagement and adoption by the wider community, and consulting and content creation for industry. In 2017 she set up AR/VR Africa, which holds large XR events on the continent, the most recent being the 2022 AR/VR Africa hackathon with participants from 42 African countries. In 2021 Imìsí 3D organized the first African Delegation to a global XR event, the African Delegation at Laval Virtual 2021. Judith is a member of the World Economic Forum's Global Future Council for the Metaverse, and a Chen Yidan Visiting Global Fellow at Harvard's Graduate School of Education.

Kathleen Siminyu (KE) is an AI Researcher who has focused on Natural Language Processing for African Languages. She works at Mozilla Foundation as a Machine Learning Fellow to support the development of Kiswahili Speech Recognition. In her NLP research, Kathleen has previously worked on speech transcription for Luhya languages and contributed to machine translation for Kenyan languages as part of Masakhane. Before joining Mozilla, Kathleen was Regional Coordinator of AI4D Africa, where she worked with ML and AI communities in Africa to run various programs. She has vast experience as a community organizer having co-organized the Nairobi Women in Machine Learning and Data Science community for three years and continues to organize as part of the committees of the Deep Learning Indaba and the Masakhane Research Foundation.

S+T+ARTS Prize Africa Advisors

The advisors are renowned international consultants with expertise in this field. They recommend projects and encourage a wide range of potential participants to submit proposals.

Tegan Bristow is Director of Education for Diriyah Art Futures, a soon to be opened new media art and art & technology center launched by the Ministry of Culture in Saudi Arabia. Bristow has a research position at Wits University's School of Arts, where she was previously a principal researcher and senior lecturer in the Digital Arts Department, specializing in African Art, Culture and Technology. Bristow additionally acted as editor in chief and digital editor of the *Ellipses Journal for Creative Research* in this role. In 2021 Bristow won the National Science and Technology Forum Award for Sustainable Development in the Creative Industries for her work in co-founding and developing the Fak'ugesi Festival that she directed from 2016 to 2020. This was further developed in GIZ supported research mapping landscape of the digital cultural industry in Africa. Beyond development, research, curation, and directing festivals, Bristow is a developer of interactive digital media in installation, interactive-performance screen-based and online media, exhibiting a *School for Vernacular Algorithms* with the University of African Futures, curated by Oulimata Gueye at Le Lieu Unique in Nantes, France in 2021.

Eduardo Cachucho is the Creative Director of the Fak'ugesi African Digital Innovation Festival. He is a program consultant, artist, and ex-architect. He has worked in digital innovation in the creative sector for over a decade both locally and internationally, believing that digital creative practices are the key to sustainable empowerment in South Africa and across the countries of Africa.

Letaru Dralega is a Ugandan Jamaican British artist and curator interested in the material/immaterial dichotomy, particularly in African and Afro-diasporic ontologies. She experiments across collage, painting, installation, and sound to examine themes of memory, belonging, and the postcolonial condition. A social scientist by training she holds a masters in International Development with African studies (2019) from Sciences Po Paris, France. She co-founded Afropocene Studio Lab, an interdisciplinary research space in Kampala dedicated to exploring the cultural aesthetics and philosophies of science that are borne of the developing intersection of African/Afro-diaspora culture with technology. She co-directs Afropocene: The Capsule, an Independent public art platform established in 2023 to promote experimental, immersive, and alternative exhibition formats in Kampala.

Femi Johnson is a digital heritage specialist and part of the project at the Museum of West African Art, collaborating with museums like RJM Koln, Oxford Pitt Rivers, Cambridge MAA, and The Swiss Benin Initiative, preserving African heritage through digitization. Beyond that, Femi excels as a filmmaker. His dedication has earned him global recognition, culminating in a fellowship at Basel House of Film, Switzerland. In visual art, talent breaks forth with a GAS Foundation Fellowship as well as works, exhibited internationally from Kunstraum Aarau to AAF Lagos. Femi is a guest lecturer at HFBK Hamburg, exploring the ephemerality of human nature. Femi strives to integrate African culture into emerging technology. He believes in leveraging technology to share African stories innovatively, preserving the continent's vibrant heritage.

Marcus Neustetter (*1976, Johannesburg) earned his master's degree in Fine Arts (2001, University of the Witwatersrand, South Africa). Interested in cross-disciplinary practice, site-specificity, and socially engaged interventions at the intersection of art and activism, Neustetter has produced artworks and projects across Africa, Europe, America, and Asia. Searching for a balance between poetic form and asking critical questions, his media fluctuates in response to concept and context. Ideas often circle the intersection of art, science and technology in an attempt to find new perspectives on his process. As artistic director, facilitator, researcher, and strategist, he finds himself building opportunities and networks that develop interest beyond his personal artistic practice into seeking alternative cultural ecosystems through his 23-year collaboration as director of the contemporary art production team The Trinity Session. Neustetter is an adjunct professor (Nelson Mandela University) and currently moves between his studios in Johannesburg and Vienna.

Azu Nwagbogu is an internationally acclaimed curator, interested in evolving new models of engagement with questions of decolonization, restitution, and repatriation. In his practice, the exhibition becomes an experimental site for reflection, civic engagement, ecology, and repatriation—both tangible and symbolic. Nwagbogu is the founder and director of the African Artists' Foundation (AAF), a non-profit organization based in Lagos, Nigeria. He also serves as founder and director of LagosPhoto Festival, an annual international arts festival of photography held in Lagos. He is the publisher of Art Base Africa, a virtual space to discover and learn about contemporary art from Africa and its diasporas. In 2021, Nwagbogu was awarded "Curator of Year 2021" by the Royal Photographic Society, UK, and also listed amongst the hundred most influential people in the art world by *ArtReview.* In 2021, Nwagbogu launched the project *Dig Where You Stand (DWYS)—From Coast to Coast,* which offers a new model for institutional building and engagement, with questions of decolonization, restitution, and repatriation. The exhibition took place in Ibrahim's Mahama's culture hub SCCA in Tamale, Ghana. Most recently, in 2023, Nwagbogu became a National Geographic "Explorer at Large"—a title bestowed on exceptional global changemakers—serving as an ambassador for the organization and receiving support to continue his storytelling work across Africa and globally. Nwagbogu's primary interest is in reinventing the idea of the museum and its role as a civic space for engagement of society at large.

Rosie Olang' Odhiambo is a curator, writer, and artist based in Nairobi, Kenya. Her artistic and curatorial approach aims to cultivate generative collaborative processes, centering local context and deep research, all thoughtfully deployed to develop exhibitions, publications, and programming that is accessible, sustainable, ambitious, and liberatory. She is currently exploring workshops, zines, and artists' books as curatorial formats to play across various disciplines engaging with decolonial, queer, feminist, and black radical traditions. More recently alongside *Down River Road* and friends, she has been experimenting with sound art and installation formats. Rosie has worked in research, editorial, communication, writing, and project management roles with literary and visual arts organizations in East Africa and the United States and has previously served as Head of Programs at the Nairobi Contemporary Art Institute (NCAI).

Azza Satti is a creative producer, curator, and social change advocate, passionate about creating experiences that inspire and foster connection. She's currently the program developer for The Rest Residency, a space for Sudanese artists displaced by the war and now based in Nairobi, Kenya. Formerly the Head of Community Engagement at African Crossroads with Hivos in the Netherlands, Azza played a pivotal role in nurturing a community of thinkers and doers. She produced the Hivos funded documentary *Water, Urban Transformation, and African Heritage,* exploring the impact of the *LAPSSET Corridor* project on Lamu Island's environment and identity in Kenya. Beyond documentaries, Azza is a founding member of the African Art in Venice Forum, a two-day forum that provides a platform for artists, critics, researchers, academics, and others to meet and discuss African Art. Empowering creative minds is central to Azza's work. In 2018, she facilitated the African Crossroads gathering in Marrakech, bringing together 120 creatives, entrepreneurs, and innovators for workshops. Azza's decade in NYC produced an MA in Art and Public Policy from New York University and a BA in Media and Film from Hunter College.

Neri Torcello is an international art consultant, independent researcher, and writer with a focus on cultural dignity, a concept encompassing those of migration, the right to freedom of artistic expression and creation, and cultural democracy. He is committed to developing participative and synergistic projects and networks to foster and support the ecosystem for the promotion of the arts from marginalized communities. Neri is co-founder of the African Art Dialogues not-for-profit organization in Italy, and founder of the African Art in Venice Forum, a public and free discursive platform presented every two years during the opening week of the Biennale Arte di Venezia. He is a columnist for *art-frame* magazine.

ARS ELECTRONICA 2024
Festival for Art, Technology & Society

Organization
Ars Electronica Linz GmbH & Co KG

Co-CEOs
Markus Jandl, Gerfried Stocker
Ars-Electronica-Straße 1, 4040 Linz, Austria
Tel: +4373272720
Fax: +4373272722
info@ars.electronica.art

Artistic Director: Gerfried Stocker
Managing & Festival Director: Veronika Liebl
Technical Director: Karl Julian Schmidinger

Head of Festival: Christl Baur
Head of create your world: Hans Christian Merten
Head of European Collaboration:
Vanessa Hannesschläger
Head of Operations: Xenia Kentz

Production Team: Magdalena Bauer, Pablo Bes Alonso, Fabiana Braunstorfer, Leo Breneis, Chris Busch, Catalina Cano, Ana Maria Carabelea, Alexandra Crasnaru, Chiara Croci, Jaia Davis-Thomas, Yusra Dellali, Stefan Doepner, Daniela Duca De Tey, Alexander Dyurkowitsch, Elwin Ebmer, Jaka Erjavec, Julian Erk, Hannes Franks, Jessica Galirow, Magdalena Giegler, Katerina Gnafaki, Christoph Graf, David Grohe, Antonia Gschwendtner, Max Haarich, Lukas Haider, Katharina Haim, Rita Hainzl, Randolf Helmstetter, Alexander Hens, Manuela Hillmann, Leo Holzweber, Holger Hörtnagl, Magdalena Hrnicek, Melchior Jahn, Michaela Keplinger, Nina Kneidinger, Andrea Kohut, Maria Koller, Simon Kopfberger, Patrick Köppl, Eunji Kwon, Marek Ledzinski, Johanna Lenhart, Lisa Lepschi, Johanna Liska, Moritz Merten, Elisabeth Mürzl, Philipp Nelweg, Pamela Neuwirth, Emiko Ogawa, Alisa Pashkova, Nathalie Pinter, Nilesh Pinto, Christina Radner, Daniel Renner, Annika Rohde, Daniel Schöngruber, Armin Seidl, Karl Seiringer, Daniela Silvestrin, Lisa Shchegolkova, Blanca Somarriba, Helmut Steinecker, Philip Steiner, Katsiaryna Suryna, Laura Torres, Lukas Traxler, Anna Tretyakova, Josipa Trupina, Edin Turalic, Leon Wagner, Matthias Weghofer, Martin Weidinger, Jan Weiler, Laura Welzenbach, Philip Wolfsohn, Carlos Velandia, Joschi Viteka, Helena Viteka, Alisa Verbina, Alexandre Zolotov, Masha Zolotova

Press
Hannah Bachl, Joan Bairam, Nina Ebner, Mario Romera Goméz, Marlene Grinner, Martin Hieslmair, Katia Kreuzhuber, Mario Schmidhumer, Thomas Schwarz, Christopher Sonnleitner, Amelie Steininger, Yazdan Zand

Marketing
Meli Posch, Christina Holzmeier

Co-Curatorial Team:
Curators of Ars Electronica Festival Programs
Artistic Director: Gerfried Stocker
Head of Programming: Christl Baur
Curatorial Advisor: Hideaki Ogawa

Theme Exhibition: Olga Tykhonova
Prix Ars Electronica Exhibition: Emiko Ogawa
STARTS Exhibition: Masha Zolotova
create your world: Hans Christian Merten
Deep Space 8K: Melinda File, Katrin Fenninger, Christoph Kremer
Open Futurelab: Anna Oelsch, Marianne Eisl
Futurelab Night: Alexandre Bezri
Ars Electronica Solutions
Ars Electronica Symposium 2024: Ana Maria Carabelea, Daniela Silvestrin, The Catalysts
Animation Festival: Jürgen Hagler (Director Animation Festival), Daniela Duca De Tey
Anton Bruckner 2024: Norbert Trawöger
Ars Electronica Nightline: Nicholas Schärer
Expanded Animation: Juergen Hagler, Michael Lankes, Jeremiah Diephuis
University of Arts Linz: Manuela Naveau
Anton Bruckner Private University: Enrique Mendoza, Angélica Castelló, Tobias Leibetseder
JKU LIT Exhibition: Jury des LIT-Calls (Stefan Koch, Alberta Bonanni, Gerfried Stocker, Veronika Liebl)

Prix Ars Electronica 2024
Idea: Hannes Leopoldseder
Conception: Christine Schöpf, Gerfried Stocker
Managing Director: Veronika Liebl
Technical Director: Karl Julian Schmidinger

Head of Prix Ars Electronica: Emiko Ogawa

Production Team: Christl Baur, Pablo Bes Alonso, Daniela Duca De Tey, Magdalena Giegler, Vanessa Hannesschläger, Manuela Hillmann, Xenia Kentz, Michaela Keplinger, Hans Christian Merten, Elisabeth Mürzl, Annika Rohde, Jutta Schmiederer, Lisa Shchegolkova, Blanca Somarriba, Helmut Steinecker, Joschi Viteka, Laura Welzenbach, Masha Zolotova

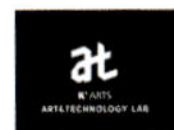
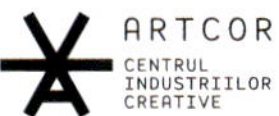
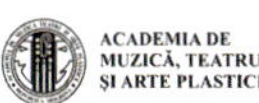
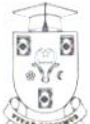

American University of Sharjah

Art and Technology Lab, Korea
National University of Arts

Artcor — Creative Industries Center

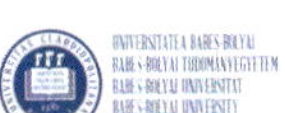
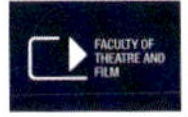
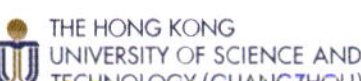

Babeş-Bolyai University Cluj-Napoca, Romania,
Faculty of Theater and Film

Bauhaus University Weimar -
Media Art and Design

Computational Media and Arts, Hong Kong
University of Science & Technology (Guangzhou)

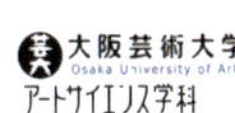
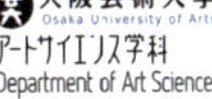
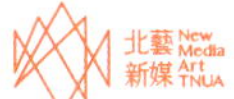
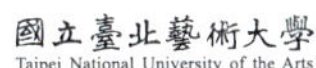
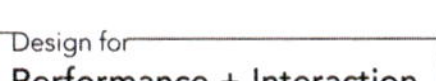
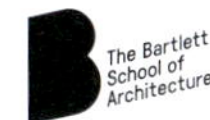

Department of Art Science,
Osaka University of Arts

Department of New Media Art,
Taipei National University of the Arts

Design for Performance and Interaction. The Bartlett
School of Architecture, University College London

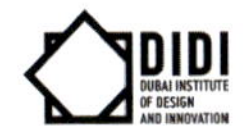
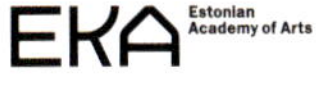
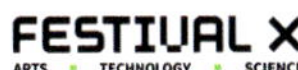
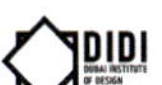
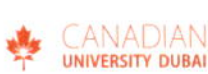
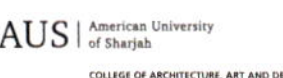

Dubai Institute of Design and
Innovation (DIDI)

EKA - Estonian Academy
of Arts

Festival X Next Gen in Collaboration with Dubai Institute for
Design and Innovation, and American University of Sharjah

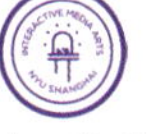
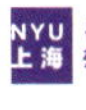
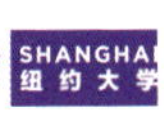
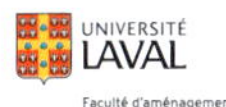

I. L. Caragiale National
University of Theatre and Film

Interactive Media Arts (IMA), New York
University, Shanghai (NYU Shanghai)

Laval University

London College of
Communication, UAL

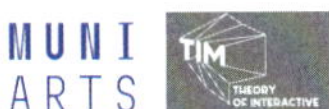
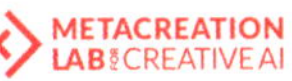
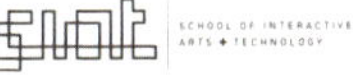
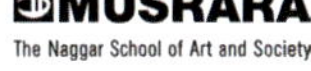

Masaryk University,
Faculty of Arts

Metacreation Lab for Creative AI, School of Interactive
Arts and Technology, Simon Fraser University

Musrara, the Naggar School
of Art and Society, Jerusalem

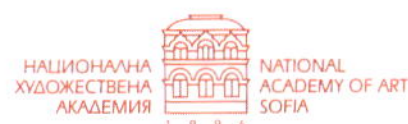
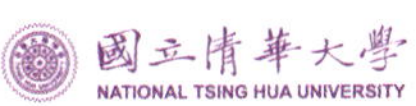
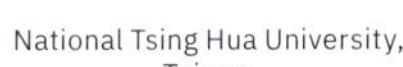
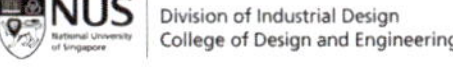
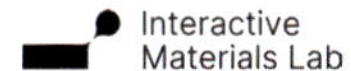

National Academy of Art
Sofia

National Tsing Hua University,
Taiwan

National University of Singapore,
Interactive Materials Lab

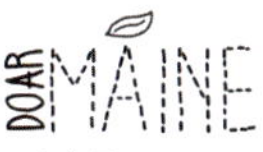
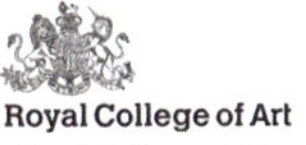
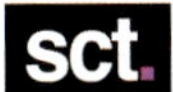
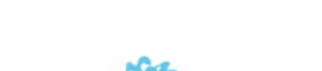
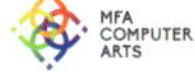

Only Tomorrow
Association

Royal College of Art

School of Cultural Technology, Xi'an
Jiaotong Liverpool University

School of Visual Arts,
MFA Computer Arts

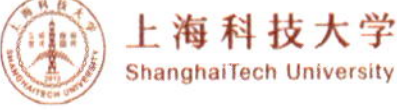
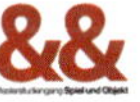
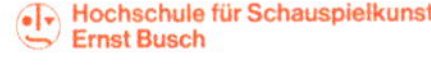
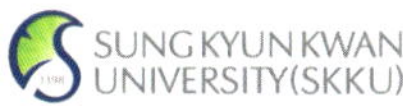
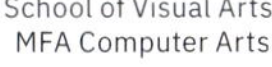

ShanghaiTech University

Spiel und Objekt Master Studio, Ernst Busch
University of Theatre Arts Berlin

Sungkyunkwan University

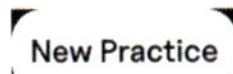
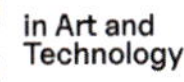
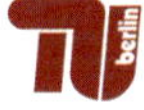
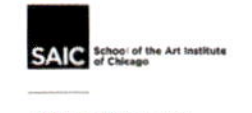
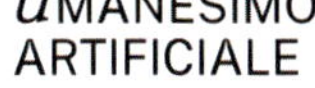
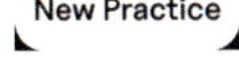
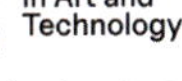
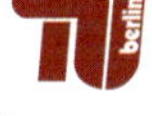
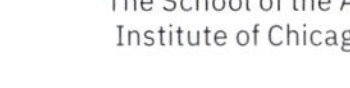

Technical University Berlin

The Pontifical Catholic University
Chile

The School of the Art
Institute of Chicago

Umanesimo Artificiale

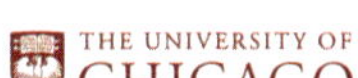
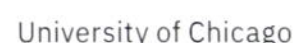

Universität der Künste Berlin

University of Applied Science Berlin – School of Culture and Design
& Department Computer Science, Communication and Business

University of Chicago

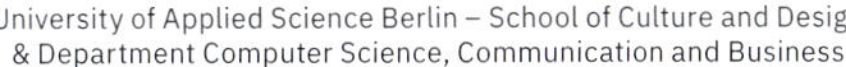
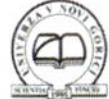
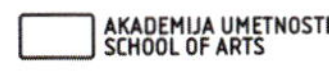
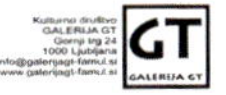
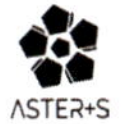
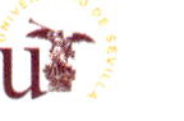
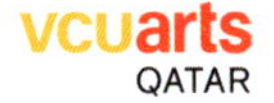
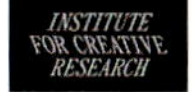
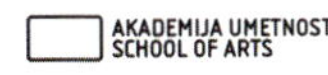

University of Nova Gorica
School of Arts

University of Seville

Virginia Commonwealth University
School of the Arts in Qatar

ARS ELECTRONICA RECEIVES SUPPORT FROM

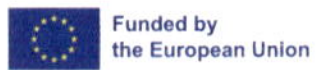

Horizon Europe /
Erasmus+ 2021-2027

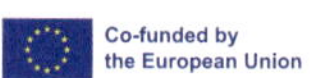

Creative Europe
2021-2027

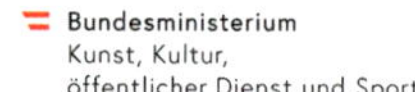

Bundesministerium für Kunst,
Kultur, öffentlichen Dienst
und Sport

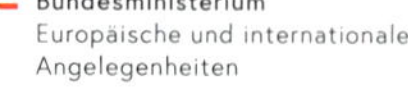

Bundesministerium für
europäische und internationale
Angelegenheiten

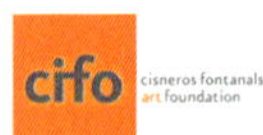

Bundesministerium für
Bildung, Wissenschaft und
Forschung

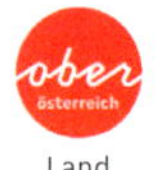

Land
Oberösterreich

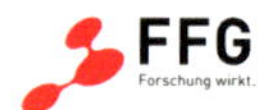

Austrian Research
Promotion Agency (FFG)

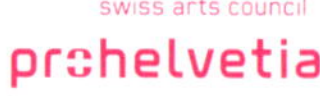

Pro Helvetia

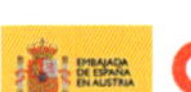 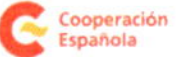

Cisneros Fontanals
Art Foundation

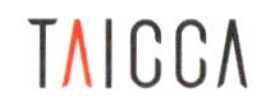

Taiwan Creative Content
Agency (TAICCA)

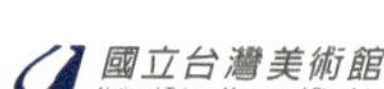

National Taiwan Museum
of Fine Arts

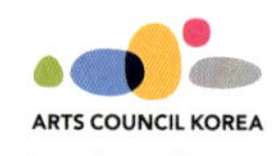

Arts Council Korea

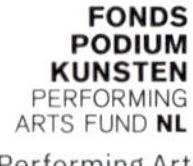

Embajada de España
en Austria

Ministerio de las Culturas, las
Artes y el Partimonio Chile

Ministerio de Relaciones Exteriores,
Dirección de Asuntos Culturales Chile

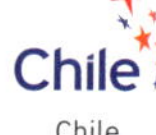

Chile

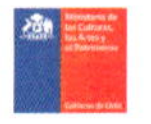

Performing Arts
Fund NL

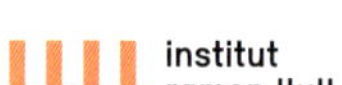

Institut Ramon Llull

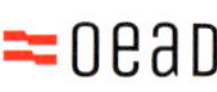

OeAD-GmbH

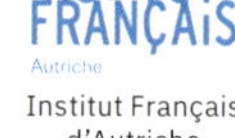

Institut Français
d'Autriche

Verwertungsgesellschaft der
Filmschaffenden GenmbH

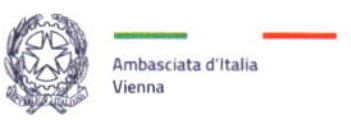

Italienische Botschaft

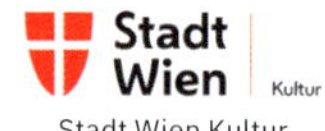

Istituto Italiano di
Cultura

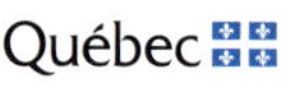

Québec Government
Office in Berlin

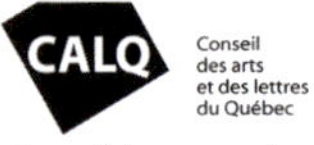

Conseil des arts et des
lettres du Québec

Stadt Wien Kultur

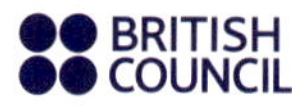

British Council Austria

MOBILITY PARTNER

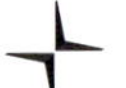

Polestar Automotive Austria GmbH

MEDIA PARTNERS

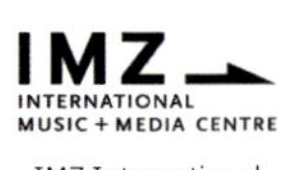

IMZ International
Music + Media Centre

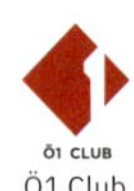

Ö1 Club

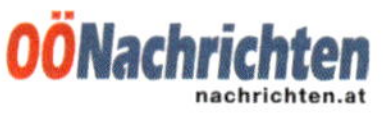

OÖ Nachrichten

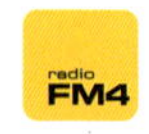

radio FM4

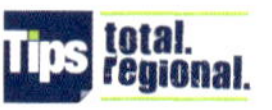

Tips

Academy for Theatre and Digitality Dortmund

Antre Peaux

Art2M/Makery

Atelierhaus Salzamt

AUTO-WELF workshop (Stockholm)

AWS - Austria Wirtschaftsservice

BeyondC

Bildrecht

Bozar

Bruckner Orchester Linz

Bundesdenkmalamt

Buni Hub

C³ Center for Culture & Communication Foundation

CCIS - Chamber of Commerce and Industry Slovenia

Centro Azkuna de Ocio y Cultura

Changemaker Educations

Chroniques

CIKE - Creative Industry Košice

Cluj Cultural Centre

Creative FED - European Federation for Creative Economy

Creative Prague

Creative Region

Crossing Europe Filmfestival Linz

Cyens Centre of Excellence

Dark Euphoria

Department of Visual Computing at Masaryk University

De Toneelmakerij

Det Norske Teatret

Deutsches Theater Berlin

DH5

Die pädagogische Hochschule Oberösterreich

Digital Media Department at the University of Applied Sciences Upper Austria

Diözese Linz

Ecopolis

Emerging Communities Africa

European Alternatives

European Science Engagement Association EUSEA

European Theatre Convention ETC

FIFTITU%

Fondazione Giorgio Cini

Fondazione Musei Civici di Venezia

Francisco Carolinum Linz

Fraunhofer ENAS

Fraunhofer Institute for Digital Medicine MEVIS

Fraunhofer IWU

GLUON

Goethe Institut

Hac Te Art, Science and Technology Hub

Hapa Foundation

Hexagone Scène Nationale

IDIZ - Institute for Social Research in Zagreb

iMAL Art Center for Digital Cultures & Technology

Innovationshauptplatz Linz

INOVA+

ISEA INTERNATIONAL

Kaiserschild-Stiftung

Kepler Salon – Verein zur Förderung von Wissensvermittlung

KILOWATT

King's College London

Klima- und Energiefonds

Klub Solitaer

KONTEJNER | bureau of contemporary art praxis

KUKA

Kulturhauptstadt Bad Ischl Salzkammergut 2024 GmbH

Kunstraum MEMPHIS

L.E.V. Festival

La Biennale di Venezia

La French Tech Grande Provence

LABoral Centro de Arte y Creación

Landestheater Linz

LATRA Innovation Lab

Łaźnia Centre for Contemporary Art

Leonardo OLATS

LINZ CENTER OF MECHATRONICS GMBH

LIVA

m-cult

Mariendom Linz

mb21 - Medienkulturzentrum Dresden

Media Solution Center Baden-Württemberg

Medizinische Universität Graz

MEET | Digital Culture Center

MKD – Meisterschule für Kommunikationsdesign Linz

Museo Nacional Thyssen-Bornemisza

Nähküche Linz

NeMe Arts Centre

NESTA

Onassis Stegi

Only Tomorrow Association (Asociația Doar Mâine)

OÖ Landeskultur GmbH

Open Commons Linz

Österreichische Akademie der Wissenschaften

Otelo eGen

Oulu University of Applied Sciences

Parlament Österreich I Parlamentsdirektion

Picha asbl

Pro Progressione

Projekt Atol

QUO ARTIS

RIXC Centre for New Media Culture

Rotes Kreuz Oberösterreich

Runway AI Film Festival

Salzburger Festspiele

Saxion University of Applied Sciences

Science for Change

Shiga University

SIGGRAPH

Silent Green

Sineglossa

Slovensko narodno gledališče Nova Gorica

Sónar

Stadtgärten

Stadtwerkstadt

T6 Ecosystems

Tactical Tech

Teatrul Național "Marin Sorescu"

Technical University Dresden

Technische Universität Wien

Technisches Museum Wien

The Center for the Promotion of Science (CPN)

The Culture Yard

The Digital Hub/Beta Festival

The Northern Photographic Centre

The University of Shiga Prefecture

Theater Phönix

Théâtre de Liège

Theatro Circo de Braga

Trinity College Dublin

TUKE - Technical University of Košice

Universität Innsbruck

University of Barcelona

University of Oulu

Vienna Center for Quantum Science and Technology

Waag Futurelab

Werkleitz Centre for Media Art

WRO Art Center

Zabala Innovation

Zaragoza City of Knowledge Foundation / Etopia (FZC)

Prix Ars Electronica 2024

Prix Ars Electronica 2024
New Animation Art
Interactive Art +
AI in Art Award
u19–create your world

Ars Electronica Award for Digital Humanity

European Union Prize for Citizen Science

S+T+ARTS Prize '24

S+T+ARTS Prize Africa

Ars Electronica Linz GmbH & Co KG
Ars-Electronica-Straße 1
4040 Linz, Austria
ars.electronica.art

CEOs: Gerfried Stocker, Markus Jandl

Editors: Gerfried Stocker, Markus Jandl

Editing: Jutta Schmiederer
Translations: Catherine Lewis (German—English)
Copyediting: Catherine Lewis, Jutta Schmiederer, Ingrid Fischer-Schreiber
Graphic design and production: Gerhard Kirchschläger, Ivan Sukhov
Typeface: IBM Plex Sans
Printed by: Gutenberg Werbering Gesellschaft m.b.H., Linz
Paper: Claro Bulk, 135 g/m², 300 g/m²

Distribution worldwide by
Hatje Cantz Verlag GmbH
Mommsenstr. 27
10629 Berlin
Germany
www.hatjecantz.com
A Ganske Publishing Group Company

ISBN 978-3-7757-5823-9
Printed in Austria

Cover illustrations:
Front: Paul Trillo, *Washed Out "The Hardest Part";* photo: courtesy of the artist
Thomas Feuerstein, *METABOLICA;* photo Atelier T. Feuerstein
Back: Beatie Wolfe, *Smoke and Mirrors;* photo: courtesy of the artist
Diane Cescutti, *Nosukaay;* photo: Blanche Lafargue

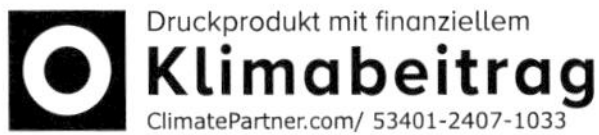